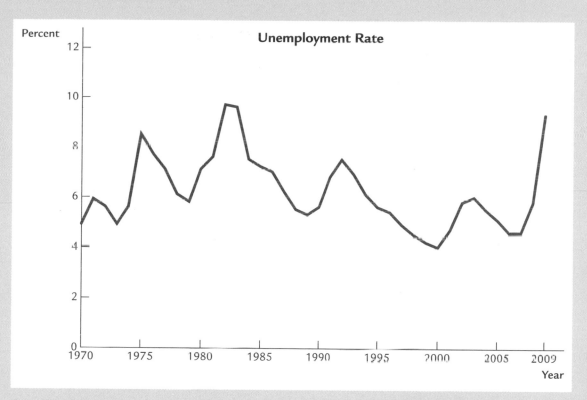

Unemployment Rate

Percent

Source: Bureau of Labor Statistics

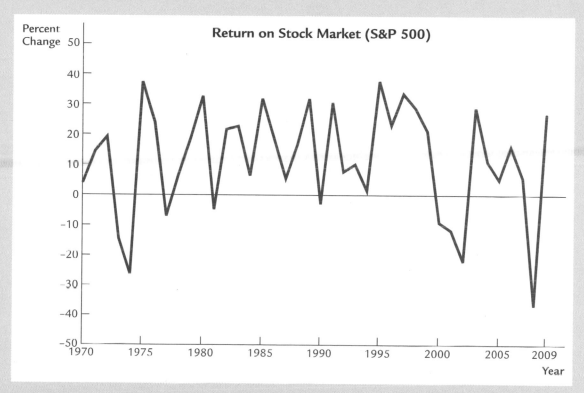

Return on Stock Market (S&P 500)

Percent
Change

Source: Global Financial Data

MACROECONOMICS
and the FINANCIAL SYSTEM

MACROECONOMICS
and the FINANCIAL SYSTEM

N. GREGORY MANKIW
Harvard University

LAURENCE M. BALL
Johns Hopkins University

Worth Publishers

Senior Publisher: Catherine Woods

Executive Editor: Charles Linsmeier

Senior Acquisitions Editor: Sarah Dorger

Executive Marketing Manager: Scott Guile

Consulting Editor: Paul Shensa

Senior Development Editor: Marie McHale

Development Editors: Jane Tufts and Barbara Brooks

Associate Media Editor: Tom Acox

Editorial Assistant: Mary Walsh

Associate Managing Editor: Tracey Kuehn

Project Editor: Dana Kasowitz

Photo Editor: Ted Szczepanski

Art Director: Babs Reingold

Cover and Text Designer: Kevin Kall

Production Manager: Barbara Anne Seixas

Composition: MPS Limited, a Macmillan Company

Printing and Binding: Quad/Graphics Versailles

Cover Artist: George Mamos

Library of Congress Cataloging-in-Publication Number: 2010932595

ISBN-13: 978-1-4292-5367-3

ISBN-10: 1-4292-5367-3

© 2011 by Worth Publishers

Printed in the United States of America

First Printing 2010

Worth Publishers

41 Madison Avenue

New York, NY 10010

www.worthpublishers.com

To Deborah and Patricia

about the authors

Christina Micek

N. Gregory Mankiw (pictured on the left) is Professor of Economics at Harvard University. He began his study of economics at Princeton University, where he received an A.B. in 1980. After earning a Ph.D. in economics from MIT, he began teaching at Harvard in 1985 and was promoted to full professor in 1987. Today, he regularly teaches both undergraduate and graduate courses in macroeconomics. He is also author of *Macroeconomics* (Worth Publishers) and *Principles of Economics* (Cengage Learning).

Professor Mankiw is a regular participant in academic and policy debates. His research ranges across macroeconomics and includes work on price adjustment, consumer behavior, financial markets, monetary and fiscal policy, and economic growth. In addition to his duties at Harvard, he has been a research associate of the National Bureau of Economic Research, a member of the Brookings Panel on Economic Activity, and an adviser to the Congressional Budget Office and the Federal Reserve Banks of Boston and New York. From 2003 to 2005 he was chairman of the President's Council of Economic Advisers.

Professor Mankiw lives in Wellesley, Massachusetts, with his wife, Deborah; children, Catherine, Nicholas, and Peter; and their border terrier, Tobin.

Laurence M. Ball (pictured on the right) is Professor of Economics at Johns Hopkins University. He received a B.A. in economics from Amherst College in 1980 and a Ph.D. in economics from MIT in 1986. He taught at New York University and Princeton University before his appointment at Johns Hopkins in 1994. He teaches both undergraduate and graduate courses in macroeconomics and is the author of *Money, Banking, and Financial Markets* (Worth Publishers).

Professor Ball's research areas include price adjustment and inflation, monetary and fiscal policy, and unemployment. He and Professor Mankiw have coauthored nine academic papers. Professor Ball is a research associate of the National Bureau of Economic Research and has been a visiting scholar at the Federal Reserve, the Bank of England, the Bank of Japan, the Central Bank of Norway, the Reserve Bank of Australia, the Reserve Bank of New Zealand, the Hong Kong Monetary Authority, and the International Monetary Fund.

Professor Ball lives in Baltimore with his wife, Patricia; son, Leverett; and their German shepherd, Bamboo.

brief contents

contents

preface

Economists have long understood that developments in the overall economy and developments in the financial system are inextricably intertwined. But if we needed reminding, the financial crisis and economic downturn that started in 2007 provided a wake-up call that is hard to ignore.

This book is designed for courses in intermediate-level macroeconomics that include ample coverage of the role of the economy's financial system. It is born of two parents. One of those parents is Greg Mankiw's text *Macroeconomics*. The other is Larry Ball's *Money, Banking, and Financial Markets*. Like any child, this book resembles both its parents but also has a personality of its own. As with a traditional book in macroeconomics, it covers such topics as monetary theory, growth theory, and the study of short-run economic fluctuations. But it also includes substantial material on asset prices, securities markets, banking, and financial crises. The integration of this material will foster interest in macroeconomics, especially among students looking toward careers in business and finance.

The great British economist John Maynard Keynes once remarked that an economist must be "mathematician, historian, statesman, philosopher, in some degree . . . as aloof and incorruptible as an artist, yet sometimes as near the earth as a politician." As this assessment suggests, students who aim to learn economics need to draw on many disparate talents. The job of helping students find and develop these talents falls to instructors and textbook authors.

When writing this book, our goal was to make macroeconomics understandable, relevant, and (believe it or not) fun. Those of us who have chosen to be professional macroeconomists have done so because we are fascinated by the field. More important, we believe that the study of macroeconomics and the financial system can illuminate much about the world and that the lessons learned, if properly applied, can make the world a better place. We hope this book conveys not only our profession's accumulated wisdom but also its enthusiasm and sense of purpose.

The Arrangement of Topics

Our strategy for teaching macroeconomics is first to examine the long run when prices are flexible and then to examine the short run when prices are sticky. This approach has several advantages. First, because the classical dichotomy permits the separation of real and monetary issues, the long-run material is easier for students to understand. Second, when students begin studying short-run fluctuations, they understand fully the long-run equilibrium around which the economy is fluctuating. Third, beginning with market-clearing models makes clearer the link between macroeconomics and microeconomics. Fourth, students learn first the material that is less controversial among macroeconomists. For all these reasons, the strategy of beginning with long-run classical models simplifies the teaching of macroeconomics.

Let's now move from strategy to tactics. What follows is a whirlwind tour of the book.

Part One, Introduction

The introductory material in Part One is brief so that students can get to the core topics quickly. Chapter 1 discusses the broad questions that macroeconomists address and the economist's approach of building models to explain the world. Chapter 2 introduces the key data of macroeconomics, emphasizing gross domestic product, the consumer price index, and the unemployment rate.

Part Two, Classical Theory: The Economy in the Long Run

Part Two examines the long run over which prices are flexible. Chapter 3 presents the basic classical model of national income. In this model, the factors of production and the production technology determine the level of income, and the marginal products of the factors determine its distribution to households. In addition, the model shows how fiscal policy influences the allocation of the economy's resources among consumption, investment, and government purchases, and it highlights how the real interest rate equilibrates the supply and demand for goods and services.

Money and the price level are introduced in Chapter 4. Because prices are assumed to be fully flexible, the chapter presents the prominent ideas of classical monetary theory: the quantity theory of money, the inflation tax, the Fisher effect, the social costs of inflation, and the causes and costs of hyperinflation.

Chapter 5 introduces the study of open-economy macroeconomics. Maintaining the assumption of full employment, this chapter presents models to explain the trade balance and the exchange rate. Various policy issues are addressed: the relationship between the budget deficit and the trade deficit, the macroeconomic impact of protectionist trade policies, and the effect of monetary policy on the value of a currency in the market for foreign exchange.

Chapter 6 relaxes the assumption of full employment by discussing the dynamics of the labor market and the natural rate of unemployment. It examines various causes of unemployment, including job search, minimum-wage laws, union power, and efficiency wages. It also presents some important facts about patterns of unemployment.

Part Three, Growth Theory: The Economy in the Very Long Run

Part Three makes the classical analysis of the economy dynamic by developing the tools of modern growth theory. Chapter 7 introduces the Solow growth model as a description of how the economy evolves over time. This chapter emphasizes the roles of capital accumulation and population growth. Chapter 8 then adds technological progress to the Solow model. It uses the model to discuss growth experiences around the world as well as public policies that influence the level and growth of the standard of living. Finally, Chapter 8 introduces students to the modern theories of endogenous growth.

Part Four, Business Cycle Theory: The Economy in the Short Run

Part Four examines the short run when prices are sticky. It begins in Chapter 9 by examining some of the key facts that describe short-run fluctuations in economic activity. The chapter then introduces the model of aggregate supply and aggregate demand as well as the role of stabilization policy. Subsequent chapters refine the ideas introduced in this chapter.

Chapters 10 and 11 look more closely at aggregate demand. Chapter 10 presents the Keynesian cross and the theory of liquidity preference and uses these models as building blocks for developing the *IS–LM* model. Chapter 11 uses the *IS–LM* model to explain economic fluctuations and the aggregate demand curve. It concludes with an extended case study of the Great Depression.

Chapter 12 looks more closely at aggregate supply. It examines various approaches to explaining the short-run aggregate supply curve and discusses the short-run tradeoff between inflation and unemployment.

Part Five, Macroeconomic Policy Debates

Once the student has command of standard long-run and short-run models of the economy, the book uses these models as the foundation for discussing some of the key debates over economic policy. Chapter 13 considers the debate over how policymakers should respond to short-run economic fluctuations. It emphasizes two broad questions: Should monetary and fiscal policy be active or passive? Should policy be conducted by rule or by discretion? The chapter presents arguments on both sides of these questions.

Chapter 14 focuses on the various debates over government debt and budget deficits. It gives some sense about the magnitude of government indebtedness, discusses why measuring budget deficits is not always straightforward, recaps the traditional view of the effects of government debt, presents Ricardian equivalence as an alternative view, and discusses various other perspectives on government debt. As in the previous chapter, students are not handed conclusions but are given the tools to evaluate the alternative viewpoints on their own.

Part Six, The Financial System and the Economy

Part Six enriches students' understanding of macroeconomics by exploring the financial system. Chapter 15 introduces financial markets and banks, emphasizing their roles in channeling funds from savers to investors and thereby spurring economic growth. It also discusses problems of asymmetric information in the financial system and how banks help overcome these problems.

Chapter 16 analyzes asset prices and interest rates. It discusses both classical theory, in which asset prices equal the present value of expected asset income, and the possibility of asset-price bubbles and crashes. The chapter also shows students how to calculate interest rates and returns on assets and explores the term structure of interest rates.

Chapter 17 surveys the markets for securities, including stocks, bonds, and derivatives. It addresses the mechanics of how securities markets operate and the decisions facing market participants, such as firms' decisions about which securities to issue and savers' decisions about which to buy. The chapter also presents a balanced discussion of a perennial debate: can anyone beat the market?

Chapter 18 discusses the banking industry: the different types of banks, how banks seek to earn profits and contain risk, the problem of bank runs, and government regulation of banking. The chapter also examines two key developments in recent history: subprime lending and the securitization of bank loans.

Finally, Chapter 19 examines financial crises. It starts with a general discussion of what happens in a financial crisis and how it affects the economy, then moves to a detailed analysis of the U.S. crisis of 2007–2009. The discussion emphasizes debates over government and central bank policies: How can policymakers contain crises when they occur? What regulatory reforms can prevent future crises? The chapter builds on what students have learned from earlier chapters about economic fluctuations, monetary and fiscal policy, and the financial system.

Alternative Routes Through the Text

We have organized the material in the way that we prefer to teach intermediate-level macroeconomics, but we understand that other instructors have different preferences. We tried to keep this in mind as we wrote the book so that it would offer a degree of flexibility. Here are a few ways that instructors might consider rearranging the material:

> ➤ Some instructors are eager to cover short-run economic fluctuations. For such a course, we recommend covering Chapters 1 through 4 so students are grounded in the basics of classical theory and then jumping to Chapters 9 through 12 to cover the model of aggregate demand and aggregate supply.

> ➤ Some instructors are eager to cover long-run economic growth. These instructors can cover Chapters 7 and 8 immediately after Chapter 3.

> ➤ An instructor who wants to defer (or even skip) open-economy macroeconomics can put off Chapter 5 without loss of continuity.

> ➤ An instructor who wants to emphasize the financial system can move to Chapters 15 through 19 immediately after covering Chapters 1 through 4 and 9 through 11.

We hope and believe that this text complements well a variety of approaches to the field.

Learning Tools

We have included a variety of features to ensure that the text is student-friendly. Here is a brief overview.

Case Studies

Economics comes to life when it is applied to understanding actual events. Therefore, the numerous case studies are an important learning tool, integrated closely with the theoretical material presented in each chapter. The frequency with which these case studies occur ensures that students do not have to grapple with an overdose of theory before seeing the theory applied.

FYI Boxes

These boxes present ancillary material "for your information." We use these boxes to clarify difficult concepts, to provide additional information about the tools of economics, and to show how economics relates to our daily lives.

Graphs

Understanding graphical analysis is a key part of learning macroeconomics, and we have worked hard to make the figures easy to follow. We often use comment boxes within figures that describe briefly and draw attention to the important points that the figures illustrate. They should help students both learn and review the material.

Mathematical Notes

We use occasional mathematical footnotes to keep more difficult material out of the body of the text. These notes make an argument more rigorous or present a proof of a mathematical result. They can easily be skipped by those students who have not been introduced to the necessary mathematical tools.

Chapter Summaries

Every chapter ends with a brief, nontechnical summary of its major lessons. Students can use the summaries to place the material in perspective and to review for exams.

Key Concepts

Learning the language of a field is a major part of any course. Within the chapter, each key concept is in **boldface** when it is introduced. At the end of the chapter, the key concepts are listed for review.

Questions for Review

After studying a chapter, students can immediately test their understanding of its basic lessons by answering the Questions for Review.

Problems and Applications

Every chapter includes Problems and Applications designed for homework assignments. Some of these are numerical applications of the theory in the chapter. Others encourage the student to go beyond the material in the chapter by addressing new issues that are closely related to the chapter topics.

Glossary

To help students become familiar with the language of macroeconomics, a glossary of more than 300 terms is provided at the back of the book.

Acknowledgments

We are grateful to the many reviewers and colleagues in the economics profession whose input helped to shape the two parents of this book, *Macroeconomics* (Mankiw) and *Money, Banking, and Financial Markets* (Ball). The former has been through seven editions, making the reviewers too numerous to list in their entirety. However, we are grateful for their willingness to have given up their scarce time to help improve the economics and pedagogy of this text.

We would like to mention those instructors whose recent input shaped the seventh edition of *Macroeconomics*, the first edition of *Money, Banking, and Financial Markets*, and this new book:

Burton Abrams
University of Delaware

Douglas Agbetsiafa
Indiana University at South Bend

Francis Ahking
University of Connecticut at Storrs

Ehsan Ahmed
James Madison University

Jack Aschkenazi
American InterContinental University

Jinhui Bai
Georgetown University

Clare Battista
California Polytechnic State University

Joydeep Bhattacharya
Iowa State University

Peter Bondarenko
University of Chicago

Michael Brandl
University of Texas at Austin

James Butkiewicz
University of Delaware

Tina Carter
Florida State University

Jin Choi
DePaul University

Ronald Cronovich
Carthage College

Massimiliano De Santis
Dartmouth College

Ranjit Dighe
State University of New York at Oswego

Aimee Dimmerman
George Washington University

John Driscoll
Federal Reserve Board

Ding Du
South Dakota State University

John Duca
Southern Methodist University

Fisheha Eshete
Bowie State University

Robert Eyler
Sonoma State University

James Fackler
University of Kentucky

Imran Farooqi
University of Iowa

David Flynn
University of North Dakota

Chris Foote
Federal Reserve Bank of Boston

Yee-Tien Fu
Stanford University

Doris Geide-Stevenson
Weber State University

Ismail Genc
University of Idaho

Rebecca Gonzalez
University of North Carolina at Pembroke

David R. Hakes
University of Northern Iowa

David Hammes
University of Hawaii at Hilo

Jane Himarios
University of Texas at Arlington

David Hineline
Miami University

Christopher House
University of Michigan

Aaron Jackson
Bentley College

Nancy Jianakoplos
Colorado State University

Bryce Kanago
University of Northern Iowa

George Karras
University of Illinois at Chicago

Roger Kaufman
Smith College

Manfred W. Keil
Claremont McKenna College

Elizabeth Sawyer Kelly
University of Wisconsin

Kathy Kelly
University of Texas at Arlington

Faik Koray
Louisiana State University

John Krieg
Western Washington University

Kristin Kucsma
Seton Hall University

Gary F. Langer
Roosevelt University

John Leahy
New York University

Mary Lesser
Iona College

Christopher Magee
Bucknell University

Michael Marlow
*California Polytechnic State
University*

Robert Martel
University of Connecticut

W. Douglas McMillin
Louisiana State University

Jianjun Miao
Boston University

Meghan Millea
Mississippi State University

Robert Murphy
Boston College

John Neri
University of Maryland

Robert Pennington
University of Central Florida

Christina Peters
*University of Colorado at
Boulder*

Ronnie Phillips
Colorado State University

Dennis Placone
Clemson University

Robert Reed
University of Kentucky

Jeffrey Reynolds
Northern Illinois University

David Romer
*University of California at
Berkeley*

Brian Rosario
American River College

Joseph Santos
*South Dakota State
University*

Naveen Sarna
*Northern Virginia
Community College*

Mark Siegler
*California State University at
Sacramento*

Robert Sonora
Fort Lewis College

David Spencer
Brigham Young University

Richard Stahl
Louisiana State University

Frank Steindl
Oklahoma State University

James Swofford
University of South Alabama

Henry S. Terrell
University of Maryland

Sven Thommesen
Auburn University

Brian Trinque
University of Texas at Austin

Nora Underwood
University of Central Florida

Kristin Van Gaasbeck
*California State University at
Sacramento*

Rubina Vohra
New Jersey City University

Qingbin Wang
University at Albany

Charles Weise
Gettysburg College

Jaejoon Woo
DePaul University

Paul Woodburne
Clarion University

Bill Yang
Georgia Southern University

Noam Yuchtman
Harvard University

In addition, we are grateful for excellent research assistance from Stacy Carlson and Daniel Norris, students at Harvard, and Hai Nguyen, a student at Johns Hopkins.

The people at Worth Publishers have continued to be congenial and dedicated. We would like to thank Catherine Woods, Senior Publisher; Charles Linsmeier, Executive Editor; Sarah Dorger, Senior Acquisitions Editor; Scott Guile, Executive Marketing Manager; Marie McHale, Senior Development Editor; Paul Shensa, Consulting Editor; Tom Acox, Associate Media and Supplements Editor; Mary Walsh, Editorial Assistant; Steven Rigolosi, Director of Market Research and Development; Dana Kasowitz, Project Editor; Tracey Kuehn, Associate Managing Editor; Barbara Seixas, Production Manager; Barbara Reingold, Art Director; Vicki Tomaselli, Design Manager; Kevin Kall, Layout Designer; Karen Osborne, Copyeditor; Laura McGinn, Supplements Editor; and Stacey Alexander, Supplements Manager.

Many other people made valuable contributions as well. Most important, Jane Tufts, freelance developmental editor, worked her magic on this book, confirming that she's the best in the business. We are also grateful to Barbara Brooks for her invaluable editorial input. Alexandra Nickerson did a great job preparing the index. Deborah Mankiw and Patricia Bovers, our wives, provided invaluable suggestions and encouragement and graciously tolerated our absence as we spent many hours in front of our computer screens writing, editing, and fine-tuning this text.

Finally, we would like to thank our children, Catherine, Nicholas, and Peter Mankiw and Leverett Ball. They helped immensely with this book—both by providing a pleasant distraction and by reminding us that textbooks are written for the next generation.

N. Gregory Mankiw

Laurence Ball

August 2010

Supplements and Media

Worth Publishers has worked closely with Greg Mankiw, Larry Ball, and a team of talented economics instructors to put together a variety of supplements to aid instructors and students. We have been delighted at the positive feedback we have received on these supplements. Here is a summary of the resources available.

For Instructors

Instructor's Resources

Robert G. Murphy (Boston College) has written a comprehensive resource manual for instructors to appear on the instructor's portion of the Web site. For each chapter of this book, the manual contains notes to the instructor, a detailed lecture outline, additional case studies, and coverage of advanced topics. Instructors can use the manual to prepare their lectures, and they can reproduce whatever pages they choose as handouts for students. Professor Murphy has also created a Dismal Scientist Activity (www.dismalscientist.com) for each chapter. Each activity challenges students to combine the chapter knowledge with a high-powered business database and analysis service that offers real-time monitoring of the global economy.

Solutions Manual

Nora Underwood (University of Central Florida) has written the *Solutions Manual* for all of the Questions for Review and Problems and Applications.

Test Bank

Nancy Jianakoplos (Colorado State University) has written the *Test Bank*, which includes nearly 2,100 multiple-choice questions, numerical problems, and short-answer graphical questions to accompany each chapter of the text. The *Test Bank* is available on a CD-ROM. The CD includes our flexible test-generating software, which instructors can use to easily write and edit questions as well as create and print tests.

PowerPoint Slides

Ronald Cronovich (Carthage College) has prepared PowerPoint presentations of the material in each chapter. They feature animated graphs with careful explanations and additional case studies, data, and helpful notes to the instructor. Designed to be customized or used "as is," they include easy instructions for those who have little experience with PowerPoint. They are available on the companion Web site.

Online Offerings

Companion Web Site for Students and Instructors
(www.worthpublishers.com/mankiwball)

The companion site is a virtual study guide for students and an excellent resource for instructors. Robert G. Murphy (Boston College) and Brian Rosario (American River College) have updated the innovative software package for students. For each chapter in the textbook, the tools on the companion Web site include the following:

➤ *Self-Tests.* Students can test their knowledge of the material in the book by taking multiple-choice tests on any chapter. After the student responds, the program explains the answer and directs the student to specific sections in the book for additional study. Students may also test their knowledge of key terms using the flashcards.

➤ *Data Plotter.* Originally created by David Weil, Brown University, this tool enables students to explore macroeconomic data with time-series graphs and scatterplots.

➤ *Macro Models.* These modules provide simulations of the models presented in the book. Students can change the exogenous variables and see the outcomes in terms of shifting curves and recalculated numerical values of the endogenous variables. Each module contains exercises that instructors can assign as homework.

➤ *A Game for Macroeconomists.* Also originally created by David Weil, Brown University, the game allows students to become president of the United States in the year 2012 and to make macroeconomic policy decisions based on news events, economic statistics, and approval ratings. It gives students a sense of the complex interconnections that influence the economy. It is also fun to play.

➤ *Flashcards.* Students can test their knowledge of the definitions in the glossary with these virtual flashcards.

Along with the Instructor's Resources (see p. xxxi), the following additional instructor support material is available:

➤ *PowerPoint Lecture Presentations.* As mentioned earlier, these customizable PowerPoint slides, prepared by Ronald Cronovich (Carthage College), are designed to assist instructors with lecture preparation and presentations.

➤ *Images from the Textbook.* Instructors have access to a complete set of figures and tables from the textbook in high-resolution and low-resolution JPEG formats. The textbook art has been processed for "high-resolution" (150 dpi). These figures and photographs have been especially formatted for maximum readability in large lecture halls and follow standards that were set and tested in a real university auditorium.

➤ *Solutions Manual.* Instructors have access to an electronic version of the printed manual, which consists of detailed solutions to the Questions for Review and Problems and Applications.

BlackBoard

The Mankiw/Ball BlackBoard course cartridge makes it possible to combine Black-Board's popular tools and easy-to-use interface with the text's Web content, including preprogrammed quizzes and tests. The result is an interactive, comprehensive online course that allows for effortless implementation, management, and use. The files are organized and prebuilt to work within the BlackBoard software.

Additional Offerings

i-clicker

Developed by a team of University of Illinois physicists, i-clicker is the most flexible and most reliable classroom response system available. It is the only solution created *for* educators, *by* educators—with continuous product improvements made through direct classroom testing and faculty feedback. No matter their level of technical expertise, instructors will appreciate the i-clicker because the focus remains on teaching, not the technology. To learn more about packaging i-clicker with this textbook, please contact your local sales representative or visit www.iclicker.com.

Financial Times Edition

For adopters of this text, Worth Publishers and the *Financial Times* are offering a 15-week subscription to students at a tremendous savings. Instructors also receive their own free *Financial Times* subscription for one year. Students and instructors may access research and archived information at www.ft.com.

Dismal Scientist

A high powered business database and analysis service comes to the classroom! Dismal Scientist offers real-time monitoring of the global economy, produced locally by economists and other professionals at Moody's Economy.com around the world. Dismal Scientist is *free* when packaged with this text. Please contact your local sales representative or go to www.dismalscientist.com.

The Economist

The Economist has partnered with Worth Publishers to create an exclusive offer we believe will enhance the classroom experience. Faculty receive a complimentary 15-week subscription when 10 or more students purchase a subscription. Students get 15 issues of *The Economist* for just $15. That's a savings of 85 percent off the cover price.

Inside and outside the classroom, *The Economist* provides a global perspective that helps students keep abreast of what's going on in the world and provides insight into how the world views the United States.

Each subscription includes:

► *Special Reports.* Approximately 20 times a year, *The Economist* publishes a Special Report providing in-depth analysis that highlights a specific country, industry, or hot-button issue.

➤ *Technology Quarterly Supplements.* This supplement analyzes new technology that could potentially transform lives, business models, industries, governments, and financial markets.

➤ *Economist.com.* Unlimited access to *The Economist*'s Web site is *free* with a print subscription.

Included on *The Economist* Web site:

➤ *Searchable Archive.* Subscribers have full access to 28,000+ articles.

➤ *Exclusive Online Research Tools.* Tools include Articles by Subject, Backgrounders, Surveys, Economics A–Z, Style Guide, Weekly Indicators, and Currency Converter.

➤ *The Full Audio Edition.* The entire magazine or specific sections are available for download.

➤ The Economist *Debate Series.* The essence of Oxford-style debate is available in an interactive online forum.

➤ *Daily Columns.* These feature columns are available exclusively online, covering views on business, the market, personal technology, the arts, and much more.

➤ *Correspondent's Diary.* Each week, an *Economist* writer from a different country details experiences and offers opinions.

➤ *Blogs.* Blogs cover economics as well as U.S. and European politics.

To get 15 issues of *The Economist* for just $15, go to www.economistacademic.com/worth.

PART I

Introduction

CHAPTER **1**

The Science of Macroeconomics

The whole of science is nothing more than the refinement of everyday thinking.

—*Albert Einstein*

1-1 What Macroeconomists Study

Why have some countries experienced rapid growth in incomes over the past century while others stay mired in poverty? Why do some countries have high rates of inflation while others maintain stable prices? Why do all countries experience recessions and depressions—recurrent periods of falling incomes and rising unemployment—and how can government policy reduce the frequency and severity of these episodes? **Macroeconomics**, the study of the economy as a whole, attempts to answer these and many related questions.

To appreciate the importance of macroeconomics, you need only read the newspaper or listen to the news. Every day you can see headlines such as INCOME GROWTH REBOUNDS, FED MOVES TO COMBAT INFLATION, or RECESSION FEARS MOUNT. These macroeconomic events may seem abstract, but they touch all of our lives. Business executives forecasting the demand for their products must guess how fast consumers' incomes will grow. Senior citizens living on fixed incomes wonder how fast prices will rise. Recent college graduates looking for jobs hope that the economy will boom and that firms will be hiring.

Macroeconomic events are closely linked with developments in the nation's financial markets. When the economy is booming, firms are profitable, and the value of those companies is reflected in higher stock prices. When the economy heads into recession, declining stock prices are often an early warning sign. At the same time that they reflect economic developments, movements in financial markets can influence the path of the economy. Fluctuations in stock prices affect households' wealth and spending decisions, which in turn can lead to fluctuations in production and employment.

The nation's banks and other financial institutions are also intertwined with the overall economy, once again with causation running in both directions. A declining economy can reduce the profitability and health of the banking system, and a booming economy can enhance it. In addition, as was evidenced during the financial crisis of 2008–2009, problems in the nation's financial institutions can make it harder for households and businesses to obtain credit, adversely affecting the economy more broadly. Conversely, when the financial system is working well, it contributes to economic prosperity by helping to allocate the economy's scarce resources to those industries and businesses that can put them to their best use.

Because the state of the economy affects everyone, macroeconomic and financial issues play a central role in national political debates. Voters are aware of how the economy is doing, and they know that government policy can affect the economy in powerful ways. As a result, the popularity of the incumbent president often rises when the economy is doing well and falls when it is doing poorly. These issues are also central to world politics, and when world leaders meet, a discussion of macroeconomic and financial policy is often high on their agenda.

Although the job of making policy belongs to world leaders, the job of explaining the workings of the economy as a whole falls to macroeconomists. Toward this end, macroeconomists collect data on incomes, prices, unemployment, and many other variables from different time periods and different countries. They then attempt to formulate general theories to explain these data. Like astronomers studying the evolution of stars or biologists studying the evolution of species, macroeconomists cannot conduct controlled experiments in a laboratory. Instead, they must make use of the data that history gives them. Macroeconomists observe that economies differ across countries and that they change over time. These observations provide both the motivation for developing macroeconomic theories and the data for testing them.

To be sure, macroeconomics is a young and imperfect science. The macroeconomist's ability to predict the future course of economic events is no better than the meteorologist's ability to predict next month's weather. But, as you will see, macroeconomists know quite a lot about how economies work. This knowledge is useful both for explaining economic events and for formulating economic policy.

Every era has its own economic problems. In the 1970s, Presidents Richard Nixon, Gerald Ford, and Jimmy Carter all wrestled in vain with a rising rate of inflation. In the 1980s, inflation subsided, but Presidents Ronald Reagan and George Bush presided over large federal budget deficits. In the 1990s, with President Bill Clinton in the Oval Office, the economy and stock market enjoyed a remarkable boom, and the federal budget turned from deficit to surplus. But as Clinton left office, the stock market was in retreat, and the economy was heading into recession. In 2001 President George W. Bush reduced taxes to help end the recession, but the tax cuts also contributed to a reemergence of budget deficits.

President Barack Obama moved into the White House in 2009 in a period of heightened economic turbulence. The economy was reeling from a financial crisis, driven by a large drop in housing prices and a steep rise in mortgage defaults. The financial crisis was spreading to other sectors and pushing the overall economy into a deep recession. In some minds, the financial crisis raised the specter of the Great Depression of the 1930s, when in its worst year one out of four Americans who wanted to work could not find a job. In 2008 and 2009, officials in the Treasury, Federal Reserve, and other parts of government acted vigorously to prevent a recurrence of that outcome. They also debated which reforms of the financial system would reduce the likelihood of future crises.

Macroeconomic history is not a simple story, but it provides a rich motivation for macroeconomic theory. While the basic principles of macroeconomics do not change from decade to decade, the macroeconomist must apply these principles with flexibility and creativity to meet changing circumstances.

CASE STUDY

The Historical Performance of the U.S. Economy

Economists use many types of data to measure the performance of an economy. Three macroeconomic variables are especially important: real gross domestic product (GDP), the inflation rate, and the unemployment rate. **Real GDP** measures the total income of everyone in the economy (adjusted for the level of prices). The **inflation rate** measures how fast prices are rising. The **unemployment rate** measures the fraction of the labor force that is out of work. Macroeconomists study how these variables are determined, why they change over time, and how they interact with one another.

Figure 1-1 shows real GDP per person in the United States. Two aspects of this figure are noteworthy. First, real GDP grows over time. Real GDP per person today is about eight times higher than it was in 1900. This growth in average income allows us to enjoy a much higher standard of living than our great-grandparents did. Second, although real GDP rises in most years, this growth is

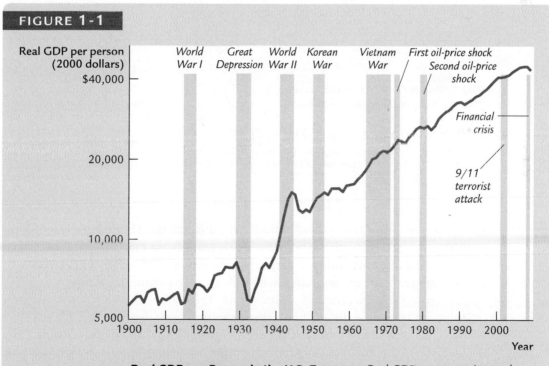

FIGURE 1-1

Real GDP per Person in the U.S. Economy Real GDP measures the total income of everyone in the economy, and real GDP per person measures the income of the average person in the economy. This figure shows that real GDP per person tends to grow over time and that this normal growth is sometimes interrupted by periods of declining income, called recessions or depressions.

Note: Real GDP is plotted here on a logarithmic scale. On such a scale, equal distances on the vertical axis represent equal *percentage* changes. Thus, the distance between $5,000 and $10,000 (a 100 percent change) is the same as the distance between $10,000 and $20,000 (a 100 percent change).

Source: U.S. Department of Commerce and Economic History Services.

FIGURE 1-2

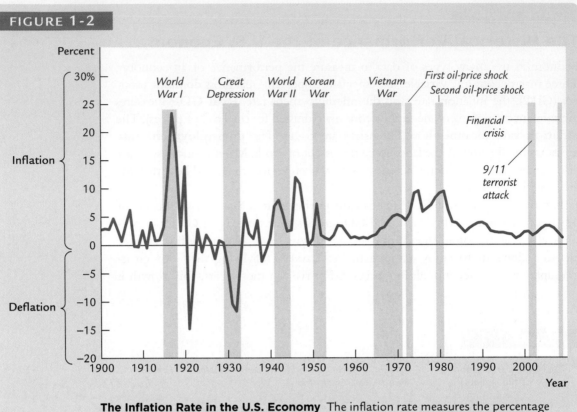

The Inflation Rate in the U.S. Economy The inflation rate measures the percentage change in the average level of prices from the year before. When the inflation rate is above zero, prices are rising. When it is below zero, prices are falling. If the inflation rate declines but remains positive, prices are rising but at a slower rate.

Note: The inflation rate is measured here using the GDP deflator.
Source: U.S. Department of Commerce and Economic History Services.

not steady. There are repeated periods during which real GDP falls, the most dramatic instance being the early 1930s. Such periods are called **recessions** if they are mild and **depressions** if they are more severe. Not surprisingly, periods of declining income are associated with substantial economic hardship.

Figure 1-2 shows the U.S. inflation rate. You can see that inflation varies substantially over time. In the first half of the twentieth century, the inflation rate averaged only slightly above zero. Periods of falling prices, called **deflation**, were almost as common as periods of rising prices. By contrast, inflation has been the norm during the past half century. Inflation became most severe during the late 1970s, when prices rose at a rate of almost 10 percent per year. In recent years, the inflation rate has been about 2 or 3 percent per year, indicating that prices have been fairly stable.

Figure 1-3 shows the U.S. unemployment rate. Three things are notable about the unemployment rate: there is always some unemployment in the economy; the unemployment rate has no long-term trend; and the unemployment rate varies substantially from year to year. Recessions and depressions are associated with unusually

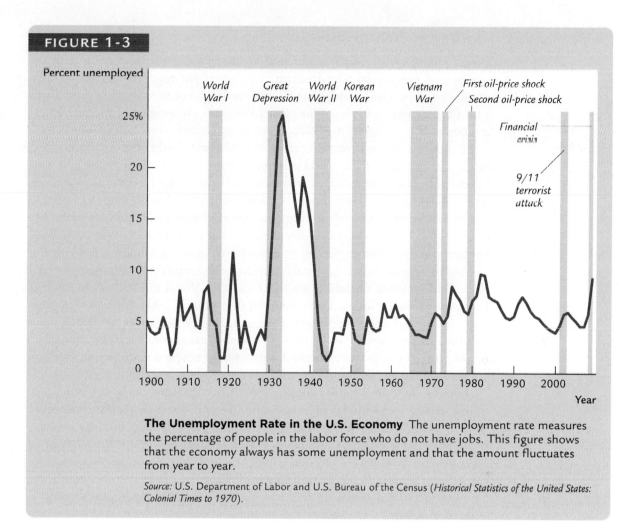

FIGURE 1-3

The Unemployment Rate in the U.S. Economy The unemployment rate measures the percentage of people in the labor force who do not have jobs. This figure shows that the economy always has some unemployment and that the amount fluctuates from year to year.

Source: U.S. Department of Labor and U.S. Bureau of the Census (*Historical Statistics of the United States: Colonial Times to 1970*).

high unemployment. The highest rates of unemployment were reached during the Great Depression of the 1930s.

These three figures offer a glimpse at the history of the U.S. economy. In the chapters that follow, we first discuss how these variables are measured and then develop theories to explain how they behave. ■

1-2 How Economists Think

Economists often study politically charged issues, but they try to address these issues with a scientist's objectivity. Like any science, economics has its own set of tools—terminology, data, and a way of thinking—that can seem foreign and arcane to the layman. The best way to become familiar with these tools is to practice using them, and this book affords you ample opportunity to do so. To make these tools less forbidding, however, let's discuss a few of them here.

Theory as Model Building

Young children learn much about the world around them by playing with toy versions of real objects. For instance, they often put together models of cars, trains, or planes. These models are far from realistic, but the model-builder learns a lot from them nonetheless. The model illustrates the essence of the real object it is designed to resemble. (In addition, for many children, building models is fun.)

Economists also use **models** to understand the world, but an economist's model is more likely to be made of symbols and equations than plastic and glue. Economists build their "toy economies" to help explain economic variables, such as GDP, inflation, and unemployment. Economic models illustrate, often in mathematical terms, the relationships among the variables. Models are useful because they help us to dispense with irrelevant details and to focus on underlying connections. (In addition, for many economists, building models is fun.)

Models have two kinds of variables: endogenous variables and exogenous variables. **Endogenous variables** are those variables that a model tries to explain. **Exogenous variables** are those variables that a model takes as given. The purpose of a model is to show how the exogenous variables affect the endogenous variables. In other words, as Figure 1-4 illustrates, exogenous variables come from outside the model and serve as the model's input, whereas endogenous variables are determined within the model and are the model's output.

To make these ideas more concrete, let's review the most celebrated of all economic models—the model of supply and demand. Imagine that an economist wanted to figure out what factors influence the price of pizza and the quantity of pizza sold. He or she would develop a model that described the behavior of pizza buyers, the behavior of pizza sellers, and their interaction in the market for pizza. For example, the economist supposes that the quantity of pizza demanded by consumers Q^d depends on the price of pizza P and on aggregate income Y. This relationship is expressed in the equation

$$Q^d = D(P, Y),$$

where $D(\ )$ represents the demand function. Similarly, the economist supposes that the quantity of pizza supplied by pizzerias Q^s depends on the price of pizza

FIGURE 1-4

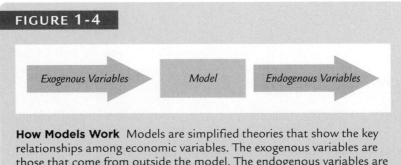

Exogenous Variables   Model   Endogenous Variables

How Models Work Models are simplified theories that show the key relationships among economic variables. The exogenous variables are those that come from outside the model. The endogenous variables are those that the model explains. The model shows how changes in the exogenous variables affect the endogenous variables.

P and on the price of materials P_m, such as cheese, tomatoes, flour, and anchovies. This relationship is expressed as

$$Q^s = S(P, P_m),$$

where $S(\ )$ represents the supply function. Finally, the economist assumes that the price of pizza adjusts to bring the quantity supplied and quantity demanded into balance:

$$Q^s = Q^d.$$

These three equations compose a model of the market for pizza.

The economist illustrates the model with a supply-and-demand diagram, as in Figure 1-5. The demand curve shows the relationship between the quantity of pizza demanded and the price of pizza, holding aggregate income constant. The demand curve slopes downward because a higher price of pizza encourages consumers to switch to other foods and buy less pizza. The supply curve shows the relationship between the quantity of pizza supplied and the price of pizza, holding the price of materials constant. The supply curve slopes upward because a higher price of pizza makes selling pizza more profitable, which encourages pizzerias to produce more of it. The equilibrium for the market is the price and quantity at which the supply and demand curves intersect. At the equilibrium price, consumers choose to buy the amount of pizza that pizzerias choose to produce.

This model of the pizza market has two exogenous variables and two endogenous variables. The exogenous variables are aggregate income and the price of materials. The model does not attempt to explain them but instead takes them as given (perhaps to be explained by another model). The endogenous variables are

FIGURE 1-5

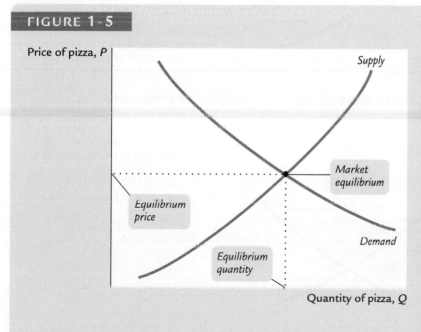

The Model of Supply and Demand The most famous economic model is that of supply and demand for a good or service—in this case, pizza. The demand curve is a downward-sloping curve relating the price of pizza to the quantity of pizza that consumers demand. The supply curve is an upward-sloping curve relating the price of pizza to the quantity of pizza that pizzerias supply. The price of pizza adjusts until the quantity supplied equals the quantity demanded. The point where the two curves cross is the market equilibrium, which shows the equilibrium price of pizza and the equilibrium quantity of pizza.

the price of pizza and the quantity of pizza exchanged. These are the variables that the model attempts to explain.

The model can be used to show how a change in one of the exogenous variables affects both endogenous variables. For example, if aggregate income increases, then the demand for pizza increases, as in panel (a) of Figure 1-6. The model shows that both the equilibrium price and the equilibrium quantity of pizza rise. Similarly, if the price of materials increases, then the supply of pizza decreases, as in panel (b) of Figure 1-6. The model shows that in this case the equilibrium price of pizza rises and the equilibrium quantity of pizza falls. Thus, the model shows how changes either in aggregate income or in the price of materials affect price and quantity in the market for pizza.

FIGURE 1-6

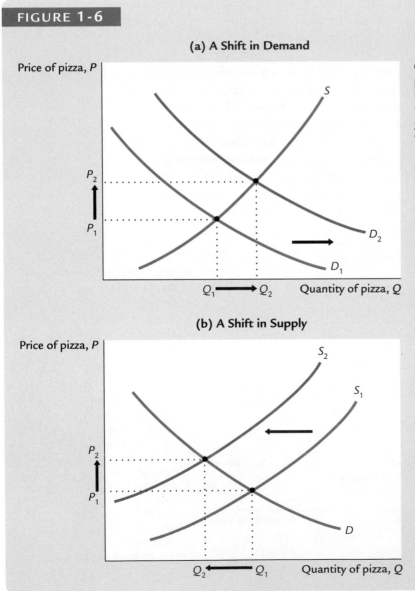

(a) A Shift in Demand

(b) A Shift in Supply

Changes in Equilibrium In panel (a), a rise in aggregate income causes the demand for pizza to increase: at any given price, consumers now want to buy more pizza. This is represented by a rightward shift in the demand curve from D_1 to D_2. The market moves to the new intersection of supply and demand. The equilibrium price rises from P_1 to P_2, and the equilibrium quantity of pizza rises from Q_1 to Q_2. In panel (b), a rise in the price of materials decreases the supply of pizza: at any given price, pizzerias find that the sale of pizza is less profitable and therefore choose to produce less pizza. This is represented by a leftward shift in the supply curve from S_1 to S_2. The market moves to the new intersection of supply and demand. The equilibrium price rises from P_1 to P_2, and the equilibrium quantity falls from Q_1 to Q_2.

Like all models, this model of the pizza market makes simplifying assumptions. The model does not take into account, for example, that every pizzeria is in a different location. For each customer, one pizzeria is more convenient than the others, and thus pizzerias have some ability to set their own prices. The model assumes that there is a single price for pizza, but in fact there could be a different price at every pizzeria.

How should we react to the model's lack of realism? Should we discard the simple model of pizza supply and demand? Should we attempt to build a more complex model that allows for diverse pizza prices? The answers to these questions depend on our purpose. If our goal is to explain how the price of cheese affects the average price of pizza and the amount of pizza sold, then the diversity of pizza prices is probably not important. The simple model of the pizza market does a good job of addressing that issue. But if our goal is to explain why towns with ten pizzerias have lower pizza prices than towns with two, the simple model is less useful.

The art in economics is in judging when a simplifying assumption (such as assuming a single price of pizza) clarifies our thinking and when it misleads us. Simplification is a necessary part of building a useful model: any model constructed to be completely realistic would be too complicated for anyone to understand. Yet

---

FYI

Using Functions to Express Relationships Among Variables

All economic models express relationships among economic variables. Often, these relationships are expressed as functions. A *function* is a mathematical concept that shows how one variable depends on a set of other variables. For example, in the model of the pizza market, we said that the quantity of pizza demanded depends on the price of pizza and on aggregate income. To express this, we use functional notation to write

$$Q^d = D(P, Y).$$

This equation says that the quantity of pizza demanded Q^d is a function of the price of pizza P and aggregate income Y. In functional notation, the variable preceding the parentheses denotes the function. In this case, $D(\ )$ is the function expressing how the variables in parentheses determine the quantity of pizza demanded.

If we knew more about the pizza market, we could give a numerical formula for the quantity of pizza demanded. For example, we might be able to write

$$Q^d = 60 - 10P + 2Y.$$

In this case, the demand function is

$$D(P, Y) = 60 - 10P + 2Y.$$

For any price of pizza and aggregate income, this function gives the corresponding quantity of pizza demanded. For example, if aggregate income is $10 and the price of pizza is $2, then the quantity of pizza demanded is 60 pies; if the price of pizza rises to $3, the quantity of pizza demanded falls to 50 pies.

Functional notation allows us to express the general idea that variables are related, even when we do not have enough information to indicate the precise numerical relationship. For example, we might know that the quantity of pizza demanded falls when the price rises from $2 to $3, but we might not know by how much it falls. In this case, functional notation is useful: as long as we know that a relationship among the variables exists, we can express that relationship using functional notation.

models lead to incorrect conclusions if they assume away features of the economy that are crucial to the issue at hand. Economic modeling therefore requires care and common sense.

The Use of Multiple Models

Macroeconomists study many facets of the economy. For example, they examine the role of saving in economic growth, the impact of minimum-wage laws on unemployment, the effect of inflation on interest rates, the influence of trade policy on the trade balance and exchange rate, and the impact of a financial crisis on production and employment.

Economists use models to address all of these issues, but no single model can answer every question. Just as carpenters use different tools for different tasks, economists use different models to explain different economic phenomena. Students of macroeconomics, therefore, must keep in mind that there is no single "correct" model that applies to all situations. Instead, there are many models, each of which is useful for shedding light on a different facet of the economy. The field of macroeconomics is like a Swiss army knife—a set of complementary but distinct tools that can be applied in different ways in different circumstances.

This book presents many different models that address different questions and make different assumptions. Remember that a model is only as good as its assumptions and that an assumption that is useful for some purposes may be misleading for others. When using a model to address a question, the economist must keep in mind the underlying assumptions and judge whether they are reasonable for studying the matter at hand.

Prices: Flexible Versus Sticky

Throughout this book, one group of assumptions will prove especially important—those concerning the speed at which wages and prices adjust to changing economic conditions. Economists normally presume that the price of a good or a service moves quickly to bring quantity supplied and quantity demanded into balance. In other words, they assume that markets are normally in equilibrium, so the price of any good or service is found where the supply and demand curves intersect. This assumption, called **market clearing**, is central to the model of the pizza market discussed earlier. For answering most questions, economists use market-clearing models.

Yet the assumption of *continuous* market clearing is not entirely realistic. For markets to clear continuously, prices must adjust instantly to changes in supply and demand. In fact, many wages and prices adjust slowly. Labor contracts often set wages for up to three years. Many firms leave their product prices the same for long periods of time—for example, magazine publishers typically change their newsstand prices only every three or four years. Although market-clearing models assume that all wages and prices are **flexible**, in the real world some wages and prices are **sticky**.

The apparent stickiness of prices does not make market-clearing models useless. After all, prices are not stuck forever; eventually, they adjust to changes in supply and demand. Market-clearing models might not describe the economy at every instant, but they do describe the equilibrium toward which the economy gravitates. Therefore, most macroeconomists believe that price flexibility is a good assumption for studying long-run issues, such as the growth in real GDP that we observe from decade to decade.

For studying short-run issues, such as year-to-year fluctuations in real GDP and unemployment, the assumption of price flexibility is less plausible. Over short periods, many prices in the economy are fixed at predetermined levels. Therefore, most macroeconomists believe that price stickiness is a better assumption for studying the short-run behavior of the economy.

Microeconomic Thinking and Macroeconomic Models

Microeconomics is the study of how households and firms make decisions and how these decisionmakers interact in the marketplace. A central principle of microeconomics is that households and firms *optimize*—they do the best they can for themselves given their objectives and the constraints they face. In microeconomic models, households choose their purchases to maximize their level of satisfaction, which economists call *utility*, and firms make production decisions to maximize their profits.

Because economy-wide events arise from the interaction of many households and firms, macroeconomics and microeconomics are inextricably linked. When we study the economy as a whole, we must consider the decisions of individual economic actors. For example, to understand what determines total consumer spending, we must think about a family deciding how much to spend today and how much to save for the future. To understand what determines total investment spending, we must think about a firm deciding whether to build a new factory. Because aggregate variables are the sum of the variables describing many individual decisions, macroeconomic theory rests on a microeconomic foundation.

Although microeconomic decisions underlie all economic models, in many models the optimizing behavior of households and firms is implicit rather than explicit. The model of the pizza market we discussed earlier is an example. Households' decisions about how much pizza to buy underlie the demand for pizza, and pizzerias' decisions about how much pizza to produce underlie the supply of pizza. Presumably, households make their decisions to maximize utility, and pizzerias make their decisions to maximize profit. Yet the model does not focus on how these microeconomic decisions are made; instead, it leaves these decisions in the background. Similarly, although microeconomic decisions underlie macroeconomic phenomena, macroeconomic models do not necessarily focus on the optimizing behavior of households and firms, but instead sometimes leave that behavior in the background.

1-3 How This Book Proceeds

This book has six parts. This chapter and the next make up Part One, the "Introduction." Chapter 2 discusses how economists measure economic variables, such as aggregate income, the inflation rate, and the unemployment rate.

Part Two, "Classical Theory: The Economy in the Long Run," presents the classical model of how the economy works. The key assumption of the classical model is that prices are flexible. That is, with rare exceptions, the classical model assumes that markets clear. Because the assumption of price flexibility describes the economy only in the long run, classical theory is best suited for analyzing a time horizon of at least several years.

Part Three, "Growth Theory: The Economy in the Very Long Run," builds on the classical model. It maintains the assumptions of price flexibility and market clearing but adds a new emphasis on growth in the capital stock, the labor force, and technological knowledge. Growth theory is designed to explain how the economy evolves over a period of several decades.

Part Four, "Business Cycle Theory: The Economy in the Short Run," examines the behavior of the economy when prices are sticky. The non-market-clearing model developed here is designed to analyze short-run issues, such as the reasons for economic fluctuations and the influence of government policy on those fluctuations. It is best suited for analyzing the changes in the economy we observe from month to month or from year to year.

Part Five, "Macroeconomic Policy Debates," builds on the previous analysis to consider what role the government should have in the economy. It considers how, if at all, the government should respond to short-run fluctuations in real GDP and unemployment. It also examines the various views of how government debt affects the economy.

Part Six, "The Financial System," presents additional material at the intersection between macroeconomics and finance. In particular, it discusses banks and other financial institutions, financial markets for stocks and bonds, and the causes of and policy responses to financial crises. As the financial crisis of 2008–2009 has vividly reminded us, the financial system is a key piece of the larger macroeconomic picture. The goal of studying the financial system in detail is to refine our understanding of the aggregate economy.

Summary

1. Macroeconomics is the study of the economy as a whole, including growth in incomes, changes in prices, and the rate of unemployment. Macroeconomists attempt both to explain economic events and to devise policies to improve economic performance.

2. To understand the economy, economists use models—theories that simplify reality in order to reveal how exogenous variables influence endogenous variables. The art in the science of economics is in judging whether a

model captures the important economic relationships for the matter at hand. Because no single model can answer all questions, macroeconomists use different models to look at different issues.

3. A key feature of a macroeconomic model is whether it assumes that prices are flexible or sticky. According to most macroeconomists, models with flexible prices describe the economy in the long run, whereas models with sticky prices offer a better description of the economy in the short run.

4. Microeconomics is the study of how firms and individuals make decisions and how these decisionmakers interact. Because macroeconomic events arise from many microeconomic interactions, all macroeconomic models must be consistent with microeconomic foundations, even if those foundations are only implicit.

KEY CONCEPTS

Macroeconomics	Recession	Exogenous variables
Real GDP	Depression	Market clearing
Inflation and deflation	Models	Flexible and sticky prices
Unemployment	Endogenous variables	Microeconomics

QUESTIONS FOR REVIEW

1. Explain the difference between macroeconomics and microeconomics. How are these two fields related?

2. Why do economists build models?

3. What is a market-clearing model? When is it appropriate to assume that markets clear?

PROBLEMS AND APPLICATIONS

1. What macroeconomic issues have been in the news lately?

2. What do you think are the defining characteristics of a science? Does the study of the economy have these characteristics? Do you think macroeconomics should be called a science? Why or why not?

3. Use the model of supply and demand to explain how a fall in the price of frozen yogurt would

affect the price of ice cream and the quantity of ice cream sold. In your explanation, identify the exogenous and endogenous variables.

4. How often does the price you pay for a haircut change? What does your answer imply about the usefulness of market-clearing models for analyzing the market for haircuts?

CHAPTER 2

The Data of Macroeconomics

It is a capital mistake to theorize before one has data. Insensibly one begins to twist facts to suit theories, instead of theories to fit facts.

—Sherlock Holmes

Scientists, economists, and detectives have much in common: they all want to figure out what's going on in the world around them. To do this, they rely on theory and observation. They build theories in an attempt to make sense of what they see happening. They then turn to more systematic observation to evaluate the theories' validity. Only when theory and evidence come into line do they feel they understand the situation. This chapter discusses the types of observation that economists use to develop and test their theories.

Casual observation is one source of information about what's happening in the economy. When you go shopping, you see how fast prices are rising. When you look for a job, you learn whether firms are hiring. Because we are all participants in the economy, we get some sense of economic conditions as we go about our lives.

A century ago, economists monitoring the economy had little more to go on than casual observations. Such fragmentary information made economic policy-making all the more difficult. One person's anecdote would suggest the economy was moving in one direction, while a different person's anecdote would suggest it was moving in another. Economists needed some way to combine many individual experiences into a coherent whole. There was an obvious solution: as the old quip goes, the plural of "anecdote" is "data."

Today, economic data offer a systematic and objective source of information, and almost every day the newspaper has a story about some newly released statistic. Most of these statistics are produced by the government. Various government agencies survey households and firms to learn about their economic activity—how much they are earning, what they are buying, what prices they are charging, whether they have a job or are looking for work, and so on. From these surveys, various statistics are computed that summarize the state of the economy. Economists use these statistics to study the economy; policymakers use them to monitor developments and formulate policies.

This chapter focuses on the three statistics that economists and policymakers use most often. Gross domestic product, or GDP, tells us the nation's total income and the total expenditure on its output of goods and services. The consumer price index, or CPI, measures the level of prices. The unemployment rate tells us the fraction of workers who are unemployed. In the following pages, we see how these statistics are computed and what they tell us about the economy.

2-1 Measuring the Value of Economic Activity: Gross Domestic Product

Gross domestic product, or **GDP**, is often considered the best measure of how well the economy is performing. This statistic is computed every three months by the Bureau of Economic Analysis, a part of the U.S. Department of Commerce, from a large number of primary data sources. The primary sources include both administrative data, which are by-products of government functions such as tax collection, education programs, defense, and regulation, and statistical data, which come from government surveys of, for example, retail establishments, manufacturing firms, and farm activity. The purpose of GDP is to summarize all these data with a single number representing the dollar value of economic activity in a given period of time.

There are two ways to view this statistic. One way to view GDP is as *the total income of everyone in the economy*. Another way to view GDP is as *the total expenditure on the economy's output of goods and services*. From either viewpoint, it is clear why GDP is a gauge of economic performance. GDP measures something people care about—their incomes. Similarly, an economy with a large output of goods and services can better satisfy the demands of households, firms, and the government.

How can GDP measure both the economy's income and its expenditure on output? The reason is that these two quantities are really the same: for the economy as a whole, income must equal expenditure. That fact, in turn, follows from an even more fundamental one: because every transaction has a buyer and a seller, every dollar of expenditure by a buyer must become a dollar of income to a seller. When Joe paints Jane's house for $1,000, that $1,000 is income for Joe and expenditure by Jane. The transaction contributes $1,000 to GDP, regardless of whether we are adding up all income or all expenditure.

To understand the meaning of GDP more fully, we turn to **national income accounting**, the accounting system used to measure GDP and many related statistics.

Income, Expenditure, and the Circular Flow

Imagine an economy that produces a single good, bread, from a single input, labor. Figure 2-1 illustrates all the economic transactions that occur between households and firms in this economy.

The inner loop in Figure 2-1 represents the flows of bread and labor. The households sell their labor to the firms. The firms use the labor of their workers to produce bread, which the firms in turn sell to the households. Hence, labor flows from households to firms, and bread flows from firms to households.

FIGURE 2-1

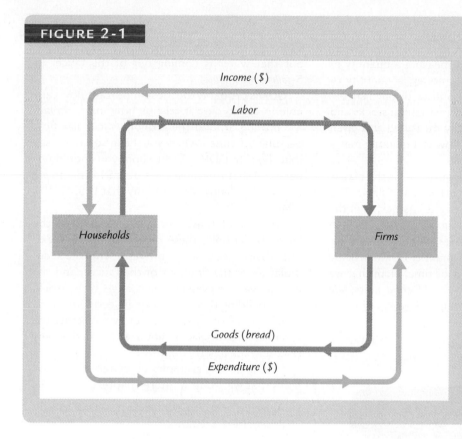

Income ($)

Labor

Households

Firms

Goods (bread)

Expenditure ($)

The Circular Flow
This figure illustrates the flows between firms and households in an economy that produces one good, bread, from one input, labor. The inner loop represents the flows of labor and bread: households sell their labor to firms, and the firms sell the bread they produce to households. The outer loop represents the corresponding flows of dollars: households pay the firms for the bread, and the firms pay wages and profit to the households. In this economy, GDP is both the total expenditure on bread and the total income from the production of bread.

The outer loop in Figure 2-1 represents the corresponding flow of dollars. The households buy bread from the firms. The firms use some of the revenue from these sales to pay the wages of their workers, and the remainder is the profit belonging to the owners of the firms (who themselves are part of the household sector). Hence, expenditure on bread flows from households to firms, and income in the form of wages and profit flows from firms to households.

GDP measures the flow of dollars in this economy. We can compute it in two ways. GDP is the total income from the production of bread, which equals the sum of wages and profit—the top half of the circular flow of dollars. GDP is also the total expenditure on purchases of bread—the bottom half of the circular flow of dollars. To compute GDP, we can look at either the flow of dollars from firms to households or the flow of dollars from households to firms.

These two ways of computing GDP must be equal because, by the rules of accounting, the expenditure of buyers on products is income to the sellers of those products. Every transaction that affects expenditure must affect income, and every transaction that affects income must affect expenditure. For example, suppose that a firm produces and sells one more loaf of bread to a household. Clearly this transaction raises total expenditure on bread, but it also has an equal effect on total income. If the firm produces the extra loaf without hiring any more labor (such as by making the production process more efficient), then profit increases. If the firm produces the extra loaf by hiring more labor, then wages increase. In both cases, expenditure and income increase equally.

Stocks and Flows

Many economic variables measure a quantity of something—a quantity of money, a quantity of goods, and so on. Economists distinguish between two types of quantity variables: stocks and flows. A **stock** is a quantity measured at a given point in time, whereas a **flow** is a quantity measured per unit of time.

A bathtub, shown in Figure 2-2, is the classic example used to illustrate stocks and flows. The amount of water in the tub is a stock: it is the quantity of water in the tub at a given point in time. The amount of water coming out of the faucet is a flow: it is the quantity of water being added to the tub per unit of time. Note that we measure stocks and flows in different units. We say that the bathtub contains 50 *gallons* of water but that water is coming out of the faucet at 5 *gallons per minute*.

GDP is probably the most important flow variable in economics: it tells us how many dollars are flowing around the economy's circular flow per unit of time. When you hear someone say that the U.S. GDP is $14 trillion, you should understand that this means that it is $14 trillion *per year*. (Equivalently, we could say that U.S. GDP is $444,000 per second.)

Stocks and flows are often related. In the bathtub example, these relationships are clear. The stock of water in the tub represents the accumulation of the flow out of the faucet, and the flow of water represents the change in the stock. When building theories to explain economic variables, it is often useful to determine whether the variables are stocks or flows and whether any relationships link them.

Here are some examples of related stocks and flows that we study in future chapters:

➤ A person's wealth is a stock; his income and expenditure are flows.

➤ The number of unemployed people is a stock; the number of people losing their jobs is a flow.

➤ The amount of capital in the economy is a stock; the amount of investment is a flow.

➤ The government debt is a stock; the government budget deficit is a flow.

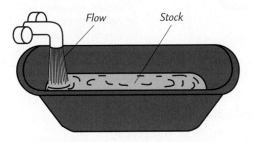

Flow   *Stock*

Figure 2-2 Stocks and Flows The amount of water in a bathtub is a stock: it is a quantity measured at a given moment in time. The amount of water coming out of the faucet is a flow: it is a quantity measured per unit of time.

Rules for Computing GDP

In an economy that produces only bread, we can compute GDP by adding up the total expenditure on bread. Real economies, however, include the production and sale of a vast number of goods and services. To compute GDP for such a complex economy, it will be helpful to have a more precise definition: *Gross domestic product (GDP) is the market value of all final goods and services produced within an economy in a given period of time.* To see how this definition is applied, let's discuss some of the rules that economists follow in constructing this statistic.

Adding Apples and Oranges The U.S. economy produces many different goods and services—hamburgers, haircuts, cars, computers, and so on. GDP combines the value of these goods and services into a single measure. The diversity of products in the economy complicates the calculation of GDP because different products have different values.

Suppose, for example, that the economy produces four apples and three oranges. How do we compute GDP? We could simply add apples and oranges and conclude that GDP equals seven pieces of fruit. But this makes sense only if we think apples and oranges have equal value, which is generally not true. (This would be even clearer if the economy had produced four watermelons and three grapes.)

To compute the total value of different goods and services, the national income accounts use market prices because these prices reflect how much people are willing to pay for a good or service. Thus, if apples cost $0.50 each and oranges cost $1.00 each, GDP would be

$$
\begin{aligned}
\text{GDP} &= (\text{Price of Apples} \times \text{Quantity of Apples}) \\
&\quad + (\text{Price of Oranges} \times \text{Quantity of Oranges}) \\
&= (\$0.50 \times 4) + (\$1.00 \times 3) \\
&= \$5.00.
\end{aligned}
$$

GDP equals $5.00—the value of all the apples, $2.00, plus the value of all the oranges, $3.00.

Used Goods When the Topps Company makes a package of baseball cards and sells it for 50 cents, that 50 cents is added to the nation's GDP. But what about when a collector sells a rare Mickey Mantle card to another collector for $500? That $500 is not part of GDP. GDP measures the value of currently produced goods and services. The sale of the Mickey Mantle card reflects the transfer of an asset, not an addition to the economy's income. Thus, the sale of used goods is not included as part of GDP.

The Treatment of Inventories Imagine that a bakery hires workers to produce more bread, pays their wages, and then fails to sell the additional bread. How does this transaction affect GDP?

The answer depends on what happens to the unsold bread. Let's first suppose that the bread spoils. In this case, the firm has paid more in wages but has not received any additional revenue, so the firm's profit is reduced by the amount that wages have increased. Total expenditure in the economy hasn't changed because no one buys the bread. Total income hasn't changed either—although more is distributed as wages and less as profit. Because the transaction affects neither expenditure nor income, it does not alter GDP.

Now suppose, instead, that the bread is put into inventory to be sold later. In this case, the transaction is treated differently. The owners of the firm are assumed to have "purchased" the bread for the firm's inventory, and the firm's profit is not reduced by the additional wages it has paid. Because the higher wages raise total income, and greater spending on inventory raises total expenditure, the economy's GDP rises.

What happens later when the firm sells the bread out of inventory? This case is much like the sale of a used good. There is spending by bread consumers, but there is inventory disinvestment by the firm. This negative spending by the firm offsets the positive spending by consumers, so the sale out of inventory does not affect GDP.

The general rule is that when a firm increases its inventory of goods, this investment in inventory is counted as an expenditure by the firm owners. Thus, production for inventory increases GDP just as much as production for final sale. A sale out of inventory, however, is a combination of positive spending (the purchase) and negative spending (inventory disinvestment), so it does not influence GDP. This treatment of inventories ensures that GDP reflects the economy's current production of goods and services.

Intermediate Goods and Value Added Many goods are produced in stages: raw materials are processed into intermediate goods by one firm and then sold to another firm for final processing. How should we treat such products when computing GDP? For example, suppose a cattle rancher sells one-quarter pound of meat to McDonald's for $0.50, and then McDonald's sells you a hamburger for $1.50. Should GDP include both the meat and the hamburger (a total of $2.00), or just the hamburger ($1.50)?

The answer is that GDP includes only the value of final goods. Thus, the hamburger is included in GDP but the meat is not: GDP increases by $1.50, not by $2.00. The reason is that the value of intermediate goods is already included as part of the market price of the final goods in which they are used. To add the intermediate goods to the final goods would be double counting—that is, the meat would be counted twice. Hence, GDP is the total value of final goods and services produced.

One way to compute the value of all final goods and services is to sum the value added at each stage of production. The **value added** of a firm equals the value of the firm's output less the value of the intermediate goods that the firm purchases. In the case of the hamburger, the value added of the rancher is $0.50 (assuming that the rancher bought no intermediate goods), and the value added of McDonald's is $1.50 − $0.50, or $1.00. Total value added is $0.50 + $1.00, which equals $1.50. For the economy as a whole, the sum of all value added must equal the value of all final goods and services. Hence, GDP is also the total value added of all firms in the economy.

Housing Services and Other Imputations Although most goods and services are valued at their market prices when computing GDP, some are not sold in the marketplace and therefore do not have market prices. If GDP is to include the value of these goods and services, we must use an estimate of their value. Such an estimate is called an **imputed value**.

Imputations are especially important for determining the value of housing. A person who rents a house is buying housing services and providing income for the landlord; the rent is part of GDP, both as expenditure by the renter and as income for the landlord. Many people, however, live in their own homes. Although they do not pay rent to a landlord, they are enjoying housing services similar to those that renters purchase. To take account of the housing services enjoyed by homeowners, GDP includes the "rent" that these homeowners "pay" to themselves. Of course, homeowners do not in fact pay themselves this rent.

The Department of Commerce estimates what the market rent for a house would be if it were rented and includes that imputed rent as part of GDP. This imputed rent is included both in the homeowner's expenditure and in the homeowner's income.

Imputations also arise in valuing government services. For example, police officers, firefighters, and senators provide services to the public. Giving a value to these services is difficult because they are not sold in a marketplace and therefore do not have a market price. The national income accounts include these services in GDP by valuing them at their cost. That is, the wages of these public servants are used as a measure of the value of their output.

In many cases, an imputation is called for in principle but, to keep things simple, is not made in practice. Because GDP includes the imputed rent on owner-occupied houses, one might expect it also to include the imputed rent on cars, lawn mowers, jewelry, and other durable goods owned by households. Yet the value of these rental services is left out of GDP. In addition, some of the output of the economy is produced and consumed at home and never enters the marketplace. For example, meals cooked at home are similar to meals cooked at a restaurant, yet the value added in meals at home is left out of GDP.

Finally, no imputation is made for the value of goods and services sold in the *underground economy*. The underground economy is the part of the economy that people hide from the government either because they wish to evade taxation or because the activity is illegal. Examples include domestic workers paid "off the books" and the illegal drug trade.

Because the imputations necessary for computing GDP are only approximate, and because the value of many goods and services is left out altogether, GDP is an imperfect measure of economic activity. These imperfections are most problematic when comparing standards of living across countries. The size of the underground economy, for instance, varies widely from country to country. Yet as long as the magnitude of these imperfections remains fairly constant over time, GDP is useful for comparing economic activity from year to year.

Real GDP Versus Nominal GDP

Economists use the rules just described to compute GDP, which values the economy's total output of goods and services. But is GDP a good measure of economic well-being? Consider once again the economy that produces only apples and oranges. In this economy GDP is the sum of the value of all the apples produced and the value of all the oranges produced. That is,

$$GDP = (\text{Price of Apples} \times \text{Quantity of Apples}) + (\text{Price of Oranges} \times \text{Quantity of Oranges}).$$

Economists call the value of goods and services measured at current prices **nominal GDP**. Notice that nominal GDP can increase either because prices rise or because quantities rise.

It is easy to see that GDP computed this way is not a good gauge of economic well-being. That is, this measure does not accurately reflect how well the economy can satisfy the demands of households, firms, and the government. If all prices doubled without any change in quantities, nominal GDP would double. Yet it would be misleading to say that the economy's ability to satisfy demands has doubled, because the quantity of every good produced remains the same.

A better measure of economic well-being would tally the economy's output of goods and services without being influenced by changes in prices. For this purpose, economists use **real GDP**, which is the value of goods and services measured using a constant set of prices. That is, real GDP shows what would have happened to expenditure on output if quantities had changed but prices had not.

To see how real GDP is computed, imagine we wanted to compare output in 2009 with output in subsequent years for our apple-and-orange economy. We could begin by choosing a set of prices, called *base-year prices*, such as the prices that prevailed in 2009. Goods and services are then added up using these base-year prices to value the different goods in each year. Real GDP for 2009 would be

Real GDP = (2009 Price of Apples × 2009 Quantity of Apples)
+ (2009 Price of Oranges × 2009 Quantity of Oranges).

Similarly, real GDP in 2010 would be

Real GDP = (2009 Price of Apples × 2010 Quantity of Apples)
+ (2009 Price of Oranges × 2010 Quantity of Oranges).

And real GDP in 2011 would be

Real GDP = (2009 Price of Apples × 2011 Quantity of Apples)
+ (2009 Price of Oranges × 2011 Quantity of Oranges).

Notice that 2009 prices are used to compute real GDP for all three years. Because the prices are held constant, real GDP varies from year to year only if the quantities produced vary. Because a society's ability to provide economic satisfaction for its members ultimately depends on the quantities of goods and services produced, real GDP provides a better measure of economic well-being than nominal GDP.

The GDP Deflator

From nominal GDP and real GDP we can compute a third statistic: the GDP deflator. The **GDP deflator**, also called the *implicit price deflator for GDP*, is the ratio of nominal GDP to real GDP:

$$\text{GDP Deflator} = \frac{\text{Nominal GDP}}{\text{Real GDP}}.$$

The GDP deflator reflects what's happening to the overall level of prices in the economy.

To better understand this, consider again an economy with only one good, bread. If P is the price of bread and Q is the quantity sold, then nominal GDP is the total number of dollars spent on bread in that year, $P \times Q$. Real GDP is the number of loaves of bread produced in that year times the price of bread in some base year, $P_{base} \times Q$. The GDP deflator is the price of bread in that year relative to the price of bread in the base year, P/P_{base}.

The definition of the GDP deflator allows us to separate nominal GDP into two parts: one part measures quantities (real GDP) and the other measures prices (the GDP deflator). That is,

$$\text{Nominal GDP} = \text{Real GDP} \times \text{GDP Deflator}.$$

Nominal GDP measures the current dollar value of the output of the economy. Real GDP measures output valued at constant prices. The GDP deflator measures the price of output relative to its price in the base year. We can also write this equation as

$$\text{Real GDP} = \frac{\text{Nominal GDP}}{\text{GDP Deflator}}.$$

In this form, you can see how the deflator earns its name: it is used to deflate (that is, take inflation out of) nominal GDP to yield real GDP.

Chain-Weighted Measures of Real GDP

We have been discussing real GDP as if the prices used to compute this measure never change from their base-year values. If this were truly the case, over time the prices would become more and more dated. For instance, the price of computers has fallen substantially in recent years, while the price of a year at college has risen. When valuing the production of computers and education, it would be misleading to use the prices that prevailed ten or twenty years ago.

To solve this problem, the Bureau of Economic Analysis used to periodically update the prices used to compute real GDP. About every five years, a new base year was chosen. The prices were then held fixed and used to measure year-to-year changes in the production of goods and services until the base year was updated once again.

In 1995, the Bureau announced a new policy for dealing with changes in the base year. In particular, it now uses *chain-weighted* measures of real GDP. With these new measures, the base year changes continuously over time. In essence, average prices in 2009 and 2010 are used to measure real growth from 2009 to 2010, average prices in 2010 and 2011 are used to measure real growth from 2010 to 2011, and so on. These various year-to-year growth rates are then put together to form a "chain" that can be used to compare the output of goods and services between any two dates.

This new chain-weighted measure of real GDP is better than the more traditional measure because it ensures that the prices used to compute real GDP are never far out of date. For most purposes, however, the differences are not significant. It turns out that the two measures of real GDP are highly correlated with each other. As a practical matter, both measures of real GDP reflect the same thing: economy-wide changes in the production of goods and services.

Two Arithmetic Tricks for Working With Percentage Changes

For manipulating many relationships in economics, there is an arithmetic trick that is useful to know: *the percentage change of a product of two variables is approximately the sum of the percentage changes in each of the variables.*

To see how this trick works, consider an example. Let P denote the GDP deflator and Y denote real GDP. Nominal GDP is $P \times Y$. The trick states that

$$\text{Percentage Change in } (P \times Y)$$
$$\approx (\text{Percentage Change in } P)$$
$$+ (\text{Percentage Change in } Y).$$

For instance, suppose that in one year, real GDP is 100 and the GDP deflator is 2; the next year, real GDP is 103 and the GDP deflator is 2.1. We can calculate that real GDP rose by 3 percent and that the GDP deflator rose by 5 percent. Nominal GDP rose from 200 the first year to 216.3 the second year, an increase of 8.15 percent. Notice that the growth in nominal GDP (8.15 percent) is approximately the sum of the growth in the GDP deflator (5 percent) and the growth in real GDP (3 percent).[1]

A second arithmetic trick follows as a corollary to the first: *the percentage change of a ratio is approximately the percentage change in the numerator minus the percentage change in the denominator.* Again, consider an example. Let Y denote GDP and L denote the population, so that Y/L is GDP per person. The second trick states that

$$\text{Percentage Change in } (Y/L)$$
$$\approx (\text{Percentage Change in } Y)$$
$$- (\text{Percentage Change in } L).$$

For instance, suppose that in the first year, Y is 100,000 and L is 100, so Y/L is 1,000; in the second year, Y is 110,000 and L is 103, so Y/L is 1,068. Notice that the growth in GDP per person (6.8 percent) is approximately the growth in income (10 percent) minus the growth in population (3 percent).

The Components of Expenditure

Economists and policymakers care not only about the economy's total output of goods and services but also about the allocation of this output among alternative uses. The national income accounts divide GDP into four broad categories of spending:

- Consumption (C)
- Investment (I)
- Government purchases (G)
- Net exports (NX).

Thus, letting Y stand for GDP,

$$Y = C + I + G + NX.$$

---

[1] *Mathematical note:* The proof that this trick works begins with the product rule from calculus:
$$d(PY) = Y\,dP + P\,dY.$$
Now divide both sides of this equation by PY to obtain:
$$d(PY)/(PY) = dP/P + dY/Y.$$
Notice that all three terms in this equation are percentage changes.

GDP is the sum of consumption, investment, government purchases, and net exports. Each dollar of GDP falls into one of these categories. This equation is an *identity* — an equation that must hold because of the way the variables are defined. It is called the **national income accounts identity**.

Consumption consists of the goods and services bought by households. It is divided into three subcategories: nondurable goods, durable goods, and services. Nondurable goods are goods that last only a short time, such as food and clothing. Durable goods are goods that last a long time, such as cars and TVs. Services include the work done for consumers by individuals and firms, such as haircuts and doctor visits.

Investment consists of goods bought for future use. Investment is also divided into three subcategories: business fixed investment, residential fixed investment, and inventory investment. Business fixed investment is the purchase of new plant and equipment by firms. Residential investment is the purchase of new housing by households and landlords. Inventory investment is the increase in firms' inventories of goods (if inventories are falling, inventory investment is negative).

Government purchases are the goods and services bought by federal, state, and local governments. This category includes such items as military equipment, highways, and the services provided by government workers. It does not include transfer payments to individuals, such as Social Security and welfare. Because transfer payments reallocate existing income and are not made in exchange for goods and services, they are not part of GDP.

FYI

What Is Investment?

Newcomers to macroeconomics are sometimes confused by how macroeconomists use familiar words in new and specific ways. One example is the term "investment." The confusion arises because what looks like investment for an individual may not be investment for the economy as a whole. The general rule is that the economy's investment does not include purchases that merely reallocate existing assets among different individuals. Investment, as macroeconomists use the term, creates new capital.

Let's consider some examples. Suppose we observe these two events:

➤ Smith buys himself a 100-year-old Victorian house.

➤ Jones builds herself a brand-new contemporary house.

What is total investment here? Two houses, one house, or zero?

A macroeconomist seeing these two transactions counts only the Jones house as investment.

Smith's transaction has not created new housing for the economy, it has merely reallocated existing housing. Smith's purchase is investment for Smith, but it is disinvestment for the person selling the house. By contrast, Jones has added new housing to the economy; her new house is counted as investment.

Similarly, consider these two events:

➤ Gates buys $5 million in IBM stock from Buffett on the New York Stock Exchange.

➤ General Motors sells $10 million in stock to the public and uses the proceeds to build a new car factory.

Here, investment is $10 million. In the first transaction, Gates is investing in IBM stock, and Buffett is disinvesting; there is no investment for the economy. By contrast, General Motors is using some of the economy's output of goods and services to add to its stock of capital; hence, its new factory is counted as investment.

The last category, **net exports**, accounts for trade with other countries. Net exports are the value of goods and services sold to other countries (exports) minus the value of goods and services that foreigners sell us (imports). Net exports are positive when the value of our exports is greater than the value of our imports and negative when the value of our imports is greater than the value of our exports. Net exports represent the net expenditure from abroad on our goods and services, which provides income for domestic producers.

CASE STUDY

GDP and Its Components

In 2009 the GDP of the United States totaled about $14.3 trillion. This number is so large that it is almost impossible to comprehend. We can make it easier to understand by dividing it by the 2009 U.S. population of 307 million. In this way, we obtain GDP per person—the amount of expenditure for the average American—which equaled $46,372 in 2009.

How did this GDP get used? Table 2-1 shows that about two-thirds of it, or $32,823 per person, was spent on consumption. Investment was $5,278 per

TABLE 2-1

GDP and the Components of Expenditure: 2009

	Total (billions of dollars)	Per Person (dollars)
Gross Domestic Product	14,259	46,372
Consumption	10,093	32,823
Nondurable goods	2,223	7,231
Durable goods	1,034	3,364
Services	6,835	22,229
Investment	1,623	5,278
Nonresidential fixed investment	1,387	4,510
Residential fixed investment	361	1,175
Inventory investment	−125	−407
Government Purchases	2,933	9,540
Federal	1,145	3,723
Defense	779	2,534
Nondefense	366	1,190
State and local	1,788	5,816
Net Exports	−390	−1,269
Exports	1,560	5,073
Imports	1,950	6,342

Source: U.S. Department of Commerce.

person. Government purchases were $9,540 per person, $2,534 of which was spent by the federal government on national defense.

The average American bought $6,342 of goods imported from abroad and produced $5,073 of goods that were exported to other countries. Because the average American imported more than he exported, net exports were negative. Furthermore, because the average American earned less from selling to foreigners than he spent on foreign goods, he must have financed the difference by taking out loans from foreigners (or, equivalently, by selling them some of his assets). Thus, the average American borrowed $1,269 from abroad in 2009. ∎

Other Measures of Income

The national income accounts include other measures of income that differ slightly in definition from GDP. It is important to be aware of the various measures, because economists and the press often refer to them.

To see how the alternative measures of income relate to one another, we start with GDP and add or subtract various quantities. To obtain *gross national product (GNP)*, we add receipts of factor income (wages, profit, and rent) from the rest of the world and subtract payments of factor income to the rest of the world:

GNP = GDP + Factor Payments from Abroad − Factor Payments to Abroad.

Whereas GDP measures the total income produced *domestically*, GNP measures the total income earned by *nationals* (residents of a nation). For instance, if a Japanese resident owns an apartment building in New York, the rental income he earns is part of U.S. GDP because it is earned in the United States. But because this rental income is a factor payment to abroad, it is not part of U.S. GNP. In the United States, factor payments from abroad and factor payments to abroad are similar in size—each representing about 3 percent of GDP—so GDP and GNP are quite close.

To obtain *net national product (NNP)*, we subtract the depreciation of capital—the amount of the economy's stock of plants, equipment, and residential structures that wears out during the year:

$$NNP = GNP - Depreciation.$$

In the national income accounts, depreciation is called the *consumption of fixed capital*. It equals about 10 percent of GNP. Because the depreciation of capital is a cost of producing the output of the economy, subtracting depreciation shows the net result of economic activity.

Net national product is approximately equal to another measure called *national income*. The two differ by a small correction called the *statistical discrepancy*, which arises because different data sources may not be completely consistent. National income is another measure of how much everyone in the economy has earned.

The national income accounts divide national income into six components, depending on who earns the income. The six categories, and the percentage of national income paid in each category in 2008, are

- *Compensation of employees* (63.6%). The wages and fringe benefits earned by workers.

- *Proprietors' income* (8.8%). The income of noncorporate businesses, such as small farms, mom-and-pop stores, and law partnerships.

- *Rental income* (1.7%). The income that landlords receive, including the imputed rent that homeowners "pay" to themselves, less expenses, such as depreciation.

- *Corporate profits* (10.8%). The income of corporations after payments to their workers and creditors.

- *Net interest* (6.5%). The interest domestic businesses pay minus the interest they receive, plus interest earned from foreigners.

- *Indirect business taxes* (8.3%). Certain taxes on businesses, such as sales taxes, less offsetting business subsidies. These taxes place a wedge between the price that consumers pay for a good and the price that firms receive.

A series of adjustments takes us from national income to *personal income*, the amount of income that households and noncorporate businesses receive. Four of these adjustments are most important. First, we subtract indirect business taxes, because these taxes never enter anyone's income. Second, we reduce national income by the amount that corporations earn but do not pay out, either because the corporations are retaining earnings or because they are paying taxes to the government. This adjustment is made by subtracting corporate profits (which equals the sum of corporate taxes, dividends, and retained earnings) and adding back dividends. Third, we increase national income by the net amount the government pays out in transfer payments. This adjustment equals government transfers to individuals minus social insurance contributions paid to the government. Fourth, we adjust national income to include the interest that households earn rather than the interest that businesses pay. This adjustment is made by adding personal interest income and subtracting net interest. (The difference between personal interest and net interest arises in part because interest on the government debt is part of the interest that households earn but is not part of the interest that businesses pay out.) Thus,

$$
\begin{aligned}
\text{Personal Income} = {} & \text{National Income} \\
& - \text{Indirect Business Taxes} \\
& - \text{Corporate Profits} \\
& - \text{Social Insurance Contributions} \\
& - \text{Net Interest} \\
& + \text{Dividends} \\
& + \text{Government Transfers to Individuals} \\
& + \text{Personal Interest Income.}
\end{aligned}
$$

Next, if we subtract personal tax payments and certain nontax payments to the government (such as parking tickets), we obtain *disposable personal income*:

Disposable Personal Income
= Personal Income − Personal Tax and Nontax Payments.

We are interested in disposable personal income because it is the amount households and noncorporate businesses have available to spend after satisfying their tax obligations to the government.

Seasonal Adjustment

Because real GDP and the other measures of income reflect how well the economy is performing, economists are interested in studying the quarter-to-quarter fluctuations in these variables. Yet when we start to do so, one fact leaps out: all these measures of income exhibit a regular seasonal pattern. The output of the economy rises during the year, reaching a peak in the fourth quarter (October, November, and December) and then falling in the first quarter (January, February, and March) of the next year. These regular seasonal changes are substantial. From the fourth quarter to the first quarter, real GDP falls on average about 8 percent.[2]

It is not surprising that real GDP follows a seasonal cycle. Some of these changes are attributable to changes in our ability to produce: for example, building homes is more difficult during the cold weather of winter than during other seasons. In addition, people have seasonal tastes: they have preferred times for such activities as vacations and Christmas shopping.

When economists study fluctuations in real GDP and other economic variables, they often want to eliminate the portion of fluctuations due to predictable seasonal changes. You will find that most of the economic statistics reported in the newspaper are *seasonally adjusted*. This means that the data have been adjusted to remove the regular seasonal fluctuations. (The precise statistical procedures used are too elaborate to bother with here, but in essence they involve subtracting those changes in income that are predictable just from the change in season.) Therefore, when you observe a rise or fall in real GDP or any other data series, you must look beyond the seasonal cycle for the explanation.

2-2 Measuring the Cost of Living: The Consumer Price Index

A dollar today doesn't buy as much as it did twenty years ago. The cost of almost everything has gone up. This increase in the overall level of prices is called *inflation*, and it is one of the primary concerns of economists and policymakers. In later chapters we examine in detail the causes and effects of inflation. Here we discuss how economists measure changes in the cost of living.

---

[2] Robert B. Barsky and Jeffrey A. Miron, "The Seasonal Cycle and the Business Cycle," *Journal of Political Economy* 97 (June 1989): 503–534.

The Price of a Basket of Goods

The most commonly used measure of the level of prices is the **consumer price index (CPI)**. The Bureau of Labor Statistics, which is part of the U.S. Department of Labor, has the job of computing the CPI. It begins by collecting the prices of thousands of goods and services. Just as GDP turns the quantities of many goods and services into a single number measuring the value of production, the CPI turns the prices of many goods and services into a single index measuring the overall level of prices.

How should economists aggregate the many prices in the economy into a single index that reliably measures the price level? They could simply compute an average of all prices. Yet this approach would treat all goods and services equally. Because people buy more chicken than caviar, the price of chicken should have a greater weight in the CPI than the price of caviar. The Bureau of Labor Statistics weights different items by computing the price of a basket of goods and services purchased by a typical consumer. The CPI is the price of this basket of goods and services relative to the price of the same basket in some base year.

For example, suppose that the typical consumer buys 5 apples and 2 oranges every month. Then the basket of goods consists of 5 apples and 2 oranges, and the CPI is

$$\text{CPI} = \frac{(5 \times \text{Current Price of Apples}) + (2 \times \text{Current Price of Oranges})}{(5 \times 2009 \text{ Price of Apples}) + (2 \times 2009 \text{ Price of Oranges})}.$$

In this CPI, 2009 is the base year. The index tells us how much it costs now to buy 5 apples and 2 oranges relative to how much it cost to buy the same basket of fruit in 2009.

The consumer price index is the most closely watched index of prices, but it is not the only such index. Another is the producer price index, which measures the price of a typical basket of goods bought by firms rather than consumers. In addition to these overall price indexes, the Bureau of Labor Statistics computes price indexes for specific types of goods, such as food, housing, and energy. Another statistic, sometimes called *core inflation*, measures the increase in price of a consumer basket that excludes food and energy products. Because food and energy prices exhibit substantial short-run volatility, core inflation is sometimes viewed as a better gauge of ongoing inflation trends.

The CPI Versus the GDP Deflator

Earlier in this chapter we saw another measure of prices—the implicit price deflator for GDP, which is the ratio of nominal GDP to real GDP. The GDP deflator and the CPI give somewhat different information about what's happening to the overall level of prices in the economy. There are three key differences between the two measures.

The first difference is that the GDP deflator measures the prices of all goods and services produced, whereas the CPI measures the prices of only the goods and services bought by consumers. Thus, an increase in the price of goods bought only by firms or the government will show up in the GDP deflator but not in the CPI.

The second difference is that the GDP deflator includes only those goods produced domestically. Imported goods are not part of GDP and do not show up in the GDP deflator. Hence, an increase in the price of a Toyota made in Japan and sold in this country affects the CPI, because the Toyota is bought by consumers, but it does not affect the GDP deflator.

The third and most subtle difference results from the way the two measures aggregate the many prices in the economy. The CPI assigns fixed weights to the prices of different goods, whereas the GDP deflator assigns changing weights. In other words, the CPI is computed using a fixed basket of goods, whereas the GDP deflator allows the basket of goods to change over time as the composition of GDP changes. The following example shows how these approaches differ. Suppose that major frosts destroy the nation's orange crop. The quantity of oranges produced falls to zero, and the price of the few oranges that remain on grocers' shelves is driven sky-high. Because oranges are no longer part of GDP, the increase in the price of oranges does not show up in the GDP deflator. But because the CPI is computed with a fixed basket of goods that includes oranges, the increase in the price of oranges causes a substantial rise in the CPI.

Economists call a price index with a fixed basket of goods a *Laspeyres index* and a price index with a changing basket a *Paasche index*. Economic theorists have studied the properties of these different types of price indexes to determine which is a better measure of the cost of living. The answer, it turns out, is that neither is clearly superior. When prices of different goods are changing by different amounts, a Laspeyres (fixed basket) index tends to overstate the increase in the cost of living because it does not take into account the fact that consumers have the opportunity to substitute less expensive goods for more expensive ones. By contrast, a Paasche (changing basket) index tends to understate the increase in the cost of living. Although it accounts for the substitution of alternative goods, it does not reflect the reduction in consumers' welfare that may result from such substitutions.

The example of the destroyed orange crop shows the problems with Laspeyres and Paasche price indexes. Because the CPI is a Laspeyres index, it overstates the impact of the increase in orange prices on consumers: by using a fixed basket of goods, it ignores consumers' ability to substitute apples for oranges. By contrast, because the GDP deflator is a Paasche index, it understates the impact on consumers: the GDP deflator shows no rise in prices, yet surely the higher price of oranges makes consumers worse off.[3]

Luckily, the difference between the GDP deflator and the CPI is usually not large in practice. Figure 2-3 shows the percentage change in the GDP deflator and the percentage change in the CPI for each year from 1948 to 2009. Both measures usually tell the same story about how quickly prices are rising.

---

[3] Because a Laspeyres index overstates inflation and a Paasche index understates inflation, one might strike a compromise by taking an average of the two measured rates of inflation. This is the approach taken by another type of index, called a *Fisher index*.

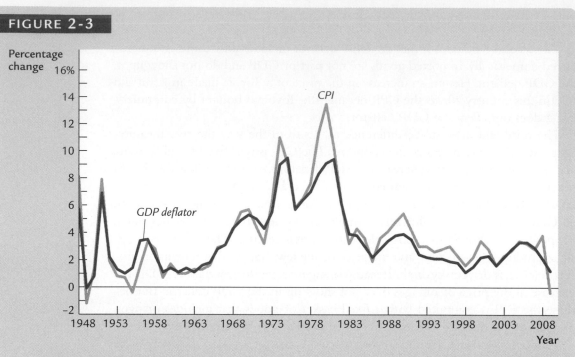

FIGURE 2-3

Percentage
change 16%

CPI

GDP deflator

14
12
10
8
6
4
2
0
-2

1948 1953 1958 1963 1968 1973 1978 1983 1988 1993 1998 2003 2008

Year

The GDP Deflator and the CPI This figure shows the percentage change in the GDP deflator and in the CPI for every year from 1948 to 2009. Although these two measures of prices diverge at times, they usually tell the same story about how quickly prices are rising. Both the CPI and the GDP deflator show that prices rose slowly in most of the 1950s and 1960s, that they rose much more quickly in the 1970s, and that they have risen slowly again since the mid-1980s.

Source: U.S. Department of Commerce and U.S. Department of Labor.

CASE STUDY

Does the CPI Overstate Inflation?

The consumer price index is a closely watched measure of inflation. Policymakers in the Federal Reserve monitor the CPI when choosing monetary policy. In addition, many laws and private contracts have cost-of-living allowances, called *COLAs*, which use the CPI to adjust for changes in the price level. For instance, Social Security benefits are adjusted automatically every year so that inflation will not erode the living standard of the elderly.

Because so much depends on the CPI, it is important to ensure that this measure of the price level is accurate. Many economists believe that, for a number of reasons, the CPI tends to overstate inflation.

One problem is the substitution bias we have already discussed. Because the CPI measures the price of a fixed basket of goods, it does not reflect the ability of consumers to substitute toward goods whose relative prices have fallen. Thus, when relative prices change, the true cost of living rises less rapidly than the CPI.

A second problem is the introduction of new goods. When a new good is introduced into the marketplace, consumers are better off, because they have more products from which to choose. In effect, the introduction of new goods increases the real value of the dollar. Yet this increase in the purchasing power of the dollar is not reflected in a lower CPI.

A third problem is unmeasured changes in quality. When a firm changes the quality of a good it sells, not all of the good's price change reflects a change in the cost of living. The Bureau of Labor Statistics does its best to account for changes in the quality of goods over time. For example, if Ford increases the horsepower of a particular car model from one year to the next, the CPI will reflect the change: the quality-adjusted price of the car will not rise as fast as the unadjusted price. Yet many changes in quality, such as comfort or safety, are hard to measure. If unmeasured quality improvement (rather than unmeasured quality deterioration) is typical, then the measured CPI rises faster than it should.

Because of these measurement problems, some economists have suggested revising laws to reduce the degree of indexation. For example, Social Security benefits could be indexed to CPI inflation minus 1 percent. Such a change would provide a rough way of offsetting these measurement problems. At the same time, it would automatically slow the growth in government spending.

In 1995, the Senate Finance Committee appointed a panel of five noted economists—Michael Boskin, Ellen Dulberger, Robert Gordon, Zvi Griliches, and Dale Jorgenson—to study the magnitude of the measurement error in the CPI. The panel concluded that the CPI was biased upward by 0.8 to 1.6 percentage points per year, with their "best estimate" being 1.1 percentage points. This report led to some changes in the way the CPI is calculated, so the bias is now thought to be under 1 percentage point. The CPI still overstates inflation, but not by as much as it once did.[4] ■

2-3 Measuring Joblessness: The Unemployment Rate

One aspect of economic performance is how well an economy uses its resources. Because an economy's workers are its chief resource, keeping workers employed is a paramount concern of economic policymakers. The unemployment rate is the statistic that measures the percentage of those people wanting to work who do not have jobs. Every month, the U.S. Bureau of Labor Statistics computes the unemployment rate and many other statistics that economists and policymakers use to monitor developments in the labor market.

---

[4] For further discussion of these issues, see Matthew Shapiro and David Wilcox, "Mismeasurement in the Consumer Price Index: An Evaluation," *NBER Macroeconomics Annual*, 1996, and the symposium on "Measuring the CPI" in the Winter 1998 issue of *The Journal of Economic Perspectives*.

The Household Survey

The unemployment rate comes from a survey of about 60,000 households called the Current Population Survey. Based on the responses to survey questions, each adult (age 16 and older) in each household is placed into one of three categories:

- *Employed*: This category includes those who at the time of the survey worked as paid employees, worked in their own business, or worked as unpaid workers in a family member's business. It also includes those who were not working but who had jobs from which they were temporarily absent because of, for example, vacation, illness, or bad weather.

- *Unemployed*: This category includes those who were not employed, were available for work, and had tried to find employment during the previous four weeks. It also includes those waiting to be recalled to a job from which they had been laid off.

- *Not in the labor force*: This category includes those who fit neither of the first two categories, such as a full-time student, homemaker, or retiree.

Notice that a person who wants a job but has given up looking—a *discouraged worker*—is counted as not being in the labor force.

The **labor force** is defined as the sum of the employed and unemployed, and the **unemployment rate** is defined as the percentage of the labor force that is unemployed. That is,

$$\text{Labor Force} = \text{Number of Employed} + \text{Number of Unemployed},$$

and

$$\text{Unemployment Rate} = \frac{\text{Number of Unemployed}}{\text{Labor Force}} \times 100.$$

A related statistic is the **labor-force participation rate**, the percentage of the adult population that is in the labor force:

$$\text{Labor-Force Participation Rate} = \frac{\text{Labor Force}}{\text{Adult Population}} \times 100.$$

The Bureau of Labor Statistics computes these statistics for the overall population and for groups within the population: men and women, whites and blacks, teenagers and prime-age workers.

Figure 2-4 shows the breakdown of the population into the three categories for December 2009. The statistics broke down as follows:

$$\text{Labor Force} = 137.8 + 15.3 = 153.1 \text{ million.}$$

$$\text{Unemployment Rate} = (15.3/153.1) \times 100 = 10.0\%.$$

$$\text{Labor-Force Participation Rate} = (153.1/236.9) \times 100 = 64.6\%.$$

Hence, about two-thirds of the adult population was in the labor force, and about 10 percent of those in the labor force did not have a job.

FIGURE 2-4

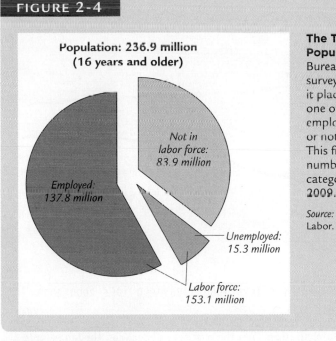

Population: 236.9 million
(16 years and older)

Not in
labor force:
83.9 million

Employed:
137.8 million

Unemployed:
15.3 million

Labor force:
153.1 million

The Three Groups of the Population When the Bureau of Labor Statistics surveys the population, it places all adults into one of three categories: employed, unemployed, or not in the labor force. This figure shows the number of people in each category in December 2009.

Source: U.S. Department of Labor.

CASE STUDY

Trends in Labor-Force Participation

The data on the labor market collected by the Bureau of Labor Statistics reflect not only economic developments, such as the booms and busts of the business cycle, but also a variety of social changes. Longer-term social changes in the roles of men and women in society, for example, are evident in the data on labor-force participation.

Figure 2-5 shows the labor-force participation rates of men and women in the United States from 1950 to 2009. Just after World War II, men and women had very different economic roles. Only 34 percent of women were working or looking for work, in contrast to 86 percent of men. Since then, the difference between the participation rates of men and women has gradually diminished, as growing numbers of women have entered the labor force and some men have left it. Data for 2009 show that 59 percent of women were in the labor force, in contrast to 72 percent of men. As measured by labor-force participation, men and women are now playing a more equal role in the economy.

There are many reasons for this change. In part, it is due to new technologies, such as the washing machine, clothes dryer, refrigerator, freezer, and dishwasher, that have reduced the amount of time required to complete routine household tasks. In part, it is due to improved birth control, which has reduced the number of children born to the typical family. And in part, this change in women's role is due to changing political and social attitudes. Together these developments have had a profound impact, as demonstrated by these data.

Although the increase in women's labor-force participation is easily explained, the fall in men's participation may seem puzzling. There are several developments

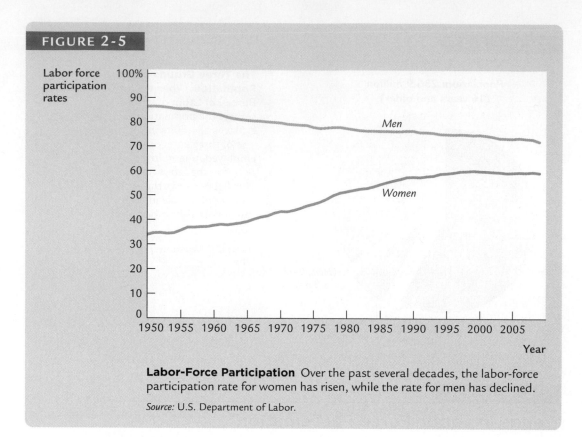

FIGURE 2-5

Labor force participation rates

Labor-Force Participation Over the past several decades, the labor-force participation rate for women has risen, while the rate for men has declined.

Source: U.S. Department of Labor.

at work. First, young men now stay in school longer than their fathers and grand-fathers did. Second, older men now retire earlier and live longer. Third, with more women employed, more fathers now stay at home to raise their children. Full-time students, retirees, and stay-at-home fathers are all counted as out of the labor force.

Looking ahead, many economists believe that labor-force participation for both men and women may gradually decline over the next several decades. The reason is demographic. People today are living longer and having fewer children than did their counterparts in previous generations. As a result, the elderly are representing an increasing share of the population. Because the elderly are more often retired and less often members of the labor force, the rising elderly share of the population will tend to reduce the economy's labor-force participation rate. ■

The Establishment Survey

When the Bureau of Labor Statistics (BLS) reports the unemployment rate every month, it also reports a variety of other statistics describing conditions in the labor market. Some of these statistics, such as the labor-force participation rate, are derived from the Current Population Survey. Other statistics come from a separate survey of about 160,000 business establishments that employ over 40 million workers. When you read a headline that says the economy created a certain number of jobs last month, that statistic is the change in the number of workers that businesses report having on their payrolls.

Because the BLS conducts two surveys of labor-market conditions, it produces two measures of total employment. From the household survey, it obtains an estimate of the number of people who say they are working. From the establishment survey, it obtains an estimate of the number of workers firms have on their payrolls.

One might expect these two measures of employment to be identical, but that is not the case. Although they are positively correlated, the two measures can diverge, especially over short periods of time. A particularly large divergence occurred in the early 2000s, as the economy recovered from the recession of 2001. From November 2001 to August 2003, the establishment survey showed a decline in employment of 1.0 million, while the household survey showed an increase of 1.4 million. Some commentators said the economy was experiencing a "jobless recovery," but this description applied only to the establishment data, not to the household data.

Why might these two measures of employment diverge? Part of the explanation is that the surveys measure different things. For example, a person who runs his or her own business is self-employed. The household survey counts that person as working, whereas the establishment survey does not, because that person does not show up on any firm's payroll. As another example, a person who holds two jobs is counted as one employed person in the household survey but is counted twice in the establishment survey, because that person would show up on the payroll of two firms.

Another part of the explanation for the divergence is that surveys are imperfect. For example, when new firms start up, it may take some time before those firms are included in the establishment survey. The BLS tries to estimate employment at start-ups, but the model it uses to produce these estimates is one possible source of error. A different problem arises from how the household survey extrapolates employment among the surveyed households to the entire population. If the BLS uses incorrect estimates of the size of the population, these errors will be reflected in its estimates of household employment. One possible source of incorrect population estimates is changes in the rate of immigration, both legal and illegal.

In the end, the divergence between the household and establishment surveys from 2001 to 2003 remains a mystery. Some economists believe that the establishment survey is the more accurate one because it has a larger sample. Yet one recent study suggests that the best measure of employment is an average of the two surveys.[5]

More important than the specifics of these surveys or this particular episode when they diverged is the broader lesson: all economic statistics are imperfect. Although they contain valuable information about what is happening in the economy, each one should be interpreted with a healthy dose of caution and a bit of skepticism.

---

[5] George Perry, "Gauging Employment: Is the Professional Wisdom Wrong?," *Brookings Papers on Economic Activity* (2005): 2.

2-4 Conclusion: From Economic Statistics to Economic Models

The three statistics discussed in this chapter—gross domestic product, the consumer price index, and the unemployment rate—quantify the performance of the economy. Public and private decisionmakers use these statistics to monitor changes in the economy and to formulate appropriate policies. Economists use these statistics to develop and test theories about how the economy works.

In the chapters that follow, we examine some of these theories. That is, we build models that explain how these variables are determined and how economic policy affects them. Having learned how to measure economic performance, we are now ready to learn how to explain it.

Summary

1. Gross domestic product (GDP) measures the income of everyone in the economy and, equivalently, the total expenditure on the economy's output of goods and services.

2. Nominal GDP values goods and services at current prices. Real GDP values goods and services at constant prices. Real GDP rises only when the amount of goods and services has increased, whereas nominal GDP can rise either because output has increased or because prices have increased.

3. GDP is the sum of four categories of expenditure: consumption, investment, government purchases, and net exports.

4. The consumer price index (CPI) measures the price of a fixed basket of goods and services purchased by a typical consumer. Like the GDP deflator, which is the ratio of nominal GDP to real GDP, the CPI measures the overall level of prices.

5. The labor-force participation rate shows the fraction of adults who are working or want to work. The unemployment rate shows what fraction of those who would like to work do not have a job.

KEY CONCEPTS

Gross domestic product (GDP)	GDP deflator	Net exports
National income accounting	National income accounts identity	Consumer price index (CPI)
Stocks and flows		Labor force
Value added	Consumption	Unemployment rate
Imputed value	Investment	Labor-force participation rate
Nominal versus real GDP	Government purchases	

QUESTIONS FOR REVIEW

1. List the two things that GDP measures. How can GDP measure two things at once?

2. What does the consumer price index measure?

3. List the three categories used by the Bureau of Labor Statistics to classify everyone in the economy. How does the Bureau compute the unemployment rate?

4. Describe the two ways the Bureau of Labor Statistics measures total employment.

PROBLEMS AND APPLICATIONS

1. Look at the newspapers for the past few days. What new economic statistics have been released? How do you interpret these statistics?

2. A farmer grows a bushel of wheat and sells it to a miller for $1.00. The miller turns the wheat into flour and then sells the flour to a baker for $3.00. The baker uses the flour to make bread and sells the bread to an engineer for $6.00. The engineer eats the bread. What is the value added by each person? What is GDP?

3. Suppose a woman marries her butler. After they are married, her husband continues to wait on her as before, and she continues to support him as before (but as a husband rather than as an employee). How does the marriage affect GDP? How should it affect GDP?

4. Place each of the following transactions in one of the four components of expenditure: consumption, investment, government purchases, and net exports.

   a. Boeing sells an airplane to the Air Force.

   b. Boeing sells an airplane to American Airlines.

   c. Boeing sells an airplane to Air France.

   d. Boeing sells an airplane to Amelia Earhart.

   e. Boeing builds an airplane to be sold next year.

5. Find data on GDP and its components, and compute the percentage of GDP for the following components for 1950, 1980, and the most recent year available.

   a. Personal consumption expenditures

   b. Gross private domestic investment

   c. Government purchases

   d. Net exports

   e. National defense purchases

   f. State and local purchases

   g. Imports

   Do you see any stable relationships in the data? Do you see any trends? (*Hint:* A good place to look for data is the statistical appendices of the *Economic Report of the President*, which is written each year by the Council of Economic Advisers. Alternatively, you can go to www.bea.gov, which is the Web site of the Bureau of Economic Analysis.)

6. Consider an economy that produces and consumes bread and automobiles. In the following table are data for two different years:

	2000		2010	
Good	Quantity	Price	Quantity	Price
Automobiles	100	$50,000	120	$60,000
Bread	500,000	$10	400,000	$20

   a. Using the year 2000 as the base year, compute the following statistics for each year: nominal GDP, real GDP, the implicit price deflator for GDP, and a fixed-weight price index such as the CPI.

   b. How much did prices rise between 2000 and 2010? Compare the answers given by the Laspeyres and Paasche price indexes. Explain the difference.

   c. Suppose you are a senator writing a bill to index Social Security and federal pensions. That is, your bill will adjust these benefits to offset changes in the cost of living. Will you use the GDP deflator or the CPI? Why?

7. Abby consumes only apples. In year 1, red apples cost $1 each, green apples cost $2 each, and Abby buys 10 red apples. In year 2, red apples cost $2, green apples cost $1, and Abby buys 10 green apples.

   a. Compute a consumer price index for apples for each year. Assume that year 1 is the base year in which the consumer basket is fixed. How does your index change from year 1 to year 2?

   b. Compute Abby's nominal spending on apples in each year. How does it change from year 1 to year 2?

   c. Using year 1 as the base year, compute Abby's real spending on apples in each year. How does it change from year 1 to year 2?

   d. Defining the implicit price deflator as nominal spending divided by real spending, compute the deflator for each year. How does the deflator change from year 1 to year 2?

   e. Suppose that Abby is equally happy eating red or green apples. How much has the true cost of living increased for Abby? Compare this answer to your answers to parts (a) and (d). What does this example tell you about Laspeyres and Paasche price indexes?

8. Consider how each of the following events is likely to affect real GDP. Do you think the change in real GDP reflects a similar change in economic well-being?

   a. A hurricane in Florida forces Disney World to shut down for a month.

   b. The discovery of a new, easy-to-grow strain of wheat increases farm harvests.

   c. Increased hostility between unions and management sparks a rash of strikes.

   d. Firms throughout the economy experience falling demand, causing them to lay off workers.

   e. Congress passes new environmental laws that prohibit firms from using production methods that emit large quantities of pollution.

   f. More high-school students drop out of school to take jobs mowing lawns.

   g. Fathers around the country reduce their workweeks to spend more time with their children.

9. In a speech that Senator Robert Kennedy gave when he was running for president in 1968, he said the following about GDP:

   > [It] does not allow for the health of our children, the quality of their education, or the joy of their play. It does not include the beauty of our poetry or the strength of our marriages, the intelligence of our public debate or the integrity of our public officials. It measures neither our courage, nor our wisdom, nor our devotion to our country. It measures everything, in short, except that which makes life worthwhile, and it can tell us everything about America except why we are proud that we are Americans.

   Was Robert Kennedy right? If so, why do we care about GDP?

PART II

Classical Theory: The Economy in the Long Run

National Income: Where It Comes From and Where It Goes

A large income is the best recipe for happiness I ever heard of.

—*Jane Austen*

The most important macroeconomic variable is gross domestic product (GDP). As we have seen, GDP measures both a nation's total output of goods and services and its total income. To appreciate the significance of GDP, one need only take a quick look at international data: compared with their poorer counterparts, nations with a high level of GDP per person have everything from better childhood nutrition to more televisions per household. A large GDP does not ensure that all of a nation's citizens are happy, but it may be the best recipe for happiness that macroeconomists have to offer.

This chapter addresses four groups of questions about the sources and uses of a nation's GDP:

- How much do the firms in the economy produce? What determines a nation's total income?

- Who gets the income from production? How much goes to compensate workers, and how much goes to compensate owners of capital?

- Who buys the output of the economy? How much do households purchase for consumption, how much do households and firms purchase for investment, and how much does the government buy for public purposes?

- What equilibrates the demand for and supply of goods and services? What ensures that desired spending on consumption, investment, and government purchases equals the level of production?

To answer these questions, we must examine how the various parts of the economy interact.

A good place to start is the circular flow diagram. In Chapter 2 we traced the circular flow of dollars in a hypothetical economy that used one input (labor services) to produce one output (bread). Figure 3-1 more accurately reflects how real economies function. It shows the linkages among the economic actors—households, firms, and the government—and how dollars flow among them through the various markets in the economy.

FIGURE 3-1

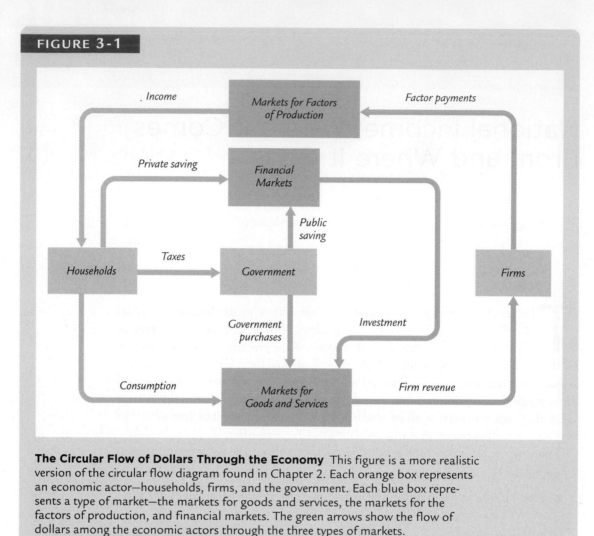

The Circular Flow of Dollars Through the Economy This figure is a more realistic version of the circular flow diagram found in Chapter 2. Each orange box represents an economic actor—households, firms, and the government. Each blue box represents a type of market—the markets for goods and services, the markets for the factors of production, and financial markets. The green arrows show the flow of dollars among the economic actors through the three types of markets.

Let's look at the flow of dollars from the viewpoints of these economic actors. Households receive income and use it to pay taxes to the government, to consume goods and services, and to save through the financial markets. Firms receive revenue from the sale of goods and services and use it to pay for the factors of production. Households and firms borrow in financial markets to buy investment goods, such as houses and factories. The government receives revenue from taxes and uses it to pay for government purchases. Any excess of tax revenue over government spending is called *public saving*, which can be either positive (a *budget surplus*) or negative (a *budget deficit*).

In this chapter we develop a basic classical model to explain the economic interactions depicted in Figure 3-1. We begin with firms and look at what determines their level of production (and, thus, the level of national income). Then we examine how the markets for the factors of production distribute this income to households. Next, we consider how much of this income households consume and how much they save. In addition to discussing the demand for goods and services arising from the consumption of households, we discuss the demand arising from investment and government purchases. Finally, we come full circle and examine how the demand for goods and services (the sum of consumption, investment, and government purchases) and the supply of goods and services (the level of production) are brought into balance.

3-1 What Determines the Total Production of Goods and Services?

An economy's output of goods and services—its GDP—depends on (1) its quantity of inputs, called the factors of production, and (2) its ability to turn inputs into output, as represented by the production function. We discuss each of these in turn.

The Factors of Production

Factors of production are the inputs used to produce goods and services. The two most important factors of production are capital and labor. *Capital* is the set of tools that workers use: the construction worker's crane, the accountant's calculator, and this author's personal computer. *Labor* is the time people spend working. We use the symbol K to denote the amount of capital and the symbol L to denote the amount of labor.

In this chapter we take the economy's factors of production as given. In other words, we assume that the economy has a fixed amount of capital and a fixed amount of labor. We write

$$K = \overline{K}.$$

$$L = \overline{L}.$$

The overbar means that each variable is fixed at some level. In Chapter 7 we examine what happens when the factors of production change over time, as they do in the real world. For now, to keep our analysis simple, we assume fixed amounts of capital and labor.

We also assume here that the factors of production are fully utilized—that is, that no resources are wasted. Again, in the real world, part of the labor force is unemployed, and some capital lies idle. In Chapter 6 we examine the reasons for unemployment, but for now we assume that capital and labor are fully employed.

The Production Function

The available production technology determines how much output is produced from given amounts of capital and labor. Economists express this relationship using a **production function**. Letting Y denote the amount of output, we write the production function as

$$Y = F(K, L).$$

This equation states that output is a function of the amount of capital and the amount of labor.

The production function reflects the available technology for turning capital and labor into output. If someone invents a better way to produce a good, the result is more output from the same amounts of capital and labor. Thus, technological change alters the production function.

Many production functions have a property called **constant returns to scale**. A production function has constant returns to scale if an increase of an equal percentage in all factors of production causes an increase in output of the same percentage. If the production function has constant returns to scale, then we get 10 percent more output when we increase both capital and labor by 10 percent. Mathematically, a production function has constant returns to scale if

$$zY = F(zK, zL)$$

for any positive number z. This equation says that if we multiply both the amount of capital and the amount of labor by some number z, output is also multiplied by z. In the next section we see that the assumption of constant returns to scale has an important implication for how the income from production is distributed.

As an example of a production function, consider production at a bakery. The kitchen and its equipment are the bakery's capital, the workers hired to make the bread are its labor, and the loaves of bread are its output. The bakery's production function shows that the number of loaves produced depends on the amount of equipment and the number of workers. If the production function has constant returns to scale, then doubling the amount of equipment and the number of workers doubles the amount of bread produced.

The Supply of Goods and Services

We can now see that the factors of production and the production function together determine the quantity of goods and services supplied, which in turn equals the economy's output. To express this mathematically, we write

$$Y = F(\overline{K}, \overline{L})$$
$$= \overline{Y}.$$

In this chapter, because we assume that the supplies of capital and labor and the technology are fixed, output is also fixed (at a level denoted here as $\overline{Y}$). When we discuss economic growth in Chapters 7 and 8, we will examine how increases in capital and labor and advances in technology lead to growth in the economy's output.

3-2 How Is National Income Distributed to the Factors of Production?

As we discussed in Chapter 2, the total output of an economy equals its total income. Because the factors of production and the production function together determine the total output of goods and services, they also determine national income. The circular flow diagram in Figure 3-1 shows that this national income flows from firms to households through the markets for the factors of production.

In this section we continue to develop our model of the economy by discussing how these factor markets work. Economists have long studied factor markets to understand the distribution of income. For example, Karl Marx, the noted nineteenth-century economist, spent much time trying to explain the incomes of capital and labor. The political philosophy of communism was in part based on Marx's now-discredited theory.

Here we examine the modern theory of how national income is divided among the factors of production. It is based on the classical (eighteenth-century) idea that prices adjust to balance supply and demand, applied here to the markets for the factors of production, together with the more recent (nineteenth-century) idea that the demand for each factor of production depends on the marginal productivity of that factor. This theory, called the *neoclassical theory of distribution*, is accepted by most economists today as the best place to start in understanding how the economy's income is distributed from firms to households.

Factor Prices

The distribution of national income is determined by factor prices. **Factor prices** are the amounts paid to the factors of production. In an economy where the two factors of production are capital and labor, the two factor prices are the wage workers earn and the rent the owners of capital collect.

As Figure 3-2 illustrates, the price each factor of production receives for its services is in turn determined by the supply and demand for that factor. Because we have assumed that the economy's factors of production are fixed, the factor supply curve in Figure 3-2 is vertical. Regardless of the factor price, the quantity of the factor supplied to the market is the same. The intersection of the downward-sloping factor demand curve and the vertical supply curve determines the equilibrium factor price.

FIGURE 3-2

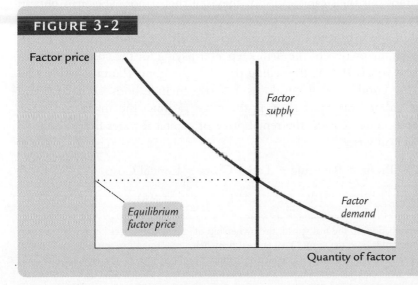

How a Factor of Production Is Compensated The price paid to any factor of production depends on the supply and demand for that factor's services. Because we have assumed that supply is fixed, the supply curve is vertical. The demand curve is downward sloping. The intersection of supply and demand determines the equilibrium factor price.

To understand factor prices and the distribution of income, we must examine the demand for the factors of production. Because factor demand arises from the thousands of firms that use capital and labor, we start by examining the decisions a typical firm makes about how much of these factors to employ.

The Decisions Facing the Competitive Firm

The simplest assumption to make about a typical firm is that it is competitive. A **competitive firm** is small relative to the markets in which it trades, so it has little influence on market prices. For example, our firm produces a good and sells it at the market price. Because many firms produce this good, our firm can sell as much as it wants without causing the price of the good to fall, or it can stop selling altogether without causing the price of the good to rise. Similarly, our firm cannot influence the wages of the workers it employs because many other local firms also employ workers. The firm has no reason to pay more than the market wage, and if it tried to pay less, its workers would take jobs elsewhere. Therefore, the competitive firm takes the prices of its output and its inputs as given by market conditions.

To make its product, the firm needs two factors of production, capital and labor. As we did for the aggregate economy, we represent the firm's production technology with the production function

$$Y = F(K, L),$$

where Y is the number of units produced (the firm's output), K the number of machines used (the amount of capital), and L the number of hours worked by the firm's employees (the amount of labor). Holding constant the technology as expressed in the production function, the firm produces more output only if it uses more machines or if its employees work more hours.

The firm sells its output at a price P, hires workers at a wage W, and rents capital at a rate R. Notice that when we speak of firms renting capital, we are assuming that households own the economy's stock of capital. In this analysis, households rent out their capital, just as they sell their labor. The firm obtains both factors of production from the households that own them.[1]

The goal of the firm is to maximize profit. **Profit** is equal to revenue minus costs; it is what the owners of the firm keep after paying for the costs of production. Revenue equals $P \times Y$, the selling price of the good P multiplied by the amount of the good the firm produces Y. Costs include both labor costs and capital costs. Labor costs equal $W \times L$, the wage W times the amount of labor L. Capital costs equal $R \times K$, the rental price of capital R times the amount of capital K. We can write

$$\text{Profit} = \text{Revenue} - \text{Labor Costs} - \text{Capital Costs}$$

$$= PY - WL - RK.$$

---

[1] This is a simplification. In the real world, the ownership of capital is indirect because firms own capital and households own the firms. That is, real firms have two functions: owning capital and producing output. To help us understand how the factors of production are compensated, however, we assume that firms only produce output and that households own capital directly.

To see how profit depends on the factors of production, we use the production function $Y = F(K, L)$ to substitute for Y to obtain

$$\text{Profit} = PF(K, L) - WL - RK.$$

This equation shows that profit depends on the product price P, the factor prices W and R, and the factor quantities L and K. The competitive firm takes the product price and the factor prices as given and chooses the amounts of labor and capital that maximize profit.

The Firm's Demand for Factors

We now know that our firm will hire labor and rent capital in the quantities that maximize profit. But what are those profit-maximizing quantities? To answer this question, we first consider the quantity of labor and then the quantity of capital.

The Marginal Product of Labor The more labor the firm employs, the more output it produces. The **marginal product of labor (MPL)** is the extra amount of output the firm gets from one extra unit of labor, holding the amount of capital fixed. We can express this using the production function:

$$MPL = F(K, L + 1) - F(K, L).$$

The first term on the right-hand side is the amount of output produced with K units of capital and $L + 1$ units of labor; the second term is the amount of output produced with K units of capital and L units of labor. This equation states that the marginal product of labor is the difference between the amount of output produced with $L + 1$ units of labor and the amount produced with only L units of labor.

Most production functions have the property of **diminishing marginal product**: holding the amount of capital fixed, the marginal product of labor decreases as the amount of labor increases. To see why, consider again the production of bread at a bakery. As a bakery hires more labor, it produces more bread. The MPL is the amount of extra bread produced when an extra unit of labor is hired. As more labor is added to a fixed amount of capital, however, the MPL falls. Fewer additional loaves are produced because workers are less productive when the kitchen is more crowded. In other words, holding the size of the kitchen fixed, each additional worker adds fewer loaves of bread to the bakery's output.

Figure 3-3 graphs the production function. It illustrates what happens to the amount of output when we hold the amount of capital constant and vary the amount of labor. This figure shows that the marginal product of labor is the slope of the production function. As the amount of labor increases, the production function becomes flatter, indicating diminishing marginal product.

From the Marginal Product of Labor to Labor Demand When the competitive, profit-maximizing firm is deciding whether to hire an additional unit of labor, it considers how that decision would affect profits. It therefore compares the extra revenue from increased production with the extra cost of higher spending on wages. The increase in revenue from an additional unit of labor depends

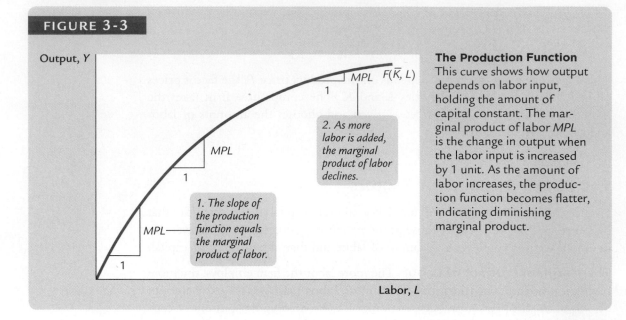

FIGURE 3-3

Output, Y

MPL $F(\bar{K}, L)$

1

MPL

1

2. As more labor is added, the marginal product of labor declines.

MPL

1. The slope of the production function equals the marginal product of labor.

1

Labor, L

The Production Function This curve shows how output depends on labor input, holding the amount of capital constant. The marginal product of labor MPL is the change in output when the labor input is increased by 1 unit. As the amount of labor increases, the production function becomes flatter, indicating diminishing marginal product.

on two variables: the marginal product of labor and the price of the output. Because an extra unit of labor produces MPL units of output and each unit of output sells for P dollars, the extra revenue is $P \times MPL$. The extra cost of hiring one more unit of labor is the wage W. Thus, the change in profit from hiring an additional unit of labor is

$$\Delta \text{Profit} = \Delta \text{Revenue} - \Delta \text{Cost}$$
$$= (P \times MPL) - W.$$

The symbol Δ (called *delta*) denotes the change in a variable.

We can now answer the question we asked at the beginning of this section: how much labor does the firm hire? The firm's manager knows that if the extra revenue $P \times MPL$ exceeds the wage W, an extra unit of labor increases profit. Therefore, the manager continues to hire labor until the next unit would no longer be profitable—that is, until the MPL falls to the point where the extra revenue equals the wage. The competitive firm's demand for labor is determined by

$$P \times MPL = W.$$

We can also write this as

$$MPL = W/P.$$

W/P is the **real wage**—the payment to labor measured in units of output rather than in dollars. To maximize profit, the firm hires up to the point at which the marginal product of labor equals the real wage.

For example, again consider a bakery. Suppose the price of bread P is $2 per loaf, and a worker earns a wage W of $20 per hour. The real wage W/P is 10 loaves per hour. In this example, the firm keeps hiring workers as long as the additional worker would produce at least 10 loaves per hour. When the MPL falls to 10 loaves per hour or less, hiring additional workers is no longer profitable.

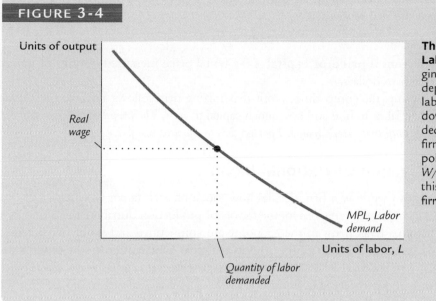

FIGURE 3-4

Units of output

Real
wage

MPL, Labor
demand

Units of labor, L

Quantity of labor
demanded

The Marginal Product of Labor Schedule The marginal product of labor *MPL* depends on the amount of labor. The *MPL* curve slopes downward because the *MPL* declines as *L* increases. The firm hires labor up to the point where the real wage *W/P* equals the *MPL*. Hence, this schedule is also the firm's labor demand curve.

Figure 3-4 shows how the marginal product of labor depends on the amount of labor employed (holding the firm's capital stock constant). That is, this figure graphs the *MPL* schedule. Because the *MPL* diminishes as the amount of labor increases, this curve slopes downward. For any given real wage, the firm hires up to the point at which the *MPL* equals the real wage. Hence, the *MPL* schedule is also the firm's labor demand curve.

The Marginal Product of Capital and Capital Demand The firm decides how much capital to rent in the same way it decides how much labor to hire. The **marginal product of capital (MPK)** is the amount of extra output the firm gets from an extra unit of capital, holding the amount of labor constant:

$$MPK = F(K + 1, L) - F(K, L).$$

Thus, the marginal product of capital is the difference between the amount of output produced with $K + 1$ units of capital and that produced with only K units of capital.

Like labor, capital is subject to diminishing marginal product. Once again consider the production of bread at a bakery. The first several ovens installed in the kitchen will be very productive. However, if the bakery installs more and more ovens, while holding its labor force constant, it will eventually contain more ovens than its employees can effectively operate. Hence, the marginal product of the last few ovens is lower than that of the first few.

The increase in profit from renting an additional machine is the extra revenue from selling the output of that machine minus the machine's rental price:

$$\Delta\text{Profit} = \Delta\text{Revenue} - \Delta\text{Cost}$$
$$= (P \times MPK) - R.$$

To maximize profit, the firm continues to rent more capital until the *MPK* falls to equal the real rental price:

$$MPK = R/P.$$

The **real rental price of capital** is the rental price measured in units of goods rather than in dollars.

To sum up, the competitive, profit-maximizing firm follows a simple rule about how much labor to hire and how much capital to rent. *The firm demands each factor of production until that factor's marginal product falls to equal its real factor price.*

The Division of National Income

Having analyzed how a firm decides how much of each factor to employ, we can now explain how the markets for the factors of production distribute the economy's total income. If all firms in the economy are competitive and profit maximizing, then each factor of production is paid its marginal contribution to the production process. The real wage paid to each worker equals the *MPL*, and the real rental price paid to each owner of capital equals the *MPK*. The total real wages paid to labor are therefore *MPL* × *L*, and the total real return paid to capital owners is *MPK* × *K*.

The income that remains after the firms have paid the factors of production is the **economic profit** of the owners of the firms. Real economic profit is

$$\text{Economic Profit} = Y - (MPL \times L) - (MPK \times K).$$

Because we want to examine the distribution of national income, we rearrange the terms as follows:

$$Y = (MPL \times L) + (MPK \times K) + \text{Economic Profit}.$$

Total income is divided among the return to labor, the return to capital, and economic profit.

How large is economic profit? The answer is surprising: if the production function has the property of constant returns to scale, as is often thought to be the case, then economic profit must be zero. That is, nothing is left after the factors of production are paid. This conclusion follows from a famous mathematical result called *Euler's theorem*,[2] which states that if the production function has constant returns to scale, then

$$F(K, L) = (MPK \times K) + (MPL \times L).$$

If each factor of production is paid its marginal product, then the sum of these factor payments equals total output. In other words, constant returns to scale, profit maximization, and competition together imply that economic profit is zero.

---

[2] *Mathematical note*: To prove Euler's theorem, we need to use some multivariate calculus. Begin with the definition of constant returns to scale: $zY = F(zK, zL)$. Now differentiate with respect to z to obtain:

$$Y = F_1(zK, zL)K + F_2(zK, zL)L,$$

where F_1 and F_2 denote partial derivatives with respect to the first and second arguments of the function. Evaluating this expression at $z = 1$, and noting that the partial derivatives equal the marginal products, yields Euler's theorem.

If economic profit is zero, how can we explain the existence of "profit" in the economy? The answer is that the term "profit" as normally used is different from economic profit. We have been assuming that there are three types of agents: workers, owners of capital, and owners of firms. Total income is divided among wages, return to capital, and economic profit. In the real world, however, most firms own rather than rent the capital they use. Because firm owners and capital owners are the same people, economic profit and the return to capital are often lumped together. If we call this alternative definition **accounting profit**, we can say that

$$\text{Accounting Profit} = \text{Economic Profit} + (MPK \times K).$$

Under our assumptions—constant returns to scale, profit maximization, and competition—economic profit is zero. If these assumptions approximately describe the world, then the "profit" in the national income accounts must be mostly the return to capital.

We can now answer the question posed at the beginning of this chapter about how the income of the economy is distributed from firms to households. Each factor of production is paid its marginal product, and these factor payments exhaust total output. *Total output is divided between the payments to capital and the payments to labor, depending on their marginal productivities.*

CASE STUDY

The Black Death and Factor Prices

According to the neoclassical theory of distribution, factor prices equal the marginal products of the factors of production. Because the marginal products depend on the quantities of the factors, a change in the quantity of any one factor alters the marginal products of all the factors. Therefore, a change in the supply of a factor alters equilibrium factor prices and the distribution of income.

Fourteenth-century Europe provides a grisly natural experiment to study how factor quantities affect factor prices. The outbreak of the bubonic plague—the Black Death—in 1348 reduced the population of Europe by about one-third within a few years. Because the marginal product of labor increases as the amount of labor falls, this massive reduction in the labor force should have raised the marginal product of labor and equilibrium real wages. (That is, the economy should have moved to the left along the curves in Figures 3-3 and 3-4.) The evidence confirms the theory: real wages approximately doubled during the plague years. The peasants who were fortunate enough to survive the plague enjoyed economic prosperity.

The reduction in the labor force caused by the plague should also have affected the return to land, the other major factor of production in medieval Europe. With fewer workers available to farm the land, an additional unit of land would have produced less additional output, and so land rents should have fallen. Once again, the theory is confirmed: real rents fell 50 percent or more during this period. While the peasant classes prospered, the landed classes suffered reduced incomes.[3] ∎

---

[3] Carlo M. Cipolla, *Before the Industrial Revolution: European Society and Economy, 1000–1700*, 2nd ed. (New York: Norton, 1980), 200–202.

The Cobb–Douglas Production Function

What production function describes how actual economies turn capital and labor into GDP? One answer to this question came from a historic collaboration between a U.S. senator and a mathematician.

Paul Douglas was a U.S. senator from Illinois from 1949 to 1966. In 1927, however, when he was still a professor of economics, he noticed a surprising fact: the division of national income between capital and labor had been roughly constant over a long period. In other words, as the economy grew more prosperous over time, the total income of workers and the total income of capital owners grew at almost exactly the same rate. This observation caused Douglas to wonder what conditions might lead to constant factor shares.

Douglas asked Charles Cobb, a mathematician, what production function, if any, would produce constant factor shares if factors always earned their marginal products. The production function would need to have the property that

$$\text{Capital Income} = MPK \times K = \alpha Y$$

and

$$\text{Labor Income} = MPL \times L = (1 - \alpha)Y,$$

where α is a constant between zero and one that measures capital's share of income. That is, α determines what share of income goes to capital and what share goes to labor. Cobb showed that the function with this property is

$$F(K, L) = AK^{\alpha}L^{1-\alpha},$$

where A is a parameter greater than zero that measures the productivity of the available technology. This function became known as the **Cobb–Douglas production function**.

Let's take a closer look at some of the properties of this production function. First, the Cobb–Douglas production function has constant returns to scale. That is, if capital and labor are increased by the same proportion, then output increases by that proportion as well.[4]

---

[4] *Mathematical note*: To prove that the Cobb–Douglas production function has constant returns to scale, examine what happens when we multiply capital and labor by a constant z:

$$F(zK, zL) = A(zK)^{\alpha}(zL)^{1-\alpha}.$$

Expanding terms on the right,

$$F(zK, zL) = Az^{\alpha} K^{\alpha}z^{1-\alpha}L^{1-\alpha}.$$

Rearranging to bring like terms together, we get

$$F(zK, zL) = Az^{\alpha}z^{1-\alpha}K^{\alpha}L^{1-\alpha}.$$

Since $z^{\alpha} z^{1-\alpha} = z$, our function becomes

$$F(zK, zL) = z AK^{\alpha}L^{1-\alpha}.$$

But $A K^{\alpha}L^{1-\alpha} = F(K, L)$. Thus,

$$F(zK, zL) = zF(K, L) = zY.$$

Hence, the amount of output Y increases by the same factor z, which implies that this production function has constant returns to scale.

Next, consider the marginal products for the Cobb–Douglas production function. The marginal product of labor is[5]

$$MPL = (1 - \alpha) AK^{\alpha}L^{-\alpha},$$

and the marginal product of capital is

$$MPK = \alpha AK^{\alpha-1}L^{1-\alpha}.$$

From these equations, recalling that α is between zero and one, we can see what causes the marginal products of the two factors to change. An increase in the amount of capital raises the MPL and reduces the MPK. Similarly, an increase in the amount of labor reduces the MPL and raises the MPK. A technological advance that increases the parameter A raises the marginal product of both factors proportionately.

The marginal products for the Cobb–Douglas production function can also be written as[6]

$$MPL = (1 - \alpha)Y/L.$$
$$MPK = \alpha Y/K.$$

The MPL is proportional to output per worker, and the MPK is proportional to output per unit of capital. Y/L is called *average labor productivity*, and Y/K is called *average capital productivity*. If the production function is Cobb–Douglas, then the marginal productivity of a factor is proportional to its average productivity.

We can now verify that if factors earn their marginal products, then the parameter α indeed tells us how much income goes to labor and how much goes to capital. The total amount paid to labor, which we have seen is $MPL \times L$, equals $(1 - \alpha)Y$. Therefore, $(1 - \alpha)$ is labor's share of output. Similarly, the total amount paid to capital, $MPK \times K$, equals αY, and α is capital's share of output. The ratio of labor income to capital income is a constant, $(1 - \alpha)/\alpha$, just as Douglas observed. The factor shares depend only on the parameter α, not on the amounts of capital or labor or on the state of technology as measured by the parameter A.

More recent U.S. data are also consistent with the Cobb–Douglas production function. Figure 3-5 shows the ratio of labor income to total income in the United States from 1960 to 2008. Despite the many changes in the economy over the past half century, this ratio has remained about 0.7. This division of income is easily explained by a Cobb–Douglas production function in which the parameter α is about 0.3. According to this parameter, capital receives 30 percent of income, and labor receives 70 percent.

---

[5] *Mathematical note:* Obtaining the formulas for the marginal products from the production function requires a bit of calculus. To find the MPL, differentiate the production function with respect to L. This is done by multiplying by the exponent $(1 - \alpha)$ and then subtracting 1 from the old exponent to obtain the new exponent, $-\alpha$. Similarly, to obtain the MPK, differentiate the production function with respect to K.

[6] *Mathematical note:* To check these expressions for the marginal products, substitute in the production function for Y to show that these expressions are equivalent to the earlier formulas for the marginal products.

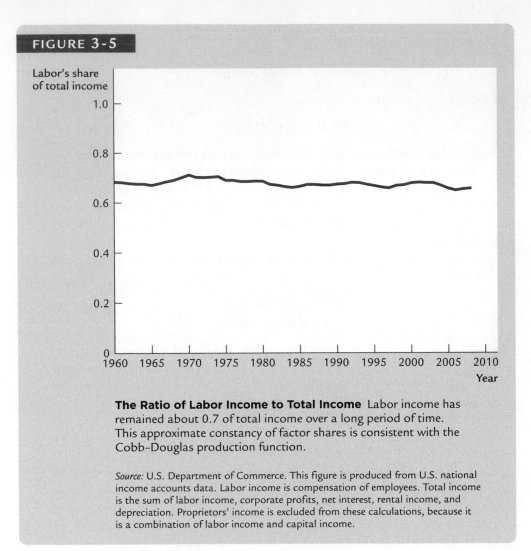

FIGURE 3-5

The Ratio of Labor Income to Total Income Labor income has remained about 0.7 of total income over a long period of time. This approximate constancy of factor shares is consistent with the Cobb–Douglas production function.

Source: U.S. Department of Commerce. This figure is produced from U.S. national income accounts data. Labor income is compensation of employees. Total income is the sum of labor income, corporate profits, net interest, rental income, and depreciation. Proprietors' income is excluded from these calculations, because it is a combination of labor income and capital income.

The Cobb–Douglas production function is not the last word in explaining the economy's production of goods and services or the distribution of national income between capital and labor. It is, however, a good place to start.

CASE STUDY

Labor Productivity as the Key Determinant of Real Wages

The neoclassical theory of distribution tells us that the real wage W/P equals the marginal product of labor. The Cobb–Douglas production function tells us that the marginal product of labor is proportional to average labor productivity Y/L. If this theory is right, then workers should enjoy rapidly rising living standards when labor productivity is growing robustly. Is this true?

> ### TABLE 3-1
>
> #### Growth in Labor Productivity and Real Wages: The U.S. Experience
>
> | Time Period | Growth Rate of Labor Productivity | Growth Rate of Real Wages |
> |---|---|---|
> | 1959–2009 | 2.1% | 1.9% |
> | 1959–1973 | 2.8 | 2.8 |
> | 1973–1995 | 1.4 | 1.2 |
> | 1995–2009 | 2.6 | 2.3 |
>
> *Source: Economic Report of the President 2009*, Table B-49, and updates from the U.S. Department of Commerce website. Growth in labor productivity is measured here as the annualized rate of change in output per hour in the nonfarm business sector. Growth in real wages is measured as the annualized change in compensation per hour in the nonfarm business sector divided by the implicit price deflator for that sector.

Table 3-1 presents some data on growth in productivity and real wages for the U.S. economy. From 1959 to 2009, productivity as measured by output per hour of work grew about 2.1 percent per year. Real wages grew at 1.9 percent—almost exactly the same rate. With a growth rate of 2 percent per year, productivity and real wages double about every 35 years.

Productivity growth varies over time. The table shows the data for three shorter periods that economists have identified as having different productivity experiences. (A case study in Chapter 8 examines the reasons for these changes in productivity growth.) Around 1973, the U.S. economy experienced a significant slowdown in productivity growth that lasted until 1995. The cause of the productivity slowdown is not well understood, but the link between productivity and real wages was exactly as standard theory predicts. The slowdown in productivity growth from 2.8 to 1.4 percent per year coincided with a slowdown in real wage growth from 2.8 to 1.2 percent per year.

Productivity growth picked up again around 1995, and many observers hailed the arrival of the "new economy." This productivity acceleration is often attributed to the spread of computers and information technology. As theory predicts, growth in real wages picked up as well. From 1995 to 2009, productivity grew by 2.6 percent per year and real wages by 2.3 percent per year.

Theory and history both confirm the close link between labor productivity and real wages. This lesson is the key to understanding why workers today are better off than workers in previous generations. ∎

3-3 What Determines the Demand for Goods and Services?

We have seen what determines the level of production and how the income from production is distributed to workers and owners of capital. We now continue our tour of the circular flow diagram, Figure 3-1, and examine how the output from production is used.

In Chapter 2 we identified the four components of GDP:

- Consumption (*C*)
- Investment (*I*)
- Government purchases (*G*)
- Net exports (*NX*).

The circular flow diagram contains only the first three components. For now, to simplify the analysis, we assume our economy is a *closed economy*—a country that does not trade with other countries. Thus, net exports are always zero. (We examine the macroeconomics of *open economies* in Chapter 5.)

A closed economy has three uses for the goods and services it produces. These three components of GDP are expressed in the national income accounts identity:

$$Y = C + I + G.$$

Households consume some of the economy's output; firms and households use some of the output for investment; and the government buys some of the output for public purposes. We want to see how GDP is allocated among these three uses.

Consumption

When we eat food, wear clothing, or go to a movie, we are consuming some of the output of the economy. All forms of consumption together make up about two-thirds of GDP. Because consumption is so large, macroeconomists have devoted much energy to studying how households decide how much to consume. Here we consider the simplest story of consumer behavior.

Households receive income from their labor and their ownership of capital, pay taxes to the government, and then decide how much of their after-tax income to consume and how much to save. As we discussed in Section 3-2, the income that households receive equals the output of the economy *Y*. The government then taxes households an amount *T*. (Although the government imposes many kinds of taxes, such as personal and corporate income taxes and sales taxes, for our purposes we can lump all these taxes together.) We define income after the payment of all taxes, $Y - T$, to be **disposable income**. Households divide their disposable income between consumption and saving.

We assume that the level of consumption depends directly on the level of disposable income. A higher level of disposable income leads to greater consumption. Thus,

$$C = C(Y - T).$$

This equation states that consumption is a function of disposable income. The relationship between consumption and disposable income is called the **consumption function**.

The **marginal propensity to consume (MPC)** is the amount by which consumption changes when disposable income increases by one dollar. The *MPC*

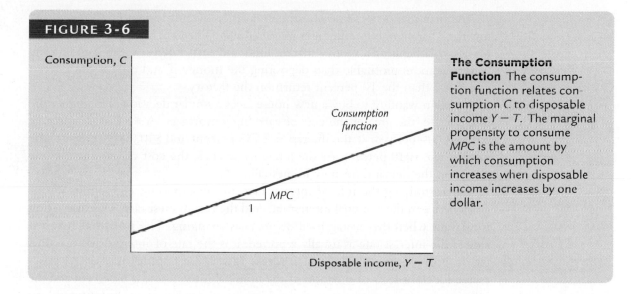

FIGURE 3-6

Consumption, C

Consumption function

MPC
1

Disposable income, Y − T

The Consumption Function The consumption function relates consumption C to disposable income Y − T. The marginal propensity to consume MPC is the amount by which consumption increases when disposable income increases by one dollar.

is between zero and one: an extra dollar of income increases consumption, but by less than one dollar. Thus, if households obtain an extra dollar of income, they save a portion of it. For example, if the MPC is 0.7, then households spend 70 cents of each additional dollar of disposable income on consumer goods and services and save 30 cents.

Figure 3-6 illustrates the consumption function. The slope of the consumption function tells us how much consumption increases when disposable income increases by one dollar. That is, the slope of the consumption function is the MPC.

Investment

Both firms and households purchase investment goods. Firms buy investment goods to add to their stock of capital and to replace existing capital as it wears out. Households buy new houses, which are also part of investment. Total investment in the United States averages about 15 percent of GDP.

The quantity of investment goods demanded depends on the **interest rate**, which measures the cost of the funds used to finance investment. For an investment project to be profitable, its return (the revenue from increased future production of goods and services) must exceed its cost (the payments for borrowed funds). If the interest rate rises, fewer investment projects are profitable, and the quantity of investment goods demanded falls.

For example, suppose a firm is considering whether it should build a $1 million factory that would yield a return of $100,000 per year, or 10 percent. The firm compares this return to the cost of borrowing the $1 million. If the interest rate is below 10 percent, the firm borrows the money in financial markets and makes the investment. If the interest rate is above 10 percent, the firm forgoes the investment opportunity and does not build the factory.

The firm makes the same investment decision even if it does not have to borrow the $1 million but rather uses its own funds. The firm can always deposit this money in a bank or a money market fund and earn interest on it. Building the factory is more profitable than depositing the money if and only if the interest rate is less than the 10 percent return on the factory.

A person wanting to buy a new house faces a similar decision. The higher the interest rate, the greater the cost of carrying a mortgage. A $100,000 mortgage costs $8,000 per year if the interest rate is 8 percent and $10,000 per year if the interest rate is 10 percent. As the interest rate rises, the cost of owning a home rises, and the demand for new homes falls.

When studying the role of interest rates in the economy, economists distinguish between the nominal interest rate and the real interest rate. This distinction is relevant when the overall level of prices is changing. The **nominal interest rate** is the interest rate as usually reported: it is the rate of interest that investors pay to borrow money. The **real interest rate** is the nominal interest rate corrected for the effects of inflation. If the nominal interest rate is 8 percent and the inflation rate is 3 percent, then the real interest rate is 5 percent. In Chapter 4 we discuss the relation between nominal and real interest rates in detail. Here it is sufficient to note that the real interest rate measures the true cost of borrowing and, thus, determines the quantity of investment.

We can summarize this discussion with an equation relating investment I to the real interest rate r:

$$I = I(r).$$

Figure 3-7 shows this investment function. It slopes downward, because as the interest rate rises, the quantity of investment demanded falls.

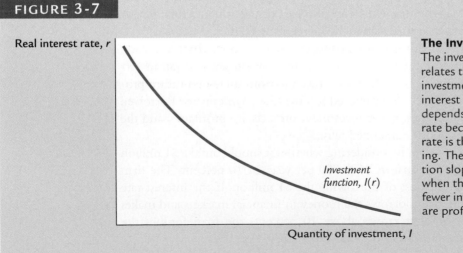

FIGURE 3-7

Real interest rate, r

Investment function, $I(r)$

Quantity of investment, I

The Investment Function The investment function relates the quantity of investment I to the real interest rate r. Investment depends on the real interest rate because the interest rate is the cost of borrowing. The investment function slopes downward: when the interest rate rises, fewer investment projects are profitable.

The Many Different Interest Rates

If you look in the business section of a newspaper, you will find many different interest rates reported. By contrast, throughout most of this book, we will talk about "the" interest rate, as if there were only one interest rate in the economy. The only distinction we will make is between the nominal interest rate (which is not corrected for inflation) and the real interest rate (which is corrected for inflation). Almost all of the interest rates reported in the newspaper are nominal.

Why does the newspaper report so many interest rates? The various interest rates differ in three ways:

➤ *Term.* Some loans in the economy are for short periods of time, even as short as overnight. Other loans are for thirty years or even longer. The interest rate on a loan depends on its term. Long-term interest rates are usually, but not always, higher than short-term interest rates.

➤ *Credit risk.* In deciding whether to make a loan, a lender must take into account the probability that the borrower will repay. The law allows borrowers to default on their loans by declaring bankruptcy. The higher the perceived probability of default, the higher the interest rate. Because the safest credit risk is the government, government bonds tend to pay a low interest rate. At the other extreme, financially shaky corporations can raise funds only by issuing *junk bonds*, which pay a high interest rate to compensate for the high risk of default.

➤ *Tax treatment.* The interest on different types of bonds is taxed differently. Most important, when state and local governments issue bonds, called *municipal bonds*, the holders of the bonds do not pay federal income tax on the interest income. Because of this tax advantage, municipal bonds pay a lower interest rate.

When you see two different interest rates in the newspaper, you can almost always explain the difference by considering the term, the credit risk, and the tax treatment of the loan.

Although there are many different interest rates in the economy, macroeconomists can usually ignore these distinctions. The various interest rates tend to move up and down together. For many purposes, we will not go far wrong by assuming there is only one interest rate.

Government Purchases

Government purchases are the third component of the demand for goods and services. The federal government buys guns, missiles, and the services of government employees. Local governments buy library books, build schools, and hire teachers. Governments at all levels build roads and other public works. All these transactions make up government purchases of goods and services, which account for about 20 percent of GDP in the United States.

These purchases are only one type of government spending. The other type is transfer payments to households, such as welfare for the poor and Social Security payments for the elderly. Unlike government purchases, transfer payments are not made in exchange for some of the economy's output of goods and services. Therefore, they are not included in the variable G.

Transfer payments do affect the demand for goods and services indirectly. Transfer payments are the opposite of taxes: they increase households' disposable income, just as taxes reduce disposable income. Thus, an increase in transfer payments financed by an increase in taxes leaves disposable income unchanged. We can now revise our definition of T to equal taxes minus transfer payments. Disposable income, $Y - T$, includes both the negative impact of taxes and the positive impact of transfer payments.

If government purchases equal taxes minus transfers, then $G = T$ and the government has a *balanced budget*. If G exceeds T, the government runs a *budget deficit*, which it funds by issuing government debt—that is, by borrowing in the financial markets. If G is less than T, the government runs a *budget surplus*, which it can use to repay some of its outstanding debt.

Here we do not try to explain the political process that leads to a particular fiscal policy—that is, to the level of government purchases and taxes. Instead, we take government purchases and taxes as exogenous variables. To denote that these variables are fixed outside of our model of national income, we write

$$G = \overline{G}.$$

$$T = \overline{T}.$$

We do, however, want to examine the impact of fiscal policy on the endogenous variables, which are determined within the model. The endogenous variables here are consumption, investment, and the interest rate.

To see how the exogenous variables affect the endogenous variables, we must complete the model. This is the subject of the next section.

3-4 What Brings the Supply and Demand for Goods and Services Into Equilibrium?

We have now come full circle in the circular flow diagram, Figure 3-1. We began by examining the supply of goods and services, and we have just discussed the demand for them. How can we be certain that all these flows balance? In other words, what ensures that the sum of consumption, investment, and government purchases equals the amount of output produced? We will see that in this classical model, the interest rate is the price that has the crucial role of equilibrating supply and demand.

There are two ways to think about the role of the interest rate in the economy. We can consider how the interest rate affects the supply and demand for goods or services. Or we can consider how the interest rate affects the supply and demand for loanable funds. As we will see, these two approaches are two sides of the same coin.

Equilibrium in the Market for Goods and Services: The Supply and Demand for the Economy's Output

The following equations summarize the discussion of the demand for goods and services in Section 3-3:

$$Y = C + I + G.$$

$$C = C(Y - T).$$

$$I = I(r).$$

$$G = \overline{G}.$$

$$T = \overline{T}.$$

The demand for the economy's output comes from consumption, investment, and government purchases. Consumption depends on disposable income; investment depends on the real interest rate; and government purchases and taxes are the exogenous variables set by fiscal policymakers.

To this analysis, let's add what we learned about the supply of goods and services in Section 3-1. There we saw that the factors of production and the production function determine the quantity of output supplied to the economy:

$$Y = F(\overline{K}, \overline{L})$$
$$= \overline{Y}.$$

Now let's combine these equations describing the supply and demand for output. If we substitute the consumption function and the investment function into the national income accounts identity, we obtain

$$Y = C(Y - T) + I(r) + G.$$

Because the variables G and T are fixed by policy, and the level of output Y is fixed by the factors of production and the production function, we can write

$$\overline{Y} = C(\overline{Y} - \overline{T}) + I(r) + \overline{G}.$$

This equation states that the supply of output equals its demand, which is the sum of consumption, investment, and government purchases.

Notice that the interest rate r is the only variable not already determined in the last equation. This is because the interest rate still has a key role to play: it must adjust to ensure that the demand for goods equals the supply. The greater the interest rate, the lower the level of investment, and thus the lower the demand for goods and services, $C + I + G$. If the interest rate is too high, then investment is too low and the demand for output falls short of the supply. If the interest rate is too low, then investment is too high and the demand exceeds the supply. *At the equilibrium interest rate, the demand for goods and services equals the supply.*

This conclusion may seem somewhat mysterious: how does the interest rate get to the level that balances the supply and demand for goods and services? The best way to answer this question is to consider how financial markets fit into the story.

Equilibrium in the Financial Markets: The Supply and Demand for Loanable Funds

Because the interest rate is the cost of borrowing and the return to lending in financial markets, we can better understand the role of the interest rate in the economy by thinking about the financial markets. To do this, rewrite the national income accounts identity as

$$Y - C - G = I.$$

The term $Y - C - G$ is the output that remains after the demands of consumers and the government have been satisfied; it is called **national saving** or simply **saving** (S). In this form, the national income accounts identity shows that saving equals investment.

To understand this identity more fully, we can split national saving into two parts—one part representing the saving of the private sector and the other representing the saving of the government:

$$S = (Y - T - C) + (T - G) = I.$$

The term $(Y - T - C)$ is disposable income minus consumption, which is **private saving**. The term $(T - G)$ is government revenue minus government spending, which is **public saving**. (If government spending exceeds government revenue, then the government runs a budget deficit and public saving is negative.) National saving is the sum of private and public saving. The circular flow diagram in Figure 3-1 reveals an interpretation of this equation: this equation states that the flows into the financial markets (private and public saving) must balance the flows out of the financial markets (investment).

To see how the interest rate brings financial markets into equilibrium, substitute the consumption function and the investment function into the national income accounts identity:

$$Y - C(Y - T) - G = I(r).$$

Next, note that G and T are fixed by policy and Y is fixed by the factors of production and the production function:

$$\overline{Y} - C(\overline{Y} - \overline{T}) - \overline{G} = I(r)$$
$$\overline{S} = I(r).$$

The left-hand side of this equation shows that national saving depends on income Y and the fiscal-policy variables G and T. For fixed values of Y, G, and T, national saving S is also fixed. The right-hand side of the equation shows that investment depends on the interest rate.

Figure 3-8 graphs saving and investment as a function of the interest rate. The saving function is a vertical line because in this model saving does not depend

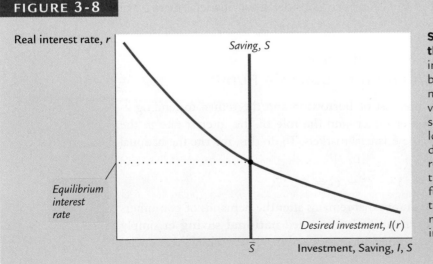

FIGURE 3-8

Real interest rate, r

Saving, S

Equilibrium interest rate

Desired investment, $I(r)$

$\overline{S}$

Investment, Saving, I, S

Saving, Investment, and the Interest Rate The interest rate adjusts to bring saving and investment into balance. The vertical line represents saving—the supply of loanable funds. The downward-sloping line represents investment—the demand for loanable funds. The intersection of these two curves determines the equilibrium interest rate.

on the interest rate (we relax this assumption later). The investment function slopes downward: as the interest rate decreases, more investment projects become profitable.

From a quick glance at Figure 3-8, one might think it was a supply-and-demand diagram for a particular good. In fact, saving and investment can be interpreted in terms of supply and demand. In this case, the "good" is **loanable funds**, and its "price" is the interest rate. Saving is the supply of loanable funds—households lend their saving to investors or deposit their saving in a bank that then loans the funds out. Investment is the demand for loanable funds—investors borrow from the public directly by selling bonds or indirectly by borrowing from banks. Because investment depends on the interest rate, the quantity of loanable funds demanded also depends on the interest rate.

The interest rate adjusts until the amount that firms want to invest equals the amount that households want to save. If the interest rate is too low, investors want more of the economy's output than households want to save. Equivalently, the quantity of loanable funds demanded exceeds the quantity supplied. When this happens, the interest rate rises. Conversely, if the interest rate is too high, households want to save more than firms want to invest; because the quantity of loanable funds supplied is greater than the quantity demanded, the interest rate falls. The equilibrium interest rate is found where the two curves cross. *At the equilibrium interest rate, households' desire to save balances firms' desire to invest, and the quantity of loanable funds supplied equals the quantity demanded.*

Changes in Saving: The Effects of Fiscal Policy

We can use our model to show how fiscal policy affects the economy. When the government changes its spending or the level of taxes, it affects the demand for the economy's output of goods and services and alters national saving, investment, and the equilibrium interest rate.

An Increase in Government Purchases Consider first the effects of an increase in government purchases by an amount ΔG. The immediate impact is to increase the demand for goods and services by ΔG. But because total output is fixed by the factors of production, the increase in government purchases must be met by a decrease in some other category of demand. Disposable income $Y - T$ is unchanged, so consumption C is unchanged as well. Therefore, the increase in government purchases must be met by an equal decrease in investment.

To induce investment to fall, the interest rate must rise. Hence, the increase in government purchases causes the interest rate to increase and investment to decrease. Government purchases are said to **crowd out** investment.

To grasp the effects of an increase in government purchases, consider the impact on the market for loanable funds. Because the increase in government purchases is not accompanied by an increase in taxes, the government finances the additional spending by borrowing—that is, by reducing public saving. With private saving unchanged, this government borrowing reduces national saving.

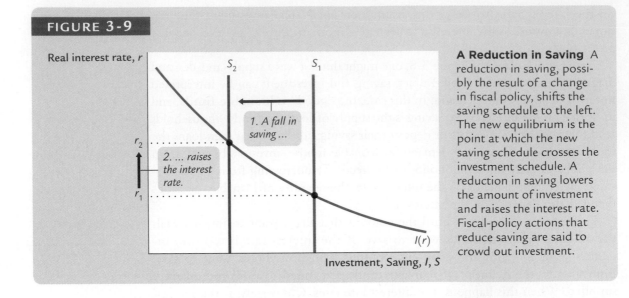

FIGURE 3-9

A Reduction in Saving A reduction in saving, possibly the result of a change in fiscal policy, shifts the saving schedule to the left. The new equilibrium is the point at which the new saving schedule crosses the investment schedule. A reduction in saving lowers the amount of investment and raises the interest rate. Fiscal-policy actions that reduce saving are said to crowd out investment.

As Figure 3-9 shows, a reduction in national saving is represented by a leftward shift in the supply of loanable funds available for investment. At the initial interest rate, the demand for loanable funds exceeds the supply. The equilibrium interest rate rises to the point where the investment schedule crosses the new saving schedule. Thus, an increase in government purchases causes the interest rate to rise from r_1 to r_2.

CASE STUDY

Wars and Interest Rates in the United Kingdom, 1730–1920

Wars are traumatic—both for those who fight them and for a nation's economy. Because the economic changes accompanying them are often large, wars provide a natural experiment with which economists can test their theories. We can learn about the economy by seeing how in wartime the endogenous variables respond to the major changes in the exogenous variables.

One exogenous variable that changes substantially in wartime is the level of government purchases. Figure 3-10 shows military spending as a percentage of GDP for the United Kingdom from 1730 to 1919. This graph shows, as one would expect, that government purchases rose suddenly and dramatically during the eight wars of this period.

Our model predicts that this wartime increase in government purchases—and the increase in government borrowing to finance the wars—should have raised the demand for goods and services, reduced the supply of loanable funds, and raised the interest rate. To test this prediction, Figure 3-10 also shows the interest rate on long-term government bonds, called *consols* in the United Kingdom. A positive association between military purchases and interest rates is apparent in

FIGURE 3-10

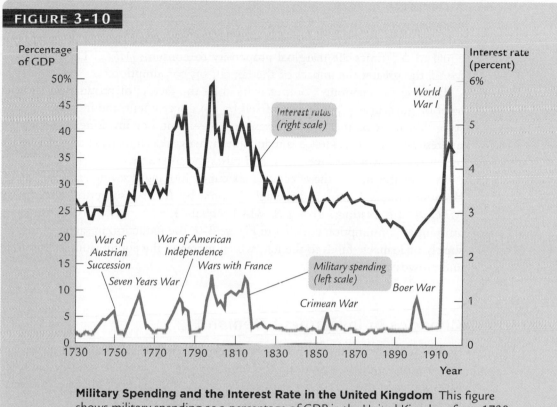

Military Spending and the Interest Rate in the United Kingdom This figure shows military spending as a percentage of GDP in the United Kingdom from 1730 to 1919. Not surprisingly, military spending rose substantially during each of the eight wars of this period. This figure also shows that the interest rate tended to rise when military spending rose.

Source: Series constructed from various sources described in Robert J. Barro, "Government Spending, Interest Rates, Prices, and Budget Deficits in the United Kingdom, 1701–1918," *Journal of Monetary Economics* 20 (September 1987): 221–248.

this figure. These data support the model's prediction: interest rates do tend to rise when government purchases increase.[7]

One problem with using wars to test theories is that many economic changes may be occurring at the same time. For example, in World War II, while government purchases increased dramatically, rationing also restricted consumption of many goods. In addition, the risk of defeat in the war and default by the government on its debt presumably increases the interest rate the government must pay. Economic models predict what happens when one exogenous variable changes and all the other exogenous variables remain constant. In the real world, however, many exogenous variables may change at once. Unlike controlled laboratory experiments, the natural experiments on which economists must rely are not always easy to interpret. ■

---

[7] Daniel K. Benjamin and Levis A. Kochin, "War, Prices, and Interest Rates: A Martial Solution to Gibson's Paradox," in M. D. Bordo and A. J. Schwartz, eds., *A Retrospective on the Classical Gold Standard, 1821–1931* (Chicago: University of Chicago Press, 1984), 587–612; Robert J. Barro, "Government Spending, Interest Rates, Prices, and Budget Deficits in the United Kingdom, 1701–1918," *Journal of Monetary Economics* 20 (September 1987): 221–248.

A Decrease in Taxes Now consider a reduction in taxes of ΔT. The immediate impact of the tax cut is to raise disposable income and thus to raise consumption. Disposable income rises by ΔT, and consumption rises by an amount equal to ΔT times the marginal propensity to consume MPC. The higher the MPC, the greater the impact of the tax cut on consumption.

Because the economy's output is fixed by the factors of production and the level of government purchases is fixed by the government, the increase in consumption must be met by a decrease in investment. For investment to fall, the interest rate must rise. Hence, a reduction in taxes, like an increase in government purchases, crowds out investment and raises the interest rate.

We can also analyze the effect of a tax cut by looking at saving and investment. Because the tax cut raises disposable income by ΔT, consumption goes up by $MPC \times \Delta T$. National saving S, which equals $Y - C - G$, falls by the same amount as consumption rises. As in Figure 3-9, the reduction in saving shifts the supply of loanable funds to the left, which increases the equilibrium interest rate and crowds out investment.

Changes in Investment Demand

So far, we have discussed how fiscal policy can change national saving. We can also use our model to examine the other side of the market—the demand for investment. In this section we look at the causes and effects of changes in investment demand.

One reason investment demand might increase is technological innovation. Suppose, for example, that someone invents a new technology, such as the railroad or the computer. Before a firm or household can take advantage of the innovation, it must buy investment goods. The invention of the railroad had no value until railroad cars were produced and tracks were laid. The idea of the computer was not productive until computers were manufactured. Thus, technological innovation leads to an increase in investment demand.

Investment demand may also change because the government encourages or discourages investment through the tax laws. For example, suppose that the government increases personal income taxes and uses the extra revenue to provide tax cuts for those who invest in new capital. Such a change in the tax laws makes more investment projects profitable and, like a technological innovation, increases the demand for investment goods.

Figure 3-11 shows the effects of an increase in investment demand. At any given interest rate, the demand for investment goods (and also for loanable funds) is higher. This increase in demand is represented by a shift in the investment schedule to the right. The economy moves from the old equilibrium, point A, to the new equilibrium, point B.

The surprising implication of Figure 3-11 is that the equilibrium amount of investment is unchanged. Under our assumptions, the fixed level of saving determines the amount of investment; in other words, there is a fixed supply of loanable funds. An increase in investment demand merely raises the equilibrium interest rate.

FIGURE 3-11

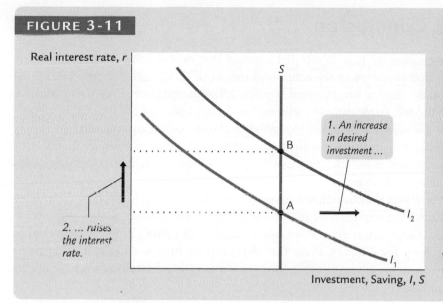

An Increase in the Demand for Investment An increase in the demand for investment goods shifts the investment schedule to the right. At any given interest rate, the amount of investment is greater. The equilibrium moves from point A to point B. Because the amount of saving is fixed, the increase in investment demand raises the interest rate while leaving the equilibrium amount of investment unchanged.

We would reach a different conclusion, however, if we modified our simple consumption function and allowed consumption (and its flip side, saving) to depend on the interest rate. Because the interest rate is the return to saving (as well as the cost of borrowing), a higher interest rate might reduce consumption and increase saving. If so, the saving schedule would be upward sloping rather than vertical.

With an upward-sloping saving schedule, an increase in investment demand would raise both the equilibrium interest rate and the equilibrium quantity of investment. Figure 3-12 shows such a change. The increase in the interest rate causes households to consume less and save more. The decrease in consumption frees resources for investment.

FIGURE 3-12

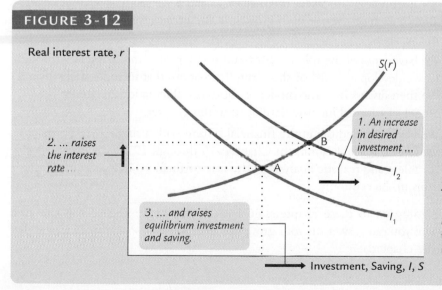

An Increase in Investment Demand When Saving Depends on the Interest Rate When saving is positively related to the interest rate, a rightward shift in the investment schedule increases the interest rate and the amount of investment. The higher interest rate induces people to increase saving, which in turn allows investment to increase.

3-5 Conclusion

In this chapter we have developed a model that explains the production, distribution, and allocation of the economy's output of goods and services. The model relies on the classical assumption that prices adjust to equilibrate supply and demand. In this model, factor prices equilibrate factor markets, and the interest rate equilibrates the supply and demand for goods and services (or, equivalently, the supply and demand for loanable funds). Because the model incorporates all the interactions illustrated in the circular flow diagram in Figure 3-1, it is sometimes called a *general equilibrium model*.

Throughout the chapter, we have discussed various applications of the model. The model can explain how income is divided among the factors of production and how factor prices depend on factor supplies. We have also used the model to discuss how fiscal policy alters the allocation of output among its alternative uses—consumption, investment, and government purchases—and how it affects the equilibrium interest rate.

At this point it is useful to review some of the simplifying assumptions we have made in this chapter. In the following chapters we relax some of these assumptions to address a greater range of questions.

- We have ignored the role of money, the asset with which goods and services are bought and sold. In Chapter 4 we discuss how money affects the economy and the influence of monetary policy.

- We have assumed that there is no trade with other countries. In Chapter 5 we consider how international interactions affect our conclusions.

- We have assumed that the labor force is fully employed. In Chapter 6 we examine the reasons for unemployment and see how public policy influences the level of unemployment.

- We have assumed that the capital stock, the labor force, and the production technology are fixed. In Chapters 7 and 8 we see how changes over time in each of these lead to growth in the economy's output of goods and services.

- We have ignored the role of short-run sticky prices. In Chapters 9 through 12 we develop a model of short-run fluctuations that includes sticky prices. We then discuss how the model of short-run fluctuations relates to the model of national income developed in this chapter.

- We have modeled the entire financial system with a single market, the market for loanable funds. In Chapters 15 through 19 we develop a more complete and realistic analysis of the role of financial markets and institutions in the economy.

Before going on to these chapters, go back to the beginning of this one and make sure you can answer the four groups of questions about national income that begin the chapter.

Summary

1. The factors of production and the production technology determine the economy's output of goods and services. An increase in one of the factors of production or a technological advance raises output.

2. Competitive, profit-maximizing firms hire labor until the marginal product of labor equals the real wage. Similarly, these firms rent capital until the marginal product of capital equals the real rental price. Therefore, each factor of production is paid its marginal product. If the production function has constant returns to scale, then according to Euler's theorem, all output is used to compensate the inputs.

3. The economy's output is used for consumption, investment, and government purchases. Consumption depends positively on disposable income. Investment depends negatively on the real interest rate. Government purchases and taxes are the exogenous variables of fiscal policy.

4. The real interest rate adjusts to equilibrate the supply and demand for the economy's output—or, equivalently, the supply of loanable funds (saving) and the demand for loanable funds (investment). A decrease in national saving, perhaps because of an increase in government purchases or a decrease in taxes, reduces the equilibrium amount of investment and raises the interest rate. An increase in investment demand, perhaps because of a technological innovation or a tax incentive for investment, also raises the interest rate. An increase in investment demand increases the quantity of investment only if higher interest rates stimulate additional saving.

KEY CONCEPTS

Factors of production

Production function

Constant returns to scale

Factor prices

Competition

Profit

Marginal product of labor (MPL)

Diminishing marginal product

Real wage

Marginal product of capital (MPK)

Real rental price of capital

Economic profit versus accounting profit

Cobb–Douglas production function

Disposable income

Consumption function

Marginal propensity to consume (MPC)

Interest rate

Nominal interest rate

Real interest rate

National saving (saving)

Private saving

Public saving

Loanable funds

Crowding out

QUESTIONS FOR REVIEW

1. What determines the amount of output an economy produces?

2. Explain how a competitive, profit-maximizing firm decides how much of each factor of production to demand.

3. What is the role of constant returns to scale in the distribution of income?

4. Write down a Cobb–Douglas production function for which capital earns one-fourth of total income.

5. What determines consumption and investment?

6. Explain the difference between government purchases and transfer payments. Give two examples of each.

7. What makes the demand for the economy's output of goods and services equal the supply?

8. Explain what happens to consumption, investment, and the interest rate when the government increases taxes.

PROBLEMS AND APPLICATIONS

1. Use the neoclassical theory of distribution to predict the impact on the real wage and the real rental price of capital of each of the following events:

   a. A wave of immigration increases the labor force.

   b. An earthquake destroys some of the capital stock.

   c. A technological advance improves the production function.

2. If a 10 percent increase in both capital and labor causes output to increase by less than 10 percent, the production function is said to exhibit *decreasing returns to scale*. If it causes output to increase by more than 10 percent, the production function is said to exhibit *increasing returns to scale*. Why might a production function exhibit decreasing or increasing returns to scale?

3. Suppose that an economy's production function is Cobb–Douglas with parameter $\alpha = 0.3$.

   a. What fractions of income do capital and labor receive?

   b. Suppose that immigration increases the labor force by 10 percent. What happens to total output (in percent)? The rental price of capital? The real wage?

   c. Suppose that a gift of capital from abroad raises the capital stock by 10 percent. What happens to total output (in percent)? The rental price of capital? The real wage?

   d. Suppose that a technological advance raises the value of the parameter A by 10 percent. What happens to total output (in percent)? The rental price of capital? The real wage?

4. Figure 3-5 shows that in U.S. data, labor's share of total income is approximately a constant over time. Table 3-1 shows that the trend in the real wage closely tracks the trend in labor productivity. How are these facts related? Could the first fact be true without the second also being true?

5. According to the neoclassical theory of distribution, the real wage earned by any worker equals that worker's marginal productivity. Let's use this insight to examine the incomes of two groups of workers: farmers and barbers.

   a. Over the past century, the productivity of farmers has risen substantially because of technological progress. According to the neoclassical theory, what should have happened to their real wage?

   b. In what units is the real wage discussed in part (a) measured?

   c. Over the same period, the productivity of barbers has remained constant. What should have happened to their real wage?

   d. In what units is the real wage in part (c) measured?

   e. Suppose workers can move freely between being farmers and being barbers. What does this mobility imply for the wages of farmers and barbers?

f. What do your previous answers imply for the price of haircuts relative to the price of food?

g. Who benefits from technological progress in farming—farmers or barbers?

6. (This problem requires the use of calculus.) Consider a Cobb–Douglas production function with three inputs. K is capital (the number of machines), L is labor (the number of workers), and H is human capital (the number of college degrees among the workers). The production function is

$$Y = K^{1/3} L^{1/3} H^{1/3}.$$

a. Derive an expression for the marginal product of labor. How does an increase in the amount of human capital affect the marginal product of labor?

b. Derive an expression for the marginal product of human capital. How does an increase in the amount of human capital affect the marginal product of human capital?

c. What is the income share paid to labor? What is the income share paid to human capital? In the national income accounts of this economy, what share of total income do you think workers would appear to receive? (*Hint*: Consider where the return to human capital shows up.)

d. An unskilled worker earns the marginal product of labor, whereas a skilled worker earns the marginal product of labor plus the marginal product of human capital. Using your answers to parts (a) and (b), find the ratio of the skilled wage to the unskilled wage. How does an increase in the amount of human capital affect this ratio? Explain.

e. Some people advocate government funding of college scholarships as a way of creating a more egalitarian society. Others argue that scholarships help only those who are able to go to college. Do your answers to the preceding questions shed light on this debate?

7. The government raises taxes by $100 billion. If the marginal propensity to consume is 0.6, what happens to the following? Do they rise or fall? By what amounts?

a. Public saving

b. Private saving

c. National saving

d. Investment

8. Suppose that an increase in consumer confidence raises consumers' expectations about their future income and thus increases the amount they want to consume today. This might be interpreted as an upward shift in the consumption function. How does this shift affect investment and the interest rate?

9. Consider an economy described by the following equations:

$$Y = C + I + G$$
$$Y = 5,000$$
$$G = 1,000$$
$$T = 1,000$$
$$C = 250 + 0.75(Y - T)$$
$$I = 1,000 - 50r.$$

a. In this economy, compute private saving, public saving, and national saving.

b. Find the equilibrium interest rate.

c. Now suppose that G rises to 1,250. Compute private saving, public saving, and national saving.

d. Find the new equilibrium interest rate.

10. Suppose that the government increases taxes and government purchases by equal amounts. What happens to the interest rate and investment in response to this balanced-budget change? Does your answer depend on the marginal propensity to consume?

11. When the government subsidizes investment, such as with an investment tax credit, the subsidy often applies to only some types of investment. This question asks you to consider the effect of such a change. Suppose there are two types of investment in the economy: business investment and residential investment. And suppose that the government institutes an investment tax credit only for business investment.

a. How does this policy affect the demand curve for business investment? The demand curve for residential investment?

b. Draw the economy's supply and demand for loanable funds. How does this policy affect the supply and demand for loanable funds? What happens to the equilibrium interest rate?

c. Compare the old and the new equilibria. How does this policy affect the total quantity of investment? The quantity of business investment? The quantity of residential investment?

12. If consumption depended on the interest rate, how would that affect the conclusions reached in this chapter about the effects of fiscal policy?

13. Macroeconomic data do not show a strong correlation between investment and interest rates. Let's examine why this might be so. Use our model in which the interest rate adjusts to equilibrate the supply of loanable funds (which is upward sloping) and the demand for loanable funds (which is downward sloping).

   a. Suppose the demand for loanable funds was stable but the supply fluctuated from year to year. What might cause these fluctuations in supply? In this case, what correlation between investment and interest rates would you find?

   b. Suppose the supply of loanable funds was stable but the demand fluctuated from year to year. What might cause these fluctuations in demand? In this case, what correlation between investment and interest rates would you find now?

   c. Suppose that both supply and demand in this market fluctuated over time. If you were to construct a scatterplot of investment and the interest rate, what would you find?

   d. Which of the above three cases seems most empirically realistic to you?

CHAPTER 4

Money and Inflation

Lenin is said to have declared that the best way to destroy the Capitalist System was to debauch the currency. . . .Lenin was certainly right. There is no subtler, no surer means of overturning the existing basis of society than to debauch the currency. The process engages all the hidden forces of economic law on the side of destruction, and does it in a manner which not one man in a million is able to diagnose.

—*John Maynard Keynes*

I n 1970 the *New York Times* cost 15 cents, the median price of a single-family home was $23,400, and the average wage in manufacturing was $3.36 per hour. In 2009 the *Times* cost $2.00, the median price of a home was $174,100, and the average wage was $20.42 per hour. This overall increase in prices is called **inflation**, which is the subject of this chapter.

The rate of inflation—the percentage change in the overall level of prices—varies greatly over time and across countries. In the United States, according to the consumer price index, prices rose an average of 2.4 percent per year in the 1960s, 7.1 percent per year in the 1970s, 5.5 percent per year in the 1980s, 3.0 percent per year in the 1990s, and 2.6 percent from 2000 to 2009. Even when the U.S. inflation problem became severe during the 1970s, however, it was nothing compared to the episodes of extraordinarily high inflation, called **hyperinflation**, that other countries have experienced from time to time. A classic example is Germany in 1923, when prices increased an average of 500 percent *per month*. In 2008, a similar hyperinflation gripped the nation of Zimbabwe.

In this chapter we examine the classical theory of the causes, effects, and social costs of inflation. The theory is "classical" in the sense that it assumes that prices are flexible. As we first discussed in Chapter 1, most economists believe this assumption describes the behavior of the economy in the long run. By contrast, many prices are thought to be sticky in the short run, and beginning in Chapter 9, we incorporate this fact into our analysis. For now, we ignore short-run price stickiness. As we will see, the classical theory of inflation not only provides a good description of the long run, it also provides a useful foundation for the short-run analysis we develop later.

The "hidden forces of economic law" that lead to inflation are not as mysterious as Keynes claims in the quotation that opens this chapter. Inflation is simply an increase in the average level of prices, and a price is the rate at which money is exchanged for a good or a service. To understand inflation, therefore, we must understand money—what it is, what affects its supply and demand, and what influence it has on the economy. Thus, Section 4-1 begins our analysis of inflation by discussing the economist's concept of "money" and how, in most modern economies, the government controls the quantity of money in the hands of the public. Section 4-2 shows that the quantity of money determines the price level and that the rate of growth in the quantity of money determines the rate of inflation.

Inflation in turn has numerous effects of its own on the economy. Section 4-3 discusses the revenue that governments can raise by printing money, sometimes called the *inflation tax*. Section 4-4 examines how inflation affects the nominal interest rate. Section 4-5 discusses how the nominal interest rate in turn affects the quantity of money people wish to hold and, thereby, the price level.

After completing our analysis of the causes and effects of inflation, in Section 4-6 we address what is perhaps the most important question about inflation: Is it a major social problem? Does inflation amount to "overturning the existing basis of society," as the chapter's opening quotation suggests?

Finally, in Section 4-7, we discuss the dramatic case of hyperinflation. Hyperinflations are interesting to examine because they show clearly the causes, effects, and costs of inflation. Just as seismologists learn much by studying earthquakes, economists learn much by studying how hyperinflations begin and end.

4-1 What Is Money?

When we say that a person has a lot of money, we usually mean that he or she is wealthy. By contrast, economists use the term "money" in a more specialized way. To an economist, money does not refer to all wealth but only to one type of it: **money** is the stock of assets that can be readily used to make transactions. Roughly speaking, the dollars in the hands of the public make up the nation's stock of money.

The Functions of Money

Money has three purposes: it is a store of value, a unit of account, and a medium of exchange.

As a **store of value**, money is a way to transfer purchasing power from the present to the future. If I work today and earn $100, I can hold the money and spend it tomorrow, next week, or next month. Of course, money is an imperfect store of value: if prices are rising, the amount you can buy with any given quantity of money is falling. Even so, people hold money because they can trade it for goods and services at some time in the future.

As a **unit of account**, money provides the terms in which prices are quoted and debts are recorded. Microeconomics teaches us that resources are allocated according to relative prices—the prices of goods relative to other goods—yet stores post their prices in dollars and cents. A car dealer tells you that a car costs $20,000, not 400 shirts (even though it may amount to the same thing). Similarly, most debts require the debtor to deliver a specified number of dollars in the future, not a specified amount of some commodity. Money is the yardstick with which we measure economic transactions.

As a **medium of exchange**, money is what we use to buy goods and services. "This note is legal tender for all debts, public and private" is printed on the U.S. dollar. When we walk into stores, we are confident that the shopkeepers will accept our money in exchange for the items they are selling. The ease with which an asset can be converted into the medium of exchange and used to buy other things—goods and services—is sometimes called the asset's *liquidity*. Because money is the medium of exchange, it is the economy's most liquid asset.

To better understand the functions of money, try to imagine an economy without it: a barter economy. In such a world, trade requires the *double coincidence of wants*—the unlikely happenstance of two people each having a good that the other wants at the right time and place to make an exchange. A barter economy permits only simple transactions.

Money makes more indirect transactions possible. A professor uses her salary to buy books; the book publisher uses its revenue from the sale of books to buy paper; the paper company uses its revenue from the sale of paper to pay the lumberjack; the lumberjack uses his income to send his child to college; and the college uses its tuition receipts to pay the salary of the professor. In a complex, modern economy, trade is usually indirect and requires the use of money.

The Types of Money

Money takes many forms. In the U.S. economy we make transactions with an item whose sole function is to act as money: dollar bills. These pieces of green paper with small portraits of famous Americans would have little value if they were not widely accepted as money. Money that has no intrinsic value is called **fiat money** because it is established as money by government decree, or fiat.

Fiat money is the norm in most economies today, but most societies in the past have used a commodity with some intrinsic value for money. This type of money is called **commodity money**. The most widespread example is gold. When people use gold as money (or use paper money that is redeemable for gold), the economy is said to be on a **gold standard**. Gold is a form of commodity money because it can be used for various purposes—jewelry, dental fillings, and so on—as well as for transactions. The gold standard was common throughout the world during the late nineteenth and early twentieth centuries.

Drawing by Bernard Schoenbaum; © 1979 The New Yorker Magazine, Inc.

"And how would you like your funny money?"

CASE STUDY

Money in a POW Camp

An unusual form of commodity money developed in some Nazi prisoner of war (POW) camps during World War II. The Red Cross supplied the prisoners with various goods—food, clothing, cigarettes, and so on. Yet these rations were allocated without close attention to personal preferences, so the allocations were often inefficient. One prisoner may have preferred chocolate, while another may have preferred cheese, and a third may have wanted a new shirt. The differing tastes and endowments of the prisoners led them to trade with one another.

Barter proved to be an inconvenient way to allocate these resources, however, because it required the double coincidence of wants. In other words, a barter system was not the easiest way to ensure that each prisoner received the goods he valued most. Even the limited economy of the POW camp needed some form of money to facilitate transactions.

Eventually, cigarettes became the established "currency" in which prices were quoted and with which trades were made. A shirt, for example, cost about 80 cigarettes. Services were also quoted in cigarettes: some prisoners offered to do other prisoners' laundry for 2 cigarettes per garment. Even nonsmokers were happy to accept cigarettes in exchange, knowing they could trade the cigarettes in the future for some good they did enjoy. Within the POW camp the cigarette became the store of value, the unit of account, and the medium of exchange.[1] ■

The Development of Fiat Money

It is not surprising that in any society, no matter how primitive, some form of commodity money arises to facilitate exchange: people are willing to accept a commodity currency such as gold because it has intrinsic value. The development of fiat money, however, is more perplexing. What would make people begin to value something that is intrinsically useless?

To understand how the evolution from commodity money to fiat money takes place, imagine an economy in which people carry around bags of gold. When a purchase is made, the buyer measures out the appropriate amount of gold. If the seller is convinced that the weight and purity of the gold are right, the buyer and seller make the exchange.

The government might first get involved in the monetary system to help people reduce transaction costs. Using raw gold as money is costly because it takes time to verify the purity of the gold and to measure the correct quantity. To reduce these costs, the government can mint gold coins of known purity and weight. The coins are easier to use than gold bullion because their values are widely recognized.

The next step is for the government to accept gold from the public in exchange for gold certificates—pieces of paper that can be redeemed for a certain quantity

---

[1] R. A. Radford, "The Economic Organisation of a P.O.W. Camp," *Economica* 12 (November 1945): 189–201. The use of cigarettes as money is not limited to this example. In the Soviet Union in the late 1980s, packs of Marlboros were preferred to the ruble in the large underground economy.

of gold. If people believe the government's promise to redeem the paper bills for gold, the bills are just as valuable as the gold itself. In addition, because the bills are lighter than gold (and gold coins), they are easier to use in transactions. Eventually, no one carries gold around at all, and these gold-backed government bills become the monetary standard.

Finally, the gold backing becomes irrelevant. If no one ever bothers to redeem the bills for gold, no one cares if the option is abandoned. As long as everyone continues to accept the paper bills in exchange, they will have value and serve as money. Thus, the system of commodity money evolves into a system of fiat money. Notice that in the end the use of money in exchange is a social convention: everyone values fiat money because they expect everyone else to value it.

CASE STUDY

Money and Social Conventions on the Island of Yap

The economy of Yap, a small island in the Pacific, once had a type of money that was something between commodity and fiat money. The traditional medium of exchange in Yap was *fei*, stone wheels up to 12 feet in diameter. These stones had holes in the center so that they could be carried on poles and used for exchange.

Large stone wheels are not a convenient form of money. The stones were heavy, so it took substantial effort for a new owner to take his *fei* home after completing a transaction. Although the monetary system facilitated exchange, it did so at great cost.

Eventually, it became common practice for the new owner of the *fei* not to bother to take physical possession of the stone. Instead, the new owner accepted a claim to the *fei* without moving it. In future bargains, he traded this claim for goods that he wanted. Having physical possession of the stone became less important than having legal claim to it.

This practice was put to a test when a valuable stone was lost at sea during a storm. Because the owner lost his money by accident rather than through negligence, everyone agreed that his claim to the *fei* remained valid. Even generations later, when no one alive had ever seen this stone, the claim to this *fei* was still valued in exchange.[2] ■

How the Quantity of Money Is Controlled

The quantity of money available in an economy is called the **money supply**. In a system of commodity money, the money supply is simply the quantity of that commodity. In an economy that uses fiat money, such as most economies today, the government controls the supply of money: legal restrictions give the government a monopoly on the printing of money. Just as the level of taxation and the level of government purchases are policy instruments of the government, so is the quantity of money. The government's control over the money supply is called **monetary policy**.

---

[2] Norman Angell, *The Story of Money* (New York: Frederick A. Stokes Company, 1929), 88–89.

In the United States and many other countries, monetary policy is delegated to a partially independent institution called the **central bank**. The central bank of the United States is the **Federal Reserve**—often called *the Fed*. If you look at a U.S. dollar bill, you will see that it is called a *Federal Reserve Note*. Decisions over monetary policy are made by the Fed's Federal Open Market Committee. This committee is made up of members of the Federal Reserve Board, who are appointed by the president and confirmed by Congress, together with the presidents of the regional Federal Reserve Banks. The Federal Open Market Committee meets about every six weeks to discuss and set monetary policy.

The primary way in which the Fed controls the supply of money is through **open-market operations**—the purchase and sale of government bonds. When the Fed wants to increase the money supply, it uses some of the dollars it has to buy government bonds from the public. Because these dollars leave the Fed and enter into the hands of the public, the purchase increases the quantity of money in circulation. Conversely, when the Fed wants to decrease the money supply, it sells some government bonds from its own portfolio. This open-market sale of bonds takes some dollars out of the hands of the public and, thus, decreases the quantity of money in circulation.

The appendix to this chapter discusses in detail how the Fed controls the supply of money. For much of our current discussion, these details are not crucial. It is sufficient to assume that the Fed (or any other central bank) directly controls the supply of money.

How the Quantity of Money Is Measured

One goal of this chapter is to determine how the money supply affects the economy; we turn to that topic in the next section. As a background for that analysis, let's first discuss how economists measure the quantity of money.

Because money is the stock of assets used for transactions, the quantity of money is the quantity of those assets. In simple economies, this quantity is easy to measure. In the POW camp, the quantity of money was the number of cigarettes in the camp. But how can we measure the quantity of money in more complex economies? The answer is not obvious, because no single asset is used for all transactions. People can use various assets, such as cash in their wallets or deposits in their checking accounts, to make transactions, although some assets are more convenient than others.

The most obvious asset to include in the quantity of money is **currency**, the sum of outstanding paper money and coins. Most day-to-day transactions use currency as the medium of exchange.

A second type of asset used for transactions is **demand deposits**, the funds people hold in their checking accounts. If most sellers accept personal checks, assets in a checking account are almost as convenient as currency. In both cases, the assets are in a form ready to facilitate a transaction. Demand deposits are therefore added to currency when measuring the quantity of money.

Once we admit the logic of including demand deposits in the measured money stock, many other assets become candidates for inclusion. Funds in savings accounts, for example, can be easily transferred into checking accounts; these assets

TABLE 4-1

The Measures of Money

Symbol	Assets Included	Amount in December 2009 (billions of dollars)
C	Currency	$ 865
M1	Currency plus demand deposits, traveler's checks, and other checkable deposits	1719
M2	M1 plus retail money market mutual fund balances, saving deposits (including money market deposit accounts), and small time deposits	8421

Source: Federal Reserve.

are almost as convenient for transactions. Money market mutual funds allow investors to write checks against their accounts, although restrictions sometimes apply with regard to the size of the check or the number of checks written. Because these assets can be easily used for transactions, they should arguably be included in the quantity of money.

Because it is hard to judge which assets should be included in the money stock, more than one measure is available. Table 4-1 presents the three measures

How Do Credit Cards and Debit Cards Fit Into the Monetary System?

Many people use credit or debit cards to make purchases. Because money is the medium of exchange, one might naturally wonder how these cards fit into the measurement and analysis of money.

Let's start with credit cards. One might guess that credit cards are part of the economy's stock of money, but in fact measures of the quantity of money do not take credit cards into account. This is because credit cards are not really a method of payment but a method of *deferring* payment. When you buy an item with a credit card, the bank that issued the card pays the store what it is due. Later, you repay the bank. When the time comes to pay your credit card bill, you will likely do so by writing a check against your checking account. The balance in this checking account is part of the economy's stock of money.

The story is different with debit cards, which automatically withdraw funds from a bank account to pay for items bought. Rather than allowing users to postpone payment for their purchases, a debit card allows users immediate access to deposits in their bank accounts. Using a debit card is similar to writing a check. The account balances that lie behind debit cards are included in measures of the quantity of money.

Even though credit cards are not a form of money, they are still important for analyzing the monetary system. Because people with credit cards can pay many of their bills all at once at the end of the month, rather than sporadically as they make purchases, they may hold less money on average than people without credit cards. Thus, the increased popularity of credit cards may reduce the amount of money that people choose to hold. In other words, credit cards are not part of the supply of money, but they may affect the demand for money.

of the money stock that the Federal Reserve calculates for the U.S. economy, together with a list of which assets are included in each measure. From the smallest to the largest, they are designated C, $M1$, and $M2$.

4-2 The Quantity Theory of Money

Having defined what money is and described how it is controlled and measured, we can now examine how the quantity of money affects the economy. To do this, we need a theory of how the quantity of money is related to other economic variables, such as prices and incomes. The theory we will now develop, called the *quantity theory of money*, has its roots in the work of the early monetary theorists, including the philosopher and economist David Hume (1711–1776). It remains the leading explanation for how money affects the economy in the long run.

Transactions and the Quantity Equation

People hold money to buy goods and services. The more money they need for such transactions, the more money they hold. Thus, the quantity of money in the economy is related to the number of dollars exchanged in transactions.

The link between transactions and money is expressed in the following equation, called the **quantity equation**:

$$\text{Money} \times \text{Velocity} = \text{Price} \times \text{Transactions}$$

$$M \quad \times \quad V \quad = \quad P \quad \times \quad T.$$

Let's examine each of the four variables in this equation.

The right-hand side of the quantity equation tells us about transactions. T represents the total number of transactions during some period of time, say, a year. In other words, T is the number of times in a year that goods or services are exchanged for money. P is the price of a typical transaction—the number of dollars exchanged. The product of the price of a transaction and the number of transactions, PT, equals the number of dollars exchanged in a year.

The left-hand side of the quantity equation tells us about the money used to make the transactions. M is the quantity of money. V, called the **transactions velocity of money**, measures the rate at which money circulates in the economy. In other words, velocity tells us the number of times a dollar bill changes hands in a given period of time.

For example, suppose that 60 loaves of bread are sold in a given year at $0.50 per loaf. Then T equals 60 loaves per year, and P equals $0.50 per loaf. The total number of dollars exchanged is

$$PT = \$0.50/\text{loaf} \times 60 \text{ loaves/year} = \$30/\text{year}.$$

The right-hand side of the quantity equation equals $30 per year, which is the dollar value of all transactions.

Suppose further that the quantity of money in the economy is $10. Then, by rearranging the quantity equation, we can compute velocity as

$$V = PT/M$$
$$= (\$30/\text{year})/(\$10)$$
$$= 3 \text{ times per year.}$$

That is, for $30 of transactions per year to take place with $10 of money, each dollar must change hands 3 times per year.

The quantity equation is an *identity*: the definitions of the four variables make it true. This type of equation is useful because it shows that if one of the variables changes, one or more of the others must also change to maintain the equality. For example, if the quantity of money increases and the velocity of money remains unchanged, then either the price or the number of transactions must rise.

From Transactions to Income

When studying the role of money in the economy, economists usually use a slightly different version of the quantity equation than the one just introduced. The problem with the first equation is that the number of transactions is difficult to measure. To solve this problem, the number of transactions T is replaced by the total output of the economy Y.

Transactions and output are related, because the more the economy produces, the more goods are bought and sold. They are not the same, however. When one person sells a used car to another person, for example, they make a transaction using money, even though the used car is not part of current output. Nonetheless, the dollar value of transactions is roughly proportional to the dollar value of output.

If Y denotes the amount of output and P denotes the price of one unit of output, then the dollar value of output is PY. We encountered measures for these variables when we discussed the national income accounts in Chapter 2: Y is real GDP; P, the GDP deflator; and PY, nominal GDP. The quantity equation becomes

$$\text{Money} \times \text{Velocity} = \text{Price} \times \text{Output}$$
$$M \quad \times \quad V \quad = \quad P \quad \times \quad Y.$$

Because Y is also total income, V in this version of the quantity equation is called the **income velocity of money**. The income velocity of money tells us the number of times a dollar bill enters someone's income in a given period of time. This version of the quantity equation is the most common, and it is the one we use from now on.

The Money Demand Function and the Quantity Equation

When we analyze how money affects the economy, it is often useful to express the quantity of money in terms of the quantity of goods and services it can buy. This amount, M/P, is called **real money balances**.

Real money balances measure the purchasing power of the stock of money. For example, consider an economy that produces only bread. If the quantity of money is $10, and the price of a loaf is $0.50, then real money balances are 20 loaves of bread. That is, at current prices, the stock of money in the economy is able to buy 20 loaves.

A **money demand function** is an equation that shows the determinants of the quantity of real money balances people wish to hold. A simple money demand function is

$$(M/P)^{\mathrm{d}} = kY,$$

where k is a constant that tells us how much money people want to hold for every dollar of income. This equation states that the quantity of real money balances demanded is proportional to real income.

The money demand function is like the demand function for a particular good. Here the "good" is the convenience of holding real money balances. Just as owning an automobile makes it easier for a person to travel, holding money makes it easier to make transactions. Therefore, just as higher income leads to a greater demand for automobiles, higher income also leads to a greater demand for real money balances.

This money demand function offers another way to view the quantity equation. To see this, add to the money demand function the condition that the demand for real money balances $(M/P)^{\mathrm{d}}$ must equal the supply M/P. Therefore,

$$M/P = kY.$$

A simple rearrangement of terms changes this equation into

$$M(1/k) = PY,$$

which can be written as

$$MV = PY,$$

where $V = 1/k$. These few steps of simple mathematics show the link between the demand for money and the velocity of money. When people want to hold a lot of money for each dollar of income (k is large), money changes hands infrequently (V is small). Conversely, when people want to hold only a little money (k is small), money changes hands frequently (V is large). In other words, the money demand parameter k and the velocity of money V are opposite sides of the same coin.

The Assumption of Constant Velocity

The quantity equation can be viewed as a definition: it defines velocity V as the ratio of nominal GDP (PY) to the quantity of money (M). Yet if we make the additional assumption that the velocity of money is constant, then the quantity equation becomes a useful theory about the effects of money, called the **quantity theory of money**.

As with many of the assumptions in economics, the assumption of constant velocity is only a simplification of reality. Velocity does change if the money demand function changes. For example, when automatic teller machines were introduced, people could reduce their average money holdings, which meant a fall in the money demand parameter k and an increase in velocity V. Nonetheless, experience shows that the assumption of constant velocity is a useful one in many situations. Let's therefore assume that velocity is constant and see what this assumption implies about the effects of the money supply on the economy.

With this assumption included, the quantity equation can be seen as a theory of what determines nominal GDP. The quantity equation says

$$M\overline{V} = PY,$$

where the bar over V means that velocity is fixed. Therefore, a change in the quantity of money (M) must cause a proportionate change in nominal GDP (PY). That is, if velocity is fixed, the quantity of money determines the dollar value of the economy's output.

Money, Prices, and Inflation

We now have a theory to explain what determines the economy's overall level of prices. The theory has three building blocks:

1. The factors of production and the production function determine the level of output Y. We borrow this conclusion from Chapter 3.

2. The money supply M determines the nominal value of output PY. This conclusion follows from the quantity equation and the assumption that the velocity of money is fixed.

3. The price level P is then the ratio of the nominal value of output PY to the level of output Y.

In other words, the productive capability of the economy determines real GDP, the quantity of money determines nominal GDP, and the GDP deflator is the ratio of nominal GDP to real GDP.

This theory explains what happens when the central bank changes the supply of money. Because velocity is fixed, any change in the money supply leads to a proportionate change in nominal GDP. Because the factors of production and the production function have already determined real GDP, nominal GDP can adjust only if the price level changes. Hence, the quantity theory implies that the price level is proportional to the money supply.

Because the inflation rate is the percentage change in the price level, this theory of the price level is also a theory of the inflation rate. The quantity equation, written in percentage-change form, is

% Change in M + % Change in V = % Change in P + % Change in Y.

Consider each of these four terms. First, the percentage change in the quantity of money M is under the control of the central bank. Second, the percentage change in velocity V reflects shifts in money demand; we have assumed that velocity is constant, so the percentage change in velocity is zero. Third, the percentage change in the price level P is the rate of inflation; this is the variable in the equation that we would like to explain. Fourth, the percentage change in output Y depends on growth in the factors of production and on technological progress, which for our present purposes we are taking as given. This analysis tells us that (except for a constant that depends on exogenous growth in output) the growth in the money supply determines the rate of inflation.

Thus, the quantity theory of money states that the central bank, which controls the money supply, has ultimate control over the rate of inflation. If the central bank keeps the money supply stable, the price level will be stable. If the central bank increases the money supply rapidly, the price level will rise rapidly.

CASE STUDY

Inflation and Money Growth

"Inflation is always and everywhere a monetary phenomenon." So wrote Milton Friedman, the great economist who won the Nobel Prize in economics in 1976. The quantity theory of money leads us to agree that the growth in the quantity of money is the primary determinant of the inflation rate. Yet Friedman's claim

FIGURE 4-1

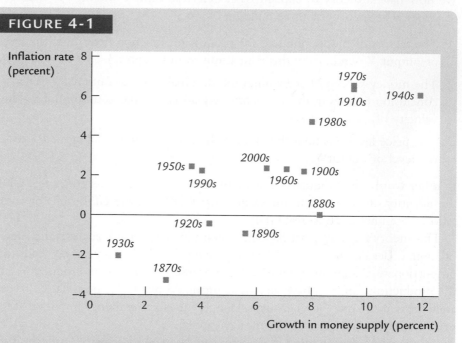

Historical Data on U.S. Inflation and Money Growth In this scatterplot of money growth and inflation, each point represents a decade. The horizontal axis shows the average growth in the money supply (as measured by *M2*) over the decade, and the vertical axis shows the average rate of inflation (as measured by the GDP deflator). The positive correlation between money growth and inflation is evidence for the quantity theory's prediction that high money growth leads to high inflation.

Source: For the data through the 1960s: Milton Friedman and Anna J. Schwartz, *Monetary Trends in the United States and the United Kingdom: Their Relation to Income, Prices, and Interest Rates 1867–1975* (Chicago: University of Chicago Press, 1982). For recent data: U.S. Department of Commerce and Federal Reserve Board.

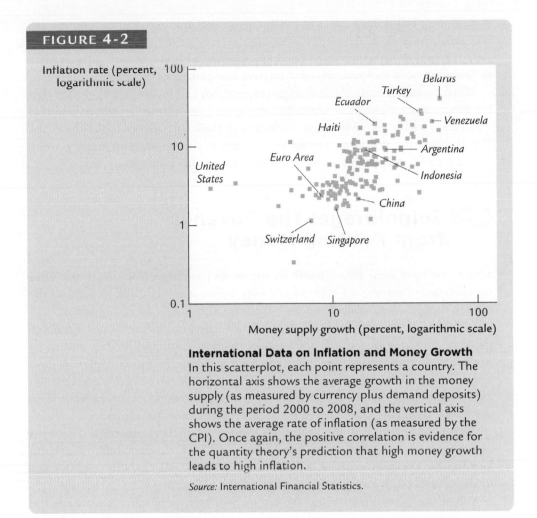

FIGURE 4-2

Inflation rate (percent, logarithmic scale)

Money supply growth (percent, logarithmic scale)

International Data on Inflation and Money Growth
In this scatterplot, each point represents a country. The horizontal axis shows the average growth in the money supply (as measured by currency plus demand deposits) during the period 2000 to 2008, and the vertical axis shows the average rate of inflation (as measured by the CPI). Once again, the positive correlation is evidence for the quantity theory's prediction that high money growth leads to high inflation.

Source: International Financial Statistics.

is empirical, not theoretical. To evaluate his claim, and to judge the usefulness of our theory, we need to look at data on money and prices.

Friedman, together with fellow economist Anna Schwartz, wrote two treatises on monetary history that documented the sources and effects of changes in the quantity of money over the past century.[3] Figure 4-1 uses some of their data and plots the average rate of money growth and the average rate of inflation in the United States over each decade since the 1870s. The data verify the link between inflation and growth in the quantity of money. Decades with high money growth (such as the 1970s) tend to have high inflation, and decades with low money growth (such as the 1930s) tend to have low inflation.

Figure 4-2 examines the same question using international data. It shows the average rate of inflation and the average rate of money growth in 158 countries

[3] Milton Friedman and Anna J. Schwartz, *A Monetary History of the United States, 1867–1960* (Princeton, NJ: Princeton University Press, 1963); Milton Friedman and Anna J. Schwartz, *Monetary Trends in the United States and the United Kingdom: Their Relation to Income, Prices, and Interest Rates, 1867–1975* (Chicago: University of Chicago Press, 1982).

during the period from 2000 to 2008. Again, the link between money growth and inflation is clear. Countries with high money growth (such as Turkey and Belarus) tend to have high inflation, and countries with low money growth (such as Singapore and Switzerland) tend to have low inflation.

If we looked at monthly data on money growth and inflation, rather than data for longer periods, we would not see as close a connection between these two variables. This theory of inflation works best in the long run, not in the short run. We examine the short-run impact of changes in the quantity of money when we turn to economic fluctuations in Part Four of this book. ■

4-3 Seigniorage: The Revenue from Printing Money

So far, we have seen how growth in the money supply causes inflation. With inflation as a consequence, what would ever induce a central bank to increase the money supply substantially? Here we examine one answer to this question.

Let's start with an indisputable fact: all governments spend money. Some of this spending is to buy goods and services (such as roads and police), and some is to provide transfer payments (for the poor and elderly, for example). A government can finance its spending in three ways. First, it can raise revenue through taxes, such as personal and corporate income taxes. Second, it can borrow from the public by selling government bonds. Third, it can print money.

The revenue raised by the printing of money is called **seigniorage**. The term comes from *seigneur,* the French word for "feudal lord." In the Middle Ages, the lord had the exclusive right on his manor to coin money. Today this right belongs to the central government, and it is one source of revenue.

When the government prints money to finance expenditure, it increases the money supply. The increase in the money supply, in turn, causes inflation. Printing money to raise revenue is like imposing an *inflation tax.*

At first it may not be obvious that inflation can be viewed as a tax. After all, no one receives a bill for this tax—the government merely prints the money it needs. Who, then, pays the inflation tax? The answer is the holders of money. As prices rise, the real value of the money in your wallet falls. Therefore, when the government prints new money for its use, it makes the old money in the hands of the public less valuable. Inflation is like a tax on holding money.

The amount of revenue raised by printing money varies from country to country. In the United States, the amount has been small: seigniorage has usually accounted for less than 3 percent of government revenue. In Italy and Greece, seigniorage has often been more than 10 percent of government revenue.[4] In countries experiencing hyperinflation, seigniorage is often the government's chief source of revenue—indeed, the need to print money to finance expenditure is a primary cause of hyperinflation.

---

[4] Stanley Fischer, "Seigniorage and the Case for a National Money," *Journal of Political Economy* 90 (April 1982): 295–313.

CASE STUDY

Paying for the American Revolution

Although seigniorage has not been a major source of revenue for the U.S. government in recent history, the situation was very different two centuries ago. Beginning in 1775, the Continental Congress needed to find a way to finance the Revolution, but it had limited ability to raise revenue through taxation. It therefore relied on the printing of fiat money to help pay for the war.

The Continental Congress's reliance on seigniorage increased over time. In 1775 new issues of continental currency were about $6 million. This amount increased to $19 million in 1776, $13 million in 1777, $63 million in 1778, and $125 million in 1779.

Not surprisingly, this rapid growth in the money supply led to massive inflation. At the end of the war, the price of gold measured in continental dollars was more than 100 times its level of only a few years earlier. The large quantity of the continental currency made the continental dollar nearly worthless. This experience also gave birth to a once-popular expression: people used to say something was "not worth a continental" to mean that the item had little real value.

When the new nation won its independence, there was a natural skepticism about fiat money. On the recommendation of the first Secretary of the Treasury, Alexander Hamilton, the Congress passed the Mint Act of 1792, which established gold and silver as the basis for a new system of commodity money. ∎

4-4 Inflation and Interest Rates

As we first discussed in Chapter 3, interest rates are among the most important macroeconomic variables. In essence, they are the prices that link the present and the future. Here we discuss the relationship between inflation and interest rates.

Two Interest Rates: Real and Nominal

Suppose you deposit your savings in a bank account that pays 8 percent interest annually. Next year, you withdraw your savings and the accumulated interest. Are you 8 percent richer than you were when you made the deposit a year earlier?

The answer depends on what "richer" means. Certainly, you have 8 percent more dollars than you had before. But if prices have risen, each dollar buys less, and your purchasing power has not risen by 8 percent. If the inflation rate was 5 percent over the year, then the amount of goods you can buy has increased by only 3 percent. And if the inflation rate was 10 percent, then your purchasing power has fallen by 2 percent.

The interest rate that the bank pays is called the **nominal interest rate**, and the increase in your purchasing power is called the **real interest rate**. If i denotes the nominal interest rate, r the real interest rate, and π the rate of inflation, then the relationship among these three variables can be written as

$$r = i - \pi.$$

The real interest rate is the difference between the nominal interest rate and the rate of inflation.[5]

The Fisher Effect

Rearranging terms in our equation for the real interest rate, we can show that the nominal interest rate is the sum of the real interest rate and the inflation rate:

$$i = r + \pi.$$

The equation written in this way is called the **Fisher equation**, after economist Irving Fisher (1867–1947). It shows that the nominal interest rate can change for two reasons: because the real interest rate changes or because the inflation rate changes.

Once we separate the nominal interest rate into these two parts, we can use this equation to develop a theory that explains the nominal interest rate. Chapter 3 showed that the real interest rate adjusts to equilibrate saving and investment. The quantity theory of money shows that the rate of money growth determines the rate of inflation. The Fisher equation then tells us to add the real interest rate and the inflation rate together to determine the nominal interest rate.

The quantity theory and the Fisher equation together tell us how money growth affects the nominal interest rate. *According to the quantity theory, an increase in the rate of money growth of 1 percent causes a 1 percent increase in the rate of inflation. According to the Fisher equation, a 1 percent increase in the rate of inflation in turn causes a 1 percent increase in the nominal interest rate.* The one-for-one relation between the inflation rate and the nominal interest rate is called the **Fisher effect**.

CASE STUDY

Inflation and Nominal Interest Rates

How useful is the Fisher effect in explaining interest rates? To answer this question, we look at two types of data on inflation and nominal interest rates.

Figure 4-3 shows the variation over time in the nominal interest rate and the inflation rate in the United States. You can see that the Fisher effect has done a good job of explaining fluctuations in the nominal interest rate over the past 50 years. When inflation is high, nominal interest rates are typically high, and when inflation is low, nominal interest rates are typically low as well.

Similar support for the Fisher effect comes from examining the variation across countries. As Figure 4-4 shows, a nation's inflation rate and its nominal interest rate

---

[5] *Mathematical note:* This equation relating the real interest rate, nominal interest rate, and inflation rate is only an approximation. The exact formula is $(1 + r) = (1 + i)/(1 + \pi)$. The approximation in the text is reasonably accurate as long as r, i, and π are relatively small (say, less than 20 percent per year).

FIGURE 4-3

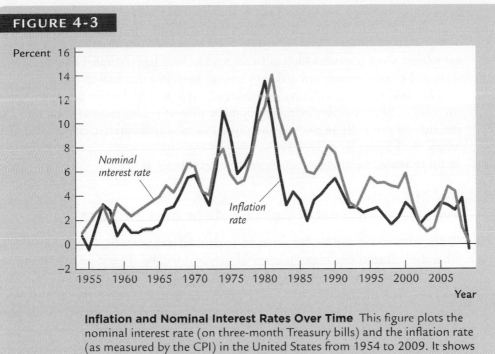

Inflation and Nominal Interest Rates Over Time This figure plots the nominal interest rate (on three-month Treasury bills) and the inflation rate (as measured by the CPI) in the United States from 1954 to 2009. It shows the Fisher effect: higher inflation leads to a higher nominal interest rate.

Source: Federal Reserve and U.S. Department of Labor.

FIGURE 4-4

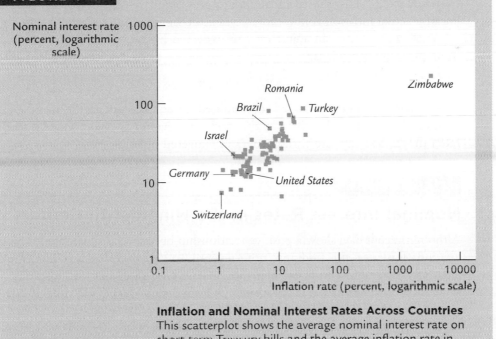

Inflation and Nominal Interest Rates Across Countries This scatterplot shows the average nominal interest rate on short-term Treasury bills and the average inflation rate in 81 countries during the period 2000 to 2008. The positive correlation between the inflation rate and the nominal interest rate is evidence for the Fisher effect.

Source: International Monetary Fund and World Bank.

are related. Countries with high inflation tend to have high nominal interest rates as well, and countries with low inflation tend to have low nominal interest rates.

The link between inflation and interest rates is well known to Wall Street investment firms. Because bond prices move inversely with interest rates, one can get rich by correctly predicting the direction in which interest rates will move. Many Wall Street firms hire *Fed watchers* to monitor monetary policy and news about inflation to anticipate changes in interest rates. ■

Two Real Interest Rates: *Ex Ante* and *Ex Post*

When a borrower and lender agree on a nominal interest rate, they do not know what the inflation rate over the term of the loan will be. Therefore, we must distinguish between two concepts of the real interest rate: the real interest rate that the borrower and lender expect when the loan is made, called the **ex ante real interest rate**, and the real interest rate that is actually realized, called the **ex post real interest rate**.

Although borrowers and lenders cannot predict future inflation with certainty, they do have some expectation about what the inflation rate will be. Let π denote actual future inflation and $E\pi$ the expectation of future inflation. The *ex ante* real interest rate is $i - E\pi$, and the *ex post* real interest rate is $i - \pi$. The two real interest rates differ when actual inflation π differs from expected inflation $E\pi$.

How does this distinction between actual and expected inflation modify the Fisher effect? Clearly, the nominal interest rate cannot adjust to actual inflation, because actual inflation is not known when the nominal interest rate is set. The nominal interest rate can adjust only to expected inflation. The Fisher effect is more precisely written as

$$i = r + E\pi.$$

The *ex ante* real interest rate r is determined by equilibrium in the market for goods and services, as described by the model in Chapter 3. The nominal interest rate i moves one-for-one with changes in expected inflation $E\pi$.

CASE STUDY

Nominal Interest Rates in the Nineteenth Century

Although recent data show a positive relationship between nominal interest rates and inflation rates, this finding is not universal. In data from the late nineteenth and early twentieth centuries, high nominal interest rates did not accompany high inflation. The apparent absence of any Fisher effect during this time puzzled Irving Fisher. He suggested that inflation "caught merchants napping."

How should we interpret the absence of an apparent Fisher effect in nineteenth-century data? Does this period of history provide evidence against the adjustment of nominal interest rates to inflation? Recent research suggests that this period has little to tell us about the validity of the Fisher effect. The reason is that the Fisher effect relates the nominal interest rate to *expected* inflation and, according to this research, inflation at this time was largely unexpected.

Although expectations are not easily observable, we can draw inferences about them by examining the persistence of inflation. In recent experience, inflation has been very persistent: when it is high one year, it tends to be high the next year as well. Therefore, when people have observed high inflation, it has been rational for them to expect high inflation in the future. By contrast, during the nineteenth century, when the gold standard was in effect, inflation had little persistence. High inflation in one year was just as likely to be followed the next year by low inflation (or even deflation) as by high inflation. Therefore, high inflation did not imply high expected inflation and did not lead to high nominal interest rates. So, in a sense, Fisher was right to say that inflation "caught merchants napping."[6] ∎

4-5 The Nominal Interest Rate and the Demand for Money

The quantity theory is based on a simple money demand function: it assumes that the demand for real money balances is proportional to income. The quantity theory is a good place to start when analyzing the effects of money on the economy, but it is not the whole story. Here we add another determinant of the quantity of money demanded—the nominal interest rate.

The Cost of Holding Money

The money you hold in your wallet does not earn interest. If, instead of holding that money, you used it to buy government bonds or deposited it in a savings account, you would earn the nominal interest rate. Therefore, the nominal interest rate is the opportunity cost of holding money: it is what you give up by holding money rather than bonds.

Another way to see that the cost of holding money equals the nominal interest rate is to compare the real returns on alternative assets. Assets other than money, such as government bonds, earn the real return r. Money earns an expected real return of $-E\pi$, because its real value declines at the rate of inflation. When you hold money, you give up the difference between these two returns. Thus, the cost of holding money is $r - (-E\pi)$, which the Fisher equation tells us is the nominal interest rate i.

Just as the quantity of bread demanded depends on the price of bread, the quantity of money demanded depends on the price of holding money. Hence, the demand for real money balances depends both on the level of income and on the nominal interest rate. We write the general money demand function as

$$(M/P)^d = L(i, Y).$$

The letter L is used to denote money demand because money is the economy's most liquid asset (the asset most easily used to make transactions). This equation

[6] Robert B. Barsky, "The Fisher Effect and the Forecastability and Persistence of Inflation," *Journal of Monetary Economics* 19 (January 1987): 3–24.

states that the demand for the liquidity of real money balances is a function of income and the nominal interest rate. The higher the level of income Y, the greater the demand for real money balances. The higher the nominal interest rate i, the lower the demand for real money balances.

Future Money and Current Prices

Money, prices, and interest rates are now related in several ways. Figure 4-5 illustrates the linkages we have discussed. As the quantity theory of money explains, money supply and money demand together determine the equilibrium price level. Changes in the price level are, by definition, the rate of inflation. Inflation, in turn, affects the nominal interest rate through the Fisher effect. But now, because the nominal interest rate is the cost of holding money, the nominal interest rate feeds back to affect the demand for money.

Consider how the introduction of this last link affects our theory of the price level. First, equate the supply of real money balances M/P to the demand $L(i,Y)$:

$$M/P = L(i,\ Y).$$

Next, use the Fisher equation to write the nominal interest rate as the sum of the real interest rate and expected inflation:

$$M/P = L(r + E\pi,\ Y).$$

This equation states that the level of real money balances depends on the expected rate of inflation.

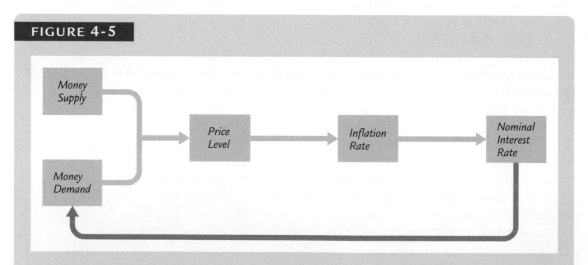

FIGURE 4-5

The Linkages Among Money, Prices, and Interest Rates This figure illustrates the relationships among money, prices, and interest rates. Money supply and money demand determine the price level. Changes in the price level determine the inflation rate. The inflation rate influences the nominal interest rate. Because the nominal interest rate is the cost of holding money, it may affect money demand. This last link (shown as a blue line) is omitted from the basic quantity theory of money.

The last equation tells a more sophisticated story about the determination of the price level than does the quantity theory. The quantity theory of money says that today's money supply determines today's price level. This conclusion remains partly true: if the nominal interest rate and the level of output are held constant, the price level moves proportionately with the money supply. Yet the nominal interest rate is not constant; it depends on expected inflation, which in turn depends on growth in the money supply. The presence of the nominal interest rate in the money demand function yields an additional channel through which money supply affects the price level.

This general money demand equation implies that the price level depends not only on today's money supply but also on the money supply expected in the future. To see why, suppose the Fed announces that it will increase the money supply in the future, but it does not change the money supply today. This announcement causes people to expect higher money growth and higher inflation. Through the Fisher effect, this increase in expected inflation raises the nominal interest rate. The higher nominal interest rate increases the cost of holding money and therefore reduces the demand for real money balances. Because the Fed has not changed the quantity of money available today, the reduced demand for real money balances leads to a higher price level. Hence, expectations of higher money growth in the future lead to a higher price level today.

The effect of money on prices is now complex. But the bottom line can be simply stated: once the role of expected inflation in money demand is incorporated into the analysis, the price level depends not only on the current money supply but on a weighted average of the current money supply and the money supply expected to prevail in the future.

4-6 The Social Costs of Inflation

Our discussion of the causes and effects of inflation does not tell us much about the social problems that result from inflation. We turn to those problems now.

The Layman's View and the Classical Response

If you ask the average person why inflation is a social problem, he will probably answer that inflation makes him poorer. "Each year my boss gives me a raise, but prices go up and that takes some of my raise away from me." The implicit assumption in this statement is that if there were no inflation, he would get the same raise and be able to buy more goods.

This complaint about inflation is a common fallacy. As we know from Chapter 3, the purchasing power of labor—the real wage—depends on the marginal productivity of labor, not on how much money the government chooses to print. If the central bank reduces inflation by slowing the rate of money growth, workers will not see their real wage increasing more rapidly. Instead, when inflation slows, firms will increase the prices of their products less each year and, as a result, will give their workers smaller raises.

According to the classical theory of money, a change in the overall price level is like a change in the units of measurement. It is as if we switched from measuring distances in feet to measuring them in inches: numbers get larger, but nothing really changes. Imagine that tomorrow morning you wake up and find that, for some reason, all dollar figures in the economy have been multiplied by ten. The price of everything you buy has increased tenfold, but so have your wage and the value of your savings. What difference would such a price increase make to your life? All numbers would have an extra zero at the end, but nothing else would change. Your economic well-being depends on relative prices, not the overall price level.

Why, then, is a persistent increase in the price level a social problem? It turns out that the costs of inflation are subtle. Indeed, economists disagree about the size of the social costs. To the surprise of many laymen, some economists argue that the costs of inflation are small—at least for the moderate rates of inflation that most countries have experienced in recent years.[7]

CASE STUDY

What Economists and the Public Say About Inflation

As we have been discussing, laymen and economists hold very different views about the costs of inflation. In 1996, economist Robert Shiller documented this difference of opinion in a survey of the two groups. The survey results are striking, because they show how the study of economics changes a person's attitudes.

In one question, Shiller asked people whether their "biggest gripe about inflation" was that "inflation hurts my real buying power, it makes me poorer." Among the general public, 77 percent agreed with this statement, compared to only 12 percent of economists. Shiller also asked people whether they agreed with the following statement: "When I see projections about how many times more a college education will cost, or how many times more the cost of living will be in coming decades, I feel a sense of uneasiness; these inflation projections really make me worry that my own income will not rise as much as such costs will." Among the general public, 66 percent said they fully agreed with this statement, whereas only 5 percent of economists agreed with it.

Survey respondents were asked to judge the seriousness of inflation as a policy problem: "Do you agree that preventing high inflation is an important national priority, as important as preventing drug abuse or preventing deterioration in the quality of our schools?" Shiller found that 52 percent of laymen, but only 18 percent of economists, fully agreed with this view. Apparently, inflation worries the public much more than it does the economics profession.

The public's distaste for inflation may be psychological. Shiller asked those surveyed if they agreed with the following statement: "I think that if my pay

---

[7] See, for example, Chapter 2 of Alan Blinder, *Hard Heads, Soft Hearts: Tough-Minded Economics for a Just Society* (Reading, MA: Addison Wesley, 1987).

went up I would feel more satisfaction in my job, more sense of fulfillment, even if prices went up just as much." Among the public, 49 percent fully or partly agreed with this statement, compared to 8 percent of economists.

Do these survey results mean that laymen are wrong and economists are right about the costs of inflation? Not necessarily. But economists do have the advantage of having given the issue more thought. So let's now consider what some of the costs of inflation might be.[8] ∎

The Costs of Expected Inflation

Consider first the case of expected inflation. Suppose that every month the price level rose by 1 percent. What would be the social costs of such a steady and predictable 12 percent annual inflation?

One cost is the distortion of the inflation tax on the amount of money people hold. As we have already discussed, a higher inflation rate leads to a higher nominal interest rate, which in turn leads to lower real money balances. If people are to hold lower money balances on average, they must make more frequent trips to the bank to withdraw money—for example, they might withdraw $50 twice a week rather than $100 once a week. The inconvenience of reducing money holding is metaphorically called the **shoeleather cost** of inflation, because walking to the bank more often causes one's shoes to wear out more quickly.

A second cost of inflation arises because high inflation induces firms to change their posted prices more often. Changing prices is sometimes costly: for example, it may require printing and distributing a new catalog. These costs are called **menu costs,** because the higher the rate of inflation, the more often restaurants have to print new menus.

A third cost of inflation arises because firms facing menu costs change prices infrequently; therefore, the higher the rate of inflation, the greater the variability in relative prices. For example, suppose a firm issues a new catalog every January. If there is no inflation, then the firm's prices relative to the overall price level are constant over the year. Yet if inflation is 1 percent per month, then from the beginning to the end of the year the firm's relative prices fall by 12 percent. Sales from this catalog will tend to be low early in the year (when its prices are relatively high) and high later in the year (when its prices are relatively low). Hence, when inflation induces variability in relative prices, it leads to microeconomic inefficiencies in the allocation of resources.

A fourth cost of inflation results from the tax laws. Many provisions of the tax code do not take into account the effects of inflation. Inflation can alter individuals' tax liability, often in ways that lawmakers did not intend.

One example of the failure of the tax code to deal with inflation is the tax treatment of capital gains. Suppose you buy some stock today and sell it a year

[8] Robert J. Shiller, "Why Do People Dislike Inflation?" in Christina D. Romer and David H. Romer, eds., *Reducing Inflation: Motivation and Strategy* (Chicago: University of Chicago Press, 1997): 13–65.

from now at the same real price. It would seem reasonable for the government not to levy a tax, because you have earned no real income from this investment. Indeed, if there is no inflation, a zero tax liability would be the outcome. But suppose the rate of inflation is 12 percent and you initially paid $100 per share for the stock; for the real price to be the same a year later, you must sell the stock for $112 per share. In this case the tax code, which ignores the effects of inflation, says that you have earned $12 per share in income, and the government taxes you on this capital gain. The problem is that the tax code measures income as the nominal rather than the real capital gain. In this example, and in many others, inflation distorts how taxes are levied.

A fifth cost of inflation is the inconvenience of living in a world with a changing price level. Money is the yardstick with which we measure economic transactions. When there is inflation, that yardstick is changing in length. To continue the analogy, suppose that Congress passed a law specifying that a yard would equal 36 inches in 2010, 35 inches in 2011, 34 inches in 2012, and so on. Although the law would result in no ambiguity, it would be highly inconvenient. When someone measured a distance in yards, it would be necessary to specify whether the measurement was in 2010 yards or 2011 yards; to compare distances measured in different years, one would need to make an "inflation" correction. Similarly, the dollar is a less useful measure when its value is always changing. The changing value of the dollar requires that we correct for inflation when comparing dollar figures from different times.

For example, a changing price level complicates personal financial planning. One important decision that all households face is how much of their income to consume today and how much to save for retirement. A dollar saved today and invested at a fixed nominal interest rate will yield a fixed dollar amount in the future. Yet the real value of that dollar amount—which will determine the retiree's living standard—depends on the future price level. Deciding how much to save would be much simpler if people could count on the price level in 30 years being similar to its level today.

The Costs of Unexpected Inflation

Unexpected inflation has an effect that is more pernicious than any of the costs of steady, anticipated inflation: it arbitrarily redistributes wealth among individuals. You can see how this works by examining long-term loans. Most loan agreements specify a nominal interest rate, which is based on the rate of inflation expected at the time of the agreement. If inflation turns out differently from what was expected, the *ex post* real return that the debtor pays to the creditor differs from what both parties anticipated. On the one hand, if inflation turns out to be higher than expected, the debtor wins and the creditor loses because the debtor repays the loan with less valuable dollars. On the other hand, if inflation turns out to be lower than expected, the creditor wins and the debtor loses because the repayment is worth more than the two parties anticipated.

Consider, for example, a person taking out a mortgage in 1960. At the time, a 30-year mortgage had an interest rate of about 6 percent per year. This rate was based on a low rate of expected inflation—inflation over the previous decade had averaged only 2.5 percent. The creditor probably expected to receive a real return of about 3.5 percent, and the debtor expected to pay this real return. In fact, over the life of the mortgage, the inflation rate averaged 5 percent, so the *ex post* real return was only 1 percent. This unanticipated inflation benefited the debtor at the expense of the creditor.

Unanticipated inflation also hurts individuals on fixed pensions. Workers and firms often agree on a fixed nominal pension when the worker retires (or even earlier). Because the pension is deferred earnings, the worker is essentially providing the firm a loan: the worker provides labor services to the firm while young but does not get fully paid until old age. Like any creditor, the worker is hurt when inflation is higher than anticipated. Like any debtor, the firm is hurt when inflation is lower than anticipated.

These situations provide a clear argument against variable inflation. The more variable the rate of inflation, the greater the uncertainty that both debtors and creditors face. Because most people are *risk averse*—they dislike uncertainty—the unpredictability caused by highly variable inflation hurts almost everyone.

Given these effects of uncertain inflation, it is puzzling that nominal contracts are so prevalent. One might expect debtors and creditors to protect themselves from this uncertainty by writing contracts in real terms—that is, by indexing to some measure of the price level. In economies with high and variable inflation, indexation is often widespread; sometimes this indexation takes the form of writing contracts using a more stable foreign currency. In economies with moderate inflation, such as the United States, indexation is less common. Yet even in the United States, some long-term obligations are indexed. For example, Social Security benefits for the elderly are adjusted annually in response to changes in the consumer price index. And in 1997, the U.S. federal government issued inflation-indexed bonds for the first time.

Finally, in thinking about the costs of inflation, it is important to note a widely documented but little understood fact: high inflation is variable inflation. That is, countries with high average inflation also tend to have inflation rates that change greatly from year to year. The implication is that if a country decides to pursue a high-inflation monetary policy, it will likely have to accept highly variable inflation as well. As we have just discussed, highly variable inflation increases uncertainty for both creditors and debtors by subjecting them to arbitrary and potentially large redistributions of wealth.

CASE STUDY

The Free Silver Movement, the Election of 1896, and the Wizard of Oz

The redistributions of wealth caused by unexpected changes in the price level are often a source of political turmoil, as evidenced by the Free Silver movement in the late nineteenth century. From 1880 to 1896, the price level in the United States fell 23 percent. This deflation was good for creditors, primarily the bankers of the Northeast, but it was bad for debtors, primarily the farmers of the South and West. One proposed solution to this problem was to replace the gold standard with a bimetallic standard, under which both gold and silver could be minted into coin. The move to a bimetallic standard would increase the money supply and stop the deflation.

The silver issue dominated the presidential election of 1896. William McKinley, the Republican nominee, campaigned on a platform of preserving the gold standard. William Jennings Bryan, the Democratic nominee, supported the bimetallic standard. In a famous speech, Bryan proclaimed, "You shall not press down upon the brow of labor this crown of thorns, you shall not crucify mankind upon a cross of gold." Not surprisingly, McKinley was the candidate of the conservative eastern establishment, whereas Bryan was the candidate of the southern and western populists.

This debate over silver found its most memorable expression in a children's book, *The Wizard of Oz*. Written by a midwestern journalist, L. Frank Baum, just after the 1896 election, it tells the story of Dorothy, a girl lost in a strange land far from her home in Kansas. Dorothy (representing traditional American values) makes three friends: a scarecrow (the farmer), a tin woodman (the industrial worker), and a lion whose roar exceeds his might (William Jennings Bryan). Together, the four of them make their way along a perilous yellow brick road (the gold standard), hoping to find the Wizard who will help Dorothy return home. Eventually they arrive in Oz (Washington), where everyone sees the world through green glasses (money). The Wizard (William McKinley) tries to be all things to all people but turns out to be a fraud. Dorothy's problem is solved only when she learns about the magical power of her silver slippers.[9]

The Republicans won the election of 1896, and the United States stayed on the gold standard, but the Free Silver advocates got the inflation that they wanted. Around the time of the election, gold was discovered in Alaska, Australia, and South Africa. In addition, gold refiners devised the cyanide process, which facilitated the extraction of gold from ore. These developments led to increases in the money supply and in prices. From 1896 to 1910, the price level rose 35 percent. ■

One Benefit of Inflation

So far, we have discussed the many costs of inflation. These costs lead many economists to conclude that monetary policymakers should aim for zero inflation. Yet there is another side to the story. Some economists believe that a little bit of inflation—say, 2 or 3 percent per year—can be a good thing.

The argument for moderate inflation starts with the observation that cuts in nominal wages are rare: firms are reluctant to cut their workers' nominal wages, and workers are reluctant to accept such cuts. A 2 percent wage cut in a zero-inflation world is, in real terms, the same as a 3 percent raise with 5 percent inflation, but

---

[9] The movie made forty years later hid much of the allegory by changing Dorothy's slippers from silver to ruby. For more on this topic, see Henry M. Littlefield, "The Wizard of Oz: Parable on Populism," *American Quarterly* 16 (Spring 1964): 47–58; and Hugh Rockoff, "The Wizard of Oz as a Monetary Allegory," *Journal of Political Economy* 98 (August 1990): 739–760. It should be noted that there is no direct evidence that Baum intended his work as a monetary allegory, so some people believe that the parallels are the work of economic historians' overactive imaginations.

workers do not always see it that way. The 2 percent wage cut may seem like an insult, whereas the 3 percent raise is, after all, still a raise. Empirical studies confirm that nominal wages rarely fall.

This finding suggests that some inflation may make labor markets work better. The supply and demand for different kinds of labor are always changing. Sometimes an increase in supply or decrease in demand leads to a fall in the equilibrium real wage for a group of workers. If nominal wages can't be cut, then the only way to cut real wages is to allow inflation to do the job. Without inflation, the real wage will be stuck above the equilibrium level, resulting in higher unemployment.

For this reason, some economists argue that inflation "greases the wheels" of labor markets. Only a little inflation is needed: an inflation rate of 2 percent lets real wages fall by 2 percent per year, or 20 percent per decade, without cuts in nominal wages. Such automatic reductions in real wages are impossible with zero inflation.[10]

4-7 Hyperinflation

Hyperinflation is often defined as inflation that exceeds 50 percent per month, which is just over 1 percent per day. Compounded over many months, this rate of inflation leads to very large increases in the price level. An inflation rate of 50 percent per month implies a more than 100-fold increase in the price level over a year and a more than 2-million-fold increase over three years. Here we consider the costs and causes of such extreme inflation.

The Costs of Hyperinflation

Although economists debate whether the costs of moderate inflation are large or small, no one doubts that hyperinflation extracts a high toll on society. The costs are qualitatively the same as those we discussed earlier. When inflation reaches extreme levels, however, these costs are more apparent because they are so severe.

The shoeleather costs associated with reduced money holding, for instance, are serious under hyperinflation. Business executives devote much time and energy to cash management when cash loses its value quickly. By diverting this time and energy from more socially valuable activities, such as production and investment decisions, hyperinflation makes the economy run less efficiently.

Menu costs also become larger under hyperinflation. Firms have to change prices so often that normal business practices, such as printing and distributing catalogs with fixed prices, become impossible. In one restaurant during the German hyperinflation of the 1920s, a waiter would stand up on a table every 30 minutes to call out the new prices.

---

[10] For an examination of this benefit of inflation, see George A. Akerlof, William T. Dickens, and George L. Perry, "The Macroeconomics of Low Inflation," *Brookings Papers on Economic Activity*, 1996:1, pp. 1–76. Another argument for positive inflation is that it allows for the possibility of negative real interest rates. This issue is discussed in Chapter 11 in an FYI box on the Liquidity Trap.

Similarly, relative prices do not do a good job of reflecting true scarcity during hyperinflations. When prices change frequently by large amounts, it is hard for customers to shop around for the best price. Highly volatile and rapidly rising prices can alter behavior in many ways. According to one report, when patrons entered a pub during the German hyperinflation, they would often buy two pitchers of beer. Although the second pitcher would lose value by getting warm over time, it would lose value less rapidly than the money left sitting in the patron's wallet.

Tax systems are also distorted by hyperinflation—but in ways that are different from the distortions of moderate inflation. In most tax systems there is a delay between the time a tax is levied and the time it is actually paid to the government. In the United States, for example, taxpayers are required to make estimated income tax payments every three months. This short delay does not matter much under low inflation. By contrast, during hyperinflation, even a short delay greatly reduces real tax revenue. By the time the government gets the money it is due, the money has fallen in value. As a result, once hyperinflations start, the real tax revenue of the government often falls substantially.

Finally, no one should underestimate the sheer inconvenience of living with hyperinflation. When carrying money to the grocery store is as burdensome as carrying the groceries back home, the monetary system is not doing its best to facilitate exchange. The government tries to overcome this problem by adding more and more zeros to the paper currency, but often it cannot keep up with the exploding price level.

Eventually, these costs of hyperinflation become intolerable. Over time, money loses its role as a store of value, unit of account, and medium of exchange. Barter becomes more common. And more stable unofficial monies—cigarettes or the U.S. dollar—start to replace the official money.

CASE STUDY

Life During the Bolivian Hyperinflation

The following article from the *Wall Street Journal* shows what life was like during the Bolivian hyperinflation of 1985. What costs of inflation does this article emphasize?

Precarious Peso—Amid Wild Inflation, Bolivians Concentrate on Swapping Currency

LA PAZ, Bolivia—When Edgar Miranda gets his monthly teacher's pay of 25 million pesos, he hasn't a moment to lose. Every hour, pesos drop in value. So, while his wife rushes to market to lay in a month's supply of rice and noodles, he is off with the rest of the pesos to change them into black-market dollars.

Mr. Miranda is practicing the First Rule of Survival amid the most out-of-control inflation in the world today. Bolivia is a case study of how runaway inflation undermines a society. Price increases are so huge that the figures build up almost beyond comprehension. In one six-month period, for example, prices soared at an annual rate of 38,000%. By official count, however, last year's inflation reached 2,000%, and this year's is expected to hit 8,000%—though other estimates range many times higher. In any event, Bolivia's rate dwarfs Israel's 370% and Argentina's 1,100%—two other cases of severe inflation.

It is easier to comprehend what happens to the 38-year-old Mr. Miranda's pay if he doesn't quickly change it into dollars. The day he was paid 25 million pesos, a dollar cost 500,000 pesos. So he received $50. Just days later, with the rate at 900,000 pesos, he would have received $27.

"We think only about today and converting every peso into dollars," says Ronald MacLean, the manager of a gold-mining firm. "We have become myopic."

And intent on survival. Civil servants won't hand out a form without a bribe. Lawyers, accountants, hairdressers, even prostitutes have almost given up working to become money-changers in the streets. Workers stage repeated strikes and steal from their bosses. The bosses smuggle production abroad, take out phony loans, duck taxes—anything to get dollars for speculation.

The production at the state mines, for example, dropped to 12,000 tons last year from 18,000. The miners pad their wages by smuggling out the richest ore in their lunch pails, and the ore goes by a contraband network into neighboring Peru. Without a major tin mine, Peru now exports some 4,000 metric tons of tin a year.

"We don't produce anything. We are all currency speculators," a heavy-equipment dealer in La Paz says. "People don't know what's good and bad anymore. We have become an amoral society. . . ."

It is an open secret that practically all of the black-market dollars come from the illegal cocaine trade with the U.S. Cocaine traffickers earn an estimated $1 billion a year. . . .

But meanwhile the country is suffering from inflation largely because the government's revenues cover a mere 15% of its expenditures and its deficit has widened to nearly 25% of the country's total annual output. The revenues are hurt by a lag in tax payments, and taxes aren't being collected largely because of widespread theft and bribery.

Source: Reprinted by permission of the *Wall Street Journal.* © August 13, 1985, page 1, Dow Jones & Company, Inc. All rights reserved worldwide. ∎

The Causes of Hyperinflation

Why do hyperinflations start, and how do they end? This question can be answered at different levels.

The most obvious answer is that hyperinflations are due to excessive growth in the supply of money. When the central bank prints money, the price level rises. When it prints money rapidly enough, the result is hyperinflation. To stop the hyperinflation, the central bank must reduce the rate of money growth.

This answer is incomplete, however, because it leaves open the question of why central banks in hyperinflating economics choose to print so much money. To address this deeper question, we must turn our attention from monetary to fiscal policy. Most hyperinflations

"I told you the Fed should have tightened."

begin when the government has inadequate tax revenue to pay for its spending. Although the government might prefer to finance this budget deficit by issuing debt, it may find itself unable to borrow, perhaps because lenders view the government as a bad credit risk. To cover the deficit, the government turns to the only mechanism at its disposal—the printing press. The result is rapid money growth and hyperinflation.

Once the hyperinflation is under way, the fiscal problems become even more severe. Because of the delay in collecting tax payments, real tax revenue falls as inflation rises. Thus, the government's need to rely on seigniorage is self-reinforcing. Rapid money creation leads to hyperinflation, which leads to a larger budget deficit, which leads to even more rapid money creation.

The ends of hyperinflations almost always coincide with fiscal reforms. Once the magnitude of the problem becomes apparent, the government musters the political will to reduce government spending and increase taxes. These fiscal reforms reduce the need for seigniorage, which allows a reduction in money growth. Hence, even if inflation is always and everywhere a monetary phenomenon, the end of hyperinflation is often a fiscal phenomenon as well.[11]

CASE STUDY

Hyperinflation in Interwar Germany

After World War I, Germany experienced one of history's most spectacular examples of hyperinflation. At the war's end, the Allies demanded that Germany pay substantial reparations. These payments led to fiscal deficits in Germany, which the German government eventually financed by printing large quantities of money.

Panel (a) of Figure 4-6 shows the quantity of money and the general price level in Germany from January 1922 to December 1924. During this period, both money and prices rose at an amazing rate. For example, the price of a daily newspaper rose from 0.30 mark in January 1921 to 1 mark in May 1922, to 8 marks in October 1922, to 100 marks in February 1923, and to 1,000 marks in September 1923. Then, in the fall of 1923, prices took off: the newspaper sold for 2,000 marks on October 1, 20,000 marks on October 15, 1 million marks on October 29, 15 million marks on November 9, and 70 million marks on November 17. In December 1923 the money supply and prices abruptly stabilized.[12]

Just as fiscal problems caused the German hyperinflation, a fiscal reform ended it. At the end of 1923, the number of government employees was cut by one-third, and the reparations payments were temporarily suspended and eventually reduced. At the same time, a new central bank, the Rentenbank, replaced the old central bank, the Reichsbank. The Rentenbank was committed to not financing the government by printing money.

---

[11] For more on these issues, see Thomas J. Sargent, "The End of Four Big Inflations," in Robert Hall, ed., *Inflation* (Chicago: University of Chicago Press, 1983), 41–98; and Rudiger Dornbusch and Stanley Fischer, "Stopping Hyperinflations: Past and Present," *Weltwirtschaftliches Archiv* 122 (April 1986): 1–47.

[12] The data on newspaper prices are from Michael Mussa, "Sticky Individual Prices and the Dynamics of the General Price Level," *Carnegie-Rochester Conference on Public Policy* 15 (Autumn 1981): 261–296.

FIGURE 4-6

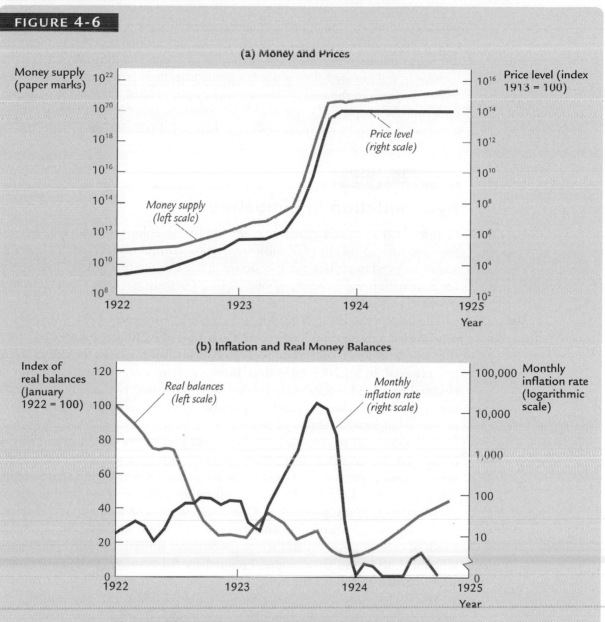

(a) Money and Prices

Money supply (paper marks) — left scale

Money supply (left scale)

Price level (right scale)

Price level (index 1913 = 100) — right scale

Year: 1922, 1923, 1924, 1925

(b) Inflation and Real Money Balances

Index of real balances (January 1922 = 100) — left scale

Real balances (left scale)

Monthly inflation rate (right scale)

Monthly inflation rate (logarithmic scale) — right scale

Year: 1922, 1923, 1924, 1925

Money and Prices in Interwar Germany Panel (a) shows the money supply and the price level in Germany from January 1922 to December 1924. The immense increases in the money supply and the price level provide a dramatic illustration of the effects of printing large amounts of money. Panel (b) shows inflation and real money balances. As inflation rose, real money balances fell. When the inflation ended at the end of 1923, real money balances rose.

Source: Adapted from Thomas J. Sargent, "The End of Four Big Inflations," in Robert Hall, ed., *Inflation* (Chicago: University of Chicago Press, 1983), 41–98.

According to our theoretical analysis of money demand, an end to a hyperinflation should lead to an increase in real money balances as the cost of holding money falls. Panel (b) of Figure 4-6 shows that real money balances in Germany did fall as inflation increased and then increased again as inflation fell. Yet the increase in real money balances was not immediate. Perhaps the adjustment of real money balances to the cost of holding money is a gradual process. Or perhaps it took time for people in Germany to believe that the inflation had ended, causing expected inflation to fall more gradually than actual inflation. ■

Hyperinflation in Zimbabwe

In 1980, after years of colonial rule, the old British colony of Rhodesia became the new African nation of Zimbabwe. A new currency, the Zimbabwe dollar, was introduced to replace the Rhodesian dollar. For the first decade, inflation in the new nation was modest—about 10 to 20 percent per year. That, however, would soon change.

The hero of the Zimbabwe independence movement was Robert Mugabe. In general elections in 1980, he became the nation's first prime minister and later, after a government reorganization, its president. Over the years, he continued to get reelected. In his 2008 reelection, however, there were widespread claims of electoral fraud and threats against voters who supported rival candidates. At the age of 84, Mugabe was no longer as popular as he once was, but he gave no sign of any willingness to relinquish power.

Throughout his tenure, Mugabe's economic philosophy was Marxist, and one of his goals was to redistribute wealth. In the 1990s his government instituted a series of land reforms with the ostensible purpose of redistributing land from the white minority who ruled Zimbabwe during the colonial era to the historically disenfranchised black population. One result of these reforms was widespread corruption. Many abandoned and expropriated white farms ended up in the hands of cabinet ministers and senior government officials. Another result was a substantial decline in farm output. Productivity fell as many of the experienced white farmers fled the country.

The decline in the economy's output led to a fall in the government's tax revenue. The government responded to this revenue shortfall by printing money to pay the salaries of government employees. As textbook economic theory predicts, the monetary expansion led to higher inflation.

Mugabe tried to deal with inflation by imposing price controls. Once again, the result was predictable: a shortage of many goods and the growth of an underground economy in which price controls and tax collection were evaded. The government's tax revenue declined further, inducing even more monetary expansion and yet higher inflation. In July 2008, the officially reported inflation rate was 231 million percent. Other observers put the inflation rate even higher.

The repercussions of the hyperinflation were widespread. In an article in the *Washington Post*, one Zimbabwean citizen describes the situation as follows:

"If you don't get a bill collected in 48 hours, it isn't worth collecting, because it is worthless. Whenever we get money, we must immediately spend it, just go and buy what we can. Our pension was destroyed ages ago. None of us have any savings left."

The Zimbabwe hyperinflation finally ended in March 2009, when the government abandoned its own money. The U.S. dollar became the nation's official currency. ■

4-8 Conclusion: The Classical Dichotomy

We have finished our discussion of money and inflation. Let's now step back and examine a key assumption that has been implicit in our discussion.

In Chapter 3 we explained many macroeconomic variables. Some of these variables were *quantities*, such as real GDP and the capital stock; others were *relative prices*, such as the real wage and the real interest rate. But all of these variables had one thing in common—they measured a physical (rather than a monetary) quantity. Real GDP is the quantity of goods and services produced in a given year, and the capital stock is the quantity of machines and structures available at a given time. The real wage is the quantity of output a worker earns for each hour of work, and the real interest rate is the quantity of output a person earns in the future by lending one unit of output today. All variables measured in physical units, such as quantities and relative prices, are called **real variables**.

In this chapter we examined **nominal variables**—variables expressed in terms of money. The economy has many nominal variables, such as the price level, the inflation rate, and the dollar wage a person earns.

At first it may seem surprising that we were able to explain real variables without introducing nominal variables or the existence of money. In Chapter 3 we studied the level and allocation of the economy's output without mentioning the price level or the rate of inflation. Our theory of the labor market explained the real wage without explaining the nominal wage.

Economists call this theoretical separation of real and nominal variables the **classical dichotomy**. It is the hallmark of classical macroeconomic theory. The classical dichotomy is an important insight because it simplifies economic theory. In particular, it allows us to examine real variables, as we have done, while ignoring nominal variables. The classical dichotomy arises because, in classical economic theory, changes in the money supply do not influence real variables. This irrelevance of money for real variables is called **monetary neutrality**. For many purposes—in particular for studying long-run issues—monetary neutrality is approximately correct.

Yet monetary neutrality does not fully describe the world in which we live. Beginning in Chapter 9, we discuss departures from the classical model and monetary neutrality. These departures are crucial for understanding many macroeconomic phenomena, such as short-run economic fluctuations.

Summary

1. Money is the stock of assets used for transactions. It serves as a store of value, a unit of account, and a medium of exchange. Different sorts of assets are used as money: commodity money systems use an asset with intrinsic value, whereas fiat money systems use an asset whose sole function is to serve as money. In modern economies, a central bank such as the Federal Reserve is responsible for controlling the supply of money.

2. The quantity theory of money assumes that the velocity of money is stable and concludes that nominal GDP is proportional to the stock of money. Because the factors of production and the production function determine real GDP, the quantity theory implies that the price level is proportional to the quantity of money. Therefore, the rate of growth in the quantity of money determines the inflation rate.

3. Seigniorage is the revenue that the government raises by printing money. It is a tax on money holding. Although seigniorage is quantitatively small in most economies, it is often a major source of government revenue in economies experiencing hyperinflation.

4. The nominal interest rate is the sum of the real interest rate and the inflation rate. The Fisher effect says that the nominal interest rate moves one-for-one with expected inflation.

5. The nominal interest rate is the opportunity cost of holding money. Thus, one might expect the demand for money to depend on the nominal interest rate. If it does, then the price level depends on both the current quantity of money and the quantities of money expected in the future.

6. The costs of expected inflation include shoeleather costs, menu costs, the cost of relative price variability, tax distortions, and the inconvenience of making inflation corrections. In addition, unexpected inflation causes arbitrary redistributions of wealth between debtors and creditors. One possible benefit of inflation is that it improves the functioning of labor markets by allowing real wages to reach equilibrium levels without cuts in nominal wages.

7. During hyperinflations, most of the costs of inflation become severe. Hyperinflations typically begin when governments finance large budget deficits by printing money. They end when fiscal reforms eliminate the need for seigniorage.

8. According to classical economic theory, money is neutral: the money supply does not affect real variables. Therefore, classical theory allows us to study how real variables are determined without any reference to the money supply. The equilibrium in the money market then determines the price level and, as a result, all other nominal variables. This theoretical separation of real and nominal variables is called the classical dichotomy.

KEY CONCEPTS

Inflation	Central bank	Seigniorage
Hyperinflation	Federal Reserve	Nominal and real interest rates
Money	Open-market operations	Fisher equation and Fisher effect
Store of value	Currency	*Ex ante and ex post* real interest rates
Unit of account	Demand deposits	Shoeleather costs
Medium of exchange	Quantity equation	Menu costs
Fiat money	Transactions velocity of money	Real and nominal variables
Commodity money	Income velocity of money	Classical dichotomy
Gold standard	Real money balances	Monetary neutrality
Money supply	Money demand function	
Monetary policy	Quantity theory of money	

QUESTIONS FOR REVIEW

1. Describe the functions of money.

2. What is fiat money? What is commodity money?

3. Who controls the money supply and how?

4. Write the quantity equation and explain it.

5. What does the assumption of constant velocity imply?

6. Who pays the inflation tax?

7. If inflation rises from 6 to 8 percent, what happens to real and nominal interest rates according to the Fisher effect?

8. List all the costs of inflation you can think of, and rank them according to how important you think they are.

9. Explain the roles of monetary and fiscal policy in causing and ending hyperinflations.

10. Define the terms "real variable" and "nominal variable," and give an example of each.

PROBLEMS AND APPLICATIONS

1. What are the three functions of money? Which of the functions do the following items satisfy? Which do they not satisfy?

   a. A credit card

   b. A painting by Rembrandt

   c. A subway token

2. In the country of Wiknam, the velocity of money is constant. Real GDP grows by 5 percent per year, the money stock grows by 14 percent per year, and the nominal interest rate is 11 percent. What is the real interest rate?

3. A newspaper article once reported that the U.S. economy was experiencing a low rate of inflation. It said that "low inflation has a downside: 45 million recipients of Social Security and other benefits will see their checks go up by just 2.8 percent next year."

   a. Why does inflation affect the increase in Social Security and other benefits?

   b. Is this effect a cost of inflation, as the article suggests? Why or why not?

4. Suppose a country has a money demand function $(M/P)^d = kY$, where k is a constant

parameter. The money supply grows by 12 per year, and real income grows by 4 percent per year.

   a. What is the average inflation rate?

   b. How would inflation be different if real income growth was higher? Explain.

   c. Suppose, instead of a constant money demand function, the velocity of money in this economy was growing steadily because of financial innovation. How would that affect the inflation rate? Explain.

5. Suppose you are advising a small country (such as Bermuda) on whether to print its own money or to use the money of its larger neighbor (such as the United States). What are the costs and benefits of a national money? Does the relative political stability of the two countries have any role in this decision?

6. During World War II, both Germany and England had plans for a paper weapon: they each printed the other's currency, with the intention of dropping large quantities by airplane. Why might this have been an effective weapon?

7. Suppose that the money demand function takes the form

$$(M/P)^d = L(i, Y) = Y/(5i)$$

   a. If output grows at rate g, at what rate will the demand for real balances grow (assuming constant nominal interest rates)?

   b. What is the velocity of money in this economy?

   c. If inflation and nominal interest rates are constant, at what rate, if any, will velocity grow?

   d. How will a permanent (once-and-for-all) increase in the level of interest rates affect the level of velocity? How will it affect the subsequent growth rate of velocity?

8. Calvin Coolidge once said that "inflation is repudiation." What might he have meant by this? Do you agree? Why or why not? Does it matter whether the inflation is expected or unexpected?

9. Some economic historians have noted that during the period of the gold standard, gold discoveries were most likely to occur after a long deflation. (The discoveries of 1896 are an example.) Why might this be true?

10. Suppose that consumption depends on the level of real money balances (on the grounds that real money balances are part of wealth). Show that if real money balances depend on the nominal interest rate, then an increase in the rate of money growth affects consumption, investment, and the real interest rate. Does the nominal interest rate adjust more than one-for-one or less than one-for-one to expected inflation?

This deviation from the classical dichotomy and the Fisher effect is called the *Mundell–Tobin effect*. How might you decide whether the Mundell–Tobin effect is important in practice?

11. Use the Internet to identify a country that has had high inflation over the past year and another country that has had low inflation. (*Hint*: One useful Web site is http://www.economist.com/markets/indicators/.) For these two countries, find the rate of money growth and the current level of the nominal interest rate. Relate your findings to the theories presented in this chapter.

The Money Supply and the Banking System

The body of this chapter introduced the concept of "money supply" in a highly simplified manner. We defined the quantity of money as the number of dollars held by the public, and we assumed that the Federal Reserve controls the supply of money by increasing or decreasing the number of dollars in circulation through open-market operations. This explanation is a good starting point for understanding what determines the supply of money, but it is incomplete, because it omits the role of the banking system in this process. We now present a more complete explanation.

In this appendix we see that the money supply is determined not only by Fed policy but also by the behavior of households (which hold money) and banks (in which money is held). We begin by recalling that the money supply includes both currency in the hands of the public and deposits at banks that households can use on demand for transactions, such as checking account deposits. That is, letting M denote the money supply, C denote currency, and D denote demand deposits, we can write

$$\text{Money Supply} = \text{Currency} + \text{Demand Deposits}$$
$$M \quad = \quad C \quad + \quad D.$$

To understand the money supply, we must understand the interaction between currency and demand deposits and how Fed policy influences these two components of the money supply.

100-Percent-Reserve Banking

We begin by imagining a world without banks. In such a world, all money takes the form of currency, and the quantity of money is simply the amount of currency that the public holds. For this discussion, suppose that there is $1,000 of currency in the economy.

Now introduce banks. At first, suppose that banks accept deposits but do not make loans. The only purpose of the banks is to provide a safe place for depositors to keep their money.

The deposits that banks have received but have not lent out are called *reserves*. Some reserves are held in the vaults of local banks throughout the country, but most are held at a central bank, such as the Federal Reserve. In our hypothetical economy, all deposits are held as reserves: banks simply accept deposits, place the money in reserve, and leave the money there until the depositor makes a withdrawal or writes a check against the balance. This system is called *100-percent-reserve banking*.

Suppose that households deposit the economy's entire $1,000 in Firstbank. Firstbank's *balance sheet*—its accounting statement of assets and liabilities—looks like this:

Firstbank's Balance Sheet

Assets		Liabilities	
Reserves	$1,000	Deposits	$1,000

The bank's assets are the $1,000 it holds as reserves; the bank's liabilities are the $1,000 it owes to depositors. Unlike banks in our economy, this bank is not making loans, so it will not earn profit from its assets. The bank presumably charges depositors a small fee to cover its costs.

What is the money supply in this economy? Before the creation of Firstbank, the money supply was the $1,000 of currency. After the creation of Firstbank, the money supply is the $1,000 of demand deposits. A dollar deposited in a bank reduces currency by one dollar and raises deposits by one dollar, so the money supply remains the same. *If banks hold 100 percent of deposits in reserve, the banking system does not affect the supply of money.*

Fractional-Reserve Banking

Now imagine that banks start to use some of their deposits to make loans—for example, to families who are buying houses or to firms that are investing in new plants and equipment. The advantage to banks is that they can charge interest on the loans. The banks must keep some reserves on hand so that reserves are available whenever depositors want to make withdrawals. But as long as the amount of new deposits approximately equals the amount of withdrawals, a bank need not keep all its deposits in reserve. Thus, bankers have an incentive to make loans. When they do so, we have *fractional-reserve banking*, a system under which banks keep only a fraction of their deposits in reserve.

Here is Firstbank's balance sheet after it makes a loan:

Firstbank's Balance Sheet

Assets		Liabilities	
Reserves	$200	Deposits	$1,000
Loans	$800		

This balance sheet assumes that the *reserve–deposit ratio*—the fraction of deposits kept in reserve—is 20 percent. Firstbank keeps $200 of the $1,000 in deposits in reserve and lends out the remaining $800.

Notice that Firstbank increases the supply of money by $800 when it makes this loan. Before the loan is made, the money supply is $1,000, equaling the deposits in Firstbank. After the loan is made, the money supply is $1,800: the depositor still has a demand deposit of $1,000, but now the borrower holds $800 in currency. *Thus, in a system of fractional-reserve banking, banks create money.*

The creation of money does not stop with Firstbank. If the borrower deposits the $800 in another bank (or if the borrower uses the $800 to pay someone who then deposits it), the process of money creation continues. Here is the balance sheet of Secondbank:

Secondbank's Balance Sheet

Assets		Liabilities	
Reserves	$160	Deposits	$800
Loans	$640		

Secondbank receives the $800 in deposits, keeps 20 percent, or $160, in reserve, and then loans out $640. Thus, Secondbank creates $640 of money. If this $640 is eventually deposited in Thirdbank, this bank keeps 20 percent, or $128, in reserve and loans out $512, resulting in this balance sheet:

Thirdbank's Balance Sheet

Assets		Liabilities	
Reserves	$128	Deposits	$640
Loans	$512		

The process goes on and on. With each deposit and loan, more money is created.

Although this process of money creation can continue forever, it does not create an infinite amount of money. Letting rr denote the reserve–deposit ratio, the amount of money that the original $1,000 creates is

$$
\begin{aligned}
\text{Original Deposit} &= \$1{,}000 \\
\text{Firstbank Lending} &= (1 - rr) \times \$1{,}000 \\
\text{Secondbank Lending} &= (1 - rr)^2 \times \$1{,}000 \\
\text{Thirdbank Lending} &= (1 - rr)^3 \times \$1{,}000 \\
\hline
\text{Total Money Supply} &= [1 + (1 - rr) + (1 - rr)^2 \\
&\quad + (1 - rr)^3 + \cdots] \times \$1{,}000 \\
&= (1/rr) \times \$1{,}000.
\end{aligned}
$$

Each $1 of reserves generates $(1/rr) of money. In our example, $rr = 0.2$, so the original $1,000 generates $5,000 of money.[13]

Note that although the system of fractional-reserve banking creates money, it does not create wealth. When a bank loans out some of its reserves, it gives borrowers the ability to make transactions and therefore increases the supply of money. The borrowers are also undertaking a debt obligation to the bank, however, so the loan does not make them wealthier. In other words, the creation of money by the banking system increases the economy's liquidity, not its wealth.

---

[13] *Mathematical note:* The last step in the derivation of the total money supply uses the algebraic result for the sum of an infinite geometric series. According to this result, if x is a number between -1 and 1, then

$$1 + x + x^2 + x^3 + \cdots = 1/(1 - x).$$

In this application, $x = (1 - rr)$.

A Model of the Money Supply

Now that we have seen how banks create money, let's examine in more detail what determines the money supply. Here we present a model of the money supply under fractional-reserve banking. The model has three exogenous variables:

■ The *monetary base B* is the total number of dollars held by the public as currency C and by the banks as reserves R. It is directly controlled by the Federal Reserve.

■ The *reserve–deposit ratio rr* is the fraction of deposits that banks hold in reserve. It is determined by the business policies of banks and the laws regulating banks.

■ The *currency–deposit ratio cr* is the amount of currency C people hold as a fraction of their holdings of demand deposits D. It reflects the preferences of households about the form of money they wish to hold.

Our model shows how the money supply depends on the monetary base, the reserve–deposit ratio, and the currency–deposit ratio. It allows us to examine how Fed policy and the choices of banks and households influence the money supply.

We begin with the definitions of the money supply and the monetary base:

$$M = C + D,$$

$$B = C + R.$$

The first equation states that the money supply is the sum of currency and demand deposits. The second equation states that the monetary base is the sum of currency and bank reserves. To solve for the money supply as a function of the three exogenous variables (B, rr, and cr), we divide the first equation by the second to obtain

$$\frac{M}{B} = \frac{C + D}{C + R}.$$

We then divide both the top and bottom of the expression on the right by D.

$$\frac{M}{B} = \frac{C/D + 1}{C/D + R/D}.$$

Note that C/D is the currency–deposit ratio *cr*, and that R/D is the reserve–deposit ratio *rr*. Making these substitutions, and bringing the B from the left to the right side of the equation, we obtain

$$M = \frac{cr + 1}{cr + rr} \times B.$$

This equation shows how the money supply depends on the three exogenous variables.

We can now see that the money supply is proportional to the monetary base. The factor of proportionality, $(cr + 1)/(cr + rr)$, is denoted m and is called the *money multiplier*. We can write

$$M = m \times B.$$

Each dollar of the monetary base produces m dollars of money. Because the monetary base has a multiplied effect on the money supply, the monetary base is sometimes called *high-powered money.*

Here's a numerical example. Suppose that the monetary base B is $800 billion, the reserve–deposit ratio rr is 0.1, and the currency–deposit ratio cr is 0.8. In this case, the money multiplier is

$$m = \frac{0.8 + 1}{0.8 + 0.1} = 2.0,$$

and the money supply is

$$M = 2.0 \times \$800 \text{ billion} = \$1,600 \text{ billion.}$$

Each dollar of the monetary base generates two dollars of money, so the total money supply is $1,600 billion.

We can now see how changes in the three exogenous variables—B, rr, and cr—cause the money supply to change.

1. The money supply is proportional to the monetary base. Thus, an increase in the monetary base increases the money supply by the same percentage.

2. The lower the reserve–deposit ratio, the more loans banks make, and the more money banks create from every dollar of reserves. Thus, a decrease in the reserve–deposit ratio raises the money multiplier and the money supply.

3. The lower the currency–deposit ratio, the fewer dollars of the monetary base the public holds as currency, the more base dollars banks hold as reserves, and the more money banks can create. Thus, a decrease in the currency–deposit ratio raises the money multiplier and the money supply.

With this model in mind, we can discuss the ways in which the Fed influences the money supply.

The Instruments of Monetary Policy

Although it is often convenient to make the simplifying assumption that the Federal Reserve controls the money supply directly, in fact the Fed controls the money supply indirectly using a variety of instruments. These instruments can be classified into two broad groups: those that influence the monetary base and those that influence the reserve–deposit ratio and thereby the money multiplier.

How the Fed Changes the Monetary Base *Open-market operations* are the purchases and sales of government bonds by the Fed. When the Fed buys bonds from the public, the dollars it pays for the bonds increase the monetary base and thereby increase the money supply. When the Fed sells bonds to the public, the dollars it receives reduce the monetary base and thus decrease the money supply. Open-market operations are the policy instrument that the Fed uses most often. In fact, the Fed conducts open-market operations in New York bond markets almost every weekday.

The Fed can also alter the monetary base and the money supply by lending reserves to banks. Banks borrow from the Fed when they think they do not have enough reserves on hand, either to satisfy bank regulators, to meet depositor withdrawals, to make new loans, or for some other business reason.

There are various ways banks can borrow from the Fed. Traditionally, banks have borrowed at the Fed's so-called *discount window*, and the *discount rate* is the interest rate that the Fed charges on these loans. The lower the discount rate, the cheaper are borrowed reserves, and the more banks borrow at the Fed's discount window. Hence, a reduction in the discount rate raises the monetary base and the money supply.

In recent years, the Federal Reserve has set up new mechanisms for banks to borrow from it. For example, under the *Term Auction Facility*, the Fed sets a quantity of funds it wants to lend to banks, and eligible banks then bid to borrow those funds. The loans go to the highest eligible bidders—that is, to the banks that have acceptable collateral and are offering to pay the highest interest rate. Unlike at the discount window, where the Fed sets the price of a loan and the banks determine the quantity of borrowing, at the Term Auction Facility the Fed sets the quantity of borrowing and a competitive bidding process among banks determines the price. The more funds the Fed makes available through this and similar facilities, the greater the monetary base and the money supply.

How the Fed Changes the Reserve–Deposit Ratio As our model of the money supply shows, the money multiplier is the link between the monetary base and the money supply. The money multiplier depends on the reserve–deposit ratio, which in turn is influenced by various Fed policy instruments.

Reserve requirements are Fed regulations that impose a minimum reserve–deposit ratio on banks. An increase in reserve requirements tends to raise the reserve–deposit ratio and thus lower the money multiplier and the money supply. Changes in reserve requirements are the least frequently used of the Fed's policy instruments. Moreover, in recent years, this particular tool has become less effective, because many banks hold more reserves than are required. Reserves above the minimum required are called *excess reserves*.

In October 2008, the Fed started paying *interest on reserves*. That is, when a bank holds reserves on deposit at the Fed, the Fed now pays the bank interest on those deposits. This change gives the Fed another tool with which to influence the economy. The higher the interest rate on reserves, the more reserve banks will choose to hold. Thus, an increase in the interest rate on reserves will tend to increase the reserve–deposit ratio, lower the money multiplier, and lower the money supply. Because the Fed has paid interest on reserves for a relatively short time, it is not yet clear how important this new instrument will be in the conduct of monetary policy.

Problems in Monetary Control These various instruments give the Fed substantial power to influence the money supply. Nonetheless, the Fed cannot control the money supply perfectly. Bank discretion in conducting business can cause the money supply to change in ways the Fed did not anticipate. For example, banks may choose to hold more excess reserves, a decision that increases the reserve–deposit ratio and lowers the money supply. As another example, the Fed cannot precisely control the amount banks borrow from the discount window. The less banks borrow, the smaller the monetary base, and the smaller the money supply. Hence, the money supply sometimes moves in ways the Fed does not intend.

CASE STUDY

Bank Failures and the Money Supply in the 1930s

Between August 1929 and March 1933, the money supply fell 28 percent. This decline in the money supply was the proximate cause of the deflation during the era. Moreover, as we will discuss in Chapter 11, some economists believe that this large decline in the money supply was the primary cause of the large decline in economic activity called the Great Depression.

Why did the money supply fall so dramatically? The three variables that determine the money supply—the monetary base, the reserve–deposit ratio, and the currency–deposit ratio—are shown in Table 4-2 for 1929 and 1933. You can see that the fall in the money supply cannot be attributed to a fall in the monetary base: in fact, the monetary base rose 18 percent over this period. Instead, the money supply fell because the money multiplier fell 38 percent. The money multiplier fell because the currency–deposit and reserve–deposit ratios both rose substantially.

Most economists attribute the fall in the money multiplier to the large number of bank failures in the early 1930s. From 1930 to 1933, more than 9,000 banks suspended operations, often defaulting on their depositors. The bank failures caused the money supply to fall by altering the behavior of both depositors and bankers.

Bank failures raised the currency–deposit ratio by reducing public confidence in the banking system. People feared that bank failures would continue, and they began to view currency as a more desirable form of money than demand deposits. When they withdrew their deposits, they drained the banks of reserves. The process of money creation reversed itself, because banks responded to lower reserves by reducing their outstanding balance of loans.

TABLE 4-2

The Money Supply and Its Determinants: 1929 and 1933

	August 1929	March 1933
Money Supply	26.5	19.0
Currency	3.9	5.5
Demand deposits	22.6	13.5
Monetary Base	7.1	8.4
Currency	3.9	5.5
Reserves	3.2	2.9
Money Multiplier	3.7	2.3
Reserve–deposit ratio	0.14	0.21
Currency–deposit ratio	0.17	0.41

Source: Adapted from Milton Friedman and Anna Schwartz, *A Monetary History of the United States, 1867–1960* (Princeton, N.J.: Princeton University Press, 1963), Appendix A.

In addition, the bank failures raised the reserve–deposit ratio by making bankers more cautious. Having just observed many bank runs, bankers became apprehensive about operating with a small amount of reserves. They therefore increased their holdings of reserves to well above the legal minimum. Just as households responded to the banking crisis by holding more currency relative to deposits, bankers responded by holding more reserves relative to loans. Together these changes caused a large fall in the money multiplier.

Although it is easy to explain why the money supply fell, it is more difficult to decide whether to blame the Federal Reserve. One might argue that the monetary base did not fall, so the Fed should not be blamed. Critics of Fed policy during this period make two counterarguments. First, they claim that the Fed should have taken a more vigorous role in preventing bank failures by acting as a *lender of last resort* when banks needed cash during bank runs. This would have helped maintain confidence in the banking system and prevented the large fall in the money multiplier. Second, they point out that the Fed could have responded to the fall in the money multiplier by increasing the monetary base even more than it did. Either of these actions would likely have prevented such a large fall in the money supply, which in turn might have reduced the severity of the Great Depression.

Since the 1930s, many policies have been put into place that make such a large and sudden fall in the money multiplier less likely today. Most important, the system of federal deposit insurance protects depositors when a bank fails. This policy is designed to maintain public confidence in the banking system and thus prevents large swings in the currency–deposit ratio. Deposit insurance has a cost: in the late 1980s and early 1990s, for example, the federal government incurred the large expense of bailing out many insolvent savings-and-loan institutions. Yet deposit insurance helps stabilize the banking system and the money supply. That is why, during the financial crisis of 2008–2009, the Federal Deposit Insurance Corporation raised the amount guaranteed from $100,000 to $250,000 per depositor. ■

MORE PROBLEMS AND APPLICATIONS

1. The money supply fell from 1929 to 1933 because both the currency–deposit ratio and the reserve–deposit ratio increased. Use the model of the money supply and the data in Table 4-2 to answer the following hypothetical questions about this episode.

   a. What would have happened to the money supply if the currency–deposit ratio had risen but the reserve–deposit ratio had remained the same?

   b. What would have happened to the money supply if the reserve–deposit ratio had risen but the currency–deposit ratio had remained the same?

   c. Which of the two changes was more responsible for the fall in the money supply?

The Open Economy

No nation was ever ruined by trade.

—*Benjamin Franklin*

Even if you never leave your hometown, you are an active participant in the global economy. When you go to the grocery store, for instance, you might choose between apples grown locally and grapes grown in Chile. When you make a deposit into your local bank, the bank might lend those funds to your next-door neighbor or to a Japanese company building a factory outside Tokyo. Because our economy is integrated with many others around the world, consumers have more goods and services from which to choose, and savers have more opportunities to invest their wealth.

In previous chapters we simplified our analysis by assuming a closed economy. In actuality, however, most economies are open: they export goods and services abroad, they import goods and services from abroad, and they borrow and lend in world financial markets. Figure 5-1 gives some sense of the importance of these international interactions by showing imports and exports as a percentage of GDP for seven major industrial countries. As the figure shows, exports from the United States are about 9 percent of GDP, and imports are about 15 percent. Trade is even more important for many other countries—in Canada and Germany, for instance, imports and exports are about a third of GDP. In these countries, international trade is central to analyzing economic developments and formulating economic policies.

This chapter begins our study of open-economy macroeconomics. We begin in Section 5-1 with questions of measurement. To understand how an open economy works, we must understand the key macroeconomic variables that measure the interactions among countries. Accounting identities reveal a key insight: the flow of goods and services across national borders is always matched by an equivalent flow of funds to finance capital accumulation.

In Section 5-2 we examine the determinants of these international flows. We develop a model of the small open economy that corresponds to our model of the closed economy in Chapter 3. The model shows the factors that determine whether a country is a borrower or a lender in world markets and how policies at home and abroad affect the flows of capital and goods.

In Section 5-3 we extend the model to discuss the prices at which a country makes exchanges in world markets. We examine what determines the price of

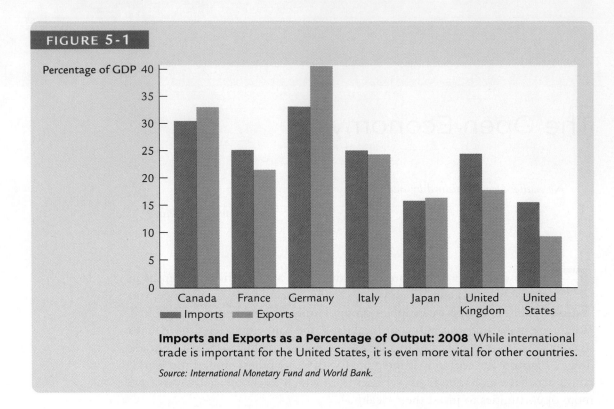

FIGURE 5-1

Imports and Exports as a Percentage of Output: 2008 While international trade is important for the United States, it is even more vital for other countries.

Source: International Monetary Fund and World Bank.

domestic goods relative to foreign goods. We also examine what determines the rate at which the domestic currency trades for foreign currencies. Our model shows how protectionist trade policies—policies designed to protect domestic industries from foreign competition—influence the amount of international trade and the exchange rate.

5-1 The International Flows of Capital and Goods

The key macroeconomic difference between open and closed economies is that, in an open economy, a country's spending in any given year need not equal its output of goods and services. A country can spend more than it produces by borrowing from abroad, or it can spend less than it produces and lend the difference to foreigners. To understand this more fully, let's take another look at national income accounting, which we first discussed in Chapter 2.

The Role of Net Exports

Consider the expenditure on an economy's output of goods and services. In a closed economy, all output is sold domestically, and expenditure is divided into three components: consumption, investment, and government purchases. In an open economy, some output is sold domestically and some is exported to be sold abroad. We can divide expenditure on an open economy's output Y into four components:

- C^d, consumption of domestic goods and services,
- I^d, investment in domestic goods and services,
- G^d, government purchases of domestic goods and services,
- X, exports of domestic goods and services.

The division of expenditure into these components is expressed in the identity

$$Y = C^d + I^d + G^d + X.$$

The sum of the first three terms, $C^d + I^d + G^d$, is domestic spending on domestic goods and services. The fourth term, X, is foreign spending on domestic goods and services.

A bit of manipulation can make this identity more useful. Note that domestic spending on *all* goods and services equals domestic spending on *domestic* goods and services plus domestic spending on *foreign* goods and services. Hence, total consumption C equals consumption of domestic goods and services C^d plus consumption of foreign goods and services C^f; total investment I equals investment in domestic goods and services I^d plus investment in foreign goods and services I^f; and total government purchases G equals government purchases of domestic goods and services G^d plus government purchases of foreign goods and services G^f. Thus,

$$C = C^d + C^f,$$

$$I = I^d + I^f,$$

$$G = G^d + G^f.$$

We substitute these three equations into the identity above:

$$Y = (C - C^f) + (I - I^f) + (G - G^f) + X.$$

We can rearrange to obtain

$$Y = C + I + G + X - (C^f + I^f + G^f).$$

The sum of domestic spending on foreign goods and services $(C^f + I^f + G^f)$ is expenditure on imports (IM). We can thus write the national income accounts identity as

$$Y = C + I + G + X - IM.$$

Because spending on imports is included in domestic spending $(C + I + G)$, and because goods and services imported from abroad are not part of a country's output, this equation subtracts spending on imports. Defining **net exports** to be exports minus imports $(NX = X - IM)$, the identity becomes

$$Y = C + I + G + NX.$$

This equation states that expenditure on domestic output is the sum of consumption, investment, government purchases, and net exports. This is the most common form of the national income accounts identity; it should be familiar from Chapter 2.

The national income accounts identity shows how domestic output, domestic spending, and net exports are related. In particular,

$$NX = Y - (C + I + G)$$

$$\text{Net Exports} = \text{Output} - \text{Domestic Spending}.$$

This equation shows that in an open economy, domestic spending need not equal the output of goods and services. *If output exceeds domestic spending, we export the difference: net exports are positive. If output falls short of domestic spending, we import the difference: net exports are negative.*

International Capital Flows and the Trade Balance

In an open economy, as in the closed economy we discussed in Chapter 3, financial markets and goods markets are closely related. To see the relationship, we must rewrite the national income accounts identity in terms of saving and investment. Begin with the identity

$$Y = C + I + G + NX.$$

Subtract C and G from both sides to obtain

$$Y - C - G = I + NX.$$

Recall from Chapter 3 that $Y - C - G$ is national saving S, which equals the sum of private saving, $Y - T - C$, and public saving, $T - G$, where T stands for taxes. Therefore,

$$S = I + NX.$$

Subtracting I from both sides of the equation, we can write the national income accounts identity as

$$S - I = NX.$$

This form of the national income accounts identity shows that an economy's net exports must always equal the difference between its saving and its investment.

Let's look more closely at each part of this identity. The easy part is the right-hand side, NX, the net export of goods and services. Another name for net exports is the **trade balance**, because it tells us how our trade in goods and services departs from the benchmark of equal imports and exports.

The left-hand side of the identity is the difference between domestic saving and domestic investment, $S - I$, which we'll call **net capital outflow**. (It's sometimes called *net foreign investment*.) Net capital outflow equals the amount that domestic residents are lending abroad minus the amount that foreigners are lending to us. If net capital outflow is positive, the economy's saving exceeds its investment, and it is lending the excess to foreigners. If the net capital outflow is negative, the economy is experiencing a capital inflow: investment exceeds saving, and the economy is financing this extra investment by borrowing from abroad. Thus, net capital outflow reflects the international flow of funds to finance capital accumulation.

The national income accounts identity shows that net capital outflow always equals the trade balance. That is,

$$\text{Net Capital Outflow} = \text{Trade Balance}$$

$$S - I = NX.$$

If $S - I$ and NX are positive, we have a **trade surplus**. In this case, we are net lenders in world financial markets, and we are exporting more goods than we are importing. If $S - I$ and NX are negative, we have a **trade deficit**. In this case, we are net borrowers in world financial markets, and we are importing more goods than we are exporting. If $S - I$ and NX are exactly zero, we are said to have **balanced trade** because the value of imports equals the value of exports.

The national income accounts identity shows that the international flow of funds to finance capital accumulation and the international flow of goods and services are two sides of the same coin. If domestic saving exceeds domestic investment, the surplus saving is used to make loans to foreigners. Foreigners require these loans because we are providing them with more goods and services than they are providing us. That is, we are running a trade surplus. If investment exceeds saving, the extra investment must be financed by borrowing from abroad. These foreign loans enable us to import more goods and services than we export. That is, we are running a trade deficit. Table 5-1 summarizes these lessons.

Note that the international flow of capital can take many forms. It is easiest to assume—as we have done so far—that when we run a trade deficit, foreigners make loans to us. This happens, for example, when the Japanese buy the debt issued by U.S. corporations or by the U.S. government. But the flow of capital can also take the form of foreigners buying domestic assets, such as when a citizen of Germany buys stock from an American on the New York Stock Exchange. Whether foreigners buy domestically issued debt or domestically owned assets, they obtain a claim to the future returns to domestic capital. In both cases, foreigners end up owning some of the domestic capital stock.

TABLE 5-1

International Flows of Goods and Capital: Summary

This table shows the three outcomes that an open economy can experience.

Trade Surplus	Balanced Trade	Trade Deficit
Exports > Imports	Exports = Imports	Exports < Imports
Net Exports > 0	Net Exports = 0	Net Exports < 0
$Y > C + I + G$	$Y = C + I + G$	$Y < C + I + G$
Saving > Investment	Saving = Investment	Saving < Investment
Net Capital Outflow > 0	Net Capital Outflow = 0	Net Capital Outflow < 0

International Flows of Goods and Capital: An Example

The equality of net exports and net capital outflow is an identity: it must hold because of how the variables are defined and the numbers are added up. But it is easy to miss the intuition behind this important relationship. The best way to understand it is to consider an example.

Imagine that Bill Gates sells a copy of the Windows operating system to a Japanese consumer for 5,000 yen. Because Mr. Gates is a U.S. resident, the sale represents an export of the United States. Other things equal, U.S. net exports rise. What else happens to make the identity hold? It depends on what Mr. Gates does with the 5,000 yen.

Suppose Mr. Gates decides to stuff the 5,000 yen into his mattress. In this case, Mr. Gates has allocated some of his saving to an investment in the Japanese economy (in the form of the Japanese currency) rather than to an investment in the U.S. economy. Thus, U.S. saving exceeds U.S. investment. The rise in U.S. net exports is matched by a rise in the U.S. net capital outflow.

If Mr. Gates wants to invest in Japan, however, he is unlikely to make currency his asset of choice. He might use the 5,000 yen to buy some stock in, say, the

The Irrelevance of Bilateral Trade Balances

The trade balance we have been discussing measures the difference between a nation's exports and its imports with the rest of the world. Sometimes you might hear in the media a report on a nation's trade balance with a specific other nation. This is called a *bilateral* trade balance. For example, the U.S. bilateral trade balance with China equals exports that the United States sells to China minus imports that the United States buys from China.

The overall trade balance is, as we have seen, inextricably linked to a nation's saving and investment. That is not true of a bilateral trade balance. Indeed, a nation can have large trade deficits and surpluses with specific trading partners, while having balanced trade overall.

For example, suppose the world has three countries: the United States, China, and Australia. The United States sells $100 billion in machine tools to Australia, Australia sells $100 billion in wheat to China, and China sells $100 billion in toys to the United States. In this case, the United States has a bilateral trade deficit with China, China has a bilateral trade deficit with Australia, and Australia has a bilateral trade deficit with the United States. But each of the three nations has balanced trade overall, exporting and importing $100 billion in goods.

Bilateral trade deficits receive more attention in the political arena than they deserve. This is in part because international relations are conducted country to country, so politicians and diplomats are naturally drawn to statistics measuring country-to-country economic transactions. Most economists, however, believe that bilateral trade balances are not very meaningful. From a macroeconomic standpoint, it is a nation's trade balance with all foreign nations put together that matters.

The same lesson applies to individuals as it does to nations. Your own personal trade balance is the difference between your income and your spending, and you may be concerned if these two variables are out of line. But you should not be concerned with the difference between your income and spending with a particular person or firm. Economist Robert Solow once explained the irrelevance of bilateral trade balances as follows: "I have a chronic deficit with my barber, who doesn't buy a darned thing from me." But that doesn't stop Mr. Solow from living within his means—or getting a haircut when he needs it.

FYI

Sony Corporation, or he might buy a bond issued by the Japanese government. In either case, some of U.S. saving is flowing abroad. Once again, U.S. net capital outflow exactly balances U.S. net exports.

The opposite situation occurs in Japan. When the Japanese consumer buys a copy of the Windows operating system, Japan's purchases of goods and services ($C + I + G$) rise, but there is no change in what Japan has produced (Y). The transaction reduces Japan's saving ($S = Y - C - G$) for a given level of investment (I). While the U.S. experiences a net capital outflow, Japan experiences a net capital inflow.

Now let's change the example. Suppose that instead of investing his 5,000 yen in a Japanese asset, Mr. Gates uses it to buy something made in Japan, such as a Sony Walkman MP3 player. In this case, imports into the United State rise. Together, the Windows export and the Walkman import represent balanced trade between Japan and the United States. Because exports and imports rise equally, net exports and net capital outflow are both unchanged.

A final possibility is that Mr. Gates exchanges his 5,000 yen for U.S. dollars at a local bank. But this doesn't change the situation: the bank now has to do something with the 5,000 yen. It can buy Japanese assets (a U.S. net capital outflow); it can buy a Japanese good (a U.S. import); or it can sell the yen to another American who wants to make such a transaction. If you follow the money, you can see that, in the end, U.S. net exports must equal U.S. net capital outflow.

5-2 Saving and Investment in a Small Open Economy

So far in our discussion of the international flows of goods and capital, we have rearranged accounting identities. That is, we have defined some of the variables that measure transactions in an open economy, and we have shown the links among these variables that follow from their definitions. Our next step is to develop a model that explains the behavior of these variables. We can then use the model to answer questions such as how the trade balance responds to changes in policy.

Capital Mobility and the World Interest Rate

In a moment we present a model of the international flows of capital and goods. Because the trade balance equals the net capital outflow, which in turn equals saving minus investment, our model focuses on saving and investment. To develop this model, we use some elements that should be familiar from Chapter 3, but in contrast to the Chapter 3 model, we do not assume that the real interest rate equilibrates saving and investment. Instead, we allow the economy to run a trade deficit and borrow from other countries or to run a trade surplus and lend to other countries.

If the real interest rate does not adjust to equilibrate saving and investment in this model, what *does* determine the real interest rate? We answer this question here by considering the simple case of a **small open economy** with perfect capital mobility. By "small" we mean that this economy is a small part of the world market and thus, by itself, can have only a negligible effect on the world interest rate. By "perfect capital mobility" we mean that residents of the country have full access to world financial markets. In particular, the government does not impede international borrowing or lending.

Because of this assumption of perfect capital mobility, the interest rate in our small open economy, r, must equal the **world interest rate** r^*, the real interest rate prevailing in world financial markets:

$$r = r^*.$$

Residents of the small open economy need never borrow at any interest rate above r^* because they can always get a loan at r^* from abroad. Similarly, residents of this economy need never lend at any interest rate below r^* because they can always earn r^* by lending abroad. Thus, the world interest rate determines the interest rate in our small open economy.

Let's discuss briefly what determines the world real interest rate. In a closed economy, the equilibrium of domestic saving and domestic investment determines the interest rate. Barring interplanetary trade, the world economy is a closed economy. Therefore, the equilibrium of world saving and world investment determines the world interest rate. Our small open economy has a negligible effect on the world real interest rate because, being a small part of the world, it has a negligible effect on world saving and world investment. Hence, our small open economy takes the world interest rate as exogenously given.

Why Assume a Small Open Economy?

The analysis in the body of this chapter assumes that the nation being studied is a small open economy. This assumption raises some questions.

Q: Is the United States well described by the assumption of a small open economy?

A: No, it is not, at least not completely. The United States does borrow and lend in world financial markets, and these markets exert a strong influence over the U.S. real interest rate, but it would be an exaggeration to say that the U.S. real interest rate is determined solely by world financial markets.

Q: So why are we assuming a small open economy?

A: Some nations, such as Canada and the Netherlands, are better described by the assumption of a small open economy. Yet the main reason for making this assumption is to develop understanding of and intuition for the macroeconomics of open economies. Remember from Chapter 1 that economic models are built with simplifying assumptions. An assumption need not be realistic to be useful. Assuming a small open economy simplifies the analysis greatly and, therefore, will help clarify our thinking.

Q: Can we relax this assumption and make the model more realistic?

A: Yes, we can, and we will. The appendix to this chapter considers the more realistic and more complicated case of a large open economy. Some instructors skip directly to this material when teaching these topics because the approach is more realistic for economies such as that of the United States. Others think that students should walk before they run and, therefore, begin with the simplifying assumption of a small open economy.

The Model

To build the model of the small open economy, we take three assumptions from Chapter 3:

- The economy's output Y is fixed by the factors of production and the production function. We write this as

$$Y = \overline{Y} = F(\overline{K}, \overline{L}).$$

- Consumption C is positively related to disposable income $Y - T$. We write the consumption function as

$$C = C(Y - T).$$

- Investment I is negatively related to the real interest rate r. We write the investment function as

$$I = I(r).$$

These are the three key parts of our model. If you do not understand these relationships, review Chapter 3 before continuing.

We can now return to the accounting identity and write it as

$$NX = (Y - C - G) - I$$

$$NX = S - I.$$

Substituting the Chapter 3 assumptions recapped above and the assumption that the interest rate equals the world interest rate, we obtain

$$NX = [\overline{Y} - C(\overline{Y} - T) - G] - I(r^*)$$

$$= \overline{S} - I(r^*).$$

This equation shows that the trade balance NX depends on those variables that determine saving S and investment I. Because saving depends on fiscal policy (lower government purchases G or higher taxes T raise national saving) and investment depends on the world real interest rate r^* (a higher interest rate makes some investment projects unprofitable), the trade balance depends on these variables as well.

In Chapter 3 we graphed saving and investment as in Figure 5-2. In the closed economy studied in that chapter, the real interest rate adjusts to equilibrate saving and investment—that is, the real interest rate is found where the saving and investment curves cross. In the small open economy, however, the real interest rate

FIGURE 5-2

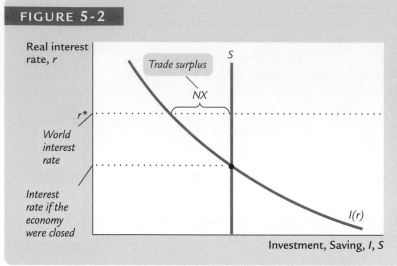

Saving and Investment in a Small Open Economy In a closed economy, the real interest rate adjusts to equilibrate saving and investment. In a small open economy, the interest rate is determined in world financial markets. The difference between saving and investment determines the trade balance. Here there is a trade surplus, because at the world interest rate, saving exceeds investment.

equals the world real interest rate. *The trade balance is determined by the difference between saving and investment at the world interest rate.*

At this point, you might wonder about the mechanism that causes the trade balance to equal the net capital outflow. The determinants of the capital flows are easy to understand. When saving falls short of investment, investors borrow from abroad; when saving exceeds investment, the excess is lent to other countries. But what causes those who import and export to behave so as to ensure that the international flow of goods exactly balances this international flow of capital? For now we leave this question unanswered, but we return to it in Section 5-3 when we discuss the determination of exchange rates.

How Policies Influence the Trade Balance

Suppose that the economy begins in a position of balanced trade. That is, at the world interest rate, investment I equals saving S, and net exports NX equal zero. Let's use our model to predict the effects of government policies at home and abroad.

Fiscal Policy at Home Consider first what happens to the small open economy if the government expands domestic spending by increasing government purchases. The increase in G reduces national saving, because $S = Y - C - G$. With an unchanged world real interest rate, investment remains the same. Therefore, saving falls below investment, and some investment must now be financed by borrowing from abroad. Because $NX = S - I$, the fall in S implies a fall in NX. The economy now runs a trade deficit.

The same logic applies to a decrease in taxes. A tax cut lowers T, raises disposable income $Y - T$, stimulates consumption, and reduces national saving. (Even though some of the tax cut finds its way into private saving, public saving falls by the full amount of the tax cut; in total, saving falls.) Because $NX = S - I$, the reduction in national saving in turn lowers NX.

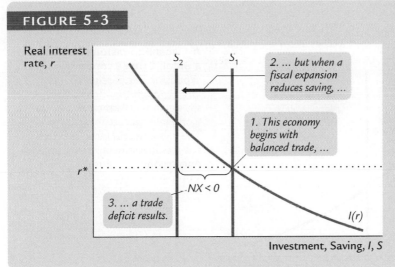

FIGURE 5-3

Real interest rate, r

S_2 S_1

2. ... but when a fiscal expansion reduces saving, ...

1. This economy begins with balanced trade, ...

r^* ....

$NX < 0$

3. ... a trade deficit results.

$I(r)$

Investment, Saving, I, S

A Fiscal Expansion at Home in a Small Open Economy An increase in government purchases or a reduction in taxes reduces national saving and thus shifts the saving schedule to the left, from S_1 to S_2. The result is a trade deficit.

Figure 5-3 illustrates these effects. A fiscal policy change that increases private consumption C or public consumption G reduces national saving $(Y - C - G)$ and, therefore, shifts the vertical line that represents saving from S_1 to S_2. Because NX is the distance between the saving schedule and the investment schedule at the world interest rate, this shift reduces NX. *Hence, starting from balanced trade, a change in fiscal policy that reduces national saving leads to a trade deficit.*

Fiscal Policy Abroad Consider now what happens to a small open economy when foreign governments increase their government purchases. If these foreign countries are a small part of the world economy, then their fiscal change has a negligible impact on other countries. But if these foreign countries are a large part of the world economy, their increase in government purchases reduces world saving. The decrease in world saving causes the world interest rate to rise, just as we saw in our closed-economy model (remember, Earth is a closed economy).

The increase in the world interest rate raises the cost of borrowing and, thus, reduces investment in our small open economy. Because there has been no change in domestic saving, saving S now exceeds investment I, and some of our saving begins to flow abroad. Because $NX = S - I$, the reduction in I must also increase NX. Hence, reduced saving abroad leads to a trade surplus at home.

Figure 5-4 illustrates how a small open economy starting from balanced trade responds to a foreign fiscal expansion. Because the policy change is occurring abroad, the domestic saving and investment schedules remain the same. The only change is an increase in the world interest rate from r_1^* to r_2^*. The trade balance is the difference between the saving and investment schedules; because saving exceeds investment at r_2^*, there is a trade surplus. *Hence, starting from balanced trade, an increase in the world interest rate due to a fiscal expansion abroad leads to a trade surplus.*

Shifts in Investment Demand Consider what happens to our small open economy if its investment schedule shifts outward—that is, if the demand for

FIGURE 5-4

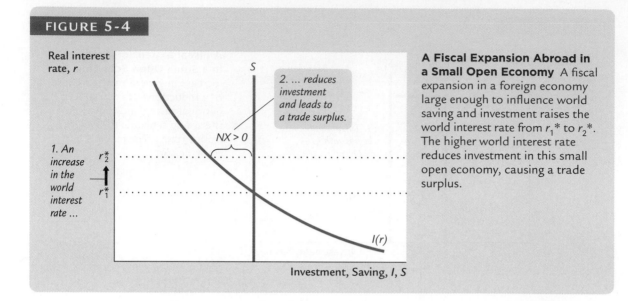

Real interest rate, r

1. An increase in the world interest rate ...

r_2^*

r_1^*

S

2. ... reduces investment and leads to a trade surplus.

$NX > 0$

$I(r)$

Investment, Saving, I, S

A Fiscal Expansion Abroad in a Small Open Economy A fiscal expansion in a foreign economy large enough to influence world saving and investment raises the world interest rate from r_1^* to r_2^*. The higher world interest rate reduces investment in this small open economy, causing a trade surplus.

investment goods at every interest rate increases. This shift would occur if, for example, the government changed the tax laws to encourage investment by providing an investment tax credit. Figure 5-5 illustrates the impact of a shift in the investment schedule. At a given world interest rate, investment is now higher. Because saving is unchanged, some investment must now be financed by borrowing from abroad. Because capital flows into the economy to finance the increased investment, the net capital outflow is negative. Put differently, because $NX = S - I$, the increase in I implies a decrease in NX. *Hence, starting from balanced trade, an outward shift in the investment schedule causes a trade deficit.*

FIGURE 5-5

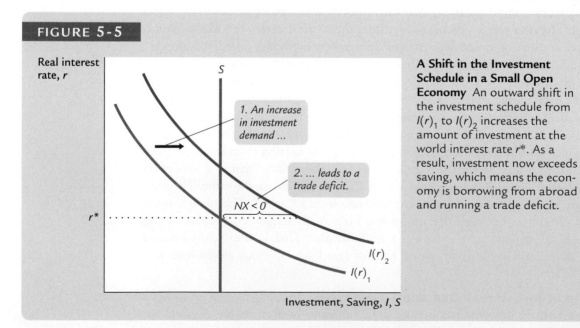

Real interest rate, r

1. An increase in investment demand ...

S

2. ... leads to a trade deficit.

$NX < 0$

r^*

$I(r)_2$

$I(r)_1$

Investment, Saving, I, S

A Shift in the Investment Schedule in a Small Open Economy An outward shift in the investment schedule from $I(r)_1$ to $I(r)_2$ increases the amount of investment at the world interest rate r^*. As a result, investment now exceeds saving, which means the economy is borrowing from abroad and running a trade deficit.

Evaluating Economic Policy

Our model of the open economy shows that the flow of goods and services measured by the trade balance is inextricably connected to the international flow of funds for capital accumulation. The net capital outflow is the difference between domestic saving and domestic investment. Thus, the impact of economic policies on the trade balance can always be found by examining their impact on domestic saving and domestic investment. Policies that increase investment or decrease saving tend to cause a trade deficit, and policies that decrease investment or increase saving tend to cause a trade surplus.

Our analysis of the open economy has been positive, not normative. That is, our analysis of how economic policies influence the international flows of capital and goods has not told us whether these policies are desirable. Evaluating economic policies and their impact on the open economy is a frequent topic of debate among economists and policymakers.

When a country runs a trade deficit, policymakers must confront the question of whether it represents a national problem. Most economists view a trade deficit not as a problem in itself, but perhaps as a symptom of a problem. A trade deficit could be a reflection of low saving. In a closed economy, low saving leads to low investment and a smaller future capital stock. In an open economy, low saving leads to a trade deficit and a growing foreign debt, which eventually must be repaid. In both cases, high current consumption leads to lower future consumption, implying that future generations bear the burden of low national saving.

Yet trade deficits are not always a reflection of an economic malady. When poor rural economies develop into modern industrial economies, they sometimes finance their high levels of investment with foreign borrowing. In these cases, trade deficits are a sign of economic development. For example, South Korea ran large trade deficits throughout the 1970s, and it became one of the success stories of economic growth. The lesson is that one cannot judge economic performance from the trade balance alone. Instead, one must look at the underlying causes of the international flows.

CASE STUDY

The U.S. Trade Deficit

During the 1980s, 1990s, and 2000s, the United States ran large trade deficits. Panel (a) of Figure 5-6 documents this experience by showing net exports as a percentage of GDP. The exact size of the trade deficit fluctuated over time, but it was large throughout these three decades. As accounting identities require, this trade deficit had to be financed by borrowing from abroad (or, equivalently, by selling U.S. assets abroad). During this period, the United States went from being the world's largest creditor to the world's largest debtor.

What caused the U.S. trade deficit? There is no single explanation. But to understand some of the forces at work, it helps to look at national saving and domestic investment, as shown in panel (b) of the figure. Keep in mind that the trade deficit is the difference between saving and investment.

FIGURE 5-6

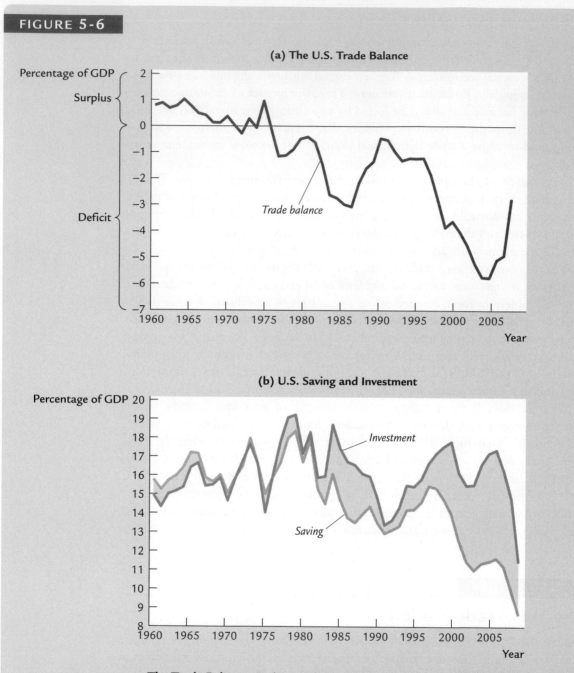

(a) The U.S. Trade Balance

Percentage of GDP

Surplus

Deficit

Trade balance

Year

(b) U.S. Saving and Investment

Percentage of GDP

Investment

Saving

Year

The Trade Balance, Saving, and Investment: The U.S. Experience
Panel (a) shows the trade balance as a percentage of GDP. Positive numbers represent a surplus, and negative numbers represent a deficit. Panel (b) shows national saving and investment as a percentage of GDP from 1960 to 2009. The trade balance equals saving minus investment.

Source: U.S. Department of Commerce.

The start of the trade deficit coincided with a fall in national saving. This development can be explained by the expansionary fiscal policy in the 1980s. With the support of President Reagan, the U.S. Congress passed legislation in 1981 that substantially cut personal income taxes over the next three years. Because these tax cuts were not met with equal cuts in government spending, the federal budget went into deficit. These budget deficits were among the largest ever experienced in a period of peace and prosperity, and they continued long after Reagan left office. According to our model, such a policy should reduce national saving, thereby causing a trade deficit. And, in fact, that is exactly what happened. Because the government budget and trade balance went into deficit at roughly the same time, these shortfalls were called the *twin deficits*.

Things started to change in the 1990s, when the U.S. federal government got its fiscal house in order. The first President Bush and President Clinton both signed tax increases, while Congress kept a lid on spending. In addition to these policy changes, rapid productivity growth in the late 1990s raised incomes and, thus, further increased tax revenue. These developments moved the U.S. federal budget from deficit to surplus, which in turn caused national saving to rise.

In contrast to what our model predicts, the increase in national saving did not coincide with a shrinking trade deficit, because domestic investment rose at the same time. The likely explanation is that the boom in information technology caused an expansionary shift in the U.S. investment function. Even though fiscal policy was pushing the trade deficit toward surplus, the investment boom was an even stronger force pushing the trade balance toward deficit.

In the early 2000s, fiscal policy once again put downward pressure on national saving. With the second President Bush in the White House, tax cuts were signed into law in 2001 and 2003, while the war on terror led to substantial increases in government spending. The federal government was again running budget deficits. National saving fell to historic lows, and the trade deficit reached historic highs.

A few years later, the trade deficit started to shrink when the economy experienced a substantial decline in housing prices and a deep recession (a phenomenon examined in Chapter 11). Both of these events caused investment to plummet. The trade deficit fell from 5.7 percent of GDP at its peak in 2006 to 2.7 percent in 2009.

The history of the U.S. trade deficit shows that this statistic, by itself, does not tell us much about what is happening in the economy. We have to look deeper at saving, investment, and the policies and events that cause them (and thus the trade balance) to change over time.[1] ∎

CASE STUDY

Why Doesn't Capital Flow to Poor Countries?

The U.S. trade deficit discussed in the previous case study represents a flow of capital into the United States from the rest of the world. What countries were the source of these capital flows? Because the world is a closed economy, the

---

[1] For more on this topic, see Catherine L. Mann, *Is the U.S. Trade Deficit Sustainable?* (Washington DC: Institute for International Economics, 1999).

capital must have been coming from those countries that were running trade surpluses. In 2009, this group included many nations that were far poorer than the United States, such as Russia, Malaysia, Venezuela, and China. In these nations, saving exceeded investment in domestic capital. These countries were sending funds abroad to countries like the United States, where investment in domestic capital exceeded saving.

From one perspective, the direction of international capital flows is a paradox. Recall our discussion of production functions in Chapter 3. There, we established that an empirically realistic production function is the Cobb–Douglas form:

$$F(K, L) = AK^\alpha L^{1-\alpha},$$

where K is capital, L is labor, A is a variable representing the state of technology, and α is a parameter that determines capital's share of total income. For this production function, the marginal product of capital is

$$MPK = \alpha A \, (K/L)^{\alpha-1}.$$

The marginal product of capital tells us how much extra output an extra unit of capital would produce. Because α is capital's share, it must be less than 1, so $\alpha - 1 < 0$. This means that an increase in K/L decreases MPK. In other words, holding other variables constant, the more capital a nation has, the less valuable an extra unit of capital is. This phenomenon of diminishing marginal product says that capital should be more valuable where capital is scarce.

This prediction, however, seems at odds with the international flow of capital represented by trade imbalances. Capital does not seem to flow to those nations where it should be most valuable. Instead of capital-rich countries like the United States lending to capital-poor countries, we often observe the opposite. Why is that?

One reason is that there are important differences among nations other than their accumulation of capital. Poor nations have not only lower levels of capital accumulation (represented by K/L) but also inferior production capabilities (represented by the variable A). For example, compared to rich nations, poor nations may have less access to advanced technologies, lower levels of education (or *human capital*), or less efficient economic policies. Such differences could mean less output for given inputs of capital and labor; in the Cobb–Douglas production function, this is translated into a lower value of the parameter A. If so, then capital need not be more valuable in poor nations, even though capital is scarce.

A second reason capital might not flow to poor nations is that property rights are often not enforced. Corruption is much more prevalent; revolutions, coups, and expropriation of wealth are more common; and governments often default on their debts. So even if capital is more valuable in poor nations, foreigners may avoid investing their wealth there simply because they are afraid of losing it. Moreover, local investors face similar incentives. Imagine that you live in a poor nation and are lucky enough to have some wealth to invest; you might well decide that putting it in a safe country like the United States is your best option, even if capital is less valuable there than in your home country.

Whichever of these two reasons is correct, the challenge for poor nations is to find ways to reverse the situation. If these nations offered the same production efficiency and legal protections as the U.S. economy, the direction of international capital flows would likely reverse. The U.S. trade deficit would become a trade surplus, and capital would flow to these emerging nations. Such a change would help the poor of the world escape poverty.[2] ■

5-3 Exchange Rates

Having examined the international flows of capital and of goods and services, we now extend the analysis by considering the prices that apply to these transactions. The *exchange rate* between two countries is the price at which residents of those countries trade with each other. In this section we first examine precisely what the exchange rate measures, and we then discuss how exchange rates are determined.

Nominal and Real Exchange Rates

Economists distinguish between two exchange rates: the nominal exchange rate and the real exchange rate. Let's discuss each in turn and see how they are related.

The Nominal Exchange Rate The **nominal exchange rate** is the relative price of the currencies of two countries. For example, if the exchange rate between the U.S. dollar and the Japanese yen is 120 yen per dollar, then you can exchange one dollar for 120 yen in world markets for foreign currency. A Japanese who wants to obtain dollars would pay 120 yen for each dollar he bought. An American who wants to obtain yen would get 120 yen for each dollar he paid. When people refer to "the exchange rate" between two countries, they usually mean the nominal exchange rate.

Notice that an exchange rate can be reported in two ways. If one dollar buys 120 yen, then one yen buys 0.00833 dollar. We can say the exchange rate is 120 yen per dollar, or we can say the exchange rate is 0.00833 dollar per yen. Because 0.00833 equals 1/120, these two ways of expressing the exchange rate are equivalent.

This book always expresses the exchange rate in units of foreign currency per dollar. With this convention, a rise in the exchange rate—say, from 120 to 125 yen per dollar—is called an *appreciation* of the dollar; a fall in the exchange rate is called a *depreciation*. When the domestic currency appreciates, it buys more of the foreign currency; when it depreciates, it buys less. An appreciation is sometimes called a *strengthening* of the currency, and a depreciation is sometimes called a *weakening* of the currency.

The Real Exchange Rate The **real exchange rate** is the relative price of the goods of two countries. That is, the real exchange rate tells us the rate at which we can trade the goods of one country for the goods of another. The real exchange rate is sometimes called the *terms of trade*.

---

[2] For more on this topic, see Robert E. Lucas, "Why Doesn't Capital Flow From Rich to Poor Countries?" *American Economic Review* 80 (May 1990): 92–96.

To see the relation between the real and nominal exchange rates, consider a single good produced in many countries: cars. Suppose an American car costs $10,000 and a similar Japanese car costs 2,400,000 yen. To compare the prices of the two cars, we must convert them into a common currency. If a dollar is worth 120 yen, then the American car costs 1,200,000 yen. Comparing the price of the American car (1,200,000 yen) and the price of the Japanese car (2,400,000 yen), we conclude that the American car costs one-half of what the Japanese car costs. In other words, at current prices, we can exchange two American cars for one Japanese car.

We can summarize our calculation as follows:

$$\frac{\text{Real Exchange}}{\text{Rate}} = \frac{(120 \text{ Yen/Dollar}) \times (10,000 \text{ Dollars/American Car})}{(2,400,000 \text{ Yen/Japanese Car})}$$

$$= 0.5 \frac{\text{Japanese Car}}{\text{American Car}}.$$

At these prices and this exchange rate, we obtain one-half of a Japanese car per American car. More generally, we can write this calculation as

$$\frac{\text{Real Exchange}}{\text{Rate}} = \frac{\text{Nominal Exchange Rate} \times \text{Price of Domestic Good}}{\text{Price of Foreign Good}}.$$

The rate at which we exchange foreign and domestic goods depends on the prices of the goods in the local currencies and on the rate at which the currencies are exchanged.

This calculation of the real exchange rate for a single good suggests how we should define the real exchange rate for a broader basket of goods. Let e be the nominal exchange rate (the number of yen per dollar), P be the price level in the United States (measured in dollars), and P^* be the price level in Japan (measured in yen). Then the real exchange rate ε is

$$\begin{array}{ccc} \text{Real} & \text{Nominal} & \text{Ratio of} \\ \text{Exchange} = \text{Exchange} & \times & \text{Price} \\ \text{Rate} & \text{Rate} & \text{Levels} \\ \varepsilon \quad = & e & \times (P/P^*). \end{array}$$

The real exchange rate between two countries is computed from the nominal exchange rate and the price levels in the two countries. *If the real exchange rate is high, foreign goods are relatively cheap, and domestic goods are relatively expensive. If the real exchange rate is low, foreign goods are relatively expensive, and domestic goods are relatively cheap.*

The Real Exchange Rate and the Trade Balance

What macroeconomic influence does the real exchange rate exert? To answer this question, remember that the real exchange rate is nothing more than a relative price. Just as the relative price of hamburgers and pizza determines which you choose for lunch, the relative price of domestic and foreign goods affects the demand for these goods.

Suppose first that the real exchange rate is low. In this case, because domestic goods are relatively cheap, domestic residents will want to purchase fewer imported goods: they will buy Fords rather than Hondas, drink Coors rather than Heineken, and vacation in Florida rather than Italy. For the same reason, foreigners will want to buy many of our goods. As a result of both of these actions, the quantity of our net exports demanded will be high.

The opposite occurs if the real exchange rate is high. Because domestic goods are expensive relative to foreign goods, domestic residents will want to buy many imported goods, and foreigners will want to buy few of our goods. Therefore, the quantity of our net exports demanded will be low.

We write this relationship between the real exchange rate and net exports as

$$NX = NX(\varepsilon).$$

This equation states that net exports are a function of the real exchange rate. Figure 5-7 illustrates the negative relationship between the trade balance and the real exchange rate.

"How about Nebraska? The dollar's still strong in Nebraska."

The Determinants of the Real Exchange Rate

We now have all the pieces needed to construct a model that explains what factors determine the real exchange rate. In particular, we combine the relationship between net exports and the real exchange rate we just discussed with the model

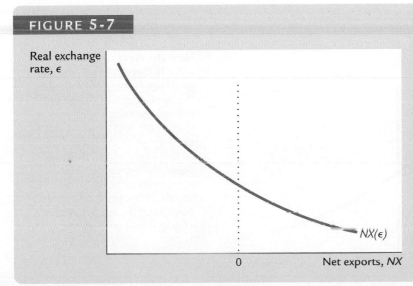

FIGURE 5-7

Real exchange rate, ϵ

$NX(\epsilon)$

0   Net exports, *NX*

Net Exports and the Real Exchange Rate The figure shows the relationship between the real exchange rate and net exports: the lower the real exchange rate, the less expensive are domestic goods relative to foreign goods, and thus the greater are our net exports. Note that a portion of the horizontal axis measures negative values of *NX*: because imports can exceed exports, net exports can be less than zero.

of the trade balance we developed earlier in the chapter. We can summarize the analysis as follows:

■ The real exchange rate is related to net exports. When the real exchange rate is lower, domestic goods are less expensive relative to foreign goods, and net exports are greater.

■ The trade balance (net exports) must equal the net capital outflow, which in turn equals saving minus investment. Saving is fixed by the consumption function and fiscal policy; investment is fixed by the investment function and the world interest rate.

Figure 5-8 illustrates these two conditions. The line showing the relationship between net exports and the real exchange rate slopes downward because a low real exchange rate makes domestic goods relatively inexpensive. The line representing the excess of saving over investment, $S - I$, is vertical because neither saving nor investment depends on the real exchange rate. The crossing of these two lines determines the equilibrium real exchange rate.

Figure 5-8 looks like an ordinary supply-and-demand diagram. In fact, you can think of this diagram as representing the supply and demand for foreign-currency exchange. The vertical line, $S - I$, represents the net capital outflow and thus the supply of dollars to be exchanged into foreign currency and invested abroad. The downward-sloping line, $NX(\varepsilon)$, represents the net demand for dollars coming from foreigners who want dollars to buy our goods. *At the equilibrium real exchange rate, the supply of dollars available from the net capital outflow balances the demand for dollars by foreigners buying our net exports.*

How Policies Influence the Real Exchange Rate

We can use this model to show how the changes in economic policy we discussed earlier affect the real exchange rate.

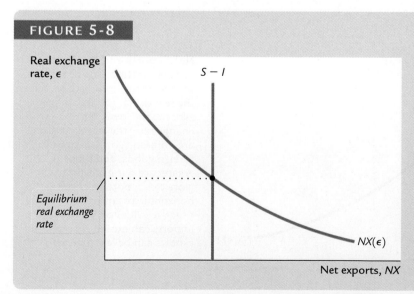

FIGURE 5-8

Real exchange rate, ϵ

$S - I$

Equilibrium real exchange rate

$NX(\epsilon)$

Net exports, NX

How the Real Exchange Rate Is Determined The real exchange rate is determined by the intersection of the vertical line representing saving minus investment and the downward-sloping net-exports schedule. At this intersection, the quantity of dollars supplied for the flow of capital abroad equals the quantity of dollars demanded for the net export of goods and services.

FIGURE 5-9

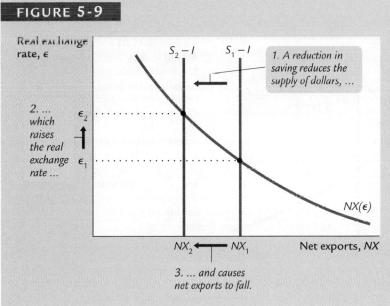

The Impact of Expansionary Fiscal Policy at Home on the Real Exchange Rate Expansionary fiscal policy at home, such as an increase in government purchases or a cut in taxes, reduces national saving. The fall in saving reduces the supply of dollars to be exchanged into foreign currency, from $S_1 - I$ to $S_2 - I$. This shift raises the equilibrium real exchange rate from ε_1 to ε_2.

Fiscal Policy at Home What happens to the real exchange rate if the government reduces national saving by increasing government purchases or cutting taxes? As we discussed earlier, this reduction in saving lowers $S - I$ and thus NX. That is, the reduction in saving causes a trade deficit.

Figure 5-9 shows how the equilibrium real exchange rate adjusts to ensure that NX falls. The change in policy shifts the vertical $S - I$ line to the left, lowering the supply of dollars to be invested abroad. The lower supply causes the equilibrium real exchange rate to rise from ε_1 to ε_2—that is, the dollar becomes more valuable. Because of the rise in the value of the dollar, domestic goods become more expensive relative to foreign goods, which causes exports to fall and imports to rise. The change in exports and the change in imports both act to reduce net exports.

Fiscal Policy Abroad What happens to the real exchange rate if foreign governments increase government purchases or cut taxes? This change in fiscal policy reduces world saving and raises the world interest rate. The increase in the world interest rate reduces domestic investment I, which raises $S - I$ and thus NX. That is, the increase in the world interest rate causes a trade surplus.

Figure 5-10 shows that this change in policy shifts the vertical $S - I$ line to the right, raising the supply of dollars to be invested abroad. The equilibrium real exchange rate falls. That is, the dollar becomes less valuable, and domestic goods become less expensive relative to foreign goods.

Shifts in Investment Demand What happens to the real exchange rate if investment demand at home increases, perhaps because Congress passes an investment tax credit? At the given world interest rate, the increase in investment demand leads to higher investment. A higher value of I means lower

FIGURE 5-10

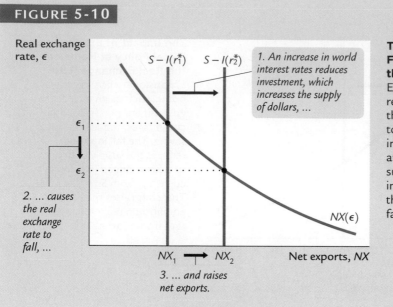

1. An increase in world interest rates reduces investment, which increases the supply of dollars, ...

2. ... causes the real exchange rate to fall, ...

3. ... and raises net exports.

The Impact of Expansionary Fiscal Policy Abroad on the Real Exchange Rate Expansionary fiscal policy abroad reduces world saving and raises the world interest rate from r_1^* to r_2^*. The increase in the world interest rate reduces investment at home, which in turn raises the supply of dollars to be exchanged into foreign currencies. As a result, the equilibrium real exchange rate falls from ε_1 to ε_2.

values of $S - I$ and NX. That is, the increase in investment demand causes a trade deficit.

Figure 5-11 shows that the increase in investment demand shifts the vertical $S - I$ line to the left, reducing the supply of dollars to be invested abroad. The equilibrium real exchange rate rises. Hence, when the investment tax credit makes investing in the United States more attractive, it also increases the value

FIGURE 5-11

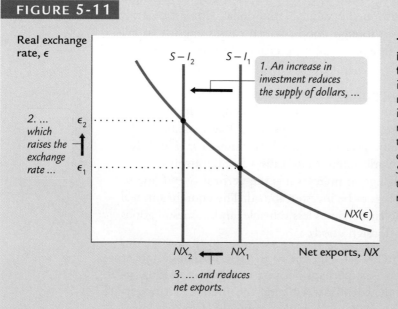

1. An increase in investment reduces the supply of dollars, ...

2. ... which raises the exchange rate ...

3. ... and reduces net exports.

The Impact of an Increase in Investment Demand on the Real Exchange Rate An increase in investment demand raises the quantity of domestic investment from I_1 to I_2. As a result, the supply of dollars to be exchanged into foreign currencies falls from $S - I_1$ to $S - I_2$. This fall in supply raises the equilibrium real exchange rate from ε_1 to ε_2.

of the U.S. dollars necessary to make these investments. When the dollar appreciates, domestic goods become more expensive relative to foreign goods, and net exports fall.

The Effects of Trade Policies

Now that we have a model that explains the trade balance and the real exchange rate, we have the tools to examine the macroeconomic effects of trade policies. Trade policies, broadly defined, are policies designed to influence directly the amount of goods and services exported or imported. Most often, trade policies take the form of protecting domestic industries from foreign competition—either by placing a tax on foreign imports (a tariff) or restricting the amount of goods and services that can be imported (a quota).

As an example of a protectionist trade policy, consider what would happen if the government prohibited the import of foreign cars. For any given real exchange rate, imports would now be lower, implying that net exports (exports minus imports) would be higher. Thus, the net-exports schedule shifts outward, as in Figure 5-12. To see the effects of the policy, we compare the old equilibrium and the new equilibrium. In the new equilibrium, the real exchange rate is higher, and net exports are unchanged. Despite the shift in the net-exports schedule, the equilibrium level of net exports remains the same, because the protectionist policy does not alter either saving or investment.

This analysis shows that protectionist trade policies do not affect the trade balance. This surprising conclusion is often overlooked in the popular debate over

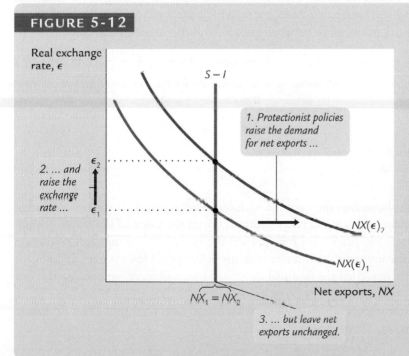

FIGURE 5-12

The Impact of Protectionist Trade Policies on the Real Exchange Rate A protectionist trade policy, such as a ban on imported cars, shifts the net-exports schedule from $NX(\varepsilon)_1$ to $NX(\varepsilon)_2$, which raises the real exchange rate from ε_1 to ε_2. Notice that, despite the shift in the net-exports schedule, the equilibrium level of net exports is unchanged.

trade policies. Because a trade deficit reflects an excess of imports over exports, one might guess that reducing imports—such as by prohibiting the import of foreign cars—would reduce a trade deficit. Yet our model shows that protectionist policies lead only to an appreciation of the real exchange rate. The increase in the price of domestic goods relative to foreign goods tends to lower net exports by stimulating imports and depressing exports. Thus, the appreciation offsets the increase in net exports that is directly attributable to the trade restriction.

Although protectionist trade policies do not alter the trade balance, they do affect the amount of trade. As we have seen, because the real exchange rate appreciates, the goods and services we produce become more expensive relative to foreign goods and services. We therefore export less in the new equilibrium. Because net exports are unchanged, we must import less as well. (The appreciation of the exchange rate does stimulate imports to some extent, but this only partly offsets the decrease in imports due to the trade restriction.) Thus, protectionist policies reduce both the quantity of imports and the quantity of exports.

This fall in the total amount of trade is the reason economists almost always oppose protectionist policies. International trade benefits all countries by allowing each country to specialize in what it produces best and by providing each country with a greater variety of goods and services. Protectionist policies diminish these gains from trade. Although these policies benefit certain groups within society— for example, a ban on imported cars helps domestic car producers—society on average is worse off when policies reduce the amount of international trade.

The Determinants of the Nominal Exchange Rate

Having seen what determines the real exchange rate, we now turn our attention to the nominal exchange rate—the rate at which the currencies of two countries trade. Recall the relationship between the real and the nominal exchange rate:

$$\begin{matrix} \text{Real} & & \text{Nominal} & & \text{Ratio of} \\ \text{Exchange} & = & \text{Exchange} & \times & \text{Price} \\ \text{Rate} & & \text{Rate} & & \text{Levels} \\ \varepsilon & = & e & & \times (P/P^*). \end{matrix}$$

We can write the nominal exchange rate as

$$e = \varepsilon \times (P^*/P).$$

This equation shows that the nominal exchange rate depends on the real exchange rate and the price levels in the two countries. Given the value of the real exchange rate, if the domestic price level P rises, then the nominal exchange rate e will fall: because a dollar is worth less, a dollar will buy fewer yen. However, if the Japanese price level P^* rises, then the nominal exchange rate will increase: because the yen is worth less, a dollar will buy more yen.

It is instructive to consider changes in exchange rates over time. The exchange rate equation can be written

% Change in e = % Change in ε + % Change in P^* − % Change in P.

The percentage change in ε is the change in the real exchange rate. The percentage change in P is the domestic inflation rate π, and the percentage change in P^* is the foreign country's inflation rate π^*. Thus, the percentage change in the nominal exchange rate is

$$\% \text{ Change in } e = \% \text{ Change in } \varepsilon + (\pi^* - \pi)$$

$$\begin{array}{c} \text{Percentage Change in} \\ \text{Nominal Exchange Rate} \end{array} = \begin{array}{c} \text{Percentage Change in} \\ \text{Real Exchange Rate} \end{array} + \begin{array}{c} \text{Difference in} \\ \text{Inflation Rates.} \end{array}$$

This equation states that the percentage change in the nominal exchange rate between the currencies of two countries equals the percentage change in the real exchange rate plus the difference in their inflation rates. *If a country has a high rate of inflation relative to the United States, a dollar will buy an increasing amount of the foreign currency over time. If a country has a low rate of inflation relative to the United States, a dollar will buy a decreasing amount of the foreign currency over time.*

This analysis shows how monetary policy affects the nominal exchange rate. We know from Chapter 4 that high growth in the money supply leads to high inflation. Here, we have just seen that one consequence of high inflation is a depreciating currency: high π implies falling e. In other words, just as growth in the amount of money raises the price of goods measured in terms of money, it also tends to raise the price of foreign currencies measured in terms of the domestic currency.

CASE STUDY

Inflation and Nominal Exchange Rates

If we look at data on exchange rates and price levels of different countries, we quickly see the importance of inflation for explaining changes in the nominal exchange rate. The most dramatic examples come from periods of very high inflation. For example, the price level in Mexico rose by 2,300 percent from 1983 to 1988. Because of this inflation, the number of pesos a person could buy with a U.S. dollar rose from 144 in 1983 to 2,281 in 1988.

The same relationship holds true for countries with more moderate inflation. Figure 5-13 is a scatterplot showing the relationship between inflation and the exchange rate for 15 countries. On the horizontal axis is the difference between each country's average inflation rate and the average inflation rate of the United States $(\pi^* - \pi)$. On the vertical axis is the average percentage change in the exchange rate between each country's currency and the U.S. dollar (percentage change in e). The positive relationship between these two variables is clear in this figure. Countries with relatively high inflation tend to have depreciating currencies (you can buy more of them with your dollars over time), and countries with relatively low inflation tend to have appreciating currencies (you can buy less of them with your dollars over time).

As an example, consider the exchange rate between Swiss francs and U.S. dollars. Both Switzerland and the United States have experienced inflation over the past thirty years, so both the franc and the dollar buy fewer goods than they once did. But, as Figure 5-13 shows, inflation in Switzerland has been lower than

FIGURE 5-13

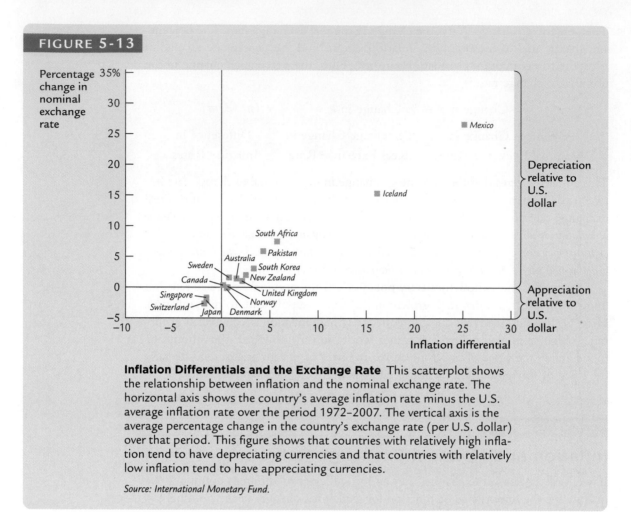

Inflation Differentials and the Exchange Rate This scatterplot shows the relationship between inflation and the nominal exchange rate. The horizontal axis shows the country's average inflation rate minus the U.S. average inflation rate over the period 1972–2007. The vertical axis is the average percentage change in the country's exchange rate (per U.S. dollar) over that period. This figure shows that countries with relatively high inflation tend to have depreciating currencies and that countries with relatively low inflation tend to have appreciating currencies.

Source: International Monetary Fund.

inflation in the United States. This means that the value of the franc has fallen less than the value of the dollar. Therefore, the number of Swiss francs you can buy with a U.S. dollar has been falling over time. ∎

The Special Case of Purchasing-Power Parity

A famous hypothesis in economics, called the *law of one price*, states that the same good cannot sell for different prices in different locations at the same time. If a bushel of wheat sold for less in New York than in Chicago, it would be profitable to buy wheat in New York and then sell it in Chicago. This profit opportunity would become quickly apparent to astute arbitrageurs—people who specialize in "buying low" in one market and "selling high" in another. As the arbitrageurs took advantage of this opportunity, they would increase the demand for wheat in New York and increase the supply of wheat in Chicago. Their actions would drive the price up in New York and down in Chicago, thereby ensuring that prices are equalized in the two markets.

The law of one price applied to the international marketplace is called **purchasing-power parity**. It states that if international arbitrage is possible, then a dollar (or any other currency) must have the same purchasing power in every country. The argument goes as follows. If a dollar could buy more wheat domestically than abroad, there would be opportunities to profit by buying wheat domestically and selling it abroad. Profit-seeking arbitrageurs would drive up the domestic price of wheat relative to the foreign price. Similarly, if a dollar could buy more wheat abroad than domestically, the arbitrageurs would buy wheat abroad and sell it domestically, driving down the domestic price relative to the foreign price. Thus, profit-seeking by international arbitrageurs causes wheat prices to be the same in all countries.

We can interpret the doctrine of purchasing-power parity using our model of the real exchange rate. The quick action of these international arbitrageurs implies that net exports are highly sensitive to small movements in the real exchange rate. A small decrease in the price of domestic goods relative to foreign goods— that is, a small decrease in the real exchange rate—causes arbitrageurs to buy goods domestically and sell them abroad. Similarly, a small increase in the relative price of domestic goods causes arbitrageurs to import goods from abroad. There- fore, as in Figure 5-14, the net-exports schedule is very flat at the real exchange rate that equalizes purchasing power among countries: any small movement in the real exchange rate leads to a large change in net exports. This extreme sensi- tivity of net exports guarantees that the equilibrium real exchange rate is always close to the level that ensures purchasing-power parity.

Purchasing-power parity has two important implications. First, because the net-exports schedule is flat, changes in saving or investment do not influence the real or nominal exchange rate. Second, because the real exchange rate is fixed, all changes in the nominal exchange rate result from changes in price levels.

Is this doctrine of purchasing-power parity realistic? Most economists believe that, despite its appealing logic, purchasing-power parity does not provide a com- pletely accurate description of the world. First, many goods are not easily traded.

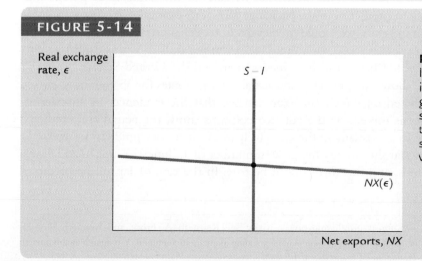

FIGURE 5-14

Real exchange rate, ϵ

$S - I$

$NX(\epsilon)$

Net exports, NX

Purchasing-Power Parity The law of one price applied to the international marketplace sug- gests that net exports are highly sensitive to small movements in the real exchange rate. This high sensitivity is reflected here with a very flat net-exports schedule.

A haircut can be more expensive in Tokyo than in New York, yet there is no room for international arbitrage because it is impossible to transport haircuts. Second, even tradable goods are not always perfect substitutes. Some consumers prefer Hondas, and others prefer Fords. Thus, the relative price of Hondas and Fords can vary to some extent without leaving any profit opportunities. For these reasons, real exchange rates do in fact vary over time.

Although the doctrine of purchasing-power parity does not describe the world perfectly, it does provide a reason why movement in the real exchange rate will be limited. There is much validity to its underlying logic: the farther the real exchange rate drifts from the level predicted by purchasing-power parity, the greater the incentive for individuals to engage in international arbitrage in goods. We cannot rely on purchasing-power parity to eliminate all changes in the real exchange rate, but this doctrine does provide a reason to expect that fluctuations in the real exchange rate will typically be small or temporary.[3]

CASE STUDY

The Big Mac Around the World

The doctrine of purchasing-power parity says that after we adjust for exchange rates, we should find that goods sell for the same price everywhere. Conversely, it says that the exchange rate between two currencies should depend on the price levels in the two countries.

To see how well this doctrine works, *The Economist*, an international news-magazine, regularly collects data on the price of a good sold in many countries: the McDonald's Big Mac hamburger. According to purchasing-power parity, the price of a Big Mac should be closely related to the country's nominal exchange rate. The higher the price of a Big Mac in the local currency, the higher the exchange rate (measured in units of local currency per U.S. dollar) should be.

Table 5-2 presents the international prices in 2009, when a Big Mac sold for $3.57 in the United States (this was the average price in New York, San Francisco, Chicago, and Atlanta). With these data, we can use the doctrine of purchasing-power parity to predict nominal exchange rates. For example, because a Big Mac cost 320 yen in Japan, we would predict that the exchange rate between the dollar and the yen was 320/3.57, or around 89.6, yen per dollar. At this exchange rate, a Big Mac would have cost the same in Japan and the United States.

Table 5-2 shows the predicted and actual exchange rates for 35 countries, ranked by the predicted exchange rate. You can see that the evidence on purchasing-power parity is mixed. As the last two columns show, the actual and predicted exchange rates are usually in the same ballpark. Our theory predicts, for instance, that a U.S. dollar should buy the greatest number of Indonesian rupiahs and fewest British pounds, and this turns out to be true. In the case of Japan, the predicted

---

[3] To learn more about purchasing-power parity, see Kenneth A. Froot and Kenneth Rogoff, "Perspectives on PPP and Long-Run Real Exchange Rates," in Gene M. Grossman and Kenneth Rogoff, eds., *Handbook of International Economics*, vol. 3 (Amsterdam: North-Holland, 1995).

TABLE 5-2

Big Mac Prices and the Exchange Rate: An Application of Purchasing-Power Parity

Country	Currency	Price of a Big Mac	Exchange rate (per U.S. dollar) Predicted	Exchange rate (per U.S. dollar) Actual
Indonesia	Rupiah	20900.00	5854	10200
South Korea	Won	3400.00	952	1315
Chile	Peso	1750.00	490	549
Hungary	Forint	720.00	202	199
Japan	Yen	320.00	89.6	92.6
Philippines	Peso	99.39	27.8	48.4
Taiwan	Dollar	75.00	21.0	33.2
Czech Republic	Koruna	67.92	19.0	18.7
Russia	Rouble	67.00	18.8	32.8
Thailand	Baht	64.49	18.1	34.2
Norway	Kroner	40.00	11.20	6.51
Sweden	Krona	39.00	10.90	7.90
Mexico	Peso	33.00	9.24	13.80
Denmark	Krone	29.50	8.26	5.34
South Africa	Rand	17.95	5.03	8.28
Isreal	Shekel	15.00	4.20	3.97
Hong Kong	Dollar	13.30	3.73	7.75
Egypt	Pound	13.00	3.64	5.58
China	Yuan	12.50	3.50	6.83
Argentina	Peso	11.50	3.22	3.81
Saudi Arabia	Riyal	11.00	3.08	3.75
UAE	Dirhams	10.00	2.80	3.67
Turkey	Lire	5.65	2.45	1.55
Peru	New Sol	8.06	2.26	3.03
Brazil	Real	8.03	2.25	2.00
Poland	Zloty	7.60	2.13	3.16
Malaysia	Ringgit	6.77	1.90	3.60
Switzerland	Franc	6.50	1.82	1.09
New Zealand	Dollar	4.90	1.37	1.59
Australia	Dollar	4.34	1.22	1.29
Singapore	Dollar	4.22	1.18	1.46
Canada	Dollar	3.89	1.09	1.16
United States	Dollar	3.57	1.00	1.00
Euro Area	Euro	3.31	0.93	0.72
United Kingdom	Pound	2.29	0.64	0.62

Note: The predicted exchange rate is the exchange rate that would make the price of a Big Mac in that country equal to its price in the United States.
Source. The Economist, July 16, 2009.

exchange rate of 89.6 yen per dollar is close to the actual exchange rate of 92.6. Yet the theory's predictions are far from exact and, in many cases, are off by 30 percent or more. Hence, although the theory of purchasing-power parity provides a rough guide to the level of exchange rates, it does not explain exchange rates completely. ■

5-4 Conclusion: The United States as a Large Open Economy

In this chapter we have seen how a small open economy works. We have examined the determinants of the international flow of funds for capital accumulation and the international flow of goods and services. We have also examined the determinants of a country's real and nominal exchange rates. Our analysis shows how various policies—monetary policies, fiscal policies, and trade policies—affect the trade balance and the exchange rate.

The economy we have studied is "small" in the sense that its interest rate is fixed by world financial markets. That is, we have assumed that this economy does not affect the world interest rate and that the economy can borrow and lend at the world interest rate in unlimited amounts. This assumption contrasts with the assumption we made when we studied the closed economy in Chapter 3. In the closed economy, the domestic interest rate equilibrates domestic saving and domestic investment, implying that policies that influence saving or investment alter the equilibrium interest rate.

Which of these analyses should we apply to an economy such as that of the United States? The answer is a little of both. The United States is neither so large nor so isolated that it is immune to developments occurring abroad. The large trade deficits of the 1980s, 1990s, and 2000s show the importance of international financial markets for funding U.S. investment. Hence, the closed-economy analysis of Chapter 3 cannot by itself fully explain the impact of policies on the U.S. economy.

Yet the U.S. economy is not so small and so open that the analysis of this chapter applies perfectly either. First, the United States is large enough that it can influence world financial markets. For example, large U.S. budget deficits were often blamed for the high real interest rates that prevailed throughout the world in the 1980s. Second, capital may not be perfectly mobile across countries. If individuals prefer holding their wealth in domestic rather than foreign assets, funds for capital accumulation will not flow freely to equate interest rates in all countries. For these two reasons, we cannot directly apply our model of the small open economy to the United States.

When analyzing policy for a country such as the United States, we need to combine the closed-economy logic of Chapter 3 and the small-open-economy logic of this chapter. The appendix to this chapter builds a model of an economy between these two extremes. In this intermediate case, there is international borrowing and lending, but the interest rate is not fixed by world financial markets. Instead, the more the economy borrows from abroad, the higher the interest rate it must offer foreign investors. The results, not surprisingly, are a mixture of the two polar cases we have already examined.

Consider, for example, a reduction in national saving due to a fiscal expansion. As in the closed economy, this policy raises the real interest rate and crowds out domestic investment. As in the small open economy, it also reduces the net capital outflow, leading to a trade deficit and an appreciation of the exchange rate. Hence, although the model of the small open economy examined here does not precisely describe an economy such as that of the United States, it does provide approximately the right answer to how policies affect the trade balance and the exchange rate.

Summary

1. Net exports are the difference between exports and imports. They are equal to the difference between what we produce and what we demand for consumption, investment, and government purchases.

2. The net capital outflow is the excess of domestic saving over domestic investment. The trade balance is the amount received for our net exports of goods and services. The national income accounts identity shows that the net capital outflow always equals the trade balance.

3. The impact of any policy on the trade balance can be determined by examining its impact on saving and investment. Policies that raise saving or lower investment lead to a trade surplus, and policies that lower saving or raise investment lead to a trade deficit.

4. The nominal exchange rate is the rate at which people trade the currency of one country for the currency of another country. The real exchange rate is the rate at which people trade the goods produced by the two countries. The real exchange rate equals the nominal exchange rate multiplied by the ratio of the price levels in the two countries.

5. Because the real exchange rate is the price of domestic goods relative to foreign goods, an appreciation of the real exchange rate tends to reduce net exports. The equilibrium real exchange rate is the rate at which the quantity of net exports demanded equals the net capital outflow.

6. The nominal exchange rate is determined by the real exchange rate and the price levels in the two countries. Other things equal, a high rate of inflation leads to a depreciating currency.

KEY CONCEPTS

Net exports	Balanced trade	Real exchange rate
Trade balance	Small open economy	Purchasing-power parity
Net capital outflow	World interest rate	
Trade surplus and trade deficit	Nominal exchange rate	

QUESTIONS FOR REVIEW

1. What are the net capital outflow and the trade balance? Explain how they are related.

2. Define the nominal exchange rate and the real exchange rate.

3. If a small open economy cuts defense spending, what happens to saving, investment, the trade balance, the interest rate, and the exchange rate?

4. If a small open economy bans the import of Japanese DVD players, what happens to saving, investment, the trade balance, the interest rate, and the exchange rate?

5. If Japan has low inflation and Mexico has high inflation, what will happen to the exchange rate between the Japanese yen and the Mexican peso?

PROBLEMS AND APPLICATIONS

1. Use the model of the small open economy to predict what would happen to the trade balance, the real exchange rate, and the nominal exchange rate in response to each of the following events:

   a. A fall in consumer confidence about the future induces consumers to spend less and save more.

   b. The introduction of a stylish line of Toyotas makes some consumers prefer foreign cars over domestic cars.

   c. The introduction of automatic teller machines reduces the demand for money.

2. Consider an economy described by the following equations:

   $$Y = C + I + G + NX,$$
   $$Y = 5,000,$$
   $$G = 1,000,$$
   $$T = 1,000,$$
   $$C = 250 + 0.75(Y - T),$$
   $$I = 1,000 - 50r,$$
   $$NX = 500 - 500\varepsilon,$$
   $$r = r^* = 5.$$

   a. In this economy, solve for national saving, investment, the trade balance, and the equilibrium exchange rate.

   b. Suppose now that G rises to 1,250. Solve for national saving, investment, the trade balance, and the equilibrium exchange rate. Explain what you find.

   c. Now suppose that the world interest rate rises from 5 to 10 percent. (G is again 1,000.)

   Solve for national saving, investment, the trade balance, and the equilibrium exchange rate. Explain what you find.

3. The country of Leverett is a small open economy. Suddenly, a change in world fashions makes the exports of Leverett unpopular.

   a. What happens in Leverett to saving, investment, net exports, the interest rate, and the exchange rate?

   b. The citizens of Leverett like to travel abroad. How will this change in the exchange rate affect them?

   c. The fiscal policymakers of Leverett want to adjust taxes to maintain the exchange rate at its previous level. What should they do? If they do this, what are the overall effects on saving, investment, net exports, and the interest rate?

4. In 2005, Federal Reserve governor (and later chairman) Ben Bernanke said in a speech: "Over the past decade a combination of diverse forces has created a significant increase in the global supply of saving—a global saving glut—which helps to explain both the increase in the U.S. current account deficit [a broad measure of the trade deficit] and the relatively low level of long-term real interest rates in the world today." Is this statement consistent with the models you have learned? Explain.

5. What will happen to the trade balance and the real exchange rate of a small open economy when government purchases increase, such as during a war? Does your answer depend on whether this is a local war or a world war?

6. A case study in this chapter concludes that if poor nations offered better production efficiency and legal protections, the trade balance in rich nations such as the United States would move toward surplus. Let's consider why this might be the case.

   a. If the world's poor nations offer better production efficiency and legal protection, what would happen to the investment demand function in those countries?

   b. How would the change you describe in part (a) affect the demand for loanable funds in world financial markets?

   c. How would the change you describe in part (b) affect the world interest rate?

   d. How would the change you describe in part (c) affect the trade balance in rich nations?

7. The president is considering placing a tariff on the import of Japanese luxury cars. Discuss the economics and politics of such a policy. In particular, how would the policy affect the U.S. trade deficit? How would it affect the exchange rate? Who would be hurt by such a policy? Who would benefit?

8. Suppose China exports TVs and uses the yuan as its currency, whereas Russia exports vodka and uses the ruble. China has a stable money supply and slow, steady technological progress in TV production, while Russia has very rapid growth in the money supply and no technological progress in vodka production. Based on this information, what would you predict for the real exchange rate (measured as bottles of vodka per TV) and the nominal exchange rate (measured as rubles per yuan)? Explain your reasoning. (*Hint*: For the real exchange rate, think about the link between scarcity and relative prices.)

9. Suppose that some foreign countries begin to subsidize investment by instituting an investment tax credit.

   a. What happens to world investment demand as a function of the world interest rate?

   b. What happens to the world interest rate?

   c. What happens to investment in our small open economy?

   d. What happens to our trade balance?

   e. What happens to our real exchange rate?

10. "Traveling in Mexico is much cheaper now than it was ten years ago," says a friend. "Ten years ago, a dollar bought 10 pesos; this year, a dollar buys 15 pesos." Is your friend right or wrong? Given that total inflation over this period was 25 percent in the United States and 100 percent in Mexico, has it become more or less expensive to travel in Mexico? Write your answer using a concrete example—such as an American hot dog versus a Mexican taco—that will convince your friend.

11. You read in a newspaper that the nominal interest rate is 12 percent per year in Canada and 8 percent per year in the United States. Suppose that the real interest rates are equalized in the two countries and that purchasing-power parity holds.

    a. Using the Fisher equation (discussed in Chapter 4), what can you infer about expected inflation in Canada and in the United States?

    b. What can you infer about the expected change in the exchange rate between the Canadian dollar and the U.S. dollar?

    c. A friend proposes a get-rich-quick scheme: borrow from a U.S. bank at 8 percent, deposit the money in a Canadian bank at 12 percent, and make a 4 percent profit. What's wrong with this scheme?

The Large Open Economy

When analyzing policy for a country such as the United States, we need to combine the closed-economy logic of Chapter 3 and the small-open-economy logic of this chapter. This appendix presents a model of an economy between these two extremes, called the *large open economy*.

Net Capital Outflow

The key difference between small and large open economies is the behavior of the net capital outflow. In the model of the small open economy, capital flows freely into or out of the economy at a fixed world interest rate r^*. The model of the large open economy makes a different assumption about international capital flows. To understand this assumption, keep in mind that the net capital outflow is the amount that domestic investors lend abroad minus the amount that foreign investors lend here.

Imagine that you are a domestic investor—such as the portfolio manager of a university endowment—deciding where to invest your funds. You could invest domestically (for example, by making loans to U.S. companies), or you could invest abroad (by making loans to foreign companies). Many factors may affect your decision, but surely one of them is the interest rate you can earn. The higher the interest rate you can earn domestically, the less attractive you would find foreign investment.

Investors abroad face a similar decision. They have a choice between investing in their home country and lending to someone in the United States. The higher the interest rate in the United States, the more willing foreigners are to lend to U.S. companies and to buy U.S. assets.

Thus, because of the behavior of both domestic and foreign investors, the net flow of capital to other countries, which we'll denote as CF, is negatively related to the domestic real interest rate r. As the interest rate rises, less of our saving flows abroad, and more funds for capital accumulation flow in from other countries. We write this as

$$CF = CF(r).$$

This equation states that the net capital outflow is a function of the domestic interest rate. Figure 5-15 illustrates this relationship. Notice that CF can be either positive or negative, depending on whether the economy is a lender or borrower in world financial markets.

To see how this CF function relates to our previous models, consider Figure 5-16. This figure shows two special cases: a vertical CF function and a horizontal CF function.

The closed economy is the special case shown in panel (a) of Figure 5-16. In the closed economy, there is no international borrowing or lending, and the

FIGURE 5-15

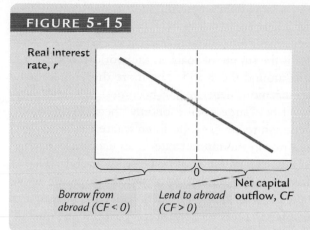

Real interest rate, r

0

Net capital outflow, CF

Borrow from abroad ($CF < 0$)

Lend to abroad ($CF > 0$)

How the Net Capital Outflow Depends on the Interest Rate A higher domestic interest rate discourages domestic investors from lending abroad and encourages foreign investors to lend here. Therefore, net capital outflow CF is negatively related to the interest rate.

interest rate adjusts to equilibrate domestic saving and investment. This means that $CF = 0$ at all interest rates. This situation would arise if investors here and abroad were unwilling to hold foreign assets, regardless of the return. It might also arise if the government prohibited its citizens from transacting in foreign financial markets, as some governments do.

The small open economy with perfect capital mobility is the special case shown in panel (b) of Figure 5-16. In this case, capital flows freely into and out of the country at the fixed world interest rate r^*. This situation would arise if investors here and abroad bought whatever asset yielded the highest return and if this economy was too small to affect the world interest rate. The economy's interest rate would be fixed at the interest rate prevailing in world financial markets.

FIGURE 5-16

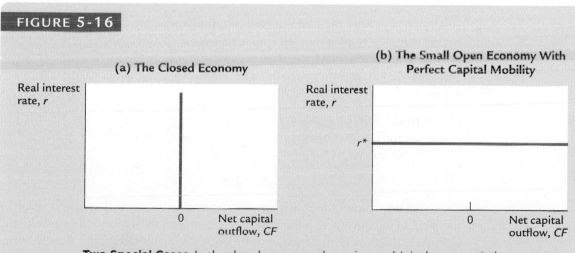

(a) The Closed Economy

Real interest rate, r

0 Net capital outflow, CF

(b) The Small Open Economy With Perfect Capital Mobility

Real interest rate, r

r^*

0 Net capital outflow, CF

Two Special Cases In the closed economy, shown in panel (a), the net capital outflow is zero for all interest rates. In the small open economy with perfect capital mobility, shown in panel (b), the net capital outflow is perfectly elastic at the world interest rate r^*.

Why isn't the interest rate of a large open economy such as the United States fixed by the world interest rate? There are two reasons. The first is that the United States is large enough to influence world financial markets. The more the United States lends abroad, the greater is the supply of loans in the world economy, and the lower interest rates become around the world. The more the United States borrows from abroad (that is, the more negative *CF* becomes), the higher are world interest rates. We use the label "large open economy" because this model applies to an economy large enough to affect world interest rates.

There is, however, a second reason the interest rate in an economy may not be fixed by the world interest rate: capital may not be perfectly mobile. That is, investors here and abroad may prefer to hold their wealth in domestic rather than foreign assets. Such a preference for domestic assets could arise because of imperfect information about foreign assets or because of government impediments to international borrowing and lending. In either case, funds for capital accumulation will not flow freely to equalize interest rates in all countries. Instead, the net capital outflow will depend on domestic interest rates relative to foreign interest rates. U.S. investors will lend abroad only if U.S. interest rates are comparatively low, and foreign investors will lend in the United States only if U.S. interest rates are comparatively high. The large-open-economy model, therefore, may apply even to a small economy if capital does not flow freely into and out of the economy.

Hence, either because the large open economy affects world interest rates, or because capital is imperfectly mobile, or perhaps for both reasons, the *CF* function slopes downward. Except for this new downward-sloping *CF* function, the model of the large open economy resembles the model of the small open economy. We put all the pieces together in the next section.

The Model

To understand how the large open economy works, we need to consider two key markets: the market for loanable funds (where the interest rate is determined) and the market for foreign exchange (where the exchange rate is determined). The interest rate and the exchange rate are two prices that guide the allocation of resources.

The Market for Loanable Funds An open economy's saving S is used in two ways: to finance domestic investment I and to finance the net capital outflow CF. We can write

$$S = I + CF.$$

Consider how these three variables are determined. National saving is fixed by the level of output, fiscal policy, and the consumption function. Investment and net capital outflow both depend on the domestic real interest rate. We can write

$$\overline{S} = I(r) + CF(r).$$

Figure 5-17 shows the market for loanable funds. The supply of loanable funds is national saving. The demand for loanable funds is the sum of the demand for

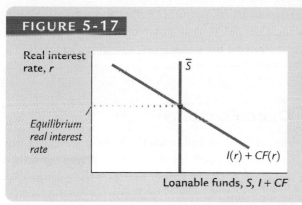

FIGURE 5-17

Real interest rate, r

$\bar{S}$

Equilibrium real interest rate

$I(r) + CF(r)$

Loanable funds, S, $I + CF$

The Market for Loanable Funds in the Large Open Economy At the equilibrium interest rate, the supply of loanable funds from saving S balances the demand for loanable funds from domestic investment I and capital investments abroad CF.

domestic investment and the demand for foreign investment (net capital outflow). The interest rate adjusts to equilibrate supply and demand.

The Market for Foreign Exchange Next, consider the relationship between the net capital outflow and the trade balance. The national income accounts identity tells us

$$NX = S - I.$$

Because NX is a function of the real exchange rate, and because $CF = S - I$, we can write

$$NX(\varepsilon) = CF.$$

Figure 5-18 shows the equilibrium in the market for foreign exchange. Once again, the real exchange rate is the price that equilibrates the trade balance and the net capital outflow.

The last variable we should consider is the nominal exchange rate. As before, the nominal exchange rate is the real exchange rate times the ratio of the price levels:

$$e = \varepsilon \times (P^*/P).$$

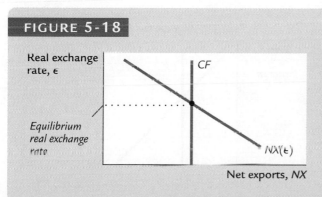

FIGURE 5-18

Real exchange rate, ϵ

CF

Equilibrium real exchange rate

$NX(\epsilon)$

Net exports, NX

The Market for Foreign-Currency Exchange in the Large Open Economy At the equilibrium exchange rate, the supply of dollars from the net capital outflow CF balances the demand for dollars from our net exports of goods and services NX.

The real exchange rate is determined as in Figure 5-18, and the price levels are determined by monetary policies here and abroad, as we discussed in Chapter 4. Forces that move the real exchange rate or the price levels also move the nominal exchange rate.

Policies in the Large Open Economy

We can now consider how economic policies influence the large open economy. Figure 5-19 shows the three diagrams we need for the analysis. Panel (a) shows the equilibrium in the market for loanable funds; panel (b) shows the relationship between the equilibrium interest rate and the net capital outflow; and panel (c) shows the equilibrium in the market for foreign exchange.

Fiscal Policy at Home Consider the effects of expansionary fiscal policy—an increase in government purchases or a decrease in taxes. Figure 5-20 shows what happens. The policy reduces national saving S, thereby reducing the supply of loanable funds and raising the equilibrium interest rate r. The higher interest rate reduces both domestic investment I and the net capital outflow CF. The fall in the net capital outflow reduces the supply of dollars to be exchanged into foreign currency. The exchange rate appreciates, and net exports fall.

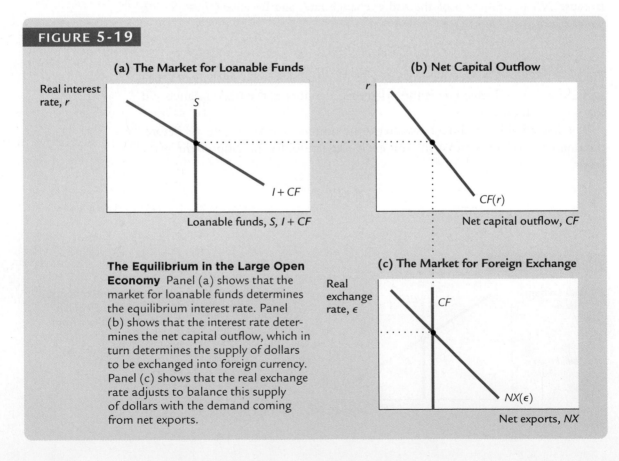

FIGURE 5-19

(a) The Market for Loanable Funds

Real interest rate, r

S

$I + CF$

Loanable funds, $S, I + CF$

(b) Net Capital Outflow

r

$CF(r)$

Net capital outflow, CF

(c) The Market for Foreign Exchange

Real exchange rate, ϵ

CF

$NX(\epsilon)$

Net exports, NX

The Equilibrium in the Large Open Economy Panel (a) shows that the market for loanable funds determines the equilibrium interest rate. Panel (b) shows that the interest rate determines the net capital outflow, which in turn determines the supply of dollars to be exchanged into foreign currency. Panel (c) shows that the real exchange rate adjusts to balance this supply of dollars with the demand coming from net exports.

FIGURE 5-20

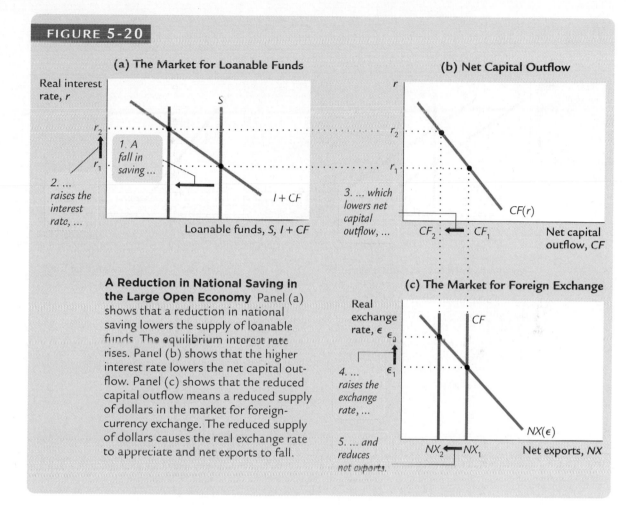

(a) The Market for Loanable Funds

Real interest rate, r

r_2

1. A fall in saving ...

r_1

2. ... raises the interest rate, ...

S

$I + CF$

Loanable funds, $S, I + CF$

(b) Net Capital Outflow

r

r_2

r_1

3. ... which lowers net capital outflow, ...

$CF(r)$

CF_2 CF_1

Net capital outflow, CF

A Reduction in National Saving in the Large Open Economy Panel (a) shows that a reduction in national saving lowers the supply of loanable funds. The equilibrium interest rate rises. Panel (b) shows that the higher interest rate lowers the net capital out-flow. Panel (c) shows that the reduced capital outflow means a reduced supply of dollars in the market for foreign-currency exchange. The reduced supply of dollars causes the real exchange rate to appreciate and net exports to fall.

(c) The Market for Foreign Exchange

Real exchange rate, ϵ

ϵ_2

CF

ϵ_1

4. ... raises the exchange rate, ...

5. ... and reduces net exports.

$NX(\epsilon)$

NX_2 NX_1

Net exports, NX

Note that the impact of fiscal policy in this model combines its impact in the closed economy and its impact in the small open economy. As in the closed economy, a fiscal expansion in a large open economy raises the interest rate and crowds out investment. As in the small open economy, a fiscal expansion causes a trade deficit and an appreciation in the exchange rate.

One way to see how the three types of economy are related is to consider the identity

$$S = I + NX.$$

In all three cases, expansionary fiscal policy reduces national saving S. In the closed economy, the fall in S coincides with an equal fall in I, and NX stays constant at zero. In the small open economy, the fall in S coincides with an equal fall in NX, and I remains constant at the level fixed by the world interest rate. The large open economy is the intermediate case: both I and NX fall, each by less than the fall in S.

Shifts in Investment Demand Suppose that the investment demand schedule shifts outward, perhaps because Congress passes an investment tax credit.

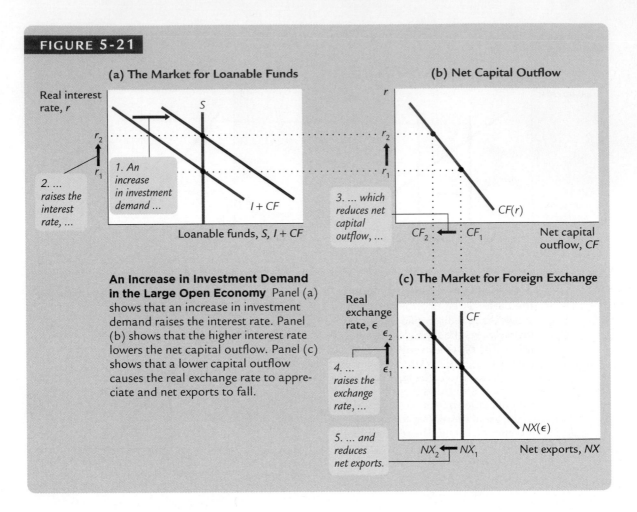

FIGURE 5-21

(a) The Market for Loanable Funds

Real interest rate, r

r_2

r_1

S

2. ... raises the interest rate, ...

1. An increase in investment demand ...

$I + CF$

Loanable funds, S, $I + CF$

(b) Net Capital Outflow

r

r_2

r_1

3. ... which reduces net capital outflow, ...

CF_2 CF_1

$CF(r)$

Net capital outflow, CF

An Increase in Investment Demand in the Large Open Economy Panel (a) shows that an increase in investment demand raises the interest rate. Panel (b) shows that the higher interest rate lowers the net capital outflow. Panel (c) shows that a lower capital outflow causes the real exchange rate to appreciate and net exports to fall.

(c) The Market for Foreign Exchange

Real exchange rate, ϵ

ϵ_2

ϵ_1

CF

4. ... raises the exchange rate, ...

5. ... and reduces net exports.

NX_2 NX_1

$NX(\epsilon)$

Net exports, NX

Figure 5-21 shows the effect. The demand for loanable funds rises, raising the equilibrium interest rate. The higher interest rate reduces the net capital outflow: Americans make fewer loans abroad, and foreigners make more loans to Americans. The fall in the net capital outflow reduces the supply of dollars in the market for foreign exchange. The exchange rate appreciates, and net exports fall.

Trade Policies Figure 5-22 shows the effect of a trade restriction, such as an import quota. The reduced demand for imports shifts the net exports schedule outward in panel (c). Because nothing has changed in the market for loanable funds, the interest rate remains the same, which in turn implies that the net capital outflow remains the same. The shift in the net-exports schedule causes the exchange rate to appreciate. The rise in the exchange rate makes U.S. goods expensive relative to foreign goods, which depresses exports and stimulates imports. In the end, the trade restriction does not affect the trade balance.

Shifts in Net Capital Outflow There are various reasons that the CF schedule might shift. One reason is fiscal policy abroad. For example, suppose that Germany pursues a fiscal policy that raises German saving. This policy reduces

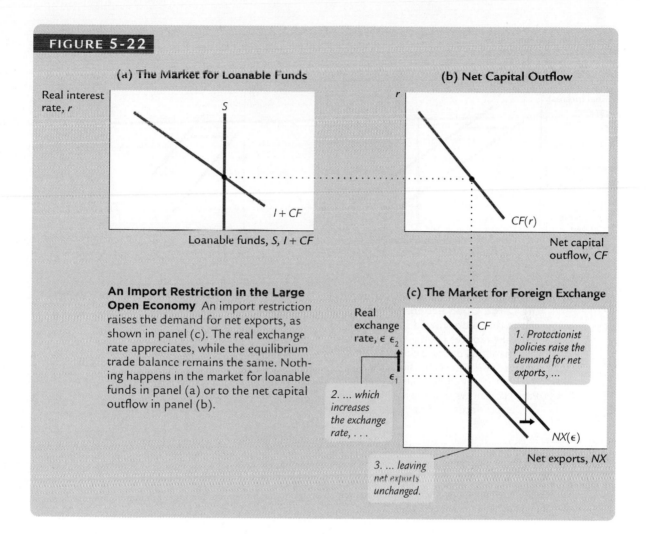

FIGURE 5-22

(a) The Market for Loanable Funds

Real interest rate, r

S

I + CF

Loanable funds, S, I + CF

(b) Net Capital Outflow

r

CF(r)

Net capital outflow, CF

An Import Restriction in the Large Open Economy An import restriction raises the demand for net exports, as shown in panel (c). The real exchange rate appreciates, while the equilibrium trade balance remains the same. Nothing happens in the market for loanable funds in panel (a) or to the net capital outflow in panel (b).

(c) The Market for Foreign Exchange

Real exchange rate, ε ϵ_2

ϵ_1

CF

1. Protectionist policies raise the demand for net exports, ...

2. ... which increases the exchange rate, . . .

NX(ε)

Net exports, NX

3. ... leaving net exports unchanged.

the German interest rate. The lower German interest rate discourages American investors from lending in Germany and encourages German investors to lend in the United States. For any given U.S. interest rate, the U.S. net capital outflow falls.

Another reason the CF schedule might shift is political instability abroad. Suppose that a war or revolution breaks out in another country. Investors around the world will try to withdraw their assets from that country and seek a "safe haven" in a stable country such as the United States. The result is a reduction in the U.S. net capital outflow.

Figure 5-23 shows the impact of a leftward shift in the CF schedule. The reduced demand for loanable funds lowers the equilibrium interest rate. The lower interest rate tends to raise net capital outflow, but because this only partly mitigates the shift in the CF schedule, CF still falls. The reduced level of net capital outflow reduces the supply of dollars in the market for foreign exchange. The exchange rate appreciates, and net exports fall.

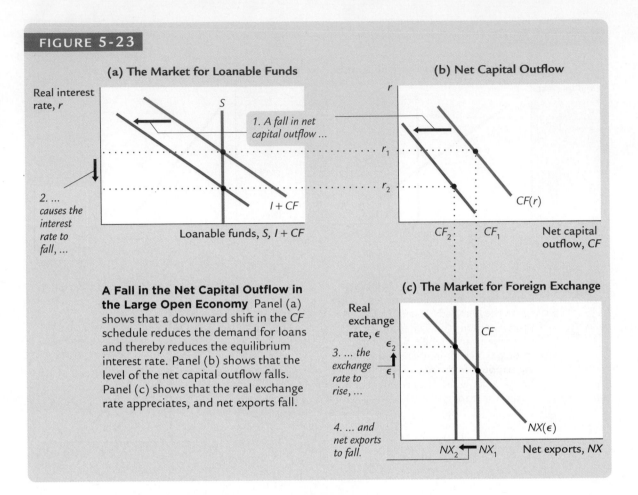

FIGURE 5-23

(a) The Market for Loanable Funds

Real interest rate, r

S

1. A fall in net capital outflow ...

r_1

r_2

I + CF

2. ... causes the interest rate to fall, ...

Loanable funds, S, I + CF

(b) Net Capital Outflow

r

r_1

r_2

CF(r)

CF_2 CF_1 Net capital outflow, CF

A Fall in the Net Capital Outflow in the Large Open Economy Panel (a) shows that a downward shift in the CF schedule reduces the demand for loans and thereby reduces the equilibrium interest rate. Panel (b) shows that the level of the net capital outflow falls. Panel (c) shows that the real exchange rate appreciates, and net exports fall.

(c) The Market for Foreign Exchange

Real exchange rate, ε

CF

ϵ_2

ϵ_1

3. ... the exchange rate to rise, ...

4. ... and net exports to fall.

NX_2 NX_1 NX(ε) Net exports, NX

Conclusion

How different are large and small open economies? Certainly, policies affect the interest rate in a large open economy, unlike in a small open economy. But, in other ways, the two models yield similar conclusions. In both large and small open economies, policies that raise saving or lower investment lead to trade surpluses. Similarly, policies that lower saving or raise investment lead to trade deficits. In both economies, protectionist trade policies cause the exchange rate to appreciate and do not influence the trade balance. Because the results are so similar, for most questions one can use the simpler model of the small open economy, even if the economy being examined is not really small.

MORE PROBLEMS AND APPLICATIONS

1. If a war broke out abroad, it would affect the U.S. economy in many ways. Use the model of the large open economy to examine each of the following effects of such a war. What happens in the United States to saving, investment, the trade balance, the interest rate, and the exchange rate? (To keep things simple, consider each of the following effects separately.)

   a. The U.S. government, fearing it may need to enter the war, increases its purchases of military equipment.

   b. Other countries raise their demand for high-tech weapons, a major export of the United States.

   c. The war makes U.S. firms uncertain about the future, and the firms delay some investment projects.

   d. The war makes U.S. consumers uncertain about the future, and the consumers save more in response.

   e. Americans become apprehensive about traveling abroad, so more of them spend their vacations in the United States.

   f. Foreign investors seek a safe haven for their portfolios in the United States.

2. On September 21, 1995, "House Speaker Newt Gingrich threatened to send the United States into default on its debt for the first time in the nation's history, to force the Clinton Administration to balance the budget on Republican terms" (*New York Times*, September 22, 1995, p. A1). That same day, the interest rate on 30-year U.S. government bonds rose from 6.46 to 6.55 percent, and the dollar fell in value from 102.7 to 99.0 yen. Use the model of the large open economy to explain this event.

Unemployment

A man willing to work, and unable to find work, is perhaps the saddest sight
that fortune's inequality exhibits under the sun.

—Thomas Carlyle

Unemployment is the macroeconomic problem that affects people most
directly and severely. For most people, the loss of a job means a reduced
living standard and psychological distress. It is no surprise that unemployment is a frequent topic of political debate and that politicians often claim
that their proposed policies would help create jobs.

Economists study unemployment to identify its causes and to help improve
the public policies that affect the unemployed. Some of these policies, such as
job-training programs, help people find employment. Others, such as unemployment insurance, alleviate some of the hardships that the unemployed face.
Still other policies affect the prevalence of unemployment inadvertently. Laws
mandating a high minimum wage, for instance, are widely thought to raise unemployment among the least skilled and experienced members of the labor
force.

Our discussions of the labor market so far have ignored unemployment. In
particular, the model of national income in Chapter 3 was built with the assumption that the economy is always at full employment. In reality, not everyone in
the labor force has a job all the time: in all free-market economies, at any moment, some people are unemployed.

Figure 6-1 shows the rate of unemployment—the percentage of the labor
force unemployed—in the United States since 1950. As the figure shows, the unemployment rate varies substantially, sometimes exceeding 10 percent, as it did
near the end of 2009. Although the rate of unemployment fluctuates from year
to year, it never gets even close to zero. The average is between 5 and 6 percent,
meaning that about 1 out of every 18 people wanting a job does not have one.

In this chapter we begin our study of unemployment by discussing why there
is always some unemployment and what determines its level. We do not study
what determines the year-to-year fluctuations in the rate of unemployment until
Part Four of this book, which examines short-run economic fluctuations. Here
we examine the determinants of the **natural rate of unemployment**—the average rate of unemployment around which the economy fluctuates. The natural

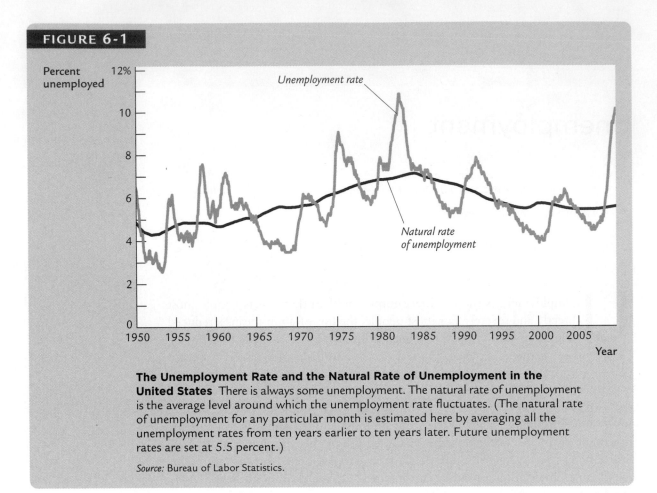

FIGURE 6-1

The Unemployment Rate and the Natural Rate of Unemployment in the United States There is always some unemployment. The natural rate of unemployment is the average level around which the unemployment rate fluctuates. (The natural rate of unemployment for any particular month is estimated here by averaging all the unemployment rates from ten years earlier to ten years later. Future unemployment rates are set at 5.5 percent.)

Source: Bureau of Labor Statistics.

rate is the rate of unemployment toward which the economy gravitates in the long run, given all the labor-market imperfections that impede workers from instantly finding jobs.

6-1 Job Loss, Job Finding, and the Natural Rate of Unemployment

Every day some workers lose or quit their jobs, and some unemployed workers are hired. This perpetual ebb and flow determines the fraction of the labor force that is unemployed. In this section we develop a model of labor-force dynamics that shows what determines the natural rate of unemployment.[1]

---

[1] Robert E. Hall, "A Theory of the Natural Rate of Unemployment and the Duration of Unemployment," *Journal of Monetary Economics* 5 (April 1979): 153–169.

CHAPTER 6 Unemployment | 167

We start with some notation. Let L denote the labor force, E the number of employed workers, and U the number of unemployed workers. Because every worker is either employed or unemployed, the labor force is the sum of the employed and the unemployed:

$$L = E + U.$$

In this notation, the rate of unemployment is U/L.

To see what factors determine the unemployment rate, we assume that the labor force L is fixed and focus on the transition of individuals in the labor force between employment E and unemployment U. This is illustrated in Figure 6-2. Let s denote the *rate of job separation*, the fraction of employed individuals who lose or leave their job each month. Let f denote the *rate of job finding*, the fraction of unemployed individuals who find a job each month. Together, the rate of job separation s and the rate of job finding f determine the rate of unemployment.

If the unemployment rate is neither rising nor falling—that is, if the labor market is in a *steady state*—then the number of people finding jobs fU must equal the number of people losing jobs sE. We can write the steady-state condition as

$$fU = sE.$$

We can use this equation to find the steady-state unemployment rate. From our definition of the labor force, we know that $E = L - U$; that is, the number of employed equals the labor force minus the number of unemployed. If we substitute $(L - U)$ for E in the steady-state condition, we find

$$fU = s(L - U).$$

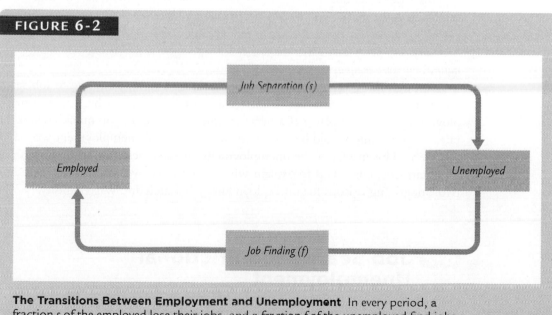

FIGURE 6-2

The Transitions Between Employment and Unemployment In every period, a fraction s of the employed lose their jobs, and a fraction f of the unemployed find jobs. The rates of job separation and job finding determine the rate of unemployment.

Next, we divide both sides of this equation by L to obtain

$$f\frac{U}{L} = s(1 - \frac{U}{L}).$$

Now we can solve for U/L to find

$$\frac{U}{L} = \frac{s}{s + f}.$$

This can also be written as

$$\frac{U}{L} = \frac{1}{1 + f/s}.$$

This equation shows that the steady-state rate of unemployment U/L depends on the rates of job separation s and job finding f. The higher the rate of job separation, the higher the unemployment rate. The higher the rate of job finding, the lower the unemployment rate.

Here's a numerical example. Suppose that 1 percent of the employed lose their jobs each month ($s = 0.01$). This means that on average jobs last 100 months, or about 8 years. Suppose further that 20 percent of the unemployed find a job each month ($f = 0.20$), so that spells of unemployment last 5 months on average. Then the steady-state rate of unemployment is

$$\frac{U}{L} = \frac{0.01}{0.01 + 0.20}$$

$$= 0.0476.$$

The rate of unemployment in this example is about 5 percent.

This simple model of the natural rate of unemployment has an important implication for public policy. *Any policy aimed at lowering the natural rate of unemployment must either reduce the rate of job separation or increase the rate of job finding. Similarly, any policy that affects the rate of job separation or job finding also changes the natural rate of unemployment.*

Although this model is useful in relating the unemployment rate to job separation and job finding, it fails to answer a central question: why is there unemployment in the first place? If a person could always find a job quickly, then the rate of job finding would be very high and the rate of unemployment would be near zero. This model of the unemployment rate assumes that job finding is not instantaneous, but it fails to explain why. In the next two sections, we examine two underlying reasons for unemployment: job search and wage rigidity.

6-2 Job Search and Frictional Unemployment

One reason for unemployment is that it takes time to match workers and jobs. The equilibrium model of the aggregate labor market discussed in Chapter 3 assumes that all workers and all jobs are identical and, therefore, that all workers are equally well suited for all jobs. If this were true and the labor market were in equilibrium, then a job loss would not cause unemployment: a laid-off worker would immediately find a new job at the market wage.

In fact, workers have different preferences and abilities, and jobs have different attributes. Furthermore, the flow of information about job candidates and job vacancies is imperfect, and the geographic mobility of workers is not instantaneous. For all these reasons, searching for an appropriate job takes time and effort, and this tends to reduce the rate of job finding. Indeed, because different jobs require different skills and pay different wages, unemployed workers may not accept the first job offer they receive. The unemployment caused by the time it takes workers to search for a job is called **frictional unemployment**.

Causes of Frictional Unemployment

Some frictional unemployment is inevitable in a changing economy. For many reasons, the types of goods that firms and households demand vary over time. As the demand for goods shifts, so does the demand for the labor that produces those goods. The invention of the personal computer, for example, reduced the demand for typewriters and the demand for labor by typewriter manufacturers. At the same time, it increased the demand for labor in the electronics industry. Similarly, because different regions produce different goods, the demand for labor may be rising in one part of the country and falling in another. An increase in the price of oil may cause the demand for labor to rise in oil-producing states such as Texas, but because expensive oil makes driving less attractive, it may decrease the demand for labor in auto-producing states such as Michigan. Economists call a change in the composition of demand among industries or regions a **sectoral shift**. Because sectoral shifts are always occurring, and because it takes time for workers to change sectors, there is always frictional unemployment.

Sectoral shifts are not the only cause of job separation and frictional unemployment. In addition, workers find themselves unexpectedly out of work when their firms fail, when their job performance is deemed unacceptable, or when their particular skills are no longer needed. Workers also may quit their jobs to change careers or to move to different parts of the country. Regardless of the cause of the job separation, it will take time and effort for the worker to find a new job. As long as the supply and demand for labor among firms are changing, frictional unemployment is unavoidable.

Public Policy and Frictional Unemployment

Many public policies seek to decrease the natural rate of unemployment by reducing frictional unemployment. Government employment agencies disseminate information about job vacancies to match jobs and workers more efficiently. Publicly funded retraining programs are designed to ease the transition of workers from declining to growing industries. If these programs succeed at increasing the rate of job finding, they decrease the natural rate of unemployment.

Other government programs inadvertently increase the amount of frictional unemployment. One of these is **unemployment insurance**. Under this program, unemployed workers can collect a fraction of their wages for a certain period after losing their jobs. Although the precise terms of the program differ from year to year and from state to state, a typical worker covered by unemployment insurance in the United States receives 50 percent of his or her former wages for 26 weeks. In many European countries, unemployment-insurance programs are significantly more generous.

By softening the economic hardship of unemployment, unemployment insurance increases the amount of frictional unemployment and raises the natural rate. The unemployed who receive unemployment-insurance benefits are less pressed to search for new employment and are more likely to turn down unattractive job offers. Both of these changes in behavior reduce the rate of job finding. In addition, because workers know that their incomes are partially protected by unemployment insurance, they are less likely to seek jobs with stable employment prospects and are less likely to bargain for guarantees of job security. These behavioral changes raise the rate of job separation.

That unemployment insurance raises the natural rate of unemployment does not necessarily imply that the policy is ill advised. The program has the benefit of reducing workers' uncertainty about their incomes. Moreover, inducing workers to reject unattractive job offers may lead to a better matching between workers and jobs. Evaluating the costs and benefits of different systems of unemployment insurance is a difficult task that continues to be a topic of much research.

Economists often propose reforms to the unemployment-insurance system that would reduce the amount of unemployment. One common proposal is to require a firm that lays off a worker to bear the full cost of that worker's unemployment benefits. Such a system is called *100 percent experience rated*, because the rate that each firm pays into the unemployment-insurance system fully reflects the unemployment experience of its own workers. Most current programs are *partially experience rated*. Under this system, when a firm lays off a worker, it is charged for only part of the worker's unemployment benefits; the remainder comes from the program's general revenue. Because a firm pays only a fraction of the cost of the unemployment it causes, it has an incentive to lay off workers when its demand for labor is temporarily low. By reducing that incentive, the proposed reform may reduce the prevalence of temporary layoffs.

CASE STUDY

Unemployment Insurance and the Rate of Job Finding

Many studies have examined the effect of unemployment insurance on job search. The most persuasive studies use data on the experiences of unemployed individuals rather than economy-wide rates of unemployment. Individual data often yield sharp results that are open to few alternative explanations.

One study followed the experience of individual workers as they used up their eligibility for unemployment-insurance benefits. It found that when unemployed workers become ineligible for benefits, they are more likely to find jobs. In particular, the probability of a person finding a job more than doubles when his or her benefits run out. One possible explanation is that an absence of benefits increases the search effort of unemployed workers. Another possibility is that workers without benefits are more likely to accept job offers that would otherwise be declined because of low wages or poor working conditions.[2]

Additional evidence on how economic incentives affect job search comes from an experiment that the state of Illinois ran in 1985. Randomly selected new claimants for unemployment insurance were each offered a $500 bonus if they found employment within 11 weeks. The subsequent experience of this group was compared to that of a control group not offered the incentive. The average duration of unemployment for the group offered the $500 bonus was 17.0 weeks, compared to 18.3 weeks for the control group. Thus, the bonus reduced the average spell of unemployment by 7 percent, suggesting that more effort was devoted to job search. This experiment shows clearly that the incentives provided by the unemployment-insurance system affect the rate of job finding.[3] ∎

6-3 Real-Wage Rigidity and Structural Unemployment

A second reason for unemployment is **wage rigidity**—the failure of wages to adjust to a level at which labor supply equals labor demand. In the equilibrium model of the labor market, as outlined in Chapter 3, the real wage adjusts to equilibrate labor supply and labor demand. Yet wages are not always flexible. Sometimes the real wage is stuck above the market-clearing level.

Figure 6-3 shows why wage rigidity leads to unemployment. When the real wage is above the level that equilibrates supply and demand, the quantity of labor supplied exceeds the quantity demanded. Firms must in some way ration the scarce jobs among workers. Real-wage rigidity reduces the rate of job finding and raises the level of unemployment.

The unemployment resulting from wage rigidity and job rationing is sometimes called **structural unemployment**. Workers are unemployed not because they are actively searching for the jobs that best suit their individual skills but because there is a fundamental mismatch between the number of people who want to work and the number of jobs that are available. At the going wage, the quantity of labor supplied exceeds the quantity of labor demanded, so many workers are simply waiting for jobs to open up.

---

[2] Lawrence F. Katz and Bruce D. Meyer, "Unemployment Insurance, Recall Expectations, and Unemployment Outcomes," *Quarterly Journal of Economics* 105 (November 1990): 973–1002.

[3] Stephen A. Woodbury and Robert G. Spiegelman, "Bonuses to Workers and Employers to Reduce Unemployment: Randomized Trials in Illinois," *American Economic Review* 77 (September 1987): 513–530.

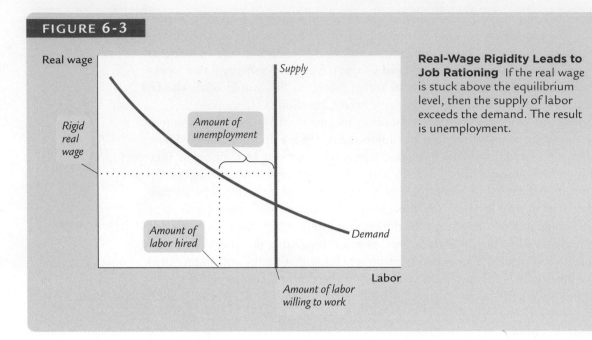

FIGURE 6-3

Real wage

Rigid
real
wage

Supply

*Amount of
unemployment*

*Amount of
labor hired*

Demand

*Amount of labor
willing to work*

Labor

**Real-Wage Rigidity Leads to
Job Rationing** If the real wage
is stuck above the equilibrium
level, then the supply of labor
exceeds the demand. The result
is unemployment.

To understand wage rigidity and structural unemployment, we must examine why the labor market does not clear. When the real wage exceeds the equilibrium level and the supply of workers exceeds the demand, we might expect firms to lower the wages they pay. Structural unemployment arises because firms fail to reduce wages despite an excess supply of labor. We now turn to three causes of this wage rigidity: minimum-wage laws, the monopoly power of unions, and efficiency wages.

Minimum-Wage Laws

The government causes wage rigidity when it prevents wages from falling to equilibrium levels. Minimum-wage laws set a legal minimum on the wages that firms pay their employees. Since the passage of the Fair Labor Standards Act of 1938, the U.S. federal government has enforced a minimum wage that has usually been between 30 and 50 percent of the average wage in manufacturing. For most workers, then, this minimum wage is not binding, because they earn well above the minimum. Yet for some workers, especially the unskilled and inexperienced, the minimum wage raises their wage above its equilibrium level and, therefore, reduces the quantity of their labor that firms demand.

Economists believe that the minimum wage has its greatest impact on teenage unemployment. The equilibrium wages of teenagers tend to be low for two reasons. First, because teenagers are among the least skilled and least experienced members of the labor force, they tend to have low marginal productivity. Second, teenagers often take some of their "compensation" in the form of on-the-job training rather than direct pay. An apprenticeship is a classic example of training offered in place of wages. For both these reasons, the wage at which the supply of teenage workers equals the demand is low. The minimum wage is therefore more often binding for teenagers than for others in the labor force.

Many economists have studied the impact of the minimum wage on teenage employment. These researchers compare the variation in the minimum wage over time with the variation in the number of teenagers with jobs. These studies find that a 10 percent increase in the minimum wage reduces teenage employment by 1 to 3 percent.[4]

The minimum wage is a perennial source of political debate. Advocates of a higher minimum wage view it as a means of raising the income of the working poor. Certainly, the minimum wage provides only a meager standard of living: in the United States, two adults working full time at minimum-wage jobs would just exceed the official poverty level for a family of four. Although minimum-wage advocates often admit that the policy causes unemployment for some workers, they argue that this cost is worth bearing to raise others out of poverty.

Opponents of a higher minimum wage claim that it is not the best way to help the working poor. They contend not only that the increased labor costs would raise unemployment but also that the minimum wage is poorly targeted. Many minimum-wage earners are teenagers from middle-class homes working for discretionary spending money, rather than heads of households working to support their families.

Many economists and policymakers believe that tax credits are a better way to increase the incomes of the working poor. The *earned income tax credit* is an amount that poor working families are allowed to subtract from the taxes they owe. For a family with very low income, the credit exceeds its taxes, and the family receives a payment from the government. Unlike the minimum wage, the earned income tax credit does not raise labor costs to firms and, therefore, does not reduce the quantity of labor that firms demand. It has the disadvantage, however, of reducing the government's tax revenue.

CASE STUDY

The Characteristics of Minimum-Wage Workers

Who earns the minimum wage? The question can be answered using the Current Population Survey—the labor-market survey used to calculate the unemployment rate and many other statistics. In 2009, the Bureau of Labor Statistics released a report describing the workers who earned at or below the minimum

[4] Charles Brown, "Minimum Wage Laws: Are They Overrated?" *Journal of Economic Perspectives* 2 (Summer 1988): 133–146. Brown presents the mainstream view of the effects of minimum wages, but it should be noted that the magnitude of employment effects is controversial. For research suggesting negligible employment effects, see David Card and Alan Krueger, *Myth and Measurement: The New Economics of the Minimum Wage* (Princeton, NJ: Princeton University Press, 1995); and Lawrence Katz and Alan Krueger, "The Effects of the Minimum Wage on the Fast-Food Industry," *Industrial and Labor Relations Review* 46 (October 1992): 6–21. For research suggesting the opposite conclusion, see David Neumark and William Wascher, "Employment Effects of Minimum and Subminimum Wages: Panel Data on State Minimum Wage Laws," *Industrial and Labor Relations Review 46* (October 1992): 55–81.

wage in 2008, when, in July, the minimum wage was raised from $5.85 to $6.55 per hour. Here is a summary:

■ About 75 million American workers are paid hourly, representing 58 percent of all wage and salary workers. Of these workers, 286,000 reported earning exactly the prevailing minimum wage, and another 1.9 million reported earning less. A reported wage below the minimum is possible because some workers are exempt from the statute (newspaper delivery workers, for example), because enforcement is imperfect, and because some workers round down when reporting their wages on surveys.

■ Minimum-wage workers are more likely to be women than men. About 2 percent of men and 4 percent of women reported wages at or below the prevailing federal minimum.

■ Minimum-wage workers tend to be young. About half of all hourly-paid workers earning the minimum wage or less were under age 25. Among employed teenagers paid by the hour, about 11 percent earned the minimum wage or less, compared with about 2 percent of workers age 25 and over.

■ Minimum-wage workers tend to be less educated. Among hourly-paid workers age 16 and over, about 3 percent of those who had only a high-school diploma earned the minimum wage or less, compared with about 2 percent of those who had obtained a college degree.

■ Minimum-wage workers are more likely to be working part time. Among part-time workers (those who usually work less than 35 hours per week), 7 percent were paid the minimum wage or less, compared with 2 percent of full-time workers.

■ The industry with the highest proportion of workers with reported hourly wages at or below the minimum wage was leisure and hospitality (about 14 percent). About three-fifths of all workers paid at or below the minimum wage were employed in this industry, primarily in food services and drinking places. For many of these workers, tips supplement the hourly wages received.

These facts by themselves do not tell us whether the minimum wage is a good or bad policy, or whether it is too high or too low. But when evaluating any public policy, it is useful to keep in mind those individuals who are affected by it.[5] ■

Unions and Collective Bargaining

A second cause of wage rigidity is the monopoly power of unions. Table 6-1 shows the importance of unions in several major countries. In the United States, only 18 percent of workers have their wages set through collective bargaining. In most European countries, unions play a much larger role.

---

[5] The figures reported here are from the Web site of the Bureau of Labor Statistics. The link is http://www.bls.gov/cps/minwage2008.htm

TABLE 6-1

Percent of Workers Covered by Collective Bargaining

United States	18 %
Japan	23
Canada	38
United Kingdom	47
Switzerland	53
New Zealand	67
Spain	68
Netherlands	71
Norway	75
Portugal	79
Australia	80
Sweden	83
Belgium	90
Germany	90
France	92
Finland	95
Austria	98

Source: OECD Employment Outlook 2004, as reported in Alberto Alesina, Edward Glaeser, and Bruce Sacerdote, "Work and Leisure in the U.S. and Europe: Why So Different?" *NBER Macroeconomics Annual 2005*.

The wages of unionized workers are determined not by the equilibrium of supply and demand but by bargaining between union leaders and firm management. Often, the final agreement raises the wage above the equilibrium level and allows the firm to decide how many workers to employ. The result is a reduction in the number of workers hired, a lower rate of job finding, and an increase in structural unemployment.

Unions can also influence the wages paid by firms whose workforces are not unionized because the threat of unionization can keep wages above the equilibrium level. Most firms dislike unions. Unions not only raise wages but also increase the bargaining power of labor on many other issues, such as hours of employment and working conditions. A firm may choose to pay its workers high wages to keep them happy and discourage them from forming a union.

The unemployment caused by unions and by the threat of unionization is an instance of conflict between different groups of workers—**insiders** and **outsiders**. Those workers already employed by a firm, the insiders, typically try to keep their firm's wages high. The unemployed, the outsiders, bear part of the cost of higher wages because at a lower wage they might be hired. These two groups inevitably have conflicting interests. The effect of any bargaining process on wages and employment depends crucially on the relative influence of each group.

The conflict between insiders and outsiders is resolved differently in different countries. In some countries, such as the United States, wage bargaining takes place at the level of the firm or plant. In other countries, such as Sweden, wage bargaining takes place at the national level—with the government often playing a key role. Despite a highly unionized labor force, Sweden has not experienced extraordinarily high unemployment throughout its history. One possible explanation is that the centralization of wage bargaining and the role of the government in the bargaining process give more influence to the outsiders, which keeps wages closer to the equilibrium level.

Efficiency Wages

Efficiency-wage theories propose a third cause of wage rigidity in addition to minimum-wage laws and unionization. These theories hold that high wages make workers more productive. The influence of wages on worker efficiency may explain the failure of firms to cut wages despite an excess supply of labor. Even though a wage reduction would lower a firm's wage bill, it would also—if these theories are correct—lower worker productivity and the firm's profits.

Economists have proposed various theories to explain how wages affect worker productivity. One efficiency-wage theory, which is applied mostly to poorer countries, holds that wages influence nutrition. Better-paid workers can afford a more nutritious diet, and healthier workers are more productive. A firm may decide to pay a wage above the equilibrium level to maintain a healthy workforce. Obviously, this consideration is not important for employers in wealthier countries, such as the United States and most of Europe, because the equilibrium wage is well above the level necessary to maintain good health.

A second efficiency-wage theory, which is more relevant for developed countries, holds that high wages reduce labor turnover. Workers quit jobs for many reasons—to accept better positions at other firms, to change careers, or to move to other parts of the country. The more a firm pays its workers, the greater is their incentive to stay with the firm. By paying a high wage, a firm reduces the frequency at which its workers quit, thereby decreasing the time and money spent hiring and training new workers.

A third efficiency-wage theory holds that the average quality of a firm's workforce depends on the wage it pays its employees. If a firm reduces its wage, the best employees may take jobs elsewhere, leaving the firm with inferior employees who have fewer alternative opportunities. Economists recognize this unfavorable sorting as an example of *adverse selection*—the tendency of people with more information (in this case, the workers, who know their own outside opportunities) to self-select in a way that disadvantages people with less information (the firm). By paying a wage above the equilibrium level, the firm may reduce adverse selection, improve the average quality of its workforce, and thereby increase productivity.

A fourth efficiency-wage theory holds that a high wage improves worker effort. This theory posits that firms cannot perfectly monitor their employees' work effort and that employees must themselves decide how hard to work. Workers can choose to work hard, or they can choose to shirk and risk getting caught and fired. Economists recognize this possibility as an example of *moral hazard*—the tendency of people to behave inappropriately when their behavior is imperfectly monitored. The firm can reduce the problem of moral hazard by paying a high wage. The higher the wage, the greater the cost to the worker of getting fired. By paying a higher wage, a firm induces more of its employees not to shirk and thus increases their productivity.

Although these four efficiency-wage theories differ in detail, they share a common theme: because a firm operates more efficiently if it pays its workers a high wage, the firm may find it profitable to keep wages above the level that balances supply and demand. The result of this higher-than-equilibrium wage is a lower rate of job finding and greater unemployment.[6]

CASE STUDY

Henry Ford's $5 Workday

In 1914 the Ford Motor Company started paying its workers $5 per day. The prevailing wage at the time was between $2 and $3 per day, so Ford's wage was well above the equilibrium level. Not surprisingly, long lines of job seekers waited outside the Ford plant gates hoping for a chance to earn this high wage.

What was Ford's motive? Henry Ford later wrote, "We wanted to pay these wages so that the business would be on a lasting foundation. We were building for the future. A low wage business is always insecure. . . . The payment of five dollars a day for an eight hour day was one of the finest cost cutting moves we ever made."

From the standpoint of traditional economic theory, Ford's explanation seems peculiar. He was suggesting that *high* wages imply *low* costs. But perhaps Ford had discovered efficiency-wage theory. Perhaps he was using the high wage to increase worker productivity.

Evidence suggests that paying such a high wage did benefit the company. According to an engineering report written at the time, "The Ford high wage does away with all the inertia and living force resistance. . . . The workingmen are absolutely docile, and it is safe to say that since the last day of 1913, every single day has seen major reductions in Ford shops' labor costs." Absenteeism fell by 75 percent, suggesting a large increase in worker effort. Alan Nevins, a historian who studied the early Ford Motor Company, wrote, "Ford and his associates freely declared on many occasions that the high wage policy had turned out to be good business. By this they meant that it had improved the discipline of the workers, given them a more loyal interest in the institution, and raised their personal efficiency."[7] ∎

---

[6] For more extended discussions of efficiency wages, see Janet Yellen, "Efficiency Wage Models of Unemployment," *American Economic Review Papers and Proceedings* (May 1984): 200–205; and Lawrence Katz, "Efficiency Wages: A Partial Evaluation," *NBER Macroeconomics Annual* (1986): 235–276.

[7] Jeremy I. Bulow and Lawrence H. Summers, "A Theory of Dual Labor Markets With Application to Industrial Policy, Discrimination, and Keynesian Unemployment," *Journal of Labor Economics* 4 (July 1986): 376–414; and Daniel M. G. Raff and Lawrence H. Summers, "Did Henry Ford Pay Efficiency Wages?" *Journal of Labor Economics* 5 (October 1987, Part 2): S57–S86.

6-4 Labor-Market Experience: The United States

So far we have developed the theory behind the natural rate of unemployment. We began by showing that the economy's steady-state unemployment rate depends on the rates of job separation and job finding. Then we discussed two reasons why job finding is not instantaneous: the process of job search (which leads to frictional unemployment) and wage rigidity (which leads to structural unemployment). Wage rigidity, in turn, arises from minimum-wage laws, unionization, and efficiency wages.

With these theories as background, we now examine some additional facts about unemployment, focusing at first on the case of American labor markets. These facts will help us to evaluate our theories and assess public policies aimed at reducing unemployment.

The Duration of Unemployment

When a person becomes unemployed, is the spell of unemployment likely to be short or long? The answer to this question is important because it indicates the reasons for the unemployment and what policy response is appropriate. On the one hand, if most unemployment is short-term, one might argue that it is frictional and perhaps unavoidable. Unemployed workers may need some time to search for the job that is best suited to their skills and tastes. On the other hand, long-term unemployment cannot easily be attributed to the time it takes to match jobs and workers: we would not expect this matching process to take many months. Long-term unemployment is more likely to be structural unemployment, representing a mismatch between the number of jobs available and the number of people who want to work. Thus, data on the duration of unemployment can affect our view about the reasons for unemployment.

The answer to our question turns out to be subtle. The data show that many spells of unemployment are short but that most weeks of unemployment are attributable to the long-term unemployed. For example, during the period from 1990 to 2006, 38 percent of unemployed people were unemployed for less than 4 weeks, while only 31 percent were unemployed for more than 15 weeks. However, 71 percent of the total amount of time spent unemployed was experienced by those who were unemployed for more than 15 weeks, while only 7 percent of the time spent unemployed was experienced by people who were unemployed for less than 4 weeks.

To see how these facts can all be true, consider an extreme but simple example. Suppose that 10 people are unemployed for part of a given year. Of these 10 people, 8 are unemployed for 1 month and 2 are unemployed for 12 months, totaling 32 months of unemployment. In this example, most spells of unemployment are short: 8 of the 10 unemployment spells, or 80 percent, end in 1 month. Yet most months of unemployment are attributable to the long-term unemployed: 24 of the 32 months of unemployment, or 75 percent, are experienced by the 2 workers who are unemployed for 12 months. Depending on whether we look at spells of unemployment or months of unemployment, most unemployment can appear to be either short-term or long-term.

This evidence on the duration of unemployment has an important implication for public policy. If the goal is to lower substantially the natural rate of unemployment, policies must aim at the long-term unemployed, because these individuals account for a large amount of unemployment. Yet policies must be carefully targeted, because the long-term unemployed constitute a small minority of those who become unemployed. Most people who become unemployed find work within a short time.

Variation in the Unemployment Rate Across Demographic Groups

The rate of unemployment varies substantially across different groups within the population. Table 6-2 presents the U.S. unemployment rates for different demographic groups in 2009, when the overall unemployment rate was 9.3 percent.

This table shows that younger workers have much higher unemployment rates than older ones. To explain this difference, recall our model of the natural rate of unemployment. The model isolates two possible causes for a high rate of unemployment: a low rate of job finding and a high rate of job separation. When economists study data on the transition of individuals between employment and unemployment, they find that those groups with high unemployment tend to have high rates of job separation. They find less variation across groups in the rate of job finding. For example, an employed white male is four times more likely to become unemployed if he is a teenager than if he is middle-aged; once unemployed, his rate of job finding is not closely related to his age.

These findings help explain the higher unemployment rates for younger workers. Younger workers have only recently entered the labor market, and they are often uncertain about their career plans. It may be best for them to try different types of jobs before making a long-term commitment to a specific occupation. If they do so, we should expect a higher rate of job separation and a higher rate of frictional unemployment for this group.

Another fact that stands out from Table 6-2 is that unemployment rates are much higher for blacks than for whites. This phenomenon is not well understood. Data on transitions between employment and unemployment show that the higher unemployment rates for blacks, especially for black teenagers, arise

TABLE 6-2				
Unemployment Rate by Demographic Group: 2009				
Age	White Men	White Women	Black Men	Black Women
16–19	25.2	18.4	46.0	33.4
20 and over	8.8	6.8	16.3	11.5

Source: Bureau of Labor Statistics.

because of both higher rates of job separation and lower rates of job finding. Possible reasons for the lower rates of job finding include less access to informal job-finding networks and discrimination by employers.

Trends in Unemployment

Over the past half century, the natural rate of unemployment in the United States has not been stable. If you look back at Figure 6-1, you will see that unemployment averaged below 5 percent in the 1950s and 1960s, rose to over 6 percent in the 1970s and 1980s, and then drifted back to around 5 percent in the 1990s and the early 2000s. Economists do not have a conclusive explanation for these changes, but they have proposed several hypotheses.

Demographics One explanation stresses the changing composition of the U.S. labor force. After World War II, birthrates rose dramatically: the number of births rose from 2.9 million in 1945 to a peak of 4.3 million in 1957, before falling back to 3.1 million in 1973. This rise in births in the 1950s led to a rise in the number of young workers in the 1970s. Younger workers have higher unemployment rates, however, so when the baby-boom generation entered the labor force, they increased the average level of unemployment. Then, as the baby-boom workers aged, the average age of the labor force increased, lowering the average unemployment rate in the 1990s.

This demographic change, however, cannot fully explain the trends in unemployment because similar trends are apparent for fixed demographic groups. For example, for men between the ages of 25 and 54, the average unemployment rate rose from 3.0 percent in the 1960s to 6.1 percent in the 1980s. Thus, although demographic changes may be part of the story of rising unemployment over this period, there must be other explanations of the long-term trend as well.

Sectoral Shifts A second explanation is based on changes in the prevalence of sectoral shifts. The greater the amount of reallocation among regions and industries, the greater the rate of job separation and the higher the level of frictional unemployment. One source of sectoral shifts during the 1970s and early 1980s was the great volatility in oil prices caused by OPEC, the international oil cartel. These large changes in oil prices may have required reallocating labor between more-energy-intensive and less-energy-intensive sectors. If so, oil-price volatility may have increased unemployment during this period. The increase in oil-price volatility in the early and mid-2000s, however, did not coincide with a similar rise in the natural rate of unemployment, but this may be because the economy is now significantly less oil-intensive (as measured by oil consumption per unit of GDP) than it was three decades ago.

Productivity A third explanation for the trends in unemployment emphasizes the link between unemployment and productivity. As Chapter 8 discusses more fully, the 1970s experienced a slowdown in productivity growth, and the 1990s experienced a pickup in productivity growth that continued into the first decade of the new century. These productivity changes roughly coincide with changes in unemployment. Perhaps slowing productivity during the 1970s raised the natural rate of unemployment, and accelerating productivity during the 1990s lowered it.

Why such an effect would occur, however, is not obvious. In standard theories of the labor market, higher productivity means greater labor demand and thus higher real wages, but unemployment is unchanged. This prediction is consistent with the long-term data, which show consistent upward trends in productivity and real wages but no trend in unemployment. Yet suppose that workers are slow to catch on to news about productivity. When productivity changes, workers may only gradually alter the real wages they ask from their employers, making real wages sluggish in response to labor demand. An acceleration in productivity growth, such as that experienced during the 1990s, will increase labor demand and, with a sluggish real wage, reduce the amount of unemployment.

In the end, the trends in the unemployment rate remain a mystery. The proposed explanations are plausible, but none seems conclusive on its own. Perhaps there is no single answer. The upward drift in the unemployment rate in the 1970s and 1980s and the downward drift in the 1990s and early 2000s may be the result of several unrelated developments.[8]

Transitions Into and Out of the Labor Force

So far we have ignored an important aspect of labor market dynamics: the movement of individuals into and out of the labor force. Our model of the natural rate of unemployment assumes that the labor force is fixed. In this case, the sole reason for unemployment is job separation, and the sole reason for leaving unemployment is job finding.

In fact, movements into and out of the labor force are important. About one-third of the unemployed have only recently entered the labor force. Some of these entrants are young workers still looking for their first jobs; others have worked before but had temporarily left the labor force. In addition, not all unemployment ends with job finding: almost half of all spells of unemployment end in the unemployed person's withdrawal from the labor market.

Individuals entering and leaving the labor force make unemployment statistics more difficult to interpret. On the one hand, some individuals calling themselves unemployed may not be seriously looking for jobs and perhaps should best be viewed as out of the labor force. Their "unemployment" may not represent a social problem. On the other hand, some individuals may want jobs but, after unsuccessful searches, have given up looking. These **discouraged workers** are counted as being out of the labor force and do not show up in unemployment statistics. Even though their joblessness is unmeasured, it may nonetheless be a social problem.

---

[8] On the role of demographics, see Robert Shimer, "Why Is the U.S. Unemployment Rate So Much Lower?" *NBER Macroeconomics Annual* 13 (1998): 11–61. On the role of sectoral shifts, see David M. Lilien, "Sectoral Shifts and Cyclical Unemployment," *Journal of Political Economy* 90 (August 1982): 777–793. On the role of productivity, see Laurence Ball and Robert Moffitt, "Productivity Growth and the Phillips Curve," in Alan B. Krueger and Robert Solow, eds., *The Roaring Nineties: Can Full Employment Be Sustained?* (New York: The Russell Sage Foundation and the Century Foundation Press, 2001).

TABLE 6-3

Alternative Measures of Labor Underutilization

Variable	Description	Rate
U-1	Persons unemployed 15 weeks or longer, as a percent of the civilian labor force (includes only very long-term unemployed)	5.9%
U-2	Job losers and persons who have completed temporary jobs, as a percent of the civilian labor force (excludes job leavers)	6.3
U-3	Total unemployed, as a percent of the civilian labor force (official unemployment rate)	10.0
U-4	Total unemployed, plus discouraged workers, as a percent of the civilian labor force plus discouraged workers	10.5
U-5	Total unemployed plus all marginally attached workers, as a percent of the civilian labor force plus all marginally attached workers	11.4
U-6	Total unemployed, plus all marginally attached workers, plus total employed part time for economic reasons, as a percent of the civilian labor force plus all marginally attached workers	17.3

Note: Marginally attached workers are persons who currently are neither working nor looking for work but indicate that they want and are available for a job and have looked for work sometime in the recent past. *Discouraged workers*, a subset of the marginally attached, have given a job-market-related reason for not currently looking for a job. *Persons employed part time for economic reasons* are those who want and are available for full-time work but have had to settle for a part-time schedule.
Source: Bureau of Labor Statistics. Data are for December 2009.

Because of these and many other issues that complicate the interpretation of the unemployment data, the Bureau of Labor Statistics calculates several measures of labor underutilization. Table 6–3 gives the definitions and their values as of December 2009, when the economy was in the midst of a deep recession and the standard unemployment rate was 10 percent. The measures range from 5.9 to 17.3 percent, depending on the characteristics one uses to classify a worker as not fully employed.

6-5 Labor-Market Experience: Europe

Although our discussion has focused largely on the United States, many fascinating and sometimes puzzling phenomena become apparent when economists compare the experiences of Americans in the labor market with those of Europeans.

The Rise in European Unemployment

Figure 6–4 shows the rate of unemployment from 1960 to 2008 in the four largest European countries—France, Germany, Italy, and the United Kingdom. As you can see, the rate of unemployment in these countries has risen substantially.

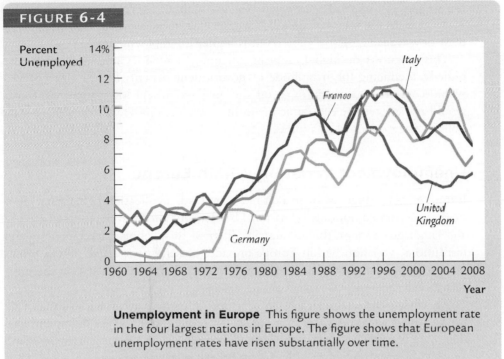

FIGURE 6-4

Unemployment in Europe This figure shows the unemployment rate in the four largest nations in Europe. The figure shows that European unemployment rates have risen substantially over time.

Source: Bureau of Labor Statistics.

For France and Germany, the change is particularly pronounced: unemployment averaged below 2 percent in the 1960s and about 9 percent in recent years.

What is the cause of rising European unemployment? No one knows for sure, but there is a leading theory. Many economists believe that the problem can be traced to the interaction between a long-standing policy and a more recent shock. The long-standing policy is generous benefits for unemployed workers. The recent shock is a technologically driven fall in the demand for unskilled workers relative to skilled workers.

There is no question that most European countries have generous programs for those without jobs. These programs go by various names: social insurance, the welfare state, or simply "the dole." Many countries allow the unemployed to collect benefits for years rather than for only a short period of time as in the United States. In some sense, those living on the dole are really out of the labor force: given the employment opportunities available, taking a job is less attractive than remaining without work. Yet these people are often counted as unemployed in government statistics.

There is also no question that the demand for unskilled workers has fallen relative to the demand for skilled workers. This change in demand is probably due to changes in technology: computers, for example, increase the demand for workers who can use them and reduce the demand for those who cannot. In the United States, this change in demand has been reflected in wages rather than unemployment: over the past three decades, the wages of unskilled workers have fallen substantially relative to the wages of skilled workers. In Europe, however, the welfare state provides unskilled workers with an alternative to working for low wages. As the wages of unskilled workers fall, more workers view the dole as their best available option. The result is higher unemployment.

This diagnosis of high European unemployment does not suggest an easy remedy. Reducing the magnitude of government benefits for the unemployed would encourage workers to get off the dole and accept low-wage jobs. But it would also exacerbate economic inequality—the very problem that welfare-state policies were designed to address.[9]

Unemployment Variation Within Europe

Europe is not a single labor market but is, instead, a collection of national labor markets, separated not only by national borders but also by differences in culture and language. Because these countries differ in their labor-market policies and institutions, variation within Europe provides a useful perspective on the causes of unemployment. Many empirical studies have, therefore, focused on these international differences.

The first noteworthy fact is that the unemployment rate varies substantially from country to country. For example, in November 2009, when the unemployment rate was 10.0 percent in the United States, it was 4.1 percent in Switzerland and 19.3 percent in Spain. Although in recent years average unemployment has been higher in Europe than in the United States, about a third of Europeans have been living in nations with unemployment rates lower than the U.S. rate.

A second notable fact is that much of the variation in unemployment rates is attributable to the long-term unemployed. The unemployment rate can be separated into two pieces—the percentage of the labor force that has been unemployed for less than a year and the percentage of the labor force that has been unemployed for more than a year. The long-term unemployment rate exhibits more variability from country to country than does the short-term unemployment rate.

National unemployment rates are correlated with a variety of labor-market policies. Unemployment rates are higher in nations with more generous unemployment insurance, as measured by the replacement rate—the percentage of previous wages that is replaced when a worker loses a job. In addition, nations tend to have higher unemployment, especially higher long-term unemployment, if benefits can be collected for longer periods of time.

Although government spending on unemployment insurance seems to raise unemployment, spending on "active" labor-market policies appears to decrease it. These active labor-market policies include job training, assistance with job search, and subsidized employment. Spain, for instance, has historically had a high rate of unemployment, a fact that can be explained by the combination of generous payments to the unemployed with minimal assistance at helping them find new jobs.

---

[9] For more discussion of these issues, see Paul Krugman, "Past and Prospective Causes of High Unemployment," in *Reducing Unemployment: Current Issues and Policy Options*, Federal Reserve Bank of Kansas City, August 1994.

The role of unions also varies from country to country, as we saw in Table 6-1. This fact also helps explain differences in labor-market outcomes. National unemployment rates are positively correlated with the percentage of the labor force whose wages are set by collective bargaining with unions. The adverse impact of unions on unemployment is smaller, however, in nations where there is substantial coordination among employers in bargaining with unions, perhaps because coordination may moderate the upward pressure on wages.

A word of warning: Correlation does not imply causation, so empirical results such as these should be interpreted with caution. But they do suggest that a nation's unemployment rate, rather than being immutable, is instead a function of the choices a nation makes.[10]

CASE STUDY

The Secrets to Happiness

Why are some people more satisfied with their lives than others? This is a deep and difficult question, most often left to philosophers, psychologists, and self-help gurus. But part of the answer is macroeconomic. Recent research has shown that people are happier when they are living in a country with low inflation and low unemployment.

From 1975 to 1991, a survey called the Euro-Barometer Survey Series asked 264,710 people living in 12 European countries about their happiness and overall satisfaction with life. One question asked, "On the whole, are you very satisfied, fairly satisfied, not very satisfied, or not at all satisfied with the life you lead?" To see what determines happiness, the answers to this question were correlated with individual and macroeconomic variables. Other things equal, people are more satisfied with their lives if they are rich, educated, married, in school, self-employed, retired, female, or either young or old (as opposed to middle-aged). They are less satisfied if they are unemployed, divorced, or living with adolescent children. (Some of these correlations may reflect the effects, rather than causes, of happiness; for example, a happy person may find it easier than an unhappy one to keep a job and a spouse.)

Beyond these individual characteristics, the economy's overall rates of unemployment and inflation also play a significant role in explaining reported happiness. An increase in the unemployment rate of 4 percentage points is large enough to move 11 percent of the population down from one life-satisfaction category to another. The overall unemployment rate reduces satisfaction even after controlling for an individual's employment status. That is, the employed in a high-unemployment nation are less happy than their counterparts in a low-unemployment nation, perhaps because they are more worried about job loss or perhaps out of sympathy with their fellow citizens.

High inflation is also associated with lower life satisfaction, although the effect is not as large. A 1.7 percentage-point increase in inflation reduces

[10] Stephen Nickell, "Unemployment and Labor Market Rigidities: Europe Versus North America," *Journal of Economic Perspectives* 11 (September 1997): 55–74.

happiness by about as much as a 1-percentage-point increase in unemployment. The commonly cited "misery index," which is the sum of the inflation and unemployment rates, apparently gives too much weight to inflation relative to unemployment.[11] ∎

The Rise of European Leisure

Higher unemployment rates in Europe are part of the larger phenomenon that Europeans typically work fewer hours than do their American counterparts. Figure 6-5 presents some data on how many hours a typical person works in the United States, France, and Germany. In the 1960s, the number of hours worked was about the same in each of these countries. But since then, the number of hours has stayed level in the United States, while it has declined substantially in Europe. Today, the typical American works many more hours than the typical resident of these two western European countries.

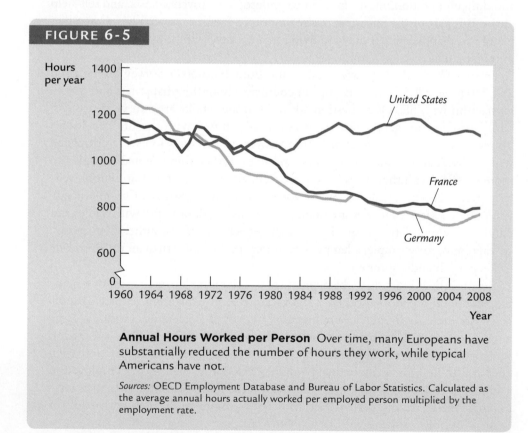

FIGURE 6-5

Annual Hours Worked per Person Over time, many Europeans have substantially reduced the number of hours they work, while typical Americans have not.

Sources: OECD Employment Database and Bureau of Labor Statistics. Calculated as the average annual hours actually worked per employed person multiplied by the employment rate.

---

[11] Rafael Di Tella, Robert J. MacCulloch, and Andrew J. Oswald, "Preferences Over Inflation and Unemployment: Evidence From Surveys of Happiness," *American Economic Review* 91 (March 2001): 335–341.

The difference in hours worked reflects two facts. First, the average employed person in the United States works more hours per year than the average employed person in Europe. Europeans typically enjoy shorter workweeks and more frequent holidays. Second, more potential workers are employed in the United States. That is, the employment-to-population ratio is higher in the United States than it is in Europe. Higher unemployment is one reason for the lower employment-to-population ratio in Europe. Another reason is earlier retirement in Europe and thus lower labor-force participation among older workers.

What is the underlying cause of these differences in work patterns? Economists have proposed several hypotheses.

Edward Prescott, the 2004 winner of the Nobel Prize in economics, has concluded that "virtually all of the large differences between U.S. labor supply and those of Germany and France are due to differences in tax systems." This hypothesis is consistent with two facts: (1) Europeans face higher tax rates than Americans, and (2) European tax rates have risen significantly over the past several decades. Some economists take these facts as powerful evidence for the impact of taxes on work effort. Yet others are skeptical, arguing that to explain the difference in hours worked by tax rates alone requires an implausibly large elasticity of labor supply.

A related hypothesis is that the difference in observed work effort may be attributable to the underground economy. When tax rates are high, people have a greater incentive to work "off the books" to evade taxes. For obvious reasons, data on the underground economy are hard to come by. But economists who study the subject believe the underground economy is larger in Europe than it is in the United States. This fact suggests that the difference in actual hours worked, including work in the underground economy, may be smaller than the difference in measured hours worked.

Another hypothesis stresses the role of unions. As we have seen, collective bargaining is more important in European than in U.S. labor markets. Unions often push for shorter workweeks in contract negotiations, and they lobby the government for a variety of labor-market regulations, such as official holidays. Economists Alberto Alesina, Edward Glaeser, and Bruce Sacerdote conclude that "mandated holidays can explain 80 percent of the difference in weeks worked between the U.S. and Europe and 30 percent of the difference in total labor supply between the two regions." They suggest that Prescott may overstate the role of taxes because, looking across countries, tax rates and unionization rates are positively correlated; as a result, the effects of high taxes and the effects of widespread unionization are hard to disentangle.

A final hypothesis emphasizes the possibility of different preferences. As technological advance and economic growth have made all advanced countries richer, people around the world must decide whether to take the greater prosperity in the form of increased consumption of goods and services or increased leisure. According to economist Olivier Blanchard, "the main difference [between the continents] is that Europe has used some of the increase in productivity to increase leisure rather than income, while the U.S. has done the opposite." Blanchard believes that Europeans simply have more taste for leisure than do Americans. (As a French economist working in the United States, he may have special insight into this phenomenon.) If Blanchard is right, this raises the even harder question of why tastes vary by geography.

Economists continue to debate the merits of these alternative hypotheses. In the end, there may be some truth to all of them.[12]

6-6 Conclusion

Unemployment represents wasted resources. Unemployed workers have the potential to contribute to national income but are not doing so. Those searching for jobs to suit their skills are happy when the search is over, and those waiting for jobs in firms that pay above-equilibrium wages are happy when positions open up.

Unfortunately, neither frictional unemployment nor structural unemployment can be easily reduced. The government cannot make job search instantaneous, and it cannot easily bring wages closer to equilibrium levels. Zero unemployment is not a plausible goal for free-market economies.

Yet public policy is not powerless in the fight to reduce unemployment. Job-training programs, the unemployment-insurance system, the minimum wage, and the laws governing collective bargaining are often topics of political debate. The policies we choose are likely to have important effects on the economy's natural rate of unemployment.

Summary

1. The natural rate of unemployment is the steady-state rate of unemployment. It depends on the rate of job separation and the rate of job finding.

2. Because it takes time for workers to search for the job that best suits their individual skills and tastes, some frictional unemployment is inevitable. Various government policies, such as unemployment insurance, alter the amount of frictional unemployment.

3. Structural unemployment results when the real wage remains above the level that equilibrates labor supply and labor demand. Minimum-wage legislation is one cause of wage rigidity. Unions and the threat of unionization are another. Finally, efficiency-wage theories suggest that, for various reasons, firms may find it profitable to keep wages high despite an excess supply of labor.

4. Whether we conclude that most unemployment is short-term or long-term depends on how we look at the data. Most spells of unemployment are short. Yet most weeks of unemployment are attributable to the small number of long-term unemployed.

---

[12] To read more about this topic, see Edward C. Prescott "Why Do Americans Work So Much More Than Europeans?" *Federal Reserve Bank of Minneapolis Quarterly Review*, 28, number 1 (July 2004): 2–13; Alberto Alesina, Edward Glaeser, and Bruce Sacerdote, "Work and Leisure in the U.S. and Europe: Why So Different?" *NBER Macroeconomics Annual* (2005); and Olivier Blanchard, "The Economic Future of Europe" *Journal of Economic Perspectives*, 18, number 4 (Fall 2004): 3–26.

5. The unemployment rates among demographic groups differ substantially. In particular, the unemployment rates for younger workers are much higher than for older workers. This results from a difference in the rate of job separation rather than from a difference in the rate of job finding.

6. The natural rate of unemployment in the United States has exhibited long-term trends. In particular, it rose from the 1950s to the 1970s and then started drifting downward again in the 1990s and early 2000s. Various explanations of the trends have been proposed, including the changing demographic composition of the labor force, changes in the prevalence of sectoral shifts, and changes in the rate of productivity growth.

7. Individuals who have recently entered the labor force, including both new entrants and reentrants, make up about one-third of the unemployed. Transitions into and out of the labor force make unemployment statistics more difficult to interpret.

8. American and European labor markets exhibit some significant differences. In recent years, Europe has experienced significantly more unemployment than the United States. In addition, because of higher unemployment, shorter workweeks, more holidays, and earlier retirement, Europeans work fewer hours than Americans.

KEY CONCEPTS

Natural rate of unemployment	Unemployment insurance	Insiders versus outsiders
Frictional unemployment	Wage rigidity	Efficiency wages
Sectoral shift	Structural unemployment	Discouraged workers

QUESTIONS FOR REVIEW

1. What determines the natural rate of unemployment?

2. Describe the difference between frictional unemployment and structural unemployment.

3. Give three explanations why the real wage may remain above the level that equilibrates labor supply and labor demand.

4. Is most unemployment long-term or short-term? Explain your answer.

5. How do economists explain the high natural rate of unemployment in the 1970s and 1980s? How do they explain the fall in the natural rate in the 1990s and early 2000s?

PROBLEMS AND APPLICATIONS

1. Answer the following questions about your own experience in the labor force:

   a. When you or one of your friends is looking for a part time job, how many weeks does it typically take? After you find a job, how many weeks does it typically last?

   b. From your estimates, calculate (in a rate per week) your rate of job finding f and your rate of job separation s. (*Hint:* If f is the rate of job finding, then the average spell of unemployment is $1/f$.)

c. What is the natural rate of unemployment for the population you represent?

2. In this chapter we saw that the steady-state rate of unemployment is $U/L = s/(s + f)$. Suppose that the unemployment rate does not begin at this level. Show that unemployment will evolve over time and reach this steady state. (*Hint:* Express the change in the number of unemployed as a function of s, f, and U. Then show that if unemployment is above the natural rate, unemployment falls, and if unemployment is below the natural rate, unemployment rises.)

3. The residents of a certain dormitory have collected the following data: People who live in the dorm can be classified as either involved in a relationship or uninvolved. Among involved people, 10 percent experience a breakup of their relationship every month. Among uninvolved people, 5 percent will enter into a relationship every month. What is the steady-state fraction of residents who are uninvolved?

4. Suppose that Congress passes legislation making it more difficult for firms to fire workers. (An example is a law requiring severance pay for fired workers.) If this legislation reduces the rate of job separation without affecting the rate of job finding, how would the natural rate of unemployment change? Do you think it is plausible that the legislation would not affect the rate of job finding? Why or why not?

5. Consider an economy with the following Cobb–Douglas production function:

$$Y = K^{1/3}L^{2/3}.$$

The economy has 1,000 units of capital and a labor force of 1,000 workers.

a. Derive the equation describing labor demand in this economy as a function of the real wage and the capital stock. (*Hint:* Review Chapter 3.)

b. If the real wage can adjust to equilibrate labor supply and labor demand, what is the real wage? In this equilibrium, what are employment, output, and the total amount earned by workers?

c. Now suppose that Congress, concerned about the welfare of the working class, passes a law requiring firms to pay workers a real wage of 1 unit of output. How does this wage compare to the equilibrium wage?

d. Congress cannot dictate how many workers firms hire at the mandated wage. Given this fact, what are the effects of this law? Specifically, what happens to employment, output, and the total amount earned by workers?

e. Will Congress succeed in its goal of helping the working class? Explain.

f. Do you think that this analysis provides a good way of thinking about a minimum-wage law? Why or why not?

6. Suppose that a country experiences a reduction in productivity—that is, an adverse shock to the production function.

a. What happens to the labor demand curve?

b. How would this change in productivity affect the labor market—that is, employment, unemployment, and real wages—if the labor market was always in equilibrium?

c. How would this change in productivity affect the labor market if unions prevented real wages from falling?

7. When workers' wages rise, their decision about how much time to spend working is affected in two conflicting ways—as you may have learned in courses in microeconomics. The *income effect* is the impulse to work less, because greater incomes mean workers can afford to consume more leisure. The *substitution effect* is the impulse to work more, because the reward for working an additional hour has risen (equivalently, the opportunity cost of leisure has gone up). Apply these concepts to Blanchard's hypothesis about American and European tastes for leisure. On which side of the Atlantic do income effects appear larger than substitution effects? On which side do the two effects approximately cancel? Do you think it is a reasonable hypothesis that tastes for leisure vary by geography? Why or why not?

8. In any city at any time, some of the stock of usable office space is vacant. This vacant office space is unemployed capital. How would you explain this phenomenon? Is it a social problem?

PART III

Growth Theory: The Economy in the Very Long Run

CHAPTER 7

Economic Growth I: Capital Accumulation and Population Growth

The question of growth is nothing new but a new disguise for an age-old issue, one which has always intrigued and preoccupied economics: the present versus the future.

— *James Tobin*

If you have ever spoken with your grandparents about what their lives were like when they were young, most likely you learned an important lesson about economic growth: material standards of living have improved substantially over time for most families in most countries. This advance comes from rising incomes, which have allowed people to consume greater quantities of goods and services.

To measure economic growth, economists use data on gross domestic product, which measures the total income of everyone in the economy. The real GDP of the United States today is more than five times its 1950 level, and real GDP per person is more than three times its 1950 level. In any given year, we also observe large differences in the standard of living among countries. Table 7-1 shows the 2008 income per person in the world's 14 most populous countries. The United States tops the list with an income of $46,970 per person. Bangladesh has an income per person of only $1,440—about 3 percent of the figure for the United States.

Our goal in this part of the book is to understand what causes these differences in income over time and across countries. In Chapter 3 we identified the factors of production—capital and labor—and the production technology as the sources of the economy's output and, thus, of its total income. Differences in income, then, must come from differences in capital, labor, and technology.

Our primary task in this chapter and the next is to develop a theory of economic growth called the **Solow growth model**. Our analysis in Chapter 3 enabled us to describe how the economy produces and uses its output at one point in time. The analysis was static—a snapshot of the economy. To explain why our national income grows, and why some economies grow faster than others, we must broaden our analysis so that it describes changes in the economy over time.

TABLE 7-1

International Differences in the Standard of Living

Country	Income per Person (2008)	Country	Income per Person (2008)
United States	$46,970	Philippines	3,900
Germany	35,940	Indonesia	3,830
Japan	35,220	India	2,960
Russia	15,630	Pakistan	2,700
Mexico	14,270	Vietnam	2,700
Brazil	10,070	Nigeria	1,940
China	6,020	Bangladesh	1,440

Source: The World Bank.

By developing such a model, we make our analysis dynamic—more like a movie than a photograph. The Solow growth model shows how saving, population growth, and technological progress affect the level of an economy's output and its growth over time. In this chapter we analyze the roles of saving and population growth. In the next chapter we introduce technological progress.[1]

7-1 The Accumulation of Capital

The Solow growth model is designed to show how growth in the capital stock, growth in the labor force, and advances in technology interact in an economy as well as how they affect a nation's total output of goods and services. We will build this model in a series of steps. Our first step is to examine how the supply and demand for goods determine the accumulation of capital. In this first step, we assume that the labor force and technology are fixed. We then relax these assumptions by introducing changes in the labor force later in this chapter and by introducing changes in technology in the next.

The Supply and Demand for Goods

The supply and demand for goods played a central role in our static model of the closed economy in Chapter 3. The same is true for the Solow model. By considering the supply and demand for goods, we can see what determines how much

[1] The Solow growth model is named after economist Robert Solow and was developed in the 1950s and 1960s. In 1987 Solow won the Nobel Prize in economics for his work on economic growth. The model was introduced in Robert M. Solow, "A Contribution to the Theory of Economic Growth," *Quarterly Journal of Economics* (February 1956): 65–94.

output is produced at any given time and how this output is allocated among alternative uses.

The Supply of Goods and the Production Function The supply of goods in the Solow model is based on the production function, which states that output depends on the capital stock and the labor force:

$$Y = F(K, L).$$

The Solow growth model assumes that the production function has constant returns to scale. This assumption is often considered realistic, and, as we will see shortly, it helps simplify the analysis. Recall that a production function has constant returns to scale if

$$zY = F(zK, zL)$$

for any positive number z. That is, if both capital and labor are multiplied by z, the amount of output is also multiplied by z.

Production functions with constant returns to scale allow us to analyze all quantities in the economy relative to the size of the labor force. To see that this is true, set $z = 1/L$ in the preceding equation to obtain

$$Y/L = F(K/L, 1).$$

This equation shows that the amount of output per worker Y/L is a function of the amount of capital per worker K/L. (The number 1 is constant and thus can be ignored.) The assumption of constant returns to scale implies that the size of the economy—as measured by the number of workers—does not affect the relationship between output per worker and capital per worker.

Because the size of the economy does not matter, it will prove convenient to denote all quantities in per-worker terms. We designate quantities per worker with lowercase letters, so $y = Y/L$ is output per worker, and $k = K/L$ is capital per worker. We can then write the production function as

$$y = f(k),$$

where we define $f(k) = F(k, 1)$. Figure 7-1 illustrates this production function.

The slope of this production function shows how much extra output a worker produces when given an extra unit of capital. This amount is the marginal product of capital MPK. Mathematically, we write

$$MPK = f(k + 1) - f(k).$$

Note that in Figure 7-1, as the amount of capital increases, the production function becomes flatter, indicating that the production function exhibits diminishing marginal product of capital. When k is low, the average worker has only a little capital to work with, so an extra unit of capital is very useful and produces a lot of additional output. When k is high, the average worker has a lot of capital already, so an extra unit increases production only slightly.

FIGURE 7-1

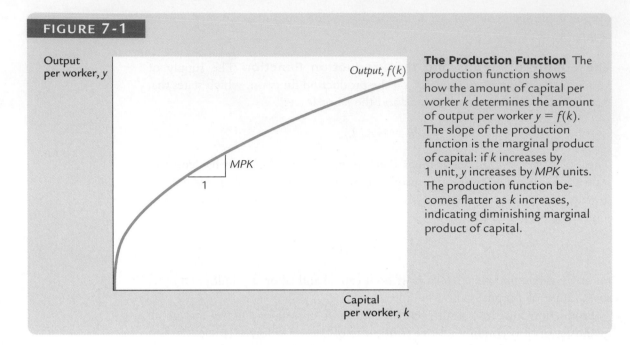

Output per worker, y

Output, $f(k)$

MPK

1

Capital per worker, k

The Production Function The production function shows how the amount of capital per worker k determines the amount of output per worker $y = f(k)$. The slope of the production function is the marginal product of capital: if k increases by 1 unit, y increases by MPK units. The production function becomes flatter as k increases, indicating diminishing marginal product of capital.

The Demand for Goods and the Consumption Function The demand for goods in the Solow model comes from consumption and investment. In other words, output per worker y is divided between consumption per worker c and investment per worker i:

$$y = c + i.$$

This equation is the per-worker version of the national income accounts identity for an economy. Notice that it omits government purchases (which for present purposes we can ignore) and net exports (because we are assuming a closed economy).

The Solow model assumes that each year people save a fraction s of their income and consume a fraction $(1 - s)$. We can express this idea with the following consumption function:

$$c = (1 - s)y,$$

where s, the saving rate, is a number between zero and one. Keep in mind that various government policies can potentially influence a nation's saving rate, so one of our goals is to find what saving rate is desirable. For now, however, we just take the saving rate s as given.

To see what this consumption function implies for investment, substitute $(1 - s)y$ for c in the national income accounts identity:

$$y = (1 - s)y + i.$$

Rearrange the terms to obtain

$$i = sy.$$

This equation shows that investment equals saving, as we first saw in Chapter 3. Thus, the rate of saving s is also the fraction of output devoted to investment.

We have now introduced the two main ingredients of the Solow model—the production function and the consumption function—which describe the economy at any moment in time. For any given capital stock k, the production function $y = f(k)$ determines how much output the economy produces, and the saving rate s determines the allocation of that output between consumption and investment.

Growth in the Capital Stock and the Steady State

At any moment, the capital stock is a key determinant of the economy's output, but the capital stock can change over time, and those changes can lead to economic growth. In particular, two forces influence the capital stock: investment and depreciation. *Investment* is expenditure on new plant and equipment, and it causes the capital stock to rise. *Depreciation* is the wearing out of old capital, and it causes the capital stock to fall. Let's consider each of these forces in turn.

As we have already noted, investment per worker i equals sy. By substituting the production function for y, we can express investment per worker as a function of the capital stock per worker:

$$i = sf(k).$$

This equation relates the existing stock of capital k to the accumulation of new capital i. Figure 7-2 shows this relationship. This figure illustrates how, for any value of k, the amount of output is determined by the production function $f(k)$, and the allocation of that output between consumption and investment is determined by the saving rate s.

FIGURE 7-2

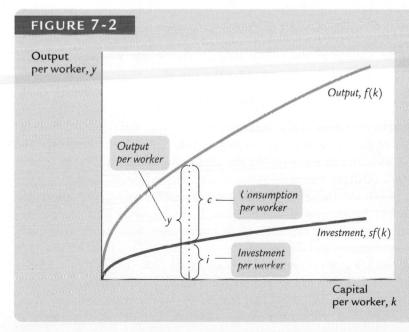

Output per worker, y

Output, $f(k)$

Output per worker

Consumption per worker

Investment, $sf(k)$

Investment per worker

Capital per worker, k

Output, Consumption, and Investment The saving rate s determines the allocation of output between consumption and investment. For any level of capital k, output is $f(k)$, investment is $sf(k)$, and consumption is $f(k) - sf(k)$.

FIGURE 7-3

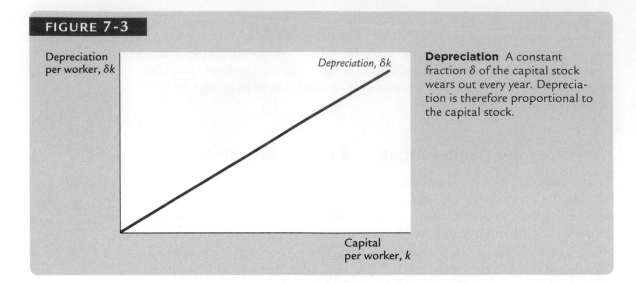

Depreciation per worker, δk

Depreciation, δk

Capital per worker, k

Depreciation A constant fraction δ of the capital stock wears out every year. Depreciation is therefore proportional to the capital stock.

To incorporate depreciation into the model, we assume that a certain fraction δ of the capital stock wears out each year. Here δ (the lowercase Greek letter delta) is called the *depreciation rate*. For example, if capital lasts an average of 25 years, then the depreciation rate is 4 percent per year ($\delta = 0.04$). The amount of capital that depreciates each year is δk. Figure 7–3 shows how the amount of depreciation depends on the capital stock.

We can express the impact of investment and depreciation on the capital stock with this equation:

$$\text{Change in Capital Stock} = \text{Investment} - \text{Depreciation}$$

$$\Delta k \qquad = \qquad i \qquad - \qquad \delta k,$$

where Δk is the change in the capital stock between one year and the next. Because investment i equals $sf(k)$, we can write this as

$$\Delta k = sf(k) - \delta k.$$

Figure 7-4 graphs the terms of this equation—investment and depreciation—for different levels of the capital stock k. The higher the capital stock, the greater the amounts of output and investment. Yet the higher the capital stock, the greater also the amount of depreciation.

As Figure 7-4 shows, there is a single capital stock k^* at which the amount of investment equals the amount of depreciation. If the economy finds itself at this level of the capital stock, the capital stock will not change because the two forces acting on it—investment and depreciation—just balance. That is, at k^*, $\Delta k = 0$, so the capital stock k and output $f(k)$ are steady over time (rather than growing or shrinking). We therefore call k^* the **steady-state** level of capital.

The steady state is significant for two reasons. As we have just seen, an economy at the steady state will stay there. In addition, and just as important, an

FIGURE 7-4

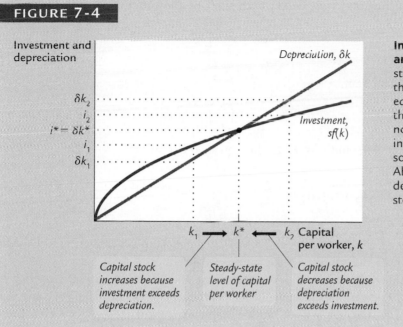

Investment, Depreciation, and the Steady State The steady-state level of capital k^* is the level at which investment equals depreciation, indicating that the amount of capital will not change over time. Below k^* investment exceeds depreciation, so the capital stock grows. Above k^* investment is less than depreciation, so the capital stock shrinks.

economy *not* at the steady state will go there. That is, regardless of the level of capital with which the economy begins, it ends up with the steady-state level of capital. In this sense, *the steady state represents the long-run equilibrium of the economy.*

To see why an economy always ends up at the steady state, suppose that the economy starts with less than the steady-state level of capital, such as level k_1 in Figure 7-4. In this case, the level of investment exceeds the amount of depreciation. Over time, the capital stock will rise and will continue to rise—along with output $f(k)$—until it approaches the steady state k^*.

Similarly, suppose that the economy starts with more than the steady-state level of capital, such as level k_2. In this case, investment is less than depreciation: capital is wearing out faster than it is being replaced. The capital stock will fall, again approaching the steady-state level. Once the capital stock reaches the steady state, investment equals depreciation, and there is no pressure for the capital stock to either increase or decrease.

Approaching the Steady State: A Numerical Example

Let's use a numerical example to see how the Solow model works and how the economy approaches the steady state. For this example, we assume that the production function is

$$Y = K^{1/2}L^{1/2}.$$

From Chapter 3, you will recognize this as the Cobb–Douglas production function with the capital-share parameter α equal to 1/2. To derive the per-worker production function $f(k)$, divide both sides of the production function by the labor force L:

$$\frac{Y}{L} = \frac{K^{1/2}L^{1/2}}{L}.$$

Rearrange to obtain

$$\frac{Y}{L} = \left(\frac{K}{L}\right)^{1/2}.$$

Because $y = Y/L$ and $k = K/L$, this equation becomes

$$y = k^{1/2},$$

which can also be written as

$$y = \sqrt{k}.$$

This form of the production function states that output per worker equals the square root of the amount of capital per worker.

To complete the example, let's assume that 30 percent of output is saved ($s = 0.3$), that 10 percent of the capital stock depreciates every year ($\delta = 0.1$), and that the economy starts off with 4 units of capital per worker ($k = 4$). Given these numbers, we can now examine what happens to this economy over time.

We begin by looking at the production and allocation of output in the first year, when the economy has 4 units of capital per worker. Here are the steps we follow.

- According to the production function $y = \sqrt{k}$, the 4 units of capital per worker (k) produce 2 units of output per worker (y).
- Because 30 percent of output is saved and invested and 70 percent is consumed, $i = 0.6$ and $c = 1.4$.
- Because 10 percent of the capital stock depreciates, $\delta k = 0.4$.
- With investment of 0.6 and depreciation of 0.4, the change in the capital stock is $\Delta k = 0.2$.

Thus, the economy begins its second year with 4.2 units of capital per worker.

We can do the same calculations for each subsequent year. Table 7-2 shows how the economy progresses. Every year, because investment exceeds depreciation, new capital is added and output grows. Over many years, the economy approaches a steady state with 9 units of capital per worker. In this steady state, investment of 0.9 exactly offsets depreciation of 0.9, so the capital stock and output are no longer growing.

Following the progress of the economy for many years is one way to find the steady-state capital stock, but there is another way that requires fewer calculations. Recall that

$$\Delta k = sf(k) - \delta k.$$

This equation shows how k evolves over time. Because the steady state is (by definition) the value of k at which $\Delta k = 0$, we know that

$$0 = sf(k^*) - \delta k^*,$$

TABLE 7-2						
Approaching the Steady State: A Numerical Example						
Assumptions: $y = \sqrt{k}$; $s = 0.3$; $\delta = 0.1$; initial $k = 4.0$						
Year	k	y	c	i	δk	Δk
1	4.000	2.000	1.400	0.600	0.400	0.200
2	4.200	2.049	1.435	0.615	0.420	0.195
3	4.395	2.096	1.467	0.629	0.440	0.189
4	4.584	2.141	1.499	0.642	0.458	0.184
5	4.768	2.184	1.529	0.655	0.477	0.178
.						
.						
.						
10	5.602	2.367	1.657	0.710	0.560	0.150
.						
.						
.						
25	7.321	2.706	1.894	0.812	0.732	0.080
.						
.						
.						
100	8.962	2.994	2.096	0.898	0.896	0.002
.						
.						
.						
∞	9.000	3.000	2.100	0.900	0.900	0.000

or, equivalently,

$$\frac{k^*}{f(k^*)} = \frac{s}{\delta}.$$

This equation provides a way of finding the steady-state level of capital per worker, k^*. Substituting in the numbers and production function from our example, we obtain

$$\frac{k^*}{\sqrt{k^*}} = \frac{0.3}{0.1}.$$

Now square both sides of this equation to find

$$k^* = 9.$$

The steady-state capital stock is 9 units per worker. This result confirms the calculation of the steady state in Table 7-2.

CASE STUDY

The Miracle of Japanese and German Growth

Japan and Germany are two success stories of economic growth. Although today they are economic superpowers, in 1945 the economies of both countries were in shambles. World War II had destroyed much of their capital stocks. In the decades after the war, however, these two countries experienced some of the most rapid growth rates on record. Between 1948 and 1972, output per person grew at 8.2 percent per year in Japan and 5.7 percent per year in Germany, compared to only 2.2 percent per year in the United States.

Are the postwar experiences of Japan and Germany so surprising from the standpoint of the Solow growth model? Consider an economy in steady state. Now suppose that a war destroys some of the capital stock. (That is, suppose the capital stock drops from k^* to k_1 in Figure 7-4.) Not surprisingly, the level of output falls immediately. But if the saving rate—the fraction of output devoted to saving and investment—is unchanged, the economy will then experience a period of high growth. Output grows because, at the lower capital stock, more capital is added by investment than is removed by depreciation. This high growth continues until the economy approaches its former steady state. Hence, although destroying part of the capital stock immediately reduces output, it is followed by higher-than-normal growth. The "miracle" of rapid growth in Japan and Germany, as it is often described in the business press, is what the Solow model predicts for countries in which war has greatly reduced the capital stock. ∎

How Saving Affects Growth

The explanation of Japanese and German growth after World War II is not quite as simple as suggested in the preceding case study. Another relevant fact is that both Japan and Germany save and invest a higher fraction of their output than does the United States. To understand more fully the international differences in economic performance, we must consider the effects of different saving rates.

Consider what happens to an economy when its saving rate increases. Figure 7-5 shows such a change. The economy is assumed to begin in a steady state with saving rate s_1 and capital stock k_1^*. When the saving rate increases from s_1 to s_2, the $sf(k)$ curve shifts upward. At the initial saving rate s_1 and the initial capital stock k_1^*, the amount of investment just offsets the amount of depreciation. Immediately after the saving rate rises, investment is higher, but the capital stock and depreciation are unchanged. Therefore, investment exceeds depreciation. The capital stock will gradually rise until the economy reaches the new steady state k_2^*, which has a higher capital stock and a higher level of output than the old steady state.

The Solow model shows that the saving rate is a key determinant of the steady-state capital stock. *If the saving rate is high, the economy will have a large capital*

FIGURE 7-5

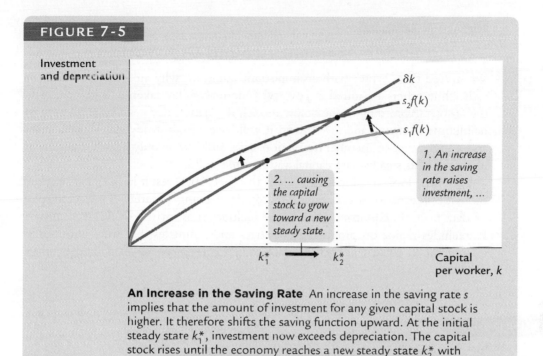

An Increase in the Saving Rate An increase in the saving rate s implies that the amount of investment for any given capital stock is higher. It therefore shifts the saving function upward. At the initial steady state k_1^*, investment now exceeds depreciation. The capital stock rises until the economy reaches a new steady state k_2^* with more capital and output.

stock and a high level of output in the steady state. If the saving rate is low, the economy will have a small capital stock and a low level of output in the steady state. This conclusion sheds light on many discussions of fiscal policy. As we saw in Chapter 3, a government budget deficit can reduce national saving and crowd out investment. Now we can see that the long-run consequences of a reduced saving rate are a lower capital stock and lower national income. This is why many economists are critical of persistent budget deficits.

What does the Solow model say about the relationship between saving and economic growth? Higher saving leads to faster growth in the Solow model, but only temporarily. An increase in the rate of saving raises growth only until the economy reaches the new steady state. If the economy maintains a high saving rate, it will maintain a large capital stock and a high level of output, but it will not maintain a high rate of growth forever. Policies that alter the steady-state growth rate of income per person are said to have a *growth effect*; we will see examples of such policies in the next chapter. By contrast, a higher saving rate is said to have a *level effect*, because only the level of income per person—not its growth rate—is influenced by the saving rate in the steady state.

Now that we understand how saving and growth interact, we can more fully explain the impressive economic performance of Germany and Japan after World War II. Not only were their initial capital stocks low because of the war, but their steady-state capital stocks were also high because of their high saving rates. Both of these facts help explain the rapid growth of these two countries in the 1950s and 1960s.

Saving and Investment Around the World

We started this chapter with an important question: why are some countries so rich while others are mired in poverty? Our analysis has taken us a step closer to the answer. According to the Solow model, if a nation devotes a large fraction of its income to saving and investment, it will have a high steady-state capital stock and a high level of income. If a nation saves and invests only a small fraction of its income, its steady-state capital and income will be low.

Let's now look at some data to see if this theoretical result in fact helps explain the large international variation in standards of living. Figure 7-6 is a scatterplot of data from 96 countries. (The figure includes most of the world's economies. It excludes major oil-producing countries and countries that were communist during much of this period, because their experiences are explained by their

FIGURE 7-6

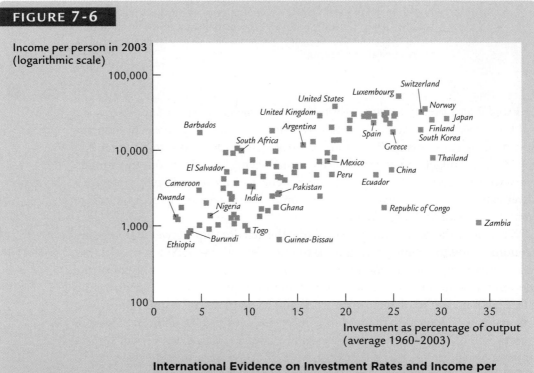

International Evidence on Investment Rates and Income per Person This scatterplot shows the experience of 96 countries, each represented by a single point. The horizontal axis shows the country's rate of investment, and the vertical axis shows the country's income per person. High investment is associated with high income per person, as the Solow model predicts.

Source: Alan Heston, Robert Summers, and Bettina Aten, Penn World Table Version 6.2, Center for International Comparisons of Production, Income, and Prices at the University of Pennsylvania, September 2006.

special circumstances.) The data show a positive relationship between the fraction of output devoted to investment and the level of income per person. That is, countries with high rates of investment, such as the United States and Japan, usually have high incomes, whereas countries with low rates of investment, such as Ethiopia and Burundi, have low incomes. Thus, the data are consistent with the Solow model's prediction that the investment rate is a key determinant of whether a country is rich or poor.

The strong correlation shown in this figure is an important fact, but it raises as many questions as it resolves. One might naturally ask, why do rates of saving and investment vary so much from country to country? There are many potential answers, such as tax policy, retirement patterns, and cultural differences. Politics may play a role: not surprisingly, rates of saving and investment tend to be low in countries with frequent wars, revolutions, and coups as well as in countries with high levels of official corruption. In addition, the development of the economy's financial system may be important. As we discuss later in this book, financial markets, banks, and other financial institutions play the crucial role of directing the economy's saving toward the best investments; whether they are performing that function well or poorly might influence an economy's propensity to save and invest. A final interpretation of the evidence in Figure 7-6 is reverse causation: perhaps high levels of income somehow foster high rates of saving and investment. Unfortunately, there is no consensus among economists about which of the many possible explanations is most important.

The association between investment rates and income per person is strong, and it is an important clue as to why some countries are rich and others poor, but it is not the whole story. The correlation between these two variables is far from perfect. The United States and Peru, for instance, have had similar investment rates, but income per person is more than eight times higher in the United States. There must be other determinants of living standards beyond saving and investment. Later in this chapter and also in the next one, we return to the international differences in income per person to see what other variables enter the picture. ∎

7-2 The Golden Rule Level of Capital

So far, we have used the Solow model to examine how an economy's rate of saving and investment determines its steady-state levels of capital and income. This analysis might lead you to think that higher saving is always a good thing because it always leads to greater income. Yet suppose a nation had a saving rate of 100 percent. That would lead to the largest possible capital stock and the largest possible income. But if all of this income is saved and none is ever consumed, what good is it?

This section uses the Solow model to discuss the optimal amount of capital accumulation from the standpoint of economic well-being. In the next chapter, we discuss how government policies influence a nation's saving rate. But first, in this section, we present the theory behind these policy decisions.

Comparing Steady States

To keep our analysis simple, let's assume that a policymaker can set the economy's saving rate at any level. By setting the saving rate, the policymaker determines the economy's steady state. What steady state should the policymaker choose?

The policymaker's goal is to maximize the well-being of the individuals who make up the society. Individuals themselves do not care about the amount of capital in the economy, or even the amount of output. They care about the amount of goods and services they can consume. Thus, a benevolent policymaker would want to choose the steady state with the highest level of consumption. The steady-state value of k that maximizes consumption is called the **Golden Rule level of capital** and is denoted k^*_{gold}.[2]

How can we tell whether an economy is at the Golden Rule level? To answer this question, we must first determine steady-state consumption per worker. Then we can see which steady state provides the most consumption.

To find steady-state consumption per worker, we begin with the national income accounts identity

$$y = c + i$$

and rearrange it as

$$c = y - i.$$

Consumption is output minus investment. Because we want to find steady-state consumption, we substitute steady-state values for output and investment. Steady-state output per worker is $f(k^*)$, where k^* is the steady-state capital stock per worker. Furthermore, because the capital stock is not changing in the steady state, investment equals depreciation δk^*. Substituting $f(k^*)$ for y and δk^* for i, we can write steady-state consumption per worker as

$$c^* = f(k^*) - \delta k^*.$$

According to this equation, steady-state consumption is what's left of steady-state output after paying for steady-state depreciation. This equation shows that an increase in steady-state capital has two opposing effects on steady-state consumption. On the one hand, more capital means more output. On the other hand, more capital also means that more output must be used to replace capital that is wearing out.

Figure 7-7 graphs steady-state output and steady-state depreciation as a function of the steady-state capital stock. Steady-state consumption is the gap between output and depreciation. This figure shows that there is one level of the capital stock—the Golden Rule level k^*_{gold}—that maximizes consumption.

When comparing steady states, we must keep in mind that higher levels of capital affect both output and depreciation. If the capital stock is below the Golden

---

[2] Edmund Phelps, "The Golden Rule of Accumulation: A Fable for Growthmen," *American Economic Review* 51 (September 1961): 638–643.

FIGURE 7-7

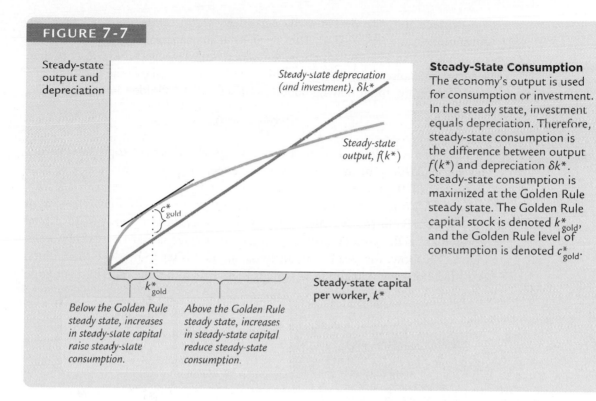

Steady-state output and depreciation

Steady-state depreciation (and investment), δk^*

Steady-state output, $f(k^*)$

c^*_{gold}

k^*_{gold}

Steady-state capital per worker, k^*

Below the Golden Rule steady state, increases in steady-state capital raise steady-state consumption.

Above the Golden Rule steady state, increases in steady-state capital reduce steady-state consumption.

Steady-State Consumption The economy's output is used for consumption or investment. In the steady state, investment equals depreciation. Therefore, steady-state consumption is the difference between output $f(k^*)$ and depreciation δk^*. Steady-state consumption is maximized at the Golden Rule steady state. The Golden Rule capital stock is denoted k^*_{gold}, and the Golden Rule level of consumption is denoted c^*_{gold}.

Rule level, an increase in the capital stock raises output more than depreciation, so consumption rises. In this case, the production function is steeper than the δk^* line, so the gap between these two curves—which equals consumption—grows as k^* rises. By contrast, if the capital stock is above the Golden Rule level, an increase in the capital stock reduces consumption, because the increase in output is smaller than the increase in depreciation. In this case, the production function is flatter than the δk^* line, so the gap between the curves—consumption—shrinks as k^* rises. At the Golden Rule level of capital, the production function and the δk^* line have the same slope, and consumption is at its greatest level.

We can now derive a simple condition that characterizes the Golden Rule level of capital. Recall that the slope of the production function is the marginal product of capital MPK. The slope of the δk^* line is δ. Because these two slopes are equal at k^*_{gold}, the Golden Rule is described by the equation

$$MPK = \delta.$$

At the Golden Rule level of capital, the marginal product of capital equals the depreciation rate.

To make the point somewhat differently, suppose that the economy starts at some steady-state capital stock k^* and that the policymaker is considering increasing the capital stock to $k^* + 1$. The amount of extra output from this increase in capital would be $f(k^* + 1) - f(k^*)$, the marginal product of capital MPK. The amount of extra depreciation from having 1 more unit of capital is the depreciation rate δ. Thus, the net effect of this extra unit of capital on consumption is $MPK - \delta$. If $MPK - \delta > 0$, then increases in capital increase consumption, so k^* must be below the Golden Rule level. If $MPK - \delta < 0$, then increases in capital decrease consumption, so k^* must be above the Golden Rule level. Therefore, the following condition describes the Golden Rule:

$$MPK - \delta = 0.$$

At the Golden Rule level of capital, the marginal product of capital net of depreciation ($MPK - \delta$) equals zero. As we will see, a policymaker can use this condition to find the Golden Rule capital stock for an economy.[3]

Keep in mind that the economy does not automatically gravitate toward the Golden Rule steady state. If we want any particular steady-state capital stock, such as the Golden Rule, we need a particular saving rate to support it. Figure 7-8 shows the steady state if the saving rate is set to produce the Golden Rule level of capital. If the saving rate is higher than the one used in this figure,

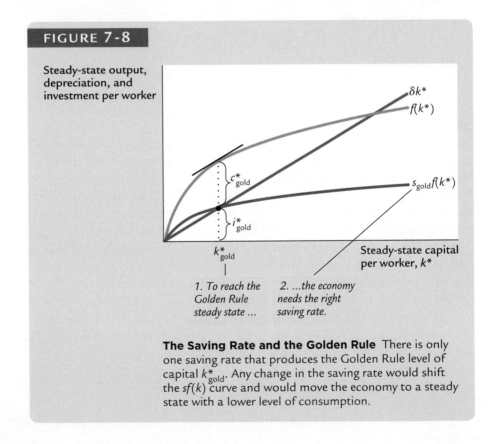

FIGURE 7-8

1. To reach the Golden Rule steady state ...

2. ...the economy needs the right saving rate.

The Saving Rate and the Golden Rule There is only one saving rate that produces the Golden Rule level of capital k^*_{gold}. Any change in the saving rate would shift the $sf(k)$ curve and would move the economy to a steady state with a lower level of consumption.

---

[3] *Mathematical note*: Another way to derive the condition for the Golden Rule uses a bit of calculus. Recall that $c^* = f(k^*) - \delta k^*$. To find the k^* that maximizes c^*, differentiate to find $dc^*/dk^* = f'(k^*) - \delta$ and set this derivative equal to zero. Noting that $f'(k^*)$ is the marginal product of capital, we obtain the Golden Rule condition in the text.

the steady-state capital stock will be too high. If the saving rate is lower, the steady-state capital stock will be too low. In either case, steady-state consumption will be lower than it is at the Golden Rule steady state.

Finding the Golden Rule Steady State: A Numerical Example

Consider the decision of a policymaker choosing a steady state in the following economy. The production function is the same as in our earlier example:

$$y = \sqrt{k}.$$

Output per worker is the square root of capital per worker. Depreciation δ is again 10 percent of capital. This time, the policymaker chooses the saving rate s and thus the economy's steady state.

To see the outcomes available to the policymaker, recall that the following equation holds in the steady state:

$$\frac{k^*}{f(k^*)} = \frac{s}{\delta}.$$

In this economy, this equation becomes

$$\frac{k^*}{\sqrt{k^*}} = \frac{s}{0.1}.$$

Squaring both sides of this equation yields a solution for the steady-state capital stock. We find

$$k^* = 100s^2.$$

Using this result, we can compute the steady-state capital stock for any saving rate.

Table 7-3 presents calculations showing the steady states that result from various saving rates in this economy. We see that higher saving leads to a higher capital stock, which in turn leads to higher output and higher depreciation. Steady-state consumption, the difference between output and depreciation, first rises with higher saving rates and then declines. Consumption is highest when the saving rate is 0.5. Hence, a saving rate of 0.5 produces the Golden Rule steady state.

Recall that another way to identify the Golden Rule steady state is to find the capital stock at which the net marginal product of capital ($MPK - \delta$) equals zero. For this production function, the marginal product is[4]

$$MPK = \frac{1}{2\sqrt{k}}.$$

---

[4] *Mathematical note:* To derive this formula, note that the marginal product of capital is the derivative of the production function with respect to k.

TABLE 7-3

Finding the Golden Rule Steady State: A Numerical Example

Assumptions: $y = \sqrt{k};$ $\delta = 0.1$

s	k*	y*	δk*	c*	MPK	MPK − δ
0.0	0.0	0.0	0.0	0.0	∞	∞
0.1	1.0	1.0	0.1	0.9	0.500	0.400
0.2	4.0	2.0	0.4	1.6	0.250	0.150
0.3	9.0	3.0	0.9	2.1	0.167	0.067
0.4	16.0	4.0	1.6	2.4	0.125	0.025
0.5	**25.0**	**5.0**	**2.5**	**2.5**	**0.100**	**0.000**
0.6	36.0	6.0	3.6	2.4	0.083	−0.017
0.7	49.0	7.0	4.9	2.1	0.071	−0.029
0.8	64.0	8.0	6.4	1.6	0.062	−0.038
0.9	81.0	9.0	8.1	0.9	0.056	−0.044
1.0	100.0	10.0	10.0	0.0	0.050	−0.050

Using this formula, the last two columns of Table 7-3 present the values of *MPK* and *MPK* − δ in the different steady states. Note that the net marginal product of capital is exactly zero when the saving rate is at its Golden Rule value of 0.5. Because of diminishing marginal product, the net marginal product of capital is greater than zero whenever the economy saves less than this amount, and it is less than zero whenever the economy saves more.

This numerical example confirms that the two ways of finding the Golden Rule steady state—looking at steady-state consumption or looking at the marginal product of capital—give the same answer. If we want to know whether an actual economy is currently at, above, or below its Golden Rule capital stock, the second method is usually more convenient, because it is relatively straightforward to estimate the marginal product of capital. By contrast, evaluating an economy with the first method requires estimates of steady-state consumption at many different saving rates; such information is harder to obtain. Thus, when we apply this kind of analysis to the U.S. economy in the next chapter, we will evaluate U.S. saving by examining the marginal product of capital. Before engaging in that policy analysis, however, we need to proceed further in our development and understanding of the Solow model.

The Transition to the Golden Rule Steady State

Let's now make our policymaker's problem more realistic. So far, we have been assuming that the policymaker can simply choose the economy's steady state and jump there immediately. In this case, the policymaker would choose the steady state with highest consumption—the Golden Rule steady state. But now suppose that the economy has reached a steady state other than the Golden Rule. What happens to consumption, investment, and capital when the economy makes the transition between steady states? Might the impact of the transition deter the policymaker from trying to achieve the Golden Rule?

We must consider two cases: the economy might begin with more capital than in the Golden Rule steady state, or with less. It turns out that the two cases offer very different problems for policymakers. (As we will see in the next chapter, the second case—too little capital—describes most actual economies, including that of the United States.)

Starting With Too Much Capital We first consider the case in which the economy begins at a steady state with more capital than it would have in the Golden Rule steady state. In this case, the policymaker should pursue policies aimed at reducing the rate of saving in order to reduce the capital stock. Suppose that these policies succeed and that at some point—call it time t_0—the saving rate falls to the level that will eventually lead to the Golden Rule steady state.

Figure 7-9 shows what happens to output, consumption, and investment when the saving rate falls. The reduction in the saving rate causes an immediate increase in consumption and a decrease in investment. Because investment and depreciation were equal in the initial steady state, investment will now be less than depreciation, which means the economy is no longer in a steady state. Gradually, the capital stock falls, leading to reductions in output, consumption, and investment. These variables continue to fall until the economy reaches the new steady state. Because we are assuming that the new steady state is the Golden Rule steady state, consumption must be higher than it was before the change in the saving rate, even though output and investment are lower.

FIGURE 7-9

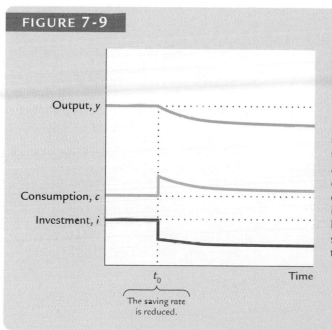

Reducing Saving When Starting With More Capital Than in the Golden Rule Steady State This figure shows what happens over time to output, consumption, and investment when the economy begins with more capital than the Golden Rule level and the saving rate is reduced. The reduction in the saving rate (at time t_0) causes an immediate increase in consumption and an equal decrease in investment. Over time, as the capital stock falls, output, consumption, and investment fall together. Because the economy began with too much capital, the new steady state has a higher level of consumption than the initial steady state.

Output, y

Consumption, c

Investment, i

t_0

Time

The saving rate is reduced.

Note that, compared to the old steady state, consumption is higher not only in the new steady state but also along the entire path to it. When the capital stock exceeds the Golden Rule level, reducing saving is clearly a good policy because it increases consumption at every point in time.

Starting With Too Little Capital When the economy begins with less capital than in the Golden Rule steady state, the policymaker must raise the saving rate to reach the Golden Rule. Figure 7-10 shows what happens. The increase in the saving rate at time t_0 causes an immediate fall in consumption and a rise in investment. Over time, higher investment causes the capital stock to rise. As capital accumulates, output, consumption, and investment gradually increase, eventually approaching the new steady-state levels. Because the initial steady state was below the Golden Rule, the increase in saving eventually leads to a higher level of consumption than that which prevailed initially.

Does the increase in saving that leads to the Golden Rule steady state raise economic welfare? Eventually it does, because the new steady-state level of consumption is higher than the initial level. But achieving that new steady state requires an initial period of reduced consumption. Note the contrast to the case in which the economy begins above the Golden Rule. *When the economy begins above the Golden Rule, reaching the Golden Rule produces higher consumption at all points in time. When the economy begins below the Golden Rule, reaching the Golden Rule requires initially reducing consumption to increase consumption in the future.*

When deciding whether to try to reach the Golden Rule steady state, policymakers have to take into account the fact that current consumers and future consumers are not always the same people. Reaching the Golden Rule achieves the highest steady-state level of consumption and thus benefits future generations. But when the economy is initially below the Golden Rule, reaching the

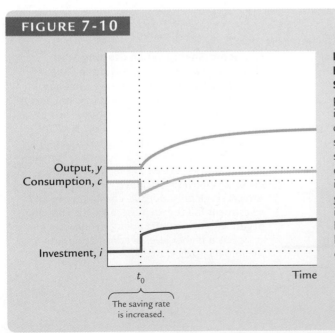

FIGURE 7-10

Increasing Saving When Starting With Less Capital Than in the Golden Rule Steady State This figure shows what happens over time to output, consumption, and investment when the economy begins with less capital than the Golden Rule level and the saving rate is increased. The increase in the saving rate (at time t_0) causes an immediate drop in consumption and an equal jump in investment. Over time, as the capital stock grows, output, consumption, and investment increase together. Because the economy began with less capital than the Golden Rule level, the new steady state has a higher level of consumption than the initial steady state.

Golden Rule requires raising investment and thus lowering the consumption of current generations. Thus, when choosing whether to increase capital accumulation, the policymaker faces a tradeoff among the welfare levels of different generations. A policymaker who cares more about current generations than about future ones may decide not to pursue policies to reach the Golden Rule steady state. By contrast, a policymaker who cares about all generations equally will choose to reach the Golden Rule. Even though current generations will consume less, an infinite number of future generations will benefit by moving to the Golden Rule.

Thus, optimal capital accumulation depends crucially on how we weigh the interests of current and future generations. The biblical Golden Rule tells us to "do unto others as you would have them do unto you." If we heed this advice, we give all generations equal weight. In this case, it is optimal to reach the Golden Rule level of capital—which is why it is called the "Golden Rule."

7-3 Population Growth

The basic Solow model shows that capital accumulation, by itself, cannot explain sustained economic growth: high rates of saving lead to high growth temporarily, but the economy eventually approaches a steady state in which capital and output are constant. To explain the sustained economic growth that we observe in most parts of the world, we must expand the Solow model to incorporate the other two sources of economic growth—population growth and technological progress. In this section we add population growth to the model.

Instead of assuming that the population is fixed, as we did in Sections 7-1 and 7-2, we now suppose that the population and the labor force grow at a constant rate n. For example, the U.S. population grows about 1 percent per year, so $n = 0.01$. This means that if 150 million people are working one year, then 151.5 million (1.01×150) are working the next year, and 153.015 million (1.01×151.5) the year after that, and so on.

The Steady State With Population Growth

How does population growth affect the steady state? To answer this question, we must discuss how population growth, along with investment and depreciation, influences the accumulation of capital per worker. As we noted before, investment raises the capital stock, and depreciation reduces it. But now there is a third force acting to change the amount of capital per worker: the growth in the number of workers causes capital per worker to fall.

We continue to let lowercase letters stand for quantities per worker. Thus, $k = K/L$ is capital per worker, and $y = Y/L$ is output per worker. Keep in mind, however, that the number of workers is growing over time.

The change in the capital stock per worker is

$$\Delta k = i - (\delta + n)k.$$

This equation shows how investment, depreciation, and population growth influence the per-worker capital stock. Investment increases k, whereas depreciation and population growth decrease k. We saw this equation earlier in this chapter for the special case of a constant population ($n = 0$).

We can think of the term $(\delta + n)k$ as defining *break-even investment*—the amount of investment necessary to keep the capital stock per worker constant. Break-even investment includes the depreciation of existing capital, which equals δk. It also includes the amount of investment necessary to provide new workers with capital. The amount of investment necessary for this purpose is nk, because there are n new workers for each existing worker and because k is the amount of capital for each worker. The equation shows that population growth reduces the accumulation of capital per worker much the way depreciation does. Depreciation reduces k by wearing out the capital stock, whereas population growth reduces k by spreading the capital stock more thinly among a larger population of workers.[5]

Our analysis with population growth now proceeds much as it did previously. First, we substitute $sf(k)$ for i. The equation can then be written as

$$\Delta k = sf(k) - (\delta + n)k.$$

To see what determines the steady-state level of capital per worker, we use Figure 7-11, which extends the analysis of Figure 7-4 to include the effects of

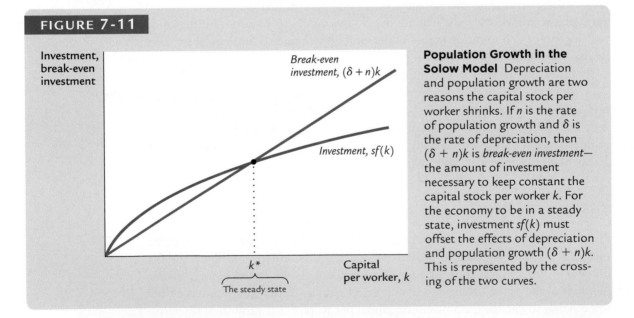

FIGURE 7-11

Investment, break-even investment

Break-even investment, $(\delta + n)k$

Investment, $sf(k)$

k^*

The steady state

Capital per worker, k

Population Growth in the Solow Model Depreciation and population growth are two reasons the capital stock per worker shrinks. If n is the rate of population growth and δ is the rate of depreciation, then $(\delta + n)k$ is *break-even investment*—the amount of investment necessary to keep constant the capital stock per worker k. For the economy to be in a steady state, investment $sf(k)$ must offset the effects of depreciation and population growth $(\delta + n)k$. This is represented by the crossing of the two curves.

---

[5] *Mathematical note*: Formally deriving the equation for the change in k requires a bit of calculus. Note that the change in k per unit of time is $dk/dt = d(K/L)/dt$. After applying the standard rules of calculus, we can write this as $dk/dt = (1/L)(dK/dt) - (K/L^2)(dL/dt)$. Now use the following facts to substitute in this equation: $dK/dt = I - \delta K$ and $(dL/dt)/L = n$. After a bit of manipulation, this produces the equation in the text.

population growth. An economy is in a steady state if capital per worker k is unchanging. As before, we designate the steady-state value of k as k^*. If k is less than k^*, investment is greater than break-even investment, so k rises. If k is greater than k^*, investment is less than break-even investment, so k falls.

In the steady state, the positive effect of investment on the capital stock per worker exactly balances the negative effects of depreciation and population growth. That is, at k^*, $\Delta k = 0$ and $i^* = \delta k^* + nk^*$. Once the economy is in the steady state, investment has two purposes. Some of it (δk^*) replaces the depreciated capital, and the rest (nk^*) provides the new workers with the steady-state amount of capital.

The Effects of Population Growth

Population growth alters the basic Solow model in three ways. First, it brings us closer to explaining sustained economic growth. In the steady state with population growth, capital per worker and output per worker are constant. Because the number of workers is growing at rate n, however, *total* capital and *total* output must also be growing at rate n. Hence, although population growth cannot explain sustained growth in the standard of living (because output per worker is constant in the steady state), it can help explain sustained growth in total output.

Second, population growth gives us another explanation for why some countries are rich and others are poor. Consider the effects of an increase in population growth. Figure 7-12 shows that an increase in the rate of population growth

---

FIGURE 7-12

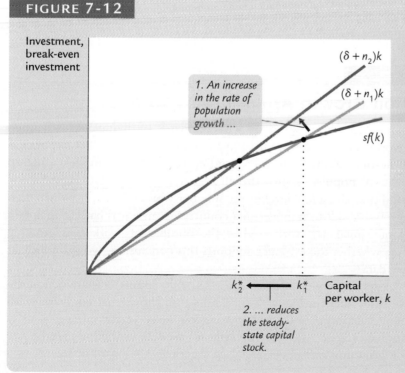

Investment, break-even investment

1. An increase in the rate of population growth ...

$(\delta + n_2)k$

$(\delta + n_1)k$

$sf(k)$

$k_2^* \longleftarrow k_1^*$ Capital per worker, k

2. ... reduces the steady-state capital stock.

The Impact of Population Growth An increase in the rate of population growth from n_1 to n_2 shifts the line representing population growth and depreciation upward. The new steady state k_2^* has a lower level of capital per worker than the initial steady state k_1^*. Thus, the Solow model predicts that economies with higher rates of population growth will have lower levels of capital per worker and therefore lower incomes.

from n_1 to n_2 reduces the steady-state level of capital per worker from k_1^* to k_2^*. Because k^* is lower and because $y^* = f(k^*)$, the level of output per worker y^* is also lower. Thus, the Solow model predicts that countries with higher population growth will have lower levels of GDP per person. Notice that a change in the population growth rate, like a change in the saving rate, has a level effect on income per person but does not affect the steady-state growth rate of income per person.

Finally, population growth affects our criterion for determining the Golden Rule (consumption-maximizing) level of capital. To see how this criterion changes, note that consumption per worker is

$$c = y - i.$$

Because steady-state output is $f(k^*)$ and steady-state investment is $(\delta + n)k^*$, we can express steady-state consumption as

$$c^* = f(k^*) - (\delta + n)k^*.$$

Using an argument largely the same as before, we conclude that the level of k^* that maximizes consumption is the one at which

$$MPK = \delta + n,$$

or equivalently,

$$MPK - \delta = n.$$

In the Golden Rule steady state, the marginal product of capital net of depreciation equals the rate of population growth.

CASE STUDY

Population Growth Around the World

Let's return now to the question of why standards of living vary so much around the world. The analysis we have just completed suggests that population growth may be one of the answers. According to the Solow model, a nation with a high rate of population growth will have a low steady-state capital stock per worker and thus also a low level of income per worker. In other words, high population growth tends to impoverish a country because it is hard to maintain a high level of capital per worker when the number of workers is growing quickly. To see whether the evidence supports this conclusion, we again look at cross-country data.

Figure 7-13 is a scatterplot of data for the same 96 countries examined in the previous case study (and in Figure 7-6). The figure shows that countries with high rates of population growth tend to have low levels of income per person. The international evidence is consistent with our model's prediction that the rate of population growth is one determinant of a country's standard of living.

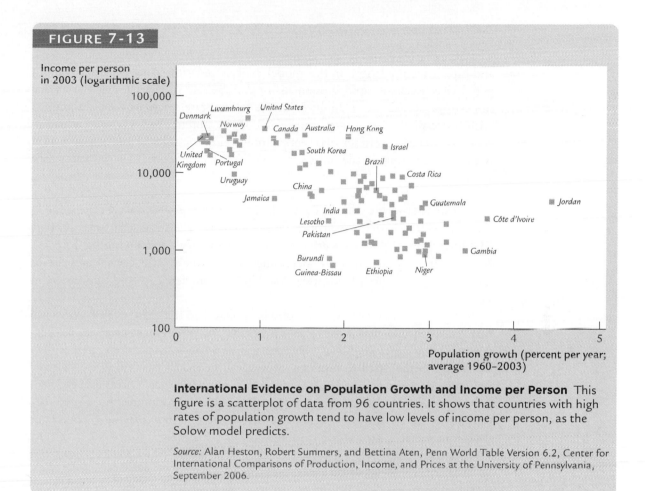

FIGURE 7-13

International Evidence on Population Growth and Income per Person This figure is a scatterplot of data from 96 countries. It shows that countries with high rates of population growth tend to have low levels of income per person, as the Solow model predicts.

Source: Alan Heston, Robert Summers, and Bettina Aten, Penn World Table Version 6.2, Center for International Comparisons of Production, Income, and Prices at the University of Pennsylvania, September 2006.

This conclusion is not lost on policymakers. Those trying to pull the world's poorest nations out of poverty, such as the advisers sent to developing nations by the World Bank, often advocate reducing fertility by increasing education about birth-control methods and expanding women's job opportunities. Toward the same end, China has followed the totalitarian policy of allowing only one child per couple. These policies to reduce population growth should, if the Solow model is right, raise income per person in the long run.

In interpreting the cross-country data, however, it is important to keep in mind that correlation does not imply causation. The data show that low population growth is typically associated with high levels of income per person, and the Solow model offers one possible explanation for this fact, but other explanations are also possible. It is conceivable that high income encourages low population growth, perhaps because birth-control techniques are more readily available in richer countries. The international data can help us evaluate a theory of growth, such as the Solow model, because they show us whether the theory's predictions are borne out in the world. But often more than one theory can explain the same facts. ∎

Alternative Perspectives on Population Growth

The Solow growth model highlights the interaction between population growth and capital accumulation. In this model, high population growth reduces output per worker because rapid growth in the number of workers forces the capital stock to be spread more thinly, so in the steady state, each worker is equipped with less capital. The model omits some other potential effects of population growth. Here we consider two—one emphasizing the interaction of population with natural resources, the other emphasizing the interaction of population with technology.

The Malthusian Model In his book *An Essay on the Principle of Population as It Affects the Future Improvement of Society,* the early economist Thomas Robert Malthus (1766–1834) offered what may be history's most chilling forecast. Malthus argued that an ever-increasing population would continually strain society's ability to provide for itself. Mankind, he predicted, would forever live in poverty.

Malthus began by noting that "food is necessary to the existence of man" and that "the passion between the sexes is necessary and will remain nearly in its present state." He concluded that "the power of population is infinitely greater than the power in the earth to produce subsistence for man." According to Malthus, the only check on population growth was "misery and vice." Attempts by charities or governments to alleviate poverty were counterproductive, he argued, because they merely allowed the poor to have more children, placing even greater strains on society's productive capabilities.

The Malthusian model may have described the world when Malthus lived, but its prediction that mankind would remain in poverty forever has proven very wrong. The world population has increased about sixfold over the past two centuries, but average living standards are much higher. Because of economic growth, chronic hunger and malnutrition are less common now than they were in Malthus's day. Famines occur from time to time, but they are more often the result of unequal income distribution or political instability than the inadequate production of food.

Malthus failed to foresee that growth in mankind's ingenuity would more than offset the effects of a larger population. Pesticides, fertilizers, mechanized farm equipment, new crop varieties, and other technological advances that Malthus never imagined have allowed each farmer to feed ever-greater numbers of people. Even with more mouths to feed, fewer farmers are necessary because each farmer is so productive. Today, fewer than 2 percent of Americans work on farms, but they produce enough food to feed the nation and some excess to export as well.

In addition, although the "passion between the sexes" is just as strong now as it was in Malthus's day, the link between passion and population growth that Malthus assumed has been broken by modern birth control. Many advanced nations, such as those in western Europe, are now experiencing fertility below replacement rates. Over the next century, shrinking populations may be more likely than rapidly expanding ones. There is now little reason to think that an ever-expanding population will overwhelm food production and doom mankind to poverty.[6]

The Kremerian Model While Malthus saw population growth as a threat to rising living standards, economist Michael Kremer has suggested that world population growth is a key driver of advancing economic prosperity. If there are more people, Kremer argues, then there are more scientists, inventors, and engineers to contribute to innovation and technological progress.

As evidence for this hypothesis, Kremer begins by noting that over the broad span of human history, world growth rates have increased together with world population. For example, world growth was more rapid when the world population was 1 billion (which occurred around the year 1800) than it was when the population was only 100 million (around 500 B.C.). This fact is consistent with the hypothesis that having more people induces more technological progress.

Kremer's second, more compelling piece of evidence comes from comparing regions of the world. The melting of the polar ice caps at the end of the ice age around 10,000 B.C. flooded the land bridges and separated the world into several distinct regions that could not communicate with one another for thousands of years. If technological progress is more rapid when there are more people to discover things, then the more populous regions should have experienced more rapid growth.

And, indeed, they did. The most successful region of the world in 1500 (when Columbus reestablished technological contact) included the "Old World" civilizations of the large Eurasia–Africa region. Next in technological development were the Aztec and Mayan civilizations in the Americas, followed by the hunter-gatherers of Australia, and then the primitive people of Tasmania, who lacked even fire-making and most stone and bone tools. The least populous isolated region was Flinders Island, a tiny island between Tasmania and Australia. With few people to contribute new innovations, Flinders Island had the least technological advance and, in fact, seemed to regress. Around 3000 B.C., human society on Flinders Island died out completely.

Kremer concludes from this evidence that a large population is a prerequisite for technological advance.[7]

---

[6] For modern analyses of the Malthusian model, see Oded Galor and David N. Weil, "Population, Technology, and Growth: From Malthusian Stagnation to the Demographic Transition and Beyond," *American Economic Review* 90 (September 2000): 806–828; and Gary D. Hansen and Edward C. Prescott, "Malthus to Solow," *American Economic Review* 92 (September 2002): 1205–1217.

[7] Michael Kremer, "Population Growth and Technological Change: One Million B.C. to 1990," *Quarterly Journal of Economics* 108 (August 1993): 681–716.

7-4 Conclusion

This chapter has started the process of building the Solow growth model. The model as developed so far shows how saving and population growth determine the economy's steady-state capital stock and its steady-state level of income per person. As we have seen, it sheds light on many features of actual growth experiences—why Germany and Japan grew so rapidly after being devastated by World War II, why countries that save and invest a high fraction of their output are richer than countries that save and invest a smaller fraction, and why countries with high rates of population growth are poorer than countries with low rates of population growth.

What the model cannot do, however, is explain the persistent growth in living standards we observe in most countries. In the model we have developed so far, output per worker stops growing when the economy reaches its steady state. To explain persistent growth, we need to introduce technological progress into the model. That is our first job in the next chapter.

Summary

1. The Solow growth model shows that in the long run, an economy's rate of saving determines the size of its capital stock and thus its level of production. The higher the rate of saving, the higher the stock of capital and the higher the level of output.

2. In the Solow model, an increase in the rate of saving has a level effect on income per person: it causes a period of rapid growth, but eventually that growth slows as the new steady state is reached. Thus, although a high saving rate yields a high steady-state level of output, saving by itself cannot generate persistent economic growth.

3. The level of capital that maximizes steady-state consumption is called the Golden Rule level. If an economy has more capital than in the Golden Rule steady state, then reducing saving will increase consumption at all points in time. By contrast, if the economy has less capital than in the Golden Rule steady state, then reaching the Golden Rule requires increased investment and thus lower consumption for current generations.

4. The Solow model shows that an economy's rate of population growth is another long-run determinant of the standard of living. According to the Solow model, the higher the rate of population growth, the lower the steady-state levels of capital per worker and output per worker. Other theories highlight other effects of population growth. Malthus suggested that population growth will strain the natural resources necessary to produce food; Kremer suggested that a large population may promote technological progress.

KEY CONCEPTS

Solow growth model   Steady state   Golden Rule level of capital

QUESTIONS FOR REVIEW

1. In the Solow model, how does the saving rate affect the steady-state level of income? How does it affect the steady-state rate of growth?

2. Why might an economic policymaker choose the Golden Rule level of capital?

3. Might a policymaker choose a steady state with more capital than in the Golden Rule steady state? With less capital than in the Golden Rule steady state? Explain your answers.

4. In the Solow model, how does the rate of population growth affect the steady-state level of income? How does it affect the steady-state rate of growth?

PROBLEMS AND APPLICATIONS

1. Country A and country B both have the production function

$$Y = F(K, L) = K^{1/2}L^{1/2}.$$

a. Does this production function have constant returns to scale? Explain.

b. What is the per-worker production function $y = f(k)$?

c. Assume that neither country experiences population growth or technological progress and that 5 percent of capital depreciates each year. Assume further that country A saves 10 percent of output each year and country B saves 20 percent of output each year. Using your answer from part (b) and the steady-state condition that investment equals depreciation, find the steady-state level of capital per worker for each country. Then find the steady-state levels of income per worker and consumption per worker.

d. Suppose that both countries start off with a capital stock per worker of 2. What are the levels of income per worker and consumption per worker? Remembering that the change in the capital stock is investment less depreciation, use a calculator or a computer spreadsheet to show how the capital stock per worker will evolve over time in both countries. For each year, calculate income per worker and consumption per worker. How many years will it be before the consumption in country B is higher than the consumption in country A?

2. In the discussion of German and Japanese postwar growth, the text describes what happens when part of the capital stock is destroyed in a war. By contrast, suppose that a war does not directly affect the capital stock but that casualties reduce the labor force. Assume the economy was in a steady state before the war, the saving rate is unchanged, and the rate of population growth after the war returns to normal.

a. What is the immediate impact of the war on total output and on output per person?

b. What happens subsequently to output per worker in the postwar economy? Is the growth rate of output per worker after the war smaller or greater than normal?

3. Consider an economy described by the production function. $Y = F(K, L) = K^{0.3}L^{0.7}$.

a. What is the per-worker production function?

b. Assuming no population growth or technological progress, find the steady-state capital stock per worker, output per worker, and consumption per worker as a function of the saving rate and the depreciation rate.

c. Assume that the depreciation rate is 10 percent per year. Make a table showing steady-state capital per worker, output per worker, and consumption per worker for saving rates of 0 percent, 10 percent, 20 percent, 30 percent, and so on. (You will need a calculator with an exponent key for this.) What saving rate maximizes output per worker? What saving rate maximizes consumption per worker?

d. (Harder) Use calculus to find the marginal product of capital. Add to your table in part (c) the marginal product of capital net of depreciation for each of the saving rates. What does your table show?

4. "Devoting a larger share of national output to investment would help restore rapid productivity growth and rising living standards." Do you agree with this claim? Explain.

5. One view of the consumption function is that workers have high propensities to consume and capitalists have low propensities to consume. To explore the implications of this view, suppose that an economy consumes all wage income and saves all capital income. Show that if the factors of production earn their marginal product, this economy reaches the Golden Rule level of capital. (*Hint:* Begin with the identity that saving equals investment. Then use the steady-state condition that investment is just enough to keep up with depreciation and population growth, and the fact that saving equals capital income in this economy.)

6. Many demographers predict that the United States will have zero population growth in the twenty-first century, in contrast to average population growth of about 1 percent per year in the twentieth century. Use the Solow model to forecast the effect of this slowdown in population growth on the growth of total output and the growth of output per person. Consider the effects both in the steady state and in the transition between steady states.

7. In the Solow model, population growth leads to steady-state growth in total output, but not in output per worker. Do you think this would still be true if the production function exhibited increasing or decreasing returns to scale? Explain. (For the definitions of increasing and decreasing returns to scale, see Chapter 3, "Problems and Applications," Problem 2.)

8. Consider how unemployment would affect the Solow growth model. Suppose that output is produced according to the production function $Y = K^\alpha[(1 - u)L]^{1-\alpha}$, where K is capital, L is the labor force, and u is the natural rate of unemployment. The national saving rate is s, the labor force grows at rate n, and capital depreciates at rate δ.

a. Express output per worker ($y = Y/L$) as a function of capital per worker ($k = K/L$) and the natural rate of unemployment. Describe the steady state of this economy.

b. Suppose that some change in government policy reduces the natural rate of unemployment. Describe how this change affects output both immediately and over time. Is the steady-state effect on output larger or smaller than the immediate effect? Explain.

9. Choose two countries that interest you—one rich and one poor. What is the income per person in each country? Find some data on country characteristics that might help explain the difference in income: investment rates, population growth rates, educational attainment, and so on. (*Hint*: The Web site of the World Bank, www.worldbank.org, is one place to find such data.) How might you figure out which of these factors is most responsible for the observed income difference?

CHAPTER 8

Economic Growth II:
Technology, Empirics, and Policy

Is there some action a government of India could take that would lead the
Indian economy to grow like Indonesia's or Egypt's? If so, what, exactly? If
not, what is it about the "nature of India" that makes it so? The consequences
for human welfare involved in questions like these are simply staggering: Once
one starts to think about them, it is hard to think about anything else.

—*Robert E. Lucas, Jr., 1988*

This chapter continues our analysis of the forces governing long-run economic growth. With the basic version of the Solow growth model as our starting point, we take on four new tasks.

Our first task is to make the Solow model more general and realistic. In Chapter 3 we saw that capital, labor, and technology are the key determinants of a nation's production of goods and services. In Chapter 7 we developed the Solow model to show how changes in capital (through saving and investment) and changes in the labor force (through population growth) affect the economy's output. We are now ready to add the third source of growth—changes in technology—to the mix. The Solow model does not explain technological progress but, instead, takes it as exogenously given and shows how it interacts with other variables in the process of economic growth.

Our second task is to move from theory to empirics. That is, we consider how well the Solow model fits the facts. Over the past two decades, a large literature has examined the predictions of the Solow model and other models of economic growth. It turns out that the glass is both half full and half empty. The Solow model can shed much light on international growth experiences, but it is far from the last word on the subject.

Our third task is to examine how a nation's public policies can influence the level and growth of its citizens' standard of living. In particular, we address five questions: Should our society save more or less? How can policy influence the rate of saving? Are there some types of investment that policy should especially encourage? What institutions ensure that the economy's resources are put to their best use? How can policy increase the rate of technological progress?

The Solow growth model provides the theoretical framework within which we consider these policy issues.

Our fourth and final task is to consider what the Solow model leaves out. As we have discussed previously, models help us understand the world by simplifying it. After completing an analysis of a model, therefore, it is important to consider whether we have oversimplified matters. In the last section, we examine a new set of theories, called *endogenous growth theories*, which help to explain the technological progress that the Solow model takes as exogenous.

8-1 Technological Progress in the Solow Model

So far, our presentation of the Solow model has assumed an unchanging relationship between the inputs of capital and labor and the output of goods and services. Yet the model can be modified to include exogenous technological progress, which over time expands society's production capabilities.

The Efficiency of Labor

To incorporate technological progress, we must return to the production function that relates total capital K and total labor L to total output Y. Thus far, the production function has been

$$Y = F(K, L).$$

We now write the production function as

$$Y = F(K, L \times E),$$

where E is a new (and somewhat abstract) variable called the **efficiency of labor**. The efficiency of labor is meant to reflect society's knowledge about production methods: as the available technology improves, the efficiency of labor rises, and each hour of work contributes more to the production of goods and services. For instance, the efficiency of labor rose when assembly-line production transformed manufacturing in the early twentieth century, and it rose again when computerization was introduced in the late twentieth century. The efficiency of labor also rises when there are improvements in the health, education, or skills of the labor force.

The term $L \times E$ can be interpreted as measuring the *effective number of workers*. It takes into account the number of actual workers L and the efficiency of each worker E. In other words, L measures the number of workers in the labor force, whereas $L \times E$ measures both the workers and the technology with which the typical worker comes equipped. This new production function states that total output Y depends on the inputs of capital K and effective workers $L \times E$.

The essence of this approach to modeling technological progress is that increases in the efficiency of labor E are analogous to increases in the labor force L. Suppose, for example, that an advance in production methods makes the efficiency of labor E double between 1980 and 2010. This means that a single worker in 2010 is, *in effect*, as productive as two workers were in 1980. That is, even if the actual number of workers (L) stays the same from 1980 to 2010, the effective number of workers ($L \times E$) doubles, and the economy benefits from the increased production of goods and services.

The simplest assumption about technological progress is that it causes the efficiency of labor E to grow at some constant rate g. For example, if $g = 0.02$, then each unit of labor becomes 2 percent more efficient each year: output increases as if the labor force had increased by 2 percent more than it really did. This form of technological progress is called *labor augmenting*, and g is called the rate of **labor-augmenting technological progress**. Because the labor force L is growing at rate n, and the efficiency of each unit of labor E is growing at rate g, the effective number of workers $L \times E$ is growing at rate $n + g$.

The Steady State With Technological Progress

Because technological progress is modeled here as labor augmenting, it fits into the model in much the same way as population growth. Technological progress does not cause the actual number of workers to increase, but because each worker in effect comes with more units of labor over time, technological progress causes the effective number of workers to increase. Thus, the analytic tools we used in Chapter 7 to study the Solow model with population growth are easily adapted to studying the Solow model with labor-augmenting technological progress.

We begin by reconsidering our notation. Previously, when there was no technological progress, we analyzed the economy in terms of quantities per worker; now we can generalize that approach by analyzing the economy in terms of quantities per effective worker. We now let $k = K/(L \times E)$ stand for capital per effective worker and $y = Y/(L \times E)$ stand for output per effective worker. With these definitions, we can again write $y = f(k)$.

Our analysis of the economy proceeds just as it did when we examined population growth. The equation showing the evolution of k over time becomes

$$\Delta k = sf(k) - (\delta + n + g)k.$$

As before, the change in the capital stock Δk equals investment $sf(k)$ minus break-even investment $(\delta + n + g)k$. Now, however, because $k = K/(L \times E)$, break-even investment includes three terms: to keep k constant, δk is needed to replace depreciating capital, nk is needed to provide capital for new workers, and gk is needed to provide capital for the new "effective workers" created by technological progress.[1]

---

[1] *Mathematical note:* This model with technological progress is a strict generalization of the model analyzed in Chapter 7. In particular, if the efficiency of labor is constant at $E = 1$, then $g = 0$, and the definitions of k and y reduce to our previous definitions. In this case, the more general model considered here simplifies precisely to the Chapter 7 version of the Solow model.

FIGURE 8-1

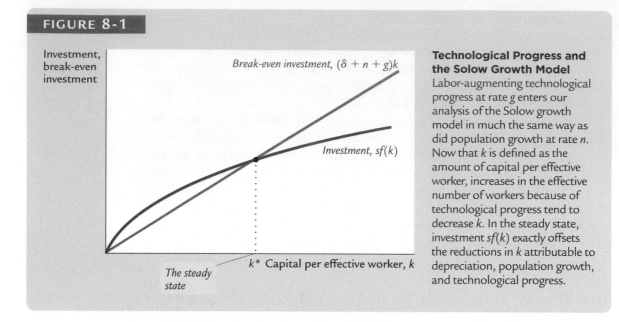

Investment, break-even investment

Break-even investment, $(\delta + n + g)k$

Investment, $sf(k)$

The steady state

k^* Capital per effective worker, k

Technological Progress and the Solow Growth Model Labor-augmenting technological progress at rate g enters our analysis of the Solow growth model in much the same way as did population growth at rate n. Now that k is defined as the amount of capital per effective worker, increases in the effective number of workers because of technological progress tend to decrease k. In the steady state, investment $sf(k)$ exactly offsets the reductions in k attributable to depreciation, population growth, and technological progress.

As shown in Figure 8-1, the inclusion of technological progress does not substantially alter our analysis of the steady state. There is one level of k, denoted k^*, at which capital per effective worker and output per effective worker are constant. As before, this steady state represents the long-run equilibrium of the economy.

The Effects of Technological Progress

Table 8-1 shows how four key variables behave in the steady state with technological progress. As we have just seen, capital per effective worker k is constant in the steady state. Because $y = f(k)$, output per effective worker is also constant. It is these quantities per effective worker that are steady in the steady state.

From this information, we can also infer what is happening to variables that are not expressed in units per effective worker. For instance, consider output per actual worker $Y/L = y \times E$. Because y is constant in the steady state and E is growing at rate g, output per worker must also be growing at rate g in the steady

TABLE 8-1

Steady-State Growth Rates in the Solow Model With Technological Progress

Variable	Symbol	Steady-State Growth Rate
Capital per effective worker	$k = K/(E \times L)$	0
Output per effective worker	$y = Y/(E \times L) = f(k)$	0
Output per worker	$Y/L = y \times E$	g
Total output	$Y = y \times (E \times L)$	$n + g$

state. Similarly, the economy's total output is $Y = y \times (E \times L)$. Because y is constant in the steady state, E is growing at rate g, and L is growing at rate n, total output grows at rate $n + g$ in the steady state.

With the addition of technological progress, our model can finally explain the sustained increases in standards of living that we observe. That is, we have shown that technological progress can lead to sustained growth in output per worker. By contrast, a high rate of saving leads to a high rate of growth only until the steady state is reached. Once the economy is in steady state, the rate of growth of output per worker depends only on the rate of technological progress. *According to the Solow model, only technological progress can explain sustained growth and persistently rising living standards.*

The introduction of technological progress also modifies the criterion for the Golden Rule. The Golden Rule level of capital is now defined as the steady state that maximizes consumption per effective worker. Following the same arguments that we have used before, we can show that steady-state consumption per effective worker is

$$c^* = f(k^*) - (\delta + n + g)k^*.$$

Steady-state consumption is maximized if

$$MPK = \delta + n + g,$$

or

$$MPK - \delta = n + g.$$

That is, at the Golden Rule level of capital, the net marginal product of capital, $MPK - \delta$, equals the rate of growth of total output, $n + g$. Because actual economies experience both population growth and technological progress, we must use this criterion to evaluate whether they have more or less capital than they would at the Golden Rule steady state.

8-2 From Growth Theory to Growth Empirics

So far in this chapter we have introduced exogenous technological progress into the Solow model to explain sustained growth in standards of living. Let's now discuss what happens when this theory is forced to confront the facts.

Balanced Growth

According to the Solow model, technological progress causes the values of many variables to rise together in the steady state. This property, called *balanced growth*, does a good job of describing the long-run data for the U.S. economy.

Consider first output per worker Y/L and the capital stock per worker K/L. According to the Solow model, in the steady state, both of these variables grow at g, the rate of technological progress. U.S. data for the past half century show that output per worker and the capital stock per worker have in fact grown at approximately the same rate—about 2 percent per year. To put it another way, the capital–output ratio has remained approximately constant over time.

Technological progress also affects factor prices. Problem 3(d) at the end of the chapter asks you to show that, in the steady state, the real wage grows at the rate of technological progress. The real rental price of capital, however, is constant over time. Again, these predictions hold true for the United States. Over the past 50 years, the real wage has increased about 2 percent per year; it has increased at about the same rate as real GDP per worker. Yet the real rental price of capital (measured as real capital income divided by the capital stock) has remained about the same.

The Solow model's prediction about factor prices—and the success of this prediction—is especially noteworthy when contrasted with Karl Marx's theory of the development of capitalist economies. Marx predicted that the return to capital would decline over time and that this would lead to economic and political crisis. Economic history has not supported Marx's prediction, which partly explains why we now study Solow's theory of growth rather than Marx's.

Convergence

If you travel around the world, you will see tremendous variation in living standards. The world's poor countries have average levels of income per person that are less than one-tenth the average levels in the world's rich countries. These differences in income are reflected in almost every measure of the quality of life—from the number of televisions and telephones per household to the infant mortality rate and life expectancy.

Much research has been devoted to the question of whether economies converge over time to one another. In particular, do economies that start off poor subsequently grow faster than economies that start off rich? If they do, then the world's poor economies will tend to catch up with the world's rich economies. This process of catch-up is called *convergence*. If convergence does not occur, then countries that start off behind are likely to remain poor.

The Solow model makes clear predictions about when convergence should occur. According to the model, whether two economies will converge depends on why they differ in the first place. On the one hand, suppose two economies happen by historical accident to start off with different capital stocks, but they have the same steady state, as determined by their saving rates, population growth rates, and efficiency of labor. In this case, we should expect the two economies to converge; the poorer economy with the smaller capital stock will naturally grow more quickly to reach the steady state. (In a case study in Chapter 7, we applied this logic to explain rapid growth in Germany and Japan after World War II.) On the other hand, if two economies have different steady states, perhaps because the economies have different rates of saving, then we should not expect convergence. Instead, each economy will approach its own steady state.

Experience is consistent with this analysis. In samples of economies with similar cultures and policies, studies find that economies converge to one another at a rate of about 2 percent per year. That is, the gap between rich and poor economies closes by about 2 percent each year. An example is the economies of individual American states. For historical reasons, such as the Civil War of the 1860s, income levels varied greatly among states at the end of the nineteenth century. Yet these differences have slowly disappeared over time.

In international data, a more complex picture emerges. When researchers examine only data on income per person, they find little evidence of convergence: countries that start off poor do not grow faster on average than countries that start off rich. This finding suggests that different countries have different steady states. If statistical techniques are used to control for some of the determinants of the steady state, such as saving rates, population growth rates, and accumulation of human capital (education), then once again the data show convergence at a rate of about 2 percent per year. In other words, the economies of the world exhibit *conditional convergence*: they appear to be converging to their own steady states, which in turn are determined by such variables as saving, population growth, and human capital.[2]

Factor Accumulation Versus Production Efficiency

As a matter of accounting, international differences in income per person can be attributed to either (1) differences in the factors of production, such as the quantities of physical and human capital, or (2) differences in the efficiency with which economies use their factors of production. That is, a worker in a poor country may be poor because he lacks tools and skills or because the tools and skills he has are not being put to their best use. To describe this issue in terms of the Solow model, the question is whether the large gap between rich and poor is explained by differences in capital accumulation (including human capital) or differences in the production function.

Much research has attempted to estimate the relative importance of these two sources of income disparities. The exact answer varies from study to study, but both factor accumulation and production efficiency appear important. Moreover, a common finding is that they are positively correlated: nations with high levels of physical and human capital also tend to use those factors efficiently.[3]

There are several ways to interpret this positive correlation. One hypothesis is that an efficient economy may encourage capital accumulation. For example, a person in a well-functioning economy may have greater resources and incentive to stay in school and accumulate human capital. Another hypothesis is that capital

[2] Robert Barro and Xavier Sala-i-Martin, "Convergence Across States and Regions," *Brookings Papers on Economic Activity* 1 (1991): 107–182; N. Gregory Mankiw, David Romer, and David N. Weil, "A Contribution to the Empirics of Economic Growth," *Quarterly Journal of Economics* (May 1992): 407–437.

[3] Robert E. Hall and Charles I. Jones, "Why Do Some Countries Produce So Much More Output per Worker Than Others?" *Quarterly Journal of Economics* 114 (February 1999): 83–116; Peter J. Klenow and Andres Rodriguez-Clare, "The Neoclassical Revival in Growth Economics: Has It Gone Too Far?" *NBER Macroeconomics Annual* (1997): 73–103.

accumulation may induce greater efficiency. If there are positive externalities to physical and human capital, then countries that save and invest more will appear to have better production functions (unless the research study accounts for these externalities, which is hard to do). Thus, greater production efficiency may cause greater factor accumulation, or the other way around.

A final hypothesis is that both factor accumulation and production efficiency are driven by a common third variable. Perhaps the common third variable is the quality of the nation's institutions, including the government's policymaking process. As one economist put it, when governments screw up, they screw up big time. Bad policies, such as high inflation, excessive budget deficits, widespread market interference, and rampant corruption, often go hand in hand. We should not be surprised that economies exhibiting these maladies both accumulate less capital and fail to use the capital they have as efficiently as they might.

CASE STUDY

Is Free Trade Good for Economic Growth?

At least since Adam Smith, economists have advocated free trade as a policy that promotes national prosperity. Here is how Smith put the argument in his 1776 classic, *The Wealth of Nations:*

> It is a maxim of every prudent master of a family, never to attempt to make at home what it will cost him more to make than to buy. The tailor does not attempt to make his own shoes, but buys them of the shoemaker. The shoemaker does not attempt to make his own clothes but employs a tailor. . . .
>
> What is prudence in the conduct of every private family can scarce be folly in that of a great kingdom. If a foreign country can supply us with a commodity cheaper than we ourselves can make it, better buy it of them with some part of the produce of our own industry employed in a way in which we have some advantage.

Today, economists make the case with greater rigor, relying on David Ricardo's theory of comparative advantage as well as more modern theories of international trade. According to these theories, a nation open to trade can achieve greater production efficiency and a higher standard of living by specializing in those goods for which it has a comparative advantage.

A skeptic might point out that this is just a theory. What about the evidence? Do nations that permit free trade in fact enjoy greater prosperity? A large body of literature addresses precisely this question.

One approach is to look at international data to see if countries that are open to trade typically enjoy greater prosperity. The evidence shows that they do. Economists Andrew Warner and Jeffrey Sachs studied this question for the period from 1970 to 1989. They report that among developed nations, the open economies grew at 2.3 percent per year, while the closed economies grew at 0.7 percent per year. Among developing nations, the open economies grew at 4.5 percent per year, while the closed economies again grew at 0.7 percent per year. These findings are consistent with Smith's view that trade enhances prosperity, but they are not conclusive. Correlation does not prove causation. Perhaps being closed to trade is correlated with various other restrictive government policies, and it is those other policies that retard growth.

A second approach is to look at what happens when closed economies remove their trade restrictions. Once again, Smith's hypothesis fares well. Throughout history, when nations open themselves up to the world economy, the typical result is a subsequent increase in economic growth. This occurred in Japan in the 1850s, South Korea in the 1960s, and Vietnam in the 1990s. But once again, correlation does not prove causation. Trade liberalization is often accompanied by other reforms, and it is hard to disentangle the effects of trade from the effects of the other reforms.

A third approach to measuring the impact of trade on growth, proposed by economists Jeffrey Frankel and David Romer, is to look at the impact of geography. Some countries trade less simply because they are geographically disadvantaged. For example, New Zealand is disadvantaged compared to Belgium because it is farther from other populous countries. Similarly, landlocked countries are disadvantaged compared to countries with their own seaports. Because these geographical characteristics are correlated with trade, but arguably uncorrelated with other determinants of economic prosperity, they can be used to identify the causal impact of trade on income. (The statistical technique, which you may have studied in an econometrics course, is called *instrumental variables*.) After analyzing the data, Frankel and Romer conclude that "a rise of one percentage point in the ratio of trade to GDP increases income per person by at least one-half percentage point. Trade appears to raise income by spurring the accumulation of human and physical capital and by increasing output for given levels of capital."

The overwhelming weight of the evidence from this body of research is that Adam Smith was right. Openness to international trade is good for economic growth.[4] ∎

8-3 Policies to Promote Growth

So far we have used the Solow model to uncover the theoretical relationships among the different sources of economic growth, and we have discussed some of the empirical work that describes actual growth experiences. We can now use the theory and evidence to help guide our thinking about economic policy.

Evaluating the Rate of Saving

According to the Solow growth model, how much a nation saves and invests is a key determinant of its citizens' standard of living. So let's begin our policy discussion with a natural question: is the rate of saving in the U.S. economy too low, too high, or about right?

---

[4] Jeffrey D. Sachs and Andrew Warner, "Economic Reform and the Process of Global Integration," *Brookings Papers on Economic Activity* (1995): 1–95; Jeffrey A. Frankel and David Romer, "Does Trade Cause Growth?" *American Economics Review* 89 (June 1999): 379–399.

As we have seen, the saving rate determines the steady-state levels of capital and output. One particular saving rate produces the Golden Rule steady state, which maximizes consumption per worker and thus economic well-being. The Golden Rule provides the benchmark against which we can compare the U.S. economy.

To decide whether the U.S. economy is at, above, or below the Golden Rule steady state, we need to compare the marginal product of capital net of depreciation ($MPK - \delta$) with the growth rate of total output ($n + g$). As we established in Section 8-1, at the Golden Rule steady state, $MPK - \delta = n + g$. If the economy is operating with less capital than in the Golden Rule steady state, then diminishing marginal product tells us that $MPK - \delta > n + g$. In this case, increasing the rate of saving will increase capital accumulation and economic growth and, eventually, lead to a steady state with higher consumption (although consumption will be lower for part of the transition to the new steady state). On the other hand, if the economy has more capital than in the Golden Rule steady state, then $MPK - \delta < n + g$. In this case, capital accumulation is excessive: reducing the rate of saving will lead to higher consumption both immediately and in the long run.

To make this comparison for a real economy, such as the U.S. economy, we need an estimate of the growth rate of output ($n + g$) and an estimate of the net marginal product of capital ($MPK - \delta$). Real GDP in the United States grows an average of 3 percent per year, so $n + g = 0.03$. We can estimate the net marginal product of capital from the following three facts:

1. The capital stock is about 2.5 times one year's GDP.

2. Depreciation of capital is about 10 percent of GDP.

3. Capital income is about 30 percent of GDP.

Using the notation of our model (and the result from Chapter 3 that capital owners earn income of MPK for each unit of capital), we can write these facts as

1. $k = 2.5y$.

2. $\delta k = 0.1y$.

3. $MPK \times k = 0.3y$.

We solve for the rate of depreciation δ by dividing equation 2 by equation 1:

$$\delta k / k = (0.1y)/(2.5y)$$

$$\delta = 0.04.$$

And we solve for the marginal product of capital MPK by dividing equation 3 by equation 1:

$$(MPK \times k)/k = (0.3y)/(2.5y)$$

$$MPK = 0.12.$$

Thus, about 4 percent of the capital stock depreciates each year, and the marginal product of capital is about 12 percent per year. The net marginal product of capital, $MPK - \delta$, is about 8 percent per year.

We can now see that the return to capital ($MPK - \delta = 8$ percent per year) is well in excess of the economy's average growth rate ($n + g = 3$ percent per year). This fact, together with our previous analysis, indicates that the capital stock in the U.S. economy is well below the Golden Rule level. In other words, if the United States saved and invested a higher fraction of its income, it would grow more rapidly and eventually reach a steady state with higher consumption.

This conclusion is not unique to the US economy. When calculations similar to those above are done for other economies, the results are similar. The possibility of excessive saving and capital accumulation beyond the Golden Rule level is intriguing as a matter of theory, but it appears not to be a problem that actual economies face. In practice, economists are more often concerned with insufficient saving. It is this kind of calculation that provides the intellectual foundation for this concern.[5]

Changing the Rate of Saving

The preceding calculations show that to move the U.S. economy toward the Golden Rule steady state, policymakers should increase national saving. But how can they do that? We saw in Chapter 3 that, as a matter of sheer accounting, higher national saving means higher public saving, higher private saving, or some combination of the two. Much of the debate over policies to increase growth centers on which of these options is likely to be most effective.

The most direct way in which the government affects national saving is through public saving—the difference between what the government receives in tax revenue and what it spends. When its spending exceeds its revenue, the government runs a *budget deficit*, which represents negative public saving. As we saw in Chapter 3, a budget deficit raises interest rates and crowds out investment; the resulting reduction in the capital stock is part of the burden of the national debt on future generations. Conversely, if it spends less than it raises in revenue, the government runs a *budget surplus*, which it can use to retire some of the national debt and stimulate investment.

The government also affects national saving by influencing private saving—the saving done by households and firms. In particular, how much people decide to save depends on the incentives they face, and these incentives are altered by a variety of public policies. Many economists argue that high tax rates on capital—including the corporate income tax, the federal income tax, the estate tax, and many state income and estate taxes—discourage private saving by reducing the rate of return that savers earn. On the other hand, tax-exempt retirement accounts, such as IRAs, are designed to encourage private saving by giving preferential treatment to income saved in these accounts. Some economists have proposed increasing the incentive to save by replacing the current system of income taxation with a system of consumption taxation.

[5] For more on this topic and some international evidence, see Andrew B. Abel, N. Gregory Mankiw, Lawrence H. Summers, and Richard J. Zeckhauser, "Assessing Dynamic Efficiency: Theory and Evidence," *Review of Economic Studies* 56 (1989): 1–19.

Many disagreements over public policy are rooted in different views about how much private saving responds to incentives. For example, suppose that the government were to increase the amount that people can put into tax-exempt retirement accounts. Would people respond to this incentive by saving more? Or, instead, would people merely transfer saving already done in other forms into these accounts—reducing tax revenue and thus public saving without any stimulus to private saving? The desirability of the policy depends on the answers to these questions. Unfortunately, despite much research on this issue, no consensus has emerged.

CASE STUDY

How to Get People to Save More

Many economists believe it would be desirable for Americans to increase the fraction of their income that they save. There are several reasons for this conclusion. From a microeconomic perspective, greater saving would mean that people would be better prepared for retirement; this goal is especially important because Social Security, the public program that provides retirement income, is projected to run into financial difficulties in the years ahead as the population ages. From a macroeconomic perspective, greater saving would increase the supply of loanable funds available to finance investment; the Solow growth model shows that increased capital accumulation leads to higher income. From an open-economy perspective, greater saving would mean that less domestic investment would be financed by capital flows from abroad; a smaller capital inflow pushes the trade balance from deficit toward surplus. Finally, in surveys, a majority of Americans say they are not saving enough; that fact may be sufficient reason to think that increased saving should be a national goal.

The difficult issue is how to get Americans to save more. The burgeoning field of behavioral economics, which infuses a bit of psychology into economics, offers some answers.

One approach is to make saving the path of least resistance. For example, consider 401(k) plans, the tax-advantaged retirement savings accounts available to many workers through their employers. In most firms, participation in the plan is an option that workers can choose by filling out a simple form. In some firms, however, workers are automatically enrolled in the plan but can opt out by filling out a simple form. Studies have shown that workers are far more likely to participate in the second case than in the first. If workers were rational maximizers, as is so often assumed in economic theory, they would choose the optimal amount of retirement saving, regardless of whether they had to choose to enroll or were enrolled automatically. In fact, workers' behavior appears to exhibit substantial inertia. Policymakers who want to increase saving can take advantage of this inertia by making automatic enrollment in these savings plans more common.

In 2009 President Obama attempted to do just that. According to legislation suggested in his first budget proposal, employers without retirement plans would be required to automatically enroll workers in direct-deposit retirement accounts. Employees would then be able to opt out of the system if they wished. Whether this proposal would become law was still unclear as this book was going to press.

A second approach to increasing saving is to give people the opportunity to control their desires for instant gratification. One intriguing possibility is the "Save More Tomorrow" program proposed by economist Richard Thaler. The essence of this program is that people commit in advance to putting a portion of their future salary increases into a retirement savings account. When a worker signs up, he or she makes no sacrifice of lower consumption today but, instead, commits to reducing consumption growth in the future. When this plan was implemented in several firms, it had a large impact. A high proportion (78 percent) of those offered the plan joined. In addition, of those enrolled, the vast majority (80 percent) stayed with the program through at least the fourth annual pay raise. The average saving rates for those in the program increased from 3.5 percent to 13.6 percent over the course of 40 months.

How successful would more widespread applications of these ideas be in increasing the U.S. national saving rate? It is impossible to say for sure. But given the importance of saving to both personal and national economic prosperity, many economists believe these proposals are worth a try.[6] ∎

Allocating the Economy's Investment

The Solow model makes the simplifying assumption that there is only one type of capital. In the world, of course, there are many types. Private businesses invest in traditional types of capital, such as bulldozers and steel plants, and newer types of capital, such as computers and robots. The government invests in various forms of public capital, called *infrastructure*, such as roads, bridges, and sewer systems.

In addition, there is *human capital*—the knowledge and skills that workers acquire through education, from early childhood programs such as Head Start to on-the-job training for adults in the labor force. Although the capital variable in the Solow model is usually interpreted as including only physical capital, in many ways human capital is analogous to physical capital. Like physical capital, human capital increases our ability to produce goods and services. Raising the level of human capital requires investment in the form of teachers, libraries, and student time. Recent research on economic growth has emphasized that human capital is at least as important as physical capital in explaining international differences in standards of living. One way of modeling this fact is to give the variable we call "capital" a broader definition that includes both human and physical capital.[7]

---

[6] James J. Choi, David I. Laibson, Brigitte Madrian, and Andrew Metrick, "Defined Contribution Pensions: Plan Rules, Participant Decisions, and the Path of Least Resistance," *Tax Policy and the Economy* 16 (2002): 67–113; Richard H. Thaler and Shlomo Benartzi, "Save More Tomorrow: Using Behavioral Economics to Increase Employee Saving," *Journal of Political Economy* 112 (2004): S164–S187.

[7] Earlier in this chapter, when we were interpreting K as only physical capital, human capital was folded into the efficiency-of-labor parameter E. The alternative approach suggested here is to include human capital as part of K instead, so E represents technology but not human capital. If K is given this broader interpretation, then much of what we call labor income is really the return to human capital. As a result, the true capital share is much larger than the traditional Cobb–Douglas value of about 1/3. For more on this topic, see N. Gregory Mankiw, David Romer, and David N. Weil, "A Contribution to the Empirics of Economic Growth," *Quarterly Journal of Economics* (May 1992): 407–437.

Policymakers trying to promote economic growth must confront the issue of what kinds of capital the economy needs most. In other words, what kinds of capital yield the highest marginal products? To a large extent, policymakers can rely on the economy's financial system to allocate the pool of saving to alternative types of investment. Those industries with the highest marginal products of capital will naturally be most willing to borrow at market interest rates to finance new investment. Many economists advocate that the government should merely create a "level playing field" for different types of capital—for example, by ensuring that the tax system treats all forms of capital equally. The government can then rely on financial markets, banks, and other financial institutions to allocate capital efficiently.

Other economists have suggested that the government should actively encourage particular forms of capital. Suppose, for instance, that technological advance occurs as a by-product of certain economic activities. This would happen if new and improved production processes were devised during the process of building capital (a phenomenon called *learning by doing*) and if these ideas became part of society's pool of knowledge. Such a by-product is called a *technological externality* (or a *knowledge spillover*). In the presence of such externalities, the social returns to capital exceed the private returns, and the benefits of increased capital accumulation to society are greater than the Solow model suggests.[8] Moreover, some types of capital accumulation may yield greater externalities than others. If, for example, installing robots yields greater technological externalities than building a new steel mill, then perhaps the government should use the tax laws to encourage investment in robots. The success of such an *industrial policy*, as it is sometimes called, requires that the government be able to accurately measure the externalities of different economic activities so it can give the correct incentive to each activity.

Most economists are skeptical about industrial policies for two reasons. First, measuring the externalities from different sectors is virtually impossible. If policy is based on poor measurements, its effects might be close to random and, thus, worse than no policy at all. Second, the political process is far from perfect. Once the government gets into the business of rewarding specific industries with subsidies and tax breaks, the rewards are as likely to be based on political clout as on the magnitude of externalities.

One type of capital that necessarily involves the government is public capital. Local, state, and federal governments are always deciding if and when they should borrow to finance new roads, bridges, and transit systems. In 2009, one of President Barack Obama's first acts was to sign a bill to increase spending on such infrastructure. This policy was motivated by a desire partly to increase short-run aggregate demand (a goal we will examine later in this book) and partly to provide public capital and enhance long-run economic growth. Among economists, this policy had both defenders and critics. Yet all of them agree that measuring the marginal product of public capital is difficult. Private capital generates an easily measured rate of profit for the firm owning the capital, whereas the benefits of

---

[8] Paul Romer, "Crazy Explanations for the Productivity Slowdown," *NBER Macroeconomics Annual* 2 (1987): 163–201.

public capital are more diffuse. Furthermore, while private capital investment is made by investors spending their own money, the allocation of resources for public capital involves the political process and taxpayer funding. It is all too common to see "bridges to nowhere" being built simply because the local senator or congressman has the political muscle to get funds approved.

Establishing the Right Institutions

As we discussed earlier, economists who study international differences in the standard of living attribute some of these differences to the inputs of physical and human capital and some to the productivity with which these inputs are used. One reason nations may have different levels of production efficiency is that they have different institutions guiding the allocation of scarce resources. Creating the right institutions is important for ensuring that resources are allocated to their best use.

A nation's legal tradition is an example of such an institution. Some countries, such as the United States, Australia, India, and Singapore, are former colonies of the United Kingdom and, therefore, have English-style common-law systems. Other nations, such as Italy, Spain, and most of those in Latin America, have legal traditions that evolved from the French Napoleonic Code. Studies have found that legal protections for shareholders and creditors are stronger in English-style than French-style legal systems. As a result, the English-style countries have better-developed capital markets. Nations with better-developed capital markets, in turn, experience more rapid growth because it is easier for small and start-up companies to finance investment projects, leading to a more efficient allocation of the nation's capital.[9]

Another important institutional difference across countries is the quality of government itself. Ideally, governments should provide a "helping hand" to the market system by protecting property rights, enforcing contracts, promoting competition, prosecuting fraud, and so on. Yet governments sometimes diverge from this ideal and act more like a "grabbing hand" by using the authority of the state to enrich a few powerful individuals at the expense of the broader community. Empirical studies have shown that the extent of corruption in a nation is indeed a significant determinant of economic growth.[10]

Adam Smith, the great eighteenth-century economist, was well aware of the role of institutions in economic growth. He once wrote, "Little else is requisite to carry a state to the highest degree of opulence from the lowest barbarism but peace, easy taxes, and a tolerable administration of justice: all the rest being brought about by the natural course of things." Sadly, many nations do not enjoy these three simple advantages.

---

[9] Rafael La Porta, Florencio Lopez-de-Silanes, Andrei Shleifer, and Robert Vishny, "Law and Finance," *Journal of Political Economy* 106 (1998): 1113–1155; Ross Levine and Robert G. King, "Finance and Growth: Schumpeter Might Be Right," *Quarterly Journal of Economics* 108 (1993): 717–737.

[10] Paulo Mauro, "Corruption and Growth," *Quarterly Journal of Economics* 110 (1995): 681–712.

The Colonial Origins of Modern Institutions

International data show a remarkable correlation between latitude and economic prosperity: nations closer to the equator typically have lower levels of income per person than nations farther from the equator. This fact is true in both the northern and southern hemispheres.

What explains the correlation? Some economists have suggested that the tropical climates near the equator have a direct negative impact on productivity. In the heat of the tropics, agriculture is more difficult, and disease is more prevalent. This makes the production of goods and services more difficult.

Although the direct impact of geography is one reason tropical nations tend to be poor, it is not the whole story. Research by Daron Acemoglu, Simon Johnson, and James Robinson has suggested an indirect mechanism—the impact of geography on institutions. Here is their explanation, presented in several steps:

1. In the seventeenth, eighteenth, and nineteenth centuries, tropical climates presented European settlers with an increased risk of disease, especially malaria and yellow fever. As a result, when Europeans were colonizing much of the rest of the world, they avoided settling in tropical areas, such as most of Africa and Central America. The European settlers preferred areas with more moderate climates and better health conditions, such as the regions that are now the United States, Canada, and New Zealand.

2. In those areas where Europeans settled in large numbers, the settlers established European-like institutions that protected individual property rights and limited the power of government. By contrast, in tropical climates, the colonial powers often set up "extractive" institutions, including authoritarian governments, so they could take advantage of the area's natural resources. These institutions enriched the colonizers, but they did little to foster economic growth.

3. Although the era of colonial rule is now long over, the early institutions that the European colonizers established are strongly correlated with the modern institutions in the former colonies. In tropical nations, where the colonial powers set up extractive institutions, there is typically less protection of property rights even today. When the colonizers left, the extractive institutions remained and were simply taken over by new ruling elites.

4. The quality of institutions is a key determinant of economic performance. Where property rights are well protected, people have more incentive to make the investments that lead to economic growth. Where property rights are less respected, as is typically the case in tropical nations, investment and growth tend to lag behind.

This research suggests that much of the international variation in living standards that we observe today is a result of the long reach of history.[11] ■

---

[11] Daron Acemoglu, Simon Johnson, and James A. Robinson, "The Colonial Origins of Comparative Development: An Empirical Investigation," *American Economic Association* 91 (December 2001): 1369–1401.

Encouraging Technological Progress

The Solow model shows that sustained growth in income per worker must come from technological progress. The Solow model, however, takes technological progress as exogenous; it does not explain it. Unfortunately, the determinants of technological progress are not well understood.

Despite this limited understanding, many public policies are designed to stimulate technological progress. Most of these policies encourage the private sector to devote resources to technological innovation. For example, the patent system gives a temporary monopoly to inventors of new products; the tax code offers tax breaks for firms engaging in research and development; and government agencies, such as the National Science Foundation, directly subsidize basic research in universities. In addition, as discussed above, proponents of industrial policy argue that the government should take a more active role in promoting specific industries that are key for rapid technological advance.

In recent years, the encouragement of technological progress has taken on an international dimension. Many of the companies that engage in research to advance technology are located in the United States and other developed nations. Developing nations such as China have an incentive to "free ride" on this research by not strictly enforcing intellectual property rights. That is, Chinese companies often use the ideas developed abroad without compensating the patent holders. The United States has strenuously objected to this practice, and China has promised to step up enforcement. If intellectual property rights were better enforced around the world, firms would have more incentive to engage in research, and this would promote worldwide technological progress.

CASE STUDY

The Worldwide Slowdown in Economic Growth: 1972–1995

Beginning in the early 1970s, and lasting until the mid 1990s, world policymakers faced a perplexing problem: a global slowdown in economic growth. Table 8-2 presents data on the growth in real GDP per person for the seven major economies. Growth in the United States fell from 2.2 percent before 1972 to 1.5 percent from 1972 to 1995. Other countries experienced similar or more severe declines. Accumulated over many years, even a small change in the rate of growth has a large effect on economic well-being. Real income in the United States today is almost 20 percent lower than it would have been had growth remained at its previous level.

Why did this slowdown occur? Studies have shown that it was attributable to a fall in the rate at which the production function was improving over time. (They establish this by constructing a measure called *total factor productivity*, which is closely related to the efficiency of labor in the Solow model.) There are many hypotheses to explain this fall in productivity growth. Here are four of them.

Measurement Problems One possibility is that the productivity slowdown did not really occur and that it shows up in the data because the data are flawed.

TABLE 8-2

Growth Around the World

Country	GROWTH IN OUTPUT PER PERSON (PERCENT PER YEAR)		
	1948–1972	1972–1995	1995–2008
Canada	2.9	1.8	2.0
France	4.3	1.6	1.6
West Germany	5.7	2.0	
Germany			1.5
Italy	4.9	2.3	1.0
Japan	8.2	2.6	1.1
United Kingdom	2.4	1.8	2.3
United States	2.2	1.5	1.9

Sources: Angus Maddison, *Phases of Capitalist Development* (Oxford: Oxford University Press, 1982); *OECD National Accounts*; and *World Bank: World Development Indicators.*

As you may recall from Chapter 2, one problem in measuring inflation is correcting for changes in the quality of goods and services. The same issue arises when measuring output and productivity. For instance, if technological advance leads to *more* computers being built, then the increase in output and productivity is easy to measure. But if technological advance leads to *faster* computers being built, then output and productivity have increased, but that increase is more subtle and harder to measure. Government statisticians try to correct for changes in quality, but despite their best efforts, the resulting data are far from perfect.

Unmeasured quality improvements mean that our standard of living is rising more rapidly than the official data indicate. This issue should make us suspicious of the data, but by itself it cannot explain the productivity slowdown. To explain a *slowdown* in growth, one must argue that the measurement problems got *worse*. There is some indication that this might be so. As history passes, fewer people work in industries with tangible and easily measured output, such as agriculture, and more work in industries with intangible and less easily measured output, such as medical services. Yet few economists believe that measurement problems were the full story.

Oil Prices When the productivity slowdown began around 1973, the obvious hypothesis to explain it was the large increase in oil prices caused by the actions of the OPEC oil cartel. The primary piece of evidence was the timing: productivity growth slowed at the same time that oil prices skyrocketed. Over time, however, this explanation has appeared less likely. One reason is that the accumulated shortfall in productivity seems too large to be explained by an increase in oil prices; petroleum-based products are not that large a fraction of a typical firm's costs. In addition, if this explanation were right, productivity should have sped up when political turmoil in OPEC caused oil prices to plummet in 1986. Unfortunately, that did not happen.

Worker Quality Some economists suggest that the productivity slowdown might have been caused by changes in the labor force. In the early 1970s, the large baby-boom generation started leaving school and taking jobs. At the same time, changing social norms encouraged many women to leave full-time housework and enter the labor force. Both of these developments lowered the average level of experience among workers, which in turn lowered average productivity.

Other economists point to changes in worker quality as gauged by human capital. Although the educational attainment of the labor force continued to rise throughout this period, it was not increasing as rapidly as it had in the past. Moreover, declining performance on some standardized tests suggests that the quality of education was declining. If so, this could explain slowing productivity growth.

The Depletion of Ideas Still other economists suggest that in the early 1970s the world started to run out of new ideas about how to produce, pushing the economy into an age of slower technological progress. These economists often argue that the anomaly is not the period since 1970 but the preceding two decades. In the late 1940s, the economy had a large backlog of ideas that had not been fully implemented because of the Great Depression of the 1930s and World War II in the first half of the 1940s. After the economy used up this backlog, the argument goes, a slowdown in productivity growth was likely. Indeed, although the growth rates in the 1970s, 1980s, and early 1990s were disappointing compared to those of the 1950s and 1960s, they were not lower than average growth rates from 1870 to 1950.

As any good doctor will tell you, sometimes a patient's illness goes away on its own, even if the doctor has failed to come up with a convincing diagnosis and remedy. This seems to be the outcome of the productivity slowdown. In the middle of the 1990s, economic growth picked up significantly in the United States and the United Kingdom. As with the slowdown in economic growth in the 1970s, the acceleration in the 1990s is hard to explain definitively. But at least part of the credit goes to advances in computer and information technology, including the Internet.[12] ∎

8-4 Beyond the Solow Model: Endogenous Growth Theory

A chemist, a physicist, and an economist are all trapped on a desert island, trying to figure out how to open a can of food.

"Let's heat the can over the fire until it explodes," says the chemist.

"No, no," says the physicist, "let's drop the can onto the rocks from the top of a high tree."

"I have an idea," says the economist. "First, we assume a can opener . . ."

---

[12] For various views on the growth slowdown, see "Symposium: The Slowdown in Productivity Growth" in the Fall 1988 issue of *The Journal of Economic Perspectives*. For a discussion of the subsequent growth acceleration and the role of information technology, see "Symposium: Computers and Productivity" in the Fall 2000 issue of *The Journal of Economic Perspectives*.

This old joke takes aim at how economists use assumptions to simplify—and sometimes oversimplify—the problems they face. It is particularly apt when evaluating the theory of economic growth. One goal of growth theory is to explain the persistent rise in living standards that we observe in most parts of the world. The Solow growth model shows that such persistent growth must come from technological progress. But where does technological progress come from? In the Solow model, it is just assumed!

The preceding case study on the productivity slowdown of the 1970s and speed-up of the 1990s suggests that changes in the pace of technological progress are tremendously important. To fully understand the process of economic growth, we need to go beyond the Solow model and develop models that explain technological advance. Models that do this often go by the label **endogenous growth theory** because they reject the Solow model's assumption of exogenous technological change. Although the field of endogenous growth theory is large and sometimes complex, here we get a quick taste of this modern research.[13]

The Basic Model

To illustrate the idea behind endogenous growth theory, let's start with a particularly simple production function:

$$Y = AK,$$

where Y is output, K is the capital stock, and A is a constant measuring the amount of output produced for each unit of capital. Notice that this production function does not exhibit the property of diminishing returns to capital. One extra unit of capital produces A extra units of output, regardless of how much capital there is. This absence of diminishing returns to capital is the key difference between this endogenous growth model and the Solow model.

Now let's see what this production function says about economic growth. As before, we assume a fraction s of income is saved and invested. We therefore describe capital accumulation with an equation similar to those we used previously:

$$\Delta K = sY - \delta K.$$

This equation states that the change in the capital stock (ΔK) equals investment (sY) minus depreciation (δK). Combining this equation with the $Y = AK$ production function, we obtain, after a bit of manipulation,

$$\Delta Y/Y = \Delta K/K = sA - \delta.$$

---

[13] This section provides a brief introduction to the large and fascinating literature on endogenous growth theory. Early and important contributions to this literature include Paul M. Romer, "Increasing Returns and Long-Run Growth," *Journal of Political Economy* 94 (October 1986): 1002–1037; and Robert E. Lucas, Jr., "On the Mechanics of Economic Development," *Journal of Monetary Economics* 22 (1988): 3–42. The reader can learn more about this topic in the undergraduate textbook by David N. Weil: *Economic Growth,* 2nd ed. (Pearson, 2008).

This equation shows what determines the growth rate of output $\Delta Y/Y$. Notice that, as long as $sA > \delta$, the economy's income grows forever, even without the assumption of exogenous technological progress.

Thus, a simple change in the production function can dramatically alter the predictions about economic growth. In the Solow model, saving temporarily leads to growth, but diminishing returns to capital eventually force the economy to approach a steady state in which growth depends only on exogenous technological progress. By contrast, in this endogenous growth model, saving and investment can lead to persistent growth.

But is it reasonable to abandon the assumption of diminishing returns to capital? The answer depends on how we interpret the variable K in the production function $Y = AK$. If we take the traditional view that K includes only the economy's stock of plants and equipment, then it is natural to assume diminishing returns. Giving ten computers to a worker does not make that worker ten times as productive as he or she is with one computer.

Advocates of endogenous growth theory, however, argue that the assumption of constant (rather than diminishing) returns to capital is more palatable if K is interpreted more broadly. Perhaps the best case can be made for the endogenous growth model by viewing knowledge as a type of capital. Clearly, knowledge is an important input into the economy's production—both its production of goods and services and its production of new knowledge. Compared to other forms of capital, however, it is less natural to assume that knowledge exhibits the property of diminishing returns. (Indeed, the increasing pace of scientific and technological innovation over the past few centuries has led some economists to argue that there are increasing returns to knowledge.) If we accept the view that knowledge is a type of capital, then this endogenous growth model with its assumption of constant returns to capital becomes a more plausible description of long-run economic growth.

A Two-Sector Model

Although the $Y = AK$ model is the simplest example of endogenous growth, the theory has gone well beyond this. One line of research has tried to develop models with more than one sector of production in order to offer a better description of the forces that govern technological progress. To see what we might learn from such models, let's sketch out an example.

The economy has two sectors, which we can call manufacturing firms and research universities. Firms produce goods and services, which are used for consumption and investment in physical capital. Universities produce a factor of production called "knowledge," which is then freely used in both sectors. The economy is described by the production function for firms, the production function for universities, and the capital-accumulation equation:

$$Y = F[K, (1 - u)LE] \quad \text{(production function in manufacturing firms),}$$

$$\Delta E = g(u)E \quad \text{(production function in research universities),}$$

$$\Delta K = sY - \delta K \quad \text{(capital accumulation),}$$

where u is the fraction of the labor force in universities (and $1 - u$ is the fraction in manufacturing), E is the stock of knowledge (which in turn determines the efficiency of labor), and g is a function that shows how the growth in knowledge depends on the fraction of the labor force in universities. The rest of the notation is standard. As usual, the production function for the manufacturing firms is assumed to have constant returns to scale: if we double both the amount of physical capital (K) and the effective number of workers in manufacturing $[(1 - u)LE]$, we double the output of goods and services (Y).

This model is a cousin of the $Y = AK$ model. Most important, this economy exhibits constant (rather than diminishing) returns to capital, as long as capital is broadly defined to include knowledge. In particular, if we double both physical capital K and knowledge E, then we double the output of both sectors in the economy. As a result, like the $Y = AK$ model, this model can generate persistent growth without the assumption of exogenous shifts in the production function. Here persistent growth arises endogenously because the creation of knowledge in universities never slows down.

At the same time, however, this model is also a cousin of the Solow growth model. If u, the fraction of the labor force in universities, is held constant, then the efficiency of labor E grows at the constant rate $g(u)$. This result of constant growth in the efficiency of labor at rate g is precisely the assumption made in the Solow model with technological progress. Moreover, the rest of the model—the manufacturing production function and the capital-accumulation equation—also resembles the rest of the Solow model. As a result, for any given value of u, this endogenous growth model works just like the Solow model.

There are two key decision variables in this model. As in the Solow model, the fraction of output used for saving and investment, s, determines the steady-state stock of physical capital. In addition, the fraction of labor in universities, u, determines the growth in the stock of knowledge. Both s and u affect the level of income, although only u affects the steady-state growth rate of income. Thus, this model of endogenous growth takes a small step in the direction of showing which societal decisions determine the rate of technological change.

The Microeconomics of Research and Development

The two-sector endogenous growth model just presented takes us closer to understanding technological progress, but it still tells only a rudimentary story about the creation of knowledge. If one thinks about the process of research and development for even a moment, three facts become apparent. First, although knowledge is largely a public good (that is, a good freely available to everyone), much research is done in firms that are driven by the profit motive. Second, research is profitable because innovations give firms temporary monopolies, either because of the patent system or because there is an advantage to being the first firm on the market with a new product. Third, when one firm innovates, other firms build on that innovation to produce the next generation of innovations. These (essentially microeconomic) facts are not easily connected with the (essentially macroeconomic) growth models we have discussed so far.

Some endogenous growth models try to incorporate these facts about research and development. Doing this requires modeling both the decisions that firms face as they engage in research and the interactions among firms that have some degree of monopoly power over their innovations. Going into more detail about these models is beyond the scope of this book, but it should be clear already that one virtue of these endogenous growth models is that they offer a more complete description of the process of technological innovation.

One question these models are designed to address is whether, from the standpoint of society as a whole, private profit-maximizing firms tend to engage in too little or too much research. In other words, is the social return to research (which is what society cares about) greater or smaller than the private return (which is what motivates individual firms)? It turns out that, as a theoretical matter, there are effects in both directions. On the one hand, when a firm creates a new technology, it makes other firms better off by giving them a base of knowledge on which to build in future research. As Isaac Newton famously remarked, "If I have seen farther than others, it is because I was standing on the shoulders of giants." On the other hand, when one firm invests in research, it can also make other firms worse off if it does little more than being the first to discover a technology that another firm would have invented in due course. This duplication of research effort has been called the "stepping on toes" effect. Whether firms left to their own devices do too little or too much research depends on whether the positive "standing on shoulders" externality or the negative "stepping on toes" externality is more prevalent.

Although theory alone is ambiguous about whether research effort is more or less than optimal, the empirical work in this area is usually less so. Many studies have suggested the "standing on shoulders" externality is important and, as a result, the social return to research is large—often in excess of 40 percent per year. This is an impressive rate of return, especially when compared to the return to physical capital, which we earlier estimated to be about 8 percent per year. In the judgment of some economists, this finding justifies substantial government subsidies to research.[14]

The Process of Creative Destruction

In his 1942 book *Capitalism, Socialism, and Democracy*, economist Joseph Schumpeter suggested that economic progress comes through a process of "creative destruction." According to Schumpeter, the driving force behind progress is the entrepreneur with an idea for a new product, a new way to produce an old product, or some other innovation. When the entrepreneur's firm enters the market, it has some degree of monopoly power over its innovation; indeed, it is the prospect of monopoly profits that motivates the entrepreneur. The entry of the new firm is good for consumers, who now have an expanded range of choices,

---

[14] For an overview of the empirical literature on the effects of research, see Zvi Griliches, "The Search for R&D Spillovers," *Scandinavian Journal of Economics* 94 (1991): 29–47.

but it is often bad for incumbent producers, who may find it hard to compete with the entrant. If the new product is sufficiently better than old ones, the incumbents may even be driven out of business. Over time, the process keeps renewing itself. The entrepreneur's firm becomes an incumbent, enjoying high profitability until its product is displaced by another entrepreneur with the next generation of innovation.

History confirms Schumpeter's thesis that there are winners and losers from technological progress. For example, in England in the early nineteenth century, an important innovation was the invention and spread of machines that could produce textiles using unskilled workers at low cost. This technological advance was good for consumers, who could clothe themselves more cheaply. Yet skilled knitters in England saw their jobs threatened by new technology, and they responded by organizing violent revolts. The rioting workers, called Luddites, smashed the weaving machines used in the wool and cotton mills and set the homes of the mill owners on fire (a less than creative form of destruction). Today, the term "Luddite" refers to anyone who opposes technological progress.

A more recent example of creative destruction involves the retailing giant Wal-Mart. Although retailing may seem like a relatively static activity, in fact it is a sector that has seen sizable rates of technological progress over the past several decades. Through better inventory-control, marketing, and personnel-management techniques, for example, Wal-Mart has found ways to bring goods to consumers at lower cost than traditional retailers. These changes benefit consumers, who can buy goods at lower prices, and the stockholders of Wal-Mart, who share in its profitability. But they adversely affect small mom-and-pop stores, which find it hard to compete when a Wal-Mart opens nearby.

Faced with the prospect of being the victims of creative destruction, incumbent producers often look to the political process to stop the entry of new, more efficient competitors. The original Luddites wanted the British government to save their jobs by restricting the spread of the new textile technology; instead, Parliament sent troops to suppress the Luddite riots. Similarly, in recent years, local retailers have sometimes tried to use local land-use regulations to stop Wal-Mart from entering their market. The cost of such entry restrictions, however, is a slower pace of technological progress. In Europe, where entry regulations are stricter than they are in the United States, the economies have not seen the emergence of retailing giants like Wal-Mart; as a result, productivity growth in retailing has been much lower.[15]

Schumpeter's vision of how capitalist economies work has merit as a matter of economic history. Moreover, it has inspired some recent work in the theory of economic growth. One line of endogenous growth theory, pioneered by economists Philippe Aghion and Peter Howitt, builds on Schumpeter's insights by modeling technological advance as a process of entrepreneurial innovation and creative destruction.[16]

---

[15] Robert J. Gordon, "Why Was Europe Left at the Station When America's Productivity Locomotive Departed?" *NBER Working Paper* No. 10661, 2004.

[16] Philippe Aghion and Peter Howitt, "A Model of Growth Through Creative Destruction," *Econometrica* 60 (1992): 323–351.

8-5 Conclusion

Long-run economic growth is the single most important determinant of the economic well-being of a nation's citizens. Everything else that macroeconomists study—unemployment, inflation, trade deficits, and so on—pales in comparison.

Fortunately, economists know quite a lot about the forces that govern economic growth. The Solow growth model and the more recent endogenous growth models show how saving, population growth, and technological progress interact in determining the level and growth of a nation's standard of living. These theories offer no magic recipe to ensure that an economy achieves rapid growth, but they give much insight, and they provide the intellectual framework for much of the debate over public policy aimed at promoting long-run economic growth.

Summary

1. In the steady state of the Solow growth model, the growth rate of income per person is determined solely by the exogenous rate of technological progress.

2. Many empirical studies have examined to what extent the Solow model can help explain long-run economic growth. The model can explain much of what we see in the data, such as balanced growth and conditional convergence. Recent studies have also found that international variation in standards of living is attributable to a combination of capital accumulation and the efficiency with which capital is used.

3. In the Solow model with population growth and technological progress, the Golden Rule (consumption-maximizing) steady state is characterized by equality between the net marginal product of capital ($MPK - \delta$) and the steady-state growth rate of total income ($n + g$). In the U.S. economy, the net marginal product of capital is well in excess of the growth rate, indicating that the U.S. economy has a lower saving rate and less capital than it would have in the Golden Rule steady state.

4. Policymakers in the United States and other countries often claim that their nations should devote a larger percentage of their output to saving and investment. Increased public saving and tax incentives for private saving are two ways to encourage capital accumulation. Policymakers can also promote economic growth by setting up the appropriate legal and financial institutions that allow resources to be allocated efficiently and by ensuring proper incentives to encourage research and technological progress.

5. In the early 1970s, the rate of growth of income per person fell substantially in most industrialized countries, including the United States. The cause of this slowdown is not well understood. In the mid-1990s, the U.S. growth rate increased, most likely because of advances in information technology.

6. Modern theories of endogenous growth attempt to explain the rate of technological progress, which the Solow model takes as exogenous. These models try to explain the decisions that determine the creation of knowledge through research and development.

KEY CONCEPTS

Efficiency of labor

Labor-augmenting technological progress

Endogenous growth theory

QUESTIONS FOR REVIEW

1. In the Solow model, what determines the steady-state rate of growth of income per worker?

2. In the steady state of the Solow model, at what rate does output per person grow? At what rate does capital per person grow? How does this compare with the U.S. experience?

3. What data would you need to determine whether an economy has more or less capital than in the Golden Rule steady state?

4. How can policymakers influence a nation's saving rate?

5. What has happened to the rate of productivity growth over the past 50 years? How might you explain this phenomenon?

6. How does endogenous growth theory explain persistent growth without the assumption of exogenous technological progress? How does this differ from the Solow model?

PROBLEMS AND APPLICATIONS

1. An economy described by the Solow growth model has the following production function:

$$y = \sqrt{k}.$$

a. Solve for the steady-state value of y as a function of s, n, g, and δ.

b. A developed country has a saving rate of 28 percent and a population growth rate of 1 percent per year. A less developed country has a saving rate of 10 percent and a population growth rate of 4 percent per year. In both countries, $g = 0.02$ and $\delta = 0.04$. Find the steady-state value of y for each country.

c. What policies might the less developed country pursue to raise its level of income?

2. In the United States, the capital share of GDP is about 30 percent, the average growth in output is about 3 percent per year, the depreciation rate is about 4 percent per year, and the capital–output ratio is about 2.5. Suppose that the production function is Cobb–Douglas, so that the capital share in output is constant, and that the United States has been in a steady state. (For a discussion of the Cobb–Douglas production function, see Chapter 3.)

a. What must the saving rate be in the initial steady state? [*Hint:* Use the steady-state relationship, $sy = (\delta + n + g)k$.]

b. What is the marginal product of capital in the initial steady state?

c. Suppose that public policy raises the saving rate so that the economy reaches the Golden Rule level of capital. What will the marginal product of capital be at the Golden Rule steady state? Compare the marginal product at the Golden Rule steady state to the marginal product in the initial steady state. Explain.

d. What will the capital–output ratio be at the Golden Rule steady state? (*Hint:* For the Cobb–Douglas production function, the capital–output ratio is related to the marginal product of capital.)

e. What must the saving rate be to reach the Golden Rule steady state?

3. Prove each of the following statements about the steady state of the Solow model with population growth and technological progress:

a. The capital–output ratio is constant.

b. Capital and labor each earn a constant share of an economy's income. [*Hint:* Recall the definition $MPK = f(k + 1) - f(k)$.]

c. Total capital income and total labor income both grow at the rate of population growth plus the rate of technological progress, $n + g$.

d. The real rental price of capital is constant, and the real wage grows at the rate of technological progress g. (*Hint:* The real rental price of capital equals total capital income divided by the capital stock, and the real wage equals total labor income divided by the labor force.)

4. Two countries, Richland and Poorland, are described by the Solow growth model. They have the same Cobb–Douglas production function, $F(K, L) = A\, K^{\alpha} L^{1-\alpha}$, but with different quantities of capital and labor. Richland saves 32 percent of its income, while Poorland saves 10 percent. Richland has population growth of 1 percent per year, while Poorland has population growth of 3 percent. (The numbers in this problem are chosen to be approximately realistic descriptions of rich and poor nations.) Both nations have technological progress at a rate of 2 percent per year and depreciation at a rate of 5 percent per year.

a. What is the per-worker production function $f(k)$?

b. Solve for the ratio of Richland's steady-state income per worker to Poorland's. (*Hint:* The parameter α will play a role in your answer.)

c. If the Cobb–Douglas parameter α takes the conventional value of about 1/3, how much higher should income per worker be in Richland compared to Poorland?

d. Income per worker in Richland is actually 16 times income per worker in Poorland. Can you explain this fact by changing the value of the parameter α? What must it be? Can you think of any way of justifying such a value for this parameter? How else might you explain the large difference in income between Richland and Poorland?

5. The amount of education the typical person receives varies substantially among countries. Suppose you were to compare a country with a highly educated labor force and a country with a less educated labor force. Assume that education affects only the level of the efficiency of labor. Also assume that the countries are otherwise the same: they have the same saving rate, the same depreciation rate, the same population growth rate, and the same rate of technological progress. Both countries are described by the Solow model and are in their steady states. What would you predict for the following variables?

a. The rate of growth of total income

b. The level of income per worker

c. The real rental price of capital

d. The real wage

6. This question asks you to analyze in more detail the two-sector endogenous growth model presented in the text.

a. Rewrite the production function for manufactured goods in terms of output per effective worker and capital per effective worker.

b. In this economy, what is break-even investment (the amount of investment needed to keep capital per effective worker constant)?

c. Write the equation of motion for k, which shows Δk as saving minus break–even investment. Use this equation to draw a graph showing the determination of steady-state k. (*Hint:* This graph will look much like those we used to analyze the Solow model.)

d. In this economy, what is the steady-state growth rate of output per worker Y/L? How do the saving rate s and the fraction of the labor force in universities u affect this steady-state growth rate?

e. Using your graph, show the impact of an increase in u. (*Hint:* This change affects both curves.) Describe both the immediate and the steady-state effects.

f. Based on your analysis, is an increase in u an unambiguously good thing for the economy? Explain.

PART IV

Business Cycle Theory: The Economy in the Short Run

CHAPTER 9

Introduction to Economic Fluctuations

The modern world regards business cycles much as the ancient Egyptians regarded the overflowing of the Nile. The phenomenon recurs at intervals, it is of great importance to everyone, and natural causes of it are not in sight.

—John Bates Clark, 1898

Economic fluctuations present a recurring problem for economists and policymakers. On average, the real GDP of the United States grows between 3 and 3.5 percent per year. But this long-run average hides the fact that the economy's output of goods and services does not grow smoothly. Growth is higher in some years than in others; sometimes the economy loses ground, and growth turns negative. These fluctuations in the economy's output are closely associated with fluctuations in employment. When the economy experiences a period of falling output and rising unemployment, the economy is said to be in *recession*.

A recent recession began in late 2007. From the third quarter of 2007 to the third quarter of 2008, the economy's production of goods and services was approximately flat, in contrast to its normal growth. Real GDP then plunged sharply in the fourth quarter of 2008 and first quarter of 2009. The unemployment rate rose from 4.7 percent in November 2007 to 10.1 percent in October 2009. Not surprisingly, the recession, along with financial crisis that led up to it, dominated the economic news of the time. Addressing the problem was high on the agenda of President Barack Obama during his first year in office.

Economists call these short-run fluctuations in output and employment the *business cycle*. Although this term suggests that economic fluctuations are regular and predictable, they are not. Recessions are actually as irregular as they are common. Sometimes they occur close together, while at other times they are much farther apart. For example, the United States fell into recession in 1982, only two years after the previous downturn. By the end of that year, the unemployment rate had reached 10.8 percent—the highest level since the Great Depression of the 1930s. But after the 1982 recession, it was eight years before the economy experienced another one.

These historical events raise a variety of related questions: What causes short-run fluctuations? What model should we use to explain them? Can policymakers avoid recessions? If so, what policy levers should they use?

In Parts Two and Three of this book, we developed theories to explain how the economy behaves in the long run. Here, in Part Four, we see how economists explain short-run fluctuations. We begin in this chapter with three tasks. First, we examine the data that describe short-run economic fluctuations. Second, we discuss the key differences between how the economy behaves in the long run and how it behaves in the short run. Third, we introduce the model of aggregate supply and aggregate demand, which most economists use to explain short-run fluctuations. Developing this model in more detail will be our primary job in the chapters that follow.

Just as Egypt now controls the flooding of the Nile Valley with the Aswan Dam, modern society tries to control the business cycle with appropriate economic policies. The model we develop over the next several chapters shows how monetary and fiscal policies influence the business cycle. We will see how these policies can potentially stabilize the economy or, if poorly conducted, make the problem of economic instability even worse.

9-1 The Facts About the Business Cycle

Before thinking about the theory of business cycles, let's look at some of the facts that describe short-run fluctuations in economic activity.

GDP and Its Components

The economy's gross domestic product measures total income and total expenditure in the economy. Because GDP is the broadest gauge of overall economic conditions, it is the natural place to start in analyzing the business cycle. Figure 9-1 shows the growth of real GDP from 1970 to 2009. The horizontal line shows the average growth rate of 3 percent per year over this period. You can see that economic growth is not at all steady and that, occasionally, it turns negative.

The shaded areas in the figure indicate periods of recession. The official arbiter of when recessions begin and end is the National Bureau of Economic Research, a nonprofit economic research group. The NBER's Business Cycle Dating Committee chooses the starting date of each recession, called the business cycle *peak*, and the ending date, called the business cycle *trough*.

What determines whether a downturn in the economy is sufficiently severe to be deemed a recession? There is no simple answer. According to an old rule of thumb, a recession is a period of at least two consecutive quarters of declining real GDP. This rule, however, does not always hold. In the most recently revised data, for example, the recession of 2001 had two quarters of negative growth, but those quarters were not consecutive. In fact, the NBER's Business Cycle Dating

FIGURE 9-1

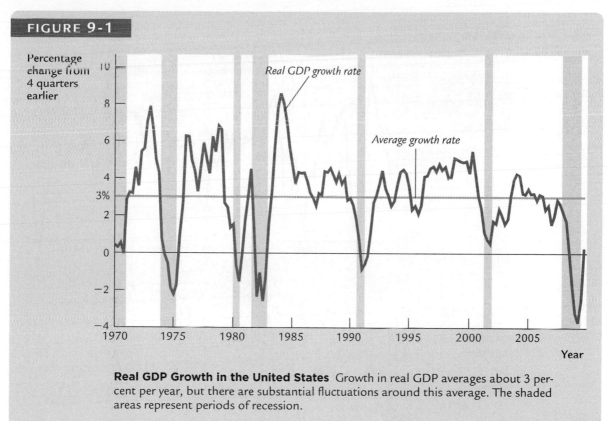

Real GDP Growth in the United States Growth in real GDP averages about 3 percent per year, but there are substantial fluctuations around this average. The shaded
areas represent periods of recession.

Source: U.S. Department of Commerce.

Committee does not follow any fixed rule but, instead, looks at a variety of economic time series and uses its judgment when picking the starting and ending
dates of recessions. As this book was going to press, the economy appeared to be
coming out of the recession of 2008–2009, although the precise ending date was
still to be determined.[1]

Figure 9-2 shows the growth in two major components of GDP—consumption
in panel (a) and investment in panel (b). Growth in both of these variables declines
during recessions. Take note, however, of the scales for the vertical axes. Investment is far more volatile than consumption over the business cycle. When the
economy heads into a recession, households respond to the fall in their incomes
by consuming less, but the decline in spending on business equipment, structures,
new housing, and inventories is even more substantial.

---

[1] Note that Figure 9-1 plots growth in real GDP from four quarters earlier, rather than from the
immediately preceding quarter. During the 2001 recession, this measure declined but never turned
negative.

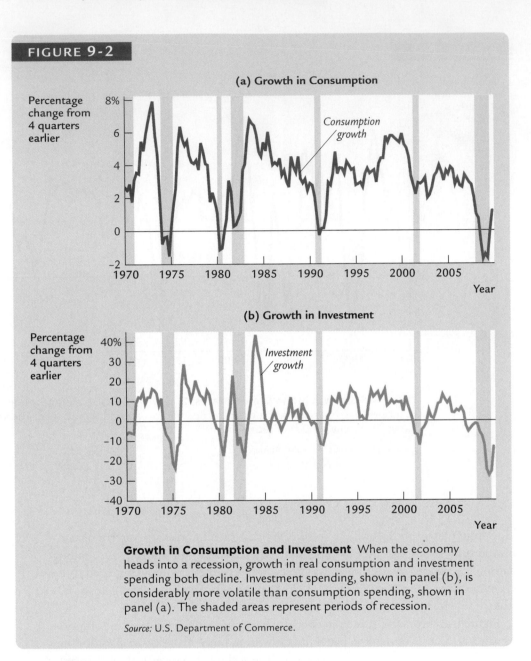

FIGURE 9-2

(a) Growth in Consumption

(b) Growth in Investment

Growth in Consumption and Investment When the economy heads into a recession, growth in real consumption and investment spending both decline. Investment spending, shown in panel (b), is considerably more volatile than consumption spending, shown in panel (a). The shaded areas represent periods of recession.

Source: U.S. Department of Commerce.

Unemployment and Okun's Law

The business cycle is apparent not only in data from the national income accounts but also in data that describe conditions in the labor market. Figure 9-3 shows the unemployment rate from 1970 to 2009, again with the shaded areas representing periods of recession. You can see that unemployment rises in each recession. Other labor-market measures tell a similar story. For example, job vacancies, as measured by the number of help-wanted ads in newspapers, decline during recessions. Put simply, during an economic downturn, jobs are harder to find.

FIGURE 9-3

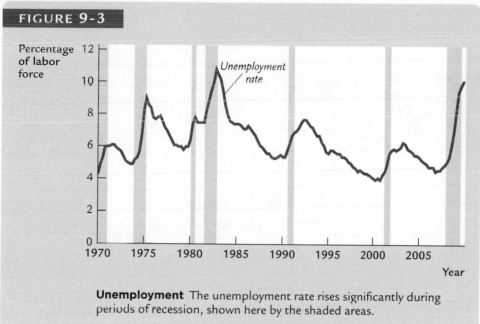

Unemployment The unemployment rate rises significantly during periods of recession, shown here by the shaded areas.

Source: U.S. Department of Labor.

What relationship should we expect to find between unemployment and real GDP? Because employed workers help to produce goods and services and unemployed workers do not, increases in the unemployment rate should be associated with decreases in real GDP. This negative relationship between unemployment and GDP is called **Okun's law**, after Arthur Okun, the economist who first studied it.[2]

Figure 9-4 uses annual data for the United States to illustrate Okun's law. In this scatterplot, each point represents the data for one year. The horizontal axis represents the change in the unemployment rate from the previous year, and the vertical axis represents the percentage change in GDP. This figure shows clearly that year-to-year changes in the unemployment rate are closely associated with year-to-year changes in real GDP.

We can be more precise about the magnitude of the Okun's law relationship. The line drawn through the scatter of points tells us that

Percentage Change in Real GDP

= 3% − 2 × Change in Unemployment Rate.

If the unemployment rate remains the same, real GDP grows by about 3 percent; this normal growth in the production of goods and services is due to growth in

[2] Arthur M. Okun, "Potential GNP: Its Measurement and Significance," in *Proceedings of the Business and Economics Statistics Section, American Statistical Association* (Washington, D.C.: American Statistical Association, 1962): 98–103; reprinted in Arthur M. Okun, *Economics for Policymaking* (Cambridge, MA: MIT Press, 1983), 145–158.

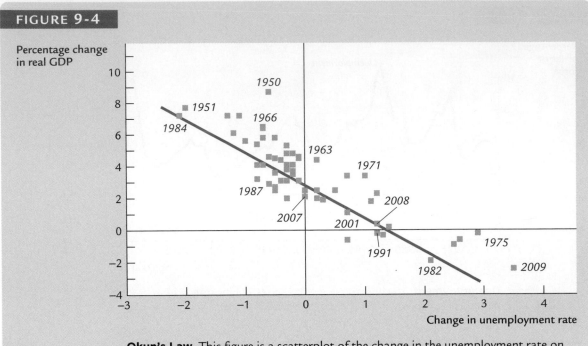

FIGURE 9-4

Okun's Law This figure is a scatterplot of the change in the unemployment rate on the horizontal axis and the percentage change in real GDP on the vertical axis, using data on the U.S economy. Each point represents one year. The negative correlation between these variables shows that increases in unemployment tend to be associated with lower-than-normal growth in real GDP.

Sources: U.S. Department of Commerce, U.S. Department of Labor.

the labor force, capital accumulation, and technological progress. In addition, for every percentage point the unemployment rate rises, real GDP growth typically falls by 2 percent. Hence, if the unemployment rate rises from 5 to 7 percent, then real GDP growth would be

$$\text{Percentage Change in Real GDP} = 3\% - 2 \times (7\% - 5\%)$$

$$= -1\%.$$

In this case, Okun's law says that GDP would fall by 1 percent, indicating that the economy is in a recession.

Okun's law is a reminder that the forces that govern the short-run business cycle are very different from those that shape long-run economic growth. As we saw in Chapters 7 and 8, long-run growth in GDP is determined primarily by technological progress. The long-run trend leading to higher standards of living from generation to generation is not associated with any long-run trend in the rate of unemployment. By contrast, short-run movements in GDP are highly correlated with the utilization of the economy's labor force. The declines in the production of goods and services that occur during recessions are always associated with increases in joblessness.

Leading Economic Indicators

Many economists, particularly those working in business and government, are engaged in the task of forecasting short-run fluctuations in the economy. Business economists are interested in forecasting to help their companies plan for changes in the economic environment. Government economists are interested in forecasting for two reasons. First, the economic environment affects the government; for example, the state of the economy influences how much tax revenue the government collects. Second, the government can affect the economy through its use of monetary and fiscal policy. Economic forecasts are, therefore, an input into policy planning.

One way that economists arrive at their forecasts is by looking at **leading indicators**, which are variables that tend to fluctuate in advance of the overall economy. Forecasts can differ in part because economists hold varying opinions about which leading indicators are most reliable.

Each month the Conference Board, a private economics research group, announces the *index of leading economic indicators*. This index includes ten data series that are often used to forecast changes in economic activity about six to nine months into the future. Here is a list of the series.

- *Average workweek of production workers in manufacturing.* Because businesses often adjust the work hours of existing employees before making new hires or laying off workers, average weekly hours is a leading indicator of employment changes. A longer workweek indicates that firms are asking their employees to work long hours because they are experiencing strong demand for their products; thus, it indicates that firms are likely to increase hiring and production in the future. A shorter workweek indicates weak demand, suggesting that firms are more likely to lay off workers and cut back production.

- *Average initial weekly claims for unemployment insurance.* The number of people making new claims on the unemployment-insurance system is one of the most quickly available indicators of conditions in the labor market. This series is inverted in computing the index of leading indicators, so that an increase in the series lowers the index. An increase in the number of people making new claims for unemployment insurance indicates that firms are laying off workers and cutting back production, which will soon show up in data on employment and production.

- *New orders for consumer goods and materials, adjusted for inflation.* This is a very direct measure of the demand that firms are experiencing. Because an increase in orders depletes a firm's inventories, this statistic typically predicts subsequent increases in production and employment.

- *New orders for nondefense capital goods.* This series is the counterpart to the previous one, but for investment goods rather than consumer goods.

- *Index of supplier deliveries.* This variable, sometimes called vendor performance, is a measure of the number of companies receiving slower deliveries from suppliers. Vendor performance is a leading indicator because deliveries slow down when companies are experiencing increased

Drawing M. Stevens; © 1980 The New Yorker Magazine, Inc.

"Well, so long Eddie, the recession's over."

demand for their products. Slower deliveries therefore indicate a future increase in economic activity.

■ *New building permits issued.* Construction of new buildings is part of investment—a particularly volatile component of GDP. An increase in building permits means that planned construction is increasing, which indicates a rise in overall economic activity.

■ *Index of stock prices.* The stock market reflects expectations about future economic conditions because stock market investors bid up prices when they expect companies to be profitable. An increase in stock prices indicates that investors expect the economy to grow rapidly; a decrease in stock prices indicates that investors expect an economic slowdown.

■ *Money supply (M2), adjusted for inflation.* Because the money supply is related to total spending, more money predicts increased spending, which in turn means higher production and employment.

■ *Interest rate spread: the yield spread between 10-year Treasury notes and 3-month Treasury bills.* This spread, sometimes called the slope of the yield curve, reflects the market's expectation about future interest rates, which in turn reflect the condition of the economy. A large spread means that interest rates are expected to rise, which typically occurs when economic activity increases.

■ *Index of consumer expectations.* This is a direct measure of expectations, based on a survey conducted by the University of Michigan's Survey Research Center. Increased optimism about future economic conditions among consumers suggests increased consumer demand for goods and services, which in turn will encourage businesses to expand production and employment to meet the demand.

The index of leading indicators is far from a precise predictor of the future, but it is one input into planning by both businesses and the government.

9-2 Time Horizons in Macroeconomics

Now that we have some sense about the facts that describe short-run economic fluctuations, we can turn to our basic task in this part of the book: building a theory to explain these fluctuations. That job, it turns out, is not a simple one. It will take us not only the rest of this chapter but also the next three chapters to develop the model of short-run fluctuations in its entirety.

Before we start building the model, however, let's step back and ask a fundamental question: Why do economists need different models for different time horizons? Why can't we stop the course here and be content with the classical models developed in Chapters 3 through 8? The answer, as this book has consistently reminded its reader, is that classical macroeconomic theory applies to the long run but not to the short run. But why is this so?

How the Short Run and Long Run Differ

Most macroeconomists believe that the key difference between the short run and the long run is the behavior of prices. *In the long run, prices are flexible and can respond to changes in supply or demand. In the short run, many prices are "sticky" at some predetermined level.* Because prices behave differently in the short run than in the long run, various economic events and policies have different effects over different time horizons.

To see how the short run and the long run differ, consider the effects of a change in monetary policy. Suppose that the Federal Reserve suddenly reduces the money supply by 5 percent. According to the classical model, the money supply affects nominal variables—variables measured in terms of money—but not real variables. As you may recall from Chapter 4, the theoretical separation of real and nominal variables is called the *classical dichotomy*, and the irrelevance of the money supply for the determination of real variables is called *monetary neutrality*. Most economists believe that these classical ideas describe how the economy works in the long run: a 5 percent reduction in the money supply lowers all prices (including nominal wages) by 5 percent while output, employment, and other real variables remain the same. Thus, in the long run, changes in the money supply do not cause fluctuations in output and employment.

In the short run, however, many prices do not respond to changes in monetary policy. A reduction in the money supply does not immediately cause all firms to cut the wages they pay, all stores to change the price tags on their goods, all mail-order firms to issue new catalogs, and all restaurants to print new menus. Instead, there is little immediate change in many prices; that is, many prices are sticky. This short-run price stickiness implies that the short run impact of a change in the money supply is not the same as the long-run impact.

A model of economic fluctuations must take into account this short-run price stickiness. We will see that the failure of prices to adjust quickly and completely to changes in the money supply (as well as to other exogenous changes in economic conditions) means that, in the short run, real variables such as output and employment must do some of the adjusting instead. In other words, during the time horizon over which prices are sticky, the classical dichotomy no longer holds: nominal variables can influence real variables, and the economy can deviate from the equilibrium predicted by the classical model.

CASE STUDY

If You Want to Know Why Firms Have Sticky Prices, Ask Them

How sticky are prices, and why are they sticky? In an intriguing study, economist Alan Blinder attacked these questions directly by surveying firms about their price-adjustment decisions.

Blinder began by asking firm managers how often they changed prices. The answers, summarized in Table 9-1, yielded two conclusions. First, sticky prices are common. The typical firm in the economy adjusts its prices once or twice a year. Second, there are large differences among firms in the frequency of price adjustment. About 10 percent of firms changed prices more often than once a week, and about the same number changed prices less often than once a year.

Blinder then asked the firm managers why they didn't change prices more often. In particular, he explained to the managers several economic theories of sticky prices and asked them to judge how well each of these theories described their firms. Table 9-2 summarizes the theories and ranks them by the percentage of managers who accepted the theory as an accurate description of their firms' pricing decisions. Notice that each of the theories was endorsed by some of the managers, but each was rejected by a large number as well. One interpretation is that different theories apply to different firms, depending on industry characteristics, and that price stickiness is a macroeconomic phenomenon without a single microeconomic explanation.

Among the dozen theories, coordination failure tops the list. According to Blinder, this is an important finding, because it suggests that the inability of firms to coordinate price changes plays a key role in explaining price stickiness and,

---

TABLE 9-1

The Frequency of Price Adjustment

This table is based on answers to the question: How often do the prices of your most important products change in a typical year?

Frequency	Percentage of Firms
Less than once	10.2
Once	39.3
1.01 to 2	15.6
2.01 to 4	12.9
4.01 to 12	7.5
12.01 to 52	4.3
52.01 to 365	8.6
More than 365	1.6

Source: Table 4.1, Alan S. Blinder, "On Sticky Prices: Academic Theories Meet the Real World," in N. G. Mankiw, ed., *Monetary Policy* (Chicago: University of Chicago Press, 1994), 117–154.

TABLE 9-2

Theories of Price Stickiness

Theory and Brief Description	Percentage of Managers Who Accepted Theory
Coordination failure: Firms hold back on price changes, waiting for others to go first	60.6
Cost-based pricing with lags: Price increases are delayed until costs rise	55.5
Delivery lags, service, etc.: Firms prefer to vary other product attributes, such as delivery lags, service, or product quality	54.8
Implicit contracts: Firms tacitly agree to stabilize prices, perhaps out of "fairness" to customers	50.4
Nominal contracts: Prices are fixed by explicit contracts	35.7
Costs of price adjustment: Firms incur costs of changing prices	30.0
Procyclical elasticity: Demand curves become less elastic as they shift in	29.7
Pricing points: Certain prices (like $9.99) have special psychological significance	24.0
Inventories: Firms vary inventory stocks instead of prices	20.9
Constant marginal cost: Marginal cost is flat and markups are constant	19.7
Hierarchical delays: Bureaucratic delays slow down decisions	13.6
Judging quality by price: Firms fear customers will mistake price cuts for reductions in quality	10.0

Source: Tables 4.3 and 4.4, Alan S. Blinder, "On Sticky Prices: Academic Theories Meet the Real World," in N. G. Mankiw, ed., *Monetary Policy* (Chicago: University of Chicago Press, 1994), 117–154.

thus, short-run economic fluctuations. He writes, "The most obvious policy implication of the model is that more coordinated wage and price setting—somehow achieved—could improve welfare. But if this proves difficult or impossible, the door is opened to activist monetary policy to cure recessions."[3] ∎

---

[3] To read more about this study, see Alan S. Blinder, "On Sticky Prices: Academic Theories Meet the Real World," in N. G. Mankiw, ed., *Monetary Policy* (Chicago: University of Chicago Press, 1994), 117–154; or Alan S. Blinder, Elie R. D. Canetti, David E. Lebow, and Jeremy E. Rudd, *Asking About Prices: A New Approach to Understanding Price Stickiness* (New York: Russell Sage Foundation, 1998).

The Model of Aggregate Supply and Aggregate Demand

How does the introduction of sticky prices change our view of how the economy works? We can answer this question by considering economists' two favorite words—supply and demand.

In classical macroeconomic theory, the amount of output depends on the economy's ability to *supply* goods and services, which in turn depends on the supplies of capital and labor and on the available production technology. This is the essence of the basic classical model in Chapter 3, as well as of the Solow growth model in Chapters 7 and 8. Flexible prices are a crucial assumption of classical theory. The theory posits, sometimes implicitly, that prices adjust to ensure that the quantity of output demanded equals the quantity supplied.

The economy works quite differently when prices are sticky. In this case, as we will see, output also depends on the economy's *demand* for goods and services. Demand, in turn, depends on a variety of factors: consumers' confidence about their economic prospects, firms' perceptions about the profitability of new investments, and monetary and fiscal policy. Because monetary and fiscal policy can influence demand, and demand in turn can influence the economy's output over the time horizon when prices are sticky, price stickiness provides a rationale for why these policies may be useful in stabilizing the economy in the short run.

In the rest of this chapter, we begin developing a model that makes these ideas more precise. The place to start is the model of supply and demand, which we used in Chapter 1 to discuss the market for pizza. This basic model offers some of the most fundamental insights in economics. It shows how the supply and demand for any good jointly determine the good's price and the quantity sold, as well as how shifts in supply and demand affect the price and quantity. We now introduce the "economy-size" version of this model—*the model of aggregate supply and aggregate demand*. This macroeconomic model allows us to study how the aggregate price level and the quantity of aggregate output are determined in the short run. It also provides a way to contrast how the economy behaves in the long run and how it behaves in the short run.

Although the model of aggregate supply and aggregate demand resembles the model of supply and demand for a single good, the analogy is not exact. The model of supply and demand for a single good considers only one good within a large economy. By contrast, as we will see in the coming chapters, the model of aggregate supply and aggregate demand is a sophisticated model that incorporates the interactions among many markets. In the remainder of this chapter we get a first glimpse at those interactions by examining the model in its most simplified form. Our goal here is not to explain the model fully but, instead, to introduce its key elements and illustrate how it can help explain short-run economic fluctuations.

9-3 Aggregate Demand

Aggregate demand (*AD*) is the relationship between the quantity of output demanded and the aggregate price level. In other words, the aggregate demand curve tells us the quantity of goods and services people want to buy at any given level of prices. We examine the theory of aggregate demand in detail in Chapters 10 and 11. Here we use the quantity theory of money to provide a simple, although incomplete, derivation of the aggregate demand curve.

The Quantity Equation as Aggregate Demand

Recall from Chapter 4 that the quantity theory says that

$$MV = PY,$$

where M is the money supply, V is the velocity of money, P is the price level, and Y is the amount of output. If the velocity of money is constant, then this equation states that the money supply determines the nominal value of output, which in turn is the product of the price level and the amount of output.

When interpreting this equation, it is useful to recall that the quantity equation can be rewritten in terms of the supply and demand for real money balances:

$$M/P = (M/P)^{\mathrm{d}} = kY,$$

where $k = 1/V$ is a parameter representing how much money people want to hold for every dollar of income. In this form, the quantity equation states that the supply of real money balances M/P equals the demand for real money balances $(M/P)^{\mathrm{d}}$ and that the demand is proportional to output Y. The velocity of money V is the "flip side" of the money demand parameter k. The assumption of constant velocity is equivalent to the assumption of a constant demand for real money balances per unit of output.

If we assume that velocity V is constant and the money supply M is fixed by the central bank, then the quantity equation yields a negative relationship between the price level P and output Y. Figure 9-5 graphs the combinations of P and Y that satisfy the quantity equation holding M and V constant. This downward-sloping curve is called the aggregate demand curve.

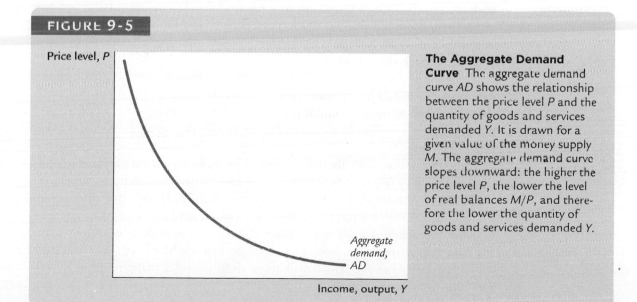

FIGURE 9-5

Price level, P

Aggregate demand, AD

Income, output, Y

The Aggregate Demand Curve The aggregate demand curve AD shows the relationship between the price level P and the quantity of goods and services demanded Y. It is drawn for a given value of the money supply M. The aggregate demand curve slopes downward: the higher the price level P, the lower the level of real balances M/P, and therefore the lower the quantity of goods and services demanded Y.

Why the Aggregate Demand Curve Slopes Downward

As a strictly mathematical matter, the quantity equation explains the downward slope of the aggregate demand curve very simply. The money supply M and the velocity of money V determine the nominal value of output PY. Once PY is fixed, if P goes up, Y must go down.

What is the economic intuition that lies behind this mathematical relationship? For a complete explanation of the downward slope of the aggregate demand curve, we have to wait for a couple of chapters. For now, however, consider the following logic: Because we have assumed the velocity of money is fixed, the money supply determines the dollar value of all transactions in the economy. (This conclusion should be familiar from Chapter 4.) If the price level rises, each transaction requires more dollars, so the number of transactions and thus the quantity of goods and services purchased must fall.

We can also explain the downward slope of the aggregate demand curve by thinking about the supply and demand for real money balances. If output is higher, people engage in more transactions and need higher real balances M/P. For a fixed money supply M, higher real balances imply a lower price level. Conversely, if the price level is lower, real money balances are higher; the higher level of real balances allows a greater volume of transactions, which means a greater quantity of output is demanded.

Shifts in the Aggregate Demand Curve

The aggregate demand curve is drawn for a fixed value of the money supply. In other words, it tells us the possible combinations of P and Y for a given value of M. If the Fed changes the money supply, then the possible combinations of P and Y change, which means the aggregate demand curve shifts.

For example, consider what happens if the Fed reduces the money supply. The quantity equation, $MV = PY$, tells us that the reduction in the money supply leads to a proportionate reduction in the nominal value of output PY. For any given price level, the amount of output is lower, and for any given amount of output, the price level is lower. As in Figure 9-6(a), the aggregate demand curve relating P and Y shifts inward.

The opposite occurs if the Fed increases the money supply. The quantity equation tells us that an increase in M leads to an increase in PY. For any given price level, the amount of output is higher, and for any given amount of output, the price level is higher. As shown in Figure 9-6(b), the aggregate demand curve shifts outward.

Although the quantity theory of money provides a very simple basis for understanding the aggregate demand curve, be forewarned that reality is more complicated. Fluctuations in the money supply are not the only source of fluctuations in aggregate demand. Even if the money supply is held constant, the aggregate demand curve shifts if some event causes a change in the velocity of money. Over the next two chapters, we develop a more general model of aggregate demand, called the *IS–LM model*, which will allow us to consider many possible reasons for shifts in the aggregate demand curve.

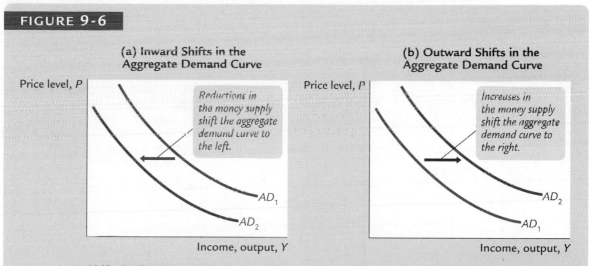

FIGURE 9-6

(a) Inward Shifts in the Aggregate Demand Curve

Price level, P

Reductions in the money supply shift the aggregate demand curve to the left.

AD_1

AD_2

Income, output, Y

(b) Outward Shifts in the Aggregate Demand Curve

Price level, P

Increases in the money supply shift the aggregate demand curve to the right.

AD_2

AD_1

Income, output, Y

Shifts in the Aggregate Demand Curve Changes in the money supply shift the aggregate demand curve. In panel (a), a decrease in the money supply M reduces the nominal value of output PY. For any given price level P, output Y is lower. Thus, a decrease in the money supply shifts the aggregate demand curve inward from AD_1 to AD_2. In panel (b), an increase in the money supply M raises the nominal value of output PY. For any given price level P, output Y is higher. Thus, an increase in the money supply shifts the aggregate demand curve outward from AD_1 to AD_2.

9-4 Aggregate Supply

By itself, the aggregate demand curve does not tell us the price level or the amount of output that will prevail in the economy; it merely gives a relationship between these two variables. To accompany the aggregate demand curve, we need another relationship between P and Y that crosses the aggregate demand curve—an aggregate supply curve. The aggregate demand and aggregate supply curves together pin down the economy's price level and quantity of output.

Aggregate supply (*AS*) is the relationship between the quantity of goods and services supplied and the price level. Because the firms that supply goods and services have flexible prices in the long run but sticky prices in the short run, the aggregate supply relationship depends on the time horizon. We need to discuss two different aggregate supply curves: the long-run aggregate supply curve *LRAS* and the short-run aggregate supply curve *SRAS*. We also need to discuss how the economy makes the transition from the short run to the long run.

The Long Run: The Vertical Aggregate Supply Curve

Because the classical model describes how the economy behaves in the long run, we derive the long-run aggregate supply curve from the classical model. Recall from Chapter 3 that the amount of output produced depends on the

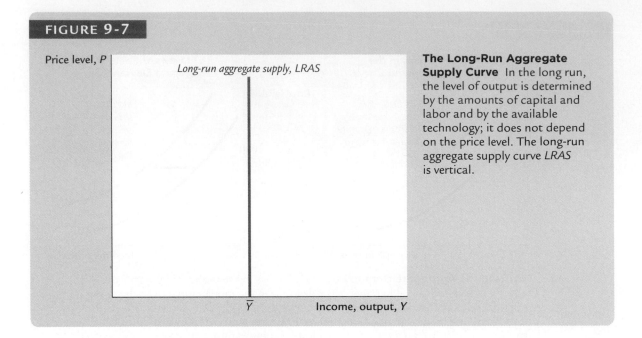

FIGURE 9-7

Price level, *P*

Long-run aggregate supply, LRAS

$\overline{Y}$ Income, output, *Y*

The Long-Run Aggregate Supply Curve In the long run, the level of output is determined by the amounts of capital and labor and by the available technology; it does not depend on the price level. The long-run aggregate supply curve *LRAS* is vertical.

fixed amounts of capital and labor and on the available technology. To show this, we write

$$Y = F(\overline{K}, \overline{L})$$
$$= \overline{Y}.$$

According to the classical model, output does not depend on the price level. To show that output is fixed at this level, regardless of the price level, we draw a vertical aggregate supply curve, as in Figure 9-7. In the long run, the intersection of the aggregate demand curve with this vertical aggregate supply curve determines the price level.

If the aggregate supply curve is vertical, then changes in aggregate demand affect prices but not output. For example, if the money supply falls, the aggregate demand curve shifts downward, as in Figure 9-8. The economy moves from the old intersection of aggregate supply and aggregate demand, point A, to the new intersection, point B. The shift in aggregate demand affects only prices.

The vertical aggregate supply curve satisfies the classical dichotomy, because it implies that the level of output is independent of the money supply. This long-run level of output, $\overline{Y}$, is called the *full-employment*, or *natural*, level of output. It is the level of output at which the economy's resources are fully employed or, more realistically, at which unemployment is at its natural rate.

The Short Run: The Horizontal Aggregate Supply Curve

The classical model and the vertical aggregate supply curve apply only in the long run. In the short run, some prices are sticky and, therefore, do not adjust to

FIGURE 9-8

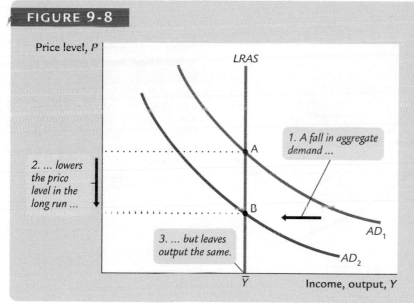

Shifts in Aggregate Demand in the Long Run A reduction in the money supply shifts the aggregate demand curve downward from AD_1 to AD_2. The equilibrium for the economy moves from point A to point B. Because the aggregate supply curve is vertical in the long run, the reduction in aggregate demand affects the price level but not the level of output.

changes in demand. Because of this price stickiness, the short-run aggregate supply curve is not vertical.

In this chapter, we will simplify things by assuming an extreme example. Suppose that all firms have issued price catalogs and that it is too costly for them to issue new ones. Thus, all prices are stuck at predetermined levels. At these prices, firms are willing to sell as much as their customers are willing to buy, and they hire just enough labor to produce the amount demanded. Because the price level is fixed, we represent this situation in Figure 9-9 with a horizontal aggregate supply curve.

The short-run equilibrium of the economy is the intersection of the aggregate demand curve and this horizontal short-run aggregate supply curve. In this case, changes in aggregate demand do affect the level of output. For example, if the Fed

FIGURE 9-9

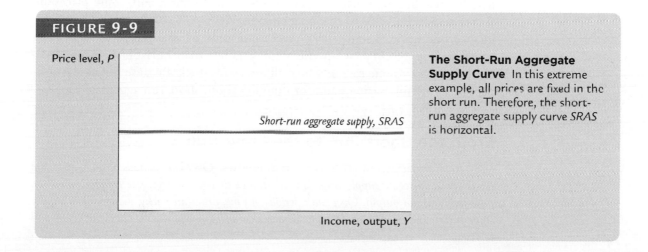

The Short-Run Aggregate Supply Curve In this extreme example, all prices are fixed in the short run. Therefore, the short-run aggregate supply curve SRAS is horizontal.

FIGURE 9-10

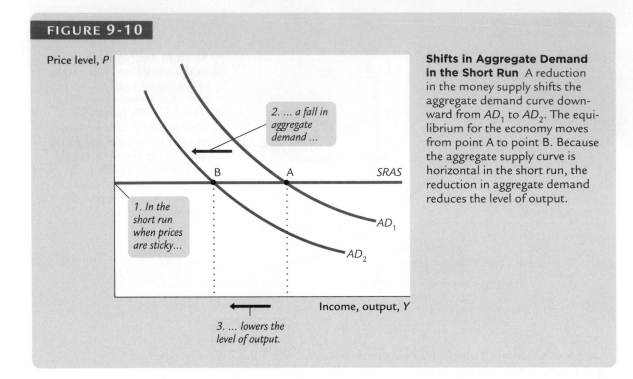

Shifts in Aggregate Demand in the Short Run A reduction in the money supply shifts the aggregate demand curve downward from AD_1 to AD_2. The equilibrium for the economy moves from point A to point B. Because the aggregate supply curve is horizontal in the short run, the reduction in aggregate demand reduces the level of output.

suddenly reduces the money supply, the aggregate demand curve shifts inward, as in Figure 9-10. The economy moves from the old intersection of aggregate demand and aggregate supply, point A, to the new intersection, point B. The movement from point A to point B represents a decline in output at a fixed price level.

Thus, a fall in aggregate demand reduces output in the short run because prices do not adjust instantly. After the sudden fall in aggregate demand, firms are stuck with prices that are too high. With demand low and prices high, firms sell less of their product, so they reduce production and lay off workers. The economy experiences a recession.

Once again, be forewarned that reality is a bit more complicated than illustrated here. Although many prices are sticky in the short run, some prices are able to respond quickly to changing circumstances. As we will see in Chapter 12, in an economy with some sticky prices and some flexible prices, the short-run aggregate supply curve is upward sloping rather than horizontal. Figure 9-10 illustrates the extreme case in which all prices are stuck. Because this case is simpler, it is a useful starting point for thinking about short-run aggregate supply.

From the Short Run to the Long Run

We can summarize our analysis so far as follows: *Over long periods of time, prices are flexible, the aggregate supply curve is vertical, and changes in aggregate demand affect the price level but not output. Over short periods of time, prices are sticky, the aggregate supply curve is flat, and changes in aggregate demand do affect the economy's output of goods and services.*

FIGURE 9-11

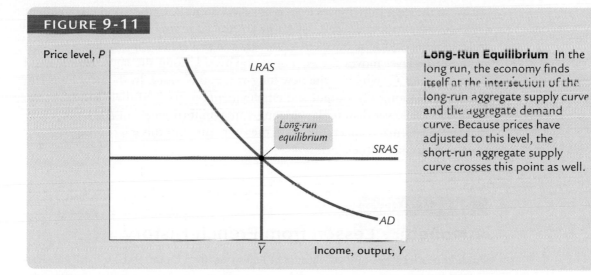

Price level, *P*

LRAS

Long-run equilibrium

SRAS

AD

$\overline{Y}$

Income, output, *Y*

Long-Run Equilibrium In the long run, the economy finds itself at the intersection of the long-run aggregate supply curve and the aggregate demand curve. Because prices have adjusted to this level, the short-run aggregate supply curve crosses this point as well.

How does the economy make the transition from the short run to the long run? Let's trace the effects over time of a fall in aggregate demand. Suppose that the economy is initially in long-run equilibrium, as shown in Figure 9-11. In this figure, there are three curves: the aggregate demand curve, the long-run aggregate supply curve, and the short-run aggregate supply curve. The long-run equilibrium is the point at which aggregate demand crosses the long-run aggregate supply curve. Prices have adjusted to reach this equilibrium. Therefore, when the economy is in its long-run equilibrium, the short-run aggregate supply curve must cross this point as well.

Now suppose that the Fed reduces the money supply and the aggregate demand curve shifts downward, as in Figure 9-12. In the short run, prices are

FIGURE 9-12

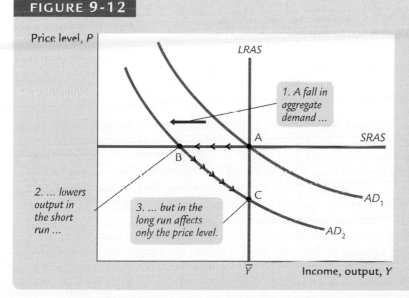

Price level, *P*

LRAS

1. A fall in aggregate demand …

A

SRAS

B

2. … lowers output in the short run …

C

3. … but in the long run affects only the price level.

AD_1

AD_2

$\overline{Y}$

Income, output, *Y*

A Reduction in Aggregate Demand The economy begins in long-run equilibrium at point A. A reduction in aggregate demand, perhaps caused by a decrease in the money supply, moves the economy from point A to point B, where output is below its natural level. As prices fall, the economy gradually recovers from the recession, moving from point B to point C.

sticky, so the economy moves from point A to point B. Output and employment fall below their natural levels, which means the economy is in a recession. Over time, in response to the low demand, wages and prices fall. The gradual reduction in the price level moves the economy downward along the aggregate demand curve to point C, which is the new long-run equilibrium. In the new long-run equilibrium (point C), output and employment are back to their natural levels, but prices are lower than in the old long-run equilibrium (point A). Thus, a shift in aggregate demand affects output in the short run, but this effect dissipates over time as firms adjust their prices.

CASE STUDY

A Monetary Lesson from French History

Finding modern examples to illustrate the lessons from Figure 9-12 is hard. Modern central banks are too smart to engineer a substantial reduction in the money supply for no good reason. They know that a recession would ensue, and they usually do their best to prevent that from happening. Fortunately, history often fills in the gap when recent experience fails to produce the right experiment.

A vivid example of the effects of monetary contraction occurred in eighteenth-century France. François Velde, an economist at the Federal Reserve Bank of Chicago, recently studied this episode in French economic history.

The story begins with the unusual nature of French money at the time. The money stock in this economy included a variety of gold and silver coins that, in contrast to modern money, did not indicate a specific monetary value. Instead, the monetary value of each coin was set by government decree, and the government could easily change the monetary value and thus the money supply. Sometimes this would occur literally overnight. It is almost as if, while you were sleeping, every $1 bill in your wallet was replaced by a bill worth only 80 cents.

Indeed, that is what happened on September 22, 1724. Every person in France woke up with 20 percent less money than he or she had the night before. Over the course of seven months of that year, the nominal value of the money stock was reduced by about 45 percent. The goal of these changes was to reduce prices in the economy to what the government considered an appropriate level.

What happened as a result of this policy? Velde reports the following consequences:

> Although prices and wages did fall, they did not do so by the full 45 percent; moreover, it took them months, if not years, to fall that far. Real wages in fact rose, at least initially. Interest rates rose. The only market that adjusted instantaneously and fully was the foreign exchange market. Even markets that were as close to fully competitive as one can imagine, such as grain markets, failed to react initially. . . .
>
> At the same time, the industrial sector of the economy (or at any rate the textile industry) went into a severe contraction, by about 30 percent. The onset of the recession may have occurred before the deflationary policy began, but it was widely believed at the time that the severity of the contraction was due to monetary policy, in particular to a resulting "credit crunch" as holders of money stopped providing credit to trade in anticipation of further price declines (the

"scarcity of money" frequently blamed by observers). Likewise, it was widely believed (on the basis of past experience) that a policy of inflation would halt the recession, and coincidentally or not, the economy rebounded once the nominal money supply was increased by 20 percent in May 1726.

This description of events from French history fits well with the lessons from modern macroeconomic theory.[4] ∎

9-5 Stabilization Policy

Fluctuations in the economy as a whole come from changes in aggregate supply or aggregate demand. Economists call exogenous events that shift these curves **shocks** to the economy. A shock that shifts the aggregate demand curve is called a **demand shock**, and a shock that shifts the aggregate supply curve is called a **supply shock**. These shocks disrupt the economy by pushing output and employment away from their natural levels. One goal of the model of aggregate supply and aggregate demand is to show how shocks cause economic fluctuations.

Another goal of the model is to evaluate how macroeconomic policy can respond to these shocks. Economists use the term **stabilization policy** to refer to policy actions aimed at reducing the severity of short-run economic fluctuations. Because output and employment fluctuate around their long-run natural levels, stabilization policy dampens the business cycle by keeping output and employment as close to their natural levels as possible.

In the coming chapters, we examine in detail how stabilization policy works and what practical problems arise in its use. Here we begin our analysis of stabilization policy using our simplified version of the model of aggregate demand and aggregate supply. In particular, we examine how monetary policy might respond to shocks. Monetary policy is an important component of stabilization policy because, as we have seen, the money supply has a powerful impact on aggregate demand.

Shocks to Aggregate Demand

Consider an example of a demand shock: the introduction and expanded availability of credit cards. Because credit cards are often a more convenient way to make purchases than using cash, they reduce the quantity of money that people choose to hold. This reduction in money demand is equivalent to an increase in the velocity of money. When each person holds less money, the money demand parameter k falls. This means that each dollar of money moves from hand to hand more quickly, so velocity $V (= 1/k)$ rises.

If the money supply is held constant, the increase in velocity causes nominal spending to rise and the aggregate demand curve to shift outward, as in Figure 9-13. In the short run, the increase in demand raises the output of the economy—it

---

[4] François R. Velde, "Chronicles of a Deflation Unforetold," Federal Reserve Bank of Chicago, November 2006.

FIGURE 9-13

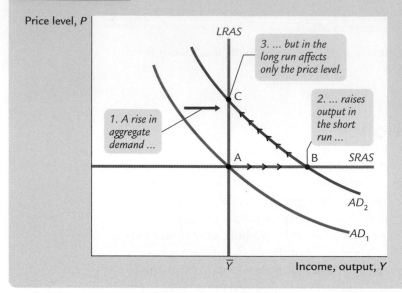

An Increase in Aggregate Demand The economy begins in long-run equilibrium at point A. An increase in aggregate demand, perhaps due to an increase in the velocity of money, moves the economy from point A to point B, where output is above its natural level. As prices rise, output gradually returns to its natural level, and the economy moves from point B to point C.

causes an economic boom. At the old prices, firms now sell more output. Therefore, they hire more workers, ask their existing workers to work longer hours, and make greater use of their factories and equipment.

Over time, the high level of aggregate demand pulls up wages and prices. As the price level rises, the quantity of output demanded declines, and the economy gradually approaches the natural level of production. But during the transition to the higher price level, the economy's output is higher than its natural level.

What can the Fed do to dampen this boom and keep output closer to the natural level? The Fed might reduce the money supply to offset the increase in velocity. Offsetting the change in velocity would stabilize aggregate demand. Thus, the Fed can reduce or even eliminate the impact of demand shocks on output and employment if it can skillfully control the money supply. Whether the Fed in fact has the necessary skill is a more difficult question, which we take up in Chapter 13.

Shocks to Aggregate Supply

Shocks to aggregate supply can also cause economic fluctuations. A supply shock is a shock to the economy that alters the cost of producing goods and services and, as a result, the prices that firms charge. Because supply shocks have a direct impact on the price level, they are sometimes called *price shocks*. Here are some examples:

- A drought that destroys crops. The reduction in food supply pushes up food prices.

- A new environmental protection law that requires firms to reduce their emissions of pollutants. Firms pass on the added costs to customers in the form of higher prices.

FIGURE 9-14

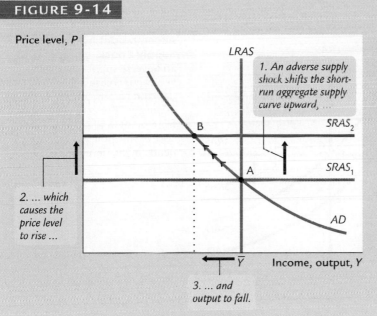

Price level, P

LRAS

1. An adverse supply shock shifts the short-run aggregate supply curve upward, ...

SRAS₂

B

A

SRAS₁

2. ... which causes the price level to rise ...

AD

$\overline{Y}$ Income, output, Y

3. ... and output to fall.

An Adverse Supply Shock An adverse supply shock pushes up costs and thus prices. If aggregate demand is held constant, the economy moves from point A to point B, leading to stagflation—a combination of increasing prices and falling output. Eventually, as prices fall, the economy returns to the natural level of output, point A.

■ An increase in union aggressiveness. This pushes up wages and the prices of the goods produced by union workers.

■ The organization of an international oil cartel. By curtailing competition, the major oil producers can raise the world price of oil.

All these events are *adverse* supply shocks, which means they push costs and prices upward. A *favorable* supply shock, such as the breakup of an international oil cartel, reduces costs and prices.

Figure 9-14 shows how an adverse supply shock affects the economy. The short-run aggregate supply curve shifts upward. (The supply shock may also lower the natural level of output and thus shift the long-run aggregate supply curve to the left, but we ignore that effect here.) If aggregate demand is held constant, the economy moves from point A to point B: the price level rises and the amount of output falls below its natural level. An experience like this is called *stagflation*, because it combines economic stagnation (falling output) with inflation (rising prices).

Faced with an adverse supply shock, a policymaker with the ability to influence aggregate demand, such as the Fed, has a difficult choice between two options. The first option, implicit in Figure 9-14, is to hold aggregate demand constant. In this case, output and employment are lower than the natural level. Eventually, prices will fall to restore full employment at the old price level (point A), but the cost of this adjustment process is a painful recession.

The second option, illustrated in Figure 9-15, is to expand aggregate demand to bring the economy toward the natural level of output more quickly. If the increase in aggregate demand coincides with the shock to aggregate supply, the

FIGURE 9-15

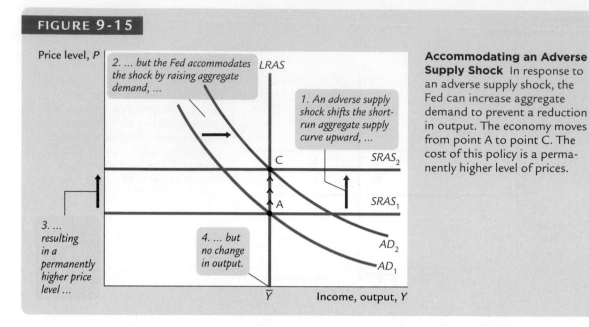

Accommodating an Adverse Supply Shock In response to an adverse supply shock, the Fed can increase aggregate demand to prevent a reduction in output. The economy moves from point A to point C. The cost of this policy is a permanently higher level of prices.

economy goes immediately from point A to point C. In this case, the Fed is said to *accommodate* the supply shock. The drawback of this option, of course, is that the price level is permanently higher. There is no way to adjust aggregate demand to maintain full employment and keep the price level stable.

CASE STUDY

How OPEC Helped Cause Stagflation in the 1970s and Euphoria in the 1980s

The most disruptive supply shocks in recent history were caused by OPEC, the Organization of Petroleum Exporting Countries. OPEC is a cartel, which is an organization of suppliers that coordinate production levels and prices. In the early 1970s, OPEC's reduction in the supply of oil nearly doubled the world price. This increase in oil prices caused stagflation in most industrial countries. These statistics show what happened in the United States:

Year	Change in Oil Prices	Inflation Rate (CPI)	Unemployment Rate
1973	11.0%	6.2%	4.9%
1974	68.0	11.0	5.6
1975	16.0	9.1	8.5
1976	3.3	5.8	7.7
1977	8.1	6.5	7.1

The 68 percent increase in the price of oil in 1974 was an adverse supply shock of major proportions. As one would have expected, this shock led to both higher inflation and higher unemployment.

A few years later, when the world economy had nearly recovered from the first OPEC recession, almost the same thing happened again. OPEC raised oil prices, causing further stagflation. Here are the statistics for the United States:

Year	Change in Oil Prices	Inflation Rate (CPI)	Unemployment Rate
1978	9.4%	7.7%	6.1%
1979	25.4	11.3	5.8
1980	47.8	13.5	7.0
1981	44.4	10.3	7.5
1982	−8.7	6.1	9.5

The increases in oil prices in 1979, 1980, and 1981 again led to double-digit inflation and higher unemployment.

In the mid-1980s, political turmoil among the Arab countries weakened OPEC's ability to restrain supplies of oil. Oil prices fell, reversing the stagflation of the 1970s and the early 1980s. Here's what happened:

Year	Changes in Oil Prices	Inflation Rate (CPI)	Unemployment Rate
1983	−7.1%	3.2%	9.5%
1984	−1.7	4.3	7.4
1985	−7.5	3.6	7.1
1986	−44.5	1.9	6.9
1987	18.3	3.6	6.1

In 1986 oil prices fell by nearly half. This favorable supply shock led to one of the lowest inflation rates experienced in recent U.S. history and to falling unemployment.

More recently, OPEC has not been a major cause of economic fluctuations. Conservation efforts and technological changes have made the U.S. economy less susceptible to oil shocks. The economy today is more service-based and less manufacturing-based, and services typically require less energy to produce than do manufactured goods. Because the amount of oil consumed per unit of real GDP has fallen by more than half over the previous three decades, it takes a much larger oil-price change to have the impact on the economy that we observed in the 1970s and 1980s. Thus, when oil prices rose precipitously in 2007 and the first half of 2008 (before retreating in the second half of 2008), these price changes had a smaller macroeconomic impact than they would have had in the past.[5] ■

9-6 Conclusion

This chapter introduced a framework to study economic fluctuations: the model of aggregate supply and aggregate demand. The model is built on the assumption that prices are sticky in the short run and flexible in the long run. It shows how shocks to the economy cause output to deviate temporarily from the level implied by the classical model.

The model also highlights the role of monetary policy. On the one hand, poor monetary policy can be a source of destabilizing shocks to the economy. On the other hand, a well-run monetary policy can respond to shocks and stabilize the economy.

In the chapters that follow, we refine our understanding of this model and our analysis of stabilization policy. Chapters 10 and 11 go beyond the quantity equation to refine our theory of aggregate demand. Chapter 12 examines aggregate supply in more detail. Chapter 13 examines the debate over the virtues and limits of stabilization policy.

Summary

1. Economies experience short-run fluctuations in economic activity, measured most broadly by real GDP. These fluctuations are associated with movement in many macroeconomic variables. In particular, when GDP growth declines, consumption growth falls (typically by a smaller amount), investment growth falls (typically by a larger amount), and unemployment rises. Although economists look at various leading indicators to forecast movements in the economy, these short-run fluctuations are largely unpredictable.

2. The crucial difference between how the economy works in the long run and how it works in the short run is that prices are flexible in the long run but sticky in the short run. The model of aggregate supply and aggregate demand provides a framework to analyze economic fluctuations and see how the impact of policies and events varies over different time horizons.

3. The aggregate demand curve slopes downward. It tells us that the lower the price level, the greater the aggregate quantity of goods and services demanded.

[5] Some economists have suggested that changes in oil prices played a major role in economic fluctuations even before the 1970s. See James D. Hamilton, "Oil and the Macroeconomy Since World War II," *Journal of Political Economy* 91 (April 1983): 228–248.

4. In the long run, the aggregate supply curve is vertical because output is determined by the amounts of capital and labor and by the available technology but not by the level of prices. Therefore, shifts in aggregate demand affect the price level but not output or employment.

5. In the short run, the aggregate supply curve is horizontal, because wages and prices are sticky at predetermined levels. Therefore, shifts in aggregate demand affect output and employment.

6. Shocks to aggregate demand and aggregate supply cause economic fluctuations. Because the Fed can shift the aggregate demand curve, it can attempt to offset these shocks to maintain output and employment at their natural levels.

KEY CONCEPTS

Okun's law

Leading indicators

Aggregate demand

Aggregate supply

Shocks

Demand shocks

Supply shocks

Stabilization policy

QUESTIONS FOR REVIEW

1. When real GDP declines during a recession, what typically happens to consumption, investment, and the unemployment rate?

2. Give an example of a price that is sticky in the short run but flexible in the long run.

3. Why does the aggregate demand curve slope downward?

4. Explain the impact of an increase in the money supply in the short run and in the long run.

5. Why is it easier for the Fed to deal with demand shocks than with supply shocks?

PROBLEMS AND APPLICATIONS

1. An economy begins in long-run equilibrium, and then a change in government regulations allows banks to start paying interest on checking accounts. Recall that the money stock is the sum of currency and demand deposits, including checking accounts, so this regulatory change makes holding money more attractive.

   a. How does this change affect the demand for money?

   b. What happens to the velocity of money?

   c. If the Fed keeps the money supply constant, what will happen to output and prices in the short run and in the long run?

   d. If the goal of the Fed is to stabilize the price level, should the Fed keep the money supply constant in response to this regulatory change? If not, what should it do? Why?

   e. If the goal of the Fed is to stabilize output, how would your answer to part (d) change?

2. Suppose the Fed reduces the money supply by 5 percent.

 a. What happens to the aggregate demand curve?

 b. What happens to the level of output and the price level in the short run and in the long run?

 c. According to Okun's law, what happens to unemployment in the short run and in the long run?

 d. What happens to the real interest rate in the short run and in the long run? (*Hint:* Use the model of the real interest rate in Chapter 3 to see what happens when output changes.)

3. Let's examine how the goals of the Fed influence its response to shocks. Suppose Fed A cares only about keeping the price level stable and Fed B cares only about keeping output and employment at their natural levels. Explain how each Fed would respond to the following:

 a. An exogenous decrease in the velocity of money

 b. An exogenous increase in the price of oil

4. The official arbiter of when recessions begin and end is the National Bureau of Economic Research, a nonprofit economics research group. Go to the NBER's Web site (www.nber.org) and find the latest turning point in the business cycle. When did it occur? Was this a switch from expansion to contraction or the other way around? List all the recessions (contractions) that have occurred during your lifetime and the dates when they began and ended.

Aggregate Demand I: Building the *IS–LM* Model

> *I shall argue that the postulates of the classical theory are applicable to a special case only and not to the general case. . . . Moreover, the characteristics of the special case assumed by the classical theory happen not to be those of the economic society in which we actually live, with the result that its teaching is misleading and disastrous if we attempt to apply it to the facts of experience.*
>
> —*John Maynard Keynes*, The General Theory

Of all the economic fluctuations in world history, the one that stands out as particularly large, painful, and intellectually significant is the Great Depression of the 1930s. During this time, the United States and many other countries experienced massive unemployment and greatly reduced incomes. In the worst year, 1933, one-fourth of the U.S. labor force was unemployed, and real GDP was 30 percent below its 1929 level.

This devastating episode caused many economists to question the validity of classical economic theory—the theory we examined in Chapters 3 through 6. Classical theory seemed incapable of explaining the Depression. According to that theory, national income depends on factor supplies and the available technology, neither of which changed substantially from 1929 to 1933. After the onset of the Depression, many economists believed that a new model was needed to explain such a large and sudden economic downturn and to suggest government policies that might reduce the economic hardship so many people faced.

In 1936 the British economist John Maynard Keynes revolutionized economics with his book *The General Theory of Employment, Interest, and Money*. Keynes proposed a new way to analyze the economy, which he presented as an alternative to classical theory. His vision of how the economy works quickly became a center of controversy. Yet, as economists debated *The General Theory*, a new understanding of economic fluctuations gradually developed.

Keynes proposed that low aggregate demand is responsible for the low income and high unemployment that characterize economic downturns. He criticized classical theory for assuming that aggregate supply alone—capital, labor, and technology—determines national income. Economists today reconcile these two views with the model of aggregate demand and aggregate supply introduced in

Chapter 9. In the long run, prices are flexible, and aggregate supply determines income. But in the short run, prices are sticky, so changes in aggregate demand influence income. In 2008 and 2009, as the United States and Europe descended into a recession, the Keynesian theory of the business cycle was often in the news. Policymakers around the world debated how best to increase aggregate demand and put their economies on the road to recovery.

In this chapter and the next, we continue our study of economic fluctuations by looking more closely at aggregate demand. Our goal is to identify the variables that shift the aggregate demand curve, causing fluctuations in national income. We also examine more fully the tools policymakers can use to influence aggregate demand. In Chapter 9 we derived the aggregate demand curve from the quantity theory of money, and we showed that monetary policy can shift the aggregate demand curve. In this chapter we see that the government can influence aggregate demand with both monetary and fiscal policy.

The model of aggregate demand developed in this chapter, called the **IS–LM model**, is the leading interpretation of Keynes's theory. The goal of the model is to show what determines national income for a given price level. There are two ways to interpret this exercise. We can view the IS–LM model as showing what causes income to change in the short run when the price level is fixed because all prices are sticky. Or we can view the model as showing what causes the aggregate demand curve to shift. These two interpretations of the model are equivalent: as Figure 10-1 shows, in the short run when the price level is fixed, shifts in the aggregate demand curve lead to changes in the equilibrium level of national income.

The two parts of the IS–LM model are, not surprisingly, the **IS curve** and the **LM curve**. IS stands for "investment" and "saving," and the IS curve represents what's going on in the market for goods and services (which we first discussed

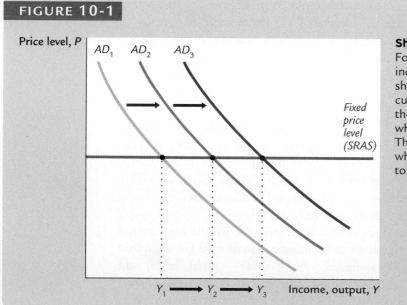

FIGURE 10-1

Price level, P

AD_1 AD_2 AD_3

Fixed price level (SRAS)

$Y_1 \longrightarrow Y_2 \longrightarrow Y_3$ Income, output, Y

Shifts in Aggregate Demand
For a given price level, national income fluctuates because of shifts in the aggregate demand curve. The IS–LM model takes the price level as given and shows what causes income to change. The model therefore shows what causes aggregate demand to shift.

in Chapter 3). *LM* stands for "liquidity" and "money," and the *LM* curve represents what's happening to the supply and demand for money (which we first discussed in Chapter 4). Because the interest rate influences both investment and money demand, it is the variable that links the two halves of the *IS–LM* model. The model shows how interactions between the goods and money markets determine the position and slope of the aggregate demand curve and, therefore, the level of national income in the short run.[1]

10-1 The Goods Market and the *IS* Curve

The *IS* curve plots the relationship between the interest rate and the level of income that arises in the market for goods and services. To develop this relationship, we start with a basic model called the **Keynesian cross**. This model is the simplest interpretation of Keynes's theory of how national income is determined and is a building block for the more complex and realistic *IS–LM* model.

The Keynesian Cross

In *The General Theory* Keynes proposed that an economy's total income is, in the short run, determined largely by the spending plans of households, businesses, and government. The more people want to spend, the more goods and services firms can sell. The more firms can sell, the more output they will choose to produce and the more workers they will choose to hire. Keynes believed that the problem during recessions and depressions is inadequate spending. The Keynesian cross is an attempt to model this insight.

Planned Expenditure We begin our derivation of the Keynesian cross by drawing a distinction between actual and planned expenditure. *Actual expenditure* is the amount households, firms, and the government spend on goods and services, and as we first saw in Chapter 2, it equals the economy's gross domestic product (GDP). *Planned expenditure* is the amount households, firms, and the government would like to spend on goods and services.

Why would actual expenditure ever differ from planned expenditure? The answer is that firms might engage in unplanned inventory investment because their sales do not meet their expectations. When firms sell less of their product than they planned, their stock of inventories automatically rises; conversely, when firms sell more than planned, their stock of inventories falls. Because these unplanned changes in inventory are counted as investment spending by firms, actual expenditure can be either above or below planned expenditure.

---

[1] The *IS–LM* model was introduced in a classic article by the Nobel Prize–winning economist John R. Hicks, "Mr. Keynes and the Classics: A Suggested Interpretation," *Econometrica* 5 (1937): 147–159.

Now consider the determinants of planned expenditure. Assuming that the economy is closed, so that net exports are zero, we write planned expenditure PE as the sum of consumption C, planned investment I, and government purchases G:

$$PE = C + I + G.$$

To this equation, we add the consumption function

$$C = C(Y - T).$$

This equation states that consumption depends on disposable income $(Y - T)$, which is total income Y minus taxes T. To keep things simple, for now we take planned investment as exogenously fixed:

$$I = \bar{I}.$$

Finally, as in Chapter 3, we assume that fiscal policy—the levels of government purchases and taxes—is fixed:

$$G = \bar{G},$$

$$T = \bar{T}.$$

Combining these five equations, we obtain

$$PE = C(Y - \bar{T}) + \bar{I} + \bar{G}.$$

This equation shows that planned expenditure is a function of income Y, the level of planned investment $\bar{I}$, and the fiscal policy variables $\bar{G}$ and $\bar{T}$.

Figure 10-2 graphs planned expenditure as a function of the level of income. This line slopes upward because higher income leads to higher consumption and thus higher planned expenditure. The slope of this line is the marginal propensity to consume, MPC: it shows how much planned expenditure increases when income rises by $1. This planned-expenditure function is the first piece of the model called the Keynesian cross.

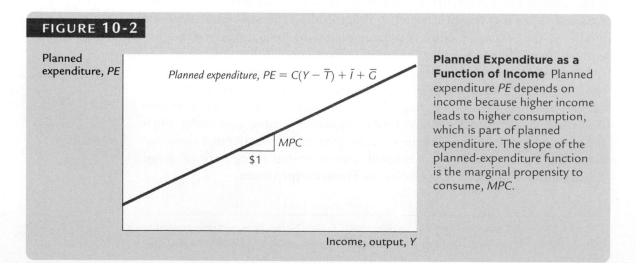

FIGURE 10-2

Planned expenditure, PE

Planned expenditure, $PE = C(Y - \bar{T}) + \bar{I} + \bar{G}$

MPC

$1

Income, output, Y

Planned Expenditure as a Function of Income Planned expenditure *PE* depends on income because higher income leads to higher consumption, which is part of planned expenditure. The slope of the planned-expenditure function is the marginal propensity to consume, *MPC*.

The Economy in Equilibrium The next piece of the Keynesian cross is the assumption that the economy is in equilibrium when actual expenditure equals planned expenditure. This assumption is based on the idea that when people's plans have been realized, they have no reason to change what they are doing. Recalling that Y as GDP equals not only total income but also total actual expenditure on goods and services, we can write this equilibrium condition as

$$\text{Actual Expenditure} = \text{Planned Expenditure}$$

$$Y = PE.$$

The 45-degree line in Figure 10-3 plots the points where this condition holds. With the addition of the planned-expenditure function, this diagram becomes the Keynesian cross. The equilibrium of this economy is at point A, where the planned-expenditure function crosses the 45-degree line.

How does the economy get to equilibrium? In this model, inventories play an important role in the adjustment process. Whenever an economy is not in equilibrium, firms experience unplanned changes in inventories, and this induces them to change production levels. Changes in production in turn influence total income and expenditure, moving the economy toward equilibrium.

For example, suppose the economy finds itself with GDP at a level greater than the equilibrium level, such as the level Y_1 in Figure 10-4. In this case, planned expenditure PE_1 is less than production Y_1, so firms are selling less than they are producing. Firms add the unsold goods to their stock of inventories. This unplanned rise in inventories induces firms to lay off workers and reduce production; these actions in turn reduce GDP. This process of unintended inventory accumulation and falling income continues until income Y falls to the equilibrium level.

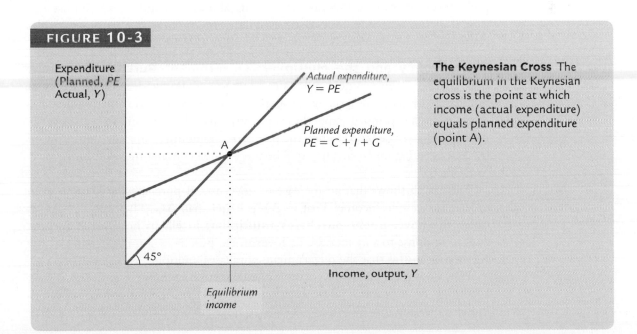

FIGURE 10-3

Expenditure (Planned, *PE* Actual, *Y*)

Actual expenditure, $Y = PE$

Planned expenditure, $PE = C + I + G$

A

45°

Income, output, *Y*

Equilibrium income

The Keynesian Cross The equilibrium in the Keynesian cross is the point at which income (actual expenditure) equals planned expenditure (point A).

FIGURE 10-4

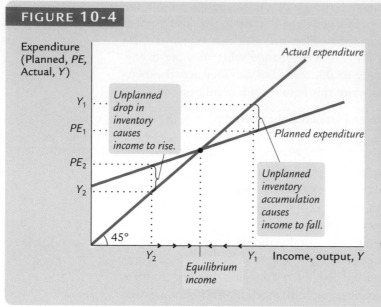

Expenditure (Planned, PE, Actual, Y)

Y_1

PE_1

PE_2

Y_2

Unplanned drop in inventory causes income to rise.

45°

Y_2

Equilibrium income

Y_1

Actual expenditure

Planned expenditure

Unplanned inventory accumulation causes income to fall.

Income, output, Y

The Adjustment to Equilibrium in the Keynesian Cross If firms are producing at level Y_1, then planned expenditure PE_1 falls short of production, and firms accumulate inventories. This inventory accumulation induces firms to decrease production. Similarly, if firms are producing at level Y_2, then planned expenditure PE_2 exceeds production, and firms run down their inventories. This fall in inventories induces firms to increase production. In both cases, the firms' decisions drive the economy toward equilibrium.

Similarly, suppose GDP is at a level lower than the equilibrium level, such as the level Y_2 in Figure 10-4. In this case, planned expenditure PE_2 is greater than production Y_2. Firms meet the high level of sales by drawing down their inventories. But when firms see their stock of inventories dwindle, they hire more workers and increase production. GDP rises, and the economy approaches equilibrium.

In summary, the Keynesian cross shows how income Y is determined for given levels of planned investment I and fiscal policy G and T. We can use this model to show how income changes when one of these exogenous variables changes.

Fiscal Policy and the Multiplier: Government Purchases Consider how changes in government purchases affect the economy. Because government purchases are one component of expenditure, higher government purchases result in higher planned expenditure for any given level of income. If government purchases rise by ΔG, then the planned-expenditure schedule shifts upward by ΔG, as in Figure 10-5. The equilibrium of the economy moves from point A to point B.

This graph shows that an increase in government purchases leads to an even greater increase in income. That is, ΔY is larger than ΔG. The ratio $\Delta Y/\Delta G$ is called the **government-purchases multiplier**; it tells us how much income rises in response to a \$1 increase in government purchases. An implication of the Keynesian cross is that the government-purchases multiplier is larger than 1.

Why does fiscal policy have a multiplied effect on income? The reason is that, according to the consumption function $C = C(Y - T)$, higher income causes higher consumption. When an increase in government purchases raises income,

FIGURE 10-5

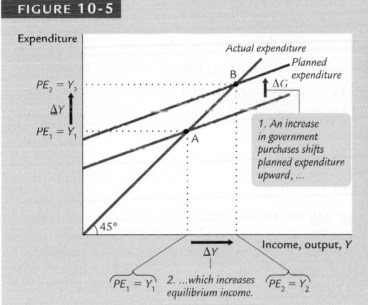

An Increase in Government Purchases in the Keynesian Cross An increase in government purchases of ΔG raises planned expenditure by that amount for any given level of income. The equilibrium moves from point A to point B, and income rises from Y_1 to Y_2. Note that the increase in income ΔY exceeds the increase in government purchases ΔG. Thus, fiscal policy has a multiplied effect on income.

it also raises consumption, which further raises income, which further raises consumption, and so on. Therefore, in this model, an increase in government purchases causes a greater increase in income.

How big is the multiplier? To answer this question, we trace through each step of the change in income. The process begins when expenditure rises by ΔG, which implies that income rises by ΔG as well. This increase in income in turn raises consumption by $MPC \times \Delta G$, where MPC is the marginal propensity to consume. This increase in consumption raises expenditure and income once again. This second increase in income of $MPC \times \Delta G$ again raises consumption, this time by $MPC \times (MPC \times \Delta G)$, which again raises expenditure and income, and so on. This feedback from consumption to income to consumption continues indefinitely. The total effect on income is

Initial Change in Government Purchases $= \quad \Delta G$

First Change in Consumption $\quad = MPC \times \Delta G$

Second Change in Consumption $\quad = MPC^2 \times \Delta G$

Third Change in Consumption $\quad = MPC^3 \times \Delta G$

$$\Delta Y = (1 + MPC + MPC^2 + MPC^3 + \cdots)\Delta G.$$

The government-purchases multiplier is

$$\Delta Y/\Delta G = 1 + MPC + MPC^2 + MPC^3 + \cdots.$$

This expression for the multiplier is an example of an *infinite geometric series*. A result from algebra allows us to write the multiplier as[2]

$$\Delta Y / \Delta G = 1 / (1 - MPC).$$

For example, if the marginal propensity to consume is 0.6, the multiplier is

$$\Delta Y / \Delta G = 1 + 0.6 + 0.6^2 + 0.6^3 + \cdots$$

$$= 1 / (1 - 0.6)$$

$$= 2.5.$$

In this case, a \$1.00 increase in government purchases raises equilibrium income by \$2.50.[3]

Fiscal Policy and the Multiplier: Taxes Consider now how changes in taxes affect equilibrium income. A decrease in taxes of ΔT immediately raises disposable income $Y - T$ by ΔT and, therefore, increases consumption by $MPC \times \Delta T$. For any given level of income Y, planned expenditure is now higher. As Figure 10-6 shows, the planned-expenditure schedule shifts upward by $MPC \times \Delta T$. The equilibrium of the economy moves from point A to point B.

Just as an increase in government purchases has a multiplied effect on income, so does a decrease in taxes. As before, the initial change in expenditure, now $MPC \times \Delta T$, is multiplied by $1 / (1 - MPC)$. The overall effect on income of the change in taxes is

$$\Delta Y / \Delta T = -MPC / (1 - MPC).$$

This expression is the **tax multiplier**, the amount income changes in response to a \$1 change in taxes. (The negative sign indicates that income moves in the

---

[2] *Mathematical note:* We prove this algebraic result as follows. For $|x| < 1$, let

$$z = 1 + x + x^2 + \cdots.$$

Multiply both sides of this equation by x:

$$xz = x + x^2 + x^3 + \cdots.$$

Subtract the second equation from the first:

$$z - xz = 1.$$

Rearrange this last equation to obtain

$$z(1 - x) = 1,$$

which implies

$$z = 1 / (1 - x).$$

This completes the proof.

[3] *Mathematical note:* The government-purchases multiplier is most easily derived using a little calculus. Begin with the equation

$$Y = C(Y - T) + I + G.$$

Holding T and I fixed, differentiate to obtain

$$dY = C'dY + dG,$$

and then rearrange to find

$$dY / dG = 1 / (1 - C').$$

This is the same as the equation in the text.

FIGURE 10-6

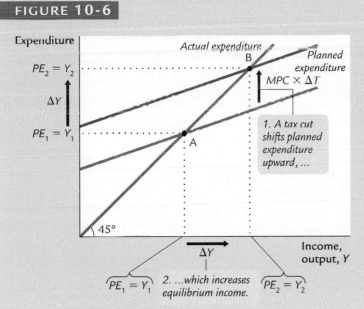

A Decrease in Taxes in the Keynesian Cross A decrease in taxes of ΔT raises planned expenditure by $MPC \times \Delta T$ for any given level of income. The equilibrium moves from point A to point B, and income rises from Y_1 to Y_2. Again, fiscal policy has a multiplied effect on income.

opposite direction from taxes.) For example, if the marginal propensity to consume is 0.6, then the tax multiplier is

$$\Delta Y / \Delta T = -0.6/(1 - 0.6) = -1.5.$$

In this example, a \$1.00 cut in taxes raises equilibrium income by \$1.50.[4]

Cutting Taxes to Stimulate the Economy: The Kennedy and Bush Tax Cuts

When John F. Kennedy became president of the United States in 1961, he brought to Washington some of the brightest young economists of the day to work on his Council of Economic Advisers. These economists, who had been schooled in the economics of Keynes, brought Keynesian ideas to discussions of economic policy at the highest level.

One of the council's first proposals was to expand national income by reducing taxes. This eventually led to a substantial cut in personal and corporate income

---

[4] *Mathematical note:* As before, the multiplier is most easily derived using a little calculus. Begin with the equation

$$Y = C(Y - T) + I + G.$$

Holding I and G fixed, differentiate to obtain

$$dY = C'(dY - dT),$$

and then rearrange to find

$$dY/dT = -C'/(1 - C').$$

This is the same as the equation in the text.

taxes in 1964. The tax cut was intended to stimulate expenditure on consumption and investment and lead to higher levels of income and employment. When a reporter asked Kennedy why he advocated a tax cut, Kennedy replied, "To stimulate the economy. Don't you remember your Economics 101?"

As Kennedy's economic advisers predicted, the passage of the tax cut was followed by an economic boom. Growth in real GDP was 5.3 percent in 1964 and 6.0 percent in 1965. The unemployment rate fell from 5.7 percent in 1963 to 5.2 percent in 1964 and then to 4.5 percent in 1965.

Economists continue to debate the source of this rapid growth in the early 1960s. A group called *supply-siders* argues that the economic boom resulted from the incentive effects of the cut in income tax rates. According to supply-siders, when workers are allowed to keep a higher fraction of their earnings, they supply substantially more labor and expand the aggregate supply of goods and services. Keynesians, however, emphasize the impact of tax cuts on aggregate demand. Most likely, both views have some truth: *tax cuts stimulate aggregate supply by improving workers' incentives and expand aggregate demand by raising households' disposable income.*

When George W. Bush was elected president in 2000, a major element of his platform was a cut in income taxes. Bush and his advisers used both supply-side and Keynesian rhetoric to make the case for their policy. (Full disclosure: One of the authors of this textbook—Mankiw—was an economic adviser to President Bush from 2003 to 2005.) During the campaign, when the economy was doing fine, they argued that lower marginal tax rates would improve work incentives. But when the economy started to slow, and unemployment started to rise, the argument shifted to emphasize that the tax cut would stimulate spending and help the economy recover from the recession.

Congress passed major tax cuts in 2001 and 2003. After the second tax cut, the weak recovery from the 2001 recession turned into a robust one. Growth in real GDP was 4.4 percent in 2004. The unemployment rate fell from its peak of 6.3 percent in June 2003 to 5.4 percent in December 2004.

When President Bush signed the 2003 tax bill, he explained the measure using the logic of aggregate demand: "When people have more money, they can spend it on goods and services. And in our society, when they demand an additional good or a service, somebody will produce the good or a service. And when somebody produces that good or a service, it means somebody is more likely to be able to find a job." The explanation could have come from an exam in Economics 101. ■

CASE STUDY

Increasing Government Purchases to Stimulate the Economy: The Obama Spending Plan

When President Barack Obama took office in January 2009, the economy was suffering from a significant recession. (The causes of this recession are discussed in a Case Study in the next chapter.) Even before he was inaugurated, the president and his advisers proposed a sizable stimulus package to increase aggregate demand. As proposed, the package would cost the federal government about $800 billion, or about 5 percent of annual GDP. The package included some tax cuts and higher transfer payments, but much of it was made up of increases in government purchases of goods and services.

Professional economists debated the merits of the plan. Advocates of the Obama plan argued that increased spending was better than reduced taxes because, according to standard Keynesian theory, the government-purchases multiplier exceeds the tax

"Your Majesty, my voyage will not only forge a new route to the spices of the East but also create over three thousand new jobs."

multiplier. The reason for this difference is simple: when the government spends a dollar, that dollar gets spent, whereas when the government gives households a tax cut of a dollar, some of that dollar might be saved. According to an analysis by Obama administration economists, the government purchases multiplier is 1.57, whereas the tax multiplier is only 0.99. Thus, they argued that increased government spending on roads, schools, and other infrastructure was the better route to increase aggregate demand and create jobs. The logic here is quintessentially Keynesian: as the economy sinks into recession, the government is acting as the demander of last resort.

The Obama stimulus proposal was controversial among economists for various reasons. One criticism was that the stimulus was not large enough given the apparent depth of the economic downturn. In March 2009, economist Paul Krugman wrote in the *New York Times:*

> The plan was too small and too cautious. . . . Employment has already fallen more in this recession than in the 1981–82 slump, considered the worst since the Great Depression. As a result, Mr. Obama's promise that his plan will create or save 3.5 million jobs by the end of 2010 looks underwhelming, to say the least. It's a credible promise—his economists used solidly mainstream estimates of the impacts of tax and spending policies. But 3.5 million jobs almost two years from now isn't enough in the face of an economy that has already lost 4.4 million jobs, and is losing 600,000 more each month.

Still other economists argued that despite the predictions of conventional Keynesian models, spending-based fiscal stimulus is not as effective as tax-based initiatives. A recent study of fiscal policy in OECD countries since 1970 examined which kinds of fiscal stimulus have historically been most successful at promoting growth in economic activity. It found that successful fiscal stimulus relies almost entirely on cuts in business and income taxes, whereas failed fiscal stimulus relies primarily on increases in government spending.[5]

---

[5] Alberto Alesina and Silvia Ardagna. "Large Changes in Fiscal Policy: Taxes Versus Spending." NBER Working Paper No. 15438, October 2009.

A related concern was that spending on infrastructure would take time, whereas tax cuts could occur more immediately. Infrastructure spending requires taking bids and signing contracts, and, even after the projects begin, they can take years to complete. The Congressional Budget Office estimated that only about 10 percent of the outlays would occur in the first nine months of 2009 and that a large fraction of outlays would be years away. By the time much of the stimulus went into effect, the recession might be well over.

In addition, some economists thought that using infrastructure spending to promote employment might conflict with the goal of obtaining the infrastructure that was most needed. Here is how economist Gary Becker explained the concern on his blog:

> Putting new infrastructure spending in depressed areas like Detroit might have a big stimulating effect since infrastructure building projects in these areas can utilize some of the considerable unemployed resources there. However, many of these areas are also declining because they have been producing goods and services that are not in great demand, and will not be in demand in the future. Therefore, the overall value added by improving their roads and other infrastructure is likely to be a lot less than if the new infrastructure were located in growing areas that might have relatively little unemployment, but do have great demand for more roads, schools, and other types of long-term infrastructure.

In the end, Congress went ahead with President Obama's proposed stimulus plans with relatively minor modifications. The president signed the $787 billion bill on February 17, 2009. In the years to come, economists will surely debate to what extent the stimulus bill contributed to economic recovery. ∎

The Interest Rate, Investment, and the *IS* Curve

The Keynesian cross is only a stepping-stone on our path to the *IS–LM* model, which explains the economy's aggregate demand curve. The Keynesian cross is useful because it shows how the spending plans of households, firms, and the government determine the economy's income. Yet it makes the simplifying assumption that the level of planned investment I is fixed. As we discussed in Chapter 3, an important macroeconomic relationship is that planned investment depends on the interest rate r.

To add this relationship between the interest rate and investment to our model, we write the level of planned investment as

$$I = I(r).$$

This investment function is graphed in panel (a) of Figure 10-7. Because the interest rate is the cost of borrowing to finance investment projects, an increase in the interest rate reduces planned investment. As a result, the investment function slopes downward.

To determine how income changes when the interest rate changes, we can combine the investment function with the Keynesian-cross diagram. Because investment is inversely related to the interest rate, an increase in the interest rate from r_1 to r_2 reduces the quantity of investment from $I(r_1)$ to $I(r_2)$. The reduction

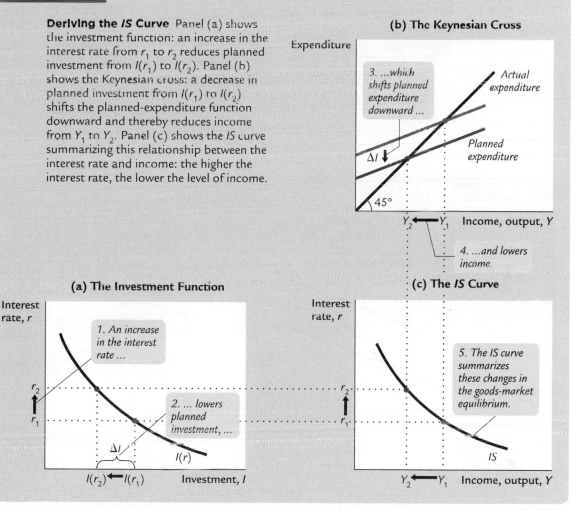

FIGURE 10-7

Deriving the *IS* Curve Panel (a) shows the investment function: an increase in the interest rate from r_1 to r_2 reduces planned investment from $I(r_1)$ to $I(r_2)$. Panel (b) shows the Keynesian cross: a decrease in planned investment from $I(r_1)$ to $I(r_2)$ shifts the planned-expenditure function downward and thereby reduces income from Y_1 to Y_2. Panel (c) shows the *IS* curve summarizing this relationship between the interest rate and income: the higher the interest rate, the lower the level of income.

in planned investment, in turn, shifts the planned-expenditure function downward, as in panel (b) of Figure 10-7. The shift in the planned-expenditure function causes the level of income to fall from Y_1 to Y_2. Hence, an increase in the interest rate lowers income.

The *IS* curve, shown in panel (c) of Figure 10-7, summarizes this relationship between the interest rate and the level of income. In essence, the *IS* curve combines the interaction between r and I expressed by the investment function and the interaction between I and Y demonstrated by the Keynesian cross. Each point on the *IS* curve represents equilibrium in the goods market, and the curve illustrates how the equilibrium level of income depends on the interest rate. Because an increase in the interest rate causes planned investment to fall, which in turn causes equilibrium income to fall, the *IS* curve slopes downward.

How Fiscal Policy Shifts the *IS* Curve

The *IS* curve shows us, for any given interest rate, the level of income that brings the goods market into equilibrium. As we learned from the Keynesian cross, the equilibrium level of income also depends on government spending G and taxes T. The *IS* curve is drawn for a given fiscal policy; that is, when we construct the *IS* curve, we hold G and T fixed. When fiscal policy changes, the *IS* curve shifts.

Figure 10-8 uses the Keynesian cross to show how an increase in government purchases ΔG shifts the *IS* curve. This figure is drawn for a given interest rate $\bar{r}$ and thus for a given level of planned investment. The Keynesian cross in

FIGURE 10-8

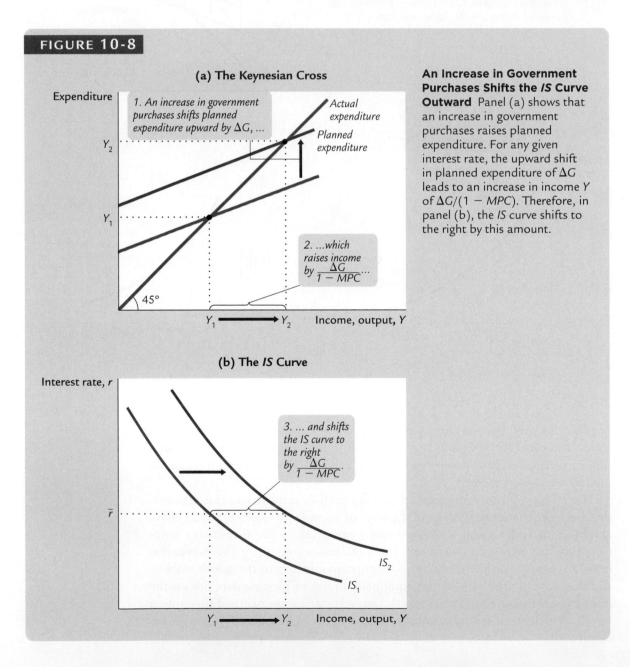

An Increase in Government Purchases Shifts the *IS* Curve Outward Panel (a) shows that an increase in government purchases raises planned expenditure. For any given interest rate, the upward shift in planned expenditure of ΔG leads to an increase in income Y of $\Delta G/(1 - MPC)$. Therefore, in panel (b), the *IS* curve shifts to the right by this amount.

panel (a) shows that this change in fiscal policy raises planned expenditure and thereby increases equilibrium income from Y_1 to Y_2. Therefore, in panel (b), the increase in government purchases shifts the *IS* curve outward.

We can use the Keynesian cross to see how other changes in fiscal policy shift the *IS* curve. Because a decrease in taxes also expands expenditure and income, it, too, shifts the *IS* curve outward. A decrease in government purchases or an increase in taxes reduces income; therefore, such a change in fiscal policy shifts the *IS* curve inward.

In summary, the IS *curve shows the combinations of the interest rate and the level of income that are consistent with equilibrium in the market for goods and services. The* IS *curve is drawn for a given fiscal policy. Changes in fiscal policy that raise the demand for goods and services shift the* IS *curve to the right. Changes in fiscal policy that reduce the demand for goods and services shift the* IS *curve to the left.*

10-2 The Money Market and the *LM* Curve

The *LM* curve plots the relationship between the interest rate and the level of income that arises in the market for money balances. To understand this relationship, we begin by looking at a theory of the interest rate, called the **theory of liquidity preference**.

The Theory of Liquidity Preference

In his classic work *The General Theory*, Keynes offered his view of how the interest rate is determined in the short run. His explanation is called the theory of liquidity preference because it posits that the interest rate adjusts to balance the supply and demand for the economy's most liquid asset—money. Just as the Keynesian cross is a building block for the *IS* curve, the theory of liquidity preference is a building block for the *LM* curve.

To develop this theory, we begin with the supply of real money balances. If M stands for the supply of money and P stands for the price level, then M/P is the supply of real money balances. The theory of liquidity preference assumes there is a fixed supply of real money balances. That is,

$$(M/P)^s = \overline{M}/\overline{P}.$$

The money supply M is an exogenous policy variable chosen by a central bank, such as the Federal Reserve. The price level P is also an exogenous variable in this model. (We take the price level as given because the *IS–LM* model—our ultimate goal in this chapter—explains the short run when the price level is fixed.) These assumptions imply that the supply of real money balances is fixed and, in particular, does not depend on the interest rate. Thus, when we plot the supply of real money balances against the interest rate in Figure 10-9, we obtain a vertical supply curve.

Next, consider the demand for real money balances. The theory of liquidity preference posits that the interest rate is one determinant of how much money people

FIGURE 10-9

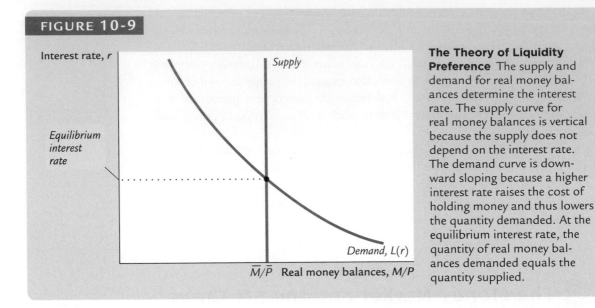

The Theory of Liquidity Preference The supply and demand for real money balances determine the interest rate. The supply curve for real money balances is vertical because the supply does not depend on the interest rate. The demand curve is downward sloping because a higher interest rate raises the cost of holding money and thus lowers the quantity demanded. At the equilibrium interest rate, the quantity of real money balances demanded equals the quantity supplied.

choose to hold. The underlying reason is that the interest rate is the opportunity cost of holding money: it is what you forgo by holding some of your assets as money, which does not bear interest, instead of as interest-bearing bank deposits or bonds. When the interest rate rises, people want to hold less of their wealth in the form of money. We can write the demand for real money balances as

$$(M/P)^{\mathrm{d}} = L(r),$$

where the function $L(\ )$ shows that the quantity of money demanded depends on the interest rate. The demand curve in Figure 10-9 slopes downward because higher interest rates reduce the quantity of real money balances demanded.[6]

According to the theory of liquidity preference, the supply and demand for real money balances determine what interest rate prevails in the economy. That is, the interest rate adjusts to equilibrate the money market. As the figure shows, at the equilibrium interest rate, the quantity of real money balances demanded equals the quantity supplied.

How does the interest rate get to this equilibrium of money supply and money demand? The adjustment occurs because whenever the money market is not in equilibrium, people try to adjust their portfolios of assets and, in the process, alter the interest rate. For instance, if the interest rate is above the equilibrium level, the quantity of real money balances supplied exceeds the quantity demanded.

---

[6] Note that r is being used to denote the interest rate here, as it was in our discussion of the *IS* curve. More accurately, it is the nominal interest rate that determines money demand and the real interest rate that determines investment. To keep things simple, we are ignoring expected inflation, which creates the difference between the real and nominal interest rates. For short-run analysis, it is often realistic to assume that expected inflation is constant, in which case real and nominal interest rates move together. The role of expected inflation in the *IS–LM* model is explored in Chapter 11.

FIGURE 10-10

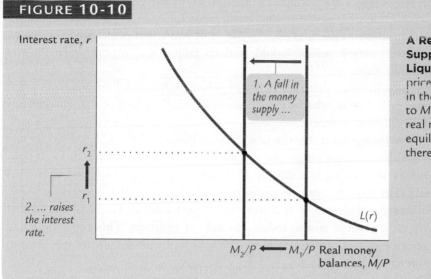

Interest rate, r

1. A fall in the money supply ...

r_2

r_1

2. ... raises the interest rate.

$L(r)$

$M_2/P \longleftarrow M_1/P$ Real money balances, M/P

A Reduction in the Money Supply in the Theory of Liquidity Preference If the price level is fixed, a reduction in the money supply from M_1 to M_2 reduces the supply of real money balances. The equilibrium interest rate therefore rises from r_1 to r_2.

Individuals holding the excess supply of money try to convert some of their non-interest-bearing money into interest-bearing bank deposits or bonds. Banks and bond issuers, who prefer to pay lower interest rates, respond to this excess supply of money by lowering the interest rates they offer. Conversely, if the interest rate is below the equilibrium level, so that the quantity of money demanded exceeds the quantity supplied, individuals try to obtain money by selling bonds or making bank withdrawals. To attract now-scarcer funds, banks and bond issuers respond by increasing the interest rates they offer. Eventually, the interest rate reaches the equilibrium level, at which people are content with their portfolios of monetary and nonmonetary assets.

Now that we have seen how the interest rate is determined, we can use the theory of liquidity preference to show how the interest rate responds to changes in the supply of money. Suppose, for instance, that the Fed suddenly decreases the money supply. A fall in M reduces M/P, because P is fixed in the model. The supply of real money balances shifts to the left, as in Figure 10-10. The equilibrium interest rate rises from r_1 to r_2, and the higher interest rate makes people satisfied to hold the smaller quantity of real money balances. The opposite would occur if the Fed had suddenly increased the money supply. Thus, according to the theory of liquidity preference, a decrease in the money supply raises the interest rate, and an increase in the money supply lowers the interest rate.

CASE STUDY

Does a Monetary Tightening Raise or Lower Interest Rates?

How does a tightening of monetary policy influence nominal interest rates? According to the theories we have been developing, the answer depends on the time horizon. Our analysis of the Fisher effect in Chapter 4 suggests that, in the long run when prices are flexible, a reduction in money growth would lower inflation, and this in turn would lead to lower nominal interest rates. Yet the theory of liquidity preference predicts that, in the short run when prices are sticky, anti-inflationary monetary policy would lead to falling real money balances and higher interest rates.

Both conclusions are consistent with experience. A good illustration occurred during the early 1980s, when the U.S. economy saw the largest and quickest reduction in inflation in recent history.

Here's the background: By the late 1970s, inflation in the U.S. economy had reached the double-digit range and was a major national problem. In 1979 consumer prices were rising at a rate of 11.3 percent per year. In October of that year, only two months after becoming the chairman of the Federal Reserve, Paul Volcker decided that it was time to change course. He announced that monetary policy would aim to reduce the rate of inflation. This announcement began a period of tight money that, by 1983, brought the inflation rate down to about 3 percent.

Let's look at what happened to nominal interest rates. If we look at the period immediately after the October 1979 announcement of tighter monetary policy, we see a fall in real money balances and a rise in the interest rate—just as the theory of liquidity preference predicts. Nominal interest rates on three-month Treasury bills rose from 10 percent just before the October 1979 announcement to 12 percent in 1980 and 14 percent in 1981. Yet these high interest rates were only temporary. As Volcker's change in monetary policy lowered inflation and expectations of inflation, nominal interest rates gradually fell, reaching 6 percent in 1986.

This episode illustrates a general lesson: to understand the link between monetary policy and nominal interest rates, we need to keep in mind both the theory of liquidity preference and the Fisher effect. A monetary tightening leads to higher nominal interest rates in the short run and lower nominal interest rates in the long run. ∎

Income, Money Demand, and the *LM* Curve

Having developed the theory of liquidity preference as an explanation for how the interest rate is determined, we can now use the theory to derive the *LM* curve. We begin by considering the following question: how does a change in the economy's level of income Y affect the market for real money balances? The answer (which should be familiar from Chapter 4) is that the level of income affects the demand for money. When income is high, expenditure is high, so people engage in more transactions that require the use of money. Thus, greater income implies greater money demand. We can express these ideas by writing the money demand function as

$$(M/P)^d = L(r, Y).$$

The quantity of real money balances demanded is negatively related to the interest rate and positively related to income.

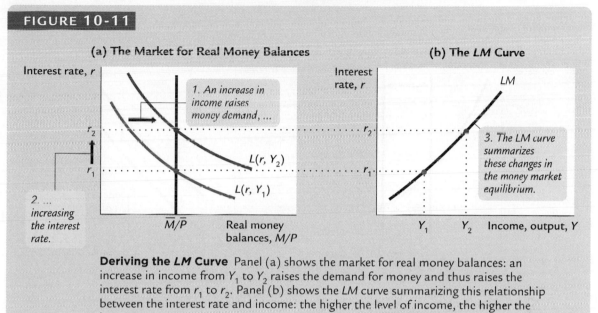

FIGURE 10-11

Deriving the *LM* Curve Panel (a) shows the market for real money balances: an increase in income from Y_1 to Y_2 raises the demand for money and thus raises the interest rate from r_1 to r_2. Panel (b) shows the *LM* curve summarizing this relationship between the interest rate and income: the higher the level of income, the higher the interest rate.

Using the theory of liquidity preference, we can figure out what happens to the equilibrium interest rate when the level of income changes. For example, consider what happens in Figure 10-11 when income increases from Y_1 to Y_2. As panel (a) illustrates, this increase in income shifts the money demand curve to the right. With the supply of real money balances unchanged, the interest rate must rise from r_1 to r_2 to equilibrate the money market. Therefore, according to the theory of liquidity preference, higher income leads to a higher interest rate.

The *LM* curve shown in panel (b) of Figure 10-11 summarizes this relationship between the level of income and the interest rate. Each point on the *LM* curve represents equilibrium in the money market, and the curve illustrates how the equilibrium interest rate depends on the level of income. The higher the level of income, the higher the demand for real money balances, and the higher the equilibrium interest rate. For this reason, the *LM* curve slopes upward.

How Monetary Policy Shifts the *LM* Curve

The *LM* curve tells us the interest rate that equilibrates the money market at any level of income. Yet, as we saw earlier, the equilibrium interest rate also depends on the supply of real money balances M/P. This means that the *LM* curve is drawn for a *given* supply of real money balances. If real money balances change—for example, if the Fed alters the money supply—the *LM* curve shifts.

We can use the theory of liquidity preference to understand how monetary policy shifts the *LM* curve. Suppose that the Fed decreases the money supply

FIGURE 10-12

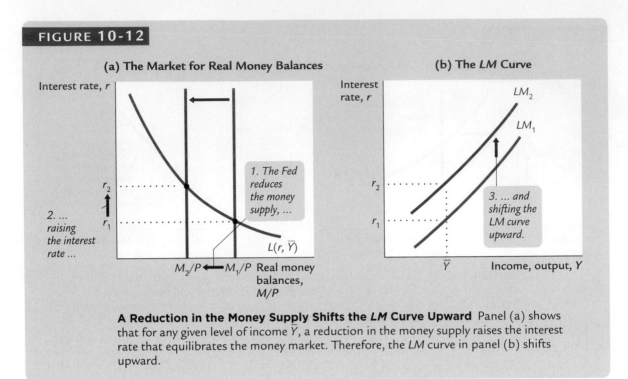

(a) The Market for Real Money Balances

Interest rate, r

1. The Fed reduces the money supply, ...

2. ... raising the interest rate ...

r_2

r_1

$L(r, \bar{Y})$

M_2/P ← M_1/P Real money balances, M/P

(b) The LM Curve

Interest rate, r

LM_2

LM_1

r_2

r_1

3. ... and shifting the LM curve upward.

$\bar{Y}$ Income, output, Y

A Reduction in the Money Supply Shifts the LM Curve Upward Panel (a) shows that for any given level of income $\bar{Y}$, a reduction in the money supply raises the interest rate that equilibrates the money market. Therefore, the LM curve in panel (b) shifts upward.

from M_1 to M_2, which causes the supply of real money balances to fall from M_1/P to M_2/P. Figure 10-12 shows what happens. Holding constant the amount of income and thus the demand curve for real money balances, we see that a reduction in the supply of real money balances raises the interest rate that equilibrates the money market. Hence, a decrease in the money supply shifts the LM curve upward.

In summary, the LM curve shows the combinations of the interest rate and the level of income that are consistent with equilibrium in the market for real money balances. The LM curve is drawn for a given supply of real money balances. Decreases in the supply of real money balances shift the LM curve upward. Increases in the supply of real money balances shift the LM curve downward.

10-3 Conclusion: The Short-Run Equilibrium

We now have all the pieces of the *IS–LM* model. The two equations of this model are

$$Y = C(Y - T) + I(r) + G \quad IS,$$

$$M/P = L(r, Y) \quad LM.$$

FIGURE 10-13

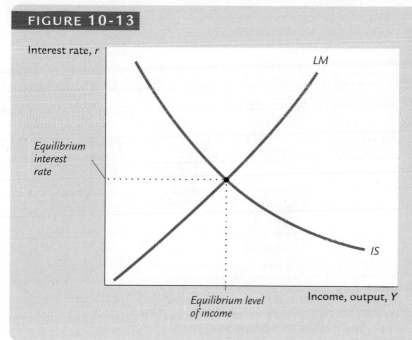

Interest rate, *r*

LM

Equilibrium interest rate

Equilibrium level of income

Income, output, *Y*

IS

Equilibrium in the *IS–LM* Model The intersection of the *IS* and *LM* curves represents simultaneous equilibrium in the market for goods and services and in the market for real money balances for given values of government spending, taxes, the money supply, and the price level.

The model takes fiscal policy *G* and *T*, monetary policy *M*, and the price level *P* as exogenous. Given these exogenous variables, the *IS* curve provides the combinations of *r* and *Y* that satisfy the equation representing the goods market, and the *LM* curve provides the combinations of *r* and *Y* that satisfy the equation representing the money market. These two curves are shown together in Figure 10-13.

The equilibrium of the economy is the point at which the *IS* curve and the *LM* curve cross. This point gives the interest rate *r* and the level of income *Y* that satisfy conditions for equilibrium in both the goods market and the money market. In other words, at this intersection, actual expenditure equals planned expenditure, and the demand for real money balances equals the supply.

As we conclude this chapter, let's recall that our ultimate goal in developing the *IS–LM* model is to analyze short-run fluctuations in economic activity. Figure 10-14 illustrates how the different pieces of our theory fit together. In this chapter we developed the Keynesian cross and the theory of liquidity preference as building blocks for the *IS–LM* model. As we see more fully in the next chapter, the *IS–LM* model helps explain the position and slope of the aggregate demand curve. The aggregate demand curve, in turn, is a piece of the model of aggregate supply and aggregate demand, which economists use to explain the short-run effects of policy changes and other events on national income.

FIGURE 10-14

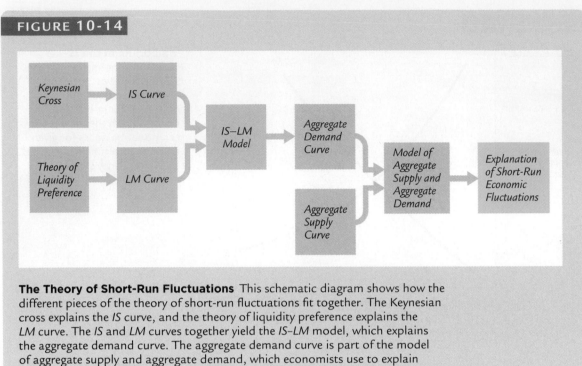

The Theory of Short-Run Fluctuations This schematic diagram shows how the different pieces of the theory of short-run fluctuations fit together. The Keynesian cross explains the *IS* curve, and the theory of liquidity preference explains the *LM* curve. The *IS* and *LM* curves together yield the *IS–LM* model, which explains the aggregate demand curve. The aggregate demand curve is part of the model of aggregate supply and aggregate demand, which economists use to explain short-run fluctuations in economic activity.

Summary

1. The Keynesian cross is a basic model of income determination. It takes fiscal policy and planned investment as exogenous and then shows that there is one level of national income at which actual expenditure equals planned expenditure. It shows that changes in fiscal policy have a multiplied impact on income.

2. Once we allow planned investment to depend on the interest rate, the Keynesian cross yields a relationship between the interest rate and national income. A higher interest rate lowers planned investment, and this in turn lowers national income. The downward-sloping *IS* curve summarizes this negative relationship between the interest rate and income.

3. The theory of liquidity preference is a basic model of the determination of the interest rate. It takes the money supply and the price level as exogenous and assumes that the interest rate adjusts to equilibrate the supply and demand for real money balances. The theory implies that increases in the money supply lower the interest rate.

4. Once we allow the demand for real money balances to depend on national income, the theory of liquidity preference yields a relationship between income and the interest rate. A higher level of income raises the demand

CHAPTER 10 Aggregate Demand I: Building the *IS–LM* Model | **303**

for real money balances, and this in turn raises the interest rate. The upward-sloping *LM* curve summarizes this positive relationship between income and the interest rate.

5. The *IS–LM* model combines the elements of the Keynesian cross and the elements of the theory of liquidity preference. The *IS* curve shows the points that satisfy equilibrium in the goods market, and the *LM* curve shows the points that satisfy equilibrium in the money market. The intersection of the *IS* and *LM* curves shows the interest rate and income that satisfy equilibrium in both markets for a given price level.

KEY CONCEPTS

IS–LM model

IS curve

LM curve

Keynesian cross

Government-purchases multiplier

Tax multiplier

Theory of liquidity preference

QUESTIONS FOR REVIEW

1. Use the Keynesian cross to explain why fiscal policy has a multiplied effect on national income.

2. Use the theory of liquidity preference to explain why an increase in the money supply lowers the

interest rate. What does this explanation assume about the price level?

3. Why does the *IS* curve slope downward?

4. Why does the *LM* curve slope upward?

PROBLEMS AND APPLICATIONS

1. Use the Keynesian cross to predict the impact on equilibrium GDP of the following:

   a. An increase in government purchases

   b. An increase in taxes

   c. Equal-sized increases in both government purchases and taxes

2. In the Keynesian cross, assume that the consumption function is given by

$$C = 200 + 0.75 \, (Y - T).$$

   Planned investment is 100; government purchases and taxes are both 100.

   a. Graph planned expenditure as a function of income.

   b. What is the equilibrium level of income?

   c. If government purchases increase to 125, what is the new equilibrium income?

   d. What level of government purchases is needed to achieve an income of 1,600?

3. Although our development of the Keynesian cross in this chapter assumes that taxes are a fixed amount, in many countries (including the United States) taxes depend on income. Let's represent the tax system by writing tax revenue as

$$T = \overline{T} + tY,$$

   where $\overline{T}$ and t are parameters of the tax code. The parameter t is the marginal tax rate: if income rises by \$1, taxes rise by $t \times$ \$1.

   a. How does this tax system change the way consumption responds to changes in GDP?

b. In the Keynesian cross, how does this tax system alter the government-purchases multiplier?

c. In the *IS–LM* model, how does this tax system alter the slope of the *IS* curve?

4. Consider the impact of an increase in thriftiness in the Keynesian cross. Suppose the consumption function is

$$C = \overline{C} + c(Y - T),$$

where $\overline{C}$ is a parameter called *autonomous consumption* and c is the marginal propensity to consume.

a. What happens to equilibrium income when the society becomes more thrifty, as represented by a decline in $\overline{C}$?

b. What happens to equilibrium saving?

c. Why do you suppose this result is called the *paradox of thrift*?

d. Does this paradox arise in the classical model of Chapter 3? Why or why not?

5. Suppose that the money demand function is

$$(M/P)^d = 1,000 - 100r,$$

where r is the interest rate in percent. The money supply M is 1,000 and the price level P is 2.

a. Graph the supply and demand for real money balances.

b. What is the equilibrium interest rate?

c. Assume that the price level is fixed. What happens to the equilibrium interest rate if the supply of money is raised from 1,000 to 1,200?

d. If the Fed wishes to raise the interest rate to 7 percent, what money supply should it set?

Aggregate Demand II: Applying the *IS–LM* Model

> *Science is a parasite: the greater the patient population the better the advance in physiology and pathology; and out of pathology arises therapy. The year 1932 was the trough of the great depression, and from its rotten soil was belatedly begot a new subject that today we call macroeconomics.*
>
> —Paul Samuelson

In Chapter 10 we assembled the pieces of the *IS–LM* model as a step toward understanding short-run economic fluctuations. We saw that the *IS* curve represents the equilibrium in the market for goods and services, that the *LM* curve represents the equilibrium in the market for real money balances, and that the *IS* and *LM* curves together determine the interest rate and national income in the short run when the price level is fixed. Now we turn our attention to applying the *IS–LM* model to analyze three issues.

First, we examine the potential causes of fluctuations in national income. We use the *IS–LM* model to see how changes in the exogenous variables (government purchases, taxes, and the money supply) influence the endogenous variables (the interest rate and national income) for a given price level. We also examine how various shocks to the goods market (the *IS* curve) and the money market (the *LM* curve) affect the interest rate and national income in the short run.

Second, we discuss how the *IS–LM* model fits into the model of aggregate supply and aggregate demand we introduced in Chapter 9. In particular, we examine how the *IS–LM* model provides a theory to explain the slope and position of the aggregate demand curve. Here we relax the assumption that the price level is fixed and show that the *IS–LM* model implies a negative relationship between the price level and national income. The model can also tell us what events shift the aggregate demand curve and in what direction.

Third, we examine the Great Depression of the 1930s. As this chapter's opening quotation indicates, this episode gave birth to short-run macroeconomic theory, for it led Keynes and his many followers to argue that aggregate demand was the key to understanding fluctuations in national income. With the benefit of hindsight, we can use the *IS–LM* model to discuss the various explanations of this traumatic economic downturn. And, as we will see throughout this chapter, the model can also be used to shed light on more recent recessions, such as those that began in 2001 and 2008.

11-1 Explaining Fluctuations With the *IS–LM* Model

The intersection of the *IS* curve and the *LM* curve determines the level of national income. When one of these curves shifts, the short-run equilibrium of the economy changes, and national income fluctuates. In this section we examine how changes in policy and shocks to the economy can cause these curves to shift.

How Fiscal Policy Shifts the *IS* Curve and Changes the Short-Run Equilibrium

We begin by examining how changes in fiscal policy (government purchases and taxes) alter the economy's short-run equilibrium. Recall that changes in fiscal policy influence planned expenditure and thereby shift the *IS* curve. The *IS–LM* model shows how these shifts in the *IS* curve affect income and the interest rate.

Changes in Government Purchases Consider an increase in government purchases of ΔG. The government-purchases multiplier in the Keynesian cross tells us that this change in fiscal policy raises the level of income at any given interest rate by $\Delta G/(1 - MPC)$. Therefore, as Figure 11-1 shows, the *IS* curve

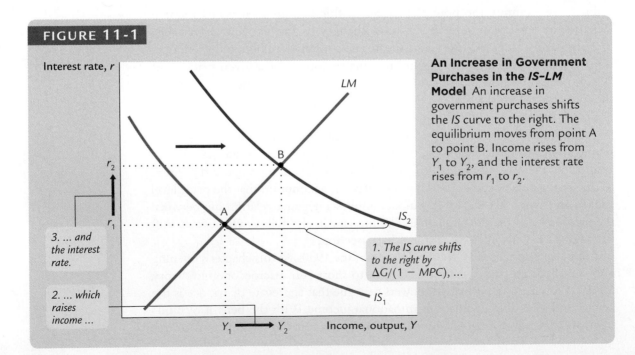

FIGURE 11-1

An Increase in Government Purchases in the *IS–LM* Model An increase in government purchases shifts the *IS* curve to the right. The equilibrium moves from point A to point B. Income rises from Y_1 to Y_2, and the interest rate rises from r_1 to r_2.

Interest rate, r

LM

r_2

B

r_1

A

IS_2

3. ... and the interest rate.

1. The IS curve shifts to the right by $\Delta G/(1 - MPC)$, ...

2. ... which raises income ...

IS_1

Y_1 Y_2 Income, output, Y

shifts to the right by this amount. The equilibrium of the economy moves from point A to point B. The increase in government purchases raises both income and the interest rate.

To understand fully what's happening in Figure 11-1, it helps to keep in mind the building blocks for the *IS–LM* model from the preceding chapter—the Keynesian cross and the theory of liquidity preference. Here is the story. When the government increases its purchases of goods and services, the economy's planned expenditure rises. The increase in planned expenditure stimulates the production of goods and services, which causes total income *Y* to rise. These effects should be familiar from the Keynesian cross.

Now consider the money market, as described by the theory of liquidity preference. Because the economy's demand for money depends on income, the rise in total income increases the quantity of money demanded at every interest rate. The supply of money has not changed, however, so higher money demand causes the equilibrium interest rate *r* to rise.

The higher interest rate arising in the money market, in turn, has ramifications back in the goods market. When the interest rate rises, firms cut back on their investment plans. This fall in investment partially offsets the expansionary effect of the increase in government purchases. Thus, the increase in income in response to a fiscal expansion is smaller in the *IS–LM* model than it is in the Keynesian cross (where investment is assumed to be fixed). You can see this in Figure 11-1. The horizontal shift in the *IS* curve equals the rise in equilibrium income in the Keynesian cross. This amount is larger than the increase in equilibrium income here in the *IS–LM* model. The difference is explained by the crowding out of investment due to a higher interest rate.

Changes in Taxes In the *IS–LM* model, changes in taxes affect the economy much the same as changes in government purchases do, except that taxes affect expenditure through consumption. Consider, for instance, a decrease in taxes of ΔT. The tax cut encourages consumers to spend more and, therefore, increases planned expenditure. The tax multiplier in the Keynesian cross tells us that this change in policy raises the level of income at any given interest rate by $\Delta T \times MPC/(1 - MPC)$. Therefore, as Figure 11-2 illustrates, the *IS* curve shifts to the right by this amount. The equilibrium of the economy moves from point A to point B. The tax cut raises both income and the interest rate. Once again, because the higher interest rate depresses investment, the increase in income is smaller in the *IS–LM* model than it is in the Keynesian cross.

How Monetary Policy Shifts the *LM* Curve and Changes the Short-Run Equilibrium

We now examine the effects of monetary policy. Recall that a change in the money supply alters the interest rate that equilibrates the money market for any given level of income and, thus, shifts the *LM* curve. The *IS–LM* model shows how a shift in the *LM* curve affects income and the interest rate.

Consider an increase in the money supply. An increase in *M* leads to an increase in real money balances M/P, because the price level *P* is fixed in the

FIGURE 11-2

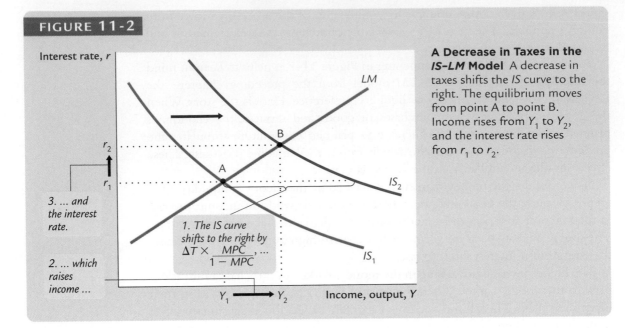

A Decrease in Taxes in the IS–LM Model A decrease in taxes shifts the *IS* curve to the right. The equilibrium moves from point A to point B. Income rises from Y_1 to Y_2, and the interest rate rises from r_1 to r_2.

3. ... and the interest rate.

2. ... which raises income ...

1. The IS curve shifts to the right by $\Delta T \times \dfrac{MPC}{1 - MPC}$, ...

short run. The theory of liquidity preference shows that for any given level of income, an increase in real money balances leads to a lower interest rate. There-fore, the *LM* curve shifts downward, as in Figure 11-3. The equilibrium moves from point A to point B. The increase in the money supply lowers the interest rate and raises the level of income.

Once again, to tell the story that explains the economy's adjustment from point A to point B, we rely on the building blocks of the *IS–LM* model—the Keynesian cross and the theory of liquidity preference. This time, we begin with

FIGURE 11-3

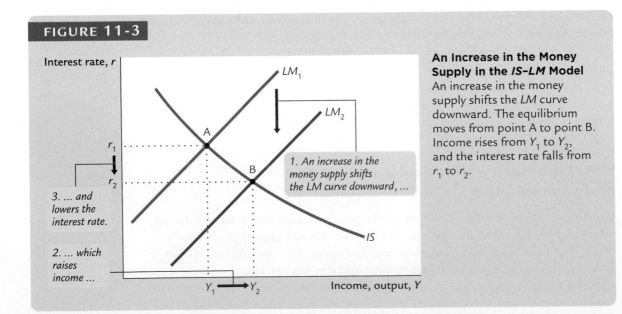

An Increase in the Money Supply in the IS–LM Model An increase in the money supply shifts the *LM* curve downward. The equilibrium moves from point A to point B. Income rises from Y_1 to Y_2, and the interest rate falls from r_1 to r_2.

3. ... and lowers the interest rate.

2. ... which raises income ...

1. An increase in the money supply shifts the LM curve downward, ...

the money market, where the monetary-policy action occurs. When the Federal Reserve increases the supply of money, people have more money than they want to hold at the prevailing interest rate. As a result, they start depositing this extra money in banks or using it to buy bonds. The interest rate r then falls until people are willing to hold all the extra money that the Fed has created; this brings the money market to a new equilibrium. The lower interest rate, in turn, has ramifications for the goods market. A lower interest rate stimulates planned investment, which increases planned expenditure, production, and income Y.

Thus, the *IS–LM* model shows that monetary policy influences income by changing the interest rate. This conclusion sheds light on our analysis of monetary policy in Chapter 9. In that chapter we showed that in the short run, when prices are sticky, an expansion in the money supply raises income. But we did not discuss *how* a monetary expansion induces greater spending on goods and services—a process called the **monetary transmission mechanism**. The *IS–LM* model shows an important part of that mechanism: *an increase in the money supply lowers the interest rate, which stimulates investment and thereby expands the demand for goods and services.*

The Interaction Between Monetary and Fiscal Policy

When analyzing any change in monetary or fiscal policy, it is important to keep in mind that the policymakers who control these policy tools are aware of what the other policymakers are doing. A change in one policy, therefore, may influence the other, and this interdependence may alter the impact of a policy change.

For example, suppose Congress raises taxes. What effect will this policy have on the economy? According to the *IS–LM* model, the answer depends on how the Fed responds to the tax increase.

Figure 11-4 shows three of the many possible outcomes. In panel (a), the Fed holds the money supply constant. The tax increase shifts the *IS* curve to the left. Income falls (because higher taxes reduce consumer spending), and the interest rate falls (because lower income reduces the demand for money). The fall in income indicates that the tax hike causes a recession.

In panel (b), the Fed wants to hold the interest rate constant. In this case, when the tax increase shifts the *IS* curve to the left, the Fed must decrease the money supply to keep the interest rate at its original level. This fall in the money supply shifts the *LM* curve upward. The interest rate does not fall, but income falls by a larger amount than if the Fed had held the money supply constant. Whereas in panel (a) the lower interest rate stimulated investment and partially offset the contractionary effect of the tax hike, in panel (b) the Fed deepens the recession by keeping the interest rate high.

In panel (c), the Fed wants to prevent the tax increase from lowering income. It must, therefore, raise the money supply and shift the *LM* curve downward enough to offset the shift in the *IS* curve. In this case, the tax increase does not cause a recession, but it does cause a large fall in the interest rate. Although the level of income is not changed, the combination of a tax increase and a monetary expansion does change the allocation of the economy's resources. The higher

FIGURE 11-4

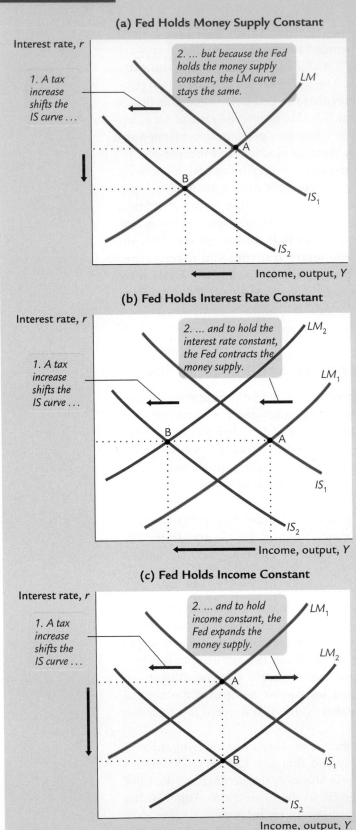

(a) Fed Holds Money Supply Constant

Interest rate, *r*

1. A tax increase shifts the IS curve . . .

2. . . . but because the Fed holds the money supply constant, the LM curve stays the same.

LM

A

B

IS_1

IS_2

Income, output, *Y*

(b) Fed Holds Interest Rate Constant

Interest rate, *r*

1. A tax increase shifts the IS curve . . .

2. . . . and to hold the interest rate constant, the Fed contracts the money supply.

LM_2

LM_1

B

A

IS_1

IS_2

Income, output, *Y*

(c) Fed Holds Income Constant

Interest rate, *r*

1. A tax increase shifts the IS curve . . .

2. . . . and to hold income constant, the Fed expands the money supply.

LM_1

LM_2

A

B

IS_1

IS_2

Income, output, *Y*

The Response of the Economy to a Tax Increase How the economy responds to a tax increase depends on how the central bank responds. In panel (a) the Fed holds the money supply constant. In panel (b) the Fed holds the interest rate constant by reducing the money supply. In panel (c) the Fed holds the level of income constant by raising the money supply. In each case, the economy moves from point A to point B.

taxes depress consumption, while the lower interest rate stimulates investment. Income is not affected because these two effects exactly balance.

From this example we can see that the impact of a change in fiscal policy depends on the policy the Fed pursues—that is, on whether it holds the money supply, the interest rate, or the level of income constant. More generally, whenever analyzing a change in one policy, we must make an assumption about its effect on the other policy. The most appropriate assumption depends on the case at hand and the many political considerations that lie behind economic policymaking.

CASE STUDY

Policy Analysis With Macroeconometric Models

The *IS–LM* model shows how monetary and fiscal policy influence the equilibrium level of income. The predictions of the model, however, are qualitative, not quantitative. The *IS–LM* model shows that increases in government purchases raise GDP and that increases in taxes lower GDP. But when economists analyze specific policy proposals, they need to know not only the direction of the effect but also the size. For example, if Congress increases taxes by $100 billion and if monetary policy is not altered, how much will GDP fall? To answer this question, economists need to go beyond the graphical representation of the *IS–LM* model.

Macroeconometric models of the economy provide one way to evaluate policy proposals. A *macroeconometric model* is a model that describes the economy quantitatively, rather than just qualitatively. Many of these models are essentially more complicated and more realistic versions of our *IS–LM* model. The economists who build macroeconometric models use historical data to estimate parameters such as the marginal propensity to consume, the sensitivity of investment to the interest rate, and the sensitivity of money demand to the interest rate. Once a model is built, economists can simulate the effects of alternative policies with the help of a computer. When interpreting such an exercise, it is important to keep in mind that the results of such a computer simulation are only as good as the macroeconometric model being simulated.

Table 11-1 shows the fiscal-policy multipliers implied by one prominent macroeconometric model, the Data Resources Incorporated (DRI) model, named for the economic forecasting firm that developed it. The multipliers are given for two assumptions about how the Fed might respond to changes in fiscal policy.

One assumption about monetary policy is that the Fed keeps the nominal interest rate constant. That is, when fiscal policy shifts the *IS* curve to the right or to the left, the Fed adjusts the money supply to shift the *LM* curve in the same direction. Because there is no crowding out of investment due to a changing interest rate, the fiscal-policy multipliers are similar to those from the Keynesian cross. The DRI model indicates that, in this case, the government-purchases multiplier is 1.93, and the tax multiplier is −1.19. That is, a $100 billion increase in government purchases raises GDP by $193 billion, and a $100 billion increase in taxes lowers GDP by $119 billion.

TABLE 11-1

The Fiscal-Policy Multipliers in the DRI Model

	VALUE OF MULTIPLIERS	
Assumption About Monetary Policy	$\Delta Y/\Delta G$	$\Delta Y/\Delta T$
Nominal interest rate held constant	1.93	−1.19
Money supply held constant	0.60	−0.26

Note: This table gives the fiscal-policy multipliers for a sustained change in government purchases or in personal income taxes. These multipliers are for the fourth quarter after the policy change is made.
Source: Otto Eckstein, *The DRI Model of the U.S. Economy* (New York: McGraw-Hill, 1983), 169.

The second assumption about monetary policy is that the Fed keeps the money supply constant so that the *LM* curve does not shift. In this case, the interest rate rises, and investment is crowded out, so the multipliers are much smaller. The government–purchases multiplier is only 0.60, and the tax multiplier is only −0.26. That is, a $100 billion increase in government purchases raises GDP by $60 billion, and a $100 billion increase in taxes lowers GDP by $26 billion.

Table 11-1 shows that the fiscal-policy multipliers are very different under the two assumptions about monetary policy. The impact of any change in fiscal policy depends crucially on how the Fed responds to that change. ∎

Shocks in the *IS–LM* Model

Because the *IS–LM* model shows how national income is determined in the short run, we can use the model to examine how various economic disturbances affect income. So far we have seen how changes in fiscal policy shift the *IS* curve and how changes in monetary policy shift the *LM* curve. Similarly, we can group other disturbances into two categories: shocks to the *IS* curve and shocks to the *LM* curve.

Shocks to the *IS* curve are exogenous changes in the demand for goods and services. Some economists, including Keynes, have emphasized that such changes

Calvin and Hobbes © 1992 Watterson. Dist. by Universal Press Syndicate.

in demand can arise from investors' *animal spirits*—exogenous and perhaps self-fulfilling waves of optimism and pessimism. For example, suppose that firms become pessimistic about the future of the economy and that this pessimism causes them to build fewer new factories. This reduction in the demand for investment goods causes a contractionary shift in the investment function: at every interest rate, firms want to invest less. The fall in investment reduces planned expenditure and shifts the *IS* curve to the left, reducing income and employment. This fall in equilibrium income in part validates the firms' initial pessimism.

Shocks to the *IS* curve may also arise from changes in the demand for consumer goods. Suppose, for instance, that the election of a popular president increases consumer confidence in the economy. This induces consumers to save less for the future and consume more today. We can interpret this change as an upward shift in the consumption function. This shift in the consumption function increases planned expenditure and shifts the *IS* curve to the right, and this raises income.

Shocks to the *LM* curve arise from exogenous changes in the demand for money. For example, suppose that new restrictions on credit-card availability increase the amount of money people choose to hold. According to the theory of liquidity preference, when money demand rises, the interest rate necessary to equilibrate the money market is higher (for any given level of income and money supply). Hence, an increase in money demand shifts the *LM* curve upward, which tends to raise the interest rate and depress income.

In summary, several kinds of events can cause economic fluctuations by shifting the *IS* curve or the *LM* curve. Remember, however, that such fluctuations are not inevitable. Policymakers can try to use the tools of monetary and fiscal policy to offset exogenous shocks. If policymakers are sufficiently quick and skillful (admittedly, a big if), shocks to the *IS* or *LM* curves need not lead to fluctuations in income or employment.

CASE STUDY

The U.S. Recession of 2001

In 2001, the U.S. economy experienced a pronounced slowdown in economic activity. The unemployment rate rose from 3.9 percent in September 2000 to 4.9 percent in August 2001, and then to 6.3 percent in June 2003. In many ways, the slowdown looked like a typical recession driven by a fall in aggregate demand.

Three notable shocks explain this event. The first was a decline in the stock market. During the 1990s, the stock market experienced a boom of historic proportions, as investors became optimistic about the prospects of the new information technology. Some economists viewed the optimism as excessive at the time, and in hindsight this proved to be the case. When the optimism faded, average stock prices fell by about 25 percent from August 2000 to August 2001. The fall in the market reduced household wealth and thus consumer spending. In addition, the declining perceptions of the profitability of the new technologies led to a fall in investment spending. In the language of the *IS–LM* model, the *IS* curve shifted to the left.

The second shock was the terrorist attacks on New York City and Washington, D.C., on September 11, 2001. In the week after the attacks, the stock market fell another 12 percent, which at the time was the biggest weekly loss since the Great Depression of the 1930s. Moreover, the attacks increased uncertainty about what the future would hold. Uncertainty can reduce spending because households and firms postpone some of their plans until the uncertainty is resolved. Thus, the terrorist attacks shifted the *IS* curve farther to the left.

The third shock was a series of accounting scandals at some of the nation's most prominent corporations, including Enron and WorldCom. The result of these scandals was the bankruptcy of some companies that had fraudulently represented themselves as more profitable than they truly were, criminal convictions for the executives who had been responsible for the fraud, and new laws aimed at regulating corporate accounting standards more thoroughly. These events further depressed stock prices and discouraged business investment—a third leftward shift in the *IS* curve.

Fiscal and monetary policymakers responded quickly to these events. Congress passed a major tax cut in 2001, including an immediate tax rebate, and a second major tax cut in 2003. One goal of these tax cuts was to stimulate consumer spending. (See the Case Study on cutting taxes in Chapter 10.) In addition, after the terrorist attacks, Congress increased government spending by appropriating funds to assist in New York's recovery and to bail out the ailing airline industry. These fiscal measures shifted the *IS* curve to the right.

At the same time, the Federal Reserve pursued expansionary monetary policy, shifting the *LM* curve to the right. Money growth accelerated, and interest rates fell. The interest rate on three-month Treasury bills fell from 6.4 percent in November 2000 to 3.3 percent in August 2001, just before the terrorist attacks. After the attacks and corporate scandals hit the economy, the Fed increased its monetary stimulus, and the Treasury bill rate fell to 0.9 percent in July 2003—the lowest level in many decades.

Expansionary monetary and fiscal policy had the intended effects. Economic growth picked up in the second half of 2003 and was strong throughout 2004. By July 2005, the unemployment rate was back down to 5.0 percent, and it stayed at or below that level for the next several years. Unemployment would begin rising again in 2008, however, when the economy experienced another recession. The causes of the 2008 recession are examined in another case study later in this chapter. ■

What Is the Fed's Policy Instrument—The Money Supply or the Interest Rate?

Our analysis of monetary policy has been based on the assumption that the Fed influences the economy by controlling the money supply. By contrast, when the media report on changes in Fed policy, they often just say that the Fed has raised or lowered interest rates. Which is right? Even though these two views may seem different, both are correct, and it is important to understand why.

In recent years, the Fed has used the **federal funds rate**—the interest rate that banks charge one another for overnight loans—as its short-term policy instrument.

When the Federal Open Market Committee meets every six weeks to set monetary policy, it votes on a target for this interest rate that will apply until the next meeting. After the meeting is over, the Fed's bond traders (who are located in New York) are told to conduct the open-market operations necessary to hit that target. These open-market operations change the money supply and shift the *LM* curve so that the equilibrium interest rate (determined by the intersection of the *IS* and *LM* curves) equals the target interest rate that the Federal Open Market Committee has chosen.

As a result of this operating procedure, Fed policy is often discussed in terms of changing interest rates. Keep in mind, however, that behind these changes in interest rates are the necessary changes in the money supply. A newspaper might report, for instance, that "the Fed has lowered interest rates." To be more precise, we can translate this statement as meaning "the Federal Open Market Committee has instructed the Fed bond traders to buy bonds in open-market operations so as to increase the money supply, shift the *LM* curve, and reduce the equilibrium interest rate to hit a new lower target."

Why has the Fed chosen to use an interest rate, rather than the money supply, as its short-term policy instrument? One possible answer is that shocks to the *LM* curve are more prevalent than shocks to the *IS* curve. When the Fed targets interest rates, it automatically offsets *LM* shocks by adjusting the money supply, although this policy exacerbates *IS* shocks. If *LM* shocks are the more prevalent type, then a policy of targeting the interest rate leads to greater economic stability than a policy of targeting the money supply. (Problem 7 at the end of this chapter asks you to analyze this issue more fully.)

One lesson from the *IS–LM* model is that when a central bank sets the money supply, it determines the equilibrium interest rate. Thus, in some ways, setting the money supply and setting the interest rate are two sides of the same coin.

11-2 *IS–LM* as a Theory of Aggregate Demand

We have been using the *IS–LM* model to explain national income in the short run when the price level is fixed. To see how the *IS–LM* model fits into the model of aggregate supply and aggregate demand introduced in Chapter 9, we now examine what happens in the *IS–LM* model if the price level is allowed to change. By examining the effects of changing the price level, we can finally deliver what was promised when we began our study of the *IS–LM* model: a theory to explain the position and slope of the aggregate demand curve.

From the *IS–LM* Model to the Aggregate Demand Curve

Recall from Chapter 9 that the aggregate demand curve describes a relationship between the price level and the level of national income. In Chapter 9 this relationship was derived from the quantity theory of money. That analysis showed that for a given money supply, a higher price level implies a lower level of income. Increases in the money supply shift the aggregate demand curve to the right, and decreases in the money supply shift the aggregate demand curve to the left.

To understand the determinants of aggregate demand more fully, we now use the *IS–LM* model, rather than the quantity theory, to derive the aggregate demand curve. First, we use the *IS–LM* model to show why national income falls as the price level rises—that is, why the aggregate demand curve is downward sloping. Second, we examine what causes the aggregate demand curve to shift.

To explain why the aggregate demand curve slopes downward, we examine what happens in the *IS–LM* model when the price level changes. This is done in Figure 11-5. For any given money supply *M*, a higher price level *P* reduces the supply of real money balances *M/P*. A lower supply of real money balances shifts the *LM* curve upward, which raises the equilibrium interest rate and lowers the equilibrium level of income, as shown in panel (a). Here the price level rises from P_1 to P_2, and income falls from Y_1 to Y_2. The aggregate demand curve in panel (b) plots this negative relationship between national income and the price level. In other words, the aggregate demand curve shows the set of equilibrium points that arise in the *IS–LM* model as we vary the price level and see what happens to income.

What causes the aggregate demand curve to shift? Because the aggregate demand curve summarizes the results from the *IS–LM* model, events that shift the *IS* curve or the *LM* curve (for a given price level) cause the aggregate demand curve to shift. For instance, an increase in the money supply raises income in the *IS–LM* model for any given price level; it thus shifts the aggregate demand curve

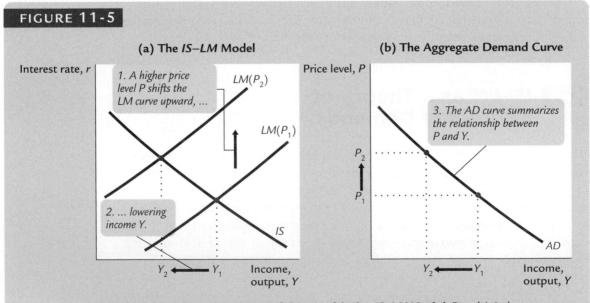

FIGURE 11-5

(a) The *IS–LM* Model

Interest rate, *r*

1. A higher price level *P* shifts the *LM* curve upward, ...

$LM(P_2)$

$LM(P_1)$

2. ... lowering income *Y*.

IS

$Y_2 \longleftarrow Y_1$ Income, output, *Y*

(b) The Aggregate Demand Curve

Price level, *P*

3. The AD curve summarizes the relationship between *P* and *Y*.

P_2

P_1

AD

$Y_2 \longleftarrow Y_1$ Income, output, *Y*

Deriving the Aggregate Demand Curve with the *IS–LM* Model Panel (a) shows the *IS–LM* model: an increase in the price level from P_1 to P_2 lowers real money balances and thus shifts the *LM* curve upward. The shift in the *LM* curve lowers income from Y_1 to Y_2. Panel (b) shows the aggregate demand curve summarizing this relationship between the price level and income: the higher the price level, the lower the level of income.

to the right, as shown in panel (a) of Figure 11-6. Similarly, an increase in government purchases or a decrease in taxes raises income in the *IS–LM* model for a given price level; it also shifts the aggregate demand curve to the right, as shown in panel (b) of Figure 11-6. Conversely, a decrease in the money supply, a decrease in government purchases, or an increase in taxes lowers income in the *IS–LM* model and shifts the aggregate demand curve to the left. Anything that

FIGURE 11-6

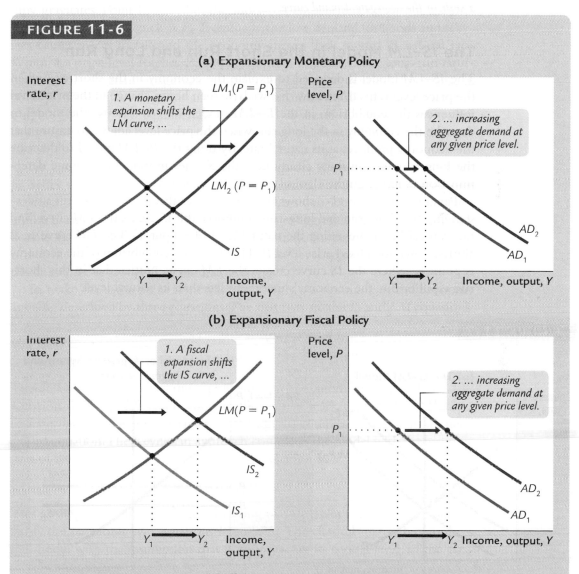

How Monetary and Fiscal Policies Shift the Aggregate Demand Curve Panel (a) shows a monetary expansion. For any given price level, an increase in the money supply raises real money balances, shifts the *LM* curve downward, and raises income. Hence, an increase in the money supply shifts the aggregate demand curve to the right. Panel (b) shows a fiscal expansion, such as an increase in government purchases or a decrease in taxes. The fiscal expansion shifts the *IS* curve to the right and, for any given price level, raises income. Hence, a fiscal expansion shifts the aggregate demand curve to the right.

TABLE 11-2

What Happened During the Great Depression?

Year	Unemployment Rate (1)	Real GNP (2)	Consumption (2)	Investment (2)	Government Purchases (2)
1929	3.2	203.6	139.6	40.4	22.0
1930	8.9	183.5	130.4	27.4	24.3
1931	16.3	169.5	126.1	16.8	25.4
1932	24.1	144.2	114.8	4.7	24.2
1933	25.2	141.5	112.8	5.3	23.3
1934	22.0	154.3	118.1	9.4	26.6
1935	20.3	169.5	125.5	18.0	27.0
1936	17.0	193.2	138.4	24.0	31.8
1937	14.3	203.2	143.1	29.9	30.8
1938	19.1	192.9	140.0	17.0	33.9
1939	17.2	209.4	148.2	24.7	35.2
1940	14.6	227.2	155.7	33.0	36.4

Source: Historical Statistics of the United States, Colonial Times to 1970, Parts I and II (Washington, DC: U.S. Department of Commerce, Bureau of Census, 1975).
Note: (1) The unemployment rate is series D9. (2) Real GNP, consumption, investment, and government purchases are series F3, F48, F52, and F66, and are measured in billions of 1958 dollars. (3) The interest rate is the prime Commercial

Which assumption is most appropriate? The answer depends on the time horizon. The classical assumption best describes the long run. Hence, our long-run analysis of national income in Chapter 3 and prices in Chapter 4 assumes that output equals its natural level. The Keynesian assumption best describes the short run. Therefore, our analysis of economic fluctuations relies on the assumption of a fixed price level.

11-3 The Great Depression

Now that we have developed the model of aggregate demand, let's use it to address the question that originally motivated Keynes: what caused the Great Depression? Even today, about eighty years after the event, economists continue to debate the cause of this major economic downturn. The Great Depression provides an extended case study to show how economists use the *IS–LM* model to analyze economic fluctuations.[1]

Before turning to the explanations economists have proposed, look at Table 11-2, which presents some statistics regarding the Depression. These statistics

---

[1] For a flavor of the debate, see Milton Friedman and Anna J. Schwartz, *A Monetary History of the United States, 1867–1960* (Princeton, N.J.: Princeton University Press, 1963); Peter Temin, *Did Monetary Forces Cause the Great Depression?* (New York: W. W. Norton, 1976); the essays in Karl Brunner, ed., *The Great Depression Revisited* (Boston: Martinus Nijhoff, 1981); and the symposium on the Great Depression in the Spring 1993 issue of the *Journal of Economic Perspectives*.

Year	Nominal Interest Rate (3)	Money Supply (4)	Price Level (5)	Inflation (6)	Real Money Balances (7)
1929	5.9	26.6	50.6	—	52.6
1930	3.6	25.8	49.3	2.6	52.3
1931	2.6	24.1	44.8	−10.1	54.5
1932	2.7	21.1	40.2	−9.3	52.5
1933	1.7	19.9	39.3	−2.2	50.7
1934	1.0	21.9	42.2	7.4	51.8
1935	0.8	25.9	42.6	0.9	60.8
1936	0.8	29.6	42.7	0.2	62.9
1937	0.9	30.9	44.5	4.2	69.5
1938	0.8	30.5	43.9	−1.3	69.5
1939	0.6	34.2	43.2	−1.6	79.1
1940	0.6	39.7	43.9	1.6	90.3

Paper rate, 4–6 months, series ×445. (4) The money supply is series ×414, currency plus demand deposits, measured in billions of dollars. (5) The price level is the GNP deflator (1958 = 100), series E1. (6) The inflation rate is the percentage change in the price level series. (7) Real money balances, calculated by dividing the money supply by the price level and multiplying by 100, are in billions of 1958 dollars.

are the battlefield on which debate about the Depression takes place. What do you think happened? An *IS* shift? An *LM* shift? Or something else?

The Spending Hypothesis: Shocks to the *IS* Curve

Table 11-2 shows that the decline in income in the early 1930s coincided with falling interest rates. This fact has led some economists to suggest that the cause of the decline may have been a contractionary shift in the *IS* curve. This view is sometimes called the *spending hypothesis,* because it places primary blame for the Depression on an exogenous fall in spending on goods and services.

Economists have attempted to explain this decline in spending in several ways. Some argue that a downward shift in the consumption function caused the contractionary shift in the *IS* curve. The stock market crash of 1929 may have been partly responsible for this shift: by reducing wealth and increasing uncertainty about the future prospects of the U.S. economy, the crash may have induced consumers to save more of their income rather than spend it.

Others explain the decline in spending by pointing to the large drop in investment in housing. Some economists believe that the residential investment boom of the 1920s was excessive and that once this "overbuilding" became apparent, the demand for residential investment declined drastically. Another possible explanation for the fall in residential investment is the reduction in immigration in the 1930s: a more slowly growing population demands less new housing.

Once the Depression began, several events occurred that could have reduced spending further. First, many banks failed in the early 1930s, in part because of inadequate bank regulation, and these bank failures may have exacerbated the fall in investment spending. Banks play the crucial role of getting the funds available for investment to those households and firms that can best use them. The closing of many banks in the early 1930s may have prevented some businesses from getting the funds they needed for capital investment and, therefore, may have led to a further contractionary shift in the investment function.[2]

In addition, the fiscal policy of the 1930s caused a contractionary shift in the *IS* curve. Politicians at that time were more concerned with balancing the budget than with using fiscal policy to keep production and employment at their natural levels. The Revenue Act of 1932 increased various taxes, especially those falling on lower- and middle-income consumers.[3] The Democratic platform of that year expressed concern about the budget deficit and advocated an "immediate and drastic reduction of governmental expenditures." In the midst of historically high unemployment, policymakers searched for ways to raise taxes and reduce government spending.

There are, therefore, several ways to explain a contractionary shift in the *IS* curve. Keep in mind that these different views may all be true. There may be no single explanation for the decline in spending. It is possible that all of these changes coincided and that together they led to a massive reduction in spending.

The Money Hypothesis: A Shock to the *LM* Curve

Table 11-2 shows that the money supply fell 25 percent from 1929 to 1933, during which time the unemployment rate rose from 3.2 percent to 25.2 percent. This fact provides the motivation and support for what is called the *money hypothesis*, which places primary blame for the Depression on the Federal Reserve for allowing the money supply to fall by such a large amount.[4] The best-known advocates of this interpretation are Milton Friedman and Anna Schwartz, who defend it in their treatise on U.S. monetary history. Friedman and Schwartz argue that contractions in the money supply have caused most economic downturns and that the Great Depression is a particularly vivid example.

Using the *IS–LM* model, we might interpret the money hypothesis as explaining the Depression by a contractionary shift in the *LM* curve. Seen in this way, however, the money hypothesis runs into two problems.

The first problem is the behavior of *real* money balances. Monetary policy leads to a contractionary shift in the *LM* curve only if real money balances fall. Yet from 1929 to 1931 real money balances rose slightly, because the fall in the

---

[2] Ben Bernanke, "Non-Monetary Effects of the Financial Crisis in the Propagation of the Great Depression," *American Economic Review* 73 (June 1983): 257–276.

[3] E. Cary Brown, "Fiscal Policy in the 'Thirties: A Reappraisal," *American Economic Review* 46 (December 1956): 857–879.

[4] We discussed the reasons for this large decrease in the money supply in the appendix to Chapter 4, where we examined the money supply process in more detail. In particular, see the Case Study "Bank Failures and the Money Supply in the 1930s."

money supply was accompanied by an even greater fall in the price level. Although the monetary contraction may be responsible for the rise in unemployment from 1931 to 1933, when real money balances did fall, it cannot easily explain the initial downturn from 1929 to 1931.

The second problem with the money hypothesis is the behavior of interest rates. If a contractionary shift in the *LM* curve triggered the Depression, we should have observed higher interest rates. Yet nominal interest rates fell continuously from 1929 to 1933.

These two reasons appear sufficient to reject the view that the Depression was instigated by a contractionary shift in the *LM* curve. But was the fall in the money stock irrelevant? Next, we turn to another mechanism through which monetary policy might have been responsible for the severity of the Depression—the deflation of the 1930s.

The Money Hypothesis Again: The Effects of Falling Prices

From 1929 to 1933 the price level fell 25 percent. Many economists blame this deflation for the severity of the Great Depression. They argue that the deflation may have turned what in 1931 was a typical economic downturn into an unprecedented period of high unemployment and depressed income. If correct, this argument gives new life to the money hypothesis. Because the falling money supply was, plausibly, responsible for the falling price level, it could have been responsible for the severity of the Depression. To evaluate this argument, we must discuss how changes in the price level affect income in the *IS–LM* model.

The Stabilizing Effects of Deflation In the *IS–LM* model we have developed so far, falling prices raise income. For any given supply of money M, a lower price level implies higher real money balances M/P. An increase in real money balances causes an expansionary shift in the *LM* curve, which leads to higher income.

Another channel through which falling prices expand income is called the **Pigou effect**. Arthur Pigou, a prominent classical economist in the 1930s, pointed out that real money balances are part of households' wealth. As prices fall and real money balances rise, consumers should feel wealthier and spend more. This increase in consumer spending should cause an expansionary shift in the *IS* curve, also leading to higher income.

These two reasons led some economists in the 1930s to believe that falling prices would help stabilize the economy. That is, they thought that a decline in the price level would automatically push the economy back toward full employment. Yet other economists were less confident in the economy's ability to correct itself. They pointed to other effects of falling prices, to which we now turn.

The Destabilizing Effects of Deflation Economists have proposed two theories to explain how falling prices could depress income rather than raise it. The first, called the **debt–deflation theory**, describes the effects of unexpected falls in the price level. The second explains the effects of expected deflation.

The debt–deflation theory begins with an observation from Chapter 4: unanticipated changes in the price level redistribute wealth between debtors and creditors. If a debtor owes a creditor $1,000, then the real amount of this debt is $1,000/P$, where P is the price level. A fall in the price level raises the real amount of this debt—the amount of purchasing power the debtor must repay the creditor. Therefore, an unexpected deflation enriches creditors and impoverishes debtors.

The debt–deflation theory then posits that this redistribution of wealth affects spending on goods and services. In response to the redistribution from debtors to creditors, debtors spend less and creditors spend more. If these two groups have equal spending propensities, there is no aggregate impact. But it seems reasonable to assume that debtors have higher propensities to spend than creditors—perhaps that is why the debtors are in debt in the first place. In this case, debtors reduce their spending by more than creditors raise theirs. The net effect is a reduction in spending, a contractionary shift in the IS curve, and lower national income.

To understand how *expected* changes in prices can affect income, we need to add a new variable to the IS–LM model. Our discussion of the model so far has not distinguished between the nominal and real interest rates. Yet we know from previous chapters that investment depends on the real interest rate and that money demand depends on the nominal interest rate. If i is the nominal interest rate and $E\pi$ is expected inflation, then the *ex ante* real interest rate is $i - E\pi$. We can now write the IS–LM model as

$$Y = C(Y - T) + I(i - E\pi) + G \quad IS,$$

$$M/P = L(i, Y) \quad LM.$$

Expected inflation enters as a variable in the IS curve. Thus, changes in expected inflation shift the IS curve.

Let's use this extended IS–LM model to examine how changes in expected inflation influence the level of income. We begin by assuming that everyone expects the price level to remain the same. In this case, there is no expected inflation ($E\pi = 0$), and these two equations produce the familiar IS–LM model. Figure 11-8 depicts this initial situation with the LM curve and the IS curve labeled IS_1. The intersection of these two curves determines the nominal and real interest rates, which for now are the same.

Now suppose that everyone suddenly expects that the price level will fall in the future, so that $E\pi$ becomes negative. The real interest rate is now higher at any given nominal interest rate. This increase in the real interest rate depresses planned investment spending, shifting the IS curve from IS_1 to IS_2. (The vertical distance of the downward shift exactly equals the expected deflation.) Thus, an expected deflation leads to a reduction in national income from Y_1 to Y_2. The nominal interest rate falls from i_1 to i_2, while the real interest rate rises from r_1 to r_2.

Here is the story behind this figure. When firms come to expect deflation, they become reluctant to borrow to buy investment goods because they believe they will have to repay these loans later in more valuable dollars. The fall in investment depresses planned expenditure, which in turn depresses income. The fall

FIGURE 11-8

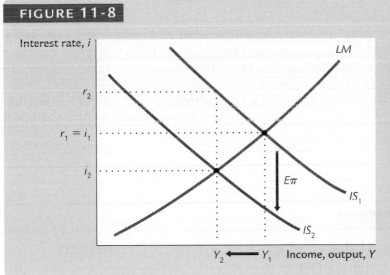

Expected Deflation in the *IS–LM* Model An expected deflation (a negative value of $E\pi$) raises the real interest rate for any given nominal interest rate, and this depresses investment spending. The reduction in investment shifts the *IS* curve downward. The level of income falls from Y_1 to Y_2. The nominal interest rate falls from i_1 to i_2, and the real interest rate rises from r_1 to r_2.

in income reduces the demand for money, and this reduces the nominal interest rate that equilibrates the money market. The nominal interest rate falls by less than the expected deflation, so the real interest rate rises.

Note that there is a common thread in these two stories of destabilizing deflation. In both, falling prices depress national income by causing a contractionary shift in the *IS* curve. Because a deflation of the size observed from 1929 to 1933 is unlikely except in the presence of a major contraction in the money supply, these two explanations assign some of the responsibility for the Depression—especially its severity—to the Fed. In other words, if falling prices are destabilizing, then a contraction in the money supply can lead to a fall in income, even without a decrease in real money balances or a rise in nominal interest rates.

Could the Depression Happen Again?

Economists study the Depression both because of its intrinsic interest as a major economic event and to provide guidance to policymakers so that it will not happen again. To state with confidence whether this event could recur, we would need to know why it happened. Because there is not yet agreement on the causes of the Great Depression, it is impossible to rule out with certainty another depression of this magnitude.

Yet most economists believe that the mistakes that led to the Great Depression are unlikely to be repeated. The Fed seems unlikely to allow the money supply to fall by one-fourth. Many economists believe that the deflation of the early 1930s was responsible for the depth and length of the Depression. And it seems likely that such a prolonged deflation was possible only in the presence of a falling money supply.

The fiscal-policy mistakes of the Depression are also unlikely to be repeated. Fiscal policy in the 1930s not only failed to help but actually further depressed aggregate demand. Few economists today would advocate such a rigid adherence to a balanced budget in the face of massive unemployment.

In addition, there are many institutions today that would help prevent the events of the 1930s from recurring. The system of Federal Deposit Insurance makes widespread bank failures less likely. The income tax causes an automatic reduction in taxes when income falls, which stabilizes the economy. Finally, economists know more today than they did in the 1930s. Our knowledge of how the economy works, limited as it still is, should help policymakers formulate better policies to combat such widespread unemployment.

CASE STUDY

The Financial Crisis and Economic Downturn of 2008 and 2009

In 2008 the U.S. economy experienced a financial crisis and a significant downturn in economic activity. We will discuss these events in detail in Chapter 19, but it is useful to get a preview here, as several of the developments during this time were reminiscent of events during the 1930s.

The story of the 2008 crisis begins a few years earlier with a substantial boom in the housing market. The boom had several sources. In part, it was fueled by low interest rates. As we saw in a previous case study in this chapter, the Federal Reserve lowered interest rates to historically low levels in the aftermath of the recession of 2001. Low interest rates helped the economy recover, but by making it less expensive to get a mortgage and buy a home, they also contributed to a rise in housing prices.

In addition, developments in the mortgage market made it easier for *subprime borrowers*—those borrowers with higher risk of default based on their income and credit history—to get mortgages to buy homes. One of these developments was securitization, the process by which a mortgage originator makes loans and then sells them to an investment bank, which in turn then bundles them together into a variety of "mortgage-backed securities." These mortgage-backed securities are then sold to other institutions (banks or insurance companies), which may not fully appreciate the risks they are taking. Some economists blame insufficient regulation for these high-risk loans. Others believe the problem was not too little regulation but the wrong kind: some government policies encouraged this high-risk lending to make the goal of homeownership more attainable for low-income families. Together, these forces drove up housing demand and housing prices. From 1995 to 2006, average housing prices in the United States more than doubled.

The high price of housing, however, proved unsustainable. From 2006 to 2009, housing prices nationwide fell about 30 percent. Such price fluctuations should not necessarily be a problem in a market economy. After all, price movements are how markets equilibrate supply and demand. But, in this case, the price decline led to a series of problematic repercussions.

The first of these repercussions was a substantial rise in mortgage defaults and home foreclosures. During the housing boom, many homeowners had bought their homes with mostly borrowed money and minimal down payments. When housing prices declined, these homeowners were *underwater*: they owed more on their mortgages than their homes were worth. Many of these homeowners stopped paying their loans. The banks servicing the mortgages responded to the defaults by taking the houses away in foreclosure procedures and then selling them off. The banks' goal was to recoup whatever they could. The increase in the number of homes for sale, however, exacerbated the downward spiral of housing prices.

A second repercussion was large losses at the various financial institutions that owned mortgage-backed securities. In essence, by borrowing large sums to buy high-risk mortgages, these companies had bet that housing prices would keep rising; when this bet turned bad, they found themselves at or near the point of bankruptcy. Even healthy banks stopped trusting one another and avoided inter-bank lending, because it was hard to discern which institution would be the next to go out of business. Because of these large losses at financial institutions and the widespread fear and distrust, the ability of the financial system to make loans even to creditworthy customers was impaired.

A third repercussion was a substantial rise in stock market volatility. Many companies rely on the financial system to get the resources they need for business expansion or to help them manage their short-term cash flows. With the financial system less able to perform its normal operations, the profitability of many companies was called into question. Because it was hard to know how bad things would get, stock market volatility reached levels not seen since the 1930s.

Higher volatility, in turn, lead to a fourth repercussion: a decline in consumer confidence. In the midst of all the uncertainty, households started putting off spending plans. Expenditure on durable goods, in particular, plummeted. As a result of all these events, the economy experienced a large contractionary shift in the *IS* curve.

The U.S government responded vigorously as the crisis unfolded. First, the Fed cut its target for the federal funds rate from 5.25 percent in September 2007 to about zero in December 2008. Second, in an even more unusual move in October 2008, Congress appropriated $700 billion for the Treasury to use to rescue the financial system. Much of this money was used for equity injections into banks. That is, the Treasury put funds into the banking system, which the banks could then use to make loans; in exchange for these funds, the U.S. government became a part owner of these banks, at least temporarily. The goal of the rescue (or "bailout," as it was sometimes called) was to stem the financial crisis on Wall Street and prevent it from causing a depression on every other street in America. Finally, as discussed in Chapter 10, one of Barack Obama's first acts when he became president in January 2009 was to support a major increase in government spending to expand aggregate demand.

As this book was going to press, the end of the story was not completely clear. These policy actions were not enough to prevent a significant downturn in economic activity. The unemployment rate rose to 10.1 percent in October 2009—the highest level in about a quarter century. But the policies put in place appear to have been sufficient to prevent the downturn from evolving into another depression. By the end of 2009, the economy was growing once again, and the unemployment rate had started to decline. ∎

The Liquidity Trap

In the United States in the 1930s, interest rates reached very low levels. As Table 11-2 shows, U.S. interest rates were well under 1 percent throughout the second half of the 1930s. A similar situation occurred in 2008. In December of that year, the Federal Reserve cut its target for the federal funds rate to the range of zero to 0.25 percent.

Some economists describe this situation as a *liquidity trap*. According to the *IS–LM* model, expansionary monetary policy works by reducing interest rates and stimulating investment spending. But if interest rates have already fallen almost to zero, then perhaps monetary policy is no longer effective. Nominal interest rates cannot fall below zero: rather than making a loan at a negative nominal interest rate, a person would just hold cash. In this environment, expansionary monetary policy raises the supply of money, making the public's asset portfolio more liquid, but because interest rates can't fall any further, the extra liquidity might not have any effect. Aggregate demand, production, and employment may be "trapped" at low levels.

Other economists are skeptical about the relevance of liquidity traps and believe that central banks continue to have tools to expand the economy, even after its interest rate target hits zero. One possibility is that the central bank could raise inflation expectations by committing itself to future monetary expansion. Even if nominal interest rates cannot fall any further, higher expected inflation can lower real interest rates by making them negative, which would stimulate investment spending. A second possibility is that monetary expansion could cause the currency to lose value in the market for foreign-currency exchange. This depreciation would make the nation's goods cheaper abroad, stimulating export demand. (This mechanism goes beyond the closed-economy *IS–LM* model we have used in this chapter, but it fits well with an open-economy version of the model.) A third possibility is that the central bank could conduct expansionary open-market operations in a larger variety of financial instruments than it normally does. For example, it could buy mortgages and corporate debt and thereby lower the interest rates on these kinds of loans. The Federal Reserve actively pursued this last option during the downturn of 2008 and 2009.

Is the liquidity trap something monetary policymakers need to worry about? Might the tools of monetary policy at times lose their power to influence the economy? There is no consensus about the answers. Skeptics say we shouldn't worry about the liquidity trap. But others say the possibility of a liquidity trap argues for a target rate of inflation greater than zero. Under zero inflation, the real interest rate, like the nominal interest, can never fall below zero. But if the normal rate of inflation is, say, 3 percent, then the central bank can easily push the real interest rate to negative 3 percent by lowering the nominal interest rate toward zero. Thus, moderate inflation gives monetary policymakers more room to stimulate the economy when needed, reducing the risk of falling into a liquidity trap.[5]

---

[5] To read more about the liquidity trap, see Paul R. Krugman, "It's Baaack: Japan's Slump and the Return of the Liquidity Trap," *Brookings Panel on Economic Activity* 2 (1998): 137–205.

11-4 Conclusion

The purpose of this chapter and the previous one has been to deepen our understanding of aggregate demand. We now have the tools to analyze the effects of monetary and fiscal policy in the long run and in the short run. In the long run, prices are flexible, and we use the classical analysis of Parts Two and Three of this book. In the short run, prices are sticky, and we use the *IS–LM* model to examine how changes in policy influence the economy.

The model in this and the previous chapter provides the basic framework for analyzing the economy in the short run, but it is not the whole story. Future chapters will refine and apply the theory. In Chapter 12 we examine the theory behind short-run aggregate supply. In Chapter 13 we consider how the theoretical framework of aggregate demand and aggregate supply should be applied to the making of stabilization policy. The *IS–LM* model presented in this and the previous chapter provides the starting point for this further analysis.

Summary

1. The *IS–LM* model is a general theory of the aggregate demand for goods and services. The exogenous variables in the model are fiscal policy, monetary policy, and the price level. The model explains two endogenous variables: the interest rate and the level of national income.

2. The *IS* curve represents the negative relationship between the interest rate and the level of income that arises from equilibrium in the market for goods and services. The *LM* curve represents the positive relationship between the interest rate and the level of income that arises from equilibrium in the market for real money balances. Equilibrium in the *IS–LM* model—the intersection of the *IS* and *LM* curves—represents simultaneous equilibrium in the market for goods and services and in the market for real money balances.

3. The aggregate demand curve summarizes the results from the *IS–LM* model by showing equilibrium income at any given price level. The aggregate demand curve slopes downward because a lower price level increases real money balances, lowers the interest rate, stimulates investment spending, and thereby raises equilibrium income.

4. Expansionary fiscal policy—an increase in government purchases or a decrease in taxes—shifts the *IS* curve to the right. This shift in the *IS* curve increases the interest rate and income. The increase in income represents a rightward shift in the aggregate demand curve. Similarly, contractionary fiscal policy shifts the *IS* curve to the left, lowers the interest rate and income, and shifts the aggregate demand curve to the left.

5. Expansionary monetary policy shifts the *LM* curve downward. This shift in the *LM* curve lowers the interest rate and raises income. The increase in

income represents a rightward shift of the aggregate demand curve. Similarly, contractionary monetary policy shifts the *LM* curve upward, raises the interest rate, lowers income, and shifts the aggregate demand curve to the left.

KEY CONCEPTS

Monetary transmission
mechanism

Federal funds rate

Pigou effect

Debt-deflation theory

QUESTIONS FOR REVIEW

1. Explain why the aggregate demand curve slopes downward.

2. What is the impact of an increase in taxes on the interest rate, income, consumption, and investment?

3. What is the impact of a decrease in the money supply on the interest rate, income, consumption, and investment?

4. Describe the possible effects of falling prices on equilibrium income.

PROBLEMS AND APPLICATIONS

1. According to the *IS–LM* model, what happens in the short run to the interest rate, income, consumption, and investment under the following circumstances?

   a. The central bank increases the money supply.

   b. The government increases government purchases.

   c. The government increases taxes.

   d. The government increases government purchases and taxes by equal amounts.

2. Use the *IS–LM* model to predict the effects of each of the following shocks on income, the interest rate, consumption, and investment. In each case, explain what the Fed should do to keep income at its initial level.

   a. After the invention of a new high-speed computer chip, many firms decide to upgrade their computer systems.

   b. A wave of credit-card fraud increases the frequency with which people make transactions in cash.

   c. A best-seller titled *Retire Rich* convinces the public to increase the percentage of their income devoted to saving.

3. Consider the economy of Hicksonia.

   a. The consumption function is given by

   $$C = 200 + 0.75(Y - T).$$

   The investment function is

   $$I = 200 - 25r.$$

   Government purchases and taxes are both 100. For this economy, graph the *IS* curve for *r* ranging from 0 to 8.

   b. The money demand function in Hicksonia is

   $$(M/P)^d = Y - 100r.$$

   The money supply *M* is 1,000 and the price level *P* is 2. For this economy, graph the *LM* curve for *r* ranging from 0 to 8.

   c. Find the equilibrium interest rate *r* and the equilibrium level of income *Y*.

   d. Suppose that government purchases are raised from 100 to 150. How much does the *IS* curve shift? What are the new equilibrium interest rate and level of income?

e. Suppose instead that the money supply is raised from 1,000 to 1,200. How much does the *LM* curve shift? What are the new equilibrium interest rate and level of income?

f. With the initial values for monetary and fiscal policy, suppose that the price level rises from 2 to 4. What happens? What are the new equilibrium interest rate and level of income?

g. Derive and graph an equation for the aggregate demand curve. What happens to this aggregate demand curve if fiscal or monetary policy changes, as in parts (d) and (e)?

4. Explain why each of the following statements is true. Discuss the impact of monetary and fiscal policy in each of these special cases.

a. If investment does not depend on the interest rate, the *IS* curve is vertical.

b. If money demand does not depend on the interest rate, the *LM* curve is vertical.

c. If money demand does not depend on income, the *LM* curve is horizontal.

d. If money demand is extremely sensitive to the interest rate, the *LM* curve is horizontal.

5. Suppose that the government wants to raise investment but keep output constant. In the *IS–LM* model, what mix of monetary and fiscal policy will achieve this goal? In the early 1980s, the U.S. government cut taxes and ran a budget deficit, while the Fed pursued a tight monetary policy. What effect should this policy mix have?

6. Use the *IS–LM* diagram to describe the short-run and long-run effects of the following changes on national income, the interest rate, the price level, consumption, investment, and real money balances:

a. An increase in the money supply

b. An increase in government purchases

c. An increase in taxes

7. The Fed is considering two alternative monetary policies:

• holding the money supply constant and letting the interest rate adjust, or

• adjusting the money supply to hold the interest rate constant.

In the *IS–LM* model, which policy will better stabilize output under the following conditions?

a. All shocks to the economy arise from exogenous changes in the demand for goods and services.

b. All shocks to the economy arise from exogenous changes in the demand for money.

8. Suppose that the demand for real money balances depends on disposable income. That is, the money demand function is

$$M/P = L(r, Y - T).$$

Using the *IS–LM* model, discuss whether this change in the money demand function alters the following:

a. The analysis of changes in government purchases.

b. The analysis of changes in taxes.

9. This problem asks you to analyze the *IS–LM* model algebraically. Suppose consumption is a linear function of disposable income:

$$C(Y - T) = a + b(Y - T),$$

where $a > 0$ and $0 < b < 1$. Suppose also that investment is a linear function of the interest rate:

$$I(r) = c - dr,$$

where $c > 0$ and $d > 0$.

a. Solve for Y as a function of r, the exogenous variables G and T, and the model's parameters $a, b, c,$ and d.

b. How does the slope of the *IS* curve depend on the parameter d, the interest rate sensitivity of investment? Refer to your answer to part (a), and explain the intuition.

c. Which will cause a bigger horizontal shift in the *IS* curve, a $100 tax cut or a $100 increase in government spending? Refer to your answer to part (a), and explain the intuition.

Now suppose demand for real money balances is a linear function of income and the interest rate:

$$L(r, Y) = eY - fr,$$

where $e > 0$ and $f > 0$.

d. Solve for r as a function of Y, M, and P and the parameters e and f.

e. Using your answer to part (d), determine whether the LM curve is steeper for large or small values of f, and explain the intuition.

f. How does the size of the shift in the LM curve resulting from a \$100 increase in M depend on

i. the value of the parameter e, the income sensitivity of money demand?

ii. the value of the parameter f, the interest sensitivity of money demand?

g. Use your answers to parts (a) and (d) to derive an expression for the aggregate demand curve. Your expression should show Y as a function of P; of exogenous policy variables M, G, and T; and of the model's parameters. This expression should not contain r.

h. Use your answer to part (g) to prove that the aggregate demand curve has a negative slope.

i. Use your answer to part (g) to prove that increases in G and M, and decreases in T, shift the aggregate demand curve to the right. How does this result change if the parameter f, the interest sensitivity of money demand, equals zero?

Aggregate Supply and the Short-Run Tradeoff Between Inflation and Unemployment

Probably the single most important macroeconomic relationship is the
Phillips curve.

—*George Akerlof*

There is always a temporary tradeoff between inflation and unemployment;
there is no permanent tradeoff. The temporary tradeoff comes not from inflation
per se, but from unanticipated inflation, which generally means, from a rising
rate of inflation.

—*Milton Friedman*

Most economists analyze short-run fluctuations in national income and the price level using the model of aggregate demand and aggregate supply. In the previous two chapters, we examined aggregate demand in some detail. The *IS–LM* model shows how changes in monetary and fiscal policy and shocks to the money and goods markets shift the aggregate demand curve. In this chapter, we turn our attention to aggregate supply and develop theories that explain the position and slope of the aggregate supply curve.

When we introduced the aggregate supply curve in Chapter 9, we established that aggregate supply behaves differently in the short run than in the long run. In the long run, prices are flexible, and the aggregate supply curve is vertical. When the aggregate supply curve is vertical, shifts in the aggregate demand curve affect the price level, but the output of the economy remains at its natural level. By contrast, in the short run, prices are sticky, and the aggregate supply curve is not vertical. In this case, shifts in aggregate demand do cause fluctuations in output. In Chapter 9 we took a simplified view of price stickiness by drawing the short-run aggregate supply curve as a horizontal line, representing the extreme situation in which all prices are fixed. Our task now is to refine this understanding of short-run aggregate supply to better reflect the real world in which some prices are sticky and others are not.

After examining the basic theory of the short-run aggregate supply curve, we establish a key implication. We show that this curve implies a tradeoff between two measures of economic performance—inflation and unemployment. This tradeoff, called the *Phillips curve*, tells us that to reduce the rate of inflation policymakers must temporarily raise unemployment, and to reduce unemployment they must accept higher inflation. As the quotation from Milton Friedman at the beginning of the chapter suggests, the tradeoff between inflation and unemployment is only temporary. One goal of this chapter is to explain why policymakers face such a tradeoff in the short run and, just as important, why they do not face it in the long run.

12-1 The Basic Theory of Aggregate Supply

When classes in physics study balls rolling down inclined planes, they often begin by assuming away the existence of friction. This assumption makes the problem simpler and is useful in many circumstances, but no good engineer would ever take this assumption as a literal description of how the world works. Similarly, this book began with classical macroeconomic theory, but it would be a mistake to assume that this model is always true. Our job now is to look more deeply into the "frictions" of macroeconomics.

We do this by examining two prominent models of aggregate supply. In both models, some market imperfection (that is, some type of friction) causes the output of the economy to deviate from its natural level. As a result, the short-run aggregate supply curve is upward sloping rather than vertical, and shifts in the aggregate demand curve cause output to fluctuate. These temporary deviations of output from its natural level represent the booms and busts of the business cycle.

Each of the two models takes us down a different theoretical route, but each route ends up in the same place. That final destination is a short-run aggregate supply equation of the form

$$Y = \overline{Y} + \alpha(P - EP), \ \alpha > 0,$$

where Y is output, $\overline{Y}$ is the natural level of output, P is the price level, and EP is the expected price level. This equation states that output deviates from its natural level when the price level deviates from the expected price level. The parameter α indicates how much output responds to unexpected changes in the price level; $1/\alpha$ is the slope of the aggregate supply curve.

Each of the models tells a different story about what lies behind this short-run aggregate supply equation. In other words, each model highlights a particular reason why unexpected movements in the price level are associated with fluctuations in aggregate output.

The Sticky-Price Model

The most widely accepted explanation for the upward-sloping short-run aggregate supply curve is called the **sticky-price model**. This model emphasizes that firms do not instantly adjust the prices they charge in response to changes in demand. Sometimes prices are set by long-term contracts between firms and customers. Even without formal agreements, firms may hold prices steady to avoid annoying their regular customers with frequent price changes. Some prices are sticky because of the way certain markets are structured: once a firm has printed and distributed its catalog or price list, it is costly to alter prices. And sometimes sticky prices can be a reflection of sticky wages: firms base their prices on the costs of production, and wages may depend on social norms and notions of fairness that evolve only slowly over time.

There are various ways to formalize the idea of sticky prices to show how they can help explain an upward-sloping aggregate supply curve. Here we examine an especially simple model. We first consider the pricing decisions of individual firms and then add together the decisions of many firms to explain the behavior of the economy as a whole. To fully understand the model, we have to depart from the assumption of perfect competition, which we have used since Chapter 3. Perfectly competitive firms are price-takers rather than price-setters. If we want to consider how firms set prices, it is natural to assume that these firms have at least some monopolistic control over the prices they charge.

Consider the pricing decision facing a typical firm. The firm's desired price p depends on two macroeconomic variables:

- The overall level of prices P. A higher price level implies that the firm's costs are higher. Hence, the higher the overall price level, the more the firm would like to charge for its product.

- The level of aggregate income Y. A higher level of income raises the demand for the firm's product. Because marginal cost increases at higher levels of production, the greater the demand, the higher the firm's desired price.

We write the firm's desired price as

$$p = P + a(Y - \overline{Y}).$$

This equation says that the desired price p depends on the overall level of prices P and on the level of aggregate output relative to the natural level $Y - \overline{Y}$. The parameter a (which is greater than zero) measures how much the firm's desired price responds to the level of aggregate output.[1]

Now assume that there are two types of firms. Some have flexible prices: they always set their prices according to this equation. Others have sticky prices: they

---

[1] *Mathematical note:* The firm cares most about its relative price, which is the ratio of its nominal price to the overall price level. If we interpret p and P as the logarithms of the firm's price and the price level, then this equation states that the desired relative price depends on the deviation of output from its natural level.

announce their prices in advance based on what they expect economic conditions to be. Firms with sticky prices set prices according to

$$p = EP + a(EY - E\overline{Y}),$$

where, as before, E represents the expected value of a variable. For simplicity, assume that these firms expect output to be at its natural level, so that the last term, $a(EY - E\overline{Y})$, is zero. Then these firms set the price

$$p = EP.$$

That is, firms with sticky prices set their prices based on what they expect other firms to charge.

We can use the pricing rules of the two groups of firms to derive the aggregate supply equation. To do this, we find the overall price level in the economy, which is the weighted average of the prices set by the two groups. If s is the fraction of firms with sticky prices and $1 - s$ is the fraction with flexible prices, then the overall price level is

$$P = sEP + (1 - s)[P + a(Y - \overline{Y})].$$

The first term is the price of the sticky-price firms weighted by their fraction in the economy; the second term is the price of the flexible-price firms weighted by their fraction. Now subtract $(1 - s)P$ from both sides of this equation to obtain

$$sP = sEP + (1 - s)[a(Y - \overline{Y})].$$

Divide both sides by s to solve for the overall price level:

$$P = EP + [(1 - s)a/s](Y - \overline{Y}).$$

The two terms in this equation are explained as follows:

- When firms expect a high price level, they expect high costs. Those firms that fix prices in advance set their prices high. These high prices cause the other firms to set high prices also. Hence, a high expected price level EP leads to a high actual price level P.

- When output is high, the demand for goods is high. Those firms with flexible prices set their prices high, which leads to a high price level. The effect of output on the price level depends on the proportion of firms with flexible prices.

Hence, the overall price level depends on the expected price level and on the level of output.

Algebraic rearrangement puts this aggregate pricing equation into a more familiar form:

$$Y = \overline{Y} + \alpha(P - EP),$$

where $\alpha = s/[(1 - s)a]$. The sticky-price model says that the deviation of output from the natural level is positively associated with the deviation of the price level from the expected price level.[2]

An Alternative Theory: The Imperfect-Information Model

Another explanation for the upward slope of the short-run aggregate supply curve is called the **imperfect-information model**. Unlike the previous model, this one assumes that markets clear—that is, all prices are free to adjust to balance supply and demand. In this model, the short-run and long-run aggregate supply curves differ because of temporary misperceptions about prices.

The imperfect-information model assumes that each supplier in the economy produces a single good and consumes many goods. Because the number of goods is so large, suppliers cannot observe all prices at all times. They monitor closely the prices of what they produce but less closely the prices of all the goods they consume. Because of imperfect information, they sometimes confuse changes in the overall level of prices with changes in relative prices. This confusion influences decisions about how much to supply, and it leads to a positive relationship between the price level and output in the short run.

Consider the decision facing a single supplier—an asparagus farmer, for instance. Because the farmer earns income from selling asparagus and uses this income to buy goods and services, the amount of asparagus she chooses to produce depends on the price of asparagus relative to the prices of other goods and services in the economy. If the relative price of asparagus is high, the farmer is motivated to work hard and produce more asparagus, because the reward is great. If the relative price of asparagus is low, she prefers to enjoy more leisure and produce less asparagus.

Unfortunately, when the farmer makes her production decision, she does not know the relative price of asparagus. As an asparagus producer, she monitors the asparagus market closely and always knows the nominal price of asparagus. But she does not know the prices of all the other goods in the economy. She must, therefore, estimate the relative price of asparagus using the nominal price of asparagus and her expectation of the overall price level.

Consider how the farmer responds if all prices in the economy, including the price of asparagus, increase. One possibility is that she expected this change in prices. When she observes an increase in the price of asparagus, her estimate of its relative price is unchanged. She does not work any harder.

The other possibility is that the farmer did not expect the price level to increase (or to increase by this much). When she observes the increase in the price

---

[2] For a more advanced development of the sticky-price model, see Julio Rotemberg, "Monopolistic Price Adjustment and Aggregate Output," *Review of Economic Studies* 49 (1982): 517–531; and Guillermo Calvo, "Staggered Prices in a Utility-Maximizing Framework," *Journal of Monetary Economics* 12, number 3 (1983): 383–398.

of asparagus, she is not sure whether other prices have risen (in which case asparagus's relative price is unchanged) or whether only the price of asparagus has risen (in which case its relative price is higher). The rational inference is that some of each has happened. In other words, the farmer infers from the increase in the nominal price of asparagus that its relative price has risen somewhat. She works harder and produces more.

Our asparagus farmer is not unique. Her decisions are similar to those of her neighbors, who produce broccoli, cauliflower, dill, endive, . . . , and zucchini. When the price level rises unexpectedly, all suppliers in the economy observe increases in the prices of the goods they produce. They all infer, rationally but mistakenly, that the relative prices of the goods they produce have risen. They work harder and produce more.

To sum up, the imperfect-information model says that when actual prices exceed expected prices, suppliers raise their output. The model implies an aggregate supply curve with the familiar form

$$Y = \overline{Y} + \alpha(P - EP).$$

Output deviates from the natural level when the price level deviates from the expected price level.

The imperfect-information story described above is the version developed originally by Nobel Prize–winning economist Robert Lucas in the 1970s. Recent work on imperfect-information models of aggregate supply has taken a somewhat different approach. Rather than emphasizing confusion about relative prices and the absolute price level, as Lucas did, this new work stresses the limited ability of individuals to incorporate information about the economy into their decisions. In this case, the friction that causes the short-run aggregate supply curve to be upward sloping is not the limited availability of information but is, instead, the limited ability of people to absorb and process information that is widely available. This information-processing constraint causes price-setters to respond slowly to macroeconomic news. The resulting equation for short-run aggregate supply is similar to those from the two models we have seen, even though the microeconomic foundations are somewhat different.[3]

---

[3] To read Lucas's description of his model, see Robert E. Lucas, Jr., "Understanding Business Cycles," *Stabilization of the Domestic and International Economy*, vol. 5 of Carnegie-Rochester Conference on Public Policy (Amsterdam: North-Holland, 1977), 7–29. Lucas was building on the work of Milton Friedman, another Nobel Prize winner. See Milton Friedman, "The Role of Monetary Policy," *American Economic Review* 58 (March 1968): 1–17. For the recent work emphasizing the role of information-processing constraints, see Michael Woodford, "Imperfect Common Knowledge and the Effects of Monetary Policy," in P. Aghion, R. Frydman, J. Stiglitz, and M. Woodford, eds., *Knowledge, Information, and Expectations in Modern Macroeconomics: In Honor of Edmund S. Phelps* (Princeton, N.J.: Princeton University Press, 2002); and N. Gregory Mankiw and Ricardo Reis, "Sticky Information Versus Sticky Prices: A Proposal to Replace the New Keynesian Phillips Curve," *Quarterly Journal of Economics* 117 (November 2002): 1295–1328.

International Differences in the Aggregate Supply Curve

Although all countries experience economic fluctuations, these fluctuations are not exactly the same everywhere. International differences are intriguing puzzles in themselves, and they often provide a way to test alternative economic theories. Examining international differences has been especially fruitful in research on aggregate supply.

When Robert Lucas proposed the imperfect-information model, he derived a surprising interaction between aggregate demand and aggregate supply: according to his model, the slope of the aggregate supply curve should depend on the volatility of aggregate demand. In countries where aggregate demand fluctuates widely, the aggregate price level fluctuates widely as well. Because most movements in prices in these countries do not represent movements in relative prices, suppliers should have learned not to respond much to unexpected changes in the price level. Therefore, the aggregate supply curve should be relatively steep (that is, α will be small). Conversely, in countries where aggregate demand is relatively stable, suppliers should have learned that most price changes are relative price changes. Accordingly, in these countries, suppliers should be more responsive to unexpected price changes, making the aggregate supply curve relatively flat (that is, α will be large).

Lucas tested this prediction by examining international data on output and prices. He found that changes in aggregate demand have the biggest effect on output in those countries where aggregate demand and prices are most stable. Lucas concluded that the evidence supports the imperfect information model.[4]

The sticky-price model also makes predictions about the slope of the short-run aggregate supply curve. In particular, it predicts that the average rate of inflation should influence the slope of the short-run aggregate supply curve. When the average rate of inflation is high, it is very costly for firms to keep prices fixed for long intervals. Thus, firms adjust prices more frequently. More frequent price adjustment in turn allows the overall price level to respond more quickly to shocks to aggregate demand. Hence, a high rate of inflation should make the short-run aggregate supply curve steeper.

International data support this prediction of the sticky-price model. In countries with low average inflation, the short-run aggregate supply curve is relatively flat: fluctuations in aggregate demand have large effects on output and are only slowly reflected in prices. High-inflation countries have steep short-run aggregate supply curves. In other words, high inflation appears to erode the frictions that cause prices to be sticky.[5]

---

[4] Robert E. Lucas, Jr., "Some International Evidence on Output-Inflation Tradeoffs," *American Economic Review* 63 (June 1973): 326–334.

[5] Laurence Ball, N. Gregory Mankiw, and David Romer, "The New Keynesian Economics and the Output-Inflation Tradeoff," *Brookings Papers on Economic Activity* 1(1988): 1–65.

Note that the sticky-price model can also explain Lucas's finding that countries with variable aggregate demand have steep aggregate supply curves. If the price level is highly variable, few firms will commit to prices in advance (s will be small). Hence, the aggregate supply curve will be steep (α will be small). ■

Implications

We have seen two models of aggregate supply and the market imperfection that each uses to explain why the short-run aggregate supply curve is upward sloping. One model assumes the prices of some goods are sticky; the second assumes information about prices is imperfect. Keep in mind that these models are not incompatible with each other. We need not accept one model and reject the other. The world may contain both of these market imperfections, as well as some others, and all of them may contribute to the behavior of short-run aggregate supply.

The two models of aggregate supply differ in their assumptions and emphases, but their implications for aggregate output are similar. Both can be summarized by the equation

$$Y = \overline{Y} + \alpha(P - EP).$$

This equation states that deviations of output from the natural level are related to deviations of the price level from the expected price level. *If the price level is higher than the expected price level, output exceeds its natural level. If the price level is lower than the expected price level, output falls short of its natural level.* Figure 12-1 graphs this equation. Notice that the short-run aggregate supply curve is drawn for a given expectation EP and that a change in EP would shift the curve.

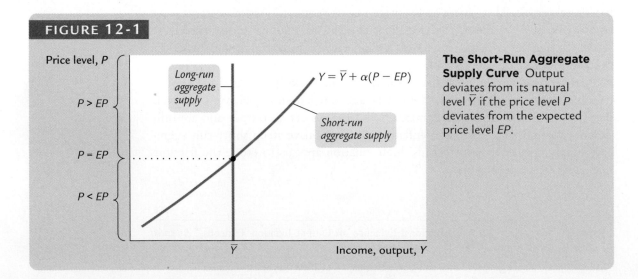

FIGURE 12-1

Price level, P

Long-run aggregate supply

$Y = \overline{Y} + \alpha(P - EP)$

$P > EP$

Short-run aggregate supply

$P = EP$

$P < EP$

$\overline{Y}$

Income, output, Y

The Short-Run Aggregate Supply Curve Output deviates from its natural level $\overline{Y}$ if the price level P deviates from the expected price level EP.

FIGURE 12-2

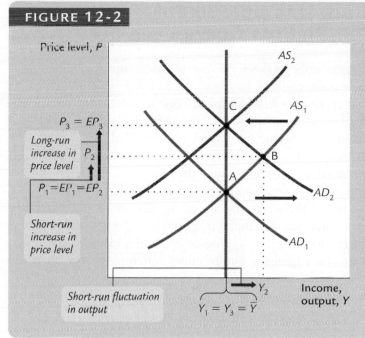

How Shifts in Aggregate Demand Lead to Short-Run Fluctuations Here the economy begins in a long-run equilibrium, point A. When aggregate demand increases unexpectedly, the price level rises from P_1 to P_2. Because the price level P_2 is above the expected price level EP_2, output rises temporarily above the natural level, as the economy moves along the short-run aggregate supply curve from point A to point B. In the long run, the expected price level rises to EP_3, causing the short-run aggregate supply curve to shift upward. The economy returns to a new long-run equilibrium, point C, where output is back at its natural level.

Now that we have a better understanding of aggregate supply, let's put aggregate supply and aggregate demand back together. Figure 12-2 uses our aggregate supply equation to show how the economy responds to an unexpected increase in aggregate demand attributable, say, to an unexpected monetary expansion. In the short run, the equilibrium moves from point A to point B. The increase in aggregate demand raises the actual price level from P_1 to P_2. Because people did not expect this increase in the price level, the expected price level remains at EP_2, and output rises from Y_1 to Y_2, which is above the natural level $\overline{Y}$. Thus, the unexpected expansion in aggregate demand causes the economy to boom.

Yet the boom does not last forever. In the long run, the expected price level rises to catch up with reality, causing the short-run aggregate supply curve to shift upward. As the expected price level rises from EP_2 to EP_3, the equilibrium of the economy moves from point B to point C. The actual price level rises from P_2 to P_3, and output falls from Y_2 to Y_3. In other words, the economy returns to the natural level of output in the long run, but at a much higher price level.

This analysis demonstrates an important principle, which holds for both models of aggregate supply: long-run monetary neutrality and short-run monetary *non*neutrality are perfectly compatible. Short-run nonneutrality is represented here by the movement from point A to point B, and long-run monetary neutrality is represented by the movement from point A to point C. We reconcile the short-run and long-run effects of money by emphasizing the adjustment of expectations about the price level.

12-2 Inflation, Unemployment, and the Phillips Curve

Two goals of economic policymakers are low inflation and low unemployment, but often these goals conflict. Suppose, for instance, that policymakers were to use monetary or fiscal policy to expand aggregate demand. This policy would move the economy along the short-run aggregate supply curve to a point of higher output and a higher price level. (Figure 12-2 shows this as the change from point A to point B.) Higher output means lower unemployment, because firms employ more workers when they produce more. A higher price level, given the previous year's price level, means higher inflation. Thus, when policymakers move the economy up along the short-run aggregate supply curve, they reduce the unemployment rate and raise the inflation rate. Conversely, when they contract aggregate demand and move the economy down the short-run aggregate supply curve, unemployment rises and inflation falls.

This tradeoff between inflation and unemployment, called the *Phillips curve*, is our topic in this section. As we have just seen (and will derive more formally in a moment), the Phillips curve is a reflection of the short-run aggregate supply curve: as policymakers move the economy along the short-run aggregate supply curve, unemployment and inflation move in opposite directions. The Phillips curve is a useful way to express aggregate supply because inflation and unemployment are such important measures of economic performance.

Deriving the Phillips Curve From the Aggregate Supply Curve

The **Phillips curve** in its modern form states that the inflation rate depends on three forces:

- Expected inflation
- The deviation of unemployment from the natural rate, called *cyclical unemployment*
- Supply shocks.

These three forces are expressed in the following equation:

$$\pi = E\pi - \beta(u - u^n) + v$$

$$\text{Inflation} = \frac{\text{Expected}}{\text{Inflation}} - \left(\beta \times \frac{\text{Cyclical}}{\text{Unemployment}} \right) + \frac{\text{Supply}}{\text{Shock}}$$

where β is a parameter measuring the response of inflation to cyclical unemployment. Notice that there is a minus sign before the cyclical unemployment term: other things equal, higher unemployment is associated with lower inflation.

Where does this equation for the Phillips curve come from? Although it may not seem familiar, we can derive it from our equation for aggregate supply. To see how, write the aggregate supply equation as

$$P = EP + (1/\alpha)(Y - \overline{Y}).$$

With one addition, one subtraction, and one substitution, we can transform this equation into the Phillips curve relationship between inflation and unemployment.

Here are the three steps. First, add to the right-hand side of the equation a supply shock v to represent exogenous events (such as a change in world oil prices) that alter the price level and shift the short-run aggregate supply curve:

$$P = EP + (1/\alpha)(Y - \overline{Y}) + v.$$

Next, to go from the price level to inflation rates, subtract last year's price level P_{-1} from both sides of the equation to obtain

$$(P - P_{-1}) = (EP - P_{-1}) + (1/\alpha)(Y - \overline{Y}) + v.$$

The term on the left-hand side, $P - P_{-1}$, is the difference between the current price level and last year's price level, which is inflation π.[6] The term on the right-hand side, $EP - P_{-1}$, is the difference between the expected price level and last year's price level, which is expected inflation $E\pi$. Therefore, we can replace $P - P_{-1}$ with π and $EP - P_{-1}$ with $E\pi$:

$$\pi = E\pi + (1/\alpha)(Y - \overline{Y}) + v.$$

Third, to go from output to unemployment, recall from Chapter 9 that Okun's law gives a relationship between these two variables. One version of Okun's law states that the deviation of output from its natural level is inversely related to the deviation of unemployment from its natural rate; that is, when output is higher than the natural level of output, unemployment is lower than the natural rate of unemployment. We can write this as

$$(1/\alpha)(Y - \overline{Y}) = -\beta(u - u^n).$$

Using this Okun's law relationship, we can substitute $-\beta(u - u^n)$ for $(1/\alpha)(Y - \overline{Y})$ in the previous equation to obtain:

$$\pi = E\pi - \beta(u - u^n) + v.$$

Thus, we can derive the Phillips curve equation from the aggregate supply equation.

All this algebra is meant to show one thing: the Phillips curve equation and the short-run aggregate supply equation represent essentially the same macroeconomic ideas. In particular, both equations show a link between real and nominal variables that causes the classical dichotomy (the theoretical separation of real

---

[6] *Mathematical note:* This statement is not precise, because inflation is really the *percentage* change in the price level. To make the statement more precise, interpret P as the logarithm of the price level. By the properties of logarithms, the change in P is roughly the inflation rate. The reason is that $dP = d(\log \text{price level}) = d(\text{price level})/\text{price level}$.

The History of the Modern Phillips Curve

The Phillips curve is named after New Zealand–born economist A. W. Phillips. In 1958 Phillips observed a negative relationship between the unemployment rate and the rate of wage inflation in data for the United Kingdom.[7] The Phillips curve that economists use today differs in three ways from the relationship Phillips examined.

First, the modern Phillips curve substitutes price inflation for wage inflation. This difference is not crucial, because price inflation and wage inflation are closely related. In periods when wages are rising quickly, prices are rising quickly as well.

Second, the modern Phillips curve includes expected inflation. This addition is due to the work of Milton Friedman and Edmund Phelps. In developing early versions of the imperfect-information model in the 1960s, these two economists emphasized the importance of expectations for aggregate supply.

Third, the modern Phillips curve includes supply shocks. Credit for this addition goes to OPEC, the Organization of Petroleum Exporting Countries. In the 1970s OPEC caused large increases in the world price of oil, which made economists more aware of the importance of shocks to aggregate supply.

and nominal variables) to break down in the short run. According to the short-run aggregate supply equation, output is related to unexpected movements in the price level. According to the Phillips curve equation, unemployment is related to unexpected movements in the inflation rate. The aggregate supply curve is more convenient when we are studying output and the price level, whereas the Phillips curve is more convenient when we are studying unemployment and inflation. But we should not lose sight of the fact that the Phillips curve and the aggregate supply curve are two sides of the same coin.

Adaptive Expectations and Inflation Inertia

To make the Phillips curve useful for analyzing the choices facing policymakers, we need to specify what determines expected inflation. A simple and often plausible assumption is that people form their expectations of inflation based on recently observed inflation. This assumption is called **adaptive expectations**. For example, suppose that people expect prices to rise this year at the same rate as they did last year. Then expected inflation $E\pi$ equals last year's inflation π_{-1}:

$$E\pi = \pi_{-1}$$

In this case, we can write the Phillips curve as

$$\pi = \pi_{-1} - \beta(u - u^n) + v,$$

which states that inflation depends on past inflation, cyclical unemployment, and a supply shock. When the Phillips curve is written in this form, the natural rate

---

[7] A. W. Phillips, "The Relationship Between Unemployment and the Rate of Change of Money Wages in the United Kingdom, 1861–1957," *Economica* 25 (November 1958): 283–299.

of unemployment is sometimes called the non-accelerating inflation rate of unemployment, or *NAIRU*.

The first term in this form of the Phillips curve, π_{-1}, implies that inflation has inertia. That is, like an object moving through space, inflation keeps going unless something acts to stop it. In particular, if unemployment is at the NAIRU and if there are no supply shocks, the continued rise in price level neither speeds up nor slows down. This inertia arises because past inflation influences expectations of future inflation and because these expectations influence the wages and prices that people set. Robert Solow captured the concept of inflation inertia well when, during the high inflation of the 1970s, he wrote, "Why is our money ever less valuable? Perhaps it is simply that we have inflation because we expect inflation, and we expect inflation because we've had it."

In the model of aggregate supply and aggregate demand, inflation inertia is interpreted as persistent upward shifts in both the aggregate supply curve and the aggregate demand curve. First, consider aggregate supply. If prices have been rising quickly, people will expect them to continue to rise quickly. Because the position of the short run aggregate supply curve depends on the expected price level, the short-run aggregate supply curve will shift upward over time. It will continue to shift upward until some event, such as a recession or a supply shock, changes inflation and thereby changes expectations of inflation.

The aggregate demand curve must also shift upward to confirm the expectations of inflation. Most often, the continued rise in aggregate demand is due to persistent growth in the money supply. If the Fed suddenly halted money growth, aggregate demand would stabilize, and the upward shift in aggregate supply would cause a recession. The high unemployment in the recession would reduce inflation and expected inflation, causing inflation inertia to subside.

Two Causes of Rising and Falling Inflation

The second and third terms in the Phillips curve equation show the two forces that can change the rate of inflation.

The second term, $\beta(u - u^n)$, shows that cyclical unemployment —the deviation of unemployment from its natural rate—exerts upward or downward pressure on inflation. Low unemployment pulls the inflation rate up. This is called **demand-pull inflation** because high aggregate demand is responsible for this type of inflation. High unemployment pulls the inflation rate down. The parameter β measures how responsive inflation is to cyclical unemployment.

The third term, v, shows that inflation also rises and falls because of supply shocks. An adverse supply shock, such as the rise in world oil prices in the 1970s, implies a positive value of v and causes inflation to rise. This is called **cost-push inflation** because adverse supply shocks are typically events that push up the costs of production. A beneficial supply shock, such as the oil glut that led to a fall in oil prices in the 1980s, makes v negative and causes inflation to fall.

CASE STUDY

Inflation and Unemployment in the United States

Because inflation and unemployment are such important measures of economic performance, macroeconomic developments are often viewed through the lens of the Phillips curve. Figure 12-3 displays the history of inflation and unemployment in the United States from 1960 to 2009. These data, spanning almost half a century, illustrate some of the causes of rising or falling inflation.

The 1960s showed how policymakers can, in the short run, lower unemployment at the cost of higher inflation. The tax cut of 1964, together with expansionary monetary policy, expanded aggregate demand and pushed the unemployment rate below 5 percent. This expansion of aggregate demand continued in the late 1960s largely as a by-product of government spending for the Vietnam War. Unemployment fell lower and inflation rose higher than policymakers intended.

The 1970s were a period of economic turmoil. The decade began with policymakers trying to lower the inflation inherited from the 1960s. President Nixon imposed temporary controls on wages and prices, and the Federal Reserve engineered a recession through contractionary monetary policy, but the inflation rate fell only slightly. The effects of wage and price controls ended when the controls were lifted, and the recession was too small to counteract the inflationary

FIGURE 12-3

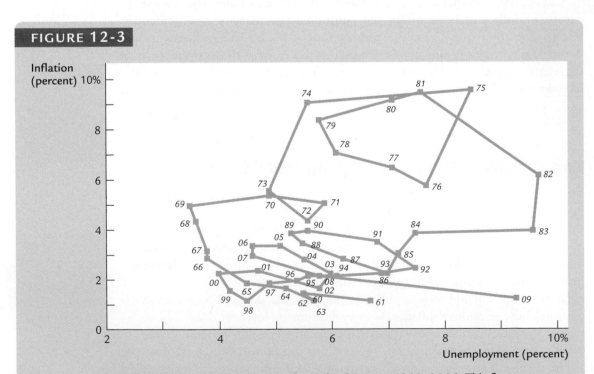

Inflation and Unemployment in the United States, 1960–2009 This figure uses annual data on the unemployment rate and the inflation rate (percentage change in the GDP deflator) to illustrate macroeconomic developments spanning almost half a century of U.S. history.

Sources: U.S. Department of Commerce and U.S. Department of Labor.

impact of the boom that had preceded it. By 1972 the unemployment rate was the same as a decade earlier, while inflation was 3 percentage points higher.

Beginning in 1973 policymakers had to cope with the large supply shocks caused by the Organization of Petroleum Exporting Countries (OPEC). OPEC first raised oil prices in the mid-1970s, pushing the inflation rate up to about 10 percent. This adverse supply shock, together with temporarily tight monetary policy, led to a recession in 1975. High unemployment during the recession reduced inflation somewhat, but further OPEC price hikes pushed inflation up again in the late 1970s.

The 1980s began with high inflation and high expectations of inflation. Under the leadership of Chairman Paul Volcker, the Federal Reserve doggedly pursued monetary policies aimed at reducing inflation. In 1982 and 1983 the unemployment rate reached its highest level in 40 years. High unemployment, aided by a fall in oil prices in 1986, pulled the inflation rate down from about 10 percent to about 3 percent. By 1987 the unemployment rate of about 6 percent was close to most estimates of the natural rate. Unemployment continued to fall through the 1980s, however, reaching a low of 5.2 percent in 1989 and beginning a new round of demand-pull inflation.

Compared to the preceding 30 years, the 1990s and early 2000s were relatively quiet. The 1990s began with a recession caused by several contractionary shocks to aggregate demand: tight monetary policy, the savings-and-loan crisis, and a fall in consumer confidence coinciding with the Gulf War. The unemployment rate rose to 7.3 percent in 1992, and inflation fell slightly. Unlike in the 1982 recession, unemployment in the 1990 recession was never far above the natural rate, so the effect on inflation was small. Similarly, a recession in 2001 (discussed in Chapter 11) raised unemployment, but the downturn was mild by historical standards, and the impact on inflation was once again slight.

A more severe recession beginning in 2008 (also discussed in Chapter 11) put more significant downward pressure on inflation. Unemployment rose significantly in 2009, and inflation fell to levels very low compared with recent history. The full magnitude of this event, however, was uncertain as this book was going to press.

Thus, U.S. macroeconomic history exhibits the two causes of changes in the inflation rate that we encountered in the Phillips curve equation. The 1960s and 1980s show the two sides of demand-pull inflation: in the 1960s low unemployment pulled inflation up, and in the 1980s high unemployment pulled inflation down. The oil-price hikes of the 1970s show the effects of cost-push inflation. ■

The Short-Run Tradeoff Between Inflation and Unemployment

Consider the options the Phillips curve gives to a policymaker who can influence aggregate demand with monetary or fiscal policy. At any moment, expected inflation and supply shocks are beyond the policymaker's immediate control. Yet, by changing aggregate demand, the policymaker can alter output, unemployment, and inflation. The policymaker can expand aggregate demand to lower unemployment and raise inflation. Or the policymaker can depress aggregate demand to raise unemployment and lower inflation.

FIGURE 12-4

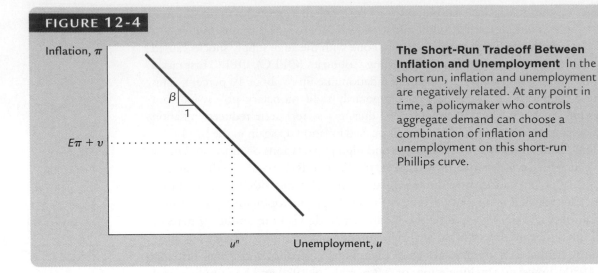

The Short-Run Tradeoff Between Inflation and Unemployment In the short run, inflation and unemployment are negatively related. At any point in time, a policymaker who controls aggregate demand can choose a combination of inflation and unemployment on this short-run Phillips curve.

Figure 12-4 plots the Phillips curve equation and shows the short-run tradeoff between inflation and unemployment. When unemployment is at its natural rate ($u = u^n$), inflation depends on expected inflation and the supply shock ($\pi = E\pi + v$). The parameter β determines the slope of the tradeoff between inflation and unemployment. In the short run, for a given level of expected inflation, policymakers can manipulate aggregate demand to choose any combination of inflation and unemployment on this curve, called the *short-run Phillips curve*.

Notice that the position of the short-run Phillips curve depends on the expected rate of inflation. If expected inflation rises, the curve shifts upward, and the policymaker's tradeoff becomes less favorable: inflation is higher for any level of unemployment. Figure 12-5 shows how the tradeoff depends on expected inflation.

FIGURE 12-5

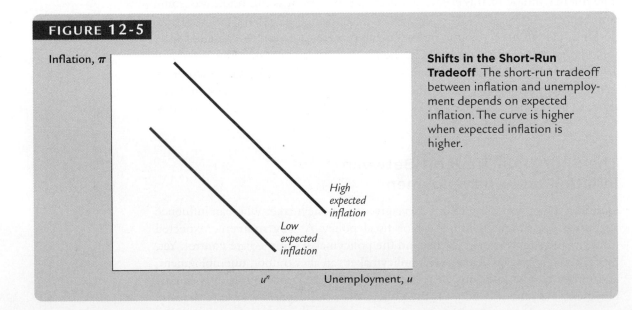

Shifts in the Short-Run Tradeoff The short-run tradeoff between inflation and unemployment depends on expected inflation. The curve is higher when expected inflation is higher.

How Precise Are Estimates of the Natural Rate of Unemployment?

If you ask an astronomer how far a particular star is from our sun, he'll give you a number, but it won't be accurate. Man's ability to measure astronomical distances is still limited. An astronomer might well take better measurements and conclude that a star is really twice or half as far away as he previously thought.

Estimates of the natural rate of unemployment, or NAIRU, are also far from precise. One problem is supply shocks. Shocks to oil supplies, farm harvests, or technological progress can cause inflation to rise or fall in the short run. When we observe rising inflation, therefore, we cannot be sure whether it is evidence that the unemployment rate is below the natural rate or evidence that the economy is experiencing an adverse supply shock.

A second problem is that the natural rate changes over time. Demographic changes (such as the aging of the baby-boom generation), policy changes (such as minimum-wage laws), and institutional changes (such as the declining role of unions) all influence the economy's normal level of unemployment. Estimating the natural rate is like hitting a moving target.

Economists deal with these problems using statistical techniques that yield a best guess about the natural rate and allow them to gauge the uncertainty associated with their estimates. In one such study, Douglas Staiger, James Stock, and Mark Watson estimated the natural rate to be 6.2 percent in 1990, with a 95 percent confidence interval from 5.1 to 7.7 percent. A 95 percent confidence interval is a range such that the statistician is 95 percent confident that the true value falls in that range. The large confidence interval here of 2.6 percentage points shows that estimates of the natural rate are not at all precise.

This conclusion has profound implications. Policymakers may want to keep unemployment close to its natural rate, but their ability to do so is limited by the fact that they cannot be sure what that natural rate is.[8]

Because people adjust their expectations of inflation over time, the tradeoff between inflation and unemployment holds only in the short run. The policymaker cannot keep inflation above expected inflation (and thus unemployment below its natural rate) forever. Eventually, expectations adapt to whatever inflation rate the policymaker has chosen. In the long run, the classical dichotomy holds, unemployment returns to its natural rate, and there is no tradeoff between inflation and unemployment.

Disinflation and the Sacrifice Ratio

Imagine an economy in which unemployment is at its natural rate and inflation is running at 6 percent. What would happen to unemployment and output if the central bank pursued a policy to reduce inflation from 6 to 2 percent?

The Phillips curve shows that in the absence of a beneficial supply shock, lowering inflation requires a period of high unemployment and reduced output.

---

[8] Douglas Staiger, James H. Stock, and Mark W. Watson, "How Precise Are Estimates of the Natural Rate of Unemployment?" in Christina D. Romer and David H. Romer, eds., *Reducing Inflation: Motivation and Strategy* (Chicago: University of Chicago Press, 1997), 195–246.

But by how much and for how long would unemployment need to rise above the natural rate? Before deciding whether to reduce inflation, policymakers must know how much output would be lost during the transition to lower inflation. This cost can then be compared with the benefits of lower inflation.

Much research has used the available data to examine the Phillips curve quantitatively. The results of these studies are often summarized in a number called the **sacrifice ratio**, the percentage of a year's real GDP that must be forgone to reduce inflation by 1 percentage point. Although estimates of the sacrifice ratio vary substantially, a typical estimate is about 5: for every percentage point that inflation is to fall, 5 percent of one year's GDP must be sacrificed.[9]

We can also express the sacrifice ratio in terms of unemployment. Okun's law says that a change of 1 percentage point in the unemployment rate translates into a change of 2 percentage points in GDP. Therefore, reducing inflation by 1 percentage point requires about 2.5 percentage points of cyclical unemployment.

We can use the sacrifice ratio to estimate by how much and for how long unemployment must rise to reduce inflation. If reducing inflation by 1 percentage point requires a sacrifice of 5 percent of a year's GDP, reducing inflation by 4 percentage points requires a sacrifice of 20 percent of a year's GDP. Equivalently, this reduction in inflation requires a sacrifice of 10 percentage points of cyclical unemployment.

This disinflation could take various forms, each totaling the same sacrifice of 20 percent of a year's GDP. For example, a rapid disinflation would lower output by 10 percent for two years: this is sometimes called the *cold-turkey* solution to inflation. A moderate disinflation would lower output by 5 percent for four years. An even more gradual disinflation would depress output by 2 percent for a decade.

Rational Expectations and the Possibility of Painless Disinflation

Because the expectation of inflation influences the short-run tradeoff between inflation and unemployment, it is crucial to understand how people form expectations. So far, we have been assuming that expected inflation depends on recently observed inflation. Although this assumption of adaptive expectations is plausible, it is probably too simple to apply in all circumstances.

An alternative approach is to assume that people have **rational expectations**. That is, we might assume that people optimally use all the available information, including information about current government policies, to forecast the future. Because monetary and fiscal policies influence inflation, expected inflation should also depend on the monetary and fiscal policies in effect. According to the theory of rational expectations, a change in monetary or fiscal policy will change

[9] Arthur M. Okun, "Efficient Disinflationary Policies," *American Economic Review* 68 (May 1978): 348–352; Robert J. Gordon and Stephen R. King, "The Output Cost of Disinflation in Traditional and Vector Autoregressive Models," *Brookings Papers on Economic Activity* 1 (1982): 205–245.

expectations, and an evaluation of any policy change must incorporate this effect on expectations. If people do form their expectations rationally, then inflation may have less inertia than it first appears.

Here is how Thomas Sargent, a prominent advocate of rational expectations, describes its implications for the Phillips curve:

> An alternative "rational expectations" view denies that there is any inherent momentum to the present process of inflation. This view maintains that firms and workers have now come to expect high rates of inflation in the future and that they strike inflationary bargains in light of these expectations. However, it is held that people expect high rates of inflation in the future precisely because the government's current and prospective monetary and fiscal policies warrant those expectations. . . . Thus inflation only seems to have a momentum of its own; it is actually the long-term government policy of persistently running large deficits and creating money at high rates which imparts the momentum to the inflation rate. An implication of this view is that inflation can be stopped much more quickly than advocates of the "momentum" view have indicated and that their estimates of the length of time and the costs of stopping inflation in terms of foregone output are erroneous. . . . [Stopping inflation] would require a change in the policy regime: there must be an abrupt change in the continuing government policy, or strategy, for setting deficits now and in the future that is sufficiently binding as to be widely believed. . . . How costly such a move would be in terms of foregone output and how long it would be in taking effect would depend partly on how resolute and evident the government's commitment was.[10]

Thus, advocates of rational expectations argue that the short-run Phillips curve does not accurately represent the options that policymakers have available. They believe that if policymakers are credibly committed to reducing inflation, rational people will understand the commitment and will quickly lower their expectations of inflation. Inflation can then come down without a rise in unemployment and fall in output. According to the theory of rational expectations, traditional estimates of the sacrifice ratio are not useful for evaluating the impact of alternative policies. Under a credible policy, the costs of reducing inflation may be much lower than estimates of the sacrifice ratio suggest.

In the most extreme case, one can imagine reducing the rate of inflation without causing any recession at all. A painless disinflation has two requirements. First, the plan to reduce inflation must be announced before the workers and firms that set wages and prices have formed their expectations. Second, the workers and firms must believe the announcement; otherwise, they will not reduce their expectations of inflation. If both requirements are met, the announcement will immediately shift the short-run tradeoff between inflation and unemployment downward, permitting a lower rate of inflation without higher unemployment.

Although the rational-expectations approach remains controversial, almost all economists agree that expectations of inflation influence the short-run tradeoff

---

[10] Thomas J. Sargent, "The Ends of Four Big Inflations," in Robert E. Hall, ed., *Inflation: Causes and Effects* (Chicago: University of Chicago Press, 1982), 41–98.

between inflation and unemployment. The credibility of a policy to reduce inflation is therefore one determinant of how costly the policy will be. Unfortunately, it is often difficult to predict whether the public will view the announcement of a new policy as credible. The central role of expectations makes forecasting the results of alternative policies far more difficult.

CASE STUDY

The Sacrifice Ratio in Practice

The Phillips curve with adaptive expectations implies that reducing inflation requires a period of high unemployment and low output. By contrast, the rational-expectations approach suggests that reducing inflation can be much less costly. What happens during actual disinflations?

Consider the U.S. disinflation in the early 1980s. This decade began with some of the highest rates of inflation in U.S. history. Yet because of the tight monetary policies the Fed pursued under Chairman Paul Volcker, the rate of inflation fell substantially in the first few years of the decade. This episode provides a natural experiment with which to estimate how much output is lost during the process of disinflation.

The first question is, how much did inflation fall? As measured by the GDP deflator, inflation reached a peak of 9.7 percent in 1981. It is natural to end the episode in 1985 because oil prices plunged in 1986—a large, beneficial supply shock unrelated to Fed policy. In 1985, inflation was 3.0 percent, so we can estimate that the Fed engineered a reduction in inflation of 6.7 percentage points over four years.

The second question is, how much output was lost during this period? Table 12-1 shows the unemployment rate from 1982 to 1985. Assuming that the natural rate of unemployment was 6 percent, we can compute the amount of cyclical unemployment in each year. In total over this period, there were 9.5 percentage points of cyclical unemployment. Okun's law says that 1 percentage point of unemployment translates into 2 percentage points of GDP. Therefore, 19.0 percentage points of annual GDP were lost during the disinflation.

TABLE 12-1

Unemployment During the Volcker Disinflation

Year	Unemployment Rate u	Natural Rate u^n	Cyclical Unemployment $u - u^n$
1982	9.5%	6.0%	3.5%
1983	9.5	6.0	3.5
1984	7.4	6.0	1.4
1985	7.1	6.0	1.1
			Total 9.5%

Now we can compute the sacrifice ratio for this episode. We know that 19.0 percentage points of GDP were lost and that inflation fell by 6.7 percentage points. Hence, 19.0/6.7, or 2.8, percentage points of GDP were lost for each percentage-point reduction in inflation. The estimate of the sacrifice ratio from the Volcker disinflation is 2.8.

This estimate of the sacrifice ratio is smaller than the estimates made before Volcker was appointed Fed chairman. In other words, Volcker reduced inflation at a smaller cost than many economists had predicted. One explanation is that Volcker's tough stand was credible enough to influence expectations of inflation directly. Yet the change in expectations was not large enough to make the disinflation painless: in 1982 unemployment reached its highest level since the Great Depression.

Although the Volcker disinflation is only one historical episode, this kind of analysis can be applied to other disinflations. One comprehensive study documented the results of 65 disinflations in 19 countries. In almost all cases, the reduction in inflation came at the cost of temporarily lower output. Yet the size of the output loss varied from episode to episode. Rapid disinflations usually had smaller sacrifice ratios than slower ones. That is, in contrast to what the Phillips curve with adaptive expectations suggests, a cold-turkey approach appears less costly than a gradual one. Moreover, countries with more flexible wage-setting institutions, such as shorter labor contracts, had smaller sacrifice ratios. These findings indicate that reducing inflation always has some cost but that policies and institutions can affect its magnitude.[11] ∎

Hysteresis and the Challenge to the Natural-Rate Hypothesis

Our discussion of the cost of disinflation—and indeed our entire discussion of economic fluctuations in the past three chapters—has been based on an assumption called the **natural-rate hypothesis**. This hypothesis is summarized in the following statement:

> *Fluctuations in aggregate demand affect output and employment only in the short run. In the long run, the economy returns to the levels of output, employment, and unemployment described by the classical model.*

The natural-rate hypothesis allows macroeconomists to study short-run and long-run developments in the economy separately. It is one expression of the classical dichotomy.

Some economists, however, have challenged the natural-rate hypothesis by suggesting that aggregate demand may affect output and employment even in the long run. They have pointed out a number of mechanisms through which recessions might leave permanent scars on the economy by altering the natural rate

---

[11] Laurence Ball, "What Determines the Sacrifice Ratio?" in N. Gregory Mankiw, ed., *Monetary Policy* (Chicago: University of Chicago Press, 1994), 155–193.

of unemployment. **Hysteresis** is the term used to describe the long-lasting influence of history on the natural rate.

A recession can have permanent effects if it changes the people who become unemployed. For instance, workers might lose valuable job skills when unemployed, lowering their ability to find a job even after the recession ends. Alternatively, a long period of unemployment may change an individual's attitude toward work and reduce his desire to find employment. In either case, the recession permanently inhibits the process of job search and raises the amount of frictional unemployment.

Another way in which a recession can permanently affect the economy is by changing the process that determines wages. Those who become unemployed may lose their influence on the wage-setting process. Unemployed workers may lose their status as union members, for example. More generally, some of the *insiders* in the wage-setting process become *outsiders*. If the smaller group of insiders cares more about high real wages and less about high employment, then the recession may permanently push real wages farther above the equilibrium level and raise the amount of structural unemployment.

Hysteresis remains a controversial theory. Some economists believe the theory helps explain persistently high unemployment in Europe, because the rise in European unemployment starting in the early 1980s coincided with disinflation but continued after inflation stabilized. Moreover, the increase in unemployment tended to be larger for those countries that experienced the greatest reductions in inflations, such as Ireland, Italy, and Spain. Yet there is still no consensus on whether the hysteresis phenomenon is significant or why it might be more pronounced in some countries than in others. (Other explanations of high European unemployment, discussed in Chapter 6, give little role to the disinflation.) If it is true, however, the theory is important, because hysteresis greatly increases the cost of recessions. Put another way, hysteresis raises the sacrifice ratio, because output is lost even after the period of disinflation is over.[12]

12-3 Conclusion

We began this chapter by discussing two models of aggregate supply, each of which focuses on a different reason why, in the short run, output rises above its natural level when the price level rises above the level that people had expected. Both models explain why the short-run aggregate supply curve is upward sloping, and both yield a short-run tradeoff between inflation and unemployment. A convenient way to express and analyze that tradeoff is with the Phillips curve

[12] Olivier J. Blanchard and Lawrence H. Summers, "Beyond the Natural Rate Hypothesis," *American Economic Review* 78 (May 1988): 182–187; Laurence Ball, "Disinflation and the NAIRU," in Christina D. Romer and David H. Romer, eds., *Reducing Inflation: Motivation and Strategy* (Chicago: University of Chicago Press, 1997), 167–185.

equation, according to which inflation depends on expected inflation, cyclical unemployment, and supply shocks.

Keep in mind that not all economists endorse all the ideas discussed here. There is widespread disagreement, for instance, about the practical importance of rational expectations and the relevance of hysteresis. If you find it difficult to fit all the pieces together, you are not alone. The study of aggregate supply remains one of the most unsettled—and therefore one of the most exciting—research areas in macroeconomics.

Summary

1. The two theories of aggregate supply—the sticky-price and imperfect-information models—attribute deviations of output and employment from their natural levels to various market imperfections. According to both theories, output rises above its natural level when the price level exceeds the expected price level, and output falls below its natural level when the price level is less than the expected price level.

2. Economists often express aggregate supply in a relationship called the Phillips curve. The Phillips curve says that inflation depends on expected inflation, the deviation of unemployment from its natural rate, and supply shocks. According to the Phillips curve, policymakers who control aggregate demand face a short-run tradeoff between inflation and unemployment.

3. If expected inflation depends on recently observed inflation, then inflation has inertia, which means that reducing inflation requires either a beneficial supply shock or a period of high unemployment and reduced output. If people have rational expectations, however, then a credible announcement of a change in policy might be able to influence expectations directly and, therefore, reduce inflation without causing a recession.

4. Most economists accept the natural-rate hypothesis, according to which fluctuations in aggregate demand have only short-run effects on output and unemployment. Yet some economists have suggested ways in which recessions can leave permanent scars on the economy by raising the natural rate of unemployment.

KEY CONCEPTS

Sticky-price model	Demand-pull inflation	Natural-rate hypothesis
Imperfect-information model	Cost-push inflation	Hysteresis
Phillips curve	Sacrifice ratio	
Adaptive expectations	Rational expectations	

QUESTIONS FOR REVIEW

1. Explain the two theories of aggregate supply. On what market imperfection does each theory rely? What do the theories have in common?

2. How is the Phillips curve related to aggregate supply?

3. Why might inflation be inertial?

4. Explain the differences between demand-pull inflation and cost-push inflation.

5. Under what circumstances might it be possible to reduce inflation without causing a recession?

6. Explain two ways in which a recession might raise the natural rate of unemployment.

PROBLEMS AND APPLICATIONS

1. In the sticky-price model, describe the aggregate supply curve in the following special cases. How do these cases compare to the short-run aggregate supply curve we discussed in Chapter 9?

    a. No firms have flexible prices ($s = 1$).

    b. The desired price does not depend on aggregate output ($a = 0$).

2. Suppose that an economy has the Phillips curve

$$\pi = \pi_{-1} - 0.5(u - 0.06).$$

    a. What is the natural rate of unemployment?

    b. Graph the short-run and long-run relationships between inflation and unemployment.

    c. How much cyclical unemployment is necessary to reduce inflation by 5 percentage points? Using Okun's law, compute the sacrifice ratio.

    d. Inflation is running at 10 percent. The Fed wants to reduce it to 5 percent. Give two scenarios that will achieve that goal.

3. According to the rational-expectations approach, if everyone believes that policymakers are committed to reducing inflation, the cost of reducing inflation—the sacrifice ratio—will be lower than if the public is skeptical about the policymakers' intentions. Why might this be true? How might credibility be achieved?

4. Suppose that the economy is initially at a long-run equilibrium. Then the Fed increases the money supply.

    a. Assuming any resulting inflation to be unexpected, explain any changes in GDP, unemployment, and inflation that are caused by the monetary expansion. Explain your conclusions using three diagrams: one for the IS–LM model, one for the AD–AS model, and one for the Phillips curve.

    b. Assuming instead that any resulting inflation is expected, explain any changes in GDP, unemployment, and inflation that are caused by the monetary expansion. Once again, explain your conclusions using three diagrams: one for the IS–LM model, one for the AD–AS model, and one for the Phillips curve.

5. Assume that people have rational expectations and that the economy is described by the sticky-price model. Explain why each of the following propositions is true.

    a. Only unanticipated changes in the money supply affect real GDP. Changes in the money supply that were anticipated when prices were set do not have any real effects.

    b. If the Fed chooses the money supply at the same time as people are setting prices, so that everyone has the same information about the state of the economy, then monetary policy cannot be used systematically to stabilize output. Hence, a policy of keeping the money supply constant will have the same real effects as a policy of adjusting the money supply in response to the state of the economy. (This is called the *policy irrelevance proposition*.)

    c. If the Fed sets the money supply well after people have set prices, so that the Fed has collected more information about the state of the economy, then monetary policy can be used systematically to stabilize output.

6. Suppose that an economy has the Phillips curve

$$\pi = \pi_{-1} - 0.5(u - u^n),$$

and that the natural rate of unemployment is given by an average of the past two years' unemployment:

$$u^n = 0.5(u_{-1} + u_{-2}).$$

a. Why might the natural rate of unemployment depend on recent unemployment (as is assumed in the preceding equation)?

b. Suppose that the Fed follows a policy to permanently reduce the inflation rate by 1 percentage point. What effect will that policy have on the unemployment rate over time?

c. What is the sacrifice ratio in this economy? Explain.

d. What do these equations imply about the short-run and long-run tradeoffs between inflation and unemployment?

7. Some economists believe that taxes have an important effect on the labor supply. They argue that higher taxes cause people to want to work less and that lower taxes cause them to want to work more. Consider how this effect alters the macroeconomic analysis of tax changes.

a. If this view is correct, how does a tax cut affect the natural level of output?

b. How does a tax cut affect the aggregate demand curve? The long-run aggregate supply curve? The short-run aggregate supply curve?

c. What is the short-run impact of a tax cut on output and the price level? How does your answer differ from the case without the labor-supply effect?

d. What is the long run impact of a tax cut on output and the price level? How does your answer differ from the case without the labor-supply effect?

8. Economist Alan Blinder, whom Bill Clinton appointed to be vice chairman of the Federal Reserve, once wrote the following:

The costs that attend the low and moderate inflation rates experienced in the United States and in other industrial countries appear to be quite modest—more like a bad cold than a cancer on society. . . . As rational individuals, we do not volunteer for a lobotomy to cure a head cold. Yet, as a collectivity, we routinely prescribe the economic equivalent of lobotomy (high unemployment) as a cure for the inflationary cold.[13]

What do you think Blinder meant by this? What are the policy implications of the viewpoint Blinder is advocating? Do you agree? Why or why not?

9. Go to the Web site of the Bureau of Labor Statistics (www.bls.gov). For each of the past five years, find the inflation rate as measured by the consumer price index for all items (sometimes called *headline inflation*) and as measured by the CPI excluding food and energy (sometimes called *core inflation*). Compare these two measures of inflation. Why might they be different? What might the difference tell you about shifts in the aggregate supply curve and in the short-run Phillips curve?

---

[13] Alan Blinder, *Hard Heads, Soft Hearts: Tough-Minded Economics for a Just Society* (Reading, Mass.: Addison-Wesley, 1987), 5.

PART V

Macroeconomic Policy Debates

CHAPTER 13

Stabilization Policy

The Federal Reserve's job is to take away the punch bowl just as the party gets going.

—William McChesney Martin

What we need is not a skilled monetary driver of the economic vehicle continuously turning the steering wheel to adjust to the unexpected irregularities of the route, but some means of keeping the monetary passenger who is in the back seat as ballast from occasionally leaning over and giving the steering wheel a jerk that threatens to send the car off the road.

—Milton Friedman

How should government policymakers respond to the business cycle? The two quotations above—the first from a former chairman of the Federal Reserve, the second from a prominent critic of the Fed—show the diversity of opinion over how this question is best answered.

Some economists, such as William McChesney Martin, view the economy as inherently unstable. They argue that the economy experiences frequent shocks to aggregate demand and aggregate supply. Unless policymakers use monetary and fiscal policy to stabilize the economy, these shocks will lead to unnecessary and inefficient fluctuations in output, unemployment, and inflation. According to the popular saying, macroeconomic policy should "lean against the wind," stimulating the economy when it is depressed and slowing the economy when it is overheated.

Other economists, such as Milton Friedman, view the economy as naturally stable. They blame bad economic policies for the large and inefficient fluctuations we have sometimes experienced. They argue that economic policy should not try to fine-tune the economy. Instead, economic policymakers should admit their limited abilities and be satisfied if they do no harm.

This debate has persisted for decades, with numerous protagonists advancing various arguments for their positions. It became especially relevant as economies around the world sank into recession in 2008. The fundamental issue is how policymakers should use the theory of short-run economic fluctuations developed in the preceding chapters.

In this chapter we ask two questions that arise in this debate. First, should monetary and fiscal policy take an active role in trying to stabilize the economy, or should policy remain passive? Second, should policymakers be free to use their discretion in responding to changing economic conditions, or should they be committed to following a fixed policy rule?

13-1 Should Policy Be Active or Passive?

Policymakers in the federal government view economic stabilization as one of their primary responsibilities. The analysis of macroeconomic policy is a regular duty of the Council of Economic Advisers, the Congressional Budget Office, the Federal Reserve, and other government agencies. As we have seen in the preceding chapters, monetary and fiscal policy can exert a powerful impact on aggregate demand and, thereby, on inflation and unemployment. When Congress or the president is considering a major change in fiscal policy, or when the Federal Reserve is considering a major change in monetary policy, foremost in the discussion are how the change will influence inflation and unemployment and whether aggregate demand needs to be stimulated or restrained.

Although the government has long conducted monetary and fiscal policy, the view that it should use these policy instruments to try to stabilize the economy is more recent. The Employment Act of 1946 was a landmark piece of legislation in which the government first held itself accountable for macroeconomic performance. The act states that "it is the continuing policy and responsibility of the Federal Government to . . . promote full employment and production." This law was written when the memory of the Great Depression was still fresh. The lawmakers who wrote it believed, as many economists do, that in the absence of an active government role in the economy, events like the Great Depression could occur regularly.

To many economists the case for active government policy is clear and simple. Recessions are periods of high unemployment, low incomes, and increased economic hardship. The model of aggregate demand and aggregate supply shows how shocks to the economy can cause recessions. It also shows how monetary and fiscal policy can prevent (or at least soften) recessions by responding to these shocks. These economists consider it wasteful not to use these policy instruments to stabilize the economy.

Other economists are critical of the government's attempts to stabilize the economy. These critics argue that the government should take a hands-off approach to macroeconomic policy. At first, this view might seem surprising. If our model shows how to prevent or reduce the severity of recessions, why do these critics want the government to refrain from using monetary and fiscal policy for economic stabilization? To find out, let's consider some of their arguments.

Lags in the Implementation and Effects of Policies

Economic stabilization would be easy if the effects of policy were immediate. Making policy would be like driving a car: policymakers would simply adjust their instruments to keep the economy on the desired path.

Making economic policy, however, is less like driving a car than it is like piloting a large ship. A car changes direction almost immediately after the steering wheel is turned. By contrast, a ship changes course long after the pilot adjusts the rudder, and once the ship starts to turn, it continues turning long after the rudder is set back to normal. A novice pilot is likely to oversteer and, after noticing the mistake, overreact by steering too much in the opposite direction. The ship's path could become unstable, as the novice responds to previous mistakes by making larger and larger corrections.

Like a ship's pilot, economic policymakers face the problem of long lags. Indeed, the problem for policymakers is even more difficult, because the lengths of the lags are hard to predict. These long and variable lags greatly complicate the conduct of monetary and fiscal policy.

Economists distinguish between two lags that are relevant for the conduct of stabilization policy: the inside lag and the outside lag. The **inside lag** is the time between a shock to the economy and the policy action responding to that shock. This lag arises because it takes time for policymakers first to recognize that a shock has occurred and then to put appropriate policies into effect. The **outside lag** is the time between a policy action and its influence on the economy. This lag arises because policies do not immediately influence spending, income, and employment.

A long inside lag is a central problem with using fiscal policy for economic stabilization. This is especially true in the United States, where changes in spending or taxes require the approval of the president and both houses of Congress. The slow and cumbersome legislative process often leads to delays, which make fiscal policy an imprecise tool for stabilizing the economy. This inside lag is shorter in countries with parliamentary systems, such as the United Kingdom, because there the party in power can often enact policy changes more rapidly.

Monetary policy has a much shorter inside lag than fiscal policy, because a central bank can decide on and implement a policy change in less than a day, but monetary policy has a substantial outside lag. Monetary policy works by changing the money supply and interest rates, which in turn influence investment and aggregate demand. Many firms make investment plans far in advance, however, so a change in monetary policy is thought not to affect economic activity until about six months after it is made.

The long and variable lags associated with monetary and fiscal policy certainly make stabilizing the economy more difficult. Advocates of passive policy argue that, because of these lags, successful stabilization policy is almost impossible. Indeed, attempts to stabilize the economy can be destabilizing. Suppose that the economy's condition changes between the beginning of a policy action and its impact on the economy. In this case, active policy may end up stimulating the economy when it is heating up or depressing the economy when it is cooling off. Advocates of active policy admit that such lags do require policymakers to be cautious. But, they argue, these lags do not necessarily mean that policy should be completely passive, especially in the face of a severe and protracted economic downturn, such as the recession that began in 2008.

Some policies, called **automatic stabilizers**, are designed to reduce the lags associated with stabilization policy. Automatic stabilizers are policies that stimulate or depress the economy when necessary without any deliberate policy change. For example, the system of income taxes automatically reduces taxes when the economy goes into a recession, without any change in the tax laws, because individuals and corporations pay less tax when their incomes fall. Similarly, the unemployment-insurance and welfare systems automatically raise transfer payments when the economy moves into a recession, because more people apply for benefits. One can view these automatic stabilizers as a type of fiscal policy without any inside lag.

The Difficult Job of Economic Forecasting

Because policy influences the economy only after a long lag, successful stabilization policy requires the ability to accurately predict future economic conditions. If we cannot predict whether the economy will be in a boom or a recession in six months or a year, we cannot evaluate whether monetary and fiscal policy should now be trying to expand or contract aggregate demand. Unfortunately, economic developments are often unpredictable, at least given our current understanding of the economy.

One way forecasters try to look ahead is with *leading indicators*. As we discussed in Chapter 9, a leading indicator is a data series that fluctuates in advance of the economy. A large fall in a leading indicator signals that a recession is more likely to occur in the coming months.

Another way forecasters look ahead is with macroeconometric models, which have been developed both by government agencies and by private firms for forecasting and policy analysis. As we discussed in Chapter 11, these large-scale computer models are made up of many equations, each representing a part of the economy. After making assumptions about the path of the exogenous variables, such as monetary policy, fiscal policy, and oil prices, these models yield predictions about unemployment, inflation, and other endogenous variables. Keep in mind, however, that the validity of these predictions is only as good as the model and the forecasters' assumptions about the exogenous variables.

Drawing by Dana Fradon; © 1988 The New Yorker Magazine, Inc.

"It's true, Caesar. Rome is declining, but I expect it to pick up in the next quarter."

CASE STUDY

Mistakes in Forecasting

"Light showers, bright intervals, and moderate winds." This was the forecast offered by the renowned British national weather service on October 14, 1987. The next day Britain was hit by its worst storm in more than two centuries.

Like weather forecasts, economic forecasts are a crucial input to private and public decisionmaking. Business executives rely on economic forecasts when deciding how much to produce and how much to invest in plant and equipment. Government policymakers also rely on forecasts when developing economic policies. Unfortunately, like weather forecasts, economic forecasts are far from precise.

The most severe economic downturn in U.S. history, the Great Depression of the 1930s, caught economic forecasters completely by surprise. Even after the stock market crash of 1929, they remained confident that the economy would not suffer a substantial setback. In late 1931, when the economy was clearly in bad shape, the eminent economist Irving Fisher predicted that it would recover quickly. Subsequent events showed that these forecasts were much too optimistic: the unemployment rate continued to rise until 1933, and it remained elevated for the rest of the decade.[1]

Figure 13-1 shows how economic forecasters did during the recession of 1982, one of the most severe economic downturns in the United States since the Great Depression. This figure shows the actual unemployment rate (in red) and six attempts to predict it for the following five quarters (in green). You can see that the forecasters did well when predicting unemployment one quarter ahead. The more distant forecasts, however, were often inaccurate. For example, in the second quarter of 1981, forecasters were predicting little change in the unemployment rate over the next five quarters; yet only two quarters later unemployment began to rise sharply. The rise in unemployment to almost 11 percent in the fourth quarter of 1982 caught the forecasters by surprise. After the depth of the recession became apparent, the forecasters failed to predict how rapid the subsequent decline in unemployment would be.

The story is much the same for the economic downturn of 2008 and 2009. The August 2008 Survey of Professional Forecasters, conducted after the recession had already begun, predicted that the downturn would be modest in size: the U.S. unemployment rate was projected to increase to only 6.0 percent in the third quarter of 2009. In fact, the unemployment rate was 9.6 percent in that quarter.

These episodes—the Great Depression, the recession and recovery of 1982, and the recent economic downturn—show that many of the most dramatic economic events are unpredictable. Although private and public decisionmakers have little choice but to rely on economic forecasts, they must always keep in mind that these forecasts come with a large margin of error. ■

Ignorance, Expectations, and the Lucas Critique

The prominent economist Robert Lucas once wrote, "As an advice-giving profession we are in way over our heads." Even many of those who advise policymakers would agree with this assessment. Economics is a young science, and

---

[1] Kathryn M. Dominguez, Ray C. Fair, and Matthew D. Shapiro, "Forecasting the Depression: Harvard Versus Yale," *American Economic Review* 78 (September 1988): 595–612. This article shows how badly economic forecasters did during the Great Depression, and it argues that they could not have done any better with the modern forecasting techniques available today.

FIGURE 13-1

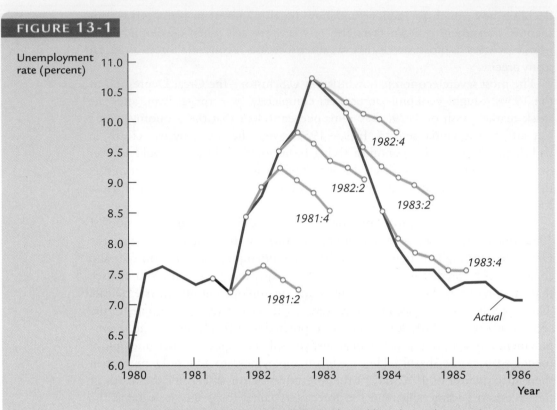

Forecasting the Recession of 1982 The red line shows the actual unemployment rate from the first quarter of 1980 to the first quarter of 1986. The green lines show the unemployment rate predicted at six points in time: the second quarter of 1981, the fourth quarter of 1981, the second quarter of 1982, and so on. For each forecast, the symbols mark the current unemployment rate and the forecast for the subsequent five quarters. Notice that the forecasters failed to predict both the rapid rise in the unemployment rate and the subsequent rapid decline.

Sources: The unemployment rate is from the Department of Labor. The predicted unemployment rate is the median forecast of about 20 forecasters surveyed by the American Statistical Association and the National Bureau of Economic Research.

there is still much that we do not know. Economists cannot be completely confident when they assess the effects of alternative policies. This ignorance suggests that economists should be cautious when offering policy advice.

In his writings on macroeconomic policymaking, Lucas has emphasized that economists need to pay more attention to the issue of how people form expectations of the future. Expectations play a crucial role in the economy because they influence all sorts of behavior. For instance, households decide how much to consume based on how much they expect to earn in the future, and firms decide how much to invest based on their expectations of future profitability. These expectations depend on many things, but one factor, according to Lucas, is especially important: the policies being pursued by the government.

When policymakers estimate the effect of any policy change, therefore, they need to know how people's expectations will respond to the policy change. Lucas has argued that traditional methods of policy evaluation—such as those that rely on standard macroeconometric models—do not adequately take into account the impact of policy on expectations. This criticism of traditional policy evaluation is known as the **Lucas critique**.[2]

An important example of the Lucas critique arises in the analysis of disinflation. As you may recall from Chapter 12, the cost of reducing inflation is often measured by the sacrifice ratio, which is the number of percentage points of GDP that must be forgone to reduce inflation by 1 percentage point. Because estimates of the sacrifice ratio are often large, they have led some economists to argue that policymakers should learn to live with inflation, rather than incur the large cost of reducing it.

According to advocates of the rational-expectations approach, however, these estimates of the sacrifice ratio are unreliable because they are subject to the Lucas critique. Traditional estimates of the sacrifice ratio are based on adaptive expectations, that is, on the assumption that expected inflation depends on past inflation. Adaptive expectations may be a reasonable premise in some circumstances, but if policymakers make a credible change in policy, workers and firms setting wages and prices will rationally respond by adjusting their expectations of inflation appropriately. This change in inflation expectations will quickly alter the short-run tradeoff between inflation and unemployment. As a result, reducing inflation can potentially be much less costly than is suggested by traditional estimates of the sacrifice ratio.

The Lucas critique leaves us with two lessons. The narrow lesson is that economists evaluating alternative policies need to consider how policy affects expectations and, thereby, behavior. The broad lesson is that policy evaluation is hard, so economists engaged in this task should be sure to show the requisite humility.

The Historical Record

In judging whether government policy should play an active or passive role in the economy, we must give some weight to the historical record. If the economy has experienced many large shocks to aggregate supply and aggregate demand, and if policy has successfully insulated the economy from these shocks, then the case for active policy should be clear. Conversely, if the economy has experienced few large shocks, and if the fluctuations we have observed can be traced to inept economic policy, then the case for passive policy should be clear. In other words, our view of stabilization policy should be influenced by whether policy has historically been stabilizing or destabilizing. For this reason, the debate over macroeconomic policy frequently turns into a debate over macroeconomic history.

---

[2] Robert E. Lucas, Jr., "Econometric Policy Evaluation: A Critique," *Carnegie Rochester Conference on Public Policy* 1 (Amsterdam: North-Holland, 1976): 19–46. Lucas won the Nobel Prize for this and other work in 1995.

Yet history does not settle the debate over stabilization policy. Disagreements over history arise because it is not easy to identify the sources of economic fluctuations. The historical record often permits more than one interpretation.

The Great Depression is a case in point. Economists' views on macroeconomic policy are often related to their views on the cause of the Depression. Some economists believe that a large contractionary shock to private spending caused the Depression. They assert that policymakers should have responded by using the tools of monetary and fiscal policy to stimulate aggregate demand. Other economists believe that the large fall in the money supply caused the Depression. They assert that the Depression would have been avoided if the Fed had been pursuing a passive monetary policy of increasing the money supply at a steady rate. Hence, depending on one's beliefs about its cause, the Great Depression can be viewed either as an example of why active monetary and fiscal policy is necessary or as an example of why it is dangerous.

CASE STUDY

Is the Stabilization of the Economy a Figment of the Data?

Keynes wrote *The General Theory* in the 1930s, and in the wake of the Keynesian revolution, governments around the world began to view economic stabilization as a primary responsibility. Some economists believe that the development of Keynesian theory has had a profound influence on the behavior of the economy. Comparing data from before World War I and after World War II, they find that real GDP and unemployment have become much more stable. This, some Keynesians claim, is the best argument for active stabilization policy: it has worked.

In a series of provocative and influential papers, economist Christina Romer has challenged this assessment of the historical record. She argues that the measured reduction in volatility reflects not an improvement in economic policy and performance but rather an improvement in the economic data. The older data are much less accurate than the newer data. Romer claims that the higher volatility of unemployment and real GDP reported for the period before World War I is largely a figment of the data.

Romer uses various techniques to make her case. One is to construct more accurate data for the earlier period. This task is difficult because data sources are not readily available. A second way is to construct *less* accurate data for the recent period—that is, data that are comparable to the older data and thus suffer from the same imperfections. After constructing new "bad" data, Romer finds that the recent period appears almost as volatile as the early period, suggesting that the volatility of the early period may be largely an artifact of how the data were assembled.

Romer's work is part of the continuing debate over whether macroeconomic policy has improved the performance of the economy. Although her work remains controversial, most economists now believe that the economy in the immediate aftermath of the Keynesian revolution was only slightly more stable than it had been before.[3] ∎

13-2 Should Policy Be Conducted by Rule or by Discretion?

A second topic debated among economists is whether economic policy should be conducted by rule or by discretion. Policy is conducted by rule if policymakers announce in advance how policy will respond to various situations and commit themselves to following through on this announcement. Policy is conducted by discretion if policymakers are free to size up events as they occur and choose whatever policy they consider appropriate at the time.

The debate over rules versus discretion is distinct from the debate over passive versus active policy. Policy can be conducted by rule and yet be either passive or active. For example, a passive policy rule might specify steady growth in the money supply of 3 percent per year. An active policy rule might specify that

$$\text{Money Growth} = 3\% + (\text{Unemployment Rate} - 6\%).$$

Under this rule, the money supply grows at 3 percent if the unemployment rate is 6 percent, but for every percentage point by which the unemployment rate exceeds 6 percent, money growth increases by an extra percentage point. This rule tries to stabilize the economy by raising money growth when the economy is in a recession.

We begin this section by discussing why policy might be improved by a commitment to a policy rule. We then examine several possible policy rules.

Distrust of Policymakers and the Political Process

Some economists believe that economic policy is too important to be left to the discretion of policymakers. Although this view is more political than economic, evaluating it is central to how we judge the role of economic policy. If politicians are incompetent or opportunistic, then we may not want to give them the discretion to use the powerful tools of monetary and fiscal policy.

Incompetence in economic policy arises for several reasons. Some economists view the political process as erratic, perhaps because it reflects the shifting power

[3] To read more about this topic, see Christina D. Romer, "Spurious Volatility in Historical Unemployment Data," *Journal of Political Economy* 94 (February 1986): 1–37; and Christina D. Romer, "Is the Stabilization of the Postwar Economy a Figment of the Data?" *American Economic Review* 76 (June 1986): 314–334. In 2009, Professor Romer became the chair of President Obama's Council of Economic Advisers.

One instance of a large increase in government debt in peacetime began in the early 1980s. When Ronald Reagan was elected president in 1980, he was committed to reducing taxes and increasing military spending. These policies, coupled with a deep recession attributable to tight monetary policy, began a long period of substantial budget deficits. The government debt expressed as a percentage of GDP roughly doubled from 26 percent in 1980 to 50 percent in 1995. The United States had never before experienced such a large increase in government debt during a period of peace and prosperity. Many economists have criticized this increase in government debt as imposing an unjustifiable burden on future generations.

The increase in government debt during the 1980s caused significant concern among many policymakers as well. The first President Bush raised taxes to reduce the deficit, breaking his "Read my lips: No new taxes" campaign pledge and, according to some political commentators, costing him reelection. In 1993, when President Clinton took office, he raised taxes yet again. These tax increases, together with spending restraint and rapid economic growth due to the information-technology boom, caused the budget deficits to shrink and eventually turn into budget surpluses. The government debt fell from 50 percent of GDP in 1995 to 33 percent in 2001.

When President George W. Bush took office in 2001, the high-tech boom in the stock market was reversing course, and the economy was heading into recession. Economic downturns automatically cause tax revenue to fall and push the budget toward deficit. In addition, tax cuts to combat the recession and increased spending for homeland security and wars in Afghanistan and Iraq further increased the budget deficit, which averaged about 3 percent of GDP during his tenure. From 2001 to 2008, government debt rose from 33 to 41 percent of GDP.

As President Barack Obama moved into the White House in 2009, the economy was in the midst of a deep recession. Tax revenues were declining as the economy shrank. In addition, one of the new president's first actions was to sign a large fiscal stimulus to prop up the aggregate demand for goods and services. (A case study in Chapter 10 examines this policy.) The federal government's budget deficit was 11 percent of GDP in 2009 and projected to be 10 percent in 2010—levels not experienced since World War II. The debt–GDP ratio was projected to continue rising, at least in the near term.

In his first budget proposal, President Obama proposed reducing the budget deficit over time to 3 percent of GDP in 2013. The success of this initiative remained to be seen as this book went to press. Regardless, these events ensured that the economic effects of government debt would remain a major policy concern in the years to come.

CASE STUDY

The Troubling Long-Term Outlook for Fiscal Policy

What does the future hold for fiscal policymakers? Economic forecasting is far from precise, and it is easy to be cynical about economic predictions. But good policy cannot be made if policymakers only look backward. As a result, economists in the Congressional Budget Office (CBO) and other government agencies are always trying to look ahead to see what problems and opportunities are likely to develop. When these economists conduct long-term projections of U.S. fiscal policy, they paint a troubling picture.

One reason is demographic. Advances in medical technology have been increasing life expectancy, while improvements in birth-control techniques and changing social norms have reduced the number of children people have. Because of these developments, the elderly are becoming a larger share of the population. In 1950, the elderly population (aged 65 and older) was about 14 percent the size of the working-age population (aged 20 to 64). Now the elderly are about 21 percent of the working-age population, and that figure will rise to about 40 percent in 2050. About one-third of the federal budget is devoted to providing the elderly with pensions (mainly through the Social Security program) and health care. As more people become eligible for these "entitlements," as they are sometimes called, government spending will automatically rise over time.

A second, related reason for the troubling fiscal picture is the rising cost of health care. The government provides health care to the elderly through the Medicare system and to the poor through Medicaid. As the cost of health care increases, government spending on these programs increases as well. Policymakers have proposed various ways to stem the rise in health care costs, such as reducing the burden of lawsuits, encouraging more competition among health care providers, and promoting greater use of information technology, but most health economists believe such measures will have only limited impact. The main reason for rising health care costs is medical advances that provide new, better, but often expensive ways to extend and improve our lives.

The combination of the aging population and rising health care costs will have a major impact on the federal budget. Government spending on Social Security, Medicare, and Medicaid has already risen from less than 1 percent of GDP in 1950 to about 9 percent today. The upward trajectory is not about to stop. The CBO estimates that if no changes are made, spending on these programs will rise to about 20 percent of GDP over the next half century.

How the United States will handle these spending pressures is an open question. Simply increasing the budget deficit is not feasible. A budget deficit just pushes the cost of government spending onto a future generation of taxpayers. In the long run, the government needs to raise tax revenue to pay for the benefits it provides.

The big question is how the required fiscal adjustment will be split between tax increases and spending reductions. Some economists believe that to pay for these commitments, we will need to raise taxes substantially as a percentage of GDP. Given the projected increases in spending on Social Security, Medicare, and Medicaid, paying for these benefits would require increasing all taxes by approximately one-third. Other economists believe that such high tax rates would impose too great a cost on younger workers. They believe that policymakers should reduce the promises now being made to the elderly of the future and that, at the same time, people should be encouraged to take a greater role in providing for themselves as they age. This might entail increasing the normal retirement age, while giving people more incentive to save during their working years as preparation for assuming their own retirement and health costs. Resolving this debate will likely be one of the great policy challenges in the decades ahead. ∎

14-2 Problems in Measurement

The government budget deficit equals government spending minus government revenue, which in turn equals the amount of new debt the government needs to issue to finance its operations. This definition may sound simple enough, but in fact debates over fiscal policy sometimes arise over how the budget deficit should be measured. Some economists believe that the deficit as currently measured is not a good indicator of the stance of fiscal policy. That is, they believe that the budget deficit does not accurately gauge either the impact of fiscal policy on today's economy or the burden being placed on future generations of taxpayers. In this section we discuss four problems with the usual measure of the budget deficit.

Measurement Problem 1: Inflation

The least controversial of the measurement issues is the correction for inflation. Almost all economists agree that the government's indebtedness should be measured in real terms, not in nominal terms. The measured deficit should equal the change in the government's real debt, not the change in its nominal debt.

The budget deficit as commonly measured, however, does not correct for inflation. To see how large an error this induces, consider the following example. Suppose that the real government debt is not changing; in other words, in real terms, the budget is balanced. In this case, the nominal debt must be rising at the rate of inflation. That is,

$$\Delta D/D = \pi,$$

where π is the inflation rate and D is the stock of government debt. This implies

$$\Delta D = \pi D.$$

The government would look at the change in the nominal debt ΔD and would report a budget deficit of πD. Hence, most economists believe that the reported budget deficit is overstated by the amount πD.

We can make the same argument in another way. The deficit is government expenditure minus government revenue. Part of expenditure is the interest paid on the government debt. Expenditure should include only the real interest paid on the debt rD, not the nominal interest paid iD. Because the difference between the nominal interest rate i and the real interest rate r is the inflation rate π, the budget deficit is overstated by πD.

This correction for inflation can be large, especially when inflation is high, and it can often change our evaluation of fiscal policy. For example, in 1979 the federal government reported a budget deficit of $28 billion. Inflation was 8.6 percent, and the government debt held at the beginning of the year by the public (excluding the Federal Reserve) was $495 billion. The deficit was therefore overstated by

$$\pi D = 0.086 \times \$495 \text{ billion}$$

$$= \$43 \text{ billion}$$

Corrected for inflation, the reported budget deficit of $28 billion turns into a budget surplus of $15 billion! In other words, even though nominal government debt was rising, real government debt was falling.

Measurement Problem 2: Capital Assets

Many economists believe that an accurate assessment of the government's budget deficit requires taking into account the government's assets as well as its liabilities. In particular, when measuring the government's overall indebtedness, we should subtract government assets from government debt. Therefore, the budget deficit should be measured as the change in debt minus the change in assets.

Certainly, individuals and firms treat assets and liabilities symmetrically. When a person borrows to buy a house, we do not say that he is running a budget deficit. Instead, we offset the increase in assets (the house) against the increase in debt (the mortgage) and record no change in net wealth. Perhaps we should treat the government's finances the same way.

A budget procedure that accounts for assets as well as liabilities is called **capital budgeting**, because it takes into account changes in capital. For example, suppose that the government sells one of its office buildings or some of its land and uses the proceeds to reduce the government debt. Under current budget procedures, the reported deficit would be lower. Under capital budgeting, the revenue received from the sale would not lower the deficit, because the reduction in debt would be offset by a reduction in assets. Similarly, under capital budgeting, government borrowing to finance the purchase of a capital good would not raise the deficit.

The major difficulty with capital budgeting is that it is hard to decide which government expenditures should count as capital expenditures. For example, should the interstate highway system be counted as an asset of the government? If so, what is its value? What about the stockpile of nuclear weapons? Should spending on education be treated as expenditure on human capital? These difficult questions must be answered if the government is to adopt a capital budget.

Economists and policymakers disagree about whether the federal government should use capital budgeting. (Many state governments already use it.) Opponents of capital budgeting argue that, although the system is superior in principle to the current system, it is too difficult to implement in practice. Proponents of capital budgeting argue that even an imperfect treatment of capital assets would be better than ignoring them altogether.

Measurement Problem 3: Uncounted Liabilities

Some economists argue that the measured budget deficit is misleading because it excludes some important government liabilities. For example, consider the pensions of government workers. These workers provide labor services to the government today, but part of their compensation is deferred to the future. In essence, these workers are providing a loan to the government. Their future pension benefits represent a government liability not very different from government debt. Yet this liability is not included as part of the government debt, and the accumulation of this liability is not included as part of the budget deficit. According to some estimates, this implicit liability is almost as large as the official government debt.

Similarly, consider the Social Security system. In some ways, the system is like a pension plan. People pay some of their income into the system when young and expect to receive benefits when old. Perhaps accumulated future Social Security benefits should be included in the government's liabilities. Estimates suggest that the government's future Social Security liabilities (less future Social Security taxes) are more than three times the government debt as officially measured.

One might argue that Social Security liabilities are different from government debt because the government can change the laws determining Social Security benefits. Yet, in principle, the government could always choose not to repay all of its debt: the government honors its debt only because it chooses to do so. Promises to pay the holders of government debt may not be fundamentally different from promises to pay the future recipients of Social Security.

A particularly difficult form of government liability to measure is the *contingent liability*—the liability that is due only if a specified event occurs. For example, the government guarantees many forms of private credit, such as student loans, mortgages for low- and moderate-income families, and deposits in banks and savings-and-loan institutions. If the borrower repays the loan, the government pays nothing; if the borrower defaults, the government makes the repayment. When the government provides this guarantee, it undertakes a liability contingent on the borrower's default. Yet this contingent liability is not reflected in the budget deficit, in part because it is not clear what dollar value to attach to it.

CASE STUDY

Accounting for TARP

In 2008, many U.S. banks found themselves in substantial trouble, and the federal government put substantial taxpayer funds into rescuing the financial system. Chapter 19 discusses the causes of this financial crisis, the ramifications, and the policy responses. But here we note one particular small side effect: it made measuring the federal government's budget deficit more difficult.

As part of the financial rescue package, called the Troubled Assets Relief Program (TARP), the U.S. Treasury bought preferred stock in many banks. In essence, the plan worked as follows. The Treasury borrowed money, gave the money to the banks, and in exchange became a part owner of those banks. In the future, the banks were expected to pay the Treasury a preferred dividend (similar to interest) and eventually to repay the initial investment as well. When that repayment occurred, the Treasury would relinquish its ownership share in the banks.

The question then arose: how should the government's accounting statements reflect these transactions?

The U.S. Treasury under the Bush administration adopted the conventional view that these TARP expenditures should be counted as current expenses, like any other form of spending. Likewise, when the banks repaid the Treasury, these funds would be counted as revenue. Accounted for in this way, TARP caused a surge in the budget deficit when the funds were distributed to the banks, but it would lead to a smaller deficit, and perhaps a surplus, in the future when repayments were received from the banks.

The Congressional Budget Office, however, took a different view. Because most of the TARP expenditures were expected to be repaid, the CBO thought it was wrong to record this expenditure like other forms of spending. Instead, the CBO believed "the equity investments for TARP should be recorded on a net present value basis adjusted for market risk, rather than on a cash basis as recorded thus far by the Treasury." That is, for this particular program, the CBO adopted a form of capital budgeting. But it took into account the possibility that these investments would not pay off. In its estimation, every dollar spent on the TARP program cost the taxpayer only about 25 cents. If the actual cost turned out to be larger than the estimated 25 cents, the CBO would record those additional costs later; if the actual cost turned out to be less than projected, the CBO would later record a gain for the government. Because of these differences in accounting, while the TARP funds were being distributed, the budget deficit as estimated by the CBO was much smaller than the budget deficit as recorded by the U.S. Treasury.

When the Obama administration came into office, it adopted an accounting treatment more similar to the one used by the CBO, but with a larger estimate of the cost of TARP funds. The president's first budget proposal said, "Estimates of the value of the financial assets acquired by the Federal Government to date suggest that the Government will get back approximately two-thirds of the money spent purchasing such assets—so the net cost to the Government is roughly 33 cents on the dollar. These transactions are typically reflected in the budget at this net cost, since that budgetary approach best reflects their impact on the Government's underlying fiscal position." ■

Measurement Problem 4: The Business Cycle

Many changes in the government's budget deficit occur automatically in response to a fluctuating economy. When the economy goes into a recession, incomes fall, so people pay less in personal income taxes. Profits fall, so corporations pay less in corporate income taxes. Fewer people are employed, so payroll tax revenue declines. More people become eligible for government assistance, such as welfare and unemployment insurance, so government spending rises. Even without any change in the laws governing taxation and spending, the budget deficit increases.

These automatic changes in the deficit are not errors in measurement, because the government truly borrows more when a recession depresses tax revenue and boosts government spending. But these changes do make it more difficult to use the deficit to monitor changes in fiscal policy. That is, the deficit can rise or fall either because the government has changed policy or because the economy has changed direction. For some purposes, it would be good to know which is occurring.

To solve this problem, the government calculates a **cyclically adjusted budget deficit** (sometimes called the *full-employment budget deficit*). The cyclically adjusted deficit is based on estimates of what government spending and tax revenue would be if the economy were operating at its natural level of output and employment. The cyclically adjusted deficit is a useful measure because it reflects policy changes but not the current stage of the business cycle.

Summing Up

Economists differ in the importance they place on these measurement problems. Some believe that the problems are so severe that the budget deficit as normally measured is almost meaningless. Most take these measurement problems seriously but still view the measured budget deficit as a useful indicator of fiscal policy.

The undisputed lesson is that to fully evaluate what fiscal policy is doing, economists and policymakers must look at more than just the measured budget deficit. And, in fact, they do. The budget documents prepared annually by the Office of Management and Budget contain much detailed information about the government's finances, including data on capital expenditures and credit programs.

No economic statistic is perfect. Whenever we see a number reported in the media, we need to know what it is measuring and what it is leaving out. This is especially true for data on government debt and budget deficits.

14-3 The Traditional View of Government Debt

Imagine that you are an economist working for the Congressional Budget Office (CBO). You receive a letter from the chair of the Senate Budget Committee:

> Dear CBO Economist:
>
> Congress is about to consider the president's request to cut all taxes by 20 percent. Before deciding whether to endorse the request, my committee would like your analysis. We see little hope of reducing government spending, so the tax cut would mean an increase in the budget deficit. How would the tax cut and budget deficit affect the economy and the economic well-being of the country?
>
> Sincerely,
> Committee Chair

Before responding to the senator, you open your favorite economics textbook—this one, of course—to see what the models predict for such a change in fiscal policy.

To analyze the long-run effects of this policy change, you turn to the models in Chapters 3 through 8. The model in Chapter 3 shows that a tax cut stimulates consumer spending and reduces national saving. The reduction in saving raises the interest rate, which crowds out investment. The Solow growth model introduced in Chapter 7 shows that lower investment eventually leads to a lower steady-state capital stock and a lower level of output. Because we concluded in Chapter 8 that the U.S. economy has less capital than in the Golden Rule steady state (the steady state with maximum consumption), the fall in steady-state capital means lower consumption and reduced economic well-being.

The open-economy model in Chapter 5 shows how international trade affects your analysis. When national saving falls, people start financing investment by borrowing from abroad, causing a trade deficit. Although the inflow of capital from abroad lessens the effect of the fiscal-policy change on U.S. capital accumulation, the United States becomes indebted to foreign countries. The fiscal-policy change also causes the dollar to appreciate, which makes foreign goods cheaper in the United States and domestic goods more expensive abroad.

To analyze the short-run effects of the policy change, you turn to the *IS–LM* model in Chapters 10 and 11. This model shows that a tax cut stimulates consumer spending, which implies an expansionary shift in the *IS* curve. If there is no change in monetary policy, the shift in the *IS* curve leads to an expansionary shift in the aggregate demand curve. In the short run, when prices are sticky, the expansion in aggregate demand leads to higher output and lower unemployment. Over time, as prices adjust, the economy returns to the natural level of output, and the higher aggregate demand results in a higher price level.

With all these models in mind, you draft a response:

Dear Senator:

A tax cut financed by government borrowing would have many effects on the economy. The immediate impact of the tax cut would be to stimulate consumer spending. Higher consumer spending affects the economy in both the short run and the long run.

In the short run, higher consumer spending would raise the demand for goods and services and thus raise output and employment. Interest rates would also rise, however, as investors competed for a smaller flow of saving. Higher interest rates would discourage investment and would encourage capital to flow in from abroad. The dollar would rise in value against foreign currencies, and U.S. firms would become less competitive in world markets.

In the long run, the smaller national saving caused by the tax cut would mean a smaller capital stock and a greater foreign debt. Therefore, the output of the nation would be smaller, and a greater share of that output would be owed to foreigners.

The overall effect of the tax cut on economic well-being is hard to judge. Current generations would benefit from higher consumption and higher employment, although inflation would likely be higher as well. Future generations would bear much of the burden of today's budget deficits: they would be born into a nation with a smaller capital stock and a larger foreign debt.

Your faithful servant,
CBO Economist

The senator replies:

Dear CBO Economist:

Thank you for your letter. It made sense to me. But yesterday my committee heard testimony from a prominent economist who called herself a "Ricardian" and who reached quite a different conclusion. She said that a tax cut by itself would not stimulate consumer spending. She concluded that the budget deficit would therefore not have all the effects you listed. What's going on here?

Sincerely,

Committee Chair

After studying the next section, you write back to the senator, explaining in detail the debate over Ricardian equivalence.

Taxes and Incentives

Throughout this book we have summarized the tax system with a single variable, *T*. In our models, the policy instrument is the level of taxation that the government chooses; we have ignored the issue of how the government raises this tax revenue. In practice, however, taxes are not lump-sum payments but are levied on some type of economic activity. The U.S. federal government raises some revenue by taxing personal income (45 percent of tax revenue in 2008), some by taxing payrolls (36 percent), some by taxing corporate profits (12 percent), and some from other sources (7 percent).

Courses in public finance spend much time studying the pros and cons of alternative types of taxes. One lesson emphasized in such courses is that taxes affect incentives. When people are taxed on their labor earnings, they have less incentive to work hard. When people are taxed on the income from owning capital, they have less incentive to save and invest in capital. As a result, when taxes change, incentives change, and this can have macroeconomic effects. If lower tax rates encourage increased work and investment, the aggregate supply of goods and services increases.

Some economists, called *supply-siders*, believe that the incentive effects of taxes are large. Some

supply-siders go so far as to suggest that tax cuts can be self-financing: a cut in tax rates induces such a large increase in aggregate supply that tax revenue increases, despite the fall in tax rates. Although all economists agree that taxes affect incentives and that incentives affect aggregate supply to some degree, most believe that the incentive effects are not large enough to make tax cuts self-financing in most circumstances.

In recent years, there has been much debate about how to reform the tax system to reduce the disincentives that impede the economy from reaching its full potential. A proposal endorsed by many economists is to move from the current income tax system toward a consumption tax. Compared to an income tax, a consumption tax would provide more incentives for saving, investment, and capital accumulation. One way of taxing consumption would be to expand the availability of tax-advantaged saving accounts, such as individual retirement accounts and 401(k) plans, which exempt saving from taxation until that saving is later withdrawn and spent. Another way of taxing consumption would be to adopt a value-added tax, a tax on consumption paid by producers rather than consumers, now used by many European countries to raise government revenue.[1]

---

[1] To read more about how taxes affect the economy through incentives, the best place to start is an undergraduate textbook in public finance, such as Harvey Rosen and Ted Gayer, *Public Finance*, 8th ed. (New York: McGraw-Hill, 2007). In the more advanced literature that links public finance and macroeconomics, a classic reference is Christophe Chamley, "Optimal Taxation of Capital Income in a General Equilibrium Model With Infinite Lives," *Econometrica* 54 (May 1986): 607–622. Chamley establishes conditions under which the tax system should not distort the incentive to save (that is, conditions under which consumption taxation is superior to income taxation). The robustness of this conclusion is investigated in Andrew Atkeson, V. V. Chari, and Patrick J. Kehoe, "Taxing Capital Income: A Bad Idea," *Federal Reserve Bank of Minneapolis Quarterly Review* 23 (Summer 1999): 3–17.

14-4 The Ricardian View of Government Debt

The traditional view of government debt presumes that when the government cuts taxes and runs a budget deficit, consumers respond to their higher after-tax income by spending more. An alternative view, called **Ricardian equivalence**, questions this presumption. According to the Ricardian view, consumers are forward-looking and, therefore, base their spending decisions not only on their current income but also on their expected future income. The forward-looking consumer is at the heart of many modern theories of consumption. The Ricardian view of government debt applies the logic of the forward-looking consumer to analyzing the effects of fiscal policy.

The Basic Logic of Ricardian Equivalence

Consider the response of a forward-looking consumer to the tax cut that the Senate Budget Committee is considering. The consumer might reason as follows:

> The government is cutting taxes without any plans to reduce government spending. Does this policy alter my set of opportunities? Am I richer because of this tax cut? Should I consume more?
>
> Maybe not. The government is financing the tax cut by running a budget deficit. At some point in the future, the government will have to raise taxes to pay off the debt and accumulated interest. So the policy really represents a tax cut today coupled with a tax hike in the future. The tax cut merely gives me transitory income that eventually will be taken back. I am not any better off, so I will leave my consumption unchanged.

The forward-looking consumer understands that government borrowing today means higher taxes in the future. A tax cut financed by government debt does not reduce the tax burden; it merely reschedules it. It therefore should not encourage the consumer to spend more.

One can view this argument another way. Suppose that the government borrows $1,000 from the typical citizen to give that citizen a $1,000 tax cut. In essence, this policy is the same as giving the citizen a $1,000 government bond as a gift. One side of the bond says, "The government owes you, the bondholder, $1,000 plus interest." The other side says, "You, the taxpayer, owe the government $1,000 plus interest." Overall, the gift of a bond from the government to the typical citizen does not make the citizen richer or poorer, because the value of the bond is offset by the value of the future tax liability.

The general principle is that government debt is equivalent to future taxes, and if consumers are sufficiently forward-looking, future taxes are equivalent to current taxes. Hence, financing the government by debt is equivalent to financing it by taxes. This view is called *Ricardian equivalence* after the famous nineteenth-century economist David Ricardo, because he first noted the theoretical argument.

The implication of Ricardian equivalence is that a debt-financed tax cut leaves consumption unaffected. Households save the extra disposable income to pay the future tax liability that the tax cut implies. This increase in private saving exactly offsets the decrease in public saving. National saving—the sum of private and public saving—remains the same. The tax cut therefore has none of the effects that the traditional analysis predicts.

The logic of Ricardian equivalence does not mean that all changes in fiscal policy are irrelevant. Changes in fiscal policy do influence consumer spending if they influence present or future government purchases. For example, suppose that the government cuts taxes today because it plans to reduce government purchases in the future. If the consumer understands that this tax cut does not require an increase in future taxes, he feels richer and raises his consumption. But note that it is the reduction in government purchases, rather than the reduction in taxes, that stimulates consumption: the announcement of a future reduction in government purchases would raise consumption today even if current taxes were unchanged, because it would imply lower taxes at some time in the future.

Consumers and Future Taxes

The essence of the Ricardian view is that when people choose their level of consumption, they rationally look ahead to the future taxes implied by government debt. But how forward-looking are consumers? Defenders of the traditional view of government debt believe that the prospect of future taxes does not have as large an influence on current consumption as the Ricardian view assumes. Here are some of their arguments.[2]

Myopia Proponents of the Ricardian view of fiscal policy assume that people are rational when making such decisions as choosing how much of their income to consume and how much to save. When the government borrows to pay for current spending, rational consumers look ahead to the future taxes required to support this debt. Thus, the Ricardian view presumes that people have substantial knowledge and foresight.

One possible argument for the traditional view of tax cuts is that people are shortsighted, perhaps because they do not fully comprehend the implications of government budget deficits. It is possible that some people follow simple and not fully rational rules of thumb when choosing how much to save. Suppose, for example, that a person acts on the assumption that future taxes will be the same as current taxes. This person will fail to take account of future changes in taxes required by current government policies. A debt-financed tax cut will lead this person to believe that his lifetime income has increased, even if it hasn't. The tax cut will therefore lead to higher consumption and lower national saving.

Borrowing Constraints The Ricardian view of government debt assumes that consumers base their spending not on their current income but on their lifetime income, which includes both current and expected future income. According to the Ricardian view, a debt-financed tax cut increases current income, but

---

[2] For a survey of the debate over Ricardian equivalence, see Douglas Bernheim, "Ricardian Equivalence: An Evaluation of Theory and Evidence," *NBER Macroeconomics Annual* (1987): 263–303. See also the symposium on budget deficits in the Spring 1989 issue of the *Journal of Economic Perspectives*.

it does not alter lifetime income or consumption. Advocates of the traditional view of government debt argue that current income is more important than lifetime income for those consumers who face binding borrowing constraints. A *borrowing constraint* is a limit on how much an individual can borrow from banks or other financial institutions.

A person who would like to consume more than his current income allows—perhaps because he expects higher income in the future—has to do so by borrowing. If he cannot borrow to finance current consumption, or can borrow only a limited amount, his current income determines his spending, regardless of what his lifetime income might be. In this case, a debt-financed tax cut raises current income and thus consumption, even though future income will be lower. In essence, when the government cuts current taxes and raises future taxes, it is giving taxpayers a loan. For a person who wanted to obtain a loan but was unable to, the tax cut expands his opportunities and stimulates consumption.

CASE STUDY

George Bush's Withholding Experiment

In early 1992, President George H.W. Bush pursued a novel policy to deal with the lingering recession in the United States. By executive order, he lowered the amount of income taxes that were being withheld from workers' paychecks. The order did not reduce the amount of taxes that workers owed; it merely delayed payment. The higher take-home pay that workers received during 1992 was to be offset by higher tax payments, or smaller tax refunds, when income taxes were due in April 1993.

What effect would you predict for this policy? According to the logic of Ricardian equivalence, consumers should realize that their lifetime resources were unchanged and, therefore, save the extra take-home pay to meet the upcoming tax liability. Yet George Bush claimed his policy would provide "money people can use to help pay for clothing, college, or to get a new car." That is, he believed that consumers would spend the extra income, thereby stimulating aggregate demand and helping the economy recover from the recession. Bush seemed to be assuming that consumers were shortsighted or faced binding borrowing constraints.

Gauging the actual effects of this policy is difficult with aggregate data, because many other things were happening at the same time. Yet some evidence comes from a survey two economists conducted shortly after the policy was announced. The survey asked people what they would do with the extra income. Fifty-seven percent of the respondents said they would save it, use it to repay debts, or adjust their withholding in order to reverse the effect of Bush's executive order. Forty-three percent said they would spend the extra income. Thus, for this policy change, a majority of the population was planning to act as Ricardian theory posits. Nonetheless, Bush was partly right: many people planned to spend the extra income, even though they understood that the following year's tax bill would be higher.[3] ∎

---

[3] Matthew D. Shapiro and Joel Slemrod, "Consumer Response to the Timing of Income: Evidence From a Change in Tax Withholding," *American Economic Review* 85 (March 1995): 274–283.

Drawing by Dave Carpenter. From the *Wall Street Journal*. Permission, Cartoon Features Syndicate.

"What's this I hear about you adults mortgaging my future?"

Future Generations Besides myopia and borrowing constraints, a third argument for the traditional view of government debt is that consumers expect the implied future taxes to fall not on them but on future generations. Suppose, for example, that the government cuts taxes today, issues 30-year bonds to finance the budget deficit, and then raises taxes in 30 years to repay the loan. In this case, the government debt represents a transfer of wealth from the next generation of taxpayers (which faces the tax hike) to the current generation of taxpayers (which gets the tax cut). This transfer raises the lifetime resources of the current generation, so it raises their consumption. In essence, a debt-financed tax cut stimulates consumption because it gives the current generation the opportunity to consume at the expense of the next generation.

Economist Robert Barro has provided a clever rejoinder to this argument to support the Ricardian view. Barro argues that because future generations are the children and grandchildren of the current generation, we should not view these various generations as independent economic actors. Instead, he argues, the appropriate assumption is that current generations care about future generations. This altruism between generations is evidenced by the gifts that many people give their children, often in the form of bequests at the time of their deaths. The existence of bequests suggests that many people are not eager to take advantage of the opportunity to consume at their children's expense.

According to Barro's analysis, the relevant decisionmaking unit is not the individual, whose life is finite, but the family, which continues forever. In other words, an individual decides how much to consume based not only on his own income but also on the income of future members of his family. A debt-financed tax cut may raise the income an individual receives in his lifetime, but it does not raise his family's overall resources. Instead of consuming the extra income from the tax cut, the individual saves it and leaves it as a bequest to his children, who will bear the future tax liability.

We can see now that the debate over government debt is really a debate over consumer behavior. The Ricardian view assumes that consumers have a long time horizon. Barro's analysis of the family implies that the consumer's time horizon, like the government's, is effectively infinite. Yet it is possible that consumers do not look ahead to the tax liabilities of future generations. Perhaps they expect their children to be richer than they are and therefore welcome the opportunity to consume at their children's expense. The fact that many people leave zero or minimal bequests to their children is consistent with this hypothesis. For these zero-bequest families, a debt-financed tax cut alters consumption by redistributing wealth among generations.[4]

---

[4] Robert J. Barro, "Are Government Bonds Net Wealth?" *Journal of Political Economy* 81 (1974): 1095–1117.

CASE STUDY

Why Do Parents Leave Bequests?

The debate over Ricardian equivalence is partly a debate over how different generations are linked to one another. Robert Barro's defense of the Ricardian view is based on the assumption that parents leave their children bequests because they care about them. But is altruism really the reason that parents leave bequests?

One group of economists has suggested that parents use bequests to control their children. Parents often want their children to do certain things for them, such as phoning home regularly and visiting on holidays. Perhaps parents use the implicit threat of disinheritance to induce their children to be more attentive.

To test this "strategic bequest motive," these economists examined data on how often children visit their parents. They found that the more wealthy the parent, the more often the children visit. Even more striking was another result: only wealth that can be left as a bequest induces more frequent visits. Wealth that cannot be bequeathed—such as pension wealth, which reverts to the pension company in the event of an early death—does not encourage children to visit. These findings suggest that there may be more to the relationships among generations than mere altruism.[5] ∎

Making a Choice

Having seen the traditional and Ricardian views of government debt, you should ask yourself two sets of questions.

First, with which view do you agree? If the government cuts taxes today, runs a budget deficit, and raises taxes in the future, how will the policy affect the economy? Will it stimulate consumption, as the traditional view holds? Or will consumers understand that their lifetime income is unchanged and, therefore, offset the budget deficit with higher private saving?

Second, why do you hold the view that you do? If you agree with the traditional view of government debt, what is the reason? Do consumers fail to understand that higher government borrowing today means higher taxes tomorrow? Or do they ignore future taxes either because they face borrowing constraints or because future taxes will fall on future generations with which they do not feel an economic link? If you hold the Ricardian view, do you believe that consumers have the foresight to see that government borrowing today will result in future taxes levied on them or their descendants? Do you believe that consumers will save the extra income to offset that future tax liability?

We might hope that the evidence could help us decide between these two views of government debt. Yet when economists examine historical episodes of large budget deficits, the evidence is inconclusive. History can be interpreted in different ways.

---

[5] B. Douglas Bernheim, Andrei Shleifer, and Lawrence H. Summers, "The Strategic Bequest Motive," *Journal of Political Economy* 93 (1985): 1045–1076.

Consider, for example, the experience of the 1980s. The large budget deficits, caused partly by the Reagan tax cut of 1981, seem to offer a natural experiment to test the two views of government debt. At first glance, this episode appears decisively to support the traditional view. The large budget deficits coincided with low national saving, high real interest rates, and a large trade deficit. Indeed, advocates of the traditional view of government debt often claim that the experience of the 1980s confirms their position.

Yet those who hold the Ricardian view of government debt interpret these events differently. Perhaps saving was low in the 1980s because people were optimistic about future economic growth—an optimism that was also reflected in a booming stock market. Or perhaps saving was low because people expected that the tax cut would eventually lead not to higher taxes but, as Reagan promised, to lower government spending. Because it is hard to rule out any of these interpretations, both views of government debt survive.

Ricardo on Ricardian Equivalence

FYI

David Ricardo was a millionaire stockbroker and one of the greatest economists of all time. His most important contribution to the field was his 1817 book *Principles of Political Economy and Taxation,* in which he developed the theory of comparative advantage, which economists still use to explain the gains from international trade. Ricardo was also a member of the British Parliament, where he put his own theories to work and opposed the corn laws, which restricted international trade in grain.

Ricardo was interested in the alternative ways in which a government might pay for its expenditure. In an 1820 article called *Essay on the Funding System*, he considered an example of a war that cost 20 million pounds. He noted that if the interest rate was 5 percent, this expense could be financed with a one-time tax of 20 million pounds, a perpetual tax of 1 million pounds, or a tax of 1.2 million pounds for 45 years. He wrote:

> In point of economy, there is no real difference in either of the modes; for twenty million in one payment, one million per annum for ever, or 1,200,000 pounds for 45 years, are precisely of the same value.

Ricardo was aware that the issue involved the linkages among generations:

> It would be difficult to convince a man possessed of 20,000 pounds, or any other sum, that a perpetual payment of 50 pounds per annum was equally burdensome with a single tax of 1000 pounds. He would have some vague notion that the 50 pounds per annum would be paid by posterity, and would not be paid by him; but if he leaves his fortune to his son, and leaves it charged with this perpetual tax, where is the difference whether he leaves him 20,000 pounds with the tax, or 19,000 pounds without it?

Although Ricardo viewed these alternative methods of government finance as equivalent, he did not think other people would view them as such:

> The people who pay taxes . . . do not manage their private affairs accordingly. We are apt to think that the war is burdensome only in proportion to what we are at the moment called to pay for it in taxes, without reflecting on the probable duration of such taxes.

Thus, Ricardo doubted that people were rational and farsighted enough to look ahead fully to their future tax liabilities.

As a policymaker, Ricardo took the government debt seriously. Before the British Parliament, he once declared:

> This would be the happiest country in the world, and its progress in prosperity would go beyond the powers of imagination to conceive, if we got rid of two great evils—the national debt and the corn laws.

It is one of the great ironies in the history of economic thought that Ricardo rejected the theory that now bears his name!

14-5 Other Perspectives on Government Debt

The policy debates over government debt have many facets. So far we have considered the traditional and Ricardian views of government debt. According to the traditional view, a government budget deficit expands aggregate demand and stimulates output in the short run but crowds out capital and depresses economic growth in the long run. According to the Ricardian view, a government budget deficit has none of these effects, because consumers understand that a budget deficit represents merely the postponement of a tax burden. With these two theories as background, we now consider several other perspectives on government debt.

Balanced Budgets Versus Optimal Fiscal Policy

In the United States, many state constitutions require the state government to run a balanced budget. A recurring topic of political debate is whether the Constitution should require a balanced budget for the federal government as well. Most economists oppose a strict rule requiring the government to balance its budget. There are three reasons why optimal fiscal policy may at times call for a budget deficit or surplus.

Stabilization A budget deficit or surplus can help stabilize the economy. In essence, a balanced-budget rule would revoke the automatic stabilizing powers of the system of taxes and transfers. When the economy goes into a recession, taxes automatically fall, and transfers automatically rise. Although these automatic responses help stabilize the economy, they push the budget into deficit. A strict balanced-budget rule would require that the government raise taxes or reduce spending in a recession, but these actions would further depress aggregate demand. Discretionary fiscal policy is more likely to move in the opposite direction over the course of the business cycle. In 2009, for example, President Barack Obama signed a stimulus bill authorizing a large increase in spending to try to reduce the severity of the recession, even though it led to the largest budget deficit in more than half a century.

Tax Smoothing A budget deficit or surplus can be used to reduce the distortion of incentives caused by the tax system. As discussed earlier, high tax rates impose a cost on society by discouraging economic activity. A tax on labor earnings, for instance, reduces the incentive that people have to work long hours. Because this disincentive becomes particularly large at very high tax rates, the total social cost of taxes is minimized by keeping tax rates relatively stable rather than making them high in some years and low in others. Economists call this policy *tax smoothing*. To keep tax rates smooth, a deficit is necessary in years of unusually low income (recessions) or unusually high expenditure (wars).

Intergenerational Redistribution A budget deficit can be used to shift a tax burden from current to future generations. For example, some economists argue that if the current generation fights a war to preserve freedom, future generations benefit as well and should bear some of the burden. To pass on some of the war's costs, the current generation can finance the war with a budget deficit. The government can later retire the debt by levying taxes on the next generation.

These considerations lead most economists to reject a strict balanced-budget rule. At the very least, a rule for fiscal policy needs to take account of the recurring episodes, such as recessions and wars, during which it is reasonable for the government to run a budget deficit.

Fiscal Effects on Monetary Policy

In 1985, Paul Volcker told Congress that "the actual and prospective size of the budget deficit . . . heightens skepticism about our ability to control the money supply and contain inflation." A decade later, Alan Greenspan claimed that "a substantial reduction in the long-term prospective deficit of the United States will significantly lower very long-term inflation expectations." Both of these Fed chairmen apparently saw a link between fiscal policy and monetary policy.

We first discussed such a possibility in Chapter 4. As we saw, one way for a government to finance a budget deficit is simply to print money—a policy that leads to higher inflation. Indeed, when countries experience hyperinflation, the typical reason is that fiscal policymakers are relying on the inflation tax to pay for some of their spending. The ends of hyperinflations almost always coincide with fiscal reforms that include large cuts in government spending and therefore a reduced need for seigniorage.

In addition to this link between the budget deficit and inflation, some economists have suggested that a high level of debt might also encourage the government to create inflation. Because most government debt is specified in nominal terms, the real value of the debt falls when the price level rises. This is the usual redistribution between creditors and debtors caused by unexpected inflation—here the debtor is the government and the creditor is the private sector. But this debtor, unlike others, has access to the monetary printing press. A high level of debt might encourage the government to print money, thereby raising the price level and reducing the real value of its debts.

Despite these concerns about a possible link between government debt and monetary policy, there is little evidence that this link is important in most developed countries. In the United States, for instance, inflation was high in the 1970s, even though government debt was low relative to GDP. Monetary policymakers got inflation under control in the early 1980s, just as fiscal policymakers started running large budget deficits and increasing the government debt. Thus, although monetary policy might be driven by fiscal policy in some situations, such as during classic hyperinflations, this situation appears not to be the norm in most countries today. There are several reasons for this. First, most governments can finance deficits by selling debt and don't need to rely on seigniorage. Second, central banks often have enough independence to resist political pressure for more expansionary monetary policy. Third, and most important, policymakers in all parts of government know that inflation is a poor solution to fiscal problems.

Debt and the Political Process

Fiscal policy is made not by angels but by an imperfect political process. Some economists worry that the possibility of financing government spending by issuing debt makes that political process all the worse.

This idea has a long history. Nineteenth-century economist Knut Wicksell claimed that if the benefit of some type of government spending exceeded its cost, it should be possible to finance that spending in a way that would receive unanimous support from the voters. He concluded that government spending should be undertaken only when support is, in fact, nearly unanimous. In the case of debt finance, however, Wicksell was concerned that "the interests [of future taxpayers] are not represented at all or are represented inadequately in the tax-approving assembly."

Many economists have echoed this theme more recently. In their 1977 book *Democracy in Deficit*, James Buchanan and Richard Wagner argued for a balanced-budget rule for fiscal policy on the grounds that it "will have the effect of bringing the real costs of public outlays to the awareness of decision makers; it will tend to dispel the illusory 'something for nothing' aspects of fiscal choice." Similarly, Martin Feldstein (once an economic adviser to Ronald Reagan and a long-time critic of budget deficits) argues that "only the 'hard budget constraint' of having to balance the budget" can force politicians to judge whether spending's "benefits really justify its costs."

These arguments have led some economists to favor a constitutional amendment requiring Congress to pass a balanced budget. Often these proposals have escape clauses for times of national emergency, such as wars and depressions, when a budget deficit is a reasonable policy response. Some critics of these proposals argue that, even with the escape clauses, such a constitutional amendment would tie the hands of policymakers too severely. Others claim that Congress would easily evade the balanced-budget requirement with accounting tricks. As this discussion makes clear, the debate over the desirability of a balanced-budget amendment is as much political as economic.

International Dimensions

Government debt may affect a nation's role in the world economy. As we first saw in Chapter 5, when a government budget deficit reduces national saving, it often leads to a trade deficit, which in turn is financed by borrowing from abroad. For instance, many observers have blamed U.S. fiscal policy for the recent switch of the United States from a major creditor in the world economy to a major debtor. This link between the budget deficit and the trade deficit leads to two further effects of government debt.

First, high levels of government debt may increase the risk that an economy will experience capital flight—an abrupt decline in the demand for a country's assets in world financial markets. International investors are aware that a government can always deal with its debt simply by defaulting. This approach was used as far back as 1335, when England's King Edward III defaulted on his debt to Italian bankers. More recently, several Latin American countries defaulted on their debts in the 1980s, and Russia did the same in 1998. The higher the level of the government debt, the greater the temptation of default. Thus, as government debt increases, international investors may come to fear default and curtail their lending. If this loss of confidence occurs suddenly, the result could be the classic symptoms of capital flight: a collapse in the value of the currency and an increase in interest rates.

Second, high levels of government debt financed by foreign borrowing may reduce a nation's political clout in world affairs. This fear was emphasized by economist Ben Friedman in his 1988 book *Day of Reckoning*. He wrote, "World power and influence have historically accrued to creditor countries. It is not coincidental that America emerged as a world power simultaneously with our transition from a debtor nation . . . to a creditor supplying investment capital to the rest of the world." Friedman suggests that if the United States continues to run large trade deficits, it will eventually lose some of its international influence. So far, the record has not been kind to this hypothesis: the United States has run trade deficits throughout the 1980s, 1990s, and the first decade of the 2000s and, nonetheless, remains a leading superpower. But perhaps other events—such as the collapse of the Soviet Union—offset the decrease in political clout that the United States would have experienced because of its increased indebtedness.

CASE STUDY

The Benefits of Indexed Bonds

In 1997, the U.S. Treasury Department started to issue bonds that pay a return based on the consumer price index. These bonds typically pay a low interest rate of about 2 percent, so a $1,000 bond pays only $20 per year in interest. But that interest payment grows with the overall price level as measured by the CPI. In addition, when the $1,000 of principal is repaid, that amount is also adjusted for changes in the CPI. The 2 percent, therefore, is a real interest rate. Professors of macroeconomics no longer need to define the real interest rate as an abstract construct. They can open the *New York Times*, point to the credit report, and say, "Look here, this is a nominal interest rate, and this is a real interest rate." (Professors in the United Kingdom and several other countries have long enjoyed this luxury because indexed bonds have been trading in other countries for years.)

Of course, making macroeconomics easier to teach was not the reason that the Treasury chose to index some of the government debt. That was just a positive externality. Its goal was to introduce a new type of government bond that would benefit bondholder and taxpayer alike. These bonds are a win–win proposition because they insulate both sides of the transaction from inflation risk. Bondholders should care about the real interest rate they earn, and taxpayers should care about the real interest rate they pay. When government bonds are specified in nominal terms, both sides take on risk that is neither productive nor necessary. The new indexed bonds eliminate this inflation risk.

In addition, the new bonds have three other benefits.

First, the bonds may encourage the private sector to begin issuing its own indexed securities. Financial innovation is, to some extent, a public good. Once an innovation has been introduced into the market, the idea is nonexcludable (people cannot be prevented from using it) and nonrival (one person's use of the idea does not diminish other people's use of it). Just as a free market will not adequately supply the public goods of national defense and basic research, it will not adequately supply financial innovation. The Treasury's new bonds can be viewed as a remedy for that market failure.

Second, the bonds reduce the government's incentive to produce surprise inflation. After the budget deficits of the past few decades, the U.S. government is now a substantial debtor, and its debts are specified almost entirely in dollar terms. What is unique about the federal government, in contrast to most debtors, is that it can print the money it needs. The greater the government's nominal debts, the more incentive the government has to inflate away its debt. The Treasury's switch toward indexed debt reduces this potentially problematic incentive.

Third, the bonds provide data that might be useful for monetary policy. Many macroeconomic theories point to expected inflation as a key variable to explain the relationship between inflation and unemployment. But what is expected inflation? One way to measure it is to survey private forecasters. Another way is to look at the difference between the yield on nominal bonds and the yield on real bonds.

The Treasury's new indexed bonds, therefore, produced many benefits: less inflation risk, more financial innovation, better government incentives, more informed monetary policy, and easier lives for students and teachers of macroeconomics.[6] ∎

14-6 Conclusion

Fiscal policy and government debt are central in the U.S. political debate. This chapter discussed some of the economic issues that lie behind the policy decisions. As we have seen, economists are not in complete agreement about the measurement or effects of government indebtedness. Nor are economists in agreement about the best budget policy. Given the profound importance of this topic, there seems little doubt that the debates will continue in the years to come.

Summary

1. The current debt of the U.S. federal government is of moderate size compared to the debt of other countries or compared to the debt that the United States has had throughout its own history. The 1980s and early 1990s were unusual in that the ratio of debt to GDP increased during a

---

[6] To read more about indexed bonds, see John Y. Campbell and Robert J. Shiller, "A Scorecard for Indexed Government Debt," *NBER Macroeconomics Annual* (1996): 155–197; and David W. Wilcox, "Policy Watch: The Introduction of Indexed Government Debt in the United States," *Journal of Economic Perspectives* 12 (Winter 1998): 219–227.

period of peace and prosperity. From 1995 to 2001, the ratio of debt to GDP declined significantly, but after 2001 it started to rise again.

2. Standard measures of the budget deficit are imperfect measures of fiscal policy because they do not correct for the effects of inflation, do not offset changes in government liabilities with changes in government assets, omit some liabilities altogether, and do not correct for the effects of the business cycle.

3. According to the traditional view of government debt, a debt-financed tax cut stimulates consumer spending and lowers national saving. This increase in consumer spending leads to greater aggregate demand and higher income in the short run, but it leads to a lower capital stock and lower income in the long run.

4. According to the Ricardian view of government debt, a debt-financed tax cut does not stimulate consumer spending because it does not raise consumers' overall resources—it merely reschedules taxes from the present to the future. The debate between the traditional and Ricardian views of government debt is ultimately a debate over how consumers behave. Are consumers rational or shortsighted? Do they face binding borrowing constraints? Are they economically linked to future generations through altruistic bequests? Economists' views of government debt hinge on their answers to these questions.

5. Most economists oppose a strict rule requiring a balanced budget. A budget deficit can sometimes be justified on the basis of short-run stabilization, tax smoothing, or intergenerational redistribution of the tax burden.

6. Government debt can potentially have other effects. Large government debt or budget deficits may encourage excessive monetary expansion and, therefore, lead to greater inflation. The possibility of running budget deficits may encourage politicians to unduly burden future generations when setting government spending and taxes. A high level of government debt may increase the risk of capital flight and diminish a nation's influence around the world. Economists differ in which of these effects they consider most important.

KEY CONCEPTS

Capital budgeting   Cyclically adjusted budget deficit   Ricardian equivalence

QUESTIONS FOR REVIEW

1. What was unusual about U.S. fiscal policy from 1980 to 1995?

2. Why do many economists project increasing budget deficits and government debt over the next several decades?

3. Describe four problems affecting measurement of the government budget deficit.

4. According to the traditional view of government debt, how does a debt-financed tax cut affect public saving, private saving, and national saving?

5. According to the Ricardian view of government debt, how does a debt-financed tax cut affect public saving, private saving, and national saving?

6. Do you find more credible the traditional or the Ricardian view of government debt? Why?

7. Give three reasons why a budget deficit might be a good policy choice.

8. Why might the level of government debt affect the government's incentives regarding money creation?

PROBLEMS AND APPLICATIONS

1. On April 1, 1996, Taco Bell, the fast-food chain, ran a full-page ad in the *New York Times* with this news: "In an effort to help the national debt, Taco Bell is pleased to announce that we have agreed to purchase the Liberty Bell, one of our country's most historic treasures. It will now be called the *Taco Liberty Bell* and will still be accessible to the American public for viewing. We hope our move will prompt other corporations to take similar action to do their part to reduce the country's debt." Would such actions by U.S. corporations actually reduce the national debt as it is now measured? How would your answer change if the U.S. government adopted capital budgeting? Do you think these actions represent a true reduction in the government's indebtedness? Do you think Taco Bell was serious about this plan? (*Hint:* Note the date.)

2. Draft a letter to the senator described in Section 14-3, explaining and evaluating the Ricardian view of government debt.

3. The Social Security system levies a tax on workers and pays benefits to the elderly. Suppose that Congress increases both the tax and the benefits.

For simplicity, assume that Congress announces that the increases will last for one year only.

 a. How do you suppose this change would affect the economy? (*Hint:* Think about the marginal propensities to consume of the young and the old.)

 b. Does your answer depend on whether generations are altruistically linked?

4. Some economists have proposed the rule that the cyclically adjusted budget deficit always be balanced. Compare this proposal to a strict balanced-budget rule. Which is preferable? What problems do you see with the rule requiring a balanced cyclically adjusted budget?

5. Using the library or the Internet, find some recent projections for the future path of the U.S. government debt as a percentage of GDP. What assumptions are made about government spending, taxes, and economic growth? Do you think these assumptions are reasonable? If the United States experiences a productivity slowdown, how will reality differ from this projection? (*Hint:* A good place to look is www.cbo.gov.)

PART VI

The Financial System and the Economy

Introduction to the Financial System

"Economists themselves have not always fully appreciated the importance of a healthy financial system for economic growth."

—*Ben Bernanke, 2010*

The financial system is part of your daily life. You buy things with debit or credit cards, and you visit ATMs to get cash. You may have borrowed money from a bank to buy a car or pay for college. You see headlines about the ups and downs of the stock market, and you or your family may own shares of stock. If you travel abroad, you depend on currency markets to change your dollars into local money at your destination.

The financial system is also an important part of the overall economy. When the system works well, it channels funds from people who have saved money to people, firms, and governments with investment projects that make the economy more productive. For example, companies obtain loans from banks to build factories, which provide new jobs for workers and produce new goods for consumers. By increasing an economy's productivity, the financial system helps the economy to grow and the living standards of its citizens to rise.

At times, however, the financial system malfunctions and damages the economy. The U.S. financial crisis of 2007–2009 is a dramatic example of such a malfunction. Losses on subprime mortgages (home loans to people with weak credit histories) led to the failure or near-failure of many large banks. Bank lending contracted severely, resulting in lower consumption and investment. The Dow Jones index of stock prices fell more than 50 percent from 2007 to early 2009, shaking confidence in the economy and further reducing consumption and investment. Financial turmoil pushed the economy into a deep recession, with the unemployment rate rising from under 5 percent at the end of 2007 to 10 percent two years later.

The next few chapters explore financial systems in the United States and around the world. We discuss the different parts of these systems, such as banks and stock markets, and their economic functions. We discover how a healthy financial system benefits the economy, why the system sometimes breaks down, and what government can do to strengthen a country's financial system. In this chapter, we begin our study of the financial system with an overview of its two main parts: financial markets and banks.

15-1 Financial Markets

In economics, a market consists of people and firms that buy and sell something. **Financial markets** are made up of people and firms that buy and sell two kinds of assets. One type of asset is currencies of various economies, such as dollars and euros. We discussed currency markets in Chapter 5 (and you can learn more about them in a course on international economics). In this chapter, we focus on the second type of asset sold in financial markets: securities.

A **security** is a claim on some future flow of income. Traditionally, this claim was recorded on a piece of paper, but today most securities exist only as records in computer systems. The most familiar kinds of securities are bonds and stocks.

Bonds

A **bond**, also called a *fixed-income security*, is a security issued by a corporation or government that promises to pay the buyer predetermined amounts of money at certain times in the future. Corporations issue bonds to finance investment projects, such as new factories. Governments issue bonds when they need funds to cover budget deficits. When a corporation or government issues bonds, it is borrowing money from those who buy the bonds. The issuer receives funds immediately and pays the buyers back in the future. Because bond issuers owe money to bond purchasers, bonds are also called *debt securities*.

For example, you might pay $100 for a bond that pays you $6 a year for 10 years and then pays back the $100 at the end of the tenth year. To introduce some terms, the *face value* of this bond is $100, and the *coupon payment* is $6; the bond's *maturity* is 10 years.

Almost always, the total payments promised by a bond—the face value plus all coupon payments—exceed the price that a buyer pays for the bond. This means that bonds pay interest: the issuer pays buyers for the use of their funds. In our example of a 10-year bond, the interest rate is the coupon payment divided by the face value: $6/$100 = 6 percent. In other cases—for example, when a bond's face value differs from the price paid by the buyer—it takes some work to determine what interest rate the buyer receives. Chapter 16 shows how to calculate interest rates on bonds.

Bonds differ in their maturities, which range from a few months to 30 years or more. Bonds with maturities of less than a year have special names: they are called *commercial paper* when issued by corporations and *Treasury bills* when issued by the U.S. government.

Bonds also differ in the stream of payments they promise. For example, a *zero-coupon bond* yields no payments until it matures. To attract buyers, it sells for less than its face value. For example, you might pay $80 for a zero-coupon bond that pays $100 at maturity. (Again, Chapter 16 shows how to calculate the interest rate on such a bond.)

In our world, promises—including promises to make payments on bonds—are not always kept. Sometimes a bond issuer **defaults:** it fails to make coupon payments or pay the face value at maturity. A corporation defaults on its bonds if it declares bankruptcy. A government defaults if it doesn't have enough revenue to make bond payments.

The risk of default varies greatly for different bonds. This risk is small for bonds issued by the U.S. government or by well-established, highly successful corporations. Default risk is larger for new corporations with unknown prospects or corporations that are losing money, because these companies may go bankrupt and stop making bond payments. The greater the risk of default, the higher the interest rate that a bond must pay to attract buyers.

Stocks

A **stock**, or *equity*, is an ownership share in a corporation. As of 2010, Exxon Mobil Corporation had issued about 5 billion shares of stock. If you own 50 million of these shares, you own 1 percent of Exxon Mobil and its oil refineries and are entitled to 1 percent of the company's future profits.

Companies issue stock for the same reason they issue bonds: to raise funds for investment. Like a bond, a share of stock produces a flow of income—but a different kind of flow. A bondholder knows exactly how much the bond will pay (unless the issuer defaults). The earnings from a company's stock are a share of profits, and profits are unpredictable. Consequently, buying stocks is usually riskier than buying bonds. People buy stocks despite the risk because stocks often produce higher returns.

Because stock is an ownership share, stockholders have ultimate control over a corporation. Stockholders elect a corporation's board of directors, which oversees the business and hires a president to run its day-to-day operations. In contrast, bondholders have no control over a corporation; a bond is simply a corporation's promise of future payments to the bond's buyer.

Stock and bond markets generate many challenging questions: How do firms decide how many bonds and shares of stock to issue, how do people decide which bonds and stocks to buy, and what determines the prices of these securities? How do developments in stock and bond markets affect the overall economy? We discuss these questions throughout the next few chapters.

15-2 Economic Functions of Financial Markets

What is the purpose of stock, bond, and other financial markets? Why do people participate in them, and why are they important for the economy? There are two main answers. First, financial markets channel funds from savers to investors with productive uses for the funds. Second, these markets help people and firms share risks.

Matching Savers and Investors

An economy's saving provides funds to finance investment. To capture this idea, Chapter 3 presented a model in which savers meet investors in a single market for loanable funds. Reality is more complicated: a system of markets and institutions helps channel funds from savers to investors. Stock and bond markets are two of the most important parts of this financial system.

We can illustrate the channeling role of securities markets with an example. Consider a young man named Britt. Unlike most people, Britt can throw a baseball 95 miles an hour, and he has a good curve ball, too. For these reasons, a baseball team pays him $10 million a year to pitch. Britt happens to be a thrifty person, so he does not spend all his salary. Over time, he accumulates a lot of savings and wonders what he should do with it.

If he just accumulates cash and puts it in a safe, Britt knows his savings will not grow. In fact, if there is inflation, the value of his money will fall over time. Britt wonders how he can use his wealth to earn more wealth.

In another city, Harriet, the owner of a software company, is pondering her future. Harriet is a person of great vision and has an idea that could make her rich: an application that sends smells from one smart phone to another.

Harriet wants to develop this app, which will let people send perfumes to their sweethearts and rotten-egg smells to their enemies. She knows this product, iSmells, will be highly profitable. Unfortunately, it is expensive to buy the computers and hire the programmers needed to make her idea a reality. Because her current business does not generate enough profits to finance this investment, Harriet fears that she won't be able to develop her great idea.

Financial markets can help both Harriet and Britt solve their problems. Harriet can obtain the funds for her investment from Britt (and people like him). Her company can issue new stock, which people like Britt will buy in the hope of sharing in Harriet's future profits. Harriet can also raise funds by selling bonds and using part of her future profits to make the payments promised by the bonds.

This is a win–win outcome. If Harriet develops iSmells and the app takes off, her company will flourish and Britt will earn large returns on the stocks and bonds that he buys. Harriet's investment will benefit other people as well: her workers will earn the high wages that a profitable business can pay, and people around the world will have fun exchanging smells.

This simple example captures the primary role of all the trillion-dollar financial markets in the real world. At any time, some people consume less than they earn and save the rest. Other people know how to use these savings for investments that earn profits, increase production and employment, and otherwise benefit the economy. When they work well, financial markets transfer funds from an economy's savers to its investors.

Risk Sharing

Financial markets have a second important role in the economy: they help people share risks. Even if investors could finance their projects without financial markets, the markets would exist to perform this risk-sharing function alone.

To see this point, let's suppose that Harriet is wealthy. If she uses most of her wealth, she could finance the expansion of her business without getting funds from anyone else and would not have to sell stocks or bonds in financial markets. She would retain full ownership of her firm and keep all the profits from iSmells.

Because the software business, like any industry, is risky, this strategy is probably unwise. Harriet's new software might be profitable, but there is no guarantee. It's possible that another firm will produce a better version of the software or that consumers will tire of smart-phone gimmicks and move on to the next technological toy.

In these cases, Harriet might not sell much software, and she could lose the funds she invested. Because of this risk, putting her money in a safe instead of into her company starts to look like a better idea. This strategy means giving up a chance for high software profits, but it is less risky.

Fortunately, Harriet does not have to choose between hoarding her money and risking it all on her company. Thanks to financial markets, she can fund her new investment, at least in part, by issuing stocks and bonds. This approach reduces the amount of her own wealth that Harriet must put into the firm and makes it possible for her to share the risk from her business with the buyers of her securities.

"Your mother called to remind you to diversify."

Harriet can use the wealth she doesn't spend on iSmells to buy stocks and bonds issued by other companies. She is likely to earn money on these assets even if her own business fares poorly. Harriet can also buy bonds issued by the U.S. and other governments. Such behavior is an example of **diversification**, the distribution of wealth among many assets.

Why is diversification desirable? Most of the time, some companies do well and others do badly. The software industry might boom while the steel industry loses money, or vice versa, and one software company may succeed while another fails. If a person's wealth is tied to one company, he loses a lot if the company is unsuccessful. If he buys the securities of many companies, bad luck and good luck tend to average out. Diversification lets savers earn healthy returns from securities while minimizing the risk of disaster.

Upcoming chapters discuss some sophisticated ideas about diversification and risk sharing, such as the markets for futures and options. At its core, however, the idea of diversification is simply common sense. The late James Tobin won the Nobel Prize in economics in 1981 largely for developing theories of asset diversification. When a newspaper reporter asked Tobin to summarize his Nobel-winning ideas, he said simply, "Don't put all your eggs in one basket."

But just because a principle reflects common sense doesn't mean that people follow it. The following case study offers an example of people who failed to heed James Tobin's advice, with disastrous consequences.

CASE STUDY

The Perils of Employee Stock Ownership

Many Americans save for their retirement through *401(k) plans*, named for the congressional act that created them. A 401(k) plan is a savings fund administered by a company for its workers. Saving through a 401(k) plan is appealing because any income contributed to the plan is not taxed. In addition, some companies match employee contributions to 401(k) plans.

A person who puts money in a 401(k) plan is offered a variety of assets to purchase. Usually the choices include shares in **mutual funds**. A mutual fund is a financial firm that buys and holds a large number of different stocks and bonds. Buying mutual fund shares is a relatively easy way to diversify your eggs into more than one basket.

A company's 401(k) asset offerings often include stock in the company itself, and some employees choose to put most of their 401(k) savings in their company's stock. As a result, their assets are not diversified. There seem to be several reasons for this behavior. Some employers encourage it, believing that workers are more loyal if they own company stock. Many workers are confident about their companies' prospects, so they view company stock as less risky than other securities. People are influenced by success stories such as that of Microsoft, where employees grew rich from owning company stock.

But putting all your eggs in one basket is disastrous if someone drops the basket, as happened at Enron, a huge energy company that went bankrupt in 2001. At Enron, 58 percent of all 401(k) funds, and all the savings of some workers, were devoted to Enron stock. During 2001, as an accounting scandal unfolded, Enron's stock price dropped from $85 to 30 cents. This drastic decline wiped out the retirement savings of many employees. One 59-year-old man saw the balance in his 401(k) account fall from $600,000 to $11,000.

The disaster was even worse because Enron laid off most of its employees. Workers lost their life savings at the same time they lost their jobs. Many suffered severe hardships such as the loss of their homes.

Since the Enron disaster, financial advisers have urged greater diversification in 401(k) plans. Many people have taken this advice to heart. One study estimates that, averaging over all companies, the percentage of 401(k) funds in company stock fell from 19 percent in 1999 to 10 percent in 2008.

The government has encouraged this trend through the Pension Reform Act of 2006, which limits companies' efforts to promote employee stock ownership. Before the act, some companies contributed their stock to 401(k) plans on the condition that workers hold on to the stock. Now employees must be allowed to sell company stock after three years of service.

Despite these changes, economists worry that too much 401(k) wealth remains in company stock. Company stock accounts for more than half of 401(k) assets at some large firms, including Procter & Gamble, Pfizer, and General Electric. In 2008–2009, GE employees saw their 401(k) balances plummet when GE Capital, a subsidiary that lends to consumers and businesses, suffered large losses. GE's stock price fell from $37.49 in December 2008 to $5.73 in March 2009, a decrease of 85 percent. In this case, the price recovered somewhat—it was $18.94 in March 2010—but the GE episode illustrates the perils of holding company stock.

Some economists think the government should take stronger action to address this problem. They propose a cap on the percentage of 401(k) money that goes to company stock. At this writing, however, no new laws appear imminent.[1] ∎

---

[1] For more on Enron's workers, see "Workers Feel Pain of Layoffs and Added Sting of Betrayal," *New York Times*, January 20, 2002, page A1. For recent trends in 401(k) plans, see Jack VanDerhei, Sarah Holden, and Luis Alonso, "401(k) Plan Asset Allocation, Account Balances, and Loan Activity in 2008," Issue Brief #335, Employee Benefit Research Institute, October 2009.

15-3 Asymmetric Information

When financial markets work well, they channel funds from savers to investors, and they help people reduce risk. But financial markets don't always work well. Sometimes they break down, harming savers, investors, and the economy. The problems of financial markets are complex, but many have the same root cause: **asymmetric information**, a situation in which one participant in an economic transaction has more information than the other participant. In financial markets, the asymmetry generally occurs because the sellers of securities have more information than the buyers.

Two types of asymmetric information exist in financial markets, *adverse selection* and *moral hazard*. These two concepts are outlined in Figure 15-1 and discussed in detail in the next sections.

Adverse Selection

In general, **adverse selection** means that the people or firms that are most eager to make a transaction are the least desirable to parties on the other side of the transaction. In securities markets, a firm is most eager to issue stocks and bonds if the values of these securities are low. That is the case if the firm's prospects are poor, which means that earnings on its stock are likely to be low and default risk on its bonds is high. Adverse selection is a problem for buyers of securities because they have less information than issuers about the securities' value. Because of their relative ignorance, buyers run a risk of overpaying for securities that will probably produce low returns.

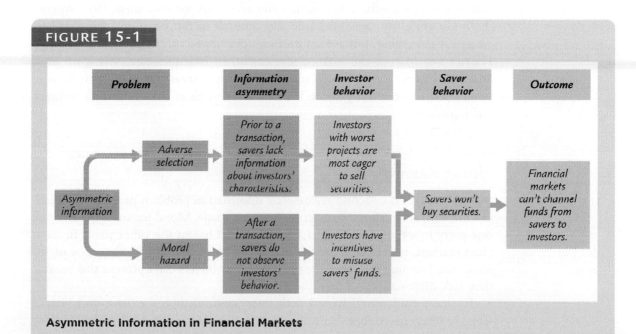

FIGURE 15-1

Asymmetric Information in Financial Markets

To illustrate adverse selection, let's return to the story of Harriet and Britt and add a third character, Martha. Like Harriet, Martha runs a software firm, and she would like to develop iSmells technology. But Martha is not as gifted as Harriet. Not only are there technical glitches in Martha's plans for the software, but she is a terrible manager. She is disorganized, and her abrasive personality results in high employee turnover. For all these reasons, Martha is less likely than Harriet to develop a successful product.

Both Martha and Harriet would like to finance their investments by selling securities to Britt. If Britt knew that Harriet is more talented than Martha, he would realize that Harriet's stock will probably produce higher earnings than Martha's and that Harriet is less likely to go bankrupt and default on her bonds. In short, he would prefer to buy Harriet's securities over Martha's. But remember: Britt's expertise is baseball, not software or business. The two women have equally glib sales pitches for their products, so both businesses seem like good bets to him. Because he doesn't know Martha or Harriet, can't evaluate their talents, and doesn't know the likelihood that each will succeed, Britt doesn't know the value of either woman's securities.

The story gets worse. Martha and Harriet understand their businesses, so they *do* know the value of their securities. They have more information than Britt. This information asymmetry produces adverse selection: Martha, the more inept businessperson, wants to issue more securities than Harriet. Why? Harriet knows that shares in her company are worth a lot. Therefore, while she wants to diversify by selling some stock to others, she wants to keep a relatively large amount for herself. Martha, on the other hand, knows her stock is not worth much because there's a good chance her company will fail. Therefore, she wants to unload all her stock onto other people and keep little or none for herself.

Britt doesn't understand software, but he does understand adverse selection. He realizes that when somebody is extremely eager to sell something, it is probably not worth much. When firms offer securities for sale, then, Britt worries that most are a bad deal. So he decides after all to put his money in a safe; he won't earn anything, but at least he won't get ripped off. Consequently, neither Harriet nor Martha can finance investment. In Martha's case, this is no great loss. But Harriet's inability to obtain financing harms the many people who would benefit from her project: Harriet, savers such as Britt, Harriet's workers, and consumers.

Moral Hazard

Moral hazard, the second asymmetric information problem prevalent in financial markets, arises after a transaction has been made. Moral hazard is the risk that one party to a transaction will act in a way that harms the other party. In securities markets, issuers of securities may take actions that reduce the value of the securities, harming buyers of the securities. The buyers can't prevent this because they lack information on the issuers' behavior.

To understand moral hazard, let's once again change the Britt-and-Harriet story. In this version, there is no adverse selection: Harriet is the only one looking for funding (there is no Martha) and everyone in securities markets, including Britt, knows that Harriet can produce great software. Britt would do well to buy Harriet's securities as long as Harriet performs as everyone expects her to and wisely uses the funds for software development.

But what if Harriet doesn't do what she's supposed to do? Software is a tough, competitive industry. Harriet has the skills to succeed, but she must work hard and keep costs low to earn profits. Unfortunately, as a human being, Harriet faces temptations. She wants to pay high salaries to herself and the friends who work for her. She wants some nice Postimpressionist paintings on her office wall. And she thinks it would be fun to leave work at 2:00 every Friday afternoon to party at trendy clubs.

If Harriet succumbs to these temptations, then costs rise, productivity falls, and her firm is less profitable. If the problems get out of hand, Harriet's firm could even go bankrupt. If Harriet had financed her business with her own wealth, she would have incentives to work hard and behave prudently because the cost of artwork and parties would come out of her own pocket. But these incentives disappear if Harriet's firm is financed by Britt. If Britt buys the firm's stock, then it is he, not Harriet, who loses if profits are low. If Britt buys bonds, it is he who loses if the firm goes bankrupt and defaults.

Asymmetric information underlies this example of moral hazard. Harriet knows how she runs her business and Britt doesn't, but he does know the fickleness of human nature. Before buying her securities, Britt might make Harriet promise to work hard and spend his money wisely. This promise would be meaningless, however, because Britt lives on the other side of the country and has no way of knowing whether Harriet is keeping her promise. If Britt could somehow see everything Harriet does, he could demand his savings back the first time she leaves work early. He could cancel her account at the art dealer and her reservations at the trendy clubs. But Britt is busy on the pitcher's mound and can't keep track of what happens at Harriet's office. So he refuses to buy Harriet's securities. Once again, Harriet cannot finance her investment, even though she has a great idea for a new product.

15-4 Banks

The story of Britt and Harriet has taken a bad turn. Because of asymmetric information, financial markets have failed to channel funds from savers to investors. But now a hero arrives on the scene: a bank. Britt deposits his money in the bank and earns interest. The bank lends money to Harriet for her investment. Ultimately, Britt's savings find their way to Harriet, and both people (and the economy as a whole) benefit.

Why can Harriet get money from a bank if she can't get it from financial markets? The answer is that banks reduce the problem of asymmetric information. We'll discuss how banks address asymmetric information later in this section. First, we need to understand some basics about banks.

What Is a Bank?

A bank is one kind of **financial institution**. A financial institution, also called a *financial intermediary*, is any firm that helps channel funds from savers to investors. A mutual fund is another example of a financial institution because it sells shares to savers and uses the proceeds to purchase securities from a number of firms.

A **bank** is a financial institution defined by two characteristics. First, it raises funds by accepting deposits. These include savings deposits and checking deposits that people and firms use to make payments. Both types of deposits earn interest, and savings deposits earn more than checking. Second, a bank uses its funds to make loans to companies and individuals. These are **private loans:** each is negotiated between one lender and one borrower. In this way, they differ from the borrowing that occurs when companies sell bonds to the public at large in financial markets.

In the past, banks were restricted to accepting deposits and making loans, but today, banks engage in many financial businesses. They trade securities, sell mutual funds and insurance, and much more. Still, what makes them banks are their deposits and loans.

There are several types of banks. For example, *savings and loan associations* are usually small, and much of their lending is to people buying homes. *Commercial banks* can be very large, and they lend for many purposes. We discuss the various types of banks in Chapter 18.

A note on terminology: in everyday language, the term "bank" is used more broadly than we have defined it. Some institutions are called banks even though they don't accept deposits or make loans. One example is an *investment bank*, a financial institution that helps companies issue new stocks and bonds. An investment bank is not really a bank in economists' sense of the term.

Banks Versus Financial Markets

Like financial markets, banks channel funds from savers to investors. Funds flow through a bank in a two-step process: savers deposit money in the bank, and then the bank lends the deposited money to investors. In financial markets, savers provide funds directly to investors by buying their stocks and bonds. For these reasons, channeling funds through banks is called **indirect finance** and channeling them through financial markets is called **direct finance.** Figure 15-2 illustrates these concepts.

Why Banks Exist

Indirect finance is costly. To cover their costs and earn some profit, banks charge higher interest on loans than they pay on deposits. In effect, banks take a cut of the funds they transfer to investors. Nonetheless, people like Britt and Harriet use banks because of the asymmetric information problems that hinder direct finance.

Banks help Harriet to expand her business, and they also help Britt because they pay him interest on his savings. The interest that Britt earns from his bank

FIGURE 15-2

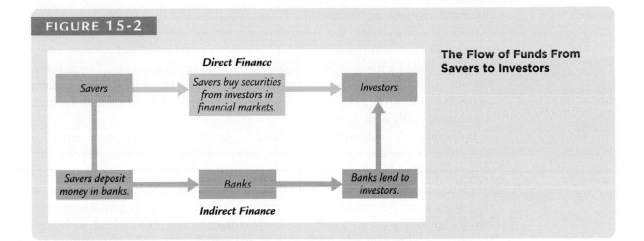

The Flow of Funds From Savers to Investors

account may be less than the return on a security, but it's more than Britt would earn by putting his money in a safe.

Banks can help Britt and Harriet because they lessen the problems of asymmetric information that hobble securities markets. Banks overcome these problems by producing information about the investors that borrow from them. Greater information reduces both adverse selection and moral hazard in financial transactions.

Reducing Adverse Selection Banks reduce adverse selection by screening potential borrowers. If both Harriet and Martha want money, Britt can't tell who has a better investment project. But a good banker can figure it out.

When the two investors apply for loans, they must provide information about their business plans, past careers, and finances. Bank loan officers are trained to evaluate this information (and information from independent sources such as credit reporting agencies) and decide whose project is likely to succeed. A firm with a bad project may go bankrupt, and bankrupt firms default not only on any bonds they've issued but also on bank loans they've taken out.

Loan officers may detect flaws in Martha's plans or see that her past projects have lost money. They turn down Martha and lend money to Harriet, who has a record of success. Because the bank has gathered information, funds flow to the most productive investment.

Reducing Moral Hazard To combat moral hazard once a loan is made, banks include covenants in their loan contracts. A **covenant** is a statement about how the bank expects the borrower to behave, and it must be agreed upon by both the bank and the borrower. For example, Harriet's lender might include a covenant requiring that she spend her loan on computers—not parties at trendy clubs.

Banks monitor their borrowers to make sure they obey covenants and don't waste money. Harriet must send her bank periodic reports on her spending. If Harriet misuses her loan—thereby increasing the risk of bankruptcy and default—the bank can demand its money back. With such monitoring in place, it is safe for the bank to finance Harriet's investment.

Who Needs Banks? Some firms can raise funds by issuing securities; those that can't depend on bank loans to fund their investments. The asymmetric information problem explains why. If a firm is large and well established (such as Microsoft or Wal-Mart), savers may know a lot about it from the media or the security analysis industry. With all this information, savers will believe they know enough to make a good decision about buying the firm's securities. Savers know less about newer or smaller firms, however, and are less willing to buy their securities. For this reason, start-ups and small businesses need to finance their investments with bank loans.

Individuals also rely on banks for funding. Again, the reason is asymmetric information. If one day you buy a house, you won't be able to finance your purchase by issuing bonds because it is likely that no one would buy them. Most savers have heard of Microsoft but probably know little or nothing about you, so they would not be willing to risk giving you their money by purchasing your bonds. Fortunately, individuals can borrow from banks. Banks lend to home-buyers after gathering information on their incomes and credit histories.

15-5 The Financial System and Economic Growth

We have seen how the financial system helps individual savers, such as Britt, and investors, such as Harriet. Financial markets and banks also benefit the economy as a whole. When funds flow to good investment projects, the economy becomes more productive and living standards rise. In other words, a strong financial system spurs economic growth.

The Allocation of Saving

In Chapters 7 and 8, we used the Solow model to study economic growth. One of the model's central ideas is that an economy's output per worker depends on its saving rate. The more people save, the more funds are available for investment. With high saving, companies can build factories and implement new technologies. The economy produces more and its people become richer.

The Solow model has large elements of truth. We saw, for example, that differences in saving rates help explain differences in income across countries. Yet the model ignores the issues discussed in this chapter. It assumes that saving flows automatically to investors with productive projects. In fact, however, the right investors get funds only if the economy has a well-functioning financial system. An economy can save a lot and still remain poor if saving is not channeled to its best uses.

Financial systems vary across countries. Some countries, including the United States, have large stock and bond markets and banks that usually have ample funds. In these countries, it is relatively easy for individuals and firms with good investment projects to raise funds. In other countries, the financial system is underdeveloped; it is difficult for firms to issue securities, and bank loans are scarce. When a financial system cannot work properly, investors have trouble financing their projects and economic growth slows.

What explains these differences? One factor is government regulation. Some governments regulate securities markets to reduce the problem of asymmetric information. In the United States, for example, companies that issue securities must publish annual reports on their investments and earnings. This information lessens adverse selection, and savers are more willing to buy securities. Some countries lack such regulations.

Government policies also affect banks. In the United States, the government provides deposit insurance, which compensates people who lose deposits because a bank fails. Not all countries have such insurance. Chapter 18 discusses governments' involvement in banking in more detail.

Evidence on the Financial System and Growth

Many economists have studied the effects of financial systems on economic growth. Much of this research has occurred at the World Bank, a large international organization that promotes economic development. The research has found that differences in financial systems help explain why some countries are richer than others.

Figure 15-3 presents a portion of World Bank data drawn from 155 countries between 1996 and 2007. Panel (a) shows *stock market capitalization* in several groups of countries. This variable is the value of all stocks issued by corporations, expressed as a percentage of GDP. For example, a figure of 50 percent means the total value of stocks is half a year's output. Stock market capitalization measures investors' success in raising funds through the stock market.

Panel (b) shows total *bank loans*, again as a percentage of GDP. This variable measures banks' success in channeling funds from savers to investors.

The figure divides countries into four groups based on their real GDP per person. The high-income group contains a quarter of all countries, those with the highest real GDP per person. Upper-middle-income countries make up the next quarter, and so on. For each group, the figure shows the average levels of stock market capitalization and bank loans.

Figure 15-3 has a simple message: richer countries—those with higher real GDP per person—tend to have more developed financial systems than poorer countries. Rich countries have larger stock markets and more bank loans. These facts support the view that financial development aids economic growth.

By themselves, these graphs are not conclusive. They show a correlation between financial development and income levels, but correlation does not prove causation. Financial development could cause economic growth, but the opposite is also possible: perhaps countries grow rich for some other reason, such as good educational systems or robust foreign trade, and this growth causes them to develop stronger financial systems. Or perhaps some third factor causes both economic growth and financial development.

Much of the World Bank's research addresses the question of causality. One strategy is to compare countries with strong and weak financial systems in some past period, such as the 1960s. Researchers find that countries with stronger systems during the 1960s had faster economic growth in the decades *after* the 1960s.

FIGURE 15-3

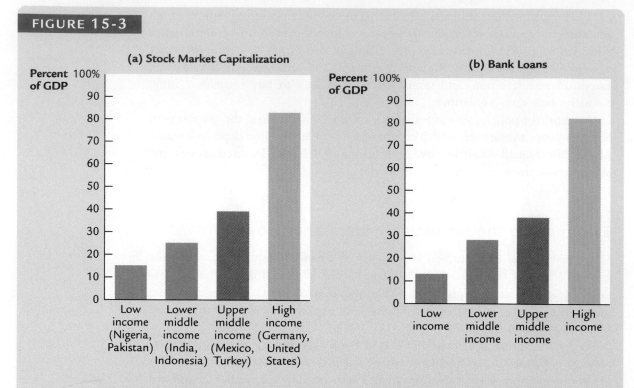

(a) Stock Market Capitalization

Percent of GDP

(b) Bank Loans

Percent of GDP

Financial Development and Economic Growth, 1996–2007 This figure compares financial development in four groups of countries, from the quarter with the lowest real GDP per capita to the quarter with the highest. Examples of countries in each group appear in parentheses in panel (a). Richer countries have higher levels of stock market capitalization and bank loans than poorer countries.

Source: World Bank.

This suggests that financial development comes first and causes growth, rather than vice versa.[2]

Let's examine two cases that illustrate how the financial system affects growth. The first, from U.S. history, discusses an unwise government policy that interfered with the financial system. The second discusses recent efforts to expand the financial systems of poor countries.

CASE STUDY

Unit Banking and Economic Growth

Today, large banks conduct business throughout the United States. You can find branches of Bank of America, for example, in most U.S. cities. This has not always been true. Before World War II, federal law allowed a bank to operate in

---

[2] Much of this research is summarized in Asli Demirguc-Kunt and Ross Levine, "Finance, Financial Sector Policies, and Economic Growth," World Bank Policy Research Working Paper 4469, January 2008.

only one state. Some states went further than federal law and restricted each bank to a single branch. A bank's customers could make deposits or seek loans at only one location. This restriction was called *unit banking*.

Proponents of unit banking believed that multiple branches would allow banks to become too large and powerful. Large banks might drive smaller banks out of business and exploit customers. Unit banking was most common in the Midwest, the home of the Populist political movement of the nineteenth century. Populists were angry at banks for seizing property from farmers who defaulted on loans.

In retrospect, most economists think unit banking was a mistake. It hurt both banks and their customers, for several reasons:

- Large banks benefit from *economies of scale*. They operate more efficiently than small banks. That is, they can offer services at a lower cost per customer. Unit banking increased costs at banks by keeping them small.

- With unit banking, a bank operated in only one town. If the town's economy did poorly, many borrowers defaulted on loans. The bank lost money and might be forced out of business. Having branches in different towns is a form of diversification: it reduces risk.

- Under unit banking, many small towns had only one bank, which operated as a monopoly. Customers had nowhere else to go if the bank charged high interest rates on their loans or provided poor service. In states that allowed multiple branches, banks from throughout the state could enter a town and increase competition.

For all these reasons, unit banking reduced the number of banks and their efficiency. The policy impeded the flow of funds from savers to investors. The result was lower economic growth.

Economists Rajeev Dehejia of Columbia University and Adriana Lleras-Muney of Princeton University analyzed the effects of unit banking. Their 2007 study compares states with unit banking to states that allowed multiple branches during the period from 1900 to 1940. As you might expect, the volume of bank loans was higher in states that permitted branching, confirming that branching helps move funds from savers to investors. The study's most important findings involve the effects of unit banking on the overall economy, including both the agricultural and manufacturing sectors. In states with branching, farms were larger in acres, and the value of farm machinery per acre was higher. Apparently the less constrained banking systems provided more funds for farmers to expand their farms and make them more productive. States with branching also had higher employment in manufacturing industries and higher manufacturing wages. Again this finding suggests that when banks were allowed to have branches, they were better able to channel funds to investors, in this case firms that wanted to build new and more productive factories. The study provides a concrete example of how policies that promote banking can contribute to a prosperous economy.[3] ∎

---

[3] Rajeev Dehejia and Adriana Lleras-Muney, "Financial Development and Pathways of Growth: State Branching and Deposit Insurance Laws in the United States from 1900 to 1940," *Journal of Law and Economics* 50 (2007) 239–272.

CASE STUDY

Microfinance

Poor countries have severe shortages of jobs that pay decent wages. As a consequence, many people seek to support themselves by starting rudimentary businesses—making furniture or clothes, running small restaurants or shops, and so on. In many countries, women are especially likely to start their own businesses because discrimination limits their other opportunities.

A business requires an initial investment; for example, a furniture maker must buy tools and raw materials. Often the necessary funds are small by the standards of high-income countries but still exceed the wealth of would-be entrepreneurs. Most banks shy away from lending to the very poor, because they fear high default rates and because the interest payments on tiny loans do not cover the costs of screening and monitoring borrowers. Discrimination can make it especially difficult for women to get loans.

Without bank loans, many people are unable to start businesses that might lift them out of poverty. Others borrow from village moneylenders at exorbitant interest rates—sometimes 10–20 percent per *day*.

Microfinance seeks to fill this gap in developing countries' banking systems by providing small loans to poor people. The idea was pioneered by Muhammad Yunus, an economics professor in Bangladesh, who founded the Grameen Bank in the village of Jobra in 1974. Since then, microfinance institutions (MFIs) have sprung up in Africa, Asia, Latin America, eastern Europe, and even poor neighborhoods in New York and other U.S. cities.

MFIs are initially funded by governments, international organizations such as the World Bank, or private foundations. Their loans can be as small as $25, but they are large enough to fund simple businesses. Microfinance has grown spectacularly since its beginnings in a single village. As of 2010, MFIs had close to 100 million borrowers around the world.

MFIs try to overcome the problems that make conventional banks wary of lending to the poor. For example, some MFIs require that people borrow money in groups. The Grameen Bank lends to five would-be entrepreneurs at a time. This practice reduces the bank's costs per loan. In addition, it reduces the problem of moral hazard—the risk that borrowers will squander their loans and default. Credit is cut off to all five borrowers if any one borrower defaults, creating peer pressure to use loans prudently.

Many MFIs lend primarily to women. In part this reflects the institutions' desire to serve a group that faces discrimination elsewhere. But MFIs also cite their self-interest: they report that women default on loans less often than men. Overall, default rates on microloans are low—less than 2 percent at many institutions.

Many people think that microfinance has helped reduce poverty. In 2006, Muhammad Yunus and the Grameen Bank were awarded the Nobel Peace Prize, making Yunus the first economist to win a Nobel Prize in an area other than economics. In explaining its choice, the Nobel committee said that "loans to poor people without any financial security had appeared to be an impossible idea," but "Yunus and Grameen Bank have shown that even the poorest of the poor can work to bring about their own development."

The microfinance industry is changing as it grows. Most MFIs are nonprofit organizations supported by donations. In recent years, however, for-profit commercial banks have taken an interest in microfinance. These banks have observed the success of MFIs, especially the low default rates on their loans, and decided that microfinance can be profitable. Commercial banks have started making microloans in countries such as India, Colombia, and Senegal. Elsewhere, commercial banks support microfinance indirectly by lending money to MFIs.

Mexico's Compartamos ("let's share" in Spanish) is one of Latin America's largest microlenders, with a million borrowers. In 2006, it transformed itself from a nonprofit organization into a commercial bank. In 2007, it raised $500 million by issuing stock that is now traded on Mexico's stock exchange. Compartamos no longer relies on donations or government funding.

Many supporters of microfinance welcome the involvement of commercial banks because it increases the availability of microloans. Others, however, criticize the "commercialization" of microfinance. They allege that for-profit lenders charge excessive interest rates and deny loans to the poorest of the poor. Muhammad Yunus has criticized Compartamos, saying it is "raking in money off poor people desperate for cash."[4] ∎

Markets Versus Central Planning

Another way to grasp the importance of the financial system is to ask what happens if an economy lacks one entirely. Imagine a country with an economy run by the government. No private firms exist; everybody works for the government, which decides what goods and services to produce and who receives them. The government also decides what investment projects are worthwhile and orders that they be undertaken. No one raises funds for investment through financial markets or private banks.

This is not a fanciful idea, but rather a basic description of a **centrally planned economy**, also known as a *command economy*. This was the economic system under communist governments in the Soviet Union and Eastern Europe, which held power until the early 1990s. The economics of Cuba and North Korea are still based primarily on central planning.

If you have studied microeconomics, you learned that its central idea is the desirability of allocating resources through free markets. Market prices provide signals about what firms should produce and consumers should buy, thus guiding the economy to efficiency. Microeconomists take a dim view of central planning because a modern economy is too complicated for government officials to run without the help of markets.

The basic principles of free markets also apply to the financial system. Prices in financial markets, such as stock prices and interest rates, help channel funds to the most productive investments. This process does not work perfectly, but it

---

[4] For more on this controversy, see "Microfinance's Success Sets Off a Debate in Mexico," *New York Times,* April 5, 2008, page C1; and Robert Cull, Asli Demirguc-Kunt, and Jonathan Morduch, "Microfinance Meets the Market," *Journal of Economic Perspectives* (Winter 2009): 167–192.

beats the alternative of central planning. History shows that government officials do a poor job of choosing investment projects. To illustrate this point, the next case study examines history's most famous example of central planning.

CASE STUDY

Investment in the Soviet Union

In 1917, a communist revolution led by V. I. Lenin overthrew Czar Nicholas II of Russia. Lenin established the Soviet Union, which eventually grew to include Russia and 14 other "republics," from Ukraine in the west to Uzbekistan in central Asia. The economy of the Soviet Union was centrally planned.

Initially, the Soviet economy was mainly agricultural, and most of its people were poor. After Lenin's death in 1924, Josef Stalin took control of the government and began a push to "industrialize." Stalin and the leaders who succeeded him hoped to achieve rapid economic growth through investment in factories and modern technologies. Because Soviet planners controlled the economy's resources, they could dictate high levels of investment. From the 1930s to the 1980s, investment as a percentage of GDP was more than twice as high in the Soviet Union as in the United States and Western Europe.

At first, high investment produced rapid economic growth. In the 1950s and 1960s, Soviet planners predicted—and Western leaders feared—that the Soviet Union would become the world's most productive economy. But growth slowed in the 1970s and 1980s. Despite high investment, the Soviet Union fell further and further behind the West. Partly because of economic failure, the Soviet Union broke apart in the early 1990s. Russia and the other former republics shifted to economic systems based on free markets.

What went wrong with the Soviet Union? While many factors led to its downfall, it is clear, in retrospect, that an important factor was a misallocation of investment. Soviet planners chose projects poorly, so high investment did not lead to high output. Economic historians point to a number of mistakes:

- Planners put too many resources into prestige sectors of the economy that symbolized economic development, mainly heavy industry. The Soviets built too many factories to produce steel and too few to produce consumer goods. They invested in an unsuccessful effort to develop large airplanes. Starting in the 1950s, they spent heavily on their space program, which boosted national pride but strained the economy.

- Soviet planners overemphasized *short-run* increases in productivity. They were too hasty in trying to reach Western output levels. In 1931, Stalin said, "We are fifty or a hundred years behind the advanced countries. We must make good the distance in ten years. Either we do it or they will crush us." This attitude caused planners to neglect investments that were important for the long term. For example, they skimped on maintenance of roads and other infrastructure. This had little immediate effect, but over time the crumbling infrastructure became a drag on productivity.

- A related problem was that factory managers were evaluated based on annual production quotas. Managers focused on meeting current quotas rather than increasing long-run productivity. For example, they were reluctant to retool factories to use new technologies because this might disrupt production temporarily.

■ The power of government bureaucrats reduced efficiency. Plant managers were rewarded for following orders, not for thinking of innovative ways to raise output. In addition, managers competed for investment funds by lobbying the government. Those who were well connected or talented at lobbying received more resources than they needed, while other managers received too few.[5] ■

15-6 Conclusion

This chapter has surveyed the main parts of the financial system: securities markets and banks. We saw how securities markets transfer funds from savers to investors and how they help people share risks. We learned that asymmetric information problems, namely adverse selection and moral hazard, reduce the effectiveness with which securities markets channel funds. We explored how banks reduce asymmetric information problems and make it possible for investors who cannot issue securities to raise funds for their investments. Finally, we saw that the strength of a country's financial system is an important factor influencing its economic growth.

The next four chapters expand our analysis of the financial system. Chapter 16 discusses how prices in securities markets, such as stock and bond prices, are determined. Chapter 17 examines choices facing participants in securities markets, such as firms' decisions about issuing securities and savers' decisions about what securities to buy. Chapter 18 turns to the banking industry, discussing how banks make profits, the risks they face, and the role of government regulation. Finally, Chapter 19 discusses financial crises, examining both their causes and their devastating effects on economies.

Summary

1. The financial system has two central parts: financial markets (the markets for currencies and securities) and banks.

2. The securities sold in financial markets include bonds and stocks. When a corporation or government issues bonds, it is borrowing money from those who buy the bonds. In return, it promises the buyers predetermined

---

[5] For more on Soviet investment, see Gur Ofer, "Soviet Economic Growth, 1928–1985," *Journal of Economic Literature* 25 (December 1987): 1767–1833. This article was published shortly before the breakup of the Soviet Union.

payments at certain times. A stock is an ownership share in a corporation. A stockholder receives a share of the corporation's earnings.

3. The primary function of financial markets is to channel funds from savers to investors with productive uses for those saved funds. Financial markets also help people diversify their asset holdings, which reduces risk.

4. Financial markets can malfunction because of asymmetric information: sellers of securities (investors) know more than buyers. Adverse selection arises from asymmetric information about investors' characteristics. Investors with low chances for success are the most eager to sell securities. Moral hazard arises from asymmetric information about investors' actions. Investors have incentives to misuse the funds they receive from savers.

5. Financial institutions such as banks and mutual funds are firms that help channel funds from savers to investors. Banks raise funds by accepting deposits and use the funds to make private loans. Banks reduce adverse selection and moral hazard by gathering information to screen borrowers, putting covenants into loan agreements, and monitoring borrower behavior.

6. Saving can spur economic growth, but only if the financial system channels savings into productive investment. Poorly conceived government policies can hinder the operation of the financial system and reduce economic growth.

KEY CONCEPTS

Financial market	Mutual fund	Private loan
Security	Asymmetric information	Indirect finance
Bond	Adverse selection	Direct finance
Interest	Moral hazard	Covenant
Default	Financial institution	Microfinance
Stock	Bank	Centrally planned economy
Diversification		

QUESTIONS FOR REVIEW

1. What is a security?

2. What are the two main functions of the financial system?

3. What is the difference between a bond and a stock?

4. What is asymmetric information, and why is it a problem in financial markets?

5. What is adverse selection? How do banks reduce this problem?

6. What is moral hazard? How do banks reduce this problem?

7. Jennifer wants to get a loan from Citizens Bank to open a hair salon, but she is sometimes tempted to visit local casinos. What type of asymmetric information problem does this example illustrate? How might the bank solve this problem?

8. Ned wants a $10,000 loan from Capital One to open a sushi bar, but he filed for bankruptcy

eight years ago. What type of asymmetric information problem does this example illustrate? How might the bank solve this problem?

9. Why is a healthy financial system important for economic growth?

10. Why have centrally planned economies failed?

PROBLEMS AND APPLICATIONS

1. When financial markets channel funds from savers to investors, who benefits? Explain.

2. Suppose the owner of a corporation needs $1 million to finance a new investment. If his total wealth is $1.2 million, would it be better to use his own funds for the investment or to issue stock in the corporation? What if the owner's wealth is $1 billion?

3. If you were required to put all your retirement savings in the securities of one company, what company would you choose, and why? Would you choose the company you work for? Would you buy stock or bonds?

4. Suppose there are two investors. One has a project to build a factory; the other has a project to visit a casino and gamble on roulette. Which investor has a greater incentive to issue bonds? Which investor's bonds are a better deal for savers?

5. A company raises funds by issuing short-term bonds (commercial paper) and uses the funds to make private loans. Such a firm is called a *finance company*. Is a finance company a type of bank?

6. Firms such as Moody's and Standard & Poor's study corporations that issue bonds. They publish "ratings" for the bonds—evaluations of the likelihood of default. Suppose these rating companies went out of business. What effect would

this have on the bond market? What effect would it have on banks?

7. National credit bureaus collect information on people's credit histories. They are likely to know whether you ever defaulted on a loan. Suppose that a new privacy law makes it illegal for credit bureaus to collect this information. What effect would this have on the banking industry?

8. When a bank makes a loan, it sometimes requires borrowers to maintain a checking account at the bank until the loan is paid off. What is the purpose of this requirement?

9. Microfinance institutions argue that (a) many traditional banks discriminate against women in lending and (b) women have lower default rates than men on loans from MFIs. Discuss how point (a) could explain point (b).

10. Go to www.planetrating.com, the site of Planet Rating, an organization that calls itself "the global microfinance rating agency." What is the main function of Planet Rating? How might its work help the microfinance industry to grow?

11. Do you know someone (such as a parent) who is working and saving for retirement? Does he or she have money in a 401(k) plan? What securities does the person hold through the plan? Does he or she follow the principle of diversification?

CHAPTER 16

Asset Prices and Interest Rates

We've long felt that the only value of stock forecasters is to make fortune tellers look good.

—Warren Buffett

At any time of the day, you can tap into financial news on your TV, computer, iPhone, or BlackBerry. You may learn, for example, that the price of Microsoft stock has risen from $35 at the start of the day to $37 at 2:00 P.M. but that it is still $8 below its high for the year. You may also see that the Dow Jones Index of stock prices has risen 89 points and that the price of a ten-year U.S. government bond has fallen from $998 to $995.

As the prices of stocks and bonds fluctuate, the owners of these assets see their wealth rise and fall. These price movements also affect the aggregate economy. In the 1990s, for example, U.S. stock prices rose rapidly and stockholders spent part of their gains on consumption goods. The boost to consumption helped fuel an economic boom in the second half of the decade. Subsequent declines in stock prices contributed to recessions in 2001 and 2007–2009.

As stock and bond prices scroll across your television or iPhone screen, their movements may appear mysterious. What economic forces determine asset prices? This chapter surveys the answers that economists give to this question. An asset entitles its owner to a future stream of income, so we first learn how to value an income stream and then examine how this valuation is used to determine an asset's price. We discuss the factors that cause asset prices to fluctuate over time, including the possibility of *bubbles* in which prices rise simply because of expectations that they will rise.

Throughout the chapter, we see that asset prices are closely related to interest rates. As a result, forces that cause interest rates to change, such as shifts in monetary policy, also help to explain asset-price movements. Finally, we examine the relationship between short-term and long-term interest rates and learn how this relationship helps us predict future interest rates.

16-1 Valuing Income Streams

Recall from Chapter 15 that a financial asset yields a stream of income in the future. The owner of a bond receives a payment when the bond matures and may receive coupon payments before then. The owner of a firm's stock receives part of the firm's future earnings. To find the value of an asset, we must determine the value of these income streams.

In making such valuations, the key principle is that payments have different values depending on when they are received. A dollar today is worth more than a dollar in the future because you can take today's dollar, put it in the bank, and earn interest on it. This process transforms one dollar today into more than one dollar in the future. Because of this principle, an economist's approach to asset pricing rests on a fundamental concept: the present value of an income stream.

Future Value

To compare payments at different times, economists begin with the concept of **future value**. The future value of a dollar is how many dollars it can produce in some future year. To understand this concept, suppose that banks pay a nominal interest rate of 4 percent. If you deposit a dollar today, it grows to $1.04 in a year. Thus, the future value of a dollar today is $1.04 in one year.

If you keep your money in the bank for a second year, it grows by another 4 percent. When $1.04 grows by 4 percent, it becomes $\$(1.04)(1.04)$, or $\$(1.04)^2 = \$1.082$. So a dollar today is worth $\$(1.04)^2$ in two years. If you keep the money in the bank for a third year, it grows by 4 percent again, becoming $\$(1.04)^3 = \$1.125$.

You should see the pattern. With a 4 percent interest rate, a dollar left in the bank for n years, where n is any number, grows to $\$(1.04)^n$. A dollar today is worth $\$(1.04)^n$ in n years.

The same principle applies to interest rates other than 4 percent. Let i be a nominal interest rate expressed in decimal form. (In decimal form, 4 percent is 0.04). A dollar today grows to $\$(1 + i)$ in one year, $\$(1 + i)^2$ in two years, and $\$(1 + i)^n$ in n years. So the future value of a dollar is given by

$$\text{Future Value of \$1 Today} = \$(1 + i)^n \text{ in } n \text{ Years.}$$

Present Value

We've seen how much a dollar today is worth in the future. Now let's turn this relation around to see how much a *future* dollar is worth *today*. This is the **present value** of a future dollar.

We can understand present value with a little algebra. We start by turning around the equation for future value:

$$\$(1 + i)^n \text{ in } n \text{ Years} = \$1 \text{ Today.}$$

Now divide both sides of the equation by $(1 + i)^n$:

$$\frac{\$(1 + i)^n}{(1 + i)^n} \text{ in } n \text{ Years} = \frac{\$1}{(1 + i)^n} \text{ Today.}$$

The left side of this equation simplifies and gives us the present value formula:

$$\text{Present Value of \$1 in } n \text{ Years} = \frac{\$1}{(1 + i)^n} \text{ Today.}$$

A dollar n years from today is worth $1/(1 + i)^n$ dollars today.

With a 4 percent interest rate, the present value of a dollar in n years is $\$1/(1.04)^n$. For example, the present value of a dollar in three years is $\$1/(1.04)^3 = \$0.889$. The present value of a dollar in twenty years is $\$1/(1.04)^{20} = \$0.456$.

Our analysis has a key implication: *a higher interest rate reduces the present value of future money.* Mathematically, a higher i reduces present value because it raises the denominator in the formula. The economic explanation is that a higher interest rate means a saver can trade a dollar today for more future dollars. Turning this around, at a higher interest rate, a future dollar is worth less today. For example, if the interest rate rises from 4 percent to 6 percent, the present value of a dollar in three years falls from $0.889 to $\$1/(1.06)^3 = \$0.840$. The present value of a dollar in twenty years falls from $0.456 to $0.312.

Series of Payments We can extend our reasoning to value a flow of money over multiple years. Suppose someone promises you $3 in two years and $5 in four years. Each dollar in two years is worth $\$1/(1 + i)^2$, so the $3 is worth $\$3/(1 + i)^2$. The $5 in four years is worth $\$5/(1 + i)^4$. Altogether, the present value of the future payments is $\$3/(1 + i)^2 + \$5/(1 + i)^4$.

To get a general formula for a series of payments, suppose you receive $\$X_1$ in one year, $\$X_2$ in two years, and so on up to $\$X_T$ in T years. The present value of this flow of money is

$$\text{Present Value} = \frac{\$X_1}{(1 + i)} + \frac{\$X_2}{(1 + i)^2} + \cdots + \frac{\$X_T}{(1 + i)^T}.$$

To practice using this formula, let's calculate the present value of a contract signed by baseball star C. C. Sabathia, a left-handed pitcher. After the 2008 season, the New York Yankees agreed to pay Sabathia $23 million per year for seven years, from 2009 through 2015. The total payments over the life of this contract are $7 \times \$23 = \$161$ million. To calculate the present value of the payments, let's assume an interest rate of 4 percent. In this case, the present value in 2008 was

$$\$23 \text{ million}/(1.04) + \$23 \text{ million}/(1.04)^2 + \cdots + \$23 \text{ million}/(1.04)^7.$$

If you plug these numbers into a financial calculator, you will find that the present value of Sabathia's salary in 2008 was about $138 million.

Payments Forever Some assets provide income indefinitely; there is no year T when the last payment is made. For example, a share of stock entitles the holder to a stream of earnings with no endpoint. A rare type of bond called a *perpetuity* pays interest forever.

In some cases, we can derive simple formulas for the present value of a perpetual income stream. One such case is a constant annual payment. If you receive a payment of $Z in all future years, the present value is[1]

$$\text{Present Value} = \frac{\$Z}{(1 + i)} + \frac{\$Z}{(1 + i)^2} + \frac{\$Z}{(1 + i)^3} + \cdots.$$

Using algebra, we can simplify this equation to

$$\text{Present Value} = \frac{\$Z}{i}.$$

Thus, a higher annual payment or lower interest rate means a higher present value. Conversely, a lower annual payment or higher interest rate means a lower present value. For example, if the interest rate is 4 percent, a payment of $100 per year forever has a present value of $100/(0.04) = $2500. If the interest rate falls to 2 percent, the present value of payments rises to $100/(0.02) = $5,000.

Another kind of perpetual income stream is a payment that grows over time at a constant rate. To analyze this case, let $Z be the payment in one year, and let g be the annual rate at which the payment grows. Each year, the payment is $(1 + g)$ times the previous payment: it is $Z(1 + g)$ in two years, $Z(1 + g)^2$ in three years, and so on. We assume the growth rate of payments is less than the interest rate ($g < i$). In this case, the present value of all payments is

$$\text{Present Value} = \frac{\$Z}{(1 + i)} + \frac{\$Z(1 + g)}{(1 + i)^2} + \frac{\$Z(1 + g)^2}{(1 + i)^3} + \cdots$$

This equation simplifies to:[2]

$$\text{Present Value} = \frac{\$Z}{(i - g)}.$$

Once again, the present value of payments depends on the initial payment Z and the interest rate i. In addition, present value depends on the growth rate g. When payments grow at a higher rate, their present value is higher. Mathematically, a higher g raises present value because it reduces $i - g$, the denominator in the formula.

Suppose again that $Z = $100 and $i = 4$ percent. If $g = 2$ percent, the present value of payments is $100/(0.04 − 0.02) = $100/(0.02) = $5,000. If g rises to 3 percent, the present value rises to $100/(0.04 − 0.03) = $100/(0.01) = $10,000.

Table 16-1 summarizes the key principles about present values that we have derived.

---

[1]*Mathematical note*: To derive this result, let $X = 1/(1 + i)$. We can write the previous equation as $PV = Z[X + X^2 + X^3 + \cdots] = ZX[1 + X + X^2 + \cdots]$. Footnote 2 on page 288 shows that $[1 + X + X^2 + \cdots] = 1/(1 − X)$. Therefore, $PV = ZX/(1 − X)$. Substituting in the definition of X and simplifying yields $PV = Z/i$.

[2] *Mathematical note*: To derive this result, let $X = (1 + g)/(1 + i)$ and write the previous equation as $PV = [Z/(1 + i)][1 + X + X^2 + \cdots]$. Footnote 2 on page 288 shows that $[1 + X + X^2 + \cdots] = 1/(1 − X)$. Therefore, $PV = Z/[(1 + i)(1 − X)]$. Substituting in the definition of X and simplifying yields $PV = Z/(i − g)$.

This derivation assumes $g < i$. If $i \geq g$, then the present value of payments is infinite.

TABLE 16-1

Present Values of Some Common Types of Payments

Payment (dollars)	Present Value (dollars)
$1 in n years	$\dfrac{1}{(1 + I)^n}$
A series of annual payments: $\$X_1, X_2, \ldots, X_T$	$\dfrac{X_1}{(1 + i)} + \dfrac{X_2}{(1 + i)^2} + \cdots + \dfrac{X_T}{(1 + i)^T}$
An annual payment of $\$Z$ forever	$\dfrac{Z}{i}$
An annual payment that equals $\$Z$ in the first year and grows at rate g	$\dfrac{Z}{(i - g)}$

16-2 The Classical Theory of Asset Prices

Now that we understand the concept of the present value of an income stream, we can use this concept to answer the question we raised earlier in this chapter: what factors determine the price of an asset, such as a stock or bond? Economists usually answer this question using the *classical theory of asset prices*, which is based on several ideas involving present values.

The Present Value of Income

An asset produces a flow of income. This flow might be a series of fixed payments (in the case of bonds) or a share of a company's profits (in the case of stock). According to the **classical theory of asset prices**, the price of an asset equals the present value of the income that people expect to receive from the asset:

> Asset Price = Present Value of Expected Asset Income.

Notice the word "expected" in the theory. In many cases, nobody knows exactly how much income an asset will produce. For example, nobody is certain of a company's future profits, which determine the income from stock. Given this uncertainty, the classical theory says that asset prices depend on people's expectations, or best guesses, about asset income.

The rationale for the classical theory is simple. People purchase an asset because it yields a future stream of income. The present value tells us how much this income stream is expected to be worth and thus how much we should be willing to pay for the asset.

Suppose an asset's price is *below* the present value of its expected income stream. If the present value of the expected income is $100 and the asset price is $80, the asset is a great deal: buyers pay less than the asset is worth. Lots of savers will purchase the asset, and high demand will push up the price until it rises to $100.

Conversely, if an asset price exceeds the present value of expected income, then sellers receive more than the asset is worth. In this situation, the asset's owners will rush to sell it, and this increase in supply will push down the price.

The classical theory applies to many types of assets. For example, it says that the price of an apartment building equals the present value of net rental income from the building. Let's look more closely at the theory's implications for the pricing of two classes of assets, bonds and stocks.

Bond Prices The income from a bond includes the periodic coupon payments (if any) and the face value received at maturity. Let's say a bond has a maturity of T years, a face value of F, and an annual coupon payment of C. Assuming no chance of default, bondholders expect to receive all the promised payments. The payments are C in years 1 through $T - 1$ and $C + F$ in year T. The bond price is the present value of these expected payments. Using the second formula in Table 16-1, this present value is

$$\text{Bond Price} = \frac{C}{(1 + i)} + \frac{C}{(1 + i)^2} + \cdots + \frac{C}{(1 + i)^{T-1}} + \frac{(C + F)}{(1 + i)^T}.$$

For example, suppose a bond's maturity is 4 years ($T = 4$), annual coupon payments are $5 ($C = \$5$), the face value F is $100, and the interest rate is 4 percent. Using the previous equation,

$$\text{Bond Price} = \frac{\$5}{1.04} + \frac{\$5}{(1.04)^2} + \frac{\$5}{(1.04)^3} + \frac{\$105}{(1.04)^4} = \$103.63.$$

Stock Prices Someone who owns a firm's stock owns a share of the firm. However, firms' earnings do not flow directly to their stockholders. Instead, firms periodically pay stockholders a portion of earnings called **dividends**. If a company with 1 million shares announces a dividend of $2 per share, it will pay stockholders a total of $2 million in dividends.

Because dividends are the income from stock, a stock's price is the present value of expected dividends. If expected dividends per share are D_1 in the next year, D_2 in the year after that, and so on, then

$$\text{Stock Price} = \frac{D_1}{(1 + i)} + \frac{D_2}{(1 + i)^2} + \frac{D_3}{(1 + i)^3} + \cdots.$$

In any year, a firm's dividends can differ from its earnings. Indeed, some firms earn healthy profits yet pay no dividends at all. Instead, they might use their earnings to finance investment projects such as new factories or the development of new products.

Over the long run, however, dividends are tied closely to earnings. If a firm uses its current earnings for investment rather than dividends, the investment boosts future earnings. These future earnings allow the firm to pay higher future dividends. Therefore, any rise in earnings raises dividends at some point in time. The present value of dividends increases, raising the firm's stock price. Because of these connections, expectations about companies' earnings have strong effects on stock prices.

What Determines Expectations?

An asset price depends on the present value of *expected* asset income. What determines what people expect? The classical theory assumes that people form *rational expectations* (introduced in Chapter 12), which means that they optimally use all available information to forecast future variables such as income flows.

To understand the implications of rational expectations, let's revisit Harriet's software company, iSmells, which we discussed in Chapter 15. The price of the company's stock depends on people's expectations of its future earnings, which will determine the dividends it can pay.

Rational expectations of earnings are based on all available information about the company. For example, if Harriet announces a new product, expected earnings rise to reflect the product's likely impact. If the economy enters a recession, expected earnings adjust based on how Harriet's firm will be affected. Expected earnings also take into account the costs of producing software, the number of competitors the firm faces, and all other factors that affect how successful Harriet's firm is likely to be.

It is important to realize that rational expectations are not always accurate or correct. Unpredictable events—changes in production costs or consumer demand, successes and failures in developing new products, and so on—can cause a firm's actual earnings to differ from the earnings people expect. If people have incorporated all relevant, available information into their expectations, however, their expectations will be as accurate as possible and the differences between expected and actual earnings will be as small as possible.

What Is the Relevant Interest Rate?

In addition to depending on expectations about earnings, asset prices depend on interest rates, which determine the present value of asset income. What interest rates should we use in present value formulas? In the classical theory, different interest rates are relevant for different assets. The riskier an asset—that is, the more uncertainty about the income flow from the asset—the higher the interest rate.

To understand this effect of risk, recall our initial discussion of present value, where we saw that a dollar today is worth $1 + i$ dollars in a year. In this discussion, i is an interest rate that savers receive for sure—say, from a safe bank account. From now on, we will call this rate the **safe interest rate**, or *risk-free rate*, i^{safe}. With this notation, a dollar today is worth a certain $\$(1 + i^{safe})$ in a year. Conversely, a certain dollar in a year is worth $\$1/(1 + i^{safe})$ today.

When determining asset prices, however, we often have to value uncertain payments. For example, suppose the expected dividend in some year from a share of stock is $10. This is the best forecast, but the dividend could range between $8 and $12. People dislike such risk. With this uncertainty, the expected dividend from the stock is worth less than a certain $10.

How does risk affect present values? A dollar today is worth $1 + i^{safe}$ certain dollars next year. This means a dollar today is worth *more* than $1 + i^{safe}$ risky dollars next year, because risky dollars are less valuable than certain dollars. To put it differently, a dollar today is worth $1 + i^{safe} + \varphi$ risky dollars in a year, where

> ### TABLE 16-2
>
> #### Ideas Behind the Classical Theory of Asset Prices
>
> · An asset price equals the present value of expected income from the asset.
> · Expectations about income are rational. Expected income is the optimal forecast based on all available information.
> · The interest rate in the present value formula is a risk-adjusted rate. It equals the safe interest rate plus a risk premium: $i = i^{\text{safe}} + \varphi$.

φ (the Greek letter phi) is a **risk premium**. A risk premium is a payment on an asset that compensates the owner for taking on risk.

The same reasoning applies to risky income at any point in the future. A dollar today is worth $(1 + i^{\text{safe}} + \varphi)^n$ risky dollars in n years. Turning this around, the present value of a risky dollar in n years is $1/(1 + i^{\text{safe}} + \varphi)^n$. In our equations for asset prices, the interest rate is the sum of the safe rate and the risk premium, $i = i^{\text{safe}} + \varphi$. We call this sum the **risk-adjusted interest rate**.

Assets carry varying degrees of risk. The greater the risk, the higher the risk premium. For example, stocks have higher risk premiums than bonds because, as we discuss in Section 16-6, the income from stocks is more volatile. A higher risk premium raises the risk-adjusted interest rate in the present value formula, reducing the present value of expected income. Therefore, a higher risk premium reduces an asset's price.

Table 16-2 summarizes the ideas behind the classical theory of asset prices.

The Gordon Growth Model of Stock Prices

Stock prices are among the most closely watched asset prices in an economy. The classical theory says a stock price is the present value of expected dividends per share. Using this idea to value stocks can be cumbersome, however, as it requires year-by-year forecasts of dividends into the distant future. Therefore, economists have sought easier ways to calculate stock prices.

One approach was proposed by Myron Gordon in 1959. Gordon pointed out that many firms raise dividends fairly steadily over time. To capture this behavior in a simple way, he assumed that expected dividends grow at a constant rate g. If expected dividends next year are D_1, expected dividends in the following years are $D_1(1 + g)$, $D_1(1 + g)^2$, and so on.

With the assumption of constant dividend growth, we can derive a firm's stock price from the last formula in Table 16-1. This formula says the present value of any steadily growing income stream is $Z/(i - g)$, where Z is the first payment and g is the payment growth rate. In Gordon's analysis, the first payment Z equals D_1, the first expected dividend, implying

$$\text{Stock Price} = \frac{D_1}{(i - g)},$$

where i is the risk-adjusted interest rate for the stock. This equation is called the **Gordon growth model** because it emphasizes the expected growth rate of dividends as a determinant of stock prices.

16-3 Fluctuations in Asset Prices

If you follow the financial news, you will notice that asset prices move around a lot. Because asset-price movements affect the value of firms and the wealth of consumers, they have significant effects on macroeconomic variables such as consumption, investment, and output. For these reasons, it is important to understand the basic forces behind asset-price movements.

Why Do Asset Prices Change?

The classical theory says an asset price is the present value of expected income from the asset. This present value changes if expected income changes or if interest rates change.

Stock prices change frequently because of changes in expected income from the stock. These changes occur when there is news (either good or bad) about a company's prospects. If a drug company patents a new wonder drug that helps people lose weight without changing their eating habits, rational expectations of the company's earnings rise. Higher expected earnings mean larger expected dividends for stockholders, so the stock price rises accordingly. If a car company's new model is recalled because of safety defects, its expected earnings and stock price fall. If there are signs that the whole economy is entering a recession, expected earnings and stock prices are likely to fall for many companies.

Such news has less effect on bond prices than on stock prices because the income from a bond is fixed as long as the issuer does not default. As a result, news about companies' prospects often has little effect on the expected income from bonds.

Changes in interest rates, however, affect the prices of both stocks and bonds. A higher interest rate reduces asset prices because it reduces the present value of any income flow. Recall that the relevant interest rate is the risk-adjusted rate, the economy's safe rate plus a risk premium ($i^{safe} + \varphi$). An asset price falls if the safe rate or the risk premium rises. The risk premium might rise because of greater uncertainty about income from the asset. For example, uncertainty about a firm's stock could rise if competitors enter its industry and people are unsure about how much business the firm will lose.

CASE STUDY

The Fed and the Stock Market

Throughout this book, we've seen that monetary policy influences many economic variables, including interest rates, output, and inflation. Monetary policy also influences asset prices. When central banks such as the Federal Reserve announce changes in policy, asset prices often react within minutes. Let's use the classical theory of asset prices to examine the reaction of stock prices.

In Chapter 11 we learned about the Fed's short-term policy instrument, *the federal funds rate*, which is the interest rate that banks charge one another for overnight loans. Suppose the Fed raises its target for this interest rate. This

FIGURE 16-1

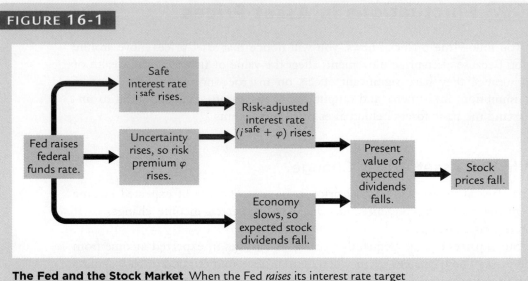

The Fed and the Stock Market When the Fed *raises* its interest rate target unexpectedly, a series of effects reduces stock prices. When the Fed *lowers* its target unexpectedly, opposite effects occur and stock prices rise.

action affects the stock market in several ways, which are summarized in Figure 16-1:

- The federal funds rate is a safe interest rate because banks are unlikely to default on overnight loans. Thus, the Fed's action raises the economy's safe interest rate. A higher safe rate reduces the present value of dividends received by stockholders, which decreases stock prices.

- The higher interest rate reduces spending by consumers and firms, which causes aggregate output to fall. Lower output reduces expected earnings for many companies. As a result, expected dividends for these companies fall, which again reduces stock prices.

- Some economists think an increase in the federal funds rate also increases risk premiums. The fall in output that results from the increase in the federal funds rate not only reduces expected earnings but also raises uncertainty, because it is hard to predict how badly companies will be hurt. Greater uncertainty means higher risk premiums, which raise the risk–adjusted interest rate and decrease present values and stock prices.

When the Fed raises its interest rate target, all three effects reduce the present value of dividends, pushing stock prices down. If the Fed reduces its target, the three effects work in reverse and stock prices rise.

A qualification: Fed actions have large effects *only when they are unexpected*. If people know the Fed is going to change interest rates, stock prices are likely to adjust in advance, and nothing happens when the Fed moves. In contrast, surprise rate changes cause sharp jumps in stock prices.

Fed Chairman Ben Bernanke studied the effects of Fed policies on the stock market during his career as an economics professor. He estimated the effects of interest rate changes on the stock market in a 2005 paper with Kenneth Kuttner of Williams College.

Bernanke and Kuttner examined the period from 1989 to 2002. They measured changes in stock prices on days when the Fed made surprise announcements about its federal-funds-rate target. On average, a rise in the target of 0.25 percent—say, from 4.0 percent to 4.25 percent—caused stock prices to drop suddenly by about 1 percent. A decrease in the target had the opposite effect: a cut of 0.25 percent *raised* stock prices by 1 percent.[3] ∎

Which Asset Prices Are Most Volatile?

All asset prices change over time, but some fluctuate more than others. Let's discuss why some asset prices are especially volatile.

Long-Term Bond Prices Changes in interest rates are the primary reason for changes in bond prices. (As noted earlier, expected income flows from a bond are constant unless default risk changes.) If interest rates in an economy rise, then all bond prices fall. But the size of the effect differs depending on bond maturities. A change in interest rates has a larger effect on prices of long-term bonds than on prices of short-term bonds.

The reason for this difference is that short-term bonds provide income only in the near future, while most payments on long-term bonds come later. The present value of payments is affected more strongly by the interest rate if the payments come later.

To illustrate this point, Table 16-3 compares bonds with maturities ranging from 1 year to 30 years. Each bond has a face value of $100 and coupon payments

TABLE 16-3

Bond Prices, Maturity, and Interest Rates

Years to Maturity	Price if $i = 4\%$	Price if $i = 6\%$	Percentage Fall in Price from Increase in i
1	$100.96	$99.06	1.89
2	101.89	98.17	3.65
3	102.78	97.33	5.30
4	103.63	96.53	6.85
5	104.45	95.79	8.29
10	108.11	92.64	14.31
15	111.12	90.29	18.75
20	113.59	88.53	22.06
25	115.62	87.22	24.57
30	117.29	86.24	26.48

Note: This table gives the prices of bonds with a face value of $100 and annual coupon payments of $5.

[3] See Ben Bernanke and Kenneth Kuttner, "What Explains the Stock Market's Reaction to Federal Reserve Policy?" *Journal of Finance* 60 (June 2005): 1221–1257.

of $5 per year. The table shows the prices of the bonds when the interest rate is 4 percent and when it is 6 percent. The longer a bond's maturity, the greater the percentage fall in the price when the interest rate rises.

For example, the owner of a 1-year bond receives a single coupon payment of $5 plus the face value of $100, both paid after 1 year. When the interest rate rises from 4 percent to 6 percent, the present value of these payments, and thus the bond's price, falls from $100.96 to $99.06. This decrease is only 1.89 percent of the bond's initial price. In contrast, the owner of a 30-year bond receives a series of coupon payments over 30 years plus the face value at the end of 30 years. When the interest rate rises, the price of this bond falls from $117.29 to $86.24, a decrease in of 26.48 percent. Because the bond's payments are stretched over a long period, a rise in the interest rate wipes out a large part of its value.

Stock Prices Prices for stocks are more volatile than prices for bonds, even long-term bonds. Stock prices fluctuate greatly for two reasons. First, like long-term bonds, stocks yield income far into the future. A firm's dividends continue indefinitely, and changes in interest rates have large effects on the present value of this long-term income. Second, as we've discussed, news about firms and the economy cause changes in expected earnings and dividends and thus in stock prices. Fluctuations in stock prices caused by changes in expected earnings add to the fluctuations caused by changes in interest rates.

16-4 Asset-Price Bubbles

The classical theory of asset prices says an asset price equals the present value of expected income from the asset. Is this just a theory, or does it explain asset-price movements in the real world?

The answer to this question is controversial. Clearly there are elements of truth in the theory. We have seen, for example, that it helps explain how stock prices react to Federal Reserve policies. However, many economists believe that changes in asset prices can occur for reasons outside the classical theory, that is, for reasons other than changes in interest rates or expected income.

Sometimes, for example, asset-price increases are part of an **asset-price bubble**. In a bubble, asset prices rise rapidly even though there is no change in interest rates or expected income to justify the rise. Let's discuss how bubbles can occur and the debate over their relevance to the asset-price movements that we observe in the economy.

How Bubbles Work

When a bubble occurs, an asset price rises simply because people *expect* it to rise. To see how this might happen, suppose a famous stock analyst announces that the stock of Acme Corporation is hot: the stock price is likely to rise rapidly in the future. Let's assume the expert doesn't really have a good reason for this view; he is just trying to get attention with a bold prediction. Nonetheless, many people believe the expert and rush to buy Acme. This increased demand pushes up the price of the stock. The expert looks smart, and a bubble has begun.

Once a bubble begins, it feeds on itself. When Acme's price starts rising, more and more people decide the stock is hot. They buy Acme stock, pushing the price higher still. The stock looks even hotter, more buyers rush in, and so on.

As the bubble expands, Acme's price rises far above the level dictated by the classical theory: the present value of dividends per share. People pay more for the stock than it is really worth. They buy it because they expect the price to rise even higher in the future, and therefore they expect to be able to sell the stock for a profit.

The problem with bubbles is that they eventually pop. At some point Acme's price will rise so high that people begin to doubt whether price increases can continue. They stop buying the stock and start to sell what they have. This fall in demand for the stock and increase in supply cause the price to fall back toward the level dictated by the classical theory. Many people who bought Acme at the height of the bubble will lose a lot when the bubble bursts.

Bubbles can arise in many kinds of asset prices. From January 2002 to July 2006, for example, the price of the average house in the United States rose 71 percent. During that period, many people bought second homes or rental properties, believing that prices would continue to rise and that they would make lots of money when they sold their property. The bubble was also fueled by an increase in the availability of home mortgage loans. Lenders relaxed their standards for borrowers' incomes and credit histories, allowing more people to enter the housing market. This development increased housing demand and pushed up prices.

The peak of the housing bubble occurred in July 2006. Between then and April 2009, the average house price fell 33 percent. The losses to homeowners produced a surge of defaults on mortgage loans, which triggered the U.S. financial crisis of 2007–2009.

In addition to stocks and houses, history has seen bubbles in the prices of bonds, foreign currencies, precious metals, and commodities such as coffee and sugar. Perhaps the oddest bubble of all time occurred in Holland in the 1630s. The asset was tulip bulbs. A fad for tulips, recently introduced from Turkey, caused the prices of bulbs to rise rapidly, and people thought they could get rich by purchasing bulbs and reselling them after prices rose further. Many people borrowed large sums of money to buy bulbs. They suffered disastrous losses in February 1637, when the bubble ended abruptly and tulip bulb prices fell 90 percent.

Looking for Bubbles

Economists often debate whether bubbles are occurring in asset prices. Discussions of stock prices sometimes focus on the **price–earnings (P/E) ratio**, the price of stock divided by earnings per share. Using earnings over the recent past, economists compute P/E ratios for individual companies and the average P/E ratio for the stock market. Some think that high P/E ratios are evidence of bubbles.

To see why, recall the classical theory: a stock price equals the present value of expected dividends per share, which depends on expected earnings. It is difficult to test this theory, because we can't directly measure expectations of future earnings. But some economists argue that earnings in the recent past are a good guide to future earnings. If a stock price is unusually high compared to past earnings—if the P/E ratio is high—then the price is probably high relative to future earnings, meaning it is higher than it should be under the classical theory. A bubble may be underway.

According to the classical theory, high P/E ratios could be explained by low interest rates. Low rates raise the present value of future income and push up stock prices. In practice, however, stocks' P/E ratios sometimes rise without changes in interest rates, indicating a possible bubble.

It is important to note that a high P/E ratio indicates a bubble *only* if recent earnings are a good predictor of future earnings. If earnings are expected to grow rapidly, then recent earnings are not a good predictor of future earnings. For example, suppose a company is developing a promising new product. The company's current earnings are low, but earnings are expected to rise a lot when the product is introduced. According to the classical theory, high expected earnings imply a high stock price. With current earnings low, the classical theory predicts a high P/E ratio.

Economists have tried to determine the correct interpretation of P/E ratios. Do high ratios usually signal a bubble? Or are they more likely to reflect expectations of high earnings growth? Some researchers address this issue by examining what happens to stock prices *after* a period of high P/E ratios. Remember that bubbles eventually end. If a bubble has pushed up the P/E ratio, stock prices are likely to fall later. In contrast, if a high P/E ratio reflects high expected earnings, there is no reason to expect stock prices to fall. Examining later stock-price movements helps to isolate why the P/E ratio was high.

This approach was introduced in a 1998 paper by John Campbell of Harvard University and Robert Shiller of Yale University. Campbell and Shiller examined the P/E ratio for a large group of companies, the S&P 500. For a given year, they defined P as the average stock price for the group and E as average earnings per share over the previous 10 years. Campbell and Shiller then compared the P/E ratio to the change in stock prices over the following 10 years.

Figure 16-2 illustrates Campbell and Shiller's comparison for the period from 1918 through 2000. In this graph, the horizontal axis is the P/E ratio and the vertical axis is the average percentage change in stock prices over the next 10 years. We see a negative relationship: when the P/E ratio is high, stock prices are likely to fall. Campbell and Shiller concluded that high P/E ratios are usually caused by bubbles that dissipate in the future.

Campbell and Shiller's research was stimulated by a rapid rise in stock prices during the 1990s. The following case study discusses this period and stock-price fluctuations since then.

CASE STUDY

The U.S. Stock Market, 1990–2010

Figure 16-3 charts the Dow Jones Index of stock prices from 1990 through 2010. We see large swings in prices, which the ideas in this chapter can help us understand. Let's examine stock-price movements over three periods: 1990 to 2003, 2003 to 2007, and 2007 to 2010.

1990–2003: The Tech Boom and Bust The 1990s were a boom period for the stock market. The Dow Jones Index rose from about 2,500 at the start of the

FIGURE 16-2

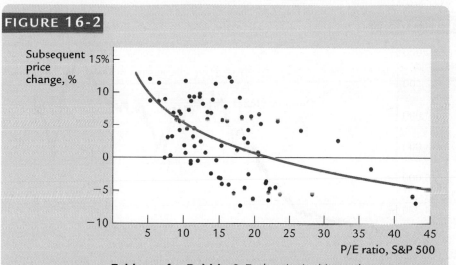

Evidence for Bubbles? Each point in this graph represents a year between 1918 and 2000. The horizontal axis is the price-earnings ratio for stocks in the S&P 500, based on average earnings over the previous 10 years. The vertical axis is the average percentage change in S&P prices over the following 10 years, adjusted for inflation. (The 10-year change after 2000 is estimated with data through 2009.) The orange "best fit" line through the data points indicates a negative relationship between these two variables: When the P/E ratio is high, stock prices are likely to grow slowly or fall over the following 10 years.

Source: Robert Shiller, Yale University (www.econ.yale.edu/~shiller/data.htm). Adapted from John Campbell and Robert Shiller, "Valuation Ratios and the Long-Run Stock Market Outlook," *Journal of Portfolio Management* 24 (Winter 1998) 11–26.

decade to over 6,000 in 1997, when Campbell and Shiller wrote their paper. The index continued to rise after that, peaking at 11,497 in the summer of 2000.

Companies' earnings rose during the 1990s, but not as fast as stock prices. This meant rising P/E ratios. From 1960 to 1995, the average P/E ratio for the Dow Jones Index was about 15. This ratio rose above 40 in 2000. P/E ratios were especially high for "tech" companies—those involved with computers, software, and the Internet. Many of these companies had P/E ratios over 100.

During the 1990s, many economists argued that a stock market bubble was under way. Federal Reserve Chairman Alan Greenspan supported this idea in a famous 1996 speech. Greenspan suggested that stock prices had been "unduly escalated" by "irrational exuberance," meaning prices had risen above the levels dictated by the classical theory.

Others argued that the high P/E ratios were in line with the classical theory. They pointed to the rapid spread of computer and Internet use in the 1990s. These technologies raised productivity and reduced costs in many industries, making it rational to expect rapid growth in companies' earnings. As we've discussed, expectations of high earnings growth imply a high P/E ratio in the classical theory.

Stock prices peaked in 2000, then fell for the next three years. The Dow Jones Index fell below 8,000 in 2003. Believers in a stock market bubble claimed

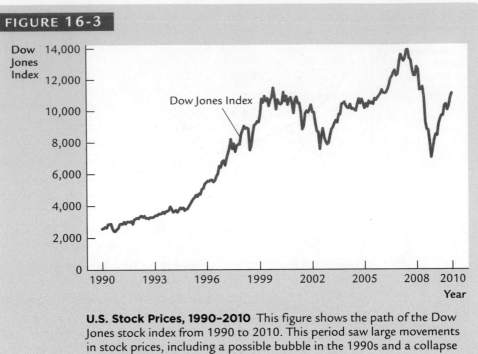

FIGURE 16-3

U.S. Stock Prices, 1990–2010 This figure shows the path of the Dow Jones stock index from 1990 to 2010. This period saw large movements in stock prices, including a possible bubble in the 1990s and a collapse in prices during the financial crisis of 2007–2009.

Source: finance.yahoo.com.

vindication. They interpreted the price declines as the bursting of the bubble and evidence that stocks were never really worth the prices of the late 1990s.

But again, not all analysts agree with this interpretation. Believers in the classical theory point to the effects of several bad-news stories between 2000 and 2003: the terrorist attacks of September 11, 2001; the discovery of false accounting at companies such as Enron; and the recession of 2001. These events reduced companies' expected earnings, possibly explaining the fall in stock prices. So the debate over stock bubbles continues.

2003–2007: Recovery As we see in Figure 16-3, stock prices started rising again in 2003. The Dow passed its 2000 peak in 2006 and reached 14,000 in mid-2007.

Initially, the rise in stock prices was driven by low interest rates. The Federal Reserve pushed rates down in 2003 because the economy remained weak after the 2001 recession. In 2004, the Fed started raising rates, but an economic recovery sustained the stock market boom. In contrast to the 1990s, the P/E ratio for the Dow was stable in the mid-2000s, suggesting that rising prices reflected increases in companies' earnings rather than a bubble.

2007–2010: The Financial Crisis and Its Aftermath Stock prices started falling in late 2007 as the housing bubble burst and disrupted financial markets. The decline accelerated after the failure of Lehman Brothers, a major investment bank, in September 2008. The Dow reached a trough of 6,547 in March 2009.

The financial crisis reduced stock prices through two channels. First, it reduced expectations of companies' future earnings and dividends. Initially, expected earnings fell for financial firms hit directly by the crisis. As the effects of the crisis spread through the economy, earnings forecasts also fell for nonfinancial firms.

Second, the financial crisis increased risk premiums. Unprecedented events created uncertainty about how bad the crisis would get. This uncertainty was reflected in large day-to-day swings in stock prices as traders reacted to the latest news. In the last four months of 2008, the Dow Jones Index rose or fell by 5 percent or more on nine different days. Uncertainty about companies' prospects raised risk premiums for their stocks.

In response to the financial crisis, the Federal Reserve pushed down the economy's safe interest rate (i^{safe}). As measured by the federal funds rate, the safe rate fell below 0.25 percent at the end of 2008. However, the decrease in the safe rate was smaller than the increase in risk premiums for stocks (φ). This difference implied an increase in risk-adjusted interest rates ($i^{safe} + \varphi$), which reduced the present value of future income. The combination of this effect and lower expected income caused stock prices to fall sharply.

In March 2009, the fall in stock prices ended. The Dow Jones Index rose over the next year and reached 11,000 in April 2010. Rising stock prices reflected a growing belief that the worst of the financial crisis was over, largely because of government and Federal Reserve efforts to save financial institutions from failure (discussed in Chapter 19). This optimism raised earnings forecasts for companies and reduced risk premiums, partially reversing the fall in stock prices during the crisis. As of April 2010, however, the Dow remained far below the 14,000 level it had reached in 2007. ∎

16-5 Asset-Price Crashes

Believers in asset-price bubbles think that bubbles eventually end and prices fall. Sometimes this occurs gradually over a period of months or years. The bubble in U.S. stock prices was reversed over the period 2000-2003 and the housing bubble over 2006-2009. At other times, however, a bubble ends with an **asset-price crash**, as prices plummet over a very short period.

As discussed earlier, Holland's tulip bubble ended with a crash in 1637. In U.S. history, the most famous asset-price crashes have occurred in the stock market. In both 1929 and 1987, stock prices fell dramatically *within a single day*. Crashes can have disastrous effects on the economy if policymakers do not handle them well. Let's discuss how crashes occur.

How Crashes Work

Crashes are hard to explain with the classical theory of asset prices. Under that theory, prices fall sharply only if there is a large drop in the present value of expected asset income. This requires either a rise in interest rates or bad news about future income, and crashes often occur without such events. For example, when the stock market crashed on October 19, 1987, prices fell by 23 percent, yet interest rates were stable on that day, and there was no significant news about companies' earnings or dividends.

A crash is easier to explain if it is preceded by an asset-price bubble. At some point during a bubble, people start worrying that it will end. They would like to hold assets as long as prices rise but sell before the bubble bursts, so they watch for the end of the bubble.

At some point, a few asset holders get especially nervous and decide to start selling. Others notice this and fear that the bubble may be ending. They sell, too, hoping to dump their assets before prices fall too much. These actions push down prices, causing more people to sell. Pessimism about prices is self-fulfilling, just as optimism was self-fulfilling during the bubble.

Once a crash starts, it can accelerate rapidly. As prices fall, panic sets in, many asset holders try to sell at the same time, and prices plummet. Eventually, prices fall far enough to make the assets attractive again. At this point, prices may be *below* the present value of expected income, so it is more profitable to hold assets than to sell them. The rush to sell abates, and prices stabilize.

According to this reasoning, a crash is a risk whenever an asset-price bubble is under way. However, nobody knows how to explain why crashes occur on particular days. Sometimes there is a small piece of news, such as a report of low company earnings, that increases the nervousness of asset holders. But often the timing of a crash appears arbitrary. Even in retrospect, we do not know why the 1987 crash occurred on October 19 rather than some other day.

CASE STUDY

The Two Big Crashes

Stock prices rose rapidly during the Roaring Twenties: the Dow Jones Index climbed from 70 in 1921 to 365 in September 1929. This performance reflected excitement about new technologies, such as cars, radios, and electric appliances. The demand for stocks was also fueled by people's ability to "buy on margin," that is, to buy stock on credit, with only a small down payment.

In retrospect the experience of the 1920s looks like a classic bubble, but economists did not recognize this at the time. On October 17, 1929, the eminent economist Irving Fisher commented that "stock prices have reached what looks like a permanently high plateau."

It is not clear why the crash occurred just when it did. Increases in interest rates in early 1929 may have made stockholders nervous, because they reduced the present values of company earnings. In any case, the stock market fluctuated erratically for several months and then plummeted. The largest one-day decline occurred on "Black Monday," October 28, when the Dow dropped by 13 percent. This crash was followed by a series of smaller declines. In July 1932, the Dow reached a low of 41.

The 1987 crash was in some ways a repeat of 1929. It followed a rapid rise in prices: the Dow climbed from 786 in 1980 to 2,655 in August 1987. Some observers suggested that a bubble was under way, but again the crash was unexpected. The market started falling on October 14, and the bottom fell out on October 19, the second Black Monday. That day the Dow dropped 23 percent, easily beating the 1929 record for a one-day drop.

The 1987 crash was exacerbated by the use of computers to trade stocks. Computers sped up trading, so prices fell more quickly than in 1929. Moreover, in 1987 large stockholders such as mutual funds had systems of *program trading,* in which computers automatically sold stock if the market fell by a certain amount. These systems were designed to get rid of stocks quickly if a crash was under way. When the crash occurred, program trading worsened the vicious circle of falling prices and heavy selling.

Despite the similarities between the two crashes, their aftermaths differed. After October 1929, stock prices stayed depressed. The Dow did not climb back to its pre-crash level until 1954. In contrast, the market bounced back quickly after the 1987 crash. The Dow reached its pre-crash level in 1989 and kept rising through the 1990s.

The two crashes also had different effects on the overall economy. The 1929 crash contributed to the Great Depression of the 1930s, while economic growth was strong after the 1987 crash. Part of the explanation is the different behavior of the Federal Reserve. The Fed responded passively to the 1929 crash and the bank panics that followed. In 1987, the Fed lent money to financial institutions threatened by the crash, thus preventing a major disruption of the financial system. ∎

Crash Prevention

Is there any way to prevent asset-price crashes? Both the federal government and stock exchanges have imposed rules for stock trading to make crashes less likely. Let's discuss two rules, one adopted after the 1929 crash and one after the 1987 crash.

Margin Requirements After the 1929 crash, Congress gave the Federal Reserve authority to establish **margin requirements**, limits on the amount that people can borrow to buy stock. Margin requirements have varied over time, but in recent years they have been around 50 percent. This means that stock purchasers must pay at least 50 percent of the cost with their own money.

This regulation tries to curtail the buildup of stock-price bubbles that precedes crashes. As we have discussed, the practice of buying on margin helped fuel the stock market boom of the 1920s. Margin requirements make such a price run up less likely. When prices don't rise as high, there is less danger they will fall sharply.

Circuit Breakers After the 1987 crash, some securities exchanges established **circuit breakers**, requirements to shut down trading temporarily if prices fall sharply. These rules are motivated by the view that crashes are a vicious circle of panic and falling prices. A circuit breaker stops this process; it gives people time to calm down and assess the true value of their assets. If the circuit breaker works, the rush to sell subsides and prices stabilize when the exchange reopens. (In other words, panicky asset traders are like naughty four-year-olds: they behave more rationally after a "time out.")

At the New York Stock Exchange, current rules mandate a suspension of trading if the Dow Jones Index falls 10 percent within a day. The length of the suspension depends on the size of the fall and the time of day. For example, trading halts for an hour if prices fall 10 to 20 percent before 2:00 P.M. Larger decreases can halt trading for the rest of the day.

So far, trading on the New York Stock Exchange has been interrupted only once, on July 27, 1997. At that time the rules set smaller price declines as triggers for circuit breakers. The Dow Jones Index fell 7 percent, which was enough to shut down the exchange for the rest of the day.

16-6 Measuring Interest Rates and Asset Returns

In the previous sections, we have studied how asset prices are determined and why they change over time. With this background, we can define two concepts that are closely related to asset prices: a bond's yield to maturity and the rate of return on a stock or bond. In the rest of this book, we will see that these variables help determine what happens in asset markets. They influence savers' decisions about what stocks and bonds (if any) to purchase and firms' decisions about issuing stocks and bonds.

Yield to Maturity

Buying a bond means lending money to the company or government that issues the bond. In deciding whether to buy a bond, people compare the interest the bond pays to the interest they could receive on other bonds or on deposits in a bank account.

Comparing interest is not as straightforward as it might seem, however. Unlike the stated interest rate on a bank account, the interest rate on a bond is not always obvious. Consider a bond with a $100 face value, 4 years to maturity, coupon payments of $5 per year, and a price of $95. If you buy this bond, what interest rate will you earn?

Economists answer this question by calculating the bond's **yield to maturity**. This concept is based on the classical theory of asset prices. Earlier, we used this theory to derive an equation for the price of a bond:

$$\text{Bond Price} = \frac{C}{(1 + i)} + \frac{C}{(1 + i)^2} + \cdots + \frac{C}{(1 + i)^{T-1}} + \frac{(C + F)}{(1 + i)^T},$$

where C is the coupon payment, F is the face value, T is the maturity, and i is the interest rate. This equation tells us that a bond's price equals the present value of payments from the bond. We can use it to calculate the price if we assume a certain interest rate.

To measure yield to maturity, we turn this calculation around. We know the payments on a bond and the bond's price, and we use the previous equation to derive an interest rate. This interest rate is the bond's yield to maturity, the rate that makes the present value of the bond's payments equal to its price.

Recall the example of a bond with a 4-year maturity, a $100 face value, and $5 coupon payments. If the bond's price is $95, our bond-price equation implies

$$95 = \frac{5}{(1 + i)} + \frac{5}{(1 + i)^2} + \frac{5}{(1 + i)^3} + \frac{105}{(1 + i)^4}.$$

The yield to maturity is the interest rate i that solves this equation. Here, the solution is $i = 0.065$, or an interest rate of 6.5 percent.

A technical note: Usually, there is no easy way to solve equations like the last one. You have to use trial and error, plugging in different values for i until you find one that makes the right side equal to the 95 on the left. Fortunately, a computer or financial calculator can do this for you quickly.

Recall that the classical theory implies that asset prices move inversely with interest rates. In the case of bonds, this principle is true by definition: it follows from how we measure the yield to maturity. If the price on the left side of our equation goes up, the interest rate on the right must go down for the equation to hold.

In our example of a 4-year bond, if the price rises from $95 to $98, the yield to maturity falls from 6.5 percent to 5.6 percent. If this happens, you might hear on the news that "bond prices rose" or that "interest rates on bonds fell." These are two ways of saying the same thing.

The Rate of Return

Suppose you buy a stock or bond and hold onto it for a year. How much have you earned by holding the security? You have potentially increased your wealth in two ways:

1. The security may pay you directly. A bond may yield a coupon payment. If you own a company's stock, you do not directly receive the company's profits, but you may receive a dividend.

2. The price of the security may change. If the price rises, you own a more valuable asset, so your wealth rises. The increase in your wealth that comes from the price increase is called a **capital gain**. If the price of the security falls, you suffer a **capital loss** and your wealth decreases.

The total amount you gain from holding the security is the capital gain or loss plus any direct payment you receive. This total is called the **return** on the security:

$$\text{Return} = (P_1 - P_0) + X,$$

where P_0 is the initial price of the security, P_1 is the price after you hold it for a year, and X represents a direct payment. (X can be a coupon payment, C, or a dividend, D.)

The **rate of return** on a security is the return expressed as a percentage of the initial price. It is calculated by dividing the return by the price:

$$\text{Rate of Return} = \frac{\text{Return}}{P_0}$$

$$= \frac{(P_1 - P_0)}{P_0} + \frac{X}{P_0}.$$

The rate of return has two parts. The first is the percentage change in the security price; the second is the direct payment divided by the initial price.

Suppose in 2020 you buy a bond for $80. In 2021, the bond makes a coupon payment of $4 and the price rises to $82. Plugging these numbers into the formula, the rate of return is

$$\frac{(82 - 80)}{80} + \frac{4}{80} = 0.075, \text{ or } 7.5\%.$$

If the bond makes a coupon payment of $4 but the price falls from $80 to $75, the rate of return is

$$\frac{(75 - 80)}{80} + \frac{4}{80} = -0.013, \text{ or } -1.3\%.$$

As this example illustrates, the rate of return can be negative if a large enough capital loss occurs.

Returns on Stocks and Bonds

Figure 16-4 traces some data on rates of return. It shows the average rates of return on U.S. stocks and Treasury bonds from 1900 through 2009. You can see immediately that stock returns are more volatile than bond returns, reflecting the fact that stock prices fluctuate more than bond prices, as we discussed in Section 16-3. Changes in stock prices cause large swings in the rate of return. Notice the disastrous rate of return on stocks (−37.2%) during the financial crisis of 2008.

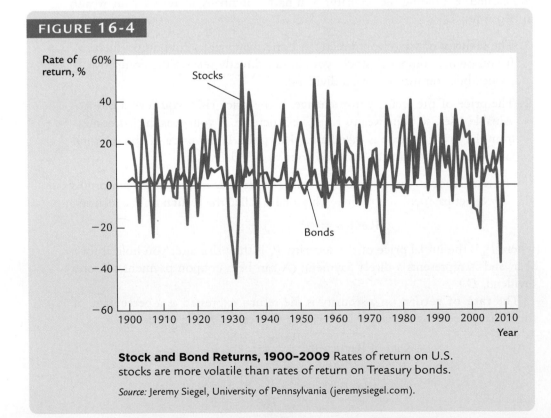

FIGURE 16-4

Stock and Bond Returns, 1900–2009 Rates of return on U.S. stocks are more volatile than rates of return on Treasury bonds.

Source: Jeremy Siegel, University of Pennsylvania (jeremysiegel.com).

While returns on stock are more volatile than those on bonds, the *average* rate of return is higher for stocks. For the period from 1900 through 2009, the average rate of return was about 11 percent for stocks and 5 percent for bonds. This difference should make sense. As we discussed earlier, savers choose assets with more uncertain (more volatile) income only if they are compensated with a risk premium—a higher average return.

Rate of Return Versus Yield to Maturity

People are often confused about the difference between the rate of return on a bond and its yield to maturity. Both variables tell us something about how much you earn by holding a bond, but they can behave quite differently. For example, a decrease in a bond's price can simultaneously cause an increase in the yield to maturity (because a bond's price and yield are inversely related) and a *negative* rate of return (because bondholders suffer capital losses). If you are thinking of buying a bond, which variable should you care about?

The answer depends on how long you are likely to hold the bond. If you hold the bond until it matures, the yield to maturity tells you what interest rate you receive. Fluctuations in the bond's price, which affect the rate of return, are irrelevant if you never sell the bond.

On the other hand, if you sell the bond after a year, you will receive the rate of return for the year. The yield to maturity does not matter if you don't hold the bond to maturity.

16-7 The Term Structure of Interest Rates

Using the concept of yield to maturity, we have seen how to measure the interest rate on a bond. In a modern economy, there are many different bonds that pay different interest rates. The FYI box "The Many Different Interest Rates" in Chapter 3 discusses why interest rates vary, including differences in credit risk and taxes. To conclude this chapter, we study one important factor that influences a bond's interest rate: its term.

"Term" is another word for time to maturity. Bond maturities range from a few months to 30 years or more. Different maturities usually imply different interest rates, even for bonds issued by the same borrower. Similarly, banks charge different interest rates on loans of different durations.

To illustrate this point, Figure 16-5 graphs the interest rates on two bonds for the period from 1960 to 2010. The securities are 10-year Treasury bonds and 90-day Treasury bills. We see that the two interest rates generally differ but that the difference is not stable. The Treasury bond rate is *usually* higher than the Treasury bill rate, but occasionally the Treasury bill rate is higher.

The relationships among interest rates on bonds with different maturities are called the **term structure of interest rates**. Let's discuss the factors that determine the term structure and why it changes over time.

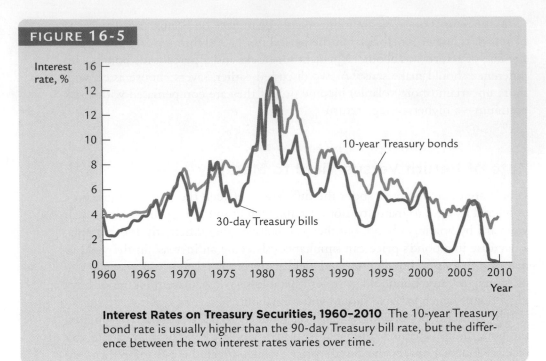

FIGURE 16-5

Interest Rates on Treasury Securities, 1960–2010 The 10-year Treasury bond rate is usually higher than the 90-day Treasury bill rate, but the difference between the two interest rates varies over time.

The Term Structure Under Certainty

To understand the term structure, we analyze savers' decisions about what bonds to buy. For now, let's make a major simplifying assumption: savers know the interest rates on all bonds, both today and in the future. For example, they know the rates on bonds that will be issued today, a year from now, and five years from now. We derive a theory of the term structure under this assumption of certainty, and then we look at what happens when savers are uncertain about future interest rates.

We start with an example involving one-year and two-year bonds. Suppose it is 2020, and Jane plans to save money for two years, until 2022. Jane is considering two ways to save: by purchasing one-year bonds and by purchasing two-year bonds. Let's compare the interest that Jane receives in the two cases.

Suppose first that Jane buys two-year bonds, and let $i_2(2020)$ denote the annual interest rate (the yield to maturity) on two-year bonds issued in 2020. Jane receives this interest rate for two years, for a total of $2i_2(2020)$. For example, if the interest rate is 4 percent, Jane receives a total of $2(4\%) = 8\%$ of her initial wealth.[4]

---

[4] This calculation uses an approximation. To see this, let's compute the earnings on a two-year bond exactly. If someone saves a dollar at an interest rate i_2, his wealth grows to $1 + i_2$ dollars after a year. His wealth after two years is $(1 + i_2)^2$ (see the discussion of future value in Section 16-1). The quantity $(1 + i_2)^2$ equals $1 + 2i_2 + (i_2)^2$. Subtracting off the saver's initial dollar yields his total earnings: $2i_2 + (i_2)^2$.

We've assumed that the earnings on a two-year bond are simply $2i_2$, which means we ignore the $(i_2)^2$ term. Economists often use this approximation because $(i_2)^2$ is small. For an interest rate of 4 percent (or 0.04 in decimal form), $(i_2)^2$ is 0.16% (0.0016). The total earnings on a two-year bond are $2i_2 + (i_2)^2 = 8\% + 0.16\% = 8.16\%$. Our approximation yields 8 percent, which is accurate enough for present purposes.

Now suppose Jane buys one-year bonds. She purchases these bonds in 2020 and they mature in 2021. At that point she can use the proceeds to buy new one-year bonds, which mature in 2022. The interest rates on one-year bonds purchased in 2020 and 2021 are $i_1(2020)$ and $i_1(2021)$, so Jane receives total interest of $i_1(2020) + i_1(2021)$. Recall that we're assuming certainty, so Jane knows both one year rates in advance.[5]

From this information, we can derive a relationship between one- and two-year interest rates. The interest earnings from a two-year bond issued in 2020 must equal the total earnings from one-year bonds issued in 2020 and 2021. That is,

$$2i_2(2020) = i_1(2020) + i_1(2021).$$

This equation must hold if borrowers issue both one- and two-year bonds. If the two-year bonds offered more interest, savers like Jane would buy only two-year bonds, and the issuers of one-year bonds would have to raise interest rates to attract buyers. If two-year bonds paid less, issuers of these bonds would have to raise rates. When savers know current and future interest rates for certain, competition to sell bonds equalizes the interest payments for different maturities.

If we divide the last equation by 2, we get a formula for the two-year interest rate:

$$i_2(2020) = \frac{1}{2}\left[i_1(2020) + i_1(2021)\right].$$

The two-year rate is the average of the current one-year rate and the one-year rate in the following year. For example, if the one-year rate is 3 percent in 2020 and 5 percent in 2021, the two-year rate in 2020 is 4 percent.

This logic applies to any year. If $i_2(t)$ is the interest rate on a two-year bond issued in year t, $i_1(t)$ the rate on a one-year bond issued in year t, and $i_1(t + 1)$ the one-year rate in the following year, then

$$i_2(t) = \frac{1}{2}\left[i_1(t) + i_1(t + 1)\right].$$

The two-year rate in year t is the average of the one-year rates in years t and $t + 1$.

This formula also holds for periods other than a year. If t is a *month* and $t + 1$ is the following month, the formula says that the two-month interest rate is the average of two one-month rates.

Our logic extends beyond one- and two-period bonds to longer-term bonds. If $i_3(t)$ is the interest rate on a *three* period bond, then

$$i_3(t) = \frac{1}{3}\left[i_1(t) + i_1(t + 1) + i_1(t + 2)\right].$$

The three-period interest rate is the average of the one-period rates in the current period, t, and the next two periods, $t + 1$ and $t + 2$.

---

[5] Once again we've used an approximation. The exact earnings from the one-year bonds are $i_1(2020) + i_1(2021) + [i_1(2020)] \times [i_1(2021)]$. We ignore the last term (the product of the two rates), which is small.

The rationale for this equation is similar to our reasoning about two-period bonds. Someone saving for three periods can buy either a three-period bond or a series of three one-period bonds. These strategies must produce the same earnings if savers buy both kinds of bonds.

Finally, we can write a general formula for any maturity. If $i_n(t)$ is the interest rate on an n-period bond in period t, then

$$i_n(t) = \frac{1}{n} \left[i_1(t) + i_1(t + 1) + \cdots + i_1(t + n - 1) \right].$$

The n-period interest rate is the average of one-period rates in the current period and the next $n - 1$ periods. For example, the ten-year interest rate in 2020 is the average of the one-year rates in 2020 and the next nine years, 2021 through 2029.

The Expectations Theory of the Term Structure

So far, we have assumed that savers know the interest rates on all bonds, current and future. This simplifying assumption is not realistic. In 2020, savers know the current interest rates for all maturities, but they do not know with certainty what rates will be in 2021 or later.

To account for this fact, economists analyze the term structure with the **expectations theory of the term structure**. In this theory, savers do not know the future with certainty, but they have expectations about future interest rates. These expectations are rational: they are optimal forecasts given current information. Savers choose among bonds of different maturities based on their rational expectations about future interest rates.

In the expectations theory of the term structure, bonds of different maturities must produce the same *expected* earnings. If they don't, nobody will buy the bonds with lower expected earnings. This reasoning leads to

$$i_n(t) = \frac{1}{n} \left[i_1(t) + E i_1(t + 1) + \cdots + E i_1(t + n - 1) \right],$$

where E means "expected." This equation expresses the expectations theory of the term structure. It is the same as the previous equation, except it replaces actual future interest rates with expected rates. The n-period interest rate is the average of the current one-period rate and expected rates from $t + 1$ to $t + n - 1$.

Accounting for Risk

The expectations theory assumes that savers choose bonds based only on expected interest rates. This assumption ignores the role of uncertainty. Modifying the theory to account for risk makes it more realistic. As we discussed in Section 16-2, savers are risk averse. When asset returns are uncertain, savers demand higher expected returns as compensation.

To see the implications of risk for the term structure, recall another point from Section 16-2: long-term bond prices respond more strongly to changes in interest rates and are therefore more volatile than short-term bond prices. This means that holders of long-term bonds may experience large capital gains or losses, and this risk makes these bonds less attractive to savers.

Therefore, once we take risk into account, it is *not* true that long- and short-term bonds yield the same expected earnings, as the basic expectations theory assumes. If they did, savers would buy only short-term bonds, which are less risky. To attract buyers, long-term bonds must offer higher expected earnings.

Economists capture this idea by modifying the expectations theory of the term structure to include a **term premium** for long-term interest rates. This premium, denoted by τ (the Greek letter tau), is the extra return that compensates the holder of a long-term bond for the bond's riskiness. The following equation summarizes the expectations theory with a term premium:

$$i_n(t) = \frac{1}{n}\left[i_1(t) + Ei_1(t+1) + \cdots + Ei_1(t+n-1)\right] + \tau_n,$$

where τ_n is the term premium for an n-period bond. This equation says that the n-period interest rate is the average of expected one-period rates *plus* the term premium.

Bonds of different maturities have different term premiums. The quantity τ_2 is the premium for two-period bonds, τ_3 is the premium for three-period bonds, and so on. The longer a bond's maturity, the higher its term premium; for example, $\tau_3 > \tau_2$ and $\tau_4 > \tau_3$. A longer maturity means a more variable bond price and requires greater compensation for risk.

The Yield Curve

The term structure of interest rates can be summarized in a graph called the **yield curve**. The yield curve shows interest rates on bonds of various maturities at a given point in time.

Figure 16-6 shows a hypothetical yield curve for January 1, 2020. On that day, bonds with longer maturities have higher interest rates. For example, the three-month interest rate is 4 percent, the one year rate is 5 percent, and the ten-year rate is 6 percent.

Yield Curve Shapes The yield curve looks different at different points in time. The shape of the curve depends on expectations about future interest rates. Figure 16-7 shows four possibilities. All assume the same one-period rate but reflect different expectations about future rates, which produce different interest rates at longer maturities.

As a first example, suppose that people expect the one-period interest rate to stay constant. The expected future rates—$Ei_1(t+1)$, $Ei_1(t+2)$, and so on—all equal the current rate $i_1(t)$. Substituting this assumption into our last formula for the n-period rate yields

$$i_n(t) = \frac{1}{n}\left[i_1(t) + i_1(t) + \cdots + i_1(t)\right] + \tau_n,$$

which simplifies to

$$i_n(t) = i_1(t) + \tau_n.$$

FIGURE 16-6

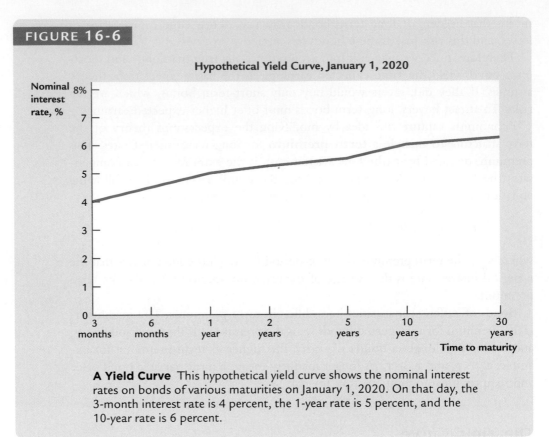

Hypothetical Yield Curve, January 1, 2020

A Yield Curve This hypothetical yield curve shows the nominal interest rates on bonds of various maturities on January 1, 2020. On that day, the 3-month interest rate is 4 percent, the 1-year rate is 5 percent, and the 10-year rate is 6 percent.

With the one-period rate expected to stay constant, the average of expected future rates equals the current one-period rate. The n-period rate is the one-period rate plus a term premium.

Recall that the term premium τ_n rises with a bond's maturity, n. Therefore, the last equation implies that the interest rate $i_n(t)$ rises with n. This case is captured by the green line in Figure 16-7. Rising term premiums cause the yield curve to slope upward.

The other lines in the figure illustrate cases in which the one-period interest rate is *not* expected to stay constant. The blue line is a yield curve that results when people expect the one-period rate to rise in the future. The average of expected future rates exceeds the current rate, pushing up long-term interest rates: they exceed the one-period rate by more than the term premium. In our graph, the yield curve is steep.

The red line is a yield curve that results when people expect the one-period interest rate to fall. The average of expected future rates is less than the current rate, reducing long-term rates and flattening the yield curve.

Finally, the orange line is an example of an **inverted yield curve**, a curve that slopes downward. This situation arises when people expect an unusually large fall in the one-period interest rate. This expectation reduces long-term rates by more than term premiums raise them, so long-term rates lie below the current one-period rate.

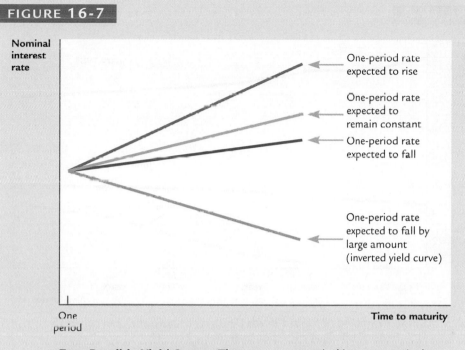

FIGURE 16-7

Four Possible Yield Curves The current one-period interest rate is the same on each of these yield curves. The slopes of the curves depend on expectations of future one-period rates.

Some Examples Figure 16-8 graphs actual yield curves for U.S. Treasury bonds in January 1981, June 1999, and December 2009. These cases illustrate some of the possible yield curves that we've discussed.

Notice first that interest rates were highest at all maturities in 1981. Inflation was high at that time, producing high nominal interest rates through the Fisher equation, $i = r + E\pi$ (discussed in Chapter 4). Interest rates were lowest in 2009, when the Federal Reserve was trying to end a deep recession.

The key features of the yield curves are their slopes. The yield curve for June 1999 has a common shape—a moderate upward slope. The interest rate is 4.6 percent at a maturity of three months, 5.6 percent at two years, and 6.0 percent at thirty years. The curve for December 2009 is steeper than usual, going from under 0.1 percent at three months to 4.5 percent at thirty years. Finally, the yield curve for January 1981 is inverted: rates fall with maturity over most of the curve.

Forecasting Interest Rates The expected path of interest rates determines the shape of the yield curve. Turning this relation around, the yield curve's shape tells us about the expected path of interest rates. An unusually steep curve, such as the one for December 2009, means that short-term interest rates are expected to rise. An inverted curve, such as the one for January 1981, means short-term rates are expected to fall sharply.

FIGURE 16-8

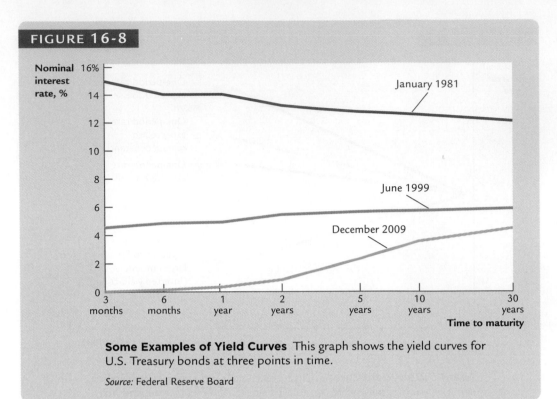

Some Examples of Yield Curves This graph shows the yield curves for U.S. Treasury bonds at three points in time.

Source: Federal Reserve Board

These facts imply a use for the yield curve: to forecast interest rates. If you are thinking of borrowing money in the future, you would like to know future interest rates. You can't know these rates for sure, but you can estimate them with the yield curve. The yield curve reveals the interest rate expectations of people who trade bonds. These are good forecasts because bond traders are well informed about interest rates.

CASE STUDY

Inverted Yield Curves

Because of term premiums, the yield curve usually has an upward slope. An inverted curve occurs only if short-term interest rates are expected to fall by a large amount. Why might this expectation arise?

Historically, most inverted yield curves have been caused by monetary policy—specifically, by efforts to reduce inflation. To fight inflation, the Federal Reserve slows the growth of the money supply, which pushes up the federal funds rate and other short-term interest rates. Higher interest rates reduce output temporarily, and lower output reduces inflation as indicated by the Phillips curve (discussed in Chapter 12).

In such an episode, the increase in short-term interest rates is temporary. People expect the Fed to reduce interest rates once inflation is under control. In fact, rates are likely to end up lower than they were before the Fed acted, because of lower inflation and the Fisher effect. The expected decrease in rates may be large enough to invert the yield curve.

In Figure 16-8, we saw that the yield curve for Treasury securities was inverted in 1981. At that time inflation was running near 10 percent, and the Federal Reserve was determined to reduce it. The Fed slowed money growth, and the three-month Treasury bill rate rose to 15 percent. The yield curve inverted because people expected large decreases in inflation and interest rates. Expectations turned out to be correct: the three-month Treasury bill rate fell to 8 percent in 1983 and 6 percent in 1986.

Another inverted yield curve occurred at the end of 2000. The Fed was worried that inflation might rise, because output had been growing at an unusually rapid pace. The Fed raised short-term interest rates to contain inflation, and the yield curve mildly inverted. In December 2000, the three-month rate was 6.0 percent, the one-year rate was 5.7 percent, and the thirty-year rate was 5.4 percent. ■

16-8 Conclusion

Fluctuations in asset prices have important effects on the economy. Changes in the prices of stocks or of houses, for example, cause changes in consumers' wealth that affect aggregate demand and output. What causes asset prices to fluctuate? In answering this question, economists typically apply the classical theory of asset prices, in which the key factors are interest rates and expected asset income. Yet the classical theory may fail to explain some asset-price movements, including price increases during bubbles and price decreases during crashes.

In earlier chapters, we discussed how "the" interest rate is determined. In this chapter we have learned that there are various interest rates, and we also learned how to calculate them and studied the relationships among them. We found that long-term interest rates depend on expectations of future short-term rates and on term premiums.

With this background, we can take a closer look at the markets for assets and their roles in the economy. The next chapter discusses the people and firms that participate in asset markets and their decisions about what to buy and sell.

Summary

1. The present value of a future dollar is its worth in today's dollars. The present value of a dollar in n years is $\$1/(1 + i)^n$. We can use this formula to find the present value of a stream of income such as that generated by a bond or a share of stock.

2. The classical theory of asset prices says an asset price equals the present value of expected future income from the asset and assumes that expectations are rational.

3. The interest rate used to compute an asset price is a risk-adjusted rate; it equals the safe rate (i^{safe}) plus a risk premium (φ). The risk premium rises with uncertainty about future asset income.

4. A rise in expected asset income raises asset prices. A rise in interest rates reduces asset prices.

5. Some economists believe that asset prices are influenced by bubbles, which occur when prices rise above the present value of asset income. In a bubble, people pay high prices for assets because they expect prices to rise even higher.

6. An asset-price bubble may dissipate gradually or end with a crash when prices plummet in a short period of time. A crash occurs when asset holders lose confidence, sparking a vicious circle of selling and declining prices.

7. The interest rate on a bond is measured by the yield to maturity, the interest rate that makes the present value of the bond's payments equal to its price. The return on an asset is the change in its price plus any current payment (a coupon payment or stock dividend). The rate of return is the return as a percentage of the initial price. The rate of return on stocks is more volatile than the rate of return on bonds, but it is higher on average.

8. The term structure is the relationship among interest rates on bonds of different maturities (terms). The yield curve summarizes the term structure at a point in time. The shape of the yield curve depends on expectations about future interest rates. Economists use the yield curve to forecast future rates.

KEY CONCEPTS

Future value	Asset-price bubble	Return
Present value	Price-earnings (P/E) ratio	Rate of return
Classical theory of asset prices	Asset-price crash	Term structure of interest rates
Dividend	Margin requirements	Expectations theory of the term structure
Safe interest rate (i^{safe})	Circuit breaker	Term premium (τ)
Risk premium (φ)	Yield to maturity	Yield curve
Risk-adjusted interest rate	Capital gain	Inverted yield curve
Gordon growth model	Capital loss	

QUESTIONS FOR REVIEW

1. What is the future value of a dollar today? What is the present value of a dollar in the future?

2. What is the classical theory of asset prices?

3. What factors cause asset prices to change?

4. Which asset prices are most volatile? Why?

5. What happens in an asset-price bubble? What happens in an asset-price crash?

6. What is the difference between the yield to maturity on a bond and its rate of return?

7. Why can yield curves be used to forecast interest rates?

PROBLEMS AND APPLICATIONS

1. Suppose you win the lottery. You have a choice between receiving $100,000 a year for twenty years or an immediate payment of $1,200,000.

   a. Which choice should you make if the interest rate is 3 percent? If it is 6 percent?

   b. For what range of interest rates should you take the immediate payment?

2. Suppose a bond has a maturity of three years, annual coupon payments of $5, and a face value of $100.

   a. If the interest rate is 4 percent, is the price of the bond higher or lower than the face value? What if the interest rate is 6 percent?

   b. For what range of interest rates does the price exceed the face value? Can you explain the answer?

3. Suppose that people expect a company's earnings to grow in the future at the same rate they have grown in the past. Does this behavior satisfy the assumption of rational expectations? Explain.

4. Describe how each of the following events affects stock and bond prices:

   a. The economy enters a recession.

   b. A genius invents a new technology that makes factories more productive.

   c. The Federal Reserve raises its target for interest rates.

   d. People learn that major news about the economy will be announced in a few days, but they don't know whether it is good news or bad news.

5. Consider two stocks. For each, the expected dividend next year is $100 and the expected growth rate of dividends is 3 percent. The risk premium is 3 percent for one stock and 8 percent for the other. The economy's safe interest rate is 5 percent.

   a. What does the difference in risk premiums tell us about the dividends from each stock?

   b. Use the Gordon growth model to compute the price of each stock. Why is one price higher than the other?

   c. Suppose the expected growth rate of dividends rises to 5 percent for both stocks. Compute the new price of each. Which stock's price changes by a larger percentage? Explain your results.

6. Consider two bonds. Each has a face value of $100 and matures in ten years. One has no coupon payments, and the other pays $10 per year.

   a. Calculate the price of each bond if the interest rate is 3 percent and if the interest rate is 6 percent.

   b. When the interest rate rises from 3 percent to 6 percent, which bond price falls by a larger percentage? Explain why.

7. Suppose a bond has a face value of $100, annual coupon payments of $4, a maturity of five years, and a price of $90.

   a. Write an equation that defines the yield to maturity on this bond.

   b. If you have the right kind of calculator or software, find the solution for the yield to maturity.

8. Suppose the price of the bond in Problem 7 falls from $90 to $85 over a year. Calculate the bond's rate of return over the year.

9. Suppose it is 2020 and the one-year interest rate is 4 percent. The expected one-year rates in the following four years (2021 to 2024) are 4 percent, 5 percent, 6 percent, and 6 percent.

   a. Assume the expectations theory of the term structure, with no term premiums. Compute the interest rates in 2020 on bonds with maturities of one, two, three, four, and five years. Draw a yield curve.

   b. Redo part (a) with term premiums. Assume the term premium for an n-year bond, τ_n, is $(n/2)$ percent. For example, the premium for a four-year bond is $(4/2)\% = 2\%$.

10. Suppose it is 2020, the one-year interest rate is 8 percent, and the ten-year rate is 6 percent.

   a. Draw a graph showing a likely path of the one-year rate from 2020 through 2029.

   b. Why might people expect such a path for the one-year rate?

11. Using the expectations theory of the term structure, derive a formula giving the four-year interest rate in 2020 as a function of *two-year* rates in 2020 and the future.

12. Suppose that some event has no effect on expected interest rates but raises uncertainty about rates. What happens to the yield curve? Explain.

13. Go to bloomberg.com, which provides daily data on the Dow Jones stock index. Find a day within the last year when the index rose or fell by at least 2 percent. Consult news reports for that day and discuss why stock prices might have changed. Was the change consistent with the classical theory of asset prices?

CHAPTER 17

Securities Markets

Markets are constantly in a state of uncertainty and flux and money is made by discounting the obvious and betting on the unexpected.

—*George Soros*

If you are a college student, you may not be a saver right now, but someday you probably will be. Perhaps your brilliance and hard work will make you rich. Even if your income is modest, you will probably set some of it aside for retirement. Either way, you will have to choose what to do with your savings.

Should you put your money in a bank? Should you buy securities such as stocks and bonds? Which securities are best? Should you buy individual securities or buy shares of a mutual fund, which owns many different securities?

People around the world face the problem of **asset allocation**, as do financial institutions that hold assets, such as banks and pension funds. Decisions about asset allocation produce the activity that we see in financial markets—the daily trading of securities worth billions of dollars.

This chapter discusses securities markets. We first meet the participants in these markets, including a variety of financial institutions. Then we discuss how the markets work—how governments and firms issue securities and how securities are traded.

Next we analyze the key choices facing securities market participants. These include firms' decisions about what securities to issue and savers' choices of asset allocation. Savers must decide how to split their wealth among broad classes of assets, such as stocks and bonds. They must also choose among individual securities, such as the stocks of different companies.

We turn last to another class of securities: *derivatives,* securities with payoffs tied to the prices of other assets. Markets for derivatives have grown rapidly in the last few decades. We discuss what derivative securities are, why they are traded, and the risks they can create.

17-1 Participants in Securities Markets

The players in securities markets include individual savers and many kinds of financial institutions. The key institutions are listed in Table 17-1. Some own large quantities of securities; some help people and firms to trade securities; some do both.

> **TABLE 17-1**
>
> ### Major Institutions in Securities Markets
>
> **Securities Firms**
>
> Mutual funds
> Hedge funds
> Brokers
> Dealers
> Investment banks
>
> **Other Financial Institutions**
>
> Pension funds
> Insurance companies
> Commercial banks

Individual Owners

Some securities are owned by individual people. In 2007 (the latest year with data available), U.S. citizens directly owned 28 percent of the stock of U.S. companies. They also owned most shares in mutual funds, which held another 25 percent of U.S. corporate stock.

Over time, stock ownership has spread to a larger fraction of the U.S. population. In 1983, only 19 percent of households owned any stock, either directly or indirectly through mutual funds. In 2008, 47 percent of households owned stock. One reason for this trend is the growth of 401(k) plans that channel workers' retirement savings into securities.

While many people own stock, a few hold disproportionately large amounts. In 2007, the wealthiest 1 percent of U.S. households owned 38 percent of stock held by individuals; the wealthiest 10 percent owned 80 percent.

Securities Firms

Among the financial institutions that participate in securities markets, one broad category is **securities firms**. These companies' primary purpose is to hold securities, trade them, or help others trade them. There are several types of securities firms: mutual funds, hedge funds, brokers and dealers, and investment banks.

Mutual Funds Recall from Chapter 15 that a mutual fund is a financial institution that holds a diversified set of securities and sells shares to savers. In effect, each shareholder owns a small part of all the securities in a fund. Buying mutual fund shares is an easy way for savers to diversify their assets, which reduces risk.

About 8,000 separate mutual funds exist in the United States. Most are run by large mutual fund companies such as Fidelity, Vanguard, and American Funds. Each company offers a menu of funds that feature different sets of securities.

Some funds hold a wide variety of stocks and bonds; others specialize. For example, some funds hold only Treasury bonds, and some hold only corporate bonds. Some specialize in stocks issued by large firms, and some specialize in small firms' stock. Some funds hold only U.S. securities, and some hold foreign securities.

Hedge Funds Like mutual funds, **hedge funds** raise pools of money to purchase securities. Unlike mutual funds, they cater only to wealthy people and institutions. Most hedge funds require clients to contribute $1 million or more.

A key difference between hedge funds and mutual funds involves government regulation. To protect small savers, the government limits the risks that mutual funds can take with shareholders' money. Hedge funds are largely unregulated because the government assumes that the funds' rich customers can look out for themselves. Light regulation means that hedge funds can make risky bets on asset prices. These bets sometimes produce large earnings, and sometimes large losses.

One common tool of hedge funds is **leverage**: funds borrow money from banks and use it to increase their security holdings. Larger security holdings magnify the funds' gains and losses when security prices change. Mutual funds are not allowed to use leverage to buy securities because of the risk of large losses. Another risky practice of hedge funds, forbidden to mutual funds, is trading derivative securities (discussed in more detail later in the chapter).

Money flowed into hedge funds in the early 2000s, and their total assets reached $3 trillion in 2007. During the ensuing financial crisis, asset values fell and savers withdrew money from hedge funds. In 2009, total hedge fund assets had fallen to $1.5 trillion.

Brokers and Dealers These firms help securities markets operate. A **broker** buys and sells securities on behalf of others. For example, if you want to acquire a share of Microsoft, a broker will buy it for you in a stock market. You pay a fee to the broker for this service.

You can choose between two types of brokers. A *full-service broker* has advisers who help clients choose which securities to buy. Leading full-service brokers include Merrill Lynch, Smith Barney, and Dean Witter. A *discount broker* provides less advice, or none at all; customers must choose securities on their own. Firms in this category include Charles Schwab, TD Ameritrade, and online brokers such as E* Trade.

A **dealer** buys securities for itself, not others, and earns profits by reselling them at higher prices. Typically, a dealer firm specializes in a narrow set of securities, such as Treasury bills or the stocks of certain companies. It holds an inventory of these securities and "makes a market" for them. The dealer stands ready to buy the securities when someone else wants to sell and to sell when someone else wants to buy.

Investment Banks This type of securities firm includes well-known names such as Goldman Sachs, Morgan Stanley, and Credit Suisse. An **investment bank** is not really a bank in economists' sense of the term, because it does not take deposits. Instead, investment banks have several functions in securities markets.

A traditional function is underwriting, a process we discuss in Section 17-2. As an **underwriter**, an investment bank helps companies issue new stocks and bonds. It advises the companies and markets the securities to potential buyers.

Investment banks also advise companies on *mergers and acquisitions*, or M&A. In these deals, two companies are combined or one company buys another. Investment banks research their client companies' potential profits from M&A and advise their clients about which deals to make and what prices to pay.

While underwriting and advising are their core functions, investment banks have also developed other ways to earn profits. Many investment banks buy and sell securities. Like hedge funds, they try to make money through risky bets on asset prices.

Investment banks also practice *financial engineering,* the development and marketing of new types of securities. One such security is the *junk bond,* a bond issued by a corporation with a low credit rating. Junk bonds were the brainchild of investment banker Michael Milken, whose firm, Drexel Burnham, started underwriting junk bonds in 1977. This innovation allowed more corporations to raise money in bond markets. More recently, investment banks have invented new derivative securities and securities backed by home mortgage loans, as discussed in upcoming case studies.

Other Financial Institutions

In addition to securities firms, several other financial institutions are important participants in securities markets because they buy large quantities of stocks and bonds.

Pension Funds Employers, both private firms and governments, establish pension funds to provide income to retired workers. Employers contribute money to the funds, and sometimes workers also make contributions. Pension funds use this money to purchase securities, and earnings from the securities provide retirement benefits.

Insurance Companies These companies sell life insurance and insurance for property, such as houses and cars. Purchasers of insurance pay premiums, which the companies use to buy securities. Earnings from the securities pay for insurance claims.

Commercial Banks In contrast to investment banks, commercial banks are institutions that accept deposits and make loans. Their primary assets are those loans—the money they are owed by borrowers. However, commercial banks also own securities, mainly government bonds. Banks hold bonds for liquidity: they can sell the bonds easily if they need cash.

Financial Industry Consolidation

In practice, the various types of institutions that participate in securities markets overlap because many firms engage in more than one business. For example, Merrill Lynch has long been a leader in both investment banking and brokerage. Over the last twenty years, mergers have produced large securities firms with multiple functions.

Two major events have contributed to consolidation in the financial industry. One was the 1999 repeal of the *Glass-Steagall Act,* which forbade commercial banks from merging with investment banks. With Glass-Steagal gone, mergers created conglomerates such as Citigroup and JP Morgan Chase, which own commercial banks and also perform most functions of securities firms. Chapter 19 discusses the reasons for these mergers.

The financial crisis of 2007–2009 was the second major event that has contributed to financial industry consolidation. During the crisis, financial institutions that were relatively healthy bought institutions in danger of failing. The following case study discusses two of these deals: the takeovers of the investment banks Bear Stearns and Merrill Lynch.

CASE STUDY

The Upheaval in Investment Banking, 2008

At the start of 2008, the five largest investment banks in the United States were Goldman Sachs, Morgan Stanley, Merrill Lynch, Lehman Brothers, and Bear Stearns. Over the course of the year, all these institutions faced crises that threatened their survival.

The story begins in the early 2000s. In that period, the five investment banks started issuing *mortgage-backed securities.* To create these securities, they purchased home mortgage loans from the original lenders and bundled them together. The buyers of the securities became entitled to shares of the interest and principal payments that borrowers made on the underlying mortgages.

Mortgage-backed securities had been issued before by other financial institutions (namely the mortgage agencies Fannie Mae and Freddie Mac, which we discuss in Chapter 18). The novel feature of the securities issued by the investment banks was that the mortgages backing them were *subprime*: they were loans to people with weak credit histories. Subprime borrowers must pay higher interest rates than traditional mortgage borrowers pay. As a result, securities backed by subprime mortgages promised high returns to their owners—as long as borrowers made their mortgage payments.

The investment banks sold some of their mortgage-backed securities to customers, but they kept others for themselves. Unfortunately, the decline in housing prices that started in 2006 caused a rash of defaults on subprime mortgages, because many borrowers couldn't afford their payments and couldn't sell their houses for enough to pay off their debts. As defaults rose, participants in financial markets realized that securities backed by subprime mortgages would produce less income than previously expected. Lower expected income reduced the prices of the securities, causing large losses to the investment banks and other owners of the securities.

Eventually, mounting losses created crises at the investment banks. In early 2008, rumors spread that Bear Stearns might go bankrupt. Other financial institutions stopped lending to Bear or buying its bonds because they feared that Bear would default on its obligations. Bear ran out of money to pay off its existing loans and commercial paper (short-term bonds) that was maturing.

In March 2008, lawyers for Bear Stearns started preparing a bankruptcy filing. At the last minute, the Federal Reserve intervened. The Fed brokered a deal in which JP Morgan Chase purchased Bear Stearns. As a result, Bear did not default on its debts. The firm ceased to exist, but many of its operations continued under the management of JP Morgan Chase.

Six months later, Lehman Brothers faced a similar crisis: doubts about its survival led other institutions to cut off lending to the firm. But in contrast to Bear's fate, nobody stepped in to save Lehman, and it declared bankruptcy on September 15, 2008. It went out of business and defaulted on its outstanding bonds and bank loans.

Lehman's failure shocked participants in financial markets and created fears that other investment banks would fail. On the same day as Lehman's bankruptcy, Bank of America purchased Merrill Lynch. Like Bear Stearns, Merrill was absorbed into a healthier institution.

Goldman Sachs and Morgan Stanley held fewer mortgage-backed securities than the other investment banks. They lost less and were able to remain independent but needed to reassure other financial institutions that they would survive. To do so, both firms became *bank holding companies (BHCs)* on September 21, 2008. This reorganization gave them the right to open commercial banks and to receive emergency loans from the Fed. In return, Goldman and Morgan accepted greater Fed regulation of their activities.

Despite these dramatic events, large investment banks still exist in the United States. As BHCs, Goldman Sachs and Morgan Stanley remain independent and continue to conduct investment-banking activities, including underwriting and securities trading. Merrill Lynch still operates as a broker and investment bank, albeit as a subsidiary of Bank of America. After losses in 2008, both Merrill and Goldman (but not Morgan Stanley) returned to profitability in 2009. ■

17-2 Stock and Bond Markets

Now that the players in securities markets have been introduced, let's discuss how they interact with one another. Savers and financial institutions participate in two kinds of markets. Firms and governments issue new securities in **primary markets**, and existing securities are traded in **secondary markets**.

Primary Markets

When a firm is founded, it can get funds from the owners' personal wealth and from bank loans. It may also attract funds from *venture capital firms*, which finance new companies in return for ownership shares. Up to this point, the firm is a *private company* with a small number of owners.

The Process of Issuing Securities As a firm grows, it may need more funds than it can raise as a private company. At that point, it turns to securities markets. It becomes a **public company**, a firm that issues stock and bonds that are traded in financial markets. A firm becomes public by making a first sale of stock, which is called an **initial public offering**, or **IPO**. Purchasers of the stock receive ownership shares in the firm. In return, the firm receives funds that it can use for investment.

Typically, a company's IPO is underwritten by investment banks. The company initiates this process by hiring a lead investment bank, which enlists other investment banks to form a *syndicate*. The syndicate members purchase the company's stock and resell it immediately to other financial institutions, such as mutual funds and pension funds. Shares are not offered directly to individual savers. Typically, investment banks sell the stock for 5 to 10 percent more than they pay for it.

A company announces an IPO in a formal document called a *prospectus,* which describes the stock being offered and the price. The prospectus also provides detailed information on the company, including financial statements and biographies of managers. The company's investment banks help prepare the prospectus. They also market the stock by sending their representatives around the country to make presentations to potential purchasers, such as mutual fund managers.

After a firm goes public, it returns to securities markets periodically to raise funds for investment. The firm can issue new stock, spreading ownership of the firm across additional buyers. It can also borrow money by issuing bonds. Investment banks underwrite these security issues, just as they underwrite IPOs.

The Need for Underwriters Investment banks earn large profits from underwriting. They receive a significant chunk of the money that firms raise by issuing securities. Why can't firms cut out investment banks and sell securities directly to the final purchasers?

The answer is that investment banks reduce the asymmetric information problem of adverse selection. Recall from Chapter 15 that firms may be most eager to issue securities when the value of the securities is low. To go public, a firm needs a track record to help people judge the value of its stock. Even then, potential stock purchasers are wary because they know less about the firm's business than the firm does. They fear that potentially unprofitable companies will try to sell securities at inflated prices.

Investment banks reduce this worry when they underwrite a firm's securities. They research the firm and try to ensure that it is sound and that its securities are priced reasonably. Investment banks convince other institutions of the securities' value by putting their own reputations on the line. If the Acme Corporation hires Goldman Sachs to underwrite its IPO, it has a better chance of selling its securities. Mutual fund managers may not have heard of Acme, but they've heard of Goldman Sachs, and they know that Goldman has a history of underwriting good securities.

Because reputation is so important, underwriting is a concentrated industry dominated by a small number of institutions. Since 2000, 10 investment banks have underwritten more than half of the securities issued around the world. It is hard for lesser-known firms to enter the underwriting business. If your friend Joe started Joe's Discount Investment Bank, he would probably have trouble selling securities. Mutual fund managers don't know Joe, so they would fear a rip-off.

We can better understand the role of underwriters by examining Google's IPO in 2004—one of the few that did *not* involve traditional underwriting.

"Damn it, I don't want to know about my love life. Tell me about the bond market."

Instead, Google sold shares through an auction in which any institution or person could submit bids. Google hired Morgan Stanley and Credit Suisse to run the auction, but these firms did not research the company's finances or market Google's stock to possible buyers. As a result, they received only 3 percent of the IPO revenue, not the usual 5 to 10 percent charged by underwriters.

Google was able to modify the traditional IPO because it is an unusually well-known and successful company. Its reputation reduced the adverse selection problem. Many people were eager to buy Google stock, so the company didn't need the usual help from investment banks.

One issuer of securities has never hired an investment bank: the U.S. government. The government is even better known than Google, so it can sell bonds directly to savers and financial institutions. Most government bonds are issued through auctions run by the Treasury department and designed to produce the highest possible prices for the bonds.

Secondary Markets

After securities are issued in primary markets, their buyers often resell them in secondary markets. Then the securities are traded repeatedly among institutions and individual savers.

To understand this process, we first discuss how brokers help people enter securities markets. Then we discuss the main types of secondary markets: exchanges and over-the-counter (OTC) markets. OTC markets can be divided into dealer markets and electronic communication networks (ECNs).

The Role of Brokers A financial institution can buy securities directly from other institutions. Individual savers can buy bonds directly from the government in auctions. However, to buy stocks or corporate bonds, individuals need assistance from brokers.

If you want to buy securities, the first step is to establish an account with a broker. You can use a traditional broker, such as Merrill-Lynch, or an online broker, such as E*trade. You deposit money in your account so it is available to buy the securities you choose.

When you want to buy or sell, you contact your broker by phone or over the Internet. You place an order—let's say you want to buy 100 shares of Boeing, the aircraft manufacturer. You can place a *market order,* which tells the broker to buy Boeing for the best price he can find. Or you can place a *limit order,* telling him to buy only if the price reaches a certain level. The broker fills your order in different ways, depending on which type of secondary market he uses.

Exchanges Your broker may fill your order at an **exchange**, a physical location where brokers and dealers meet. Exchanges are used mostly to trade stocks, not bonds. The world's largest securities exchange is the New York Stock Exchange (NYSE), located on Wall Street in lower Manhattan. The stocks of roughly 3,000 companies are traded on the NYSE. Other cities with large stock exchanges include London, Frankfurt, Tokyo, and Sao Paolo.

Figure 17-1 illustrates how stocks are traded on the NYSE. You have asked your broker, Merrill-Lynch, to buy 100 shares of Boeing. Merrill has a *seat* on the exchange, allowing it to trade there. The person you contact at Merrill sends your order to one of the firm's *commission brokers,* who work on the floor of the exchange.

The commission broker walks to the *trading post* for Boeing stock. The trading post is a desk staffed by a broker-dealer called a **specialist**. The NYSE chooses one securities firm to provide a specialist for each stock (the specialist for Boeing works for Spear, Leeds, and Kellogg). The specialist manages the trading of that stock.

Brokers tell the specialist how many shares of Boeing they want to buy or sell and what prices they will accept. The specialist records this information and

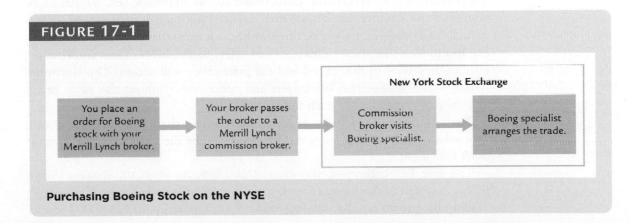

FIGURE 17-1

Purchasing Boeing Stock on the NYSE

arranges trades. Sometimes the specialist matches a broker who wants to buy stock with another who wants to sell. Other times, the specialist acts as a dealer, trading with brokers on behalf of her own firm. Either way, her job is to help brokers make the trades ordered by their customers.

Dealer Markets A secondary market that has no physical location—one that is not an exchange—is an **over-the-counter (OTC) market**. One type of OTC market is a **dealer market**, in which all trades are made with dealers. A computer network connects the dealers to brokers and other financial institutions that want to trade. Each dealer posts "bid" prices at which it will buy certain securities and "ask" prices at which it will sell.

The largest dealer market for stocks is the NASDAQ network. The initials stand for National Association of Securities Dealers Automated Quotation. Roughly 3,000 stocks are traded on the NASDAQ, the same number as on the NYSE. NASDAQ companies tend to be smaller, and many are in high-tech industries. Within the NASDAQ network, 20 or more firms may be dealers in a particular stock. If you tell your broker to buy or sell a stock for you, he looks for the dealer with the best price.

Most bonds, both corporate and government, are traded on dealer markets. Again, computer networks link dealers with other financial institutions that want to make trades. The biggest bond dealers are divisions of financial conglomerates such as Citigroup and JP Morgan Chase.

Dealers make profits from the **bid–ask spread**, the gap between the prices at which they buy and sell a security. The size of these spreads varies greatly. Spreads are smaller for more liquid securities, those that are easy to trade because there are many buyers and sellers. For the most liquid—Treasury securities—spreads are well under 0.1 percent of the price. Dealers can profit from small spreads by purchasing great numbers of securities and reselling them immediately.

Bid–ask spreads are higher for stocks, and higher still for corporate bonds. Spreads on these bonds can be several percentage points. The bond of a particular company may not be traded frequently. If a dealer buys the bond, it might take awhile to sell it, and the price could fall in the meantime. The bid–ask spread compensates the dealer for this risk.

Electronic Communication Networks An alternative to exchanges and dealer markets is an **electronic communications network (ECN)**. An ECN is an over-the-counter market in which financial institutions such as brokers and mutual funds trade directly with one another, a process that doesn't require dealers. Institutions that want to trade submit offers to the ECN. They say what securities they want to buy or sell and the prices they will accept. The electronic system automatically matches buyers and sellers who submit the same price. Traders pay a small fee for each transaction.

The advantage of trading through an ECN is that there is no bid–ask spread. The seller of a security receives the full price paid by the ultimate buyer. Dealers don't take a cut.

The first ECN, Instinet, was created in 1969. As of 2010, about a dozen ECNs operated in the United States, including Instinet, Island, and Archipelago. Trading has grown rapidly since the mid-1990s, especially for NASDAQ stocks.

More than half of all trades in these stocks occur through ECNs rather than the NASDAQ dealer network.

Finding Information on Security Prices

Suppose you are adding up your wealth and want to know the current prices of the stocks and bonds you own. Daily newspapers such as the *Wall Street Journal* report prices from the previous day. A number of Web sites provide information that is updated more frequently. One popular site is bloomberg.com. The Bloomberg company was founded in 1981 by Michael Bloomberg (more recently mayor of New York City). Its Web site reports prices for many types of U.S. and foreign stocks and bonds. It also reports prices of shares in leading mutual funds.

Panel (a) of Figure 17-2 presents a page from the Bloomberg site, one that covers the 30 stocks in the Dow Jones index. During the trading day, this page is updated about every 20 minutes. It reports the price of each stock, the change in the price since the start of the day, and the number of shares traded. Clicking on a company symbol leads to more detailed information on the company, including past movements in its stock price, the price–earnings ratio, and dividend payments. Panel (b) shows this information for Boeing.

Each day the prices of some stocks rise and others fall. The overall behavior of stock prices is measured by **stock market indexes**, which average the prices for a group of stocks.

The Dow Jones is the oldest and most famous stock index. However, because the Dow covers only 30 stocks, it may not capture the movements of the whole market. The Standard & Poor's (S&P) 500 index is better for this purpose because it covers the 500 largest U.S. companies. The Wilshire 5000 index is even broader. The NASDAQ index covers all the companies that are traded in that market and is influenced strongly by the prices of tech stocks.

Web sites such as bloomberg.com provide data on a variety of stock market indexes. In Figure 17-2(a), information on the Dow appears above the prices of individual stocks. The Bloomberg site also provides indexes for sectors of the economy, such as transportation and utilities, and indexes for foreign stocks.

17-3 Capital Structure: What Securities Should Firms Issue?

So far we've discussed the mechanics of securities trading. Now we turn to the behavior of market participants—their decisions about which securities to sell and buy. We start with firms' decisions about issuing new securities.

The basic reason that firms issue securities is to raise funds for investment. A firm can raise funds by issuing either stocks or bonds. How does it choose between the two?

The mix of stocks and bonds that a firm issues is called its **capital structure**. Economists have long debated which capital structure is best. Let's discuss some of the key ideas in this debate.

FIGURE 17-2

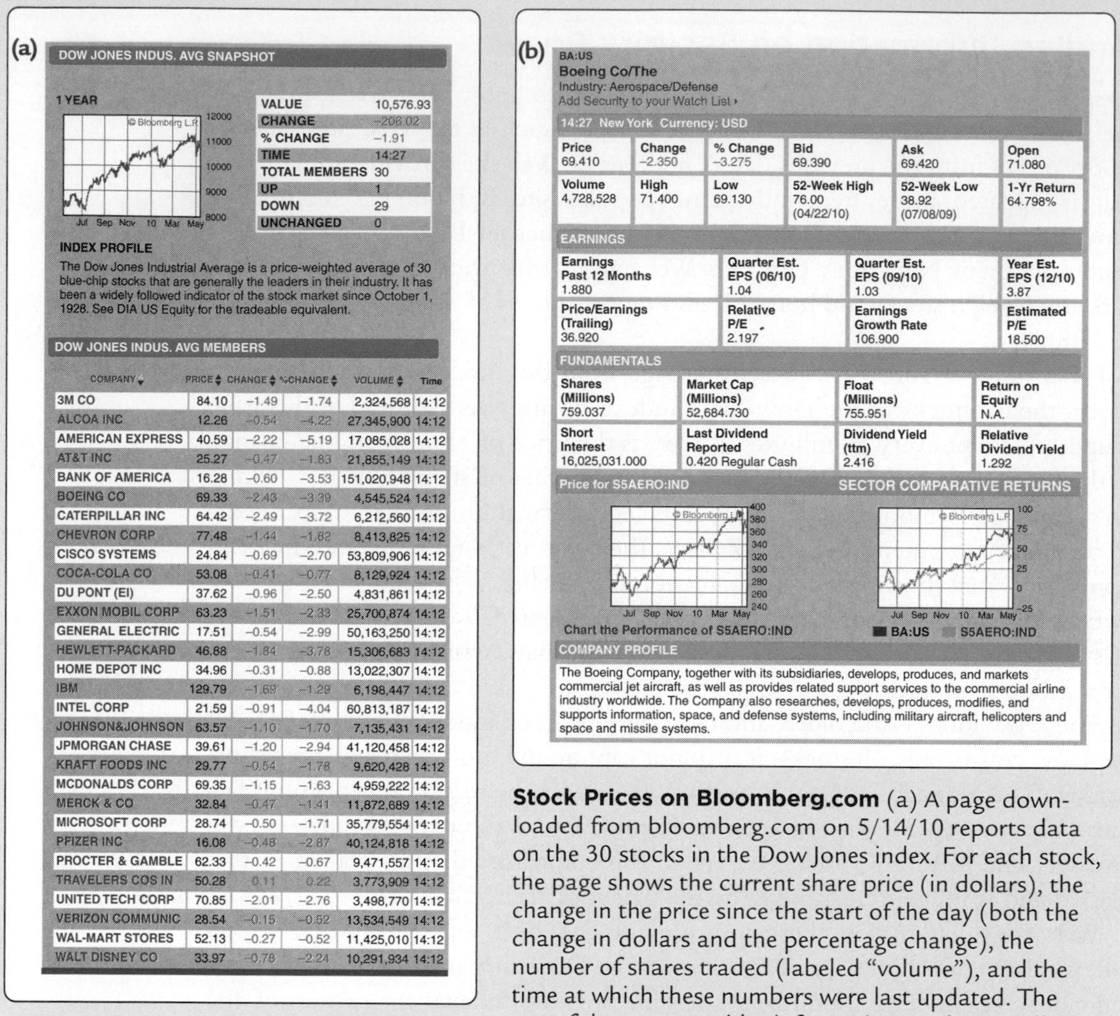

(a)

DOW JONES INDUS. AVG SNAPSHOT

1 YEAR
© Bloomberg L.P.

VALUE	10,576.93
CHANGE	−206.02
% CHANGE	−1.91
TIME	14:27
TOTAL MEMBERS	30
UP	1
DOWN	29
UNCHANGED	0

INDEX PROFILE

The Dow Jones Industrial Average is a price-weighted average of 30 blue-chip stocks that are generally the leaders in their industry. It has been a widely followed indicator of the stock market since October 1, 1928. See DIA US Equity for the tradeable equivalent.

DOW JONES INDUS. AVG MEMBERS

COMPANY	PRICE	CHANGE	%CHANGE	VOLUME	Time
3M CO	84.10	−1.49	−1.74	2,324,568	14:12
ALCOA INC	12.26	−0.54	−4.22	27,345,900	14:12
AMERICAN EXPRESS	40.59	−2.22	−5.19	17,085,028	14:12
AT&T INC	25.27	−0.47	−1.83	21,855,149	14:12
BANK OF AMERICA	16.28	−0.60	−3.53	151,020,948	14:12
BOEING CO	69.33	−2.43	−3.39	4,545,524	14:12
CATERPILLAR INC	64.42	−2.49	−3.72	6,212,560	14:12
CHEVRON CORP	77.48	−1.44	−1.82	8,413,825	14:12
CISCO SYSTEMS	24.84	−0.69	−2.70	53,809,906	14:12
COCA-COLA CO	53.08	−0.41	−0.77	8,129,924	14:12
DU PONT (EI)	37.62	−0.96	−2.50	4,831,861	14:12
EXXON MOBIL CORP	63.23	−1.51	−2.33	25,700,874	14:12
GENERAL ELECTRIC	17.51	−0.54	−2.99	50,163,250	14:12
HEWLETT-PACKARD	46.88	−1.84	−3.78	15,306,683	14:12
HOME DEPOT INC	34.96	−0.31	−0.88	13,022,307	14:12
IBM	129.79	−1.69	−1.29	6,198,447	14:12
INTEL CORP	21.59	−0.91	−4.04	60,813,187	14:12
JOHNSON&JOHNSON	63.57	−1.10	−1.70	7,135,431	14:12
JPMORGAN CHASE	39.61	−1.20	−2.94	41,120,458	14:12
KRAFT FOODS INC	29.77	−0.54	−1.78	9,620,428	14:12
MCDONALDS CORP	69.35	−1.15	−1.63	4,959,222	14:12
MERCK & CO	32.84	−0.47	−1.41	11,872,689	14:12
MICROSOFT CORP	28.74	−0.50	−1.71	35,779,554	14:12
PFIZER INC	16.08	−0.48	−2.87	40,124,818	14:12
PROCTER & GAMBLE	62.33	−0.42	−0.67	9,471,557	14:12
TRAVELERS COS IN	50.28	0.11	0.22	3,773,909	14:12
UNITED TECH CORP	70.85	−2.01	−2.76	3,498,770	14:12
VERIZON COMMUNIC	28.54	−0.15	−0.52	13,534,549	14:12
WAL-MART STORES	52.13	−0.27	−0.52	11,425,010	14:12
WALT DISNEY CO	33.97	−0.78	−2.24	10,291,934	14:12

(b)

BA:US
Boeing Co/The
Industry: Aerospace/Defense
Add Security to your Watch List ›

14:27 New York Currency: USD

Price	Change	% Change	Bid	Ask	Open
69.410	−2.350	−3.275	69.390	69.420	71.080

Volume	High	Low	52-Week High	52-Week Low	1-Yr Return
4,728,528	71.400	69.130	76.00 (04/22/10)	38.92 (07/08/09)	64.798%

EARNINGS

Earnings Past 12 Months	Quarter Est. EPS (06/10)	Quarter Est. EPS (09/10)	Year Est. EPS (12/10)
1.880	1.04	1.03	3.87

Price/Earnings (Trailing)	Relative P/E	Earnings Growth Rate	Estimated P/E
36.920	2.197	106.900	18.500

FUNDAMENTALS

Shares (Millions)	Market Cap (Millions)	Float (Millions)	Return on Equity
759.037	52,684.730	755.951	N.A.

Short Interest	Last Dividend Reported	Dividend Yield (ttm)	Relative Dividend Yield
16,025,031.000	0.420 Regular Cash	2.416	1.292

Price for S5AERO:IND
© Bloomberg L.P.

SECTOR COMPARATIVE RETURNS
© Bloomberg L.P.

Chart the Performance of S5AERO:IND   ■ BA:US   ■ S5AERO:IND

COMPANY PROFILE

The Boeing Company, together with its subsidiaries, develops, produces, and markets commercial jet aircraft, as well as provides related support services to the commercial airline industry worldwide. The Company also researches, develops, produces, modifies, and supports information, space, and defense systems, including military aircraft, helicopters and space and missile systems.

Stock Prices on Bloomberg.com (a) A page downloaded from bloomberg.com on 5/14/10 reports data on the 30 stocks in the Dow Jones index. For each stock, the page shows the current share price (in dollars), the change in the price since the start of the day (both the change in dollars and the percentage change), the number of shares traded (labeled "volume"), and the time at which these numbers were last updated. The top of the page provides information on the overall Dow index. (b) Clicking on "BOEING CO" leads to a page that gives detailed information on Boeing, including past movements in the stock price, the price–earnings ratio, and dividends.

Is Capital Structure Irrelevant?

The starting point for analyzing capital structure is the **Modigliani–Miller theorem (M and M theorem)**. This idea was proposed in 1958 by Franco Modigliani and Merton Miller, who both won the Nobel Prize in economics. Their view of capital structure is simple: capital structure doesn't matter. Stocks and bonds are equally good ways for firms to raise funds.

In making their argument, Modigliani and Miller assume that firms operate for the benefit of their stockholders. Stockholders give something up when a firm issues securities. If the firm issues new stock, current stockholders lose part of their ownership of the firm and receive smaller shares of the firm's future earnings. If the firm issues bonds, stockholders retain full ownership, but part of their earnings goes to interest payments. When firms issue securities, Modigliani and Miller argue, they should choose the type that minimizes the costs to current stockholders.

To determine these costs, Modigliani and Miller use the classical theory of asset prices. As we learned in Chapter 16, the classical theory says that the price of any security, whether a stock or a bond, equals the present value of expected income from the security.

The classical theory leads quickly to the conclusion that capital structure doesn't matter. Suppose a firm sells a share of new stock for $100. The present value of expected earnings that the buyer receives—and current stockholders give up—is $100. If the firm sells a bond for $100, the future payments again have a present value of $100. Either way, it costs $100 in present value to raise $100. Stocks and bonds are equally good deals for their issuers.

Why Capital Structure Does Matter

The M and M theorem implies that firms shouldn't care which securities they issue. However, few people take this idea literally. The theorem ignores several practical differences between stocks and bonds. Some of these factors encourage firms to issue stocks, and some favor bonds. As a result, most firms issue a mixture of the two.

Taxes Corporations pay taxes on their profits at rates up to 35 percent. In computing profits, corporations can deduct interest payments on bonds. Therefore, the more bonds a firm issues, the lower its taxes. In contrast, issuing stock does not affect corporate taxes.

These tax rules change the relative costs of securities. Ignoring taxes, the M and M theorem says it is equally costly to issue stocks and bonds. But the costs of issuing bonds are partly offset by their tax benefits, making them a cheaper way to raise funds.

Bankruptcy While issuing bonds has tax benefits, it also has a disadvantage: the risk of bankruptcy. When a firm sells bonds, it promises certain payments to bondholders. If the firm's earnings are low, it may not be able to make the payments. If it does not make the payments, it defaults, leading to bankruptcy. The more bonds a firm issues, the greater this risk.

Bankruptcy is costly. It triggers a legal process that requires expensive lawyers and accountants. Sometimes a bankrupt firm is forced to shut down, eliminating opportunities for future profits. Sometimes the firm continues to operate and eventually emerges from bankruptcy, but only after its business has been disrupted.

Firms can reduce bankruptcy risk by issuing stocks rather than bonds. If a firm's earnings are low, then stockholders receive low returns. The stockholders are disappointed, but the firm has not defaulted. Stocks don't require payments that the firm might have trouble making.

Adverse Selection As we discussed earlier, savers fear that firms will try to sell securities for more than their true value. This adverse selection problem affects capital structure because it is more severe for stocks than for bonds.

To see why, remember that adverse selection is caused by asymmetric information: buyers of securities know less than sellers. This asymmetry may be small when firms issue bonds. Buyers know exactly how much a bond pays as long as the issuer doesn't default, and they may know that default is unlikely. In contrast, stock purchasers are always uncertain about how much they will earn, and this uncertainty makes them worry about adverse selection.

The consequence is that some firms can issue bonds more easily than stock. To sell stock to nervous savers, these firms would have to accept low prices—less than the stock is really worth. In addition to the tax advantages, then, adverse selection is another reason to issue bonds.

Debt Maturity

So far, we've focused on the choice between stocks and bonds. When firms issue bonds, they must also choose the bonds' maturity. Firms can issue long-term bonds, which typically have maturities of 5 or 10 years, or commercial paper, with maturities under a year.

Generally, firms choose bond maturities based on their ability to pay off the bonds. A long-term investment project, such as a new factory, takes years to produce revenue. Firms finance these projects with long-term bonds, which they can pay off after revenue starts coming in.

Firms issue commercial paper when they need to borrow for short periods. This need often arises from the time lag between production and sales. For example, a swimwear company might produce bathing suits in the winter and sell them in the spring. It can issue three-month commercial paper to cover its winter production costs until it receives revenue in the spring.

17-4 Asset Allocation: What Assets Should Savers Hold?

We now turn from the issuers of securities to the buyers. Savers and institutions must choose their asset allocation, that is, how they split their wealth among different types of assets. We discuss the main factors in these decisions, focusing on the choice between stocks and bonds. We also touch on bank deposits, another asset held by savers.

The Risk–Return Tradeoff

Our discussion of stocks and bonds builds on Chapter 16's discussion of the rates of return on these securities. We saw that stocks have a higher average return over time. From 1900 through 2009, the nominal rate of return averaged about 11 percent for U.S. stocks and 5 percent for Treasury bonds. We can find average *real* returns by subtracting the inflation rate, which averaged 3 percent over the period 1900–2009, from the nominal rates. The real rate of return averaged 8 percent for stocks and 2 percent for bonds.

We also learned that stock returns are more volatile than bond returns: a saver can earn a lot on stocks, but she can also lose a lot. In 17 of the 110 years from 1900 through 2009, for example, nominal stock returns were less than −10 percent. In 2 years, 1932 and 2008, returns were near −40 percent. In contrast, returns on Treasury bonds have never been less than −10 percent.

When a saver chooses between stocks and bonds, she chooses between average return and safety. The choice is not all-or-nothing, however. The saver can split her wealth between the two assets, seeking a high return on part of it and keeping the rest safe. A key decision is the fraction of wealth to put into stocks. Raising this fraction raises the average return on total assets, but it also increases risk.

Calculating the Tradeoff Suppose that bonds have a real return of 2 percent (the actual average since 1900). Assume that this return is constant, so bonds are safe assets. (In reality, bond returns vary somewhat, but we assume this variation is small enough to ignore.) Stocks, by contrast, have variable returns. Assume that half the time the real return is 22 percent, and half the time it is −6 percent. The average return on stocks is

$$\frac{1}{2}[22\% + (-6\%)] = 8\%.$$

This average exceeds the return on bonds, but stocks are risky.

You have some wealth, say $100, to split between stocks and bonds. We'll use the letter s to denote the fraction of wealth you put in stocks. The fraction in bonds is $1 - s$. If $s = 0.6$, for example, you put $60 in stocks and $40 in bonds. The overall return on your wealth is a weighted average of stock and bond returns with weights of s and $1 - s$. That is,

$$\text{Return on Wealth} = s(\text{Return on Stocks})$$
$$+ (1 - s)(\text{Return on Bonds}).$$

As long as you hold some stock (s is positive), the return on your wealth is variable. If stock returns are high (22 percent), the return on your wealth is

$$\text{Return} = s(22\%) + (1 - s)(2\%)$$
$$= s(22\%) + 2\% - s(2\%)$$
$$= 2\% + s(20\%).$$

If stock returns are low (−6 percent), the return on your wealth is

$$\text{Return} = s(-6\%) + (1 - s)(2\%)$$
$$= s(-6\%) + 2\% - s(2\%)$$
$$= 2\% - s(8\%).$$

Using the last two formulas, we can see how the choice of s, the fraction of wealth in stock, affects your average return and risk. Given that high and low stock returns occur with equal probability, the average return on your wealth is

$$\text{Average Return} = \frac{1}{2}[2\% + s(20\%)] + \frac{1}{2}[2\% - s(8\%)]$$

$$= 1\% + s(10\%) + 1\% - s(4\%)$$

$$= 2\% + s(6\%).$$

The last line shows that a rise in s raises your average return.

Risk can be measured in several ways, but we will use one simple measure: the difference between the overall return on your wealth when stock returns are high and the overall return when stock returns are low. This difference shows how much your wealth can vary:

$$\text{Difference Between High and Low Returns on Wealth}$$

$$= [2\% + s(20\%)] - [2\% - s(8\%)]$$

$$= s(28\%).$$

A rise in the fraction s raises this measure of risk.[1]

Figure 17-3 shows the tradeoff you face in this example. It shows the risk and average return that result from different levels of stock ownership s. If $s = 0$ (you buy no stock), your average return is only 2 percent, but you face no risk. Both risk and return rise as s rises, reaching their highest levels at $s = 1$ (you buy only stock).

Saving in a Bank Account Buying stocks and bonds isn't the only way to save. Many people deposit some or all their wealth in bank accounts. What role do bank accounts play in asset allocation?

For present purposes, the answer is that bank accounts are similar to bonds. Bank accounts produce lower average earnings than stocks, but they are safe. In the example we just discussed, you can think of your holdings of "bonds" as your total safe assets, including bonds and bank accounts. Your key decision is how to split your wealth between these safe assets and risky stock.

Choosing the Mix

How should you respond to the risk–return tradeoff? Should you put a large fraction of your wealth in stock, accepting risk to seek high returns? Or should you play it safe and put most of your wealth in bonds and bank accounts?

These questions do not have absolute answers. The right asset allocation depends partly on personal preferences about risk. Some people are highly *risk averse:* they worry a lot about worst-case scenarios and find it painful to lose

---

[1] Economists often use another measure of risk, the standard deviation of returns. You know what this means if you have studied statistics. In our example, the standard deviation of the return on wealth is $s(14\%)$. An increase in s raises this standard deviation, as well as raising the difference in returns that we use to measure risk.

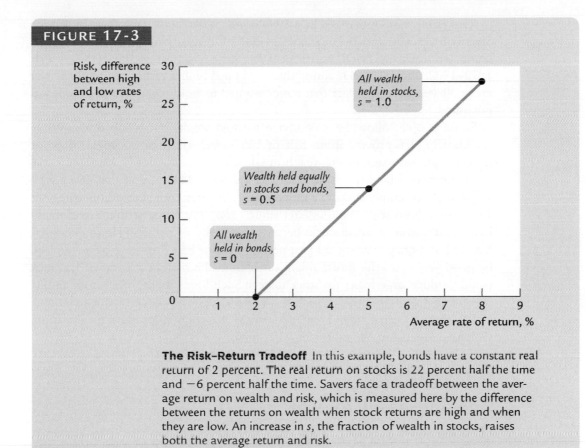

FIGURE 17-3

Risk, difference between high and low rates of return, %

All wealth held in stocks, s = 1.0

Wealth held equally in stocks and bonds, s = 0.5

All wealth held in bonds, s = 0

Average rate of return, %

The Risk–Return Tradeoff In this example, bonds have a constant real return of 2 percent. The real return on stocks is 22 percent half the time and −6 percent half the time. Savers face a tradeoff between the average return on wealth and risk, which is measured here by the difference between the returns on wealth when stock returns are high and when they are low. An increase in s, the fraction of wealth in stocks, raises both the average return and risk.

money. These individuals should hold most of their wealth in safe assets and accept low returns to avoid risk. Individuals who can better tolerate risk should put most of their wealth in stocks.

Despite this role for personal preference, most economists think that a typical individual—someone with an average level of risk aversion—should hold more stocks than bonds. Financial planners who advise savers say the same thing. A common rule of thumb is that savers should hold two-thirds of their wealth in stocks and one-third in bonds. Some advisers say the share in stocks should be even higher than two-thirds.

Two basic factors underlie this advice. First, historically, average returns are not just higher for stocks than for bonds, but *much* higher. Over long periods, the differences in returns add up. If you put $100 in bonds and they produce their average real return of 2 percent, your wealth grows to $181 in 30 years. If you put $100 in stocks and they earn 8 percent, you end up with $1006.

Second, stocks are not really as risky as they first appear. We've seen that the returns on stock vary greatly from year to year. However, these fluctuations tend to average out over time, as good years offset bad years. People who hold stock for long periods, say 20 or 30 years, are likely to do well overall.

This point was popularized by a 1994 book, *Stocks for the Long Run,* by Jeremy Siegel of the Wharton Business School at the University of Pennsylvania. Siegel compared stock and bond returns over 30-year periods since 1871 (1871–1901, 1872–1902, and so on). He found that stocks had higher returns than bonds over every 30-year period, a fact that has continued to hold true since the book was published.

Some people follow Siegel's advice to hold stock, but many don't. While stockholding has grown, about half of U.S. savers still own no stock. Many of these people have significant wealth in safe assets.

Economists debate the reasons for this behavior. Many think that savers who avoid stock are simply making a mistake, that they don't understand the true risks and returns from stock holding. Yet some economists suggest that savers might have good reasons to avoid stocks because they really *are* risky. So far, stockholders haven't lost money over any 30-year period, because bad years have been followed by good years. But the future might differ from the past, and a run of bad luck could produce large losses for stockholders. Such losses might result from an unprecedented national disaster, such as a war that destroys much of the economy.[2]

Economists' usual advice to hold stocks has one important qualification, which we discuss in the following case study.

CASE STUDY

Age and Asset Allocation

Economists such as Jeremy Siegel argue that stocks are not very risky. However, the risks from stockholding grow with age, so older people should hold less stock than younger people.

Recall Siegel's point: stocks are safe because high and low returns average out over time. This argument applies to people who hold stocks for long periods. An older person has a shorter saving horizon: he is likely to start selling his assets soon to finance retirement. If this person holds stock, a few bad years can reduce his wealth significantly, and he won't have a chance to recoup these losses.

Another difference between young and old savers is that the young expect more future income from working. This prospect reduces the risk of holding stock. To see this point, suppose a 30-year-old puts all his savings in stock and the market crashes. Even if this person's wealth is wiped out, this event is not a disaster. The 30-year-old has several decades to earn money, rebuild his savings, and finance his retirement. In contrast, a current retiree who loses his wealth is in trouble, because he has no future earnings.

For these reasons, financial advisers tell savers to change their asset allocation as they age. You should start by holding mostly stock and then shift gradually toward bonds. One rule of thumb is that the percentage of your wealth in stocks should be at least 100 minus your age—at least 70 percent at age 30, 60 percent at age 40, and so on. ∎

---

[2] This idea is discussed by Robert Barro of Harvard University in "Rare Disasters and Asset Markets in the Twentieth Century," *Quarterly Journal of Economics* 121 (August 2006): 823-866.

17-5 Which Stocks?

So far, we have discussed the allocation of wealth among broad asset classes such as stocks and bonds. A saver must also choose specific assets within each class. We now consider this decision, focusing on the choice among stocks issued by different companies.

In Chapter 15 we saw that savers need to diversify the assets that they hold. Holding too much of one company's stock can be disastrous, as we saw in the case study "The Perils of Employee Stock Ownership." To reduce risk, savers should split the wealth they allocate to stock among a sizable number of stocks. One way to do this is to buy shares in a mutual fund.

By itself, the principle of diversification does not pin down which stocks to buy. A saver can achieve diversification with around 30 or 40 stocks; with that many, one company's misfortune can't hurt too much. Thousands of companies issue stock, so the possible combinations of 30 or 40 are vast. Someone—either the saver or a mutual fund manager—must choose which stocks to buy. Here we discuss some of economists' leading ideas about stock picking.

The Efficient Markets Hypothesis

Suppose you graduate from college and get a job at a mutual fund. Your boss asks you to recommend stocks for the fund to purchase. With little experience, you're not sure what to suggest. Fortunately, you remember a friendly finance professor. You decide to consult her, figuring that a finance professor must know how to pick stocks.

You may be surprised at the professor's advice. She is likely to tell you that it doesn't matter which stocks you pick. Rather than sweating over your decision, you can choose stocks randomly. Write the names of companies on pieces of paper, put them in a hat, close your eyes, and pull out your selections.

Is your professor joking? No, her advice is sincere, because she believes the **efficient markets hypothesis**. The efficient markets hypothesis says that no stock is a better buy than any other, a conclusion that justifies random choices. The efficient markets hypothesis is a central tenet of finance theory.

The efficient markets hypothesis follows from another finance principle, the classical theory of asset prices, which we learned about in Chapter 16. To see the connection, think about how you would choose stocks if you *didn't* draw names from a hat. You would look for good deals—stocks that are worth a lot relative to their prices. Recall from Chapter 16 that a stock's worth is the present value of expected dividends, so you should buy stocks with prices below this present value. In Wall Street lingo, you should buy stocks that are **undervalued assets**.

But the classical theory of asset prices says that a stock price always equals the present value of expected dividends and that expected dividends are the best possible forecasts (due to rational expectations). Thus, according to the classical theory, the price of a stock always equals the best estimate of the stock's value. This equality implies that there are no undervalued stocks.

Prices Follow Random Walks To understand the efficient markets hypothesis another way, let's think about movements in stock prices. When you pick stocks, you might try to forecast future price changes. If you can identify stocks with prices that are likely to rise, you can buy these stocks and earn capital gains when the price increases occur. If your forecasts are correct, your returns will exceed those on a random selection of stocks.

Once again, however, the efficient markets hypothesis says your strategy won't work. A stock price reflects expectations of a firm's dividends based on all available information. The price changes when expectations change in response to new information. For this information to change expectations and price, it must be a surprise—say, an announcement that the firm's recent earnings were higher than anticipated. If the information were known in advance, it would already be accounted for in expected dividends.

By definition, you can't predict surprises. Since only surprise information affects stock prices, changes in these prices are unpredictable. In statistical language, each price follows a **random walk**. You never know which prices are likely to rise, so once again stock picking is futile.

The Critique of Stock Picking The efficient markets hypothesis is controversial. It is popular among finance professors, but there are many doubters at securities firms. Analysts for mutual funds and brokers think they can do what the efficient markets hypothesis says is impossible: identify undervalued stocks.

The dividends a company can pay depend on its earnings. In looking for undervalued stocks, analysts produce forecasts of future earnings. These forecasts are based on many factors: companies' past performances, their current investment projects, competition in their industries, and so on. When forecasts for a company's earnings are high compared to its stock price, analysts recommend the stock. The securities firms they work for buy the stock and/or recommend it to clients.

Thousands of firms perform this analysis, and they put considerable resources into it. They pay high salaries to attract talented, hardworking analysts who gather lots of data and use sophisticated statistical techniques. They monitor companies continuously, so their forecasts always take into account the latest news.

Analysts argue that this effort pays off with good stock picks. But supporters of the efficient-markets hypothesis disagree, pointing out that the analysts' research and the resulting stock trades are actually forces that make the market efficient.

We can best see this point with an example. Assume that, initially, the price of Boeing stock equals the present value of expected dividends. The stock is neither under- nor overvalued. Then Boeing announces some good news: United Airlines has ordered 50 new planes. Analysts who follow Boeing read its news release and realize that the order will raise the company's earnings. Higher earnings will lead to higher dividends, so Boeing becomes undervalued at its current price. The analysts tell their firms to buy the stock.

This scenario plays out at many firms, creating a surge in demand for Boeing stock. High demand causes the stock price to rise and quickly reach a level that equals the new present value of dividends, which incorporates the news about the United order. At this point, Boeing is no longer undervalued. The analysts' efforts to identify an undervalued stock have caused the undervaluation to disappear.

Choosing Between Two Kinds of Mutual Funds

The efficient markets hypothesis is relevant to a decision facing many savers, the choice among stock mutual funds. There are two types of funds. An **actively managed fund** employs analysts who do the kind of research on companies that we have discussed. These funds buy and sell stocks frequently based on the analysts' recommendations.

In contrast, an **index fund** doesn't try to pick stocks. Instead, it buys *all* the stocks in a broad market index, such as the S&P 500. An index fund doesn't hire analysts to study companies—someone just looks up which stocks are in the index. The fund buys these stocks and then holds onto them, so it doesn't trade as often as an actively managed fund.

If you believe the efficient markets hypothesis, you should prefer index funds. The efficient markets hypothesis says that stocks picked by analysts will do no better, on average, than an index. And actively managed funds have the disadvantage of high fees. To pay analysts and traders, the funds usually charge shareholders 1 percent or more of their assets each year. Many index funds charge around a quarter of a percent. Once fees are deducted, returns are likely to be higher for index funds than for actively managed funds.

Many economists have examined returns on mutual funds. Generally, their data support the view that index funds produce higher returns, on average, than actively managed funds. This finding suggests that the efficient markets hypothesis has a large element of truth.

For example, about 1,300 actively managed stock funds operated over the decade 1995–2005. Averaging these funds together, the rate of return was 8.2 percent. Over the same period, the return on the S&P 500 was 10.0 percent. Of the actively managed mutual funds, 15 percent had a higher return than the S&P 500, and 85 percent had a lower return.

Notice that *some* funds beat the S&P index. What accounts for this success? There are two possible answers. One is that the managers of successful funds—the top 15 percent—are unusually talented. They can identify undervalued stocks even though the average manager can't. Given this interpretation, it might make sense to buy shares in actively managed funds if you can figure out which funds have the best managers.

Believers in the efficient markets hypothesis have a different view: successful fund managers are lucky. Different funds buy different sets of stocks. There is no good reason to prefer one portfolio to another. Nonetheless, over any period, news about companies will cause some stocks to perform better than others. Mutual funds that happen to own these stocks will have above-average returns.

According to this view, it's impossible to predict which mutual funds will beat a market index. You can see which funds have done so in the past. But since these funds were just lucky, there is no reason to think their success will continue. You should reject all managed funds and put your wealth in a low-cost index fund.

Once again, research supports the predictions of the efficient markets hypothesis. A number of studies have examined mutual funds with above-average returns over periods of one to five years. The studies ask whether these funds beat an index in subsequent years—and generally find that they don't.

Can *Anyone* Beat the Market?

Some economists interpret the efficient markets hypothesis as an absolute law: anyone who tries to beat a stock market index is wasting his time. Yet other economists have a less extreme view. They think that beating the market is difficult but not impossible, because exceptions to market efficiency exist. In any case, people keep trying to beat the market—to succeed where the average mutual fund fails. Many would-be market beaters fall into one of three categories, which we now discuss.

Fast Traders One strategy for beating the market relies on speed. To understand this approach, recall the logic behind the efficient markets hypothesis. If there is good news about a company, demand rises for the company's stock. Higher demand pushes the stock price to a level that reflects current expectations about earnings and dividends.

The efficient markets hypothesis assumes that stock prices respond instantly to news, but in reality, price adjustment takes a little time. For example, suppose there is good news about a NASDAQ stock. This news prompts buy orders to dealers who trade the stock. These dealers see decreases in their inventories, realize that demand has risen, and raise their ask prices for the stock.

This process may not take long. Dealers can respond to demand shifts within minutes or even seconds. But there is a brief period before a stock price adjusts to news when the stock is undervalued. Traders can profit from this undervaluation if they get their orders in quickly.

Many investment banks have departments that specialize in fast trading. Much of the work is done by powerful computers rather than by humans. The computers are programmed to react to news that will affect security prices, such as announcements of economic statistics. When triggered by such news, some computers can buy or sell securities within 3 milliseconds (0.003 second).

Behaviorists Fast trading exploits brief deviations from market efficiency. Another strategy is based on the view that inefficiencies persist, making some stocks undervalued for long periods. People who identify these stocks can beat the market even if they aren't especially fast. This view is held by believers in **behavioral finance**.

Recall that stock prices depend on expectations about companies' future earnings and dividends. The efficient markets hypothesis assumes rational expectations: people who forecast earnings, such as stock analysts, do as well as they can given their information. Behaviorists dispute this assumption. They argue that forecasters regularly make certain kinds of mistakes that lead to over- or undervaluation of stocks.

One mistake stressed by behaviorists is that forecasts made by stock analysts are overly "anchored": analysts form opinions about companies and then are reluctant to change them. If analysts have predicted that a company will do badly, they resist evidence to the contrary. If the company reports good news, analysts grudgingly raise their earnings forecasts, but not by as much as they should. With earnings forecasts too low, the company's stock is undervalued.

Some hedge funds use behavioral theories to try to identify undervalued stocks and beat the market. These funds are fairly new, so we can't yet judge their success. Some behavioral funds have performed well in recent years, but we need more data to tell whether this record reflects good strategies or good luck.

Geniuses? Many stock pickers are neither fast traders nor behaviorists. They just study companies, forecast earnings, and decide which stocks are undervalued. We have seen that most people who follow this approach can't beat the market. But maybe a few can.

In recent history, a handful of stock pickers have gained notoriety for beating the market repeatedly. One is Peter Lynch, who ran Fidelity's Magellan Fund from 1978 to 1990. Magellan's average return during this period was 29 percent. Also famous is William Miller of Legg Mason, whose fund beat the S&P 500 for 15 straight years, from 1991 through 2005.

Hard-core believers in the efficient markets hypothesis say that Lynch and Miller were lucky. If so, they were *very, very* lucky for a long time. The efficient markets hypothesis implies that a mutual fund has no better than a 1/2 probability of beating an index each year. The probability of winning 15 years in a row is at most $(1/2)^{15} = 0.00003$. Many observers doubt that anyone beats these odds through luck alone. They conclude that people such as Lynch and Miller really can pick stocks.

How do they do it? Efficient markets supporters stress that everyone has the same information about companies. Lynch and Miller read the same annual reports as other mutual fund managers and receive the same news releases. But perhaps some people have unusual skill in *interpreting* information. If a company creates a new product, for example, everyone hears about it. But a few geniuses have special insights about the product's likely success. They can forecast earnings better than the rest of the market.

When people name the best stock pickers, Peter Lynch and William Miller are often on the list. But one man is always at the top: Warren Buffett.

CASE STUDY

The Oracle of Omaha

Warren Buffett was born in Omaha, Nebraska in 1930, the son of a stockbroker. He earned a master's degree in economics and then worked in New York for Benjamin Graham, a famous stock picker of the 1940s and 1950s. In 1957, Buffett returned to Omaha and started a fund, Buffett Partnership Ltd. Its initial wealth was $105,000 from family and friends plus $100 of Buffett's own money. Buffett bought stocks through this company and a successor, Berkshire Hathaway.

The rest is history. From 1964 through 2009, the return on Berkshire Hathaway stock averaged 20.3 percent, compared to 9.3 percent for the S&P 500. If you had put $10,000 in an S&P index fund in 1964, you would have had about

$540,000 in 2009. If you had put $10,000 in Berkshire Hathaway in the same year, you would have had $43 million in 2009.

As of 2009, Buffett owned about 30 percent of Berkshire Hathaway's stock. His total wealth was $40 billion, making him the world's second-richest person (Bill Gates had $50 billion). Despite his success, Buffett still lives in a house that he bought for $32,000 in 1957, and, at age 79, he still runs Berkshire Hathaway full time.

How does Buffett pick stocks? He says he buys "great companies" with high earnings potential. In looking for such companies, Buffett "sticks with businesses we think we understand. That means they must be relatively simple and stable in character." This principle leads Buffett to avoid tech companies, such as Microsoft, whose businesses change rapidly.

Buffett assigns great weight to the quality of companies' managers. He looks for people who are smart and dedicated to making money for shareholders. He is leery of "empire builders"—managers who maximize their companies' size rather than profits. Buffett likes to meet managers personally to judge their abilities.

Over the years, Berkshire Hathaway has purchased large stakes in many companies, including the *Washington Post* (in 1973), GEICO (1976), Coca-Cola (1988), and Gillette (1989). Most of these acquisitions have proved profitable. For example, Coca-Cola's stock price in 1988 was $11. The company's recent earnings had been mediocre, and analysts predicted that its business would stagnate. Buffett realized that Coke had untapped potential for expanding overseas, using its world-famous brand name. After he bought the company's stock, Coke did expand overseas, and other analysts raised their earnings forecasts. By 1993, Coca-Cola's stock price was $75.

Buffett's reputation for brilliance grew during the recent financial crisis. Berkshire Hathaway's stock fell 10 percent in 2008, but that was much better than the 37 percent fall in the S&P 500. In September 2008, at the height of the crisis, Berkshire Hathaway bought $5 billion in Goldman Sachs stock. As the crisis diminished over 2009, Goldman's stock rose and Buffett earned large profits.

In November 2009, Berkshire Hathaway made the largest acquisition in its history: it purchased Burlington Northern railroad for $34 billion. This deal reflected Buffett's preference for traditional, stable industries. Buffett also knew Burlington Northern well, because Berkshire had owned 23 percent of the company since 2006.

In explaining the 2009 purchase, Buffett said he expected the demand for freight-train service to rise as the economy grew and high oil prices made trucking more expensive. It's too early to judge the success of the Burlington deal, but Buffett's record suggests that, once again, he was quicker than others to recognize a company's potential. ■

17-6 Derivatives

So far, this chapter has emphasized two kinds of securities, stocks and bonds. We now turn to another, more recently developed asset called a **derivative**. The payoffs from this security are tied to the prices of other assets; that is, the value of the security is "derived" from the other assets. Common types of derivatives include futures, options, and credit default swaps.

We first define these types of derivatives and describe how they are traded; then we discuss their uses. As you will see, some savers and financial institutions use derivatives to reduce risk, while others use them to make risky bets on asset prices.

Futures

A **futures contract** is an agreement to trade an asset for a certain price at a future point in time, the *delivery date*. One party agrees to sell the asset and another agrees to buy. The oldest futures contracts are those for agricultural products, such as grain and cotton. Farmers have traded these contracts for centuries. Futures also exist for nonagricultural commodities, such as oil and natural gas, and for securities, such as bonds and stocks.

Trading futures can produce either gains or losses. Generally, one side of a contract earns money at the expense of the other. Who wins depends on the price in the futures contract and the current price of the asset on the delivery date.

Let's consider an example. On January 1, 2020, Jack sells a futures contract for a Treasury bond to Jill. Jack promises to deliver the bond on July 1, and Jill promises to pay $100 on that date. When July 1 arrives, it turns out that Treasury bonds are trading for $110. Jill is in luck. She pays Jack the $100 they agreed on six months earlier, receives a bond, and can resell it for the current price of $110. These transactions yield Jill a profit of $10. Jack, on the other hand, receives only $100 for a bond worth $110. He loses $10.

Now let's change the story. Jack and Jill make the same deal on January 1, but the price of Treasury bonds on July 1 is $90. In this case, Jack wins: he receives $100 for a bond worth $90, gaining $10. Jill pays $100 for a $90 bond, losing $10.

Futures are traded on exchanges such as the Chicago Board of Trade and the Chicago Mercantile Exchange. People who want to trade hire brokers who work at the exchanges. A broker whose client wants to sell a certain contract looks for a broker whose client wants to buy. When the brokers meet, they arrange a trade.

When a trade occurs, both buyer and seller must post deposits with the futures exchange. These deposits are called *margins*. The purpose is to ensure that both parties fulfill their contract on the delivery day. A typical margin is 10 percent of the futures price. On January 1, when Jack and Jill trade a $100 bond future, each must deposit $10 with the exchange.

Options

A futures contract requires a transaction at the delivery date. An **option**, as the name suggests, may or may not produce a later transaction. If Jack sells Jill an option, she gains the right to trade a security with him—but not an obligation. Jill pays Jack a fee to receive the option.

A **call option** allows its owner to *buy* a security at a certain price, called the *strike price*. The option holder can make this purchase at any point before the option's expiration date, which is set in the contract. If he buys the security, he is said to *exercise* the option. A **put option** allows its owner to *sell* a security. Like a call option, it specifies a strike price and an expiration date.

Call and put options for stocks and bonds are traded on exchanges such as the Chicago Board of Options Exchange. As on futures exchanges, brokers for buyers and sellers meet to make deals. An option buyer immediately pays a fee to the seller. The seller makes a margin deposit to guarantee his performance if the buyer exercises the option.

Options also come from another source. Many companies create call options on their own stock and give them to executives as part of their pay. Options are valuable if stock prices rise, as the following example illustrates.

It is January 1, 2020. The current price of Google stock is $400. You buy a call option on one share of Google, with a strike price of $450 and an expiration date of July 1. You pay $20 for this option.

As long as Google's price is below $450, you don't exercise the option. You don't choose to buy the stock for more than it's worth. If July 1 arrives and the price is still below $450, the option expires. The $20 you paid for the option is a loss.

On the other hand, suppose that Google's stock rises to $500 on April 1. At that point, you might exercise the option. You can buy the stock for $450 and resell it for $500. You come out $30 ahead after accounting for the $20 you paid initially.

It is tricky to choose when to exercise an option. In our example, you earn a profit by exercising on April 1. But you might do even better by waiting. If the stock reaches $600 on May 1, you will earn more by exercising then. On the other hand, the stock might fall after April 1. If that happens, you will wish you had cashed in when the stock was high.

Credit Default Swaps

A **credit default swap (CDS)** is a derivative tied to debt securities, such as bonds and mortgage-backed securities, that promise certain future payments. A CDS buyer pays premiums, and payments on the CDS are triggered by defaults on the original securities. For example, Jack might sell Jill a CDS on bonds issued by the Acme Corporation. In this deal, Jill agrees to pay a series of premiums over some time period—say, the next five years. In return, Jack promises to make payments to Jill if Acme defaults on its bonds.

We can sometimes interpret a CDS as an insurance policy. Jill may buy a CDS on Acme bonds because she owns some of the bonds and therefore stands to lose if Acme defaults. With the CDS, she has "swapped" her default risk to Jack. Jack will compensate Jill for losses, just as her auto insurance company will compensate her for an accident.

A CDS differs from a conventional insurance policy in an important way. Jill can buy insurance on her car, but she *cannot* buy insurance on her neighbor Joan's car. Allstate won't agree to pay Jill for Joan's accidents, because they don't cost

Jill anything. In contrast, Jill *can* buy credit default swaps on Acme bonds even if she doesn't own the bonds. She will receive money if Acme defaults even though the default does not affect her directly.

The first CDSs were issued in 1997 by Chase Manhattan Bank (now part of JP Morgan Chase). They were tied to municipal bonds, but soon others were created for corporate bonds and mortgage-backed securities. The CDS market grew explosively from 2000 to 2007: the total payments promised in case of default grew from less than $1 trillion to $62 trillion.

In contrast to futures and options, credit default swaps are *not* traded on exchanges. Each CDS is negotiated privately between a buyer and a seller, with no margin deposit by either. CDSs are traded by many financial institutions, including commercial banks, investment banks, and insurance companies. A case study later in this chapter examines the role of CDSs in the 2007–2009 financial meltdown.

Hedging With Derivatives

Why do people trade derivatives? One purpose is to reduce risk through **hedging**. To hedge is to purchase an asset that is likely to produce a high return if another of one's assets produces a low or negative return. Hedging was the original purpose of credit default swaps: a security holder can reduce his default risk by purchasing a CDS on the security. Futures and options can also be used for hedging; let's look at some examples.

Hedging With Futures Hedging was the original purpose of agricultural futures. Imagine a farmer growing wheat and a miller who will buy the wheat when it is harvested in six months. Both parties face risk from fluctuations in the price of wheat. If the price is high in six months, the farmer will earn extra income, but the miller's costs will rise. The reverse happens if the price is low.

Wheat futures eliminate this risk. The farmer can sell a contract for wheat in six months, and the miller can buy this contract. The contract locks in a price for both parties.

Like commodities futures, financial futures can reduce risk. The owners of securities experience gains and losses when security prices change. To hedge, security holders make derivatives trades that produce profits if they suffer losses elsewhere.

For example, commercial banks hold large quantities of Treasury bonds. They stand to lose a lot if bond prices fall. A bank can reduce this risk by selling Treasury bond futures. If bond prices do fall, the bank earns profits from its sale of futures (like Jack in our earlier example). The profits on futures cancel the losses on bonds. If prices rise, the bank loses on futures but gains from its bond holdings. Either way, the bank's total profits are insulated from bond-price movements.

Hedging With Options Security holders can also reduce risk by trading options. One hedging strategy is a "protective put," which means a purchase of put options on securities you own. It protects against large losses on the securities.

For example, suppose you own shares in a mutual fund that holds the S&P 500. The current level of the S&P index is 1000. The index is likely to rise, but you worry about the possibility of a stock market crash. You might sleep better if you buy puts on the index—say, with a strike price of 900. In effect this option lets you sell stocks for 90 percent of their current value, even if prices fall lower. Your potential losses are limited.

You must pay for the put options, but you never use them if the S&P index stays above 900. Nonetheless, it may be prudent to purchase the puts: it is worth paying fees to reduce risk.

Speculating With Derivatives

Derivatives are also useful for **speculation**. This practice is the opposite of hedging, which reduces risk: speculators use financial markets to make risky bets on asset prices. Speculators earn a lot if they are right and lose a lot if they are wrong.

Suppose the current price of a Treasury bond is $100. Most people expect this price to stay constant, so the six-month futures price is also $100. You, however, are more insightful than most people. You realize that the Federal Reserve is likely to lower its interest rate target, pushing up bond prices. You can bet on this belief by purchasing the $100 Treasury bond futures. You will profit if Treasury bonds are selling for more than $100 in six months.

You can also use options to bet on Treasury bonds. If you think the price will rise, you might sell put options on the bonds—say, with a strike price of $100. As long as the actual price stays above $100, nobody exercises the options. The fees you receive for the options are pure profit.

The catch, of course, is that speculation requires you to predict asset prices better than other people, something the efficient markets hypothesis says is impossible. If it's really likely that the Fed will lower interest rates, everyone else knows this information, too, and the prices of futures and options have already adjusted to it, thus eliminating profit opportunities. According to the efficient markets hypothesis, speculation is pure gambling; you might as well play the slots.

Nonetheless, many financial institutions speculate with derivatives. Leading players include investment banks and hedge funds. The term "hedge fund" is a misnomer, because hedge funds don't hedge—they speculate.

Speculating with derivatives produced large gains and losses during the financial turmoil of 2007–2009. Credit default swaps played a large role in the story, as we see in the next case study.

CASE STUDY

Credit Default Swaps and the AIG Fiasco

Many credit default swaps issued in the 2000s were tied to subprime mortgage–backed securities, which we discussed in the earlier case study on investment banks. These CDSs differed somewhat from the type we've discussed before. A traditional CDS yields a payoff if the issuer of some security defaults on payments that it owes. In contrast, the sellers of CDSs on mortgage-backed securities promised to pay CDS buyers if the market prices of the underlying securities fell, even if the securities' issuers had not yet defaulted. This feature proved important over 2006–2008, when the prices of mortgage-backed securities fell and these outcomes triggered payments on CDSs.

Some firms had used credit default swaps to hedge the risk on mortgage-backed securities. In 2006, for example, analysts at Goldman Sachs started worrying that housing prices might fall. Goldman saw that it could lose money on the mortgage-backed securities it owned, so it started buying credit default swaps to hedge against this possible loss. It did so sooner than other investment banks, and this strategy helped limit its losses during the financial crisis.

Other firms used credit default swaps to speculate. Like Goldman Sachs, some hedge funds foresaw trouble in the housing market. They bet against mortgage-backed securities by purchasing credit default swaps on securities they didn't own. These bets paid off handsomely: researchers estimate that one hedge fund, run by John Paulson, earned $15 billion on CDSs.

If hedgers and speculators were buying credit default swaps, who was selling them? The answer in many cases was the American International Group, a conglomerate that primarily owns insurance companies. AIG's swaps promised payments of hundreds of billions of dollars if prices of mortgage-backed securities fell far enough.

AIG management thought the company was getting a good deal. It received a steady flow of fees from the sale of CDSs, and managers didn't expect to pay out much in return. They didn't anticipate the fall in housing prices and its effects on mortgage-backed securities. In 2006, an AIG report to government regulators said the likelihood of losses on CDSs was "remote, even in severe recessionary market scenarios."

This view was refuted spectacularly over the next two years. As the mortgage crisis unfolded, AIG had to make larger and larger payments to holders of its CDSs. In September 2008, when Lehman Brothers went bankrupt, it seemed likely that AIG would suffer the same fate.

At that point, the Federal Reserve stepped in. The Fed feared that a collapse of AIG would magnify the financial crisis, so it kept the company afloat with more than $100 billion in loans. The Treasury department also aided AIG by purchasing its stock. AIG survived, but the Fed and Treasury were widely criticized for their use of taxpayers' money. We return to this episode in Chapter 18. ∎

17-7 Conclusion

This chapter has provided a survey of securities markets. We've examined the major types of markets, the people and firms that participate in them, and the tradeoffs they face in deciding which securities to buy and sell.

Some lessons from this chapter will likely be relevant to your financial life. If you accumulate wealth, economists believe you should hold a large share in stocks—but shift toward safer assets as you age. In choosing which stocks to buy, you should be wary of brokers or mutual fund managers who claim they can outperform the market. The evidence suggests that beating the market is very difficult.

As you can probably tell, the behavior of securities markets is a vast topic. We have highlighted key issues, but you can learn much more by taking finance courses, either in an economics department or in a business school. Courses in corporate finance, for example, examine firms' capital structure in detail. Courses in asset pricing explore the factors determining the prices of stocks, bonds, and derivatives.

Summary

1. Securities firms are companies whose primary purpose is to hold securities, trade them, or help others trade them. These firms include mutual funds, hedge funds, brokers, dealers, and investment banks.

2. Corporations and governments issue securities in primary markets. Corporations sell their stocks and bonds through investment banks. By underwriting corporations' securities, investment banks reduce the problem of adverse selection. The U.S. government sells bonds through auctions.

3. After securities are issued, they are traded in secondary markets, including exchanges, dealer markets, and electronic communications networks.

4. Firms can finance investment by issuing stocks or bonds. The mix of the two that a firm chooses is called its capital structure.

5. Savers must choose how to split their wealth among different classes of assets, such as stocks and bonds. Stocks have higher average returns than bonds, but they are also riskier.

6. According to the efficient markets hypothesis, every stock's price equals the best estimate of its value, so no stock is a better buy than any other. It is futile to look for stocks that will produce higher-than-average returns.

7. Derivative securities are securities with payoffs tied to the prices of other assets. Futures contracts, options, and credit default swaps are examples of derivative securities.

8. Some people and institutions use derivatives to hedge against possible losses: they purchase derivatives that will produce high returns if other assets they own produce low or negative returns. Other people and institutions use derivatives to speculate: they make bets on asset prices that sometimes produce large profits and sometimes large losses.

KEY CONCEPTS

Asset allocation	Exchange	Random walk
Securities firm	Specialist	Actively managed fund
Hedge fund	Over-the-counter (OTC) market	Index fund
Leverage	Dealer market	Behavioral finance
Broker	Bid–ask spread	Derivatives
Dealer	Electronic communications network (ECN)	Futures contract
Investment bank		Option
Underwriter	Stock market index	Call option
Primary markets	Capital structure	Put option
Secondary markets	Modigliani–Miller theorem	Credit default swap (CDS)
Public company	Efficient markets hypothesis	Hedging
Initial public offering (IPO)	Undervalued asset	Speculation

QUESTIONS FOR REVIEW

1. What is a mutual fund? Is buying 200 shares of a mutual fund more or less risky than buying 200 shares of Walt Disney Company?

2. How do investment banks lessen the problem of adverse selection in securities markets?

3. What is the difference between primary and secondary markets for securities?

4. What factors influence a firm's decisions about its capital structure?

5. What are the benefits and costs to a person of holding a large fraction of her wealth in stock?

6. According to the efficient markets hypothesis, how should a saver choose among the stocks of different companies?

7. James, age 59, is close to retirement and wants to allocate 80 percent of his assets to stocks so that he can maximize his returns. Is this a good decision? Explain your answer.

8. Can a firm's stock be undervalued for a long period of time? Why or why not?

9. What is a futures contract? Describe a circumstance under which a person or firm would buy a futures contract.

PROBLEMS AND APPLICATIONS

1. When investment banks underwrite IPOs, they typically sell stock for 5 to 10 percent more than they paid for it. When they underwrite new stock for companies that are already public, the typical markup is 3 percent. What explains this difference?

2. As in Section 17-4, assume that bonds pay a real return of 2 percent. Stocks pay 22 percent half the time and −6 percent half the time. Suppose you initially have wealth of $100, and let X be your wealth after 1 year. What fraction of your wealth should you hold in stock under each of the following assumptions?

   a. You want to maximize the average value of X.

   b. You want to maximize the value of X when the return on stocks is −6 percent.

   c. You want to be certain that X is at least $100 (that is, you don't lose any of your initial wealth). Subject to that constraint, you maximize the average value of X.

496 | PART VI The Financial System and the Economy

3. Suppose two people are the same age and have the same level of wealth. One has a high-paying job and the other has a low-paying job. Who should hold a higher fraction of his or her wealth in stock? Explain.

4. Chapter 16 presented the classical theory of asset prices. In this chapter, we discussed two ideas that follow from the classical theory: the Modigliani–Miller theorem and the efficient markets hypothesis. How well do these two ideas fit real-world financial markets? Where does each fit on a spectrum from literally true to completely unrealistic?

5. Suppose everyone in the world becomes convinced that the efficient markets hypothesis is true. Will it stay true? Explain.

6. Research around 1980 showed that stocks of small firms had higher average returns than stocks of large firms. This finding gained much attention because it seemed to contradict the efficient markets hypothesis. It suggested a simple way to beat the market: purchase only small-firm stocks.

   a. Can you explain this deviation from market efficiency? (*Hint:* Think about the behavior in financial markets that leads to efficiency and why this behavior might not occur.)

   b. Would you guess that small-firm stocks have done better than large-firm stocks since 1980? Why or why not?

7. Recall that U.S. mutual fund companies offer about 8,000 separate funds. Suppose each fund has a 50 percent chance of beating the S&P 500 each year.

   a. Over a 5-year period, how many funds will beat the market in every year? What about a 15-year period?

   b. Based on the performance of William Miller's mutual fund from 1981 through 2005, would you say Miller is a genius? Explain.

8. In 1989, the economist Paul Samuelson rated Warren Buffett the greatest stock picker in the country. Yet Samuelson warned against buying Berkshire Hathaway stock. He wrote that "knowledge of Buffett's skills may be already fully discounted in the marketplace. Now that B-H has gone up more than a hundredfold, it is at a premium."

   a. Explain Samuelson's reasoning in your own words.

   b. People who followed Samuelson's advice have regretted it, because the returns on B-H stock since 1989 have been similar to earlier returns. What does this tell us about Buffett and/or the efficient markets hypothesis?

9. On its Web site, one mutual fund company describes its "disciplined and sophisticated investment strategies." (The term "investment" is used to mean the choice of securities.) Let's change the company's name to "Smith." With this alteration, the site says:

   > At the center of Smith's investment process is the Smith Investment Committee. It consists of a select group of senior investment professionals who are supported by an extensive staff. This staff provides multilevel analyses of the economic and investment environments, including actual and projected corporate earnings, interest rates, and the effect of economic forecasts on market sectors, individual securities, and client portfolios.

   Does this statement convince you to buy Smith mutual funds? Why or why not?

10. Suppose you hold most of your wealth in stock. What kinds of options should you buy or sell in each of the following circumstances?

    a. You think the stock market will probably do well, but you worry about a crash.

    b. You want to get a steady return on your assets. You don't care whether you get rich from a big rise in the market.

    c. You think there will soon be big news about firms' earnings, but you don't know whether the news will be good or bad.

11. Suppose you buy call options on Microsoft stock. Each option costs $2 and has a strike price of $40 and an expiration date of July 1. Discuss whether you would exercise the options in each of the following situations and why:

    a. It is March 1 and Microsoft's stock price is $30.

    b. It is March 1 and the stock price is $40.10.

    c. It is March 1 and the stock price is $50.

    d. It is June 30 and the stock price is $50.

    e. It is June 30 and the stock price is $40.10.

12. Suppose company A has a stable stock price. The price is not likely to change much in the next year. Company B has an uncertain stock price: it could either rise or fall by a lot. Would you pay more for a call option on A's stock or B's stock? Explain.

13. Use bloomberg.com to answer the following questions:

a. Which has done better over the last year, the U.S. stock market or the Brazilian stock market?

b. Which have done better over the last year, the stocks in the Dow Jones index or the NASDAQ index?

c. What was the rate of return on Boeing stock over the last year?

14. Go to buffettsecrets.com and study Warren Buffett's principles for choosing stocks. Do you think you could beat a stock index by following these principles? Explain.

CHAPTER 18

Banking

*If you owe the bank $100, that's your problem. If you owe the bank
$100 million, that's the bank's problem.*

—J. Paul Getty

Chapter 15 described the central function of banks: reducing problems of asymmetric information. Adverse selection and moral hazard prevent some firms, especially those that are relatively unknown, from issuing securities in financial markets. These problems also prevent individuals from issuing securities. Firms and individuals that cannot raise funds by issuing securities turn to banks for loans.

In lending money, banks reduce adverse selection by screening borrowers and reduce moral hazard by establishing loan covenants and monitoring borrower behavior. Because of banks, small businesses can borrow money to expand, and people can borrow money to buy houses and cars.

This chapter takes a closer look at banking. We survey the many types of banks, from global giants such as Citigroup to banks that serve a single town. We also examine two changes in banking over the last quarter century that have had major consequences for the financial system and the macroeconomy: the growth of *subprime lenders*, a fringe of the banking industry whose customers have weak credit histories, and *securitization*, the creation of liquid securities backed by bank loans. These controversial practices both had roles in the financial crisis of 2007–2009.

We also examine banking from the point of view of bank managers. Like any business, a bank seeks to earn profits. It does so primarily by accepting deposits and lending them out at higher interest rates than it pays. We discuss banks' strategies for maximizing profits and look at the risks that banks face when they lend. We examine methods for containing risk and see what happens when risk management fails.

Finally, we discuss government regulation of banks. The main goal of regulation is to prevent bank failures. Toward that end, governments insure deposits and restrict risk taking by banks. Like the banks they supervise, regulators have experienced both successes and failures, and in the wake of the recent financial crisis there was pressure for the government to do more to regulate banks and other financial institutions.

18-1 The Banking Industry

We begin our study of banking by surveying the different types of banks, the distinct roles of large and small banks, and subprime lenders.

Types of Banks

Chapter 15 defined a *bank* as a financial institution that accepts deposits and makes loans. In the United States, this definition covers three types of institutions: commercial banks, savings institutions, and credit unions. A fourth category, finance companies, satisfies part of the definition: finance companies make loans but do not accept deposits. Figure 18-1 shows the total deposits and loans of these four types of institutions at the end of 2009.

Commercial Banks **Commercial banks** are the largest part of the banking industry. At the end of 2009, there were about 7,000 commercial banks in the United States. They had $8.3 trillion in deposits, including checking and savings deposits. They had $6.5 trillion in outstanding loans to a wide range of customers, including large corporations, small businesses, and individuals. Loans to individuals include home mortgages, car loans, student loans, and balances on credit cards.

Savings Institutions **Savings institutions** are also called *savings and loan associations (S&Ls)* or *savings banks*. At the end of 2009, savings institutions had about $900 billion in deposits and $800 billion in loans.

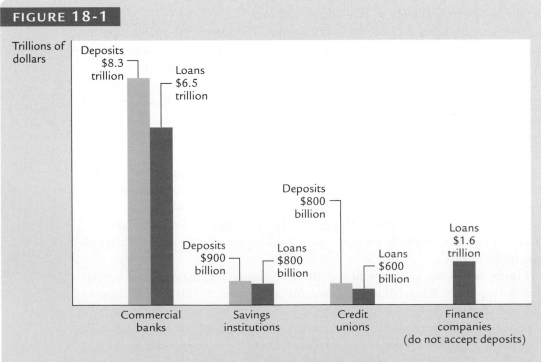

FIGURE 18-1

Loans and Deposits of U.S. Banks (December 31, 2009)

The original purpose of savings institutions was to serve households by accepting savings deposits and lending for home mortgages. Savings institutions were created in the nineteenth century, when commercial banks focused on business lending. Most savings institutions were established as *mutual banks*, meaning they were owned by their depositors and did not issue stock.

Over time, most savings institutions issued stock and ceased being mutual banks. They also expanded their businesses: today, savings institutions offer checking as well as savings accounts, and they make many types of loans. These changes have blurred the distinction between savings institutions and commercial banks, although the former still focus more on mortgages.

Credit Unions A **credit union** is a nonprofit bank. Like a mutual bank, it is owned by its depositors, who are called "members." Only members can borrow from the credit union. Membership is restricted to a group of people who have something in common. They might be employees of a company, members of a labor union, or veterans of a military service. Credit unions make several types of loans, including home mortgages, auto loans, and small personal loans. At the end of 2009, credit unions had $800 billion in deposits and $600 billion in loans.

Finance Companies Like banks, **finance companies** make loans; for example, they compete with banks in issuing mortgages and auto loans. At the end of 2009, finance companies had loans totaling $1.6 trillion. However, finance companies do *not* accept deposits. Instead, they raise funds by issuing bonds and borrowing from banks.

Many finance companies specialize in a certain kind of loan. For example, some lend to businesses for new equipment. Others are owned by manufacturing companies and lend to their customers. This group includes General Motors Acceptance Corporation (GMAC) and Ford Motor Credit Company, which make auto loans. Another market niche in which finance companies operate is subprime lending, which we discuss later in this chapter.

Large Versus Small Banks

In the United States, banks vary greatly in size. At one end of the scale are three giant commercial banks: Citibank, JP Morgan Chase, and Bank of America. Each of these banks has over a trillion dollars in total assets, which include outstanding loans and other assets, such as securities. The three banks have thousands of branches around the country and overseas. As of 2010, 15 U.S. banks had assets between $100 billion and $1 trillion, including Wells Fargo, PNC Bank, and Suntrust.

Many large banks are subsidiaries of *financial holding companies*—conglomerates that also provide the services of securities firms. For example, Citibank (a commercial bank) is part of Citigroup (a financial holding company). Citigroup has units that underwrite securities, sell mutual funds and insurance, and help people manage their wealth.

The smallest banks include **community banks**, commercial banks or savings institutions with less than $1 billion in assets. A community bank operates in a small geographic area by raising funds from local depositors and lending them to consumers and small businesses. An example is Harford Bank, based in Aberdeen, Maryland. In 2010, Harford had $250 million in assets and seven branches in Aberdeen and neighboring towns. Of the 7,000 commercial banks in the United States, more than 90 percent are community banks, but their total assets barely exceed $1 trillion. Most credit unions are also small, because they restrict membership to a narrow group of people. For example, The Johns Hopkins Federal Credit Union serves employees of the university and hospital that share its name. It has five branches and $300 million in assets.

Large and small banks coexist because each has advantages in some areas of banking. Only large banks have enough funds to lend to large corporations. In addition, large banks benefit from economies of scale: making a large number of loans reduces the cost per loan. If a bank issues credit cards, for example, it can manage the accounts of many cardholders with a single computer system.

Historically, small banks have existed because of legal restrictions on bank size. Before 1994, a bank could operate in only one state. And before World War II, some states had unit banking—a bank was restricted to a single branch (see the case study in Chapter 15).

Because these restrictions no longer exist, the number of small banks has declined as many merge with each other or are purchased by larger banks. The total number of commercial banks has fallen from a peak of 15,000 in 1984 to the current 7,000. Yet many small banks survive. Economists think the reason is that small banks are better than large banks at certain kinds of lending.

Community banks have a niche in small-business lending. Recall that lending requires information gathering. By focusing on a small area, community bankers come to know local businesses and the people who run them. As a result, they are better at screening borrowers than are banks from far away.

Credit unions reduce information problems by restricting loans to members. The fact that a borrower qualifies for membership provides information about his default risk. So does the history of his account at the credit union. This information helps loan officers screen out risky borrowers.

Subprime Lenders

Banks lend to millions of firms and individuals, yet not everyone can borrow from a bank. Loan officers deny credit to people whose default risk appears high, including people with low incomes or poor credit histories.

Government regulators encourage banks to be conservative in lending. They don't want banks to take risks that could lead to large losses. One reason is that the government insures bank deposits, so it stands to lose money if a bank fails.

People who can't borrow from banks often turn to **subprime lenders**, companies that specialize in high-risk loans. Subprime lenders include some finance companies, payday lenders, pawnshops, and illegal loan sharks. Each type of lender has methods for coping with default risk, which are summarized in Table 18-1.

Subprime Finance Companies The government regulates finance companies less heavily than banks. One reason is that finance companies do not accept

TABLE 18-1	

Subprime Lenders

Type of Lender	How Lender Copes with Default Risk
Finance company	Credit scoring; high interest rates
Payday lender	Postdated checks; very high interest rates
Pawnshop	Very high collateral
Illegal loan shark	Very high interest rates; threats to defaulters

deposits, so the government doesn't owe insurance payments if a company fails. Light regulation allows finance companies to make loans that bank regulators might deem too risky. As a result, some finance companies specialize in subprime lending.

Finance companies make subprime mortgage loans, auto loans, and personal loans. Examples of subprime lenders are Household Finance Corporation (HFC), Countrywide Financial, and CitiFinancial. Many of these companies are subsidiaries of financial holding companies that also own commercial banks. CitiFinancial, for example, is part of Citigroup, and HFC is part of the HSBC Group.

Subprime lending, especially for mortgages, grew rapidly from the 1990s to 2007. This trend reflected the development of *credit scoring*, a process that reduces asymmetric information between borrowers and lenders. Credit bureaus such as Equifax, Experian, and TransUnion collect information on people's histories of borrowing and repaying and summarize them with credit scores. During the subprime boom, lenders grew increasingly confident that credit scores were accurate measures of default risk. By knowing a borrower's default risk, finance companies could offset expected losses from defaults by charging sufficiently high interest rates.

Subprime mortgage loans, for example, typically carried interest rates two to five percentage points above the best mortgage rates. Often, lenders added to their earnings by charging fees when a loan was made. When default rates on subprime mortgages started rising in 2007, new subprime mortgage lending dried up. Other kinds of subprime lending continue, however; one growth area is subprime credit cards.

Payday Lenders **Payday lenders** are companies that make small loans to people who need cash urgently. A typical loan is a few hundred dollars for a few weeks. Payday lenders include small companies with a single office and national chains such as Advance America and ACE Cash Express.

To borrow from a payday lender, a customer writes a check with some future date on it—often the next payday. The check covers the amount of the loan plus a fee. The lender gets repaid by cashing the check on the designated day unless the borrower repays the loan with cash or pays another fee to extend the loan.

Unlike banks, payday lenders gather little information about borrowers. They lend to anyone with a checking account and a pay stub to prove employment—or, in some cases, proof of unemployment benefits from the government. Instead of screening borrowers, payday lenders rely on the postdated checks to reduce defaults. A check is written for a day when funds are likely to be available. In addition, bounced-check fees at a borrower's bank encourage the borrower to make sure the check clears.

Payday lenders also compensate for default risk with *very* high interest rates. A common fee is 15 percent of the loan amount: for $200 in cash, you write a check for $230. For a four-week loan, this fee is equivalent to an annual interest rate of 515 percent! Surveys suggest that the average annual rate on payday loans is around 400 percent.

Most states have *usury laws* that set legal limits on interest rates, often around 40 percent per year. In the 1990s, however, payday lenders lobbied state legislatures to exempt them from usury laws, and they succeeded in many states. These legal changes led to rapid growth in the industry. As of 2010, payday lenders had more than 20,000 offices in the United States, most located in low-income areas. Studies estimate that 15 percent of U.S. households have borrowed from payday lenders.

Payday lenders are controversial. Critics allege that they practice *predatory lending*: they take unfair advantage of borrowers who are poor and uninformed about financial matters. According to this view, default rates are not high enough to justify three-digit interest rates on payday loans. And people who take out the loans often get into financial trouble.

Payday loans are dangerous because a borrower may still be short on cash when the loan is due. In this case, some people take out a larger loan to "roll over" both the initial loan and the fee. Sometimes a loan is rolled over again and again. With high interest rates, the borrower quickly runs up a large debt.

Criticism of payday lending led North Carolina and Georgia to ban the practice in the early 2000s. Under a 2006 law, the federal government ended payday lending to military personnel. Aside from the military, however, payday lending remains legal in 33 states.

Payday lenders defend their business. They say their loans help people facing emergencies to stave off disaster. For example, a payday loan can be used to pay rent when someone faces eviction. Some research supports the view that payday lending has benefits. After Georgia banned the practice, the state saw a 9 percent increase in personal bankruptcies, a 13 percent increase in bounced checks, and a 64 percent increase in complaints against debt collectors.[1]

Pawnshops Like a payday lender, a **pawnshop** is a source of small, short-term loans. It protects against default with very high collateral. A borrower deposits an item he owns and receives a loan for 30 to 50 percent of the resale value. The pawnshop has the right to sell the collateral if the loan is not repaid.

---

[1] See Donald P. Morgan and Michael R. Strain, "Payday Holiday: How Households Fare After Payday Credit Bans," *Federal Reserve of New York Staff Report* #309, November 2007. For a harsh critique of payday lending, visit the Web site of the Center for Responsible Lending. For a defense, see the Web site of the Community Financial Services Association, an organization of payday lenders.

There are roughly 13,000 pawnshops in the United States. A pawnshop's typical loan is $75 to $100 for 60 or 90 days. Common collateral includes jewelry, televisions, and—in some states—guns. About 80 percent of borrowers repay their loans and get back the collateral.

Pawnshops appeared in Europe in the fifteenth century and have existed in the United States since colonial times. The industry grew rapidly from the 1970s to the 1990s. Since then, business has leveled off because of competition with payday lenders.

Illegal Loan Sharks Another source of subprime loans is illegal **loan sharks**. These lenders charge interest rates that violate usury laws. Loan-sharking is a traditional business of organized crime.

Loan sharks' disregard for the law helps them cope with default risk. They can encourage repayment with threats of violence. They can seize defaulters' property without the trouble of getting a court judgment.

Yet loan-sharking is a declining industry. Many customers have switched to legal payday lenders or pawnshops. Today loan sharks operate mainly in immigrant communities. They sometimes require immigration papers as collateral for loans.

The last organized-crime figure convicted of loan-sharking was Nicodemo Scarfo Jr., of Philadelphia. In 2002, he was sentenced to 33 months in prison for charging an interest rate of 152 percent. Scarfo's defenders point out that he charged less than most payday lenders.

18-2 Securitization

Traditionally, when a bank makes loans, the loans become assets of the bank. The flow of interest on the loans is the bank's primary source of revenue. Over the last generation, however, this basic feature of banking has changed. Today, banks sell many of the loans they make rather than holding them as assets, and the loans are transformed into securities that are traded in financial markets. This **securitization** of loans has had benefits for banks and the economy, but it also played a role in the financial crisis of 2007–2009.

The Securitization Process

Figure 18-2 illustrates the securitization process. Banks and finance companies make loans to borrowers and then sell them to a large financial institution, the securitizer. This institution gathers a pool of loans with similar characteristics; for example, a pool might be $100 million worth of mortgage loans to people with certain credit scores. The securitizer issues securities that entitle an owner to a share of the payments on the loan pool. These securities are bought by financial institutions, including commercial and investment banks, pension funds, and mutual funds. The initial buyers often resell the securities in secondary markets.

FIGURE 18-2

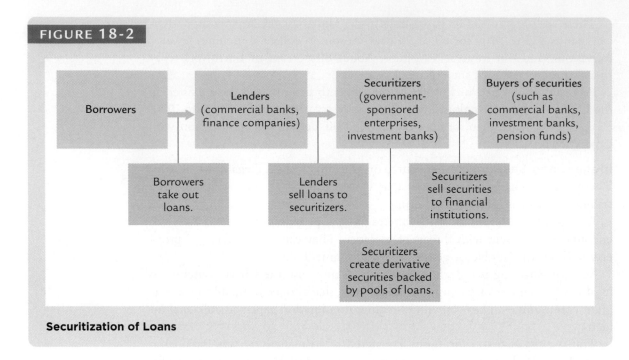

Securitization of Loans

Fannie and Freddie

Home mortgages are the type of loan most often securitized. The two largest issuers of **mortgage-backed securities** (MBSs) are the Federal National Mortgage Association, commonly known as Fannie Mae, and the Federal Home Loan Corporation, or Freddie Mac. The government created Fannie Mae in 1938 as part of President Franklin Roosevelt's New Deal; it created Freddie Mac in 1970. The purpose was to increase the supply of mortgage loans and thereby help more people achieve "the American Dream" of homeownership.

Fannie and Freddie are an unusual kind of institution called a *government-sponsored enterprise (GSE)*. They are private corporations with stocks that are traded on the New York Stock Exchange but are linked to the government: they were established by the government, the president appoints some of the directors, and they have a long-standing right to borrow money from the U.S. Treasury.

Fannie and Freddie raise funds by issuing bonds and then use the funds to purchase mortgages. Before the recent financial crisis, Fannie and Freddie were highly profitable institutions due in large part to their links to the government. In theory, Fannie or Freddie could go bankrupt, but people have long believed the government would save them if they got in trouble (as indeed happened in 2008). The belief that the government stood behind Fannie and Freddie meant their bonds were considered safe. As a result, the bonds paid low interest rates, and Fannie and Freddie could raise funds more cheaply than other financial institutions.

Initially, Fannie and Freddie held onto all the mortgages they bought with the funds they raised. In the 1970s, however, they started issuing mortgage-backed securities, which they sold to other financial institutions. This business grew rapidly, and today over half of U.S. mortgage debt is securitized by Fannie or Freddie.

From the 1970s to the early 2000s, Fannie and Freddie purchased only prime mortgages, those that appear to have low default risk based on borrowers' incomes and credit scores. In the early 2000s, they began to purchase subprime mortgages in an effort to increase the supply of mortgages to low-income people. However, the securities they sell to other institutions are still backed entirely by prime mortgages. Fannie and Freddie have held onto the subprime mortgages they purchased.

Like many financial institutions, Fannie and Freddie suffered losses in 2007 and 2008 as defaults on subprime mortgages rose. It appeared that one or both of the companies might go bankrupt, worsening the financial crisis. To prevent this outcome, the government put Fannie and Freddie under *conservatorship* in September 2008. This action meant that technically the companies remained private, but government regulators took control of their operations. We discuss this episode further in Chapter 19.

Conservatorship was meant to be a temporary arrangement, and as of the writing of this book, the future of the two companies is unclear. They might return to their pre-crisis status, or they might change from private companies into normal government agencies.

Why Securitization Occurs

Securitization occurs because banks want to sell loans and because securities backed by bank loans are attractive to many institutions. In this section we discuss the incentives for securitization, focusing on home mortgages because securitization is most common for that type of loan.

Benefits for Banks Banks sell mortgages because the possibility of default makes it risky to hold them. In addition, the loans made by a particular bank may be poorly diversified, increasing risk. If the bank lends in only one geographic area, for example, a downturn in the local economy can cause a large number of defaults. By selling loans, the bank shifts default risk to the ultimate holders of the loans.

From one point of view, selling loans might seem an odd practice. Why should a bank lend money in the first place if it plans to get rid of the loan? The answer is that the bank still performs its basic function of reducing asymmetric information. It uses its expertise to screen borrowers and design loan covenants (see Section 15-4). Because it does this work, a bank can sell a loan for more than the original amount it gave the borrower. In effect, the institution buying the loan pays the bank for reducing information problems. The bank earns a profit from the sale and avoids the default risk it would face if it held onto the loan.

Many banks both sell mortgage loans and buy mortgage-backed securities. In effect, they trade the relatively few loans they make for small pieces of many loans. They gain diversification, reducing risk. They also gain liquidity, because mortgage-backed securities can be sold more quickly than individual mortgages.

Demand for Mortgage-Backed Securities Many financial institutions buy the securities issued by Fannie Mae and Freddie Mac. Large purchasers include mutual funds and pension funds as well as banks. For these institutions,

Fannie and Freddie's securities are attractive alternatives to bonds. The securities are highly liquid, and they are considered safe because they are backed by prime mortgages and because of Fannie and Freddie's links to the government. At the same time, the securities pay a bit more interest than other safe assets, such as Treasury bonds.

Securities backed by subprime mortgages are a different matter. As we saw in Chapter 17, these securities were purchased before the financial crisis by risk-taking institutions such as investment banks and hedge funds.

The Spread of Securitization

Before the 1990s, there was little securitization of loans beyond the prime mortgage-backed securities created by Fannie Mae and Freddie Mac. Since then, investment banks have extended securitization in two directions. The first innovation was securitization of subprime mortgages. The results were sufficiently disastrous that no new securities backed by subprime mortgages are being issued as of 2010.

The second innovation, securitization of nonmortgage loans, has proven more successful. Today, financial institutions trade securities backed by auto loans, credit-card debt, and student loans. At the end of 2009, 35% of all outstanding bank loans were securitized, compared to only 6% thirty years earlier.

Securitization is sometimes called *shadow banking*, a vaguely ominous term. We've seen the benefits of securitization: it reduces risk and increases liquidity for banks, and it raises the supply of loans. Yet securitization has gained a bad name because it played a role in the financial crisis of 2007–2009, as the following case study discusses.

CASE STUDY

The Subprime Mortgage Fiasco

The crisis that gripped the financial system over 2007–2009 had its roots in a wave of mortgage defaults. This disaster stemmed from the interplay of a housing bubble, the rise of subprime lending, securitization, and gaps in government regulation. Let's review the troubling story.

The Housing Bubble As we discussed in Chapter 16, U.S. housing prices rose 71 percent from 2002 to 2006, and many people believed that prices would continue to rise. In retrospect, however, the rapid price increases were an unsustainable bubble, and prices fell by 33 percent from 2006 to 2009.

Risky Lending A basic cause of the crisis was the behavior of mortgage lenders. Eager to increase business, finance companies made loans to people who were likely to have trouble paying them back. As we've discussed, lenders believed they could measure default risk with credit scores and adjust interest rates to compensate for this risk. The reliance on credit scores led lenders to neglect traditional safeguards against defaults.

Traditional mortgages require substantial down payments. A typical borrower must pay 20 percent of the house price out of her own money to receive a mortgage for 80 percent of the price. Collateral for the mortgage—the total value of the house—exceeds the loan, reducing default risk. During the subprime boom, however, lenders reduced down payments and even offered mortgages with zero money down.

Subprime lenders also loosened rules about borrowers' incomes. For a traditional mortgage, monthly payments cannot exceed a certain percentage of income (often around 30 percent). Formally, subprime lenders adhered to this rule, but often with a "no documentation" policy: borrowers stated their incomes but weren't asked for proof such as pay stubs or past income tax forms. Some people obtained mortgages by exaggerating their incomes.

Finally, lenders tempted borrowers with low introductory interest rates, often called *teaser rates*. In many mortgage contracts, the interest rate was 4 percent or less for the first two years, but then jumped sharply. People took out loans they could afford initially but got into trouble when their payments rose.

Finance companies could engage in risky lending because they receive less attention from government regulators than do banks. Light regulation helped finance companies make loans that now seem imprudent. In 2008, the Federal Reserve banned no-documentation loans, but this was like closing the barn door after the horse had gone.

The Boom Period Risky mortgage lending didn't produce a crisis immediately. Subprime lending was profitable in the late 1990s and early 2000s because default rates were moderate. As shown in Figure 18-3, the percentage of subprime

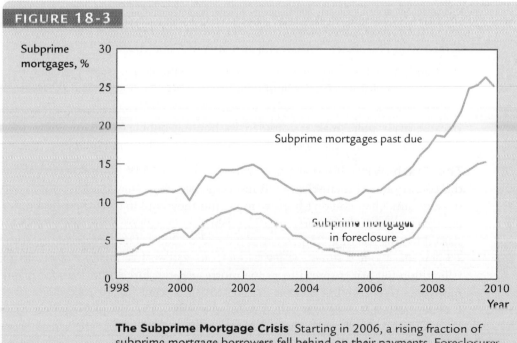

FIGURE 18-3

Subprime mortgages, %

Subprime mortgages past due

Subprime mortgages in foreclosure

Year

The Subprime Mortgage Crisis Starting in 2006, a rising fraction of subprime mortgage borrowers fell behind on their payments. Foreclosures on subprime mortgages also rose.

Source: Mortgage Bankers Association.

borrowers who were behind on their mortgage payments was about 10 percent in 2000. This delinquency rate rose during the recession of 2001, but it was back down to 10 percent in 2004. In 2005, only 3 percent of subprime mortgages were in foreclosure, meaning the lender had given up on receiving payments from the borrower and moved to seize the borrower's house. This was well above the 0.4 percent foreclosure rate for prime mortgages, but subprime interest rates were high enough to compensate lenders for defaults.

The housing bubble was a key factor behind the subprime boom. Rising housing prices made it easier for homeowners to cope with high mortgage payments. Someone short on cash could take out a second mortgage because the higher value of his home gave him more collateral. Or he could sell the home for more than he paid for it, pay off his mortgage, and earn a capital gain.

The subprime boom fed on itself. Investment banks saw the profits being made on subprime mortgages and wanted to get in on the action. As detailed in Chapter 17, the leading investment banks securitized subprime mortgages and held onto a large share of the securities. Securitization provided more funds for subprime loans. In turn, more subprime lending increased the demand for housing, fueling the rise in housing prices. As a result of these dynamics, subprime mortgages grew from almost nothing in the early 1990s to 14 percent of outstanding mortgages in 2007.

During the boom period, few people—whether investment bankers, regulators, or economists—saw the risks of subprime lending that now seem obvious. The underlying reason is that few anticipated the sharp decline in housing prices that started in 2006. A bursting bubble in Japan had reduced that country's housing prices by nearly half in the 1990s and early 2000s, but most Americans ignored this warning signal. Housing prices had also fallen in some U.S. regions when their economies weakened in the 1980s and 1990s. Yet most observers agreed with Fed chair Alan Greenspan when, in 2005, he said

> Overall, while local economies may experience significant speculative price imbalances, a national severe price distortion [that is, a national housing bubble] seems most unlikely in the United States, given its size and diversity.

Because many policymakers considered a housing bubble "most unlikely," they did not worry about the potential consequences of a bursting bubble.

The Crash When housing prices started falling in 2006, homeowners across the country found themselves with mortgage payments they couldn't afford and no way out. They couldn't borrow more and they couldn't sell their houses for enough to pay off their mortgages. The delinquency rate on subprime mortgages started to rise, reaching 25 percent at the end of 2009. The foreclosure rate was 16 percent, about 5 times the level four years earlier. Eventually, the effects of falling housing prices spread to prime mortgages: the foreclosure rate for prime mortgages rose from 0.4 percent in 2005 to 1.4 percent in late 2009.

The mortgage crisis was a disaster for the millions of people who lost their homes, and it also hurt financial institutions. The first to feel the effects were finance companies that specialized in subprime lending; two large companies, Ameriquest and New Century Financial, went bankrupt in 2007. As we saw in Chapter 17, investment banks, major holders of subprime mortgage–backed securities, faced a crisis in 2008. Eventually the crisis affected all parts of the financial system, including stock and bond markets, and it pushed the economy into a deep recession. We discuss the spread of the financial crisis and its macroeconomic effects in Chapter 19. ■

18-3 The Business of Banking

Having surveyed the banking industry, we now look at banking from the point of view of a bank manager. We examine the decisions that banks face and how they earn profits. The primary way a bank earns profits is by accepting deposits on which it pays relatively low interest and lending them out at higher rates, then either holding onto the loans or selling them. After analyzing this process, we discuss the risks that banks face, such as loan defaults, and their strategies for containing risk.

The Bank Balance Sheet

We can organize our discussion of the banking business by examining the **balance sheet** of a bank. The balance sheet summarizes a bank's financial condition at a point in time. It lists the bank's assets (what it owns) on the left side and its **liabilities** (what it owes to others) on the right. The right side of the balance sheet also includes the bank's **net worth**, defined as

$$\text{Net Worth} = \text{Assets} - \text{Liabilities}.$$

A bank's net worth is also called its *equity* or *capital*. It is the amount of assets the bank would have if it paid off all its liabilities.

Table 18-2 shows the major items on the balance sheet of Duckworth's Bank, a hypothetical commercial bank. A general way to think about the two sides of the balance sheet is that a bank's liabilities and net worth are its sources of funds and a bank's assets are its uses of funds. Let's review the balance sheet, starting with the right side.[2]

TABLE 18-2

The Balance Sheet of Duckworth's Bank

Assets		Liabilities and Net Worth	
Reserves	$ 10	Deposits	$ 70
Securities	$ 10	Borrowings	$ 20
Loans	$ 80	Net Worth	$ 10
TOTAL	$100	TOTAL	$100

---

[2] The appendix to Chapter 4 examines a similar balance sheet but ignores some items for simplicity.

Liabilities and Net Worth When banks raise funds, they incur liabilities to the people and firms that provide the funds. The primary type of liability is deposits, which come in several varieties: checking deposits, savings deposits, and certificates of deposit (CDs). CDs require depositors to leave their money in the bank for a fixed amount of time. At the start of 2010, deposits were about 65 percent of the liabilities of U.S. commercial banks.

If a bank wants more funds than it can raise in deposits, it has another source: borrowing. Banks can borrow money from one another, from corporations with spare cash, and from the Federal Reserve. Banks can also borrow in securities markets by issuing bonds.

Net worth, or capital, is the final item on the right side of the balance sheet. Like a bank's liabilities, this item is a source of funds. Initially, a bank acquires capital by issuing stock—savers provide funds to the bank in return for ownership shares. The bank's profits are added to its capital, and losses reduce capital. Capital also falls when the bank pays dividends to its stockholders.

The balance sheet in Table 18-2 shows us that Duckworth's Bank has $70 in deposits and $20 in borrowings, for a total of $90 in liabilities. The bank's net worth is $10.

Assets The asset side of the balance sheet shows how a bank uses the funds it raises. Notice that total assets must equal the sum of liabilities and net worth on the other side of the balance sheet. This equality follows from the definition of net worth as assets minus liabilities.

A bank's primary assets are the loans that it holds. These include loans it has made and not sold as well as any loans it has bought from other banks. These loans produce a flow of interest income. At the beginning of 2010, loans were 55 percent of commercial bank assets.

Banks also hold securities. Regulators restrict these holdings to safe securities, such as Treasury bonds and municipal bonds (bonds issued by state and local governments).

Finally, banks hold **reserves**, funds that are available immediately when depositors make withdrawals. Reserves include cash held in bank branches and ATMs. They also include deposits that banks make to accounts at the Federal Reserve. Every commercial bank has such an account at the Fed, which it uses to clear checks and electronic payments.

The balance sheet in Table 18-2 shows us that Duckworth's Bank has $100 in total assets divided into $10 in reserves, $10 in securities, and $80 in loans.

The primary business decisions facing a bank concern its balance sheet—what liabilities to incur, what assets to hold, and how much capital to raise. We will examine these issues after describing how banks measure profits.

Measuring Profits

For a bank, as for any firm, profits are the difference between revenue and costs. A bank's primary source of revenue is the interest it earns on its assets. Its costs include the interest it pays and the expenses of running its business, such as salaries.

Banks evaluate their profitability with two variables. One is the **return on assets** (ROA). This is the ratio of a bank's profits to its assets:

$$ROA = Profits/Assets.$$

In the example of Duckworth's Bank in Table 18-2, total assets are $100. If profits in the year 2020 are $2, the ROA for that year is $2/100 = 0.02$, or 2 percent.

The second measure of profitability is the **return on equity** (ROE). This variable is the ratio of a bank's profits to its capital:

$$ROE = Profits/Capital.$$

In our example, the bank's capital is $10, so its ROE is $2/10 = 20$ percent.

The ROE is the more important measure of profitability because it shows how much the bank earns for each dollar its stockholders put into the business. Bank managers try to produce high ROEs, just as managers in other businesses try to produce high returns for stockholders.

Figure 18-4 shows the average return on equity for all U.S. commercial banks from 1960 through 2009. In most periods, the ROE has ranged from 10 percent to 15 percent. The two exceptions were the late 1980s and 2007–2009. These two periods saw major banking crises, which we discuss later in this chapter and in Chapter 19.

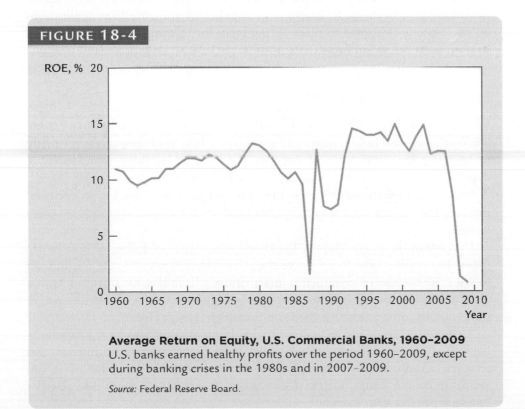

FIGURE 18-4

Average Return on Equity, U.S. Commercial Banks, 1960–2009
U.S. banks earned healthy profits over the period 1960–2009, except during banking crises in the 1980s and in 2007–2009.

Source: Federal Reserve Board.

Liability Management

As a bank seeks profits, one set of decisions it must make concerns its liabilities—the amounts of money it raises through deposits and borrowing. A key factor driving these decisions is the costs of funds.

Deposits are an inexpensive source of funds. Banks pay little or no interest on checking deposits. These deposits create expenses for processing checks and debit payments, but they are still inexpensive overall. Savings deposits and CDs pay more than checking deposits, but their interest rates are low compared to rates on bonds. Deposits are typically held by small savers, who accept low interest rates because they value the liquidity of bank accounts. In addition, some people simply don't know that higher interest rates are available from securities.

Borrowings are a relatively expensive source of funds. Banks borrow partly by issuing bonds, which carry higher interest rates than deposits. Banks also receive loans from other financial institutions, and the rates on these loans are close to bond rates. The lenders demand competitive interest rates because they could buy bonds rather than make a loan. Lenders to banks, such as other banks, are well informed about interest rates and seek the highest available rate.

Because of the varying costs of funds, many banks raise funds in two steps. First, they try to maximize deposits. They attract deposits by establishing convenient branches, providing good service, and advertising. Second, banks choose their level of borrowing. A bank can usually borrow as much as it wants, because other institutions are happy to lend if they receive sufficiently high interest rates.

Banks' choices of borrowings depend on their opportunities for using funds. For example, a bank might have a large number of attractive loan applications but lack enough deposits to make all the loans. In this situation, the bank borrows to increase its lending.

Liquidity Management

We now turn to the asset side of the balance sheet. While banks' primary assets are loans, they also hold reserves and securities. Banks hold these assets primarily to be ready for withdrawals of deposits. Reserves are available immediately if depositors demand money. And the securities held by banks are highly liquid: if banks need additional reserves, they can sell securities quickly in financial markets. For this reason, banks' securities holdings are sometimes called *secondary reserves*.

In contrast, loans are illiquid. Banks sell some types of loans, such as mortgages, but it takes time to negotiate the sales. Other types of loans are difficult to sell at all because of asymmetric information: a bank that has made a loan has gathered information about the borrower, but others have not. If a bank is eager to sell a loan, others fear that the loan has a high default risk.

Although reserves and securities provide liquidity, they also have a disadvantage: they pay low interest rates. A bank's holdings of cash pay no interest, and reserves held in accounts at the Federal Reserve pay very low rates. The safe securities held by banks, such as Treasury bonds, pay more interest than reserves but they pay less than loans.

Banks face a balancing act in choosing their asset allocation. On one hand, they want enough liquid assets to be ready to meet withdrawals. On the other hand, they want to minimize the amount of liquid assets they hold so they can earn the high interest rates paid on loans. A bank's pursuit of these potentially conflicting goals is called **liquidity management**.

Modern banks have developed a tool to ease the liquidity–return tradeoff: short-term borrowing. Although banks can borrow from various sources, they rely primarily on one another. A bank that is running short of liquid assets can borrow reserves from a bank with more liquidity than it needs. These interbank loans (which are usually *overnight loans* with a term of one day) are called **federal funds**. The federal funds market operates throughout every business day, so banks that need reserves can get them quickly.[3]

The availability of federal funds allows banks to operate with low levels of liquid assets and still be ready for withdrawals. In part because of the federal funds market, modern banks face little risk of running out of reserves—except in the extreme case of a bank run, which we discuss later in this chapter.

18-4 Risk Management at Banks

We have discussed how banks manage their assets and liabilities to maximize profits. Banks often succeed in earning healthy profits, yet their business is risky. If things go wrong, a bank can lose money and even be forced out of business. Two big risks that banks face are *credit risk* and *interest rate risk*.

Managing Credit Risk

Credit risk is another name for default risk, the risk that borrowers will not repay their loans. When a borrower defaults, her loan ceases to be an asset for the bank: the loan is worthless if it does not produce payments. When a loan is in default, the bank must *write off* the loan, which means it removes the loan from its balance sheet. A loan write-off reduces the bank's total assets and its net worth (assets minus liabilities), and the bank's stockholders lose money.

As we discussed in Chapter 15, banks seek to reduce credit risk by reducing asymmetric information problems. Screening borrowers reduces adverse selection, and monitoring them reduces moral hazard. For many loans, banks also reduce credit risk by demanding that borrowers put up some collateral before their loans are approved. **Collateral** is an asset of a borrower that the lender can seize if the borrower defaults. For home mortgages, the house serves as collateral. Collateral for business loans often includes a firm's equipment or inventories.

---

[3] Loans between banks are called federal funds because, in the past, borrowers' main motive was to meet requirements for minimum reserves set by the Fed. These requirements still exist, but they do not affect many banks. Most banks choose to hold more than the minimum level of reserves, largely because they need cash to stock their ATMs.

Collateral reduces credit risk in two ways. First, it reduces a bank's loss when a borrower defaults. By seizing collateral and selling it, the bank can recover some or all the money it is owed.

Second, collateral reduces the probability of default because it reduces information problems. Without collateral, borrowers with risky projects are eager to borrow money: they may win big, and they lose nothing if their projects fail and they default. If banks require collateral, high-risk borrowers are less likely to apply for loans because they could lose the collateral; thus, adverse selection decreases. In addition, after a borrower receives a loan, having collateral at stake is an incentive to use the loan prudently; thus, moral hazard decreases.

Banks also reduce credit risk by selling some of their loans. They sell many mortgages to Fannie Mae or Freddie Mac. When banks make very large loans, they often agree in advance to sell pieces of the loans to other banks. This arrangement is called *loan syndication*. When a loan is split among banks, no single bank loses too much from a default.

Managing Interest Rate Risk

Banks' profits are affected by short-term interest rates in financial markets, such as the Treasury bill rate. Increases in interest rates tend to reduce profits, and decreases raise profits. The resulting instability in profits is called **interest rate risk**.

Maturity Mismatch The explanation for interest rate risk involves the maturities of banks' assets and liabilities. Most liabilities have short maturities, meaning funds are not committed to the bank for long. Checking and savings deposits have zero maturities: they can be withdrawn at any moment. CDs typically mature after a year or two. Most borrowings by banks are also liabilities with short maturities. Federal funds, for example, are usually borrowed for one day at a time.

Because of these short maturities, interest rates on bank liabilities must compete with rates on securities offered for sale in financial markets. Suppose the Treasury bill rate rises. Rates on banks' borrowings rise immediately. Rates on deposits react more slowly, but they must rise before long or a substantial fraction of depositors will withdraw their money to earn higher rates on Treasury bills or other securities. Because banks must adjust the interest rates they pay when rates on securities change, bankers say their liabilities are *rate sensitive*.

In contrast, bank assets typically have long maturities. Many business loans have terms of 10 years. Traditional home mortgages have 30-year terms. If the Treasury bill rate rises, banks can charge higher rates on future loans, but the loans they hold currently have lower rates locked in for long periods. These loans are *not* rate sensitive.

To summarize, a bank's liabilities are mainly rate-sensitive and its assets are not. This *rate-sensitivity gap* means that a rise in short-term interest rates raises the interest that banks pay by more than the interest they earn. The net result is a decrease in bank profits.

Reducing Risk Banks use several techniques to reduce interest rate risk: loan sales, floating interest rates, and derivatives.

- *Loan sales.* We saw earlier that loan sales reduce credit risk. They can also reduce interest rate risk. If a bank sells long-term loans, it has fewer assets with fixed interest rates. It can use the proceeds from the loan sales to acquire assets with shorter maturities, such as Treasury bills and short-term loans, which are rate sensitive. This shift in the bank's assets reduces the rate-sensitivity gap between liabilities and assets. The smaller gap means that changes in interest rates have smaller effects on profits.

- *Floating rates.* A bank can also use **floating interest rates** for its long-term loans. A floating rate is an interest rate tied to a short-term rate. For example, the rate on a 10-year business loan might be the Treasury bill rate plus 2 percent. If Treasury bills pay 4 percent, the bank receives 6 percent on the loan. If the Treasury bill rate rises to 7 percent, the loan rate rises to 9 percent.

  Floating rates turn long-term loans into rate-sensitive assets. The loans themselves are committed for long periods, but the interest rates respond to short-term rates. Like loan sales, floating rates reduce a bank's rate-sensitivity gap. For this reason, banks charge floating rates on most business loans. Some home mortgages, called *adjustable-rate mortgages (ARMs)*, also have floating rates.

- *Derivatives.* Finally, banks can hedge interest rate risk with derivatives. For example, a bank can sell futures contracts for Treasury bonds, a transaction that yields profits if bond prices fall (see Section 17.6). Bond prices fall when interest rates rise, so higher rates produce profits for the bank. These profits offset the loss arising from the rate-sensitivity gap.

Equity and Insolvency Risk

We've seen how banks can lose money if borrowers default on loans or interest rates rise. Sometimes such losses mean only a year or two of low profits. If losses are large enough, however, a bank can face **insolvency**. This means its total assets fall below its liabilities and its net worth becomes negative.

Table 18-3 gives an example. Initially, Duckworth's Bank has the balance sheet in panel (a). It has $100 in assets, $90 in liabilities, and $10 in net worth (capital). Then disaster strikes: borrowers default on $20 of loans. The bank writes off these loans, reducing its total assets to $80, as shown in panel (b). Now the bank's net worth is -$10: the bank is insolvent.

An insolvent bank cannot stay in business. With negative net worth, it cannot pay off all its deposits and borrowings. In this situation, government regulators step in and force the bank to close. This outcome hurts the banks' stockholders because their stock becomes worthless. It also hurts bank managers, who are likely to lose their jobs. For these reasons, banks seek to avoid insolvency.

The Equity Ratio Banks can reduce their insolvency risk by holding more capital. Suppose Duckworth's Bank had started with $30 in capital rather than $10. Then capital would have stayed positive even after the bank wrote off $20 in loans. Higher capital means a deeper cushion against losses.

To be more precise, a bank's insolvency risk depends on its level of capital relative to its assets. This is measured by its **equity ratio** (ER):

$$\text{Equity Ratio} = \text{Capital}/\text{Assets}.$$

TABLE 18-3

Duckworth's Bank Becomes Insolvent

(a) Initial Balance Sheet

Assets		Liabilities and Net Worth	
Reserves	$ 10	Deposits	$ 70
Securities	$ 10	Borrowings	$ 20
Loans	$ 80	Net Worth	$ 10
TOTAL	$100	TOTAL	$100

(b) Balance Sheet After Loan Defaults

Assets		Liabilities and Net Worth	
Reserves	$10	Deposits	$ 70
Securities	$10	Borrowings	$ 20
Loans	$60	Net Worth	$−10
TOTAL	$80	TOTAL	$ 80

The equity ratio shows what percent of assets a bank would have to lose to become insolvent. In Table 18-3, the initial equity ratio for Duckworth's Bank was $10/$100 = 10 percent. Any loss exceeding 10 percent of assets was enough to make the bank insolvent. If the bank had had the same assets but $30 in capital, its equity ratio would have been a safer 30 percent.

A bank can raise its equity ratio either by raising capital (the numerator) or by reducing assets (the denominator). The bank can raise capital by issuing new stock or by reducing dividends to stockholders. It can reduce assets by making fewer loans or purchasing fewer securities. Any of these actions reduces insolvency risk.

The Equity Ratio and the Return on Equity Raising the equity ratio also has a big disadvantage: it makes a bank less profitable. Recall that profitability is measured by the return on equity (ROE), the ratio of profits to capital. This variable falls when the equity ratio rises.

We can see this effect with a little algebra. We take the formula for ROE and divide both the numerator and denominator by assets:

$$\text{ROE} = \text{Profits/Capital} = (\text{Profits/Assets})/(\text{Capital/Assets}).$$

In this formula, profits/assets is the return on assets (ROA). Capital/assets is the equity ratio (ER). So we can simplify to

$$\text{ROE} = \text{ROA/ER}.$$

The return on equity depends on the return on assets and the equity ratio. For a given ROA, raising the equity ratio reduces the ROE.

To understand this effect, suppose a bank raises its equity ratio by issuing new stock. It keeps its assets the same. With the same assets, the bank gets the same flow of profits, but now these profits are split among more stockholders. Each share of stock earns less.

To summarize, a bank faces a tradeoff when it chooses its equity ratio. A higher ratio reduces insolvency risk but also reduces the return on equity. A bank would like a ratio that is high enough to make insolvency unlikely but low enough to produce good returns for its stockholders.

CASE STUDY

The Banking Crisis of the 1980s

Figure 18-5 shows the number of U.S. bank failures from 1960 through 2009. In most years, fewer than 10 banks fail. Failures were higher in 2008 and 2009, reflecting the financial crisis and recession of those years. Yet the largest surge in failures occurred in the 1980s. Failures rose rapidly over that decade, peaking at 534 in 1989. Some of the failed institutions were commercial banks, but the majority were savings and loan associations (a type of bank discussed in Section 18-1). The episode is often called the *S&L crisis*.

Two causes of the crisis were rising interest rates and loan defaults. Examining the episode yields a deeper understanding of interest rate risk and credit risk.

Rising Interest Rates In the 1980s, banks, especially S&Ls, had large rate-sensitivity gaps. Most liabilities of S&Ls were deposits with zero maturities, and most assets were long-term, fixed-rate mortgages. Many of these loans had been made in the 1960s, when interest rates were low. In 1965, the Treasury bill rate was about 4 percent and the 30-year mortgage rate was about 6 percent.

FIGURE 18-5

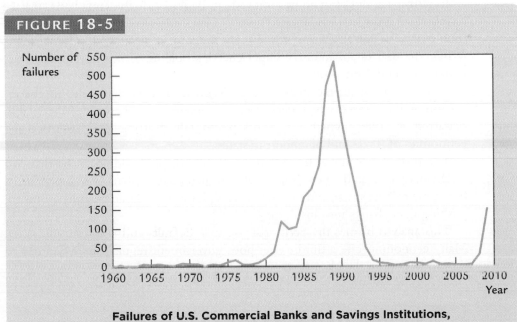

Failures of U.S. Commercial Banks and Savings Institutions, 1960–2009 The number of bank failures rose during the financial crisis of 2007–2009, but it was even higher during the savings and loan crisis of the 1980s.

Source: Federal Deposit Insurance Corporation.

Interest rates rose rapidly in the 1970s and early 1980s. Recall that the nominal interest rate is the sum of the real rate and inflation. In the 1970s real rates were low, but inflation pushed up nominal rates. At the end of the decade, the Fed raised real rates to fight inflation. It took time for inflation to respond, so both real rates *and* inflation were high in the early 80s. The nominal rate on Treasury bills peaked at 14 percent in 1981.

You can guess what happened from our earlier discussion of interest rate risk. Banks were forced to raise interest rates on deposits along with the Treasury bill rate. In the early 1980s, they paid higher rates on deposits than they received on many mortgages. So they suffered large losses.

The Commercial Real Estate Bust In the early 1980s, banks sharply raised their lending for commercial real estate projects, such as office buildings and shopping centers. This lending rose for several reasons:

- Real estate prices were high, spurring new construction. So there was a large demand for real estate loans.

- Bank loans to corporations were declining as more and more companies raised funds by issuing bonds. Banks sought new loan opportunities to offset the business they were losing.

- Regulations changed. Traditionally, S&Ls specialized in home mortgages and were forbidden to lend for commercial real estate. Congress lifted this ban in 1980, so S&Ls joined commercial banks in lending to commercial real estate developers.

In retrospect, this lending was imprudent. Banks made the same basic mistake as subprime mortgage lenders two decades later: eager for business, they relaxed their loan standards. Banks approved loans for risky projects with low collateral. When the real estate industry experienced problems, many developers went bankrupt and defaulted on loans.

Several events triggered these defaults. Many defaults occurred during the recession of 1981–1982, which decreased the demand for real estate. More defaults occurred in 1986, when world oil prices fell, hurting the oil-producing economies of Texas and neighboring states.

The final blow came at the end of the 1980s. Rapid building in the first part of the decade created an oversupply of commercial real estate. Developers had a hard time renting space, and property prices plummeted. Loan defaults mounted, pushing many banks into insolvency.

This analysis blames the S&L crisis on loan defaults and rising interest rates. Many economists cite a third cause: poor government regulation. We return to this point later in the chapter. ∎

18-5 Bank Runs, Deposit Insurance, and Moral Hazard

In any industry, a firm can fail. It can lose money, run out of funds, and be forced out of business. Often, economists think this outcome is efficient. If a firm is not profitable, its resources should be freed up for more productive uses.

When it comes to banks, however, economists have a less benign view of failure. One reason is the risk of a **bank run**, in which depositors lose confidence in a bank and make sudden, large withdrawals. A run can push a healthy bank into insolvency and cause it to fail. When that happens, both the bank's owners and its depositors suffer needless losses.

How Bank Runs Happen

The risk of a bank run is an extreme form of liquidity risk, the risk that a bank will have trouble meeting demands for withdrawals. As we saw earlier, banks manage liquidity risk by holding reserves and secondary reserves, such as Treasury bills. If they are short on reserves, they borrow federal funds from other banks. Normally these methods are sufficient to contain liquidity risk.

However, things are different when a bank experiences a run. A sudden surge in withdrawals overwhelms the bank. It runs out of liquid assets and cannot borrow enough to cover all the withdrawals.

At this point, the bank can raise additional funds by selling loans. But recall that loans are illiquid: because of asymmetric information, it is hard to sell them quickly. To quickly find buyers, the bank will likely have to accept low prices—less than the loans are really worth. In financial jargon, the bank is forced into a *fire sale* of loans.[4] Selling loans for less than their true value reduces the bank's total assets. If it loses enough, capital falls below zero and the run causes insolvency.

What causes runs? Some occur because a bank is insolvent even before the run: the bank does not have enough assets to pay off its liabilities and will likely close. In this situation, depositors fear they will lose their money. These fears are compounded by the first-come, first served nature of deposit withdrawals. The first people to withdraw get their money back, but those who act slowly may find that no funds are left. So depositors rush to withdraw before it's too late, and a run occurs.

A run can also occur at a bank that is initially solvent. This happens if depositors lose confidence in the bank, which can happen suddenly and without good reason. Suppose someone starts a rumor that a bank has lost money and become insolvent. This rumor is totally false. However, depositors hear the rumor and worry that it might be true. Some decide to play it safe and withdraw their funds.

Seeing these withdrawals, other depositors begin to fear that a run is starting. They decide to get their money out before everyone else does and the bank fails. Suddenly there are lots of withdrawals: a run *does* occur. Ultimately, the bank is forced into a fire sale of assets, and its capital is driven below zero.

Section 16-5 discussed the phenomenon of self-fulfilling expectations. We saw there how expectations can influence asset prices. If people expect stock prices to fall, then they sell stocks, causing prices to fall. Bank runs are the same kind of event: if people expect a run, then a run occurs. This can happen even if nothing is wrong at the bank before the run.

---

[4] The metaphor behind "fire sale" is a company whose warehouse has burned down, forcing it to sell goods quickly before they are stolen or damaged by the elements.

An Example

Suppose Duckworth's Bank has the balance sheet shown in Table 18-4(a). The bank has a positive level of capital, or net worth. It also has enough reserves and securities to meet normal demands for withdrawals. There is no good reason for Duckworth's Bank to go out of business.

Then a negative rumor about the bank starts circulating. Worried depositors decide to withdraw their funds. We'll assume they want to withdraw all $70 of deposits in the bank.

To pay depositors, Duckworth's Bank first uses its reserves and securities, a total of $20. Then, with its liquid assets exhausted, the bank must quickly sell its loans. We'll assume this fire sale produces only 50 cents per dollar of loans. The bank sells its $80 in loans, receives $40, and gives this money to depositors. At this point, the bank has paid off a total of $60 in deposits.

The bank's new balance sheet is shown in Table 18-4(b). The bank now has no assets. It still has $30 in liabilities, consisting of its $20 in borrowings and $10 in deposits (since it paid off only $60 of its initial $70 in deposits). The bank's net worth is negative, meaning it is insolvent. It cannot pay the $10 demanded by depositors, and it also has no funds to pay back its $20 in borrowings. As a result, Duckworth's bank goes out of business.

This example assumes that Duckworth's Bank *cannot* borrow federal funds to pay depositors. If it could, its borrowings would rise by the amount its deposits fell, and this one-for-one trade would not change its total liabilities or reduce its net worth. It is likely, however, that a bank facing a run will not be able to increase its borrowings. Other banks see the run on Duckworth's and recognize that it threatens Duckworth's solvency. They won't lend federal funds because they, along with some depositors, won't be repaid if Duckworth's is forced to close.

TABLE 18-4

A Run at Duckworth's Bank

(a) Initial Balance Sheet

Assets		Liabilities and Net Worth	
Reserves	$ 10	Deposits	$ 70
Securities	$ 10	Borrowings	$ 20
Loans	$ 80	Net Worth	$ 10
TOTAL	$100	TOTAL	$100

(b) Balance Sheet After Run

Assets		Liabilities and Net Worth	
Reserves	$0	Deposits	$ 10
Securities	$0	Borrowings	$ 20
Loans	$0	Net Worth	$−30
TOTAL	$0	TOTAL	$ 0

The run on and closure of Duckworth's Bank hurts the owners of the bank: they lose the $10 in capital that they had before the run. It also hurts the holders of the last $10 in deposits, which become worthless, and the institutions that provided Duckworth's initial $20 in borrowings, which are not repaid.

CASE STUDY

The Run on Northern Rock Bank

Since World War II, bank runs have been rare in advanced economies. Before September 2007, the United Kingdom had not experienced a run for 140 years. But suddenly, on September 14, long lines of worried depositors formed at branches of Northern Rock Bank. Depositors also jammed the banks' phone lines and crashed its Web site. Between September 14 and September 17, depositors managed to withdraw 2 billion pounds (roughly $4 billion) from Northern Rock.

Northern Rock Bank is headquartered in northern England (hence the name), and it lends primarily for home mortgages. Before the run, Northern Rock was the fifth-largest mortgage lender in the United Kingdom, and growing rapidly. The bank's lending far exceeded its deposits, so it used borrowing to finance much of the lending. A major source of funds was short-term loans from other banks (the equivalent of federal funds in the United States).

Northern Rock's problems began across the Atlantic, with the subprime mortgage crisis in the United States. In the summer of 2007, people started to realize that the U.S. crisis might spread, threatening the solvency of other countries' financial institutions. With this idea in the air, banks became wary of lending to each other—and especially wary of lending to banks that specialized in mortgages. As a result, Northern Rock had trouble raising funds as it had in the past. Other banks either refused to lend to Northern Rock or demanded high interest rates.

In a bind, Northern Rock turned to the United Kingdom's central bank, the Bank of England, asking for an emergency loan. The Bank of England approved a loan to Northern Rock and planned an announcement, but the news leaked out prematurely. On September 13, a well-known business reporter said on television that Northern Rock "has had to go cap in hand" to the Bank of England. Hearing that their bank had a problem, Northern Rock's depositors had the typical reaction: they rushed to withdraw their funds.

Deposits flowed out of Northern Rock for three days, until the British government intervened. On September 17, the government announced it would guarantee Northern Rock's deposits: if the bank failed, the government would compensate depositors. This action restored confidence enough to end the run.

Yet Northern Rock's problems were not over. The run damaged the bank's reputation, and it continued to have trouble raising funds. With fears growing about Northern Rock's solvency, the British government took over the bank in February 2008, with compensation for the bank's shareholders. As of 2010, the bank was still owned by the government. ∎

Bank Panics

Sometimes runs occur simultaneously at many individual banks. People lose confidence in the whole banking system, and depositors everywhere try to withdraw their money. Such an event is called a **bank panic**.

Nationwide bank panics were once common in the United States. Between 1873 and 1933, the country experienced an average of three panics per decade. Bank panics occur because a loss of confidence is contagious. A run at one bank causes depositors at other banks to wonder whether their money is safe. This uncertainty triggers runs at those banks, which shakes confidence further, which causes more runs, and so on.

In the United States, a typical bank panic started with runs on New York banks. These triggered runs in other parts of the East, and then the panic spread westward. The following case study discusses the last and most severe bank panics in U.S. history.

CASE STUDY

Bank Panics in the 1930s

Chapter 11 discussed the Great Depression of the 1930s, when the unemployment rate reached 25 percent. One cause of the Depression was bank failures, which disrupted the flow of funds from savers to investors. These failures were caused by a series of bank panics.

Figure 18-6 shows the percentage of all U.S. banks that failed in each year from 1876 through 1935. It shows that bank failures rose moderately in the

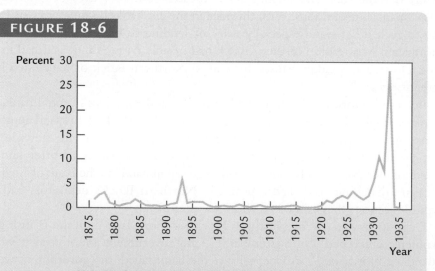

FIGURE 18-6

U.S. Bank Failure Rate, 1876–1935 The bank failure rate is failures during a year as a percentage of the total number of banks. The failure rate rose moderately during the 1920s and skyrocketed during the banking panics of the early 1930s.

Source: George J. Benston et al., *Perspectives on Safe and Sound Banking: Past, Present and Future* (Cambridge, MA: MIT Press, 1986).

1920s. Most failures occurred at small, rural banks. These banks made loans to farmers, and falling agricultural prices during the 1920s led to defaults. These failures were isolated, however; most banks appeared healthy.

Major trouble began in 1930. Failures rose at rural banks in the Midwest, and this made depositors nervous about other banks in the region. These worries were exacerbated by general unease about the economy, a result of the 1929 stock market crash. Bank runs started in the Midwest, and this time they spread eastward.

A psychological milestone was the failure of the Bank of the United States, located in New York, in December 1930. It was one of the country's largest banks, and the largest ever to fail. In addition, while it was an ordinary commercial bank, its name suggested some link to the government. Its failure shook confidence in the whole banking system.

Other events eroded confidence further. Some well-known European banks failed in 1931. In the 1932 election campaign, Democrats publicized banking problems to criticize the Republican administration. The stream of worrisome news produced a nationwide panic.

When Democrat Franklin Roosevelt became president on March 4, 1933, he quickly took charge of the banking crisis. On March 6, Roosevelt announced a *bank holiday*: across the country, all banks were required to shut down temporarily. Starting on March 13, banks were allowed to reopen, but only if the Secretary of the Treasury certified they were solvent. A quarter of all U.S. banks failed in 1933, but Roosevelt's policies ended the panic.

President Roosevelt understood the psychology of panics. His famous statement that "we have nothing to fear but fear itself" referred partly to banking and captures the fact that panics result from self-fulfilling expectations.[5] ■

Deposit Insurance

No bank panics have occurred in the United States since 1933. Runs have occurred at individual banks, but they are rare because the government figured out how to solve the problem: **deposit insurance**.

Deposit insurance is a government's promise to compensate depositors for their losses when a bank fails. In our example of Duckworth's Bank (Table 18-4), insurance would pay off the last $10 in deposits after Duckworth's runs out of assets. In addition to protecting depositors when bank failures occur, insurance makes failures less likely. This effect arises because insurance eliminates bank runs, a major cause of failures.

The reason is simple. A run occurs when depositors start worrying about the safety of their deposits and try to withdraw them. Deposit insurance eliminates the worry because depositors know they will be paid back if their bank fails. They have no reason to start a run, even if they hear bad rumors about the bank.

---

[5] For more on the bank panics of the 1930s, see Chapter 7 of Milton Friedman and Anna Schwartz, *A Monetary History of the United States, 1867–1960* (Princeton, N.J.: Princeton University Press, 1963).

In the United States, deposit insurance is provided primarily by the **Federal Deposit Insurance Corporation** (FDIC), a U.S. government agency. Congress created the FDIC in 1933 in response to the bank panics of the early 1930s. If a bank fails and depositors lose money, the FDIC compensates them up to a limit, which is currently $250,000 per bank account. In 2008 during the financial crisis, the limit was raised from $100,000 in an effort to boost confidence in the banking system.

Many countries have more limited deposit insurance than the United States. At the time of the Northern Rock bank run, the United Kingdom had deposit insurance but paid only 90 percent of losses. Northern Rock's customers ran to the bank because they stood to lose 10 percent of their deposits if the bank failed (until the fourth day of the run, when the government guaranteed deposits fully).

Moral Hazard in Banking

Deposit insurance fixes the problem of bank runs. Unfortunately, it makes another problem worse. This problem is one of moral hazard: because they do not bear the full risk of becoming insolvent, bankers have incentives to misuse deposits.

One of the basic purposes of banks is to reduce the problem of moral hazard in loan markets. Borrowers have incentives to misuse the funds they receive from lenders. Banks reduce this problem through monitoring, loan covenants, and collateral. Unfortunately, banking itself creates new moral hazard problems in which bankers are the parties with incentives to misuse funds. They can use deposits in ways that benefit themselves but hurt depositors.

One way that bankers can exploit depositors is by taking on excessive risk. Suppose a bank lends to borrowers with risky projects who are willing to pay high interest rates. If the projects succeed, the interest income produces high profits for the bank's owners. If the projects fail, the borrowers default and the bank may become insolvent.

However, not all the losses from insolvency fall on the bank. In the absence of deposit insurance, depositors also lose when the bank can't pay them back. With insurance, the government bears the cost of lost deposits. Either way, bankers have incentives to gamble because someone else pays part of the costs if their gambles fail.

We can see this point from our earlier example of insolvency (Table 18-3). In that example, Duckworth's Bank lost $20 from writing off loans. Only part of the cost was borne by the banks' owners: they lost their $10 in capital. The rest of the cost—$10 in lost deposits—fell on depositors or the government.

In addition to excessive risk taking, bankers can exploit depositors in a less subtle way: by stealing their money. The famous robber Willie Sutton was once asked why he chose to hold up banks. His response was, "That's where the money is." The same reasoning applies to white-collar crime when a bank's management is unscrupulous. Large amounts of money flow in and out of banks, creating opportunities for fraud and embezzlement. History provides many examples of bank failures caused by dishonesty.

As usual, the root of moral hazard is asymmetric information. If depositors could see what bankers do with their money, they could forbid gambling and stealing. But it isn't easy to observe what happens inside banks.

The Problem With Deposit Insurance

We can now see a drawback of deposit insurance: it exacerbates the problem of moral hazard. To see this, think about a world without deposit insurance. Depositors worry that banks may fail, costing them money. As a result, they have incentives to monitor banks. Before depositing money, prudent people will investigate a bank's safety. For example, they might check the bank's balance sheet to be sure that insolvency risk is low. After making deposits, people will watch the bank and withdraw their money if there are signs of trouble.

We saw that nervous depositors can cause bank runs. But they also have a positive effect: they discourage banks from misusing deposits. If a bank takes excessive risks or money disappears mysteriously, depositors are likely to notice and withdraw their funds. And the bank will have trouble attracting new deposits. This threat gives banks a reason to keep deposits safe.

Insurance eliminates depositors' incentives to monitor banks. Depositors know they will be compensated if banks fail, so they don't care much if bankers take risks or embezzle their money. They don't bother to check balance sheets for danger signs. This inattention gives bankers greater freedom to misuse deposits: they don't fear that bad behavior will be punished by withdrawals.

Governments recognize the problem with deposit insurance and try to reduce it by limiting the protection they provide. Recall that the FDIC limits its payments to $250,000 per account. Some deposits exceed this level, such as accounts of large corporations or state governments. Large depositors have incentives to monitor banks and withdraw their funds if banks misuse them. Yet moral hazard is still severe, given insurance for most deposits and banks' incentives to misuse funds.

18-6 Bank Regulation

Governments are keenly aware of the moral hazard problem in banking. They could reduce this problem by eliminating deposit insurance, but that might lead to bank runs. To maintain insurance and combat moral hazard, many governments heavily regulate the banking industry. Regulators do the job that depositors neglect when they are insured: they monitor banks' activities and try to prevent them from misusing depositors' funds.

The rest of this chapter surveys bank regulation. We will focus on the regulation of U.S. commercial banks as of 2010. Regulations for banks and other financial institutions are in the process of changing as a result of the recent financial crisis, as we discuss in Chapter 19.

Who Regulates Banks?

A number of government agencies regulate U.S. banks. A bank first meets regulators when it applies for a *charter*—a license to operate. Commercial banks can be chartered either by a federal agency called the Office of the Comptroller of the Currency (OCC) or a state agency such as Maryland's Office of Financial Regulation. Banks chartered by the OCC are called *national banks* and those chartered by state agencies are *state banks*.

Chartering is the first step in bank regulation. A prospective bank submits an application that describes its business plan, its expected earnings, its initial level of capital, and its top management. Regulators review the application and judge the soundness of the bank's plans. If the risk of failure appears too high, the application is denied. In the same way that banks study loan applicants' business plans to screen out borrowers who will misuse loans, regulators try to screen out banks that will misuse deposits.

After a bank is chartered, its operations are overseen by one or more regulators. Commercial banks chartered by the OCC are regulated by the OCC. Most commercial banks chartered by state agencies are regulated by those agencies *and* the Federal Reserve. A few small banks that are not members of the Federal Reserve system are regulated primarily by the Federal Deposit Insurance Corporation. The FDIC becomes involved with any bank that is near insolvency.

This complex system is not based on any logical design. Instead, it reflects the historical development of bank regulation. For example, before the Civil War, only state governments chartered and regulated banks. Concerns about corruption at those banks led to the National Bank Act of 1863, which created the OCC and national banks.

Periodically, the government has considered proposals to streamline bank regulation. In 1993, the Clinton administration proposed the creation of a Federal Banking Commission, which would have been the primary regulator of all banks. Such proposals have not been enacted, in part because of opposition from the Federal Reserve, which has not wanted to relinquish its regulatory role. However, the financial crisis of 2007–2009 rekindled interest in a simplified regulatory system, as we discuss in Chapter 19.

Restrictions on Balance Sheets

Once a bank is chartered and in business, regulators try to contain risk taking by putting restrictions on the bank's balance sheet. Regulations limit the assets that a bank can hold and mandate minimum levels of capital.

Restrictions on Assets Banks can choose among a variety of assets, including safe assets with relatively low returns and riskier assets with higher returns. As we've discussed, moral hazard distorts this choice. Banks have incentives to take on too much risk because the costs that might result are paid partly by depositors or the deposit insurance fund.

To address this problem, regulators restrict the assets that banks can hold. In the United States, there are strict limits on securities holdings. Banks can hold only the safest securities, such as government bonds and bonds issued by corporations with low default risk (as measured by bond-rating agencies). Banks cannot hold risky corporate bonds or stock in any company.

Regulators also restrict the loans that banks make. Each bank's lending must be diversified: no single loan can be too large. At national banks, loans to any one borrower cannot exceed 15 percent of the bank's capital. Loan limits at state banks vary by state. Regulators also set minimum levels of collateral for some kinds of loans, such as loans for commercial real estate.

Capital Requirements We learned earlier that when a bank chooses its level of capital, it faces a tradeoff. Lower capital raises the return on equity but it also raises the bank's insolvency risk, a tradeoff that creates moral hazard: Bank owners benefit from the higher return on equity but do not bear the full cost of insolvency. As a result, banks have incentives to choose low levels of capital, thus creating excessive risk.

Regulators address this problem by imposing **capital requirements**, rules that mandate minimum levels of capital that banks must hold. Required capital is set at levels that regulators think will keep insolvency risk low.

In the United States, capital requirements have two parts. The first is a minimum level for a bank's equity ratio (the ratio of capital to assets). Currently, this minimum is 5 percent: a bank's capital must equal at least 5 percent of its assets for regulators to consider it "well capitalized."

The second requirement is based on an international agreement about capital requirements, the 1988 *Basel Accord*. This rule takes into account the riskiness of different kinds of assets. Among the assets that banks hold, some are very safe and others are relatively risky. The riskier a bank's assets, the more capital it is required to hold. Having more capital protects banks from insolvency if risky assets lose value.

Specifically, the Basel Accord requires banks to hold capital that equals at least 8 percent of their *risk-adjusted assets*. This variable is a weighted sum of different groups of assets, with higher weights given to assets with higher risk. The safest assets, such as reserves and Treasury bonds, have weights of zero. Loans to other banks have weights of 20 percent. A number of assets have 50 percent weights, including municipal bonds and home mortgages (which were considered fairly safe when the Basel Accord was signed). The weights on most other loans are 100 percent.

Capital requirements are controversial. Banks have long complained that the rules are too restrictive. Before the recent financial crisis, the U.S. government was considering changes that would have given banks more flexibility in judging how much capital they need. In the wake of the crisis, which produced a rise in bank failures, it is likely that capital requirements will become more rather than less strict.

Supervision

Another element of government regulation is **bank supervision**, the monitoring of banks' activities. The agency that regulates a bank checks that the bank is meeting capital requirements and obeying restrictions on asset holdings. Regulators also make more subjective assessments of the bank's insolvency risk. If they perceive too much risk, they demand changes in the bank's operations.

A bank's supervisors gather information in two ways. First, they require the bank to report on its activities. The most important of these reports is the *call report*, which contains detailed information on the bank's finances, including a balance sheet and a statement of earnings and losses. A bank must submit a call report every quarter. Regulators examine call reports for signs of trouble, such as declining capital, increases in risky assets, or rising loan delinquencies.

Second, regulators gather information through *bank examinations*, in which a team of regulators visits a bank's headquarters. Every bank is visited at least once a year, more often if regulators suspect problems. Examiners sometimes arrive without warning, making it harder for banks to hide questionable activities.

Examiners review a bank's detailed financial records, study internal memos and minutes of meetings to better understand the bank's business, and interview managers about various policies, such as the criteria for approving loans. Examiners also check outside sources to verify information provided by the bank. For example, they contact some of the bank's loan customers to ensure that the loans really exist and that borrowers have the collateral reported by the bank.

After examiners visit, a bank receives a grade that summarizes its risks to solvency. The grade is based on a range of factors, including the bank's level of capital, the riskiness of its loans, its recent earnings, and the examiners' judgment of the competence of bank managers. Examination grades range from 1 to 5; a rating of 1 means a bank is "fundamentally sound," while a 5 means "imminent risk of failure."

If a bank's grade is 1 or 2, regulators leave it alone until its next examination. If the rating is 3 or worse, regulators require the bank to take action to reduce risk. This could mean tightening the loan approval process, slowing the growth of assets, cutting dividends to shareholders, or firing bad managers. Regulators can either negotiate an agreement with the bank or issue a unilateral order. If the bank's problems are severe, regulators impose fines. If they find evidence of criminal activity, such as embezzlement, they turn the case over to the FBI.

Closing Insolvent Banks

Regulators try to prevent banks from becoming insolvent, but sometimes it happens. Consequently, another task of regulators is to deal with insolvent banks. Today, U.S. regulators force these banks to close quickly. This policy reflects past experiences, such as the S&L crisis of the 1980s, in which delays in closing banks proved costly.

The Need for Government Action In most industries, an unprofitable firm cannot survive for long. If it loses enough money, it becomes insolvent: its debts to banks and bondholders exceed its assets. In this situation, the firm has trouble making debt payments, and lenders won't provide additional funds. The firm runs out of money to operate its business and is forced into bankruptcy.

However, this process may *not* occur for an insolvent bank. The reason is that the bulk of bank liabilities are insured deposits, and insurance makes depositors indifferent to their banks' fates. An insolvent bank is likely to fail eventually, but its depositors don't suffer. Indeed, the bank may be able to attract deposits and stay in business for a long time.

This outcome is dangerous for two reasons. First, the bank may continue practices that led it to insolvency, such as lax procedures for approving loans. These practices are likely to produce further losses, so the bank's net worth becomes more and more negative. Eventually the bank collapses at a high cost to the insurance fund.

Second, the bank may do risky things that it *didn't* do in the past because the moral hazard problem, which exists for all banks, is particularly severe for insolvent ones. If a bank's capital is negative, its owners have nothing left to lose if they take risks. And they have much to gain: if their gambles succeed, they may earn enough to push the bank's capital above zero. In that case, the bank stays in business and managers keep their jobs.

Forbearance Despite the dangers posed by insolvent banks, regulators have sometimes chosen *not* to shut them down. Banks have continued to operate with negative capital. A regulator's decision not to close an insolvent bank is called **forbearance**.

Forbearance occurs because bank closures are painful. Bank owners lose any chance for future profits, managers lose their jobs, and depositors lose their uninsured funds. Closures are costly for the FDIC, which must compensate insured depositors. Closures can also be embarrassing for regulators, because they suggest that bank supervision has been inadequate. For all these reasons, regulators are tempted to let insolvent banks stay open.

Forbearance is a gamble on the part of regulators. As we've discussed, an insolvent bank may start earning profits and become solvent. If that happens, everyone avoids the pain of closure. On the other hand, if the bank continues to lose money, closure is more costly when it finally occurs.

Forbearance exacerbated the savings and loan crisis of the 1980s. Many S&Ls were insolvent by the early 1980s, when interest rates peaked. In retrospect, regulators should have closed these banks promptly, but they did not. Instead, the Federal Home Loan Bank Board, which regulated S&Ls at the time, loosened regulations to help banks stay open. It reduced capital requirements in 1980 and 1982. It also changed accounting rules to allow S&Ls to report higher levels of assets, and hence higher capital. For example, it allowed banks to write off bad loans over a 10-year period rather than all at once.

This policy was unsuccessful: as we've seen, bank failures surged in the late 1980s. Ultimately the government paid $150 billion (at the time, about 3 percent of a year's GDP) to compensate depositors at failed banks. This episode motivated Congress to pass the FDIC Improvement Act of 1991, which established stringent rules for closing banks. These rules govern bank closures today.

The Closure Process Regulators monitor bank capital as part of the supervision process. Under the rules established in 1991, regulators can close a bank immediately if its capital falls below 2 percent of its assets. Note that closure can occur while the bank is still barely solvent—capital can be low but positive. Regulators try to act before capital becomes negative, a situation that creates severe moral hazard.

Regulators have a second option when capital falls below 2 percent of assets: they can give the bank a final chance to increase its capital. The bank can try to add capital by issuing new stock, which people will buy if they think the bank will be profitable in the future. Usually the bank is given three to nine months to increase capital substantially. If it can't, then it must close.

The decision to close a bank is made by the agency that granted the bank's charter (for a commercial bank, either the OCC or a state agency). This agency calls in the FDIC, which takes over the bank. In most cases, the FDIC does not simply shut down the bank; instead, it sells most of the bank's assets and liabilities to another, healthier bank. Depositors keep their deposits and bank branches stay open under new ownership.

An example is the September 2008 failure of Washington Mutual (WaMu), a victim of the subprime mortgage crisis. Before failing, WaMu was the sixth-largest bank in the country. When the FDIC took it over, its stockholders lost their money. So did financial institutions from which WaMu had borrowed—unlike deposits, loans to a bank are not insured. The FDIC sold WaMu's assets and deposits to JP Morgan Chase for $1.9 billion, a tiny amount considering that WaMu had $300 billion of assets in 2007. The day after this deal, WaMu's branches reopened as branches of JP Morgan Chase.

18-7 Conclusion

This chapter has surveyed several aspects of the financial system: the diverse banking industry, the subprime lenders that attract customers who can't borrow from banks, and the securitization of bank loans by government-sponsored enterprises and investment banks. We have seen how banks and subprime lenders earn profits and learned about the risks they face, ranging from credit risk to bank runs. We have also discussed how the government tries to prevent bank failures through deposit insurance and restrictions on risk taking by banks.

As this book is being written, the banking industry is in a state of flux as a result of the financial crisis of 2007-2009. Subprime lending has fallen drastically; the giant mortgage agencies, Fannie Mae and Freddie Mac, are temporarily under government conservatorship; and political leaders are debating a host of proposed regulatory changes to prevent future financial crises. Chapter 19 discusses where the banking industry might be headed.

Summary

1. Types of banks—institutions that make loans and accept deposits—include commercial banks, savings institutions, and credit unions. Finance companies make loans but do not accept deposits.

2. People with low incomes or poor credit histories borrow from subprime lenders, including subprime finance companies, payday lenders, pawnshops, and illegal loan sharks.

3. Many bank loans, especially home mortgages, are securitized. Securitization increases the funds available for loans and allows banks to eliminate default risk on their loans.

4. The left side of a bank's balance sheet shows its assets, including reserves, securities, and loans. The right side shows the bank's liabilities, including deposits and borrowings, and its net worth.

5. Banks face credit risk, which they seek to reduce by screening and monitoring borrowers and by demanding collateral. They also face interest rate risk, which they limit through loan sales, floating interest rates, and the trading of derivatives.

6. A bank run occurs when depositors lose confidence in a bank and make sudden, large withdrawals. A run can cause a previously healthy bank to fail. It can result from self-fulfilling expectations: people withdraw money because they expect withdrawals by others.

7. Deposit insurance, a promise by the government to compensate depositors if a bank fails, prevents bank runs because it makes depositors confident that their money is safe.

8. Bankers have incentives to misuse deposits by taking on excessive risk or by looting. Deposit insurance exacerbates this moral hazard problem because it reduces depositors' incentives to monitor banks.

9. U.S. banks are heavily regulated by a variety of federal and state agencies. Regulators seek to reduce the risk of bank failure by restricting the riskiness of banks' assets and by requiring minimum levels of capital.

10. One part of bank regulation is supervision and monitoring of banks' activities. Banks must file quarterly call reports on their finances and submit to on-site examinations at least once a year.

KEY CONCEPTS

Commercial bank	Balance sheet	Floating interest rate
Savings institution	Liabilities	Insolvency
Credit union	Net worth	Equity ratio
Finance company	Reserves	Bank run
Community bank	Return on assets	Bank panic
Subprime lender	Return on equity	Deposit insurance
Payday lender	Liquidity management	Federal Deposit Insurance Corporation
Pawnshop	Federal funds	
Loan shark	Credit risk	Capital requirements
Securitization	Collateral	Bank supervision
Mortgage-backed securities	Interest rate risk	Forbearance

QUESTIONS FOR REVIEW

1. Describe the similarities and differences between commercial banks and savings institutions.

2. Identify the four types of subprime lenders and explain how each one deals with the higher default risk of subprime loans.

3. Explain the process of how loans undergo securitization.

4. What are Fannie Mae and Freddie Mac? What are their links to the government in the past and at present?

5. Define the major items on the assets and liabilities sides of a bank's balance sheet.

6. If a bank has $100 million in assets and $80 million in liabilities, what is the bank's net worth?

7. What is credit risk? How does a bank limit its exposure to credit risk?

8. What is interest rate risk? How does a bank limit its exposure to interest rate risk?

9. Explain how deposit insurance works, the reasons that governments provide deposit insurance, and the problems that deposit insurance can create.

10. What are the main ways in which regulators try to prevent banks from misusing depositors' funds?

PROBLEMS AND APPLICATIONS

1. HSBC has $1 trillion in assets and operates in about 100 countries. It calls itself "the world's local bank." What business strategies does this phrase suggest? Why might these strategies be successful?

2. Securitization has spread from mortgages to student loans, auto loans, and credit-card debt. However, few loans to businesses have been securitized, except for loans guaranteed by the government's Small Business Administration. Explain why.

3. Suppose that loan sharks propose legislation to promote their industry. They want a legal right to break the kneecaps of loan defaulters.

   a. Suppose you were hired as a lobbyist for the loan sharks. What arguments could you make to support their proposal?

   b. How would you respond to these arguments if you oppose kneecap breaking?

4. Suppose that Duckworth's Bank starts with the balance sheet in Table 18-2. Then the bank sells $10 of loans for $10 of cash.

   a. What is the immediate effect on the balance sheet?

   b. After the loan sale, what additional transactions is the bank likely to make? What will the balance sheet look like after these transactions?

5. Suppose Hibbard's Finance Company raises most of its funds by issuing long-term bonds. It uses these funds for floating-rate loans.

   a. How does the company's rate-sensitivity gap differ from those of most banks?

   b. What deal could the company make with a bank to reduce interest rate risk for both parties?

6. Canada does not have institutions like Fannie Mae and Freddie Mac that securitize mortgages. How do you think this fact affects the types of mortgages offered by Canadian banks? (*Hint:* Think about interest rate risk.)

7. Suppose a bank has $200 million in assets, $10 million in profits, and $40 million in capital.

   a. What is the bank's return on assets?

   b. What is the bank's return on equity?

8. Suppose you are a depositor at Duckworth's Bank, which has the balance sheet shown in Table 18-2. Deposit insurance does not exist. You originally deposited your money in Duckworth's because its branch locations are more convenient than those of other banks.

   a. Suppose you know that Duckworth's other depositors plan to keep their money there. Should you do the same or withdraw your money and deposit it elsewhere?

b. Suppose you know that other depositors plan to make large withdrawals from Duckworth's. What should you do?

c. What do your answers to parts (a) and (b) tell you about the likelihood and causes of bank runs?

9. Suppose an economy has a high level of loans from one bank to another. How might this fact affect the likelihood of a bank panic?

10. Some economists suggest that banks should be charged premiums for deposit insurance based on their levels of capital. Premiums should be higher if capital is lower. What is the rationale for this proposal? Are there any drawbacks to the idea?

11. Consider an analogy (the type on the SATs): "A bank regulator is to a bank as a bank is to a borrower." In what ways is this analogy true?

12. Consider two possibilities: (i) A bank is forced to close even though there is no good reason for it to close; (ii) A bank remains open even though there *are* good reasons for it to close.

a. Explain why (i) and (ii) are possible and what regulations affect the likelihood of these outcomes.

b. Can some combination of regulations make both (i) and (ii) unlikely?

13. Many states allow payday lending but impose restrictions on the practice. For example, a state may limit the amount someone can borrow or the number of times a loan can be rolled over. Find out whether payday lending is legal in your state and, if so, what restrictions exist. How stringent are these restrictions compared to those in other states?

14. Go to the Web site of the Office of the Comptroller of the Currency and look up "enforcement actions." Find an example of a specific enforcement action against a bank. Explain what the OCC did and what problem it was trying to rectify.

CHAPTER 19

Financial Crises

There was a time when the credit markets had essentially frozen and when blue chip industrial companies were having trouble raising money. I knew then we were on the brink...We easily could have had unemployment of 25 percent."

—Henry M. Paulson (former Treasury Secretary), commenting on the state of the U.S. economy in 2008

Throughout this book, we have seen that many kinds of shocks can decrease an economy's output in the short run. Examples include increases in taxes, decreases in consumer confidence, and increases in oil prices. However, one kind of shock is especially devastating to an economy: a **financial crisis**. Such a major disruption of the financial system typically involves sharp falls in asset prices and failures of financial institutions. In the United States, a financial crisis in the early 1930s triggered the Great Depression. A U.S. crisis that started in 2007 produced a recession that by many measures was the worst since the Depression. Financial crises have also damaged economies around the world, such as those of Argentina in 2001 and Greece in 2009–2010.

Regardless of where or when they occur, financial crises are complex events; the feedbacks among different parts of the financial system and the economy make them dangerous and difficult to stop. To understand crises, we must understand the workings of financial markets and the banking system (the topics of Chapters 15–18), the short-run behavior of the aggregate economy (Chapters 9–12), and the effects of macroeconomic policies (Chapters 13–14).

In this chapter, we first look at the events in a typical financial crisis and the various ways in which governments and central banks respond to them. We then use this background to examine what happened to the United States starting in 2007 and discuss some of the reforms that have been proposed in the wake of this crisis to make future financial crises less likely or less severe. Finally, we explore financial crises in emerging economies and what makes them different from those in advanced economies, including the role of the International Monetary Fund in combating crises.

19-1 The Mechanics of Financial Crises

No two financial crises are exactly alike, but most share a few basic features. We first discuss what happens to the financial system in a crisis and then look at how a crisis affects the rest of the economy.

Events in the Financial System

At the center of most crises are declines in asset prices, failures of financial institutions caused by insolvency or liquidity crises, or some combination of these events.

Asset-Price Declines A crisis may be triggered by large decreases in the prices of stocks, real estate, or other assets. Many economists interpret these decreases as the ends of asset-price bubbles. Recall from Chapter 16 that a bubble occurs when asset prices rise far above the present value of the expected income from the assets. Then, at some point, sentiment shifts: people begin to worry that asset prices are too high and start selling the assets, pushing prices down. Falling prices shake confidence further, leading to more selling, and so on. Asset prices may fall over periods of months or years, or a crash may occur in the course of a single day.

Insolvencies In a typical crisis, decreases in asset prices are accompanied by failures of financial institutions. An institution may fail because it becomes insolvent; that is, its assets fall below its liabilities and its net worth (capital) becomes negative. A commercial bank can become insolvent because of loan defaults, increases in interest rates, and other events. When a bank becomes insolvent, regulators are likely to force its closure.

Other kinds of financial institutions can also become insolvent. Hedge funds, for example, borrow money from banks to purchase risky assets. If the prices of these assets decline, a fund's net worth can become negative. When this happens, the fund is likely to default on its debts and go out of business.

Insolvencies can spread from one institution to many others because financial institutions have debts to one another. Banks have deposits at other banks, lend to one another in the federal funds market, and lend to hedge funds and investment banks. If one institution fails, its depositors and lenders suffer losses, and they, in turn, may become insolvent.

Liquidity Crises Even if a financial institution is initially solvent, it can fail because it doesn't have enough liquid assets to make payments it has promised. The classic example of a liquidity crisis is a bank run. Depositors lose confidence in a bank, try to withdraw large amounts from their accounts, and exhaust the bank's reserves and liquid securities. To make the payments it has promised its depositors, the bank must sell its illiquid assets at fire-sale prices (less than the assets' true value), and losses on these transactions can push it into insolvency.

Liquidity crises can also occur at nondepository institutions, such as hedge funds and investment banks. These institutions often raise funds by making short-term loans and issuing *commercial paper* (short-term bonds). To stay in business, they must raise new funds continuously to pay off maturing debts. If creditors lose confidence and cut off funding, an institution can be forced into a fire sale of its illiquid assets, leading to insolvency.

Liquidity crises can spread from one financial institution to another largely for psychological reasons. If a bank experiences a run, for example, depositors at other banks start worrying about the safety of their own funds. They may start making withdrawals, thus triggering an economy-wide bank panic and widespread failures.

Financial Crises and the Economy

Financial crises have both direct and indirect costs. The direct costs include losses to asset holders when asset prices fall. They also include losses from financial institution failures. Owners of a failed institution lose their equity, and the institution's creditors lose funds they have lent. When a failed institution is a bank, losses also fall on uninsured depositors and the Federal Deposit Insurance Corporation (FDIC).

Although these direct costs can be large, the greatest costs from financial crises come from their indirect effects. A crisis can set off a chain of events that plunges the whole economy into a recession. Figure 19-1 summarizes the key parts of this process.

Lending and Spending A fall in asset prices can cause a sharp fall in aggregate demand. One reason is that asset holders suffer a loss of wealth, which leads them to reduce their consumption. Falling asset prices also shake the confidence of firms and consumers, who may interpret them as signs that the overall economy is in trouble. Uncertain of the future, they put off major decisions about spending until things settle down, and investment and consumption fall.

A fall in asset prices also makes it harder for individuals and firms to borrow. Lower prices decrease the value of borrowers' collateral, which is required to overcome adverse selection and moral hazard in loan markets. The result is a **credit crunch**, a sharp decrease in bank lending. Some borrowers are cut off from loans or face higher interest rates.

Failures of financial institutions also cause a credit crunch. When commercial banks fail, they stop lending. Surviving banks may fear failure and become more conservative in approving loans. They may also reduce loans in order to increase their liquid assets and guard against runs. When investment banks fail, securitization falls, which reduces the funds available for bank loans.

A credit crunch means less spending by firms and individuals who rely on credit. This decrease in investment and consumption reduces aggregate demand, adding to the direct effect of asset-price declines. In the short run, a fall in aggregate demand reduces output. In this way, a crisis can cause a deep recession.

A Vicious Circle Unfortunately, that's not the end of the story. If a financial crisis causes a recession, the recession can then exacerbate the crisis. Asset prices are likely to fall further. For example, stock prices fall because the recession reduces firms' expected profits, and real estate prices fall because of lower demand for real estate.

FIGURE 19-1

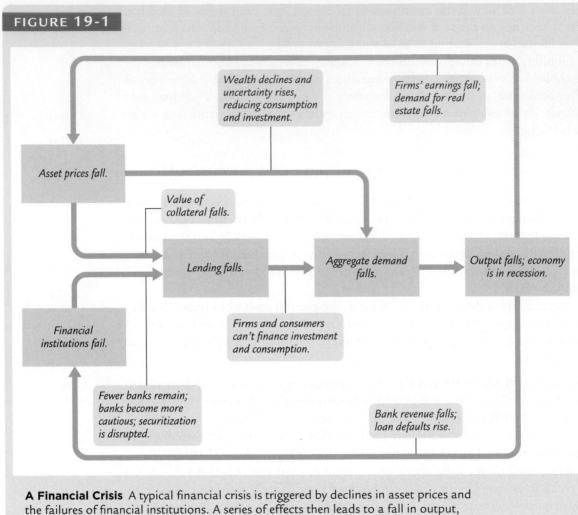

A Financial Crisis A typical financial crisis is triggered by declines in asset prices and the failures of financial institutions. A series of effects then leads to a fall in output, which reinforces the causes of the crisis.

A recession also worsens the problems of financial institutions. Banks lose revenue because a recession reduces the demand for loans. Firms go bankrupt, increasing loan defaults. Worries about these problems make bank panics more likely. For all these reasons, bank failures rise during a recession.

Because of these feedbacks, a financial crisis can trigger a vicious circle of falling output and worsening financial problems. Once a crisis starts, it can sustain itself for a long time.

So far we've discussed the most common elements of crises. Crises often have additional wrinkles—other ways they hurt the economy and build on themselves. To see how much can go wrong, let's examine the Great Depression of the 1930s. Chapter 11 analyzed that disaster using the *IS–LM* model; here, we see that our model of financial crises can shed further light on this historic event.

Disaster in the 1930s

The Depression began in the early 1930s with a financial crisis that had the classic ingredients of falling asset prices and failures of financial institutions. The fall in asset prices started with a stock market crash. on October 28, 1929, the Dow Jones Index fell 13 percent. After the crash, stock prices kept falling: the Dow Index fell from 365 before the crash to 41 in 1932, a decrease of 89 percent.

The stock market crash created great uncertainty about the economy because a crash of this size was an unprecedented event. Uncertainty led firms and consumers to postpone major purchases, such as automobiles, so aggregate demand fell.

A wave of bank failures then rolled across the country from 1930 to 1933. Midwestern banks failed when farmers defaulted on loans, and these failures made people nervous about other banks. Eventually a series of panics swept the country as depositors lost confidence and, with no deposit insurance to protect them, rushed to withdraw funds. President Franklin Roosevelt eventually ended the panics with the bank holiday of March 1933, but more than a third of all U.S. banks failed.

Falling stock prices and massive bank failures reduced bank lending dramatically, resulting in a credit crunch. Because firms and individuals couldn't borrow, investment and consumption fell, causing a decrease in aggregate demand.

As usual in crises, falling aggregate demand and hence falling output magnified the problems of the financial system, especially the stock market. With the economy depressed, firms' earnings prospects were bleak. Stock prices stayed low: it took until 1954 for the Dow Index to climb back to its 1929 level.

As we discussed in Chapter 11, a special twist in this episode was a sharp fall in the money supply, a result of the Federal Reserve's passive response to the bank panics. This development led to deflation: the aggregate price level fell by 22 percent from 1929 to 1933. Deflation in turn increased the real burden of debts, causing many borrowers, especially farmers, to default on bank loans. These defaults further weakened banks and prolonged the severe credit crunch. The Depression was made "Great" because so many problems occurred at the same time. ∎

19-2 Financial Rescues

A financial crisis is a vicious circle in which problems in the financial system and falling aggregate demand reinforce one another. Governments and central banks seek to break this cycle. They do so partly with expansionary fiscal and monetary policies, which boost demand. In crises, however, policy actions are typically not limited to these standard macroeconomic tools. Policymakers also take a range of actions aimed directly at reducing the problems of the financial system, especially the failures of financial institutions.

Generally these policies involve the use of government or central-bank funds to prevent institutions from failing or to compensate individuals or firms that are hurt by failures. In popular discussion, such policies are often called *bailouts*. This umbrella term is imprecise, however, because it is used for policies that vary widely. Bailouts range from giveaways of government money to loans or asset purchases that are costless or even profitable for taxpayers. This section explores some policy actions aimed at ending a financial crisis and looks at the debate about their benefits and costs.

Liquidity Crises and the Lender of Last Resort

Liquidity crises at financial institutions, such as bank panics, are one cause of broader financial crises. A liquidity crisis can push a solvent institution into insolvency, causing it to fail for no good reason. Most economists think policymakers should try to prevent such occurrences.

Fortunately, a central bank has a simple solution for liquidity crises. It can make emergency loans to institutions that are running out of liquid assets, allowing them to avoid fire sales of their illiquid assets. A borrowing institution remains solvent and repays the central bank when its liquidity crisis subsides. To ensure repayment, the central bank requires the borrower to pledge some of its assets as collateral for the loan.

A financial institution facing a liquidity crisis needs help from the central bank because it has trouble borrowing from other private institutions. Potential lenders are wary of an institution that could be driven into insolvency and default on its debts. When the central bank steps in, it acts as **lender of last resort** to an institution with no other source of funds.

When Congress established the Federal Reserve in 1913, the main purpose was to create a lender of last resort for U.S. banks. Unfortunately, during the bank panics of the early 1930s, the Fed underestimated the danger to the banking system and the economy and therefore did not lend to many banks. The Fed learned from this mistake and has acted quickly in more recent liquidity crises.

Deposit insurance helps prevent bank runs, thus reducing the need for a lender of last resort, but it does not eliminate the need entirely. Some banks raise most of their funds through borrowing and deposits that exceed the limit on insurance. These uninsured funds disappear quickly if depositors and lenders lose confidence in a bank. A lender of last resort is needed for such an emergency.

In the United States, a loan from the Federal Reserve to a bank is called a **discount loan**. A bank facing a liquidity crisis can apply for such a loan, which the Fed approves if it judges that the bank is solvent and can post sufficient collateral. The Fed sets the interest rate on discount loans, the *discount rate*, at a level higher than the federal funds rate, the rate on overnight loans between banks. This policy encourages banks to borrow from one another in normal times and to approach the Fed only in emergencies when they can't borrow elsewhere.

Discount loans are available only to commercial banks and savings institutions, financial institutions that fit the definition of "bank": they accept deposits and make loans. At times, however, the Fed has stretched its role as lender of last resort by providing liquidity to other financial institutions. After the terrorist attacks of September 11, 2001, for example, the Fed encouraged banks to lend to securities firms facing liquidity crises; in turn, the Fed promised to lend any necessary funds to the banks. As we discuss later in this chapter, the Fed lent money directly to securities firms during the financial crisis of 2007–2009.

Giveaways of Government Funds

When a central bank acts as lender of last resort, it helps a solvent institution facing a liquidity crisis. The loan prevents the institution from failing, and it is repaid with interest. Ultimately, there is no cost to the central bank, the government, or taxpayers.

Not all failures of financial institutions are caused by liquidity crises. Sometimes an institution simply loses money, so its assets fall below its liabilities and it becomes insolvent. Normally, this causes the institution to fail and default on its debts. In some cases, however, policymakers intervene to prevent this outcome. Instead of lending to an institution, the government or central bank gives money away. It may give funds to the failing institution to restore its solvency and keep it in business. Alternatively, it may let the institution fail but compensate other individuals and institutions that are hurt by the failure.

Deposit insurance commits the government to paying part of the costs of bank failures. The FDIC compensates depositors for their losses up to some limit. Today, few economists question the desirability of deposit insurance, at least in countries with effective bank regulation. The controversial issue is whether compensation should extend beyond promised insurance payments. When a bank fails, should the government protect uninsured depositors and creditors? Should it aid institutions with no insurance guarantees, such as investment banks and hedge funds? Let's discuss the debate over these questions.

The Pros and Cons of Giveaways When the government gives away funds beyond required insurance payments, its purpose is to prevent the problems of an insolvent financial institution from spreading. As we've discussed, banks and other institutions deposit money and lend to one another. If one institution fails, it defaults on debts to other institutions, and their losses can cause them to fail. A rash of failures can produce a financial crisis and push the economy into a recession. The government can prevent this outcome by preventing the first institution from failing or by compensating other institutions for losses from the initial failure.

Such government intervention has two kinds of costs. The first is the direct costs of payments from the government. These costs are ultimately borne by taxpayers. The second cost is a worsening of moral hazard, the problem that financial institutions may misuse the funds they raise.

In particular, the prospect of government aid makes it more likely that institutions will take excessive risks, lose money, and become insolvent. Normally, an institution's creditors and uninsured depositors monitor what happens to their money and cut off funds if the institution misuses them. But if the government intervenes when institutions face failure, everyone comes to expect protection from losses. Nobody has incentives to monitor, so institutions can easily raise funds to finance gambles. These institutions earn a lot if the gambles succeed, and if they lose, the losses fall largely on taxpayers.

When any given institution is in danger of failing, it's hard to know how badly the failure would damage the financial system. It's also hard to gauge how much a government rescue will increase moral hazard in the future. Because of these uncertainties, economists differ sharply on the desirability of government intervention.

Too Big to Fail Historically, decisions about whether to rescue an insolvent financial institution have been influenced strongly by the institution's size. A large institution has more links to other institutions than a small one does. It is likely to borrow heavily, and if it is a bank, it is likely to hold deposits from other banks. Consequently, regulators fear that the failure of a large institution threatens the financial system, whereas the failure of a small institution is relatively harmless. In other words, some financial institutions are deemed **too big to fail (TBTF)**.

This term was coined by a congressman after the rescue of Continental Illinois Bank in 1984, an episode discussed in the following case study.

CASE STUDY

The Continental Illinois Rescue

Before 1984, the U.S. government had never extended significant aid to an insolvent financial institution beyond promised payments on deposit insurance. That changed when Continental Illinois, then the nation's seventh-largest commercial bank, ran into trouble. Continental had lent heavily to energy companies and to the governments of developing countries, and both groups defaulted during a worldwide recession in the early 1980s. In May 1984, Continental was on the brink of failure.

Regulators feared that the failure of Continental Illinois would have widespread effects. Over 2,000 smaller banks had accounts at Continental. For 66 of these banks, deposits at Continental exceeded their total capital; for another 113, the deposits were more than half of their capital. Regulators feared that many of these banks would fail if they lost their deposits, shaking confidence in the financial system. The comptroller of the currency, the head regulator of national banks, said after the crisis that Continental's failure would have caused "a national, if not international, financial crisis the dimensions of which were difficult to imagine."[1]

Policymakers acted aggressively to save Continental. Despite the bank's insolvency, the Fed lent it $3.6 billion to keep it in operation. The FDIC promised to protect all of Continental's creditors and depositors, waiving the usual limit on insurance. Eventually, the FDIC bought Continental from its shareholders, added capital, and sold it to Bank of America. In the process, the FDIC lost about $1 billion.

These actions were controversial at the time, and they remain so. Critics stress the moral hazard problem and argue that policymakers overstated the risks from

[1] Todd Conover, testimony before House Banking Committee, September 19, 1984.

a failure of Continental. The debate over treating some institutions as too big to fail continued in the years after the Continental rescue and intensified during the financial crisis of 2007–2009. ■

Risky Rescues

The potential failure of a large financial institution creates a dilemma for policymakers. Letting the institution fail and default on its debts can damage the financial system, but preventing this outcome is costly for taxpayers and creates moral hazard. Policymakers wrestled with this dilemma repeatedly during the financial crisis of 2007–2009. Looking for a compromise between inaction and giveaways of government funds, they developed two new ways to aid troubled financial institutions: risky loans and equity injections. Unlike loans to solvent institutions facing liquidity crises, these policies expose taxpayers to a risk of losing money. On the other hand, unlike traditional giveaways of government funds, risky loans and equity injections *may not* cost the government anything and might even earn money. Let's discuss these policies and the rationale for using them.

Risky Loans In this type of rescue, the central bank moves beyond its traditional role as lender of last resort, in which it makes *riskless* loans to solvent institutions. When the central bank makes risky loans to prevent failures of financial institutions, it is not certain the loans will be paid back.

Chapter 17 touched on examples of risky loans by the Federal Reserve. In some cases, the Fed has taken on risk by lending to institutions that might fail. In September 2008, for example, it lent $85 billion to the insurance conglomerate AIG, which was near bankruptcy because of losses on credit default swaps. This loan prevented AIG from defaulting immediately on debts to other institutions, but it meant the Fed was on the hook for $85 billion if, as many feared, AIG declared bankruptcy later.

In other cases, the Fed has taken on risk by lending against collateral of uncertain value. In March 2008, it lent $29 billion to JP Morgan Chase to finance the takeover of the investment bank Bear Stearns. The collateral was some of Bear's holdings of subprime mortgage backed securities—the securities whose decline in value had pushed Bear to the brink of bankruptcy. Crucially, the loan to JP Morgan was made *without recourse*: if the value of the collateral declined further, the Fed would be entitled only to the collateral, not the $29 billion it had lent. The Fed stood to lose if the subprime crisis worsened.

During the crisis of 2007–2009, many economists and politicians criticized the Fed for risking money on troubled financial institutions. Fed officials argued, however, that the risks were modest. Part of their rationale was that the Fed's actions would ease the financial crisis, which in turn would reduce the risk that its debtors would default or that the value of their collateral would fall. That is, by agreeing to accept some of the potential losses from the financial crisis, the Fed hoped to prevent these losses from occurring. This strategy was similar to the logic of deposit insurance: by agreeing to bear the costs of a harmful event (bank runs), the government makes the event less likely.

Equity Injections A financial institution becomes insolvent when its capital or equity falls below zero. It can restore solvency and stay in business if it raises new capital by issuing stock. If an institution is troubled, however, individuals and private firms may not be willing to buy its stock. This problem is the rationale for **equity injections**, or purchases of stock, by the government. The U.S. Treasury Department pioneered this rescue policy in 2008 and 2009.

In buying the stock of a financial institution, the government provides the institution with capital to ensure its solvency. Like any purchaser of stock, the government receives an ownership share in the institution and it takes on risk. If the institution ultimately fails, or if it requires further assistance to survive, the government can lose money. On the other hand, the government can earn a profit on behalf of taxpayers if the institution recovers and its stock price rises. Equity injections are controversial because opinions vary on the government's likely gains or losses.

Government purchases of stock are also controversial because they deviate from a financial system based on free markets. Critics argue that the behavior of government-owned institutions may be influenced by politics. In 2008, for example, the Treasury imposed restrictions on executive pay as a condition for purchasing stock. Many voters supported such restrictions, believing that executives who had played a role in the financial crisis should not receive huge salaries and bonuses. Critics argued that high pay was needed to retain the most talented executives and that the government should not interfere with the market forces determining salaries.

19-3 The U.S. Financial Crisis of 2007–2009

The Great Depression of the 1930s showed how a financial crisis can have devastating macroeconomic repercussions. For many years after World War II, however, no such crisis caused an economic upheaval in the United States. Bank failures during the savings-and-loan crisis of the 1980s cost the government $124 billion and embarrassed regulators, but the episode had modest effects on the overall economy. In the 1990s and into the 2000s, failures of financial institutions were rare. Many economists credited the bank regulation described in Chapter 18 for keeping the financial system safe.

More generally, the 1990s and early 2000s were a period of stability in the U.S. economy. The high inflation of the 1970s and the deep recession caused by the disinflation of the 1980s joined the Great Depression in the history books. Economists often referred to the 1990s and 2000s as the "Great Moderation" because of its low inflation and steady output growth.

Over 2007–2009, everything changed. The United States experienced a 55 percent fall in the stock market, the failures of some of the country's most prestigious financial institutions, and a disruption in lending throughout the economy. The worst recession since the 1930s pushed the unemployment rate from under 5 percent in 2007 to over 10 percent in late 2009.

As with any disaster, controversy abounds about what events were critical and who deserves the blame. With hindsight, however, we can see that a series of adverse events had central roles in the financial crisis. The timeline in Figure 19-2 summarizes these events and also shows the unprecedented responses of the government and Federal Reserve to the crisis. Some economists have bitterly criticized these actions, although others think they saved the economy from an even worse fate—a collapse that could have rivaled the 1930s for the worst economic disaster in U.S. history.

2006–2007

The Subprime Crisis and the First Signs of Panic

In 2006 and 2007, as housing prices fell and defaults on subprime mortgages rose, it became increasingly clear that institutions that had made subprime loans would suffer large losses. Two large finance companies that specialized in subprime mortgages, New Century Financial and Ameriquest, declared bankruptcy in April and August 2007, respectively. Other financial institutions that held securities backed by subprime mortgages suffered billions of dollars of losses, leading firms such as Citigroup and Morgan Stanley to fire their chief executives in 2007.

Yet few saw the subprime crisis as a threat to the entire financial system or economy. In mid-2007, economists estimated that financial institutions might lose a total of $150 billion on subprime mortgages—not pocket change, but not a lot compared to the U.S. annual GDP of $14 trillion.

The Liquidity Crisis of August 2007 Warning signs of the economic disaster to come showed up in the summer of 2007. As losses on subprime mortgages rose, banks started to worry about one another. Could losses grow to the point that they pushed major institutions into insolvency? On August 9, the huge French investment bank BNP Paribus announced large losses on subprime mortgages, news that ratcheted up the fears of U.S. bankers. These fears showed up in the federal funds market, in which banks lend to one another. Lenders suddenly became scarce because banks questioned whether borrowers would be able to repay their loans.

On August 9 and 10, the scarcity of lenders pushed the federal funds rate far above the Federal Reserve's target of 5.25 percent. The Fed responded to this development with *open-market operations* in which it purchased large amounts of government bonds, pushing cash into the banking system and reducing interest rates.

Banks around the world remained worried about one another's solvency for the rest of 2007 and into 2008, causing some banks to have trouble raising funds. In September 2007, Northern Rock Bank in the United Kingdom ran short of liquid assets and asked the Bank of England, the nation's central bank, for a loan. News of this request caused depositors to lose confidence in Northern Rock, producing the United Kingdom's first bank run in over a century (see Chapter 18).

The Fed's Response In the United States, the Federal Reserve responded to the disruption of interbank lending by vigorously playing its role as lender of last

FIGURE 19-2 A Timeline of the U.S. Financial Crisis, 2007–2009

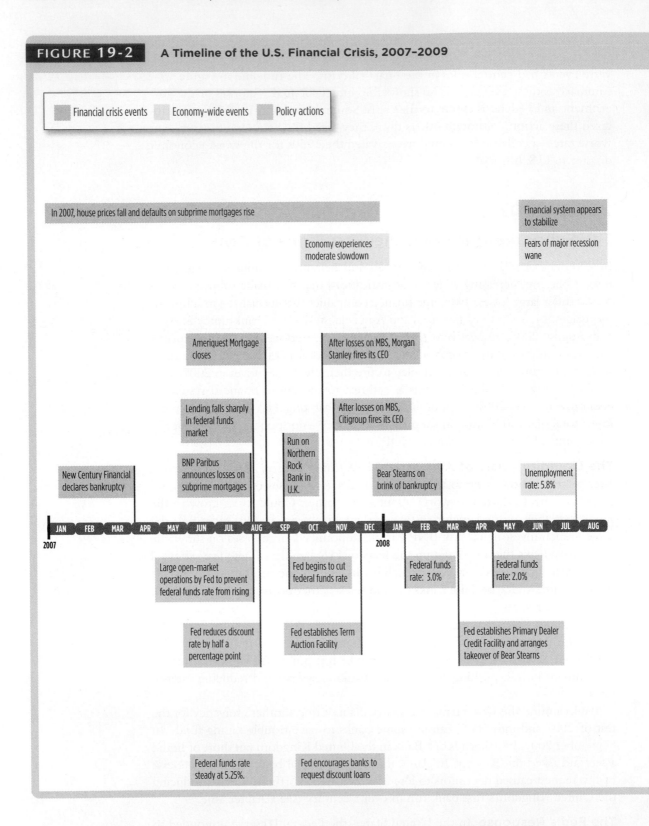

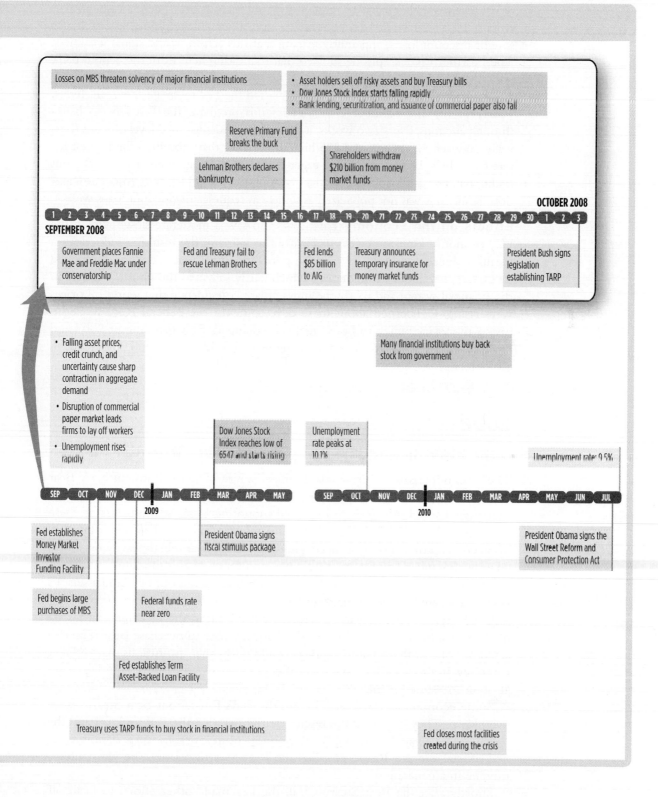

Losses on MBS threaten solvency of major financial institutions

- Asset holders sell off risky assets and buy Treasury bills
- Dow Jones Stock Index starts falling rapidly
- Bank lending, securitization, and issuance of commercial paper also fall

Reserve Primary Fund breaks the buck

Lehman Brothers declares bankruptcy

Shareholders withdraw $210 billion from money market funds

OCTOBER 2008

1 2 3 4 5 6 7 8 9 10 11 12 13 14 15 16 17 18 19 20 21 22 23 24 25 26 27 28 29 30 1 2 3

SEPTEMBER 2008

Government places Fannie Mae and Freddie Mac under conservatorship

Fed and Treasury fail to rescue Lehman Brothers

Fed lends $85 billion to AIG

Treasury announces temporary insurance for money market funds

President Bush signs legislation establishing TARP

- Falling asset prices, credit crunch, and uncertainty cause sharp contraction in aggregate demand
- Disruption of commercial paper market leads firms to lay off workers
- Unemployment rises rapidly

Many financial institutions buy back stock from government

Dow Jones Stock Index reaches low of 6547 and starts rising

Unemployment rate peaks at 10.1%

Unemployment rate: 9.5%

SEP OCT NOV DEC JAN FEB MAR APR MAY

2009

SEP OCT NOV DEC JAN FEB MAR APR MAY JUN JUL

2010

Fed establishes Money Market Investor Funding Facility

President Obama signs fiscal stimulus package

President Obama signs the Wall Street Reform and Consumer Protection Act

Fed begins large purchases of MBS

Federal funds rate near zero

Fed establishes Term Asset-Backed Loan Facility

Treasury uses TARP funds to buy stock in financial institutions

Fed closes most facilities created during the crisis

resort. It encouraged banks to request discount loans if they needed cash, and on August 16 it reduced the discount rate by half a percentage point. Yet few banks sought discount loans, apparently fearing that this action would signal weakness. The Northern Rock episode showed that requesting help from the central bank could backfire.

The low level of discount lending prompted the Fed to create the *Term Auction Facility (TAF)* in December 2007. Under this program, the Fed lent to banks through auctions. Every two weeks, it provided a predetermined level of loans (typically between $25 billion and $75 billion) to banks that submitted the highest interest rate bids. Banks were more eager to bid in these auctions than to take out traditional discount loans because the Fed took the lead in lending. Also, participation in auctions was not publicized as widely as requests for discount loans were.

Effects on the Economy Late 2007 also saw a moderate slowdown in the U.S. economy. Housing prices had started to fall, and the resulting reduction in wealth reduced consumption. Consumption and investment were also dampened by uncertainty about the economy, which partly reflected the signs of trouble in the financial system and partly the unfortunate coincidence that world oil prices were rising. Concerned about these developments, the Federal Reserve began easing monetary policy to boost aggregate demand. Between August 2007 and January 2008, it reduced its target for the federal funds rate from 5.25 percent to 3.0 percent.

2008

Bear Stearns and the Calm Before the Storm

The next unpleasant surprise was the near-failure of the investment bank Bear Stearns. As we discussed in Chapter 17, Bear held large quantities of subprime mortgage–backed securities and suffered mounting losses as the prices of these securities fell over 2007. In March 2008, rumors spread that Bear might become insolvent, and these fears produced a liquidity crisis. Bear relied heavily on short-term borrowing to fund its asset holdings, and much of this funding disappeared as lenders lost confidence in the firm. As Bear Stearns ran out of liquid assets, its lawyers prepared to file for bankruptcy.

On March 16, Bear Stearns's predicament produced the first financial rescue of the crisis: the Fed's risky loan to JP Morgan Chase to purchase Bear. The Fed acted out of fear that a failure of Bear would hurt other institutions that had lent it money. It also feared a blow to confidence that would trigger liquidity crises at other investment banks.

Some economists, however, thought the Fed's fears about Bear Stearns were overblown. They criticized the rescue for the risk that the Fed took on and the moral hazard created by saving Bear's creditors from losses. In April 2008, former Fed official Vincent Reinhart called the Bear Stearns rescue "the worst policy mistake in a generation."

Shortly after the Bear Stearns deal, the Fed made other efforts to head off problems in the financial system and economy. It once again reduced its target for the federal funds rate, taking it down to 2.0 percent at the end of March 2008. In the same month, the Fed sought to prevent liquidity crises by expanding its role as lender of last resort. It established the *Primary Dealer Credit Facility (PDCF)*, which offered loans to *primary dealers* in the government securities market—the institutions that trade with the Fed when it performs open-market operations. Primary dealers include the largest investment banks as well as commercial banks, so investment banks also became eligible for emergency loans from the Fed.

After the Bearn Stearns rescue, no major shocks hit the financial system for six months. Over the summer of 2008, fears about the solvency of financial institutions receded, and policymakers became hopeful that the economic damage from the financial drama would be modest. In June, Fed Chair Ben Bernanke said, "The risk that the economy has entered a substantial downturn appears to have diminished over the last month or so."

Disaster Strikes: September 7–19, 2008

Over two weeks in September 2008, optimism about the economy vanished as the financial crisis exploded. Bad news arrived at a dizzying pace.

Fannie and Freddie Face Insolvency Mounting losses on mortgage-backed securities threatened the solvency of Fannie Mae and Freddie Mac, the government-sponsored enterprises that securitize a large share of U.S. mortgages. On September 7, the government took Fannie and Freddie into conservatorship. Under this arrangement, the Treasury promised to cover Fannie and Freddie's losses with public funds so they wouldn't default on bonds they had issued. Default would have caused catastrophic losses to commercial banks and other financial institutions that held trillions of dollars of Fannie's and Freddie's bonds. A bankruptcy of Fannie or Freddie would also have disrupted mortgage lending, because many banks made loans with the expectation of selling them to Fannie or Freddie.

The government received stock that gave it 80 percent ownership stakes in Fannie and Freddie. Nonetheless, its action was in essence a pure giveaway of government funds. It was clear that Fannie and Freddie were insolvent and that the government would be giving them more money than their stock was worth. As of 2010, the Fannie and Freddie rescues had cost the government more than $200 billion.

Lehman Brothers' Bankruptcy Then came what many now consider the key blow to the financial system: the declaration of bankruptcy by the investment bank Lehman Brothers on September 15. Like Bear Stearns, Lehman had had large losses on mortgage-backed securities, taking it to the brink of failure. And once again, the Federal Reserve sought to arrange a takeover, in this case by the British bank Barclay's. But the deal fell through at the last minute, in part because of objections from British bank regulators.

It is unclear whether the Fed or the Treasury could still have saved Lehman. Ben Bernanke and Henry Paulson, the Secretary of the Treasury at the time, have said they did not have the legal authority to provide funds to Lehman after the Barclay's deal fell through. Critics contend that policymakers could have done something and that they misjudged the harm of letting Lehman fail. The Fed and the Treasury may have hesitated about acting aggressively because of the earlier negative reaction to the Bear Stearns rescue. A new rescue would have sparked harsh criticism that policymakers were worsening moral hazard yet again.

Lehman's failure shocked financial markets. The firm had been a pillar of the U.S. financial system since 1850, and it was the largest U.S. firm in any industry ever to file for bankruptcy. Everyone on Wall Street knew that Lehman was in trouble in September 2008, but many presumed that, like Bear Stearns, the firm would be taken over by a healthier institution.

Bankruptcy meant that Lehman defaulted on its borrowings from other financial institutions. Few people knew exactly how much Lehman owed or what institutions were its creditors, so fears arose that many institutions could suffer losses that threatened their solvency. In addition to the direct effects of Lehman's defaults, the failure of such a prestigious firm suggested that *any* financial institution could fail.

The events that followed Lehman's failure were sufficiently dire that it was the last big institution to declare bankruptcy throughout the crisis. Seeking to stem the financial panic, the Fed and the Treasury acted aggressively to save other institutions from Lehman's fate.

The Rescue of AIG Policymakers' new activism began on September 16, the day after the Lehman bankruptcy. The American International Group (AIG), the giant insurance conglomerate, was the next institution in line to fail until the Fed made an emergency loan of $85 billion. In explaining this action, Ben Bernanke said that a failure of AIG "could have resulted in a 1930s-style global financial and economic meltdown, with catastrophic implications for production, income, and jobs."

A bankrupt AIG would have defaulted on the $20 billion of commercial paper that it had issued. In addition, it would not have made promised payments on the credit default swaps it had sold on mortgage-backed securities. As a result, other institutions would not have been compensated for losses on the securities. Individuals and businesses that had purchased insurance policies from AIG would have seen their insurance coverage disappear suddenly.

The Money Market Crisis A final part of the September 2008 debacle involved money market mutual funds. These funds hold Treasury bills (short-term government bonds) and commercial paper (short-term corporate bonds) and sell shares to savers. The funds generally yield low returns but are considered safe because their assets have short maturities and low default rates. Since money market funds were invented in the 1970s, almost nobody who put a dollar in a money market fund ended up with less than a dollar. Many people have come to view money market funds as similar to bank accounts, which also yield low but safe returns.

The same day as the AIG rescue, however, one large money market fund, the Reserve Primary Fund, *broke the buck*: the value of a share in the fund, which originally cost $1, fell to 97 cents. The reason was simple: the fund owned large quantities of Lehman Brothers' commercial paper, which plummeted in value when Lehman declared bankruptcy. Suddenly people were reminded that a money market fund was *not* a bank account with a guaranteed return. And unlike bank deposits, government insurance does not cover shares in money market funds.

The result of the Reserve Primary Fund's breaking of the buck was a run on money market funds. In two days, September 17 and 18, panicked holders of money market shares withdrew $210 billion from the funds, reducing the funds' total assets by approximately 22 percent. This outflow slowed on September 19, when the Treasury Department announced it would temporarily offer insurance to money market funds. But confidence remained shaky, and the funds' assets slipped further over the next few months.

A Flight to Safety The quick succession of crises at major institutions created panic. Nobody knew what shock would come next, when the crisis would end, or how devastating it would be for the economy. This atmosphere led to a *flight to safety*. Financial institutions became fearful of any assets that appeared risky, including stocks, the bonds of corporations without top credit ratings, and securities backed by any kind of bank loans. Institutions dumped these assets and bought those they considered safest: three- and six-month Treasury bills. These Treasury bills were considered safe because it was unlikely that the government would default on its debt over the next six months, even in a financial crisis.

We can see some effects of the flight to safety in Figure 19-3, which shows data from financial markets over the period 2007–2009. Starting in September 2008, the Dow Jones Index of stock prices plummeted for six months, shown in panel (a). Securitization fell dramatically as demand for securitized loans disappeared, shown in panel (b). The prices of BAA-rated corporate bonds (bonds with moderate default risk) fell, which implied a sharp rise in their interest rates as measured by yield to maturity, shown in panel (c). In contrast, the flight to Treasury bills pushed their prices up and interest rates on them fell almost to zero, shown in panel (d).

An Economy in Freefall

Much of the financial crisis played out in the Wall Street area of lower Manhattan and in Washington, D.C., where financial institutions and policymakers grappled with the crisis. In the fall of 2008, however, the problems of Wall Street spread to Main Streets across the country, plunging the economy into a deep recession.

The story followed the broad pattern outlined in our basic model of a financial crisis, Figure 19-1, and in our review of the Great Depression of the 1930s. The stock market plunge and the accelerating decline in housing prices reduced consumers' wealth. The dramatic news from the financial system hit consumer confidence hard: from September to November 2008, the University of Michigan's survey of consumer confidence revealed one of the largest drops in the survey's 60-year history. Falling wealth and falling confidence caused a contraction in consumption spending.

Financial panic also caused a credit crunch with many dimensions. Banks became fearful of lending because losses on mortgages had reduced their capital,

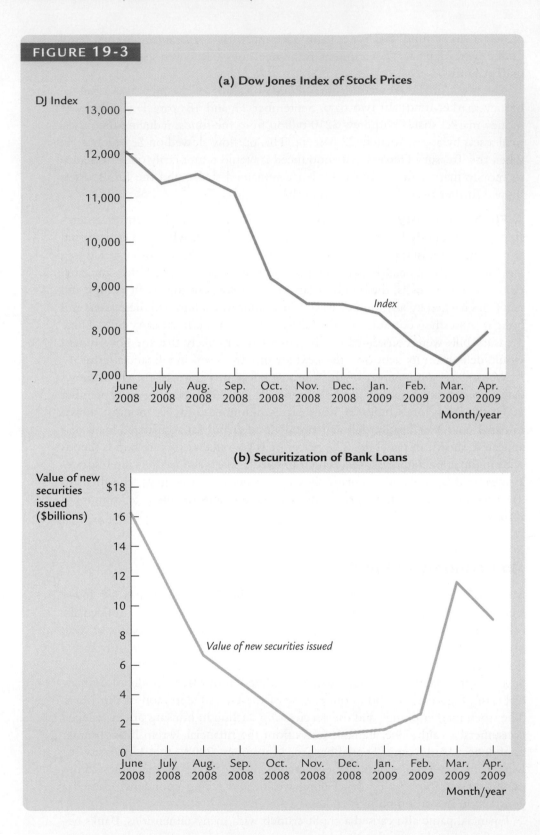

FIGURE 19-3

(a) Dow Jones Index of Stock Prices

FIGURE 19-3 *(continued)*

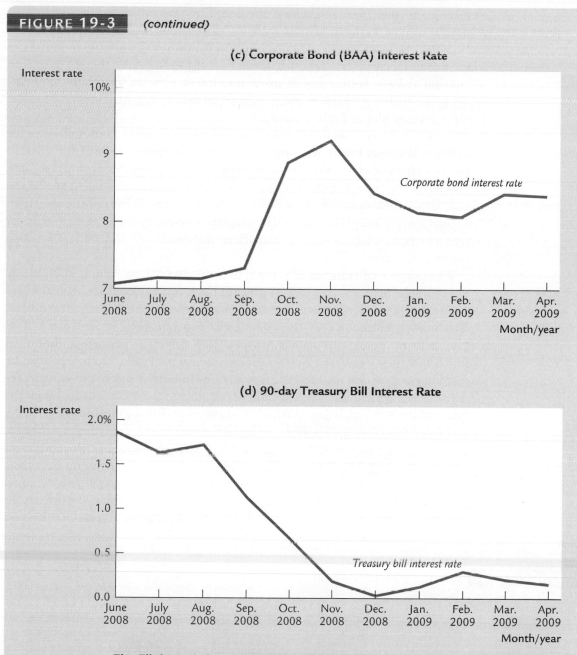

The Flight to Safety, Fall 2008 In the panic following the failure of Lehman Brothers, financial institutions dumped any assets that appeared risky, causing a sharp fall in stock prices (panel a), a collapse in securitization of bank loans (panel b), and higher interest rates on corporate bonds with moderate default risk (panel c). A surge in the demand for Treasury bills, a safe asset, pushed the interest rate on Treasury bill near zero (panel d).

Sources: finance.yahoo.com, Securities Industry and Financial Market Association, and Federal Reserve Bank of St. Louis.

meaning further losses could push them into insolvency. With financial institutions fearful of securities backed by bank loans, investment banks stopped securitizing auto loans, credit-card debt, and student loans. Because they could not sell loans to securitizers, banks had fewer funds to lend. Finally, the rise in interest rates on risky corporate bonds made investment projects too costly for many firms. With both investment and consumption falling, aggregate demand fell and the economy plunged into a recession.

Some economists think the run on money market mutual funds following the Lehman Brothers failure was one of the most damaging events of the crisis. It set off a chain of effects that are summarized in Figure 19-4. Money market funds needed to make large payments to panicked shareholders, and this depleted the cash they would normally have used to purchase new commercial paper from corporations. Companies across the country—including those in industries far removed from finance, such as manufacturing—suddenly had difficulty selling commercial paper.

The purpose of commercial paper is to cover firms' short-term needs for cash. For example, firms use commercial paper to cover production costs, such as wages and materials, while they wait for revenue to come in from selling their output. The sudden breakdown of the commercial paper market in September 2008 caused firms around the country to join Wall Street in panicking. Businesses feared that they wouldn't have enough cash to pay their bills. They responded by slashing costs, which required sharp reductions in output and layoffs of workers. The unemployment rate started rising, which added yet another channel from the financial crisis to aggregate demand: consumption fell among laid-off workers and those who feared they might be laid off next.

Through the end of 2008 and into 2009, the vicious circle of a financial crisis was in full swing. The deteriorating economy had feedback effects on the financial system: it caused stock and housing prices to continue to fall and it caused more borrowers to default on bank loans, increasing banks' risk of insolvency. In turn, the worsening problems of the financial system pushed aggregate demand even lower and caused unemployment to rise rapidly.

FIGURE 19-4

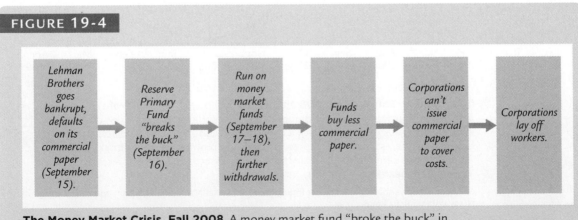

The Money Market Crisis, Fall 2008 A money market fund "broke the buck" in September 2008 and triggered a series of effects that worsened the financial crisis and increased unemployment.

The Policy Response

As the financial crisis accelerated in late 2008, so did the response of policymakers. Worries about excessive government interference in the economy were swept aside as the Federal Reserve and the Bush and Obama administrations took unprecedented actions to stave off disaster.

The TARP On October 3, 2008—18 days after the Lehman failure—President Bush signed an emergency Act of Congress establishing the *Troubled Asset Relief Program (TARP)*. The TARP committed $700 billion of government funds to rescue financial institutions.

The initial plan behind the TARP was for the government to purchase "troubled assets," primarily mortgage-backed securities. After the program was established, however, the Treasury decided to use most of the funds for equity injections: instead of purchasing the assets of financial institutions, it purchased shares in the institutions themselves. In late 2008 and early 2009, the Treasury became a major shareholder in most of the country's large financial institutions, ranging from Citigroup to Goldman Sachs to AIG.

Federal Reserve Programs Before the Lehman panic, the Fed had already sought to support the financial system with the Term Auction Facility (TAF) and the Primary Dealer Credit Facility (PDCF). In the fall of 2008, the Fed added half a dozen new programs, most with the bureaucratic title of "facility" in their names and with ugly acronyms. (This flurry of activity was reflected in the title of a speech by Fed Governor Kevin Warsh: "Longer Days and No Weekends.") The goals of the Fed's programs included repairing the commercial paper market, rejuvenating securitization, and pushing down interest rates on mortgages.

Monetary and Fiscal Policy Policymakers also sought to counter the economic downturn with the traditional tools of monetary and fiscal policy. From September to December 2008, the Federal Reserve cut its target for the federal funds rate from 2 percent to almost zero. The target was still near zero in the summer of 2010, as this book was going to press.

When President Obama took office in January 2009, one of his first priorities was fiscal stimulus. The next month, he signed a fiscal package passed by Congress that allocated about 5 percent of GDP to tax cuts and spending on infrastructure, such as roads and schools. The effects of the stimulus package are controversial, but one nonpartisan source, the Congressional Budget Office, estimated that it boosted real GDP by 1.5 to 3.5 percent.

2009 and Beyond

The Aftermath

Economists and policymakers will long debate the wisdom of Fed and Treasury actions during the financial crisis. Whatever the role of these policies, the financial system started returning to normal in 2009. Yet the broader economy remained troubled.

FYI

Specifics of Some Federal Reserve Responses to the Financial Crisis

The Federal Reserve's many actions in the fall of 2008 included the following:

➤ In October 2008, the Fed established the Money Market Investor Funding Facility (MMIFF). This program addressed the disruption of the commercial paper market after the run on money market funds. Under the MMIFF, the Fed lent money to banks that agreed to purchase commercial paper from money market funds. This arrangement helped the funds ensure that they could raise cash if their shareholders demanded it. In turn, as funds became less worried about withdrawals, they became more willing to buy commercial paper from corporations.

➤ In November, the Fed established the Term Asset-Backed Loan Facility (TALF). Under this program, the Fed lent to financial institutions such as hedge funds to finance purchases of securities backed by bank loans. The goal was to ease the credit crunch by encouraging the securitization process, which broke down during the post-Lehman panic. The Fed accepted the securities purchased under the program as collateral and its loans were without recourse, which meant the Fed took on the risk that the securities would fall in value.

➤ Also in November 2008, the Fed began purchasing mortgage-backed securities issued by Fannie Mae and Freddie Mac. The goal was to drive down interest rates on these securities and ultimately reduce rates on the mortgages behind the securities. Over a year, the Fed bought more than a trillion dollars' worth of mortgage-backed securities. Studies estimate that these purchases reduced mortgage rates by three- or four-tenths of a percentage point. The Fed hoped that lower rates would increase the demand for housing and help slow the fall in U.S. housing prices.[2]

The Financial Crisis Eases One sign that the financial system was beginning to recover was found in stock prices. The Dow Jones Index of stock prices hit a low of 6,547 in March 2009 and then rose 65 percent over the following 12 months. Fears of further failures of financial institutions waned, and institutions such as Goldman Sachs and Citigroup, which had lost billions of dollars in 2008, returned to profitability in 2009.

As the financial crisis eased, so did the need for the Federal Reserve's emergency lending programs. Borrowing under such programs as the TAF and PDCF dwindled over 2009, and the Fed quietly ended the programs in early 2010. Many financial institutions bought back the stock they had sold to the government under TARP. In the end, the government made money on many of these transactions, selling back the stock at higher prices than it paid.

Much of the money that the Fed and the Treasury poured into the most troubled institutions, including AIG, Fannie Mae, and Freddie Mac, will probably never be recouped. But overall, the direct costs of financial rescues proved modest relative to the economic damage (in terms of lost output and high unemployment) caused by the financial crisis. A government audit of TARP in 2010 estimated that it will eventually cost taxpayers $40 billion, a small fraction of the $700 billion put into the program.

---

[2] "Credit and Liquidity Policies," a page on the Fed Web site, www.frb.gov, catalogs the full range of Fed responses to the crisis.

Unemployment Persists After rising from under 5 percent before the crisis to 10 percent in late 2009, unemployment stayed high. In July 2010 (as this book was going to press), the unemployment rate was 9.5 percent, and economic forecasters predicted rates of 8 to 9 percent into 2011 and beyond.

Because the unemployment rate stayed high, more and more people found themselves jobless for long periods. In July 2010, workers who had been unemployed more than half a year accounted for 4.3 percent of the labor force, up from 0.7 percent two years earlier.

In most models of economic fluctuations—including those in Chapters 9–12 of this book—a recession causes a short-run rise in unemployment, but in the long run, unemployment returns to an unchanged natural rate. Since World War II, most U.S. recessions have followed this pattern. For example, unemployment rose from 6 percent in 1980 to over 10 percent in 1982, but then fell to 7 percent in 1984 and to 6 percent in 1987. The crisis of 2007–2009, however, may have longer-lasting effects. Chapter 12 discussed the theory of *hysteresis*, which posits that a recession can leave permanent scars on the economy, causing unemployment rates to remain high. Time will tell whether the aftermath of the financial crisis leads to a more prominent role for hysteresis in macroeconomic theory.

Constraints on Macroeconomic Policy With unemployment lingering at a high level, one might think that policymakers would seek to reduce it through expansionary fiscal or monetary policy. Unfortunately, in 2009–2010, both types of policy were severely constrained. The combination of the recession and the fiscal stimulus pushed the 2009 government budget deficit to about 10 percent of GDP, by far the highest level since World War II. This deficit exacerbated the problem of rising government debt, a long-term trend resulting from the costs of Social Security, Medicare, and Medicaid (see Chapter 14). Most economists and political leaders believed that the government couldn't afford further fiscal stimulus.

Starting in October 2008, monetary policy was constrained by the simple fact that the Fed's target for the federal funds rate was close to zero. As discussed in Chapter 11, a nominal interest rate cannot fall below zero because nobody would make a loan in return for negative interest. In 2009 and 2010, this **zero-bound problem** (also known as the *liquidity trap*) prevented the Fed from stimulating the economy. A zero interest rate was not low enough to produce a surge in aggregate demand that would push down unemployment.

As shown in Figure 13-2, a simple formula based on output and inflation—the Taylor rule—captures the broad movements in the federal funds rate from the mid-1980s until 2007. In 2009–2010, economists who used this rule to compute the appropriate federal funds rate came up with numbers around −3 or −4 percent. In effect, the zero bound was forcing the Federal Reserve to keep interest rates several points above the level needed to restore full employment.

Moral Hazard Problems Another legacy of the crisis was the precedent set by the government's rescues of financial institutions. Economists and political leaders agreed that these actions had worsened the problem of moral hazard, potentially setting the stage for increased risk taking and future crises. A consensus emerged that new government regulations were needed to protect the financial system and the economy.

19-4 The Future of Financial Regulation

The crisis of 2007–2009 sparked intense debate about government regulation of financial institutions. How can the government prevent future crises or at least minimize the damage they inflict on the economy? Unfortunately, although many economists and political leaders advocate reform, there is little consensus about *what* new regulations are desirable. This section outlines the major ideas for financial reform in recent debates. Some of these ideas are being implemented under the Dodd-Frank Act (formally named the Wall Street Reform and Consumer Protection Act), which President Obama signed into law in July, 2010.

We can classify many proposals for financial reform within four broad categories: increased regulation of nonbank financial institutions, policies to prevent institutions from becoming too big to fail, rules that discourage excessive risk taking, and new structures for regulatory agencies. Table 19-1 lists some of the major reform proposals in each category.

Regulating Nonbank Financial Institutions

Commercial banks are heavily regulated in the United States. To reduce the risk of bank failures, regulators restrict the assets that banks can hold, impose capital

TABLE 19-1

Financial Reform Proposals

Problem	Proposed Reforms
Nonbank financial institutions are insufficiently regulated.	Impose regulations similar to those for commercial banks: restrictions on assets, capital requirements, supervision.
	Give a government agency resolution authority over failing institutions.
Some institutions are considered too big to fail.	Limit size of institutions.
	Tie capital requirements to size.
	Limit scope of institutions.
Financial institutions have incentives to take too much risk.	Require security issuers to have skin in the game.
	Reform ratings agencies.
	Restrict executive pay.
Multiple regulators lead to gaps in regulation.	Consolidate agencies that regulate financial institutions.
	Create new agency to oversee existing agencies and address systemic risk.
	Tighten regulation of financial holding companies.

requirements, and subject banks to frequent examinations to be sure they are not taking on too much risk. Nonbank financial institutions, such as investment banks, hedge funds, and insurance companies, do not face the same regulations. As a result, they have been able to engage in riskier behavior. They have held low levels of capital and high levels of risky assets, such as subprime mortgage–backed securities.

Why are banks and nonbank financial institutions treated differently? Part of the justification for bank regulation is the existence of government deposit insurance. The government is committed to compensating depositors if a commercial bank fails, so it has an interest in preventing risky behavior that might lead to failure. In addition, deposit insurance makes risky behavior more likely because it eliminates the incentive of depositors to monitor banks. In contrast, institutions such as investment banks have no deposits, so the government has not promised to pay anyone if the institutions fail. And without insurance, lenders to nonbank financial institutions have incentives to monitor their behavior.

The financial crisis has led economists and policymakers to question this traditional thinking. The crises at investment banks such as Bear Stearns and Lehman Brothers and at insurance giant AIG revealed that lenders to these institutions had not monitored them well enough to prevent excessive risk taking. And the absence of insurance did not mean the government could be indifferent to failures. The aftermath of the Lehman bankruptcy showed that the failure of an investment bank can potentially have significant adverse repercussions. To keep the financial crisis from getting worse, the government felt it had to rescue other institutions even though it was not obligated to them for any insurance payments.

To prevent this situation from recurring, many economists argue that the types of regulations previously reserved for commercial banks should be extended to other financial institutions. In the future, institutions such as investment banks and hedge funds may be required to hold more capital and fewer risky assets, and regulators may scrutinize their activities more closely.

Not surprisingly, financial institutions generally dislike the idea of greater regulation because restrictions on risky activities limit their profit-seeking opportunities. In addition, financial institutions and some economists argue that stricter regulation could stifle financial innovation. When financial engineers create new securities, their actions may appear risky but may actually improve the functioning of the financial system.

An example is the invention of junk bonds, an innovation of the 1970s that increased the number of corporations that could fund investment through the bond market. Securitization is another innovation that has, in some cases, been beneficial to borrowers and asset holders. Although the securitization of subprime mortgages proved disastrous, securitization of auto loans and student loans appears to have been a success. Securitization has provided funds for people to buy cars and go to school, and owners of securities have earned healthy returns. Overly restrictive regulations could impede such innovations, making the financial system less effective in channeling funds from savers to investors.

Ideally, regulations should be strict enough to prevent excessive risk taking yet not so restrictive that they impede productive financial innovation. Implementing this principle is difficult, however, because it is hard to predict which innovations will be successful and which will cause problems.

Another proposed reform would change how the government deals with failed financial institutions. Once again, the basic idea is to treat nonbank institutions more like commercial banks. As discussed in Chapter 18, an insolvent bank is taken over by the FDIC, which attempts to minimize the costs to taxpayers and the disruption of the economy. The FDIC can take time, for example, to find another institution that will take over the failed bank and keep the profitable parts of its business running.

In contrast, when a nonbank financial institution fails, it declares bankruptcy. This outcome may be inefficient, because it triggers a complicated legal process and increases uncertainty about the ultimate losses to creditors. Bankruptcy is also likely to bring the business of the financial institution to a halt, thus disrupting the activities of other institutions with which it does business. Bankruptcy can shake confidence in the whole financial system, as the Lehman bankruptcy revealed.

In the crisis of 2007–2009, Fed and Treasury officials felt it necessary to save financial institutions from failure with emergency loans and equity injections. Such risky rescues might become unnecessary if a regulatory agency gains *resolution authority* over nonbank institutions such as investment banks and hedge funds—the right to take them over when they become insolvent. Regulators could close or sell troubled institutions in an orderly fashion and potentially avoid a panic that threatens the financial system and the economy.

Addressing Too Big To Fail

Starting with Continental Illinois in 1984, policymakers have rescued institutions they deemed too big to fail. Institutions such as Continental, and later Bear Stearns and AIG, had large debts to other institutions and agreements such as promised payments on credit default swaps. The size of these firms and their interconnectedness with other institutions meant that their failure could trigger insolvencies throughout the financial system. Failures of smaller institutions may be less likely to pose this *systemic risk*.

One way for regulators to address TBTF is to prevent financial institutions from becoming too large or interconnected. Possible tools include restrictions on institutions' size or restrictions on their scope.

Restricting Size Some economists suggest limits on the amounts of assets or liabilities held by financial institutions. Currently, if a U.S. bank holds more than 10 percent of all deposits in the country, it cannot expand by acquiring another commercial bank. As of 2010, Bank of America was the only institution that had hit the 10 percent limit. To lessen the too-big-to-fail problem, this limit could be reduced to a level such as 5 or 2 percent. In addition, limits on assets or liabilities could be extended to nonbank institutions.

Regulators could also adopt less rigid policies. Rather than banning institutions above a certain size, they could create disincentives to growth. For example, capital requirements might be more stringent at larger institutions. The need to have more capital would reduce the risk that large institutions will fail. It would also discourage institutions from becoming overly large in the first place, because higher capital requirements reduce an institution's return on equity (see Chapter 18).

Such regulations would counter a half-century-long trend in which financial institutions have grown larger through mergers. The trend was facilitated by the repeal of past regulations, such as limits on the number of branches a bank can have and on interstate banking. Deregulation was motivated by a belief in *economies of scale*, the idea that large banks have lower costs per customer than small banks. Today, some economists argue that the danger that large banks pose to the financial system outweighs the benefits from economies of scale.

Restricting Scope Other proposed reforms would limit the scope of financial institutions by restricting the range of different financial businesses that one firm can operate. Such regulation would reduce the danger that problems in one part of an institution will hurt the other parts.

Arguably, such spillovers exacerbated the financial crisis of 2007–2009. For example, the investment banking unit within Citigroup, a giant financial conglomerate, lost billions of dollars on subprime mortgage–backed securities, reducing Citigroup's capital. The shortage of capital reduced lending in Citigroup's commercial banking units. These units include Citibank and the Student Loan Corporation, which stopped lending to students at two-year colleges. If Citigroup's investment banking and commercial banking divisions had been separate companies, the mistakes of investment bankers might not have made it harder for college students to borrow.

Like restrictions on institutions' size, restrictions on their scope would reverse a historical trend. The financial crisis of the early 1930s led to the Glass–Steagall Act of 1933, which required the separation of commercial banks from investment banks and insurance companies. This law was repealed in 1999, however, and many commercial banks merged with nonbank institutions to create conglomerates like Citigroup. Supporters of such mergers suggest that they create *economies of scope*: a conglomerate can operate as a *financial supermarket* where customers efficiently receive a range of financial services. For example, a corporation can establish a relationship with a single institution that lends to it and also underwrites its securities.

Once again, the recent financial crisis has led some economists to advocate reregulation in which conglomerates are required to break up or reduce their range of activities. Others believe that limits on institutions' scope are not necessary if regulation is improved along other dimensions.

Discouraging Excessive Risk Taking

In the view of most economists, excessive risk taking by financial institutions is a key cause of financial crises. In addition to extending regulation to more institutions and limiting their size and scope, reformers have proposed a variety of curbs on risky behavior. Here, we briefly review three of these ideas.

Requiring "Skin in the Game" Some financial reformers think that institutions that arrange risky transactions should take on some of the risk themselves: these firms should be required to have "skin in the game." For example, an investment bank that securitizes loans should have to hold a certain amount of the securities it creates. Behind this idea is the view that before the financial crisis, buyers of mortgage-backed securities were unaware of how risky the securities were. Requiring skin in the game gives financial institutions a disincentive to create overly risky products.

Reforming Ratings Agencies This idea, too, arises from the belief that buyers of mortgage-backed securities did not understand their risks. *Ratings agencies* such as Moody's Investor Services and Standard & Poor's evaluate the risk of securities and assign them letter grades. Before the financial crisis, ratings agencies gave many subprime mortgage–backed securities the highest possible rating, AAA, which greatly understated their riskiness.

Critics suggest that one reason this happened stemmed from the way ratings agencies earn money: they are hired and paid by the issuers of the securities they rate. Raters are likely to get more business if they inflate the grades they assign. This conflict of interest could be lessened through a new source of revenue for ratings agencies—a tax on financial institutions is one idea—or by having regulators review the agencies' ratings.

Reforming Executive Compensation Executives at many financial institutions receive annual bonuses of millions of dollars if profits for the year are high. This practice encourages the executives to take high-risk gambles that may yield high returns. (They aren't required to pay millions of dollars if the gambles fail.) Recall that in 2008 the Treasury imposed limits on executive compensation as a condition for equity injections under the TARP. Some economists and Congress members think that such limits should exist all the time, while others object to allowing the government to regulate pay at private firms.

Changing Regulatory Structure

A variety of federal and state agencies regulate banks in a complex system that reflects the historical evolution of regulation rather than any logical plan. At the federal level alone, some commercial banks are regulated by the Office of the Comptroller of the Currency and some by the Federal Reserve. Until 2010, the Office of Thrift Supervision regulated savings institutions.

Investment banks are regulated by the federal Securities and Exchange Commission (SEC). The Federal Reserve has sometimes resisted calls to restrict risk taking by investment banks on the grounds that they are the SEC's responsibility. Yet the SEC's main objective has been to prevent fraudulent activities by securities market participants, such as the falsification of accounting information by companies that issue stock. The SEC has not focused on ensuring the solvency of nonbank financial institutions.

Many economists argue that gaps and inconsistencies in regulation enabled the risky behavior that produced the financial crisis of 2007–2009. Some believe the government should abolish existing regulatory agencies and consolidate their responsibilities in one new agency. An alternative is to preserve existing agencies but add one that coordinates regulation. The creation of such an agency, the Financial Services Oversight Council (FSOC), was a centerpiece of the 2010 regulatory reforms. The FSOC will watch for dangers to the entire financial system, not just insolvency risk at individual institutions.

One gap in current regulation involves *financial holding companies (FHCs)*, conglomerates such as Citigroup that have units in different financial businesses. The Federal Reserve is responsible for regulating FHCs, but in the past it has largely confined itself to reviewing FHC mergers with and acquisitions of other institutions. Different units of FHCs are regulated by different agencies—commercial banking units by various bank regulators, investment banking by the SEC, and insurance businesses by state insurance commissions. As we have discussed, problems in one unit of an FHC can hurt other units. In the future, the Federal Reserve may take responsibility for monitoring risky activities in all parts of an FHC.

CASE STUDY

The Financial Reforms of 2010

In July 2010, Congress passed the Dodd-Frank Act and President Obama signed it into law. The act puts into practice some of the reform ideas discussed in this section. Its most important provisions include the following:

- As mentioned earlier, a new Financial Services Oversight Council (FSOC) will coordinate financial regulation. The Secretary of the Treasury will chair the council and it will include representatives from the Federal Reserve, the SEC, the FDIC, the Office of the Comptroller of the Currency, and other agencies. To streamline regulation, the Office of Thrift Supervision is abolished.

- A new Office of Credit Ratings will examine rating agencies annually and publish reports on their performance.

- The FDIC gains the authority to take over and close a nonbank financial institution if its troubles create systemic risk. Costs to the FDIC will be repaid through fees from financial institutions. Most failures of financial institutions—failures that do not endanger the financial system—will still trigger traditional bankruptcy proceedings.

- Financial holding companies that own banks are prohibited from sponsoring hedge funds, a step toward separating banks and securities firms.

- Issuers of certain risky securities, including mortgage-backed securities, must have skin in the game: they must retain at least 5 percent of the default risk on the securities.

The new legislation also empowers the FSOC and the Federal Reserve to create additional regulations, including stricter capital requirements and supervision of nonbank financial institutions. The FSOC and Fed can also force a large financial holding company to break up if it poses a grave threat to the financial system. The Office of Credit Ratings has the right to create new regulations governing rating agencies. In the coming years, we will see how aggressively the FSOC, Fed, and Office of Credit Ratings use their new authority.

The Senate passed the financial reforms by a vote of 60 to 39 and the House of Representatives by 237 to 192. Almost all Democrats supported the act and almost all Republicans opposed it. Democrats hailed the act as a foundation for a healthy financial system; Republicans predicted it would reduce efficiency and innovation at financial institutions.[3] ■

19-5 Financial Crises in Emerging Economies

Previous sections in this chapter have emphasized financial crises in the United States, but crises occur all over the world. They are especially common in *emerging-market economies*—countries in the middle of the world income distribution (not as rich as the United States, but not as poor as many African countries). Crises occurred in Mexico in 1994, many East Asian countries in 1997–1998, Russia in 1998, and Argentina in 2001. In 2008–2009, the U.S. financial crisis spread around the world, and many emerging economies were hit hard.

Emerging-economy crises have much in common with U.S. crises, including bank failures and declines in asset prices. However, they also have another key element: **capital flight**, a sharp increase in net capital outflow that occurs when asset holders lose confidence in an economy. Capital flight creates additional channels in the vicious circle of a financial crisis.

Capital Flight

As discussed in Chapter 5, a country's net capital outflow is its capital outflow (purchases of foreign assets by the country's citizens and firms) minus its capital inflow (purchases of the country's assets by foreigners). In many emerging economies, net capital outflow is negative: inflow exceeds outflow. Capital inflow is high because foreigners expect the economies to grow and their assets to yield high returns.

Capital flight occurs when asset holders (typically led by foreigners) lose confidence in a country's economy. They sharply cut their purchases of the country's assets and start selling the ones they own. This decrease in capital inflow typically shifts net outflow from negative to positive, because inflow becomes less than outflow.

Asset holders' loss of confidence can have various causes, and financial crises often involve more than one. Some leading causes of capital flight are the following:

- *Government debt.* Rising debt levels create fears that the government will default, so foreign financial institutions stop buying government bonds. Foreigners also worry that default will hurt the economy, so they stop buying corporate securities.

---

[3] For more on the Dodd-Frank Act, see David Huntington, "Summary of Dodd-Frank Financial Regulation Legislation," Harvard Law School Forum on Corporate Governance and Financial Regulation, blogs.law.harvard.edu/corpgov/, posted 7/7/2010.

- *Political risk*. Political instability can bring bad governments to power or produce armed conflicts that disrupt the economy. Signs of instability make a country's assets more risky, which can spark capital flight.

- *Banking problems*. Loans to a country's banks from foreign banks are one kind of capital inflow. This source of funds is cut off if domestic banks encounter trouble, such as threats to their solvency from defaults on loans they have made.

Effects on Interest Rates and Exchange Rates When a loss of confidence causes foreigners to sell a country's assets, it drives down asset prices, including bond prices. As we learned in Chapter 16, lower bond prices imply higher interest rates on bonds.

Capital flight typically affects a country's exchange rate as well. Foreigners that sell the country's assets are paid in the country's currency, which they then trade for foreign currency to obtain foreign assets. Sales of the domestic currency cause the currency to depreciate; that is, it falls in value relative to other currencies.[4]

Contagion Just as a bank run can trigger runs at other banks, capital flight can spread from one country to others in a process called **contagion**. When asset holders see that one country's exchange rate and asset prices have fallen, they worry that the same thing could happen in countries in the same region or in countries with similar problems. Capital flight hits these countries as asset holders try to sell before prices fall.

For example, in July 1997, the East Asian financial crisis began in Thailand when capital flight caused the value of the Thai bhat to collapse. In the following months, capital flight spread to countries including South Korea, Indonesia, and the Philippines, driving down exchange rates and raising interest rates throughout the region.

Capital Flight and Financial Crises

Capital flight is often part of a broader financial crisis. It interacts with the basic causes of crises summarized in Figure 19-1. One of the typical causes—banking problems—can trigger capital flight. At the same time, capital flight causes declines in asset prices, another key feature of crises.

The increases in interest rates caused by capital flight are often dramatic; in South Korea, for example, short-term rates jumped from 12 percent in November 1997 to 31 percent in December 1997. Higher interest rates cause investment to fall sharply. In addition, lower confidence in the economy works to reduce both consumption and investment.

The currency depreciation caused by capital flight also has deleterious effects. In emerging economies, foreign loans to the government and to domestic banks

---

[4] The effects of capital flight on a country's interest rate and exchange rate can be captured in the model of a large open economy in the appendix to Chapter 5. Specifically, Figure 5-23 shows that a *fall* in net capital outflow reduces the interest rate and raises the exchange rate. Capital flight is a *rise* in net capital outflow and therefore has the opposite effects: the interest rate rises and the exchange rate falls.

and firms are usually made in U.S. dollars, so many debts are fixed in dollars. When the exchange rate falls, each dollar costs more in local currency, so debt levels rise when measured in local currency. Higher debts hurt the economy by worsening the problems of banks and pushing corporations into bankruptcy. Higher government debt increases fears of default, worsening capital flight.

In sum, capital flight adds a number of channels through which financial crises reduce aggregate demand and build on themselves. The vicious circle becomes more vicious, and economies rarely escape without a deep recession. The following case study recounts a particularly traumatic financial crisis.

CASE STUDY

Argentina's Financial Crisis, 2001–2002

Argentina has a long history of economic crises. For decades, a central problem has been large government budget deficits. The government has sometimes financed deficits with bank loans or bonds, but at other times it has not been able to borrow. In these periods, it has financed deficits with seignorage revenue—by printing money. Rapid money growth causes high inflation, which in turn hurts economic efficiency and long-run growth.

In the 1980s, Argentina's budget deficits produced annual inflation rates in the hundreds of percent. The situation deteriorated at the end of the decade, with inflation over 2,000 percent per year in both 1989 and 1990. In 1991, a new president, Carlos Menem, decided that Argentina needed major reforms. His government attacked the budget deficit with spending cuts and higher taxes. It also sought to make the economy more productive by privatizing government-owned industries and eliminating barriers to international trade.

The government's most radical action was to create a *currency board*, an arrangement that rigidly fixed the exchange rate between Argentina's peso and the U.S. dollar at 1.0. The government promised to maintain this exchange rate by holding large quantities of dollars—enough so it could trade a dollar for a peso with anyone who asked. Policymakers believed that the currency board would curb inflation: the value of the peso could not fall rapidly if it was tied to the dollar, because the value of the dollar was stable.

Initially, Menem's policies were highly successful. Inflation fell to 25 percent in 1992 and 4 percent in 1994. At the same time, output grew rapidly. Confidence in Argentina's economy soared, and capital flowed into the country. Foreign financial institutions started buying Argentine government debt, which they had shunned in the 1980s.

But then several problems developed:

- Budget deficits started to rise again. This resulted largely from spending by the governments of Argentina's provinces, which the national government could not control.

- Argentine inflation, although falling, remained above U.S. inflation for several years, affecting Argentina's *real* exchange rate. This variable equals $e \times (P/P^*)$, where e is the nominal exchange rate, P is the domestic price level, and P^* is the foreign price level (see Chapter 5). The real exchange rate rose because the nominal rate e was fixed at 1.0 and P (Argentina's price level) rose faster than P^* (the U.S. price level). The rising real exchange rate made Argentina's goods more expensive relative to foreign goods and reduced Argentina's net exports, thus slowing output growth and raising unemployment.

- A financial crisis in Mexico in 1994 produced contagion. Capital flight occurred throughout Latin America, including Argentina, pushing up interest rates and reducing consumption and investment. Combined with the fall in net exports, lower consumption and investment produced a recession in the mid-1990s.

As usual in a financial crisis, all these different problems reinforced one another. In the late 1990s, the recession reduced tax revenue, worsening the problem of budget deficits. The currency board precluded expansionary monetary policy: policymakers could not create additional pesos because they did not hold enough U.S. dollars to back them. Without monetary stimulus, the recession worsened and the unemployment rate rose above 15 percent. Capital flight increased because of worries about rising government debt and about a possible end of the currency board. In 1999, Fernando de la Rua replaced Carlos Menem as president, but it made little difference for the deteriorating economy.

In late 2001, Argentina's problems spiraled out of control. In October, the government defaulted by failing to make promised payments on its debt. November brought a banking crisis. Argentina's banks had been weakened by the long recession and by losses on their holdings of government bonds. Fearing bank failures, and with no deposit insurance, Argentines rushed to withdraw their money.

The government's response to the bank panic was drastic: it imposed a limit on withdrawals. A depositor could withdraw only $250 in cash per week. This policy provoked a political crisis. The long recession had made many Argentines furious at the government, and the denial of access to their money was the last straw. Riots and looting erupted in December 2001: 26 people died and President de la Rua resigned. In January 2002, an interim president, Eduardo Duhalde, ended the currency board.

The immediate economic consequences were disastrous. The value of a peso fell from its fixed level of $1 to 27 cents in 2002. This exchange-rate collapse caused a large rise in import prices, reducing living standards for Argentine consumers. It also caused a huge rise in the peso values of dollar-denominated debts, leading to a wave of corporate bankruptcies. Output fell by 15 percent from 2000 to 2002, and unemployment rose above 20 percent.

At the time, some economists predicted a long depression for Argentina. However, the fall in the exchange rate set the stage for more-rapid-than-expected recovery. It made Argentine goods cheap relative to foreign goods, and exports boomed. From 2003 to 2007, output grew rapidly and unemployment fell below 10 percent. During this period, the government also managed to reduce budget deficits, the problem underlying Argentina's history of instability. Time will tell whether strong growth and low budget deficits prove to be durable. ∎

Recent Crises

The U.S. financial crisis of 2007–2009 triggered crises in many other countries, largely by causing capital flight. As we discussed, the panic following the failure of Lehman Brothers produced a flight to safety, with financial institutions selling any assets that appeared risky. These assets included many in emerging economies, where assets are generally considered risky because the economies are less stable than advanced economies. Countries in eastern Europe and Asia, for example, experienced capital flight and sharp recessions.

In 2009–2010, a financial crisis struck Greece (which is sometimes categorized as an emerging economy, because its income is low by western European standards). The trigger for this crisis was rising government budget deficits, which produced fears that Greece might default on its debt. Asset holders around the world dumped Greek debt, pushing up the interest rates that Greece had to pay on new debt. In May 2010, Greek long-term government bonds paid 8.0 percent, compared to 2.7 percent for German government bonds (see Figure 19-5).

In the summer of 2010, it appeared that Greece was heading for a severe recession. Making matters worse, Greek policymakers could not support their economy with traditional policy tools. They could not pursue expansionary fiscal policy because that would worsen the problem of rising debt; indeed, Greece's government was trying to cut its spending. Policymakers could not

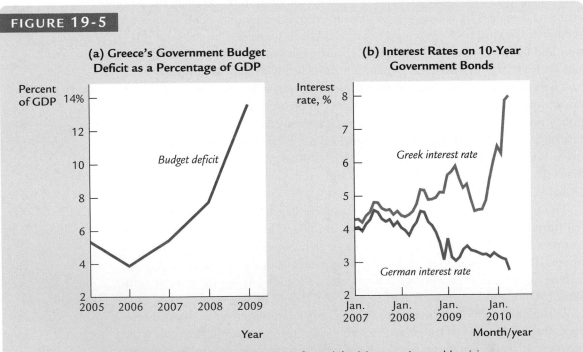

FIGURE 19-5

(a) Greece's Government Budget Deficit as a Percentage of GDP

(b) Interest Rates on 10-Year Government Bonds

Greece's Crisis, 2009–2010 Greece's financial crisis was triggered by rising government debt, which created fears of default and pushed interest rates on Greek government bonds above other European bond rates.

Source: OECD.

pursue expansionary monetary policy because Greece does not have its own currency. Its currency is the euro, which it shares with 15 other European countries. Monetary policy for all euro countries is set by the European Central Bank, so Greece has no independent policy tool to wield against recession.

As Greece's government struggled to make debt payments, Europeans worried that the crisis would worsen dramatically if the government actually defaulted. In addition to wrecking Greece's economy, a default could produce contagion. Some other European countries, such as Spain and Portugal, also have high debt levels. Default by Greece would shake confidence in these countries' debt, and they could be hit by capital flight. Uncertainty hangs over Europe's economies as this book goes to press.

The Role of the International Monetary Fund

When financial crises threaten the United States, the Federal Reserve and Treasury Department try to contain them. When emerging economies experience crises, governments and central banks often don't have the resources to respond. In particular, they lack foreign currency, which is needed to pay debts set in dollars. Therefore, countries in crisis often seek help from the **International Monetary Fund (IMF)**, an international institution that lends to countries experiencing financial crises.

The IMF was established in 1944 to oversee a system of fixed exchange rates among 44 nations, including the United States and other leading economies. That system ended in the 1970s, and since then aiding countries in financial crises has been the IMF's primary function. Most of the world's countries are members of the IMF and contribute funds to it, but rich countries provide most of the money. A country's votes on the IMF board of directors are proportional to its financial contribution, so rich countries hold most of the power.

In recent decades, the IMF has intervened in most crises involving capital flight, including those in Argentina and Greece. As we've seen, private financial institutions are wary of lending to countries in crisis. These countries turn to the IMF for emergency loans, which are made in dollars. The IMF is sometimes called the "international lender of last resort."

Countries use IMF loans in various ways depending on their circumstances:

- The government can use the loans to make payments on its debt, preventing default.

- If a country's banks have debts denominated in dollars, the central bank can lend them dollars to repay those debts.

- The central bank can use dollars to buy its own currency in foreign-exchange markets (if, unlike Greece, the country has its own currency). Increased demand for the currency dampens the fall in the exchange value of the currency.

Each of these actions attacks a part of the financial crisis. In addition, IMF loans are intended to boost confidence in the economy, reducing capital flight. The overall goal is to slow down the vicious circle and hasten financial and economic recovery.

Most IMF loans have strings attached. To obtain a loan, a country must sign an economic agreement with the IMF. The country agrees to reforms that address the problems underlying its crisis. For example, a government with a high debt level may be required to cut spending. This condition was a key part of the IMF's agreement with Greece in May 2010. Loan provisions may also include stricter bank regulation, monetary tightening to control inflation, or privatization of government-owned industries.

IMF loans are controversial. Some economists believe they significantly reduce the damage caused by financial crises, for example, by curbing the length of recessions. Others criticize the IMF on the grounds that it creates moral hazard. They criticize IMF loans to countries for essentially the same reason that many criticize rescues of U.S. financial institutions by the Federal Reserve and the Treasury. Aid to countries that get in trouble encourages other countries to behave the same way. Still others criticize the IMF for the conditions it imposes on loans, which can be painful. Reducing budget deficits, for example, may force governments to cut spending on antipoverty programs. The IMF argues that painful reforms are needed for long-run economic growth, but again, not everyone agrees.

19-6 Conclusion

Financial crises have caused many of history's worst recessions and highest unemployment rates, both in the United States and around the world. Often monetary and fiscal policies are inadequate tools for ending these recessions. To stem crises, governments and central banks take drastic actions, ranging from a bank holiday to emergency loans and equity injections for financial institutions. When emerging economies face a financial crisis, the International Monetary Fund lends to the countries' governments.

The events of 2007–2009 drove home the lesson that, despite its strong financial institutions and extensive regulatory system, the United States is susceptible to severe financial crises. Seeking to reduce this risk, economists and political leaders have proposed many reforms of financial regulation. Some of these proposals, such as a new government agency to monitor financial risk, were enacted in 2010. It remains to be seen how greatly these reforms will change the behavior of financial institutions, how effective they will be in preventing crises, and whether further changes in regulation will occur. You will surely hear much about these issues in the years to come.

Summary

1. A financial crisis typically begins with declines in asset prices, failures of financial institutions, or both. Failures can result from insolvency or liquidity crises. A financial crisis can produce a credit crunch and reduce aggregate demand, causing a recession. The recession reinforces the causes of the crisis.

2. Policymakers may seek to stem a crisis by rescuing troubled financial institutions. Rescues range from riskless loans to institutions facing liquidity

crises to giveaways of government funds. Risky rescues, including risky loans and equity injections, are an intermediate type of policy that may or may not cost the government money.

3. Financial rescues are controversial because of their potential costs to taxpayers and because they increase moral hazard: firms may take on more risk, thinking the government will bail them out if they get in trouble.

4. Over 2007–2009, the subprime mortgage crisis evolved into a broad financial and economic crisis in the United States. The stock market fell drastically, some of the country's most prestigious financial institutions failed or came close to failing, lending was disrupted throughout the economy, and the unemployment rate rose to 10 percent.

5. The 2007–2009 crisis produced an intense debate about government regulation of financial institutions. Many proposals for financial reform fall into four broad categories: increased regulation of nonbank financial institutions, policies to prevent institutions from becoming too big to fail, rules that discourage excessive risk taking, and new structures for regulatory agencies.

6. Financial crises in emerging-market economies typically include capital flight and sharp decreases in exchange rates. Causes of capital flight include high government debt, political instability, and banking problems. Capital flight adds new channels to the vicious circle of a financial crisis. The International Monetary Fund makes emergency loans to countries struck by capital flight.

KEY CONCEPTS

Financial crisis	Too big to fail (TBTF)	Contagion
Credit crunch	Equity injection	International Monetary
Lender of last resort	Zero-bound problem	Fund (IMF)
Discount loan	Capital flight	

QUESTIONS FOR REVIEW

1. What two types of events are the typical triggers for financial crises?

2. Explain how a financial crisis leads to a fall in aggregate demand and a recession.

3. Explain how the central bank can ease liquidity crises at solvent financial institutions.

4. How can the central bank or government prevent failures of insolvent financial institutions or reduce the costs of failures to the economy?

5. Why are some financial institutions "too big to fail" and what are the implications for central bank and government policy?

6. Is the following statement true or false? Explain your answer. "The only costs of financial rescues are the direct payments from the government."

7. List the four broad categories of financial reform. Describe a proposed reform in each category and explain how it would help prevent a financial crisis.

8. What effects does capital flight have on interest rates and exchange rates? Explain these effects.

9. What are the leading causes of capital flight?

10. Describe the IMF's role in the financial crises of emerging economies.

PROBLEMS AND APPLICATIONS

1. Many economists argue that a rescue of a financial institution should protect the institution's creditors from losses but *not* protect its owners: they should lose their equity. Supporters of this idea say it reduces the moral hazard created by rescues.

    a. Explain how this approach reduces moral hazard compared to a rescue that protects both creditors and equity holders.

    b. Does this approach eliminate the moral hazard problem completely? Explain.

2. What could U.S. policymakers have done to prevent the Great Depression or at least reduce its severity? Specifically:

    a. What government or Fed policies might have prevented the stock market crash and bank panics that started the financial crisis? (*Hint:* Think of policies that exist today.)

    b. Once the crisis began, what could policymakers have done to dampen the effects on the financial system and economy? Explain.

3. Some Congress members think the government should not risk taxpayer money to rescue financial firms whose highly paid executives have behaved irresponsibly. Instead, the government should aid middle- and low-income people hurt by the financial crisis, such as homeowners facing foreclosure. Discuss the arguments for this position and against it.

4. In 2010, Senator Blanche Lincoln (D-AR) proposed that commercial banks be forbidden to trade derivative securities. Discuss the arguments for and against this proposal.

5. Of the proposed financial reforms discussed in Section 19-4, which would have significantly dampened the financial crisis of 2007–2009 if they had been in place before the crisis? Could any of the reforms have prevented the crisis entirely? Explain.

6. Draw an expanded version of Figure 19-1 (the outline of a typical financial crisis) for emerging economies. The figure should include capital flight and show how this phenomenon interacts with the other elements of a crisis.

7. In the late 1990s, some economists advised Argentina to dollarize, that is, to eliminate the peso and use the U.S. dollar as its currency. Discuss how dollarization might have changed the course of events in 2001–2002.

8. Find out what has happened to Greece's financial system and economy since this book was published. Has Greece's crisis worsened or eased? Has the crisis affected other European or non-European economies? Have events followed the typical pattern of financial crises described in this chapter? Explain.

Accommodating policy: A policy that yields to the effect of a shock and thereby prevents the shock from being disruptive; for example, a policy that raises aggregate demand in response to an adverse supply shock, sustaining the effect of the shock on prices and keeping output at its natural level.

Accounting profit: The amount of revenue remaining for the owners of a firm after all the factors of production except capital have been compensated. (Cf. economic profit, profit.)

Actively managed fund: A mutual fund that picks stocks based on analysts' research.

Acyclical: Moving in no consistent direction over the business cycle. (Cf. countercyclical, procyclical.)

Adaptive expectations: An approach that assumes that people form their expectation of a variable based on recently observed values of the variable. (Cf. rational expectations.)

Adverse selection: An unfavorable sorting of individuals by their own choices; for example, in efficiency-wage theory, when a wage cut induces good workers to quit and bad workers to remain with the firm; the problem that the people or firms that are most eager to make a transaction are the least desirable to parties on the other side of the transaction.

Aggregate: Total for the whole economy.

Aggregate demand curve: The negative relationship between the price level and the aggregate quantity of output demanded that arises from the interaction between the goods market and the money market.

Aggregate supply curve: The relationship between the price level and the aggregate quantity of output firms produce.

Animal spirits: Exogenous and perhaps self-fulfilling waves of optimism and pessimism about the state of the economy that, according to some economists, influence the level of investment.

Appreciation: A rise in the value of a currency relative to other currencies in the market for foreign exchange. (Cf. depreciation.)

Arbitrage: The act of buying an item in one market and selling it at a higher price in another market in order to profit from the price differential in the two markets.

Asset allocation: Decisions by individuals or institutions about what assets to hold.

Asset-price bubble: A rapid rise in asset prices that is not justified by changes in interest rates or expected asset income.

Asset-price crash: A large, rapid fall in asset prices.

Asymmetric information: The problem that one side of an economic transaction knows more than the other.

Automatic stabilizer: A policy that reduces the amplitude of economic fluctuations without regular and deliberate changes in economic policy; for example, an income tax system that automatically reduces taxes when income falls.

Balance sheet: An accounting statement that shows assets and liabilities.

Balanced budget: A budget in which receipts equal expenditures.

Balanced growth: The condition under which many economic variables—such as income per person, capital per person, and the real wage—all grow at the same rate.

Balanced trade: A situation in which the value of imports equals the value of exports, so net exports equal zero.

Bank: A financial institution that accepts deposits and makes private loans.

Bank panic: Simultaneous runs at many individual banks.

Bank run: Sudden, large withdrawals by depositors who lose confidence in a bank.

Bank supervision: The monitoring of banks' activities by government regulators.

Behavioral finance: A field that uses ideas from psychology to study how deviations from rational behavior affect asset prices.

Bid-ask spread: A gap between the prices at which a dealer buys and sells a security.

Bond: *(fixed income security)* A document representing an interest-bearing debt of the issuer, usually a corporation or the government.

Broker: A firm that buys and sells securities for others.

Budget deficit: A shortfall of receipts from expenditure.

Budget surplus: An excess of receipts over expenditure.

Business cycle: Economy-wide fluctuations in output, incomes, and employment.

Business fixed investment: Equipment and structures that businesses buy for use in future production.

Call option: An option to buy a security.

Capital: 1. The stock of equipment and structures used in production. 2. The funds to finance the accumulation of equipment and structures. 3. The difference between assets and liabilities.

Capital budgeting: An accounting procedure that measures both assets and liabilities.

Capital flight: The sharp rise in a country's net capital outflows that occurs when asset holders lose confidence in a country's economy.

Capital gain: An increase in an asset holder's wealth from an increase in the asset's price.

Capital loss: A decrease in an asset holder's wealth from a decrease in the asset's price.

Capital requirements: Regulations setting minimum levels of capital that banks must hold.

Capital structure: The mix of stocks and bonds that a firm issues.

Central bank: The institution responsible for the conduct of monetary policy, such as the Federal Reserve in the United States.

Centrally planned economy: *(command economy)* A system in which the government decides what goods and services are produced, who receives them, and what investment projects are undertaken.

Circuit breaker: The requirement that a securities exchange shut down temporarily if prices drop by a specified percentage.

Classical dichotomy: The theoretical separation of real and nominal variables in the classical model, which implies that nominal variables do not influence real variables. (Cf. neutrality of money.)

Classical theory of asset prices: The theory that the price of an asset equals the present value of expected income from the asset.

Classical model: A model of the economy derived from the ideas of the classical, or pre-Keynesian, economists; a model based on the assumptions that wages and prices adjust to clear markets and that monetary policy does not influence real variables. (Cf. Keynesian model.)

Closed economy: An economy that does not engage in international trade. (Cf. open economy.)

Cobb–Douglas production function: A production function of the form $F(K, L) = AK^{\alpha}L^{1-\alpha}$,

where K is capital, L is labor, and A and α are parameters.

Collateral: An asset of a borrower that a bank can seize if the borrower defaults.

Commercial bank: An institution that accepts checking and savings deposits and lends to individuals and firms.

Commodity money: Money that is intrinsically useful and would be valued even if it did not serve as money. (Cf. fiat money, money.)

Community bank: A commercial bank with less than $1 billion in assets that operates in a small geographic area.

Competition: A situation in which there are many individuals or firms, so that the actions of any one of them do not influence market prices.

Conditional convergence: The tendency of economies with different initial levels of income, but similar economic policies and institutions, to become more similar in income over time.

Constant returns to scale: A property of a production function whereby a proportionate increase in all factors of production leads to an increase in output of the same proportion.

Consumer price index (CPI): A measure of the overall level of prices that shows the cost of a fixed basket of consumer goods relative to the cost of the same basket in a base year.

Consumption: Goods and services purchased by consumers.

Consumption function: A relationship showing the determinants of consumption; for example, a relationship between consumption and disposable income, $C = C(Y - T)$.

Contagion: The spread of capital flight from one country to others.

Contractionary policy: A policy that reduces aggregate demand, real income, and employment. (Cf. expansionary policy.)

Convergence: The tendency of economies with different initial levels of income to become more similar in income over time.

Cost-push inflation: Inflation resulting from shocks to aggregate supply. (Cf. demand-pull inflation.)

Countercyclical: Moving in the opposite direction from output, incomes, and employment over the business cycle; rising during recessions and falling during recoveries. (Cf. acyclical, procyclical.)

Covenant: A provision in a loan contract that restricts the borrower's behavior.

CPI: *See* consumer price index.

Credit crunch: A change in conditions at financial institutions that causes a sharp decrease in bank lending and makes it hard for potential borrowers to obtain loans.

Credit default swap (CDS): A derivative with payouts triggered by defaults on certain debt securities.

Credit risk: *(default risk)* The risk that loans will not be repaid.

Credit union: A nonprofit bank owned by its depositor members, who are drawn from a group of people with something in common.

Crowding out: The reduction in investment that results when expansionary fiscal policy raises the interest rate.

Currency: The sum of outstanding paper money and coins.

Currency board: A fixed exchange rate system under which a central bank backs all of the nation's currency with the currency of another country.

Cyclical unemployment: The unemployment associated with short-run economic fluctuations; the deviation of the unemployment rate from the natural rate.

Cyclically adjusted budget deficit: The budget deficit adjusted for the influence of the business cycle on government spending and tax revenue; the budget deficit that would occur if the economy's production and employment were at their natural levels. Also called full-employment budget deficit.

Dealer: A firm that buys and sells certain securities for itself.

Dealer market: An OTC market in which all trades are made with dealers

Debt–deflation: A theory according to which an unexpected fall in the price level redistributes real wealth from debtors to creditors and, therefore, reduces total spending in the economy.

Default: Failure to make promised payments on debts.

Deflation: A decrease in the overall level of prices. (Cf. disinflation, inflation.)

Deflator: *See* GDP deflator.

Demand deposits: Assets that are held in banks and can be used on demand to make transactions, such as checking accounts.

Demand-pull inflation: Inflation resulting from shocks to aggregate demand. (Cf. cost-push inflation.)

Demand shocks: Exogenous events that shift the aggregate demand curve.

Depreciation: 1. The reduction in the capital stock that occurs over time because of aging and use. 2. A fall in the value of a currency relative to other currencies in the market for foreign exchange. (Cf. appreciation.)

Deposit insurance: A government guarantee to compensate depositors for their losses when a bank fails.

Depression: A very severe recession.

Derivatives: Securities with payoffs tied to the prices of other assets.

Diminishing marginal product: A characteristic of a production function whereby the marginal product of a factor falls as the amount of the factor increases while all other factors are held constant.

Direct finance: A situation in which savers provide funds to investors by buying securities in financial markets.

Discount loan: A loan from the Federal Reserve to a bank.

Discount rate: The interest rate that the Federal Reserve charges when it makes loans to banks.

Discouraged workers: Individuals who have left the labor force because they believe that there is little hope of finding a job.

Disinflation: A reduction in the rate at which prices are rising. (Cf. deflation, inflation.)

Disposable income: Income remaining after the payment of taxes.

Diversification: The distribution of wealth among many assets, such as securities issued by different firms and governments.

Dividend: A firm's payment of a portion of its earnings to its stockholders.

Dollarization: The adoption of the U.S. dollar as the currency in another country.

Double coincidence of wants: A situation in which two individuals each have precisely the good that the other wants.

Economic profit: The amount of revenue remaining for the owners of a firm after all the factors of production have been compensated. (Cf. accounting profit, profit.)

Efficient markets hypothesis: The theory that the price of every stock equals the value of the stock, so no stock is a better buy than any other.

Efficiency of labor: A variable in the Solow growth model that measures the health, education, skills, and knowledge of the labor force.

Efficiency units of labor: A measure of the labor force that incorporates both the number of workers and the efficiency of each worker.

Efficiency-wage theories: Theories of real-wage rigidity and unemployment according to which firms raise labor productivity and profits by keeping real wages above the equilibrium level.

Elasticity: The percentage change in a variable caused by a 1-percent change in another variable.

Electronic communications network (ECN): OTC market in which financial institutions trade securities with one another directly, rather than through dealers.

Endogenous growth theory: Models of economic growth that try to explain the rate of technological change.

Endogenous variable: A variable that is explained by a particular model; a variable whose value is determined by the model's solution. (Cf. exogenous variable.)

Equilibrium: A state of balance between opposing forces, such as the balance of supply and demand in a market.

Equity injection: The purchase of a troubled institution's stock by the government.

Equity ratio (ER): The ratio of a bank's capital to its assets; ER = capital/assets.

Euler's theorem: The mathematical result economists use to show that economic profit must be zero if the production function has constant returns to scale and if factors are paid their marginal products.

Ex ante real interest rate: The real interest rate anticipated when a loan is made; the nominal interest rate minus expected inflation. (Cf. ex post real interest rate.)

Ex post real interest rate: The real interest rate actually realized; the nominal interest rate minus actual inflation. (Cf. ex ante real interest rate.)

Excess reserves: Reserves held by banks above the amount mandated by reserve requirements.

Exchange: A physical location where brokers and dealers meet to trade securities.

Exchange rate: The rate at which a country makes exchanges in world markets. (Cf. nominal exchange rate, real exchange rate.)

Expectations theory of the term structure: The hypothesis according to which the n-period interest rate is the average of the current one-period rate and expected rates over the next $n - 1$ periods.

Exogenous variable: A variable that a particular model takes as given; a variable whose value is independent of the model's solution. (Cf. endogenous variable.)

Expansionary policy: A policy that raises aggregate demand, real income, and employment. (Cf. contractionary policy.)

Exports: Goods and services sold to other countries.

Factor of production: An input used to produce goods and services; for example, capital or labor.

Factor price: The amount paid for one unit of a factor of production.

Factor share: The proportion of total income being paid to a factor of production.

Federal Deposit Insurance Corporation (FDIC): The government agency that insures deposits at U.S. commercial banks and savings institutions.

Federal funds: Loans from one bank to another, usually for one day.

Federal funds rate: The overnight interest rate at which banks lend to one another.

Federal Reserve (the Fed): The central bank of the United States.

Fiat money: Money that is not intrinsically useful and is valued only because it is used as money. (Cf. commodity money, money.)

Finance company: A nonbank financial institution that makes loans but does not accept deposits.

Financial crisis: A major disruption of the financial system; usually involves sharp falls in asset prices and failures of financial institutions.

Financial institution: (financial intermediary) A firm that helps channel funds from savers to investors.

Financial intermediation: The process by which resources are allocated from those individuals who wish to save some of their income for future consumption to those individuals and firms who wish to borrow to buy investment goods for future production.

Financial market: A collection of people and firms that buy and sell securities or currencies.

Fiscal policy: The government's choice regarding levels of spending and taxation.

Fisher effect: The one-for-one influence of expected inflation on the nominal interest rate.

Fisher equation: The equation stating that the nominal interest rate is the sum of the real interest rate and expected inflation ($i = r + E\pi$).

Flexible prices: Prices that adjust quickly to equilibrate supply and demand. (Cf. sticky prices.)

Floating interest rate: An interest rate on a long-term loan that is tied to a short-term rate.

Flow: A variable measured as a quantity per unit of time. (Cf. stock.)

Forbearance: A regulator's decision to allow an insolvent bank to remain open.

Fractional-reserve banking: A system in which banks keep only some of their deposits on reserve. (Cf. 100-percent-reserve banking.)

Frictional unemployment: The unemployment that results because it takes time for workers to search for the jobs that best suit their skills and tastes. (Cf. structural unemployment.)

Full-employment budget deficit: *See* cyclically-adjusted budget deficit.

Futures contract: An agreement to trade an asset for a certain price at a future point in time.

Future value: The value of a dollar today in terms of dollars at some future time, $1 today = $(1 + i)^n$ in n years.

GDP: *See* gross domestic product.

GDP deflator: The ratio of nominal GDP to real GDP; a measure of the overall level of prices that shows the cost of the currently produced basket of goods relative to the cost of that basket in a base year.

General equilibrium: The simultaneous equilibrium of all the markets in the economy.

GNP: *See* gross national product.

Gold standard: A monetary system in which gold serves as money or in which all money is convertible into gold at a fixed rate.

Golden rule: The saving rate in the Solow growth model that leads to the steady state in which consumption per worker (or consumption per efficiency unit of labor) is maximized.

Gordon growth model: The theory in which a stock price P is determined by an initial expected dividend, the expected growth rate of dividends, and the risk-adjusted interest rate: $P = D_1/(i - g)$.

Government purchases: Goods and services bought by the government. (Cf. transfer payments.)

Government-purchases multiplier: The change in aggregate income resulting from a one-dollar change in government purchases.

Gross domestic product (GDP): The total income earned domestically, including the income earned by foreign-owned factors of production; the total expenditure on domestically produced goods and services.

Gross national product (GNP): The total income of all residents of a nation, including the income from factors of production used abroad; the total expenditure on the nation's output of goods and services.

Hedge fund: A fund that raises money from wealthy people and institutions to make risky bets on asset prices.

Hedging: Reducing risk by purchasing an asset that is likely to produce a high return if another of one's assets produces low or negative returns.

High-powered money: The sum of currency and bank reserves; also called the monetary base.

Human capital: The accumulation of investments in people, such as education.

Hyperinflation: Extremely high inflation.

Hysteresis: The long lasting influence of history, such as on the natural rate of unemployment.

Imperfect-information model: The model of aggregate supply emphasizing that individuals do not always know the overall price level because they cannot observe the prices of all goods and services in the economy.

Import quota: A legal limit on the amount of a good that can be imported.

Imports: Goods and services bought from other countries.

Imputed value: An estimate of the value of a good or service that is not sold in the marketplace and therefore does not have a market price.

Income velocity of money: The ratio of the economy's total nominal income to the quantity of money. (Cf. transactions velocity of money.)

Index fund: A mutual fund that buys all the stocks in a broad market index.

Index of leading indicators: *See* leading indicators

Indirect finance: A situation in which savers deposit money in banks that then lend to investors.

Inflation: An increase in the overall level of prices. (Cf. deflation, disinflation.)

Inflation targeting: A monetary policy under which the central bank announces a specific target, or target range, for the inflation rate.

Inflation tax: The revenue raised by the government through the creation of money; also called *seigniorage*.

Initial public offering (IPO): The sale of stock when a firm becomes public.

Inside lag: The time between a shock hitting the economy and the policy action taken to respond to the shock. (Cf. outside lag.)

Insiders: Workers who are already employed and therefore have an influence on wage bargaining. (Cf. outsiders.)

Insolvency: A situation in which liabilities exceed assets, producing negative net worth.

Interest rate: The market price at which resources are transferred between the present and the future; the return to saving and the cost of borrowing.

Interest-rate risk: Instability in bank profits caused by fluctuations in short-term interest rates.

Intermediation: *See* financial intermediation.

International Monetary Fund (IMF): An international institution that lends to countries experiencing financial crises.

Intertemporal budget constraint: The budget constraint applying to expenditure and income in more than one period of time. (Cf. budget constraint.)

Inventory investment: The change in the quantity of goods that firms hold in storage, including materials and supplies, work in process, and finished goods.

Investment: Goods purchased by individuals and firms to add to their stock of capital.

Investment bank: A financial institution that serves as an underwriter and advises companies on mergers and acquisitions.

IS curve: The negative relationship between the interest rate and the level of income that arises in the market for goods and services. (Cf. *IS–LM* model, *LM* curve.)

IS–LM model: A model of aggregate demand that shows what determines aggregate income for a given price level by analyzing the interaction between the goods market and the money market. (Cf. *IS* curve, *LM* curve.)

Keynesian cross: A simple model of income determination, based on the ideas in Keynes's *General Theory*, which shows how changes in spending can have a multiplied effect on aggregate income.

Keynesian model: A model derived from the ideas of Keynes's *General Theory*; a model based on the assumptions that wages and prices do not adjust to clear markets and that aggregate demand determines the economy's output and employment. (Cf. classical model.)

Labor-augmenting technological progress: Advances in productive capability that raise the efficiency of labor.

Labor force: Those in the population who have a job or are looking for a job.

Labor-force participation rate: The percentage of the adult population in the labor force.

Labor hoarding: The phenomenon of firms employing workers whom they do not need when the demand for their products is low, so that they will still have these workers when demand recovers.

Large open economy: An open economy that can influence its domestic interest rate; an economy that, by virtue of its size, can have a substantial impact on world markets and, in particular, on the world interest rate. (Cf. small open economy.)

Laspeyres price index: A measure of the level of prices based on a fixed basket of goods. (Cf. Paasche price index.)

Leading indicators: Economic variables that fluctuate in advance of the economy's output and thus signal the direction of economic fluctuations.

Lender of last resort: The central bank's role as emergency lender to financial institutions with no other source of funds.

Leverage: Borrowing money to purchase assets.

Liabilities: Amounts of money owed to others.

Liquid: Readily convertible into the medium of exchange; easily used to make transactions.

Liquidity constraint: A restriction on the amount a person can borrow from a financial institution, which limits the person's ability to spend his future income today; also called a borrowing constraint.

Liquidity management: A bank's efforts to maximize the interest it receives from loans while holding enough liquid assets to be ready for withdrawals.

Liquidity-preference theory: A simple model of the interest rate, based on the ideas in Keynes's *General Theory*, which says that the interest rate adjusts to equilibrate the supply and demand for real money balances.

LM curve: The positive relationship between the interest rate and the level of income (while holding the price level fixed) that arises in the market for real money balances. (Cf. *IS–LM* model, *IS* curve.)

Loan shark: Lender that violates usury laws and collects debts through illegal means.

Loanable funds: The flow of resources available to finance capital accumulation.

Lucas critique: The argument that traditional policy analysis does not adequately take into account the impact of policy changes on people's expectations.

M1, M2, M3: Various measures of the stock of money, where larger numbers signify a broader definition of money.

Macroeconometric model: A model that uses data and statistical techniques to describe the economy quantitatively, rather than just qualitatively.

Macroeconomics: The study of the economy as a whole. (Cf. microeconomics.)

Margin requirements: Limits on the use of credit to purchase stocks.

Marginal product of capital (MPK): The amount of extra output produced when the capital input is increased by one unit.

Marginal product of labor (MPL): The amount of extra output produced when the labor input is increased by one unit.

Marginal propensity to consume (MPC): The increase in consumption resulting from a one-dollar increase in disposable income.

Market-clearing model: A model that assumes that prices freely adjust to equilibrate supply and demand.

Medium of exchange: The item widely accepted in transactions for goods and services; one of the functions of money. (Cf store of value, unit of account.)

Menu cost: The cost of changing a price.

Microeconomics: The study of individual markets and decisionmakers. (Cf. macroeconomics.)

Microfinance: Small loans that allow poor people to start businesses.

Model: A simplified representation of reality, often using diagrams or equations, that shows how variables interact.

Modigliani-Miller Theorem (M and M Theorem): The proposition that a firm's capital structure doesn't matter.

Monetarism: The doctrine according to which changes in the money supply are the primary cause of economic fluctuations, implying that a stable money supply would lead to a stable economy.

Monetary base: The sum of currency and bank reserves; also called high-powered money.

Monetary neutrality: *See* neutrality of money.

Monetary policy: The central bank's choice regarding the supply of money.

Monetary transmission mechanism: The process by which changes in the money supply influence the amount that households and firms wish to spend on goods and services.

Monetary union: A group of economies that have decided to share a common currency and thus a common monetary policy.

Money: The stock of assets used for transactions. (Cf. commodity money, fiat money.)

Money demand function: A function showing the determinants of the demand for real money balances; for example, $(M/P)^d = L(i, Y)$.

Money multiplier: The increase in the money supply resulting from a one-dollar increase in the monetary base.

Moral hazard: The possibility of dishonest or otherwise undesirable behavior in situations in which behavior is imperfectly monitored; for example, in efficiency-wage theory, the possibility that low-wage workers may shirk their responsibilities and risk getting caught and fired; the risk that one party to a transaction will take actions that harm another party.

Mortgage-backed securities: Securities that entitle an owner to a share of payments on a pool of bank loans.

Multiplier: *See* government-purchases multiplier, money multiplier, or tax multiplier.

Mutual fund: A financial institution that holds a diversified set of securities and sells shares to savers.

Mundell–Tobin effect: The fall in the real interest rate that results when an increase in expected inflation raises the nominal interest rate, lowers real money balances and real wealth, and thereby reduces consumption and raises saving.

NAIRU: Non-accelerating inflation rate of unemployment.

National income accounting: The accounting system that measures GDP and many other related statistics.

National income accounts identity: The equation showing that GDP is the sum of consumption, investment, government purchases, and net exports.

National saving: A nation's income minus consumption and government purchases; the sum of private and public saving.

Natural rate of unemployment: The steady-state rate of unemployment; the rate of unemployment toward which the economy gravitates in the long run.

Natural-rate hypothesis: The premise that fluctuations in aggregate demand influence output, employment, and unemployment only in the short run, and that in the long run these variables return to the levels implied by the classical model.

Net capital outflow: The net flow of funds being invested abroad; domestic saving minus domestic investment; also called net foreign investment.

Net exports: Exports minus imports.

Net foreign investment: *See* net capital outflow.

Net worth: *(equity or capital)* The difference between assets and liabilities.

Neutrality of money: The property that a change in the money supply does not influence real variables. (Cf. classical dichotomy.)

Nominal: Measured in current dollars; not adjusted for inflation. (Cf. real.)

Nominal exchange rate: The rate at which one country's currency trades for another country's currency. (Cf. exchange rate, real exchange rate.)

Nominal interest rate: The return to saving and the cost of borrowing without adjustment for inflation. (Cf. real interest rate.)

Okun's law: The negative relationship between unemployment and real GDP, according to which a decrease in unemployment of one percentage point is associated with additional growth in real GDP of approximately 2 percent.

100-percent-reserve banking: A system in which banks keep all deposits on reserve. (Cf. fractional-reserve banking.)

Open economy: An economy in which people can freely engage in international trade in goods and capital. (Cf. closed economy.)

Open-market operations: The purchase or sale of government bonds by the central bank for the purpose of increasing or decreasing the money supply.

Optimize: To achieve the best possible outcome subject to a set of constraints.

Option: The right to trade a security at a certain price any time before an expiration date.

Outside lag: The time between a policy action and its influence on the economy. (Cf. inside lag.)

Outsiders: Workers who are not employed and therefore have no influence on wage bargaining. (Cf. insiders.)

Over-the-counter (OTC) market: A secondary securities market with no physical location.

Paasche price index: A measure of the level of prices based on a changing basket of goods. (Cf. Laspeyres price index.)

Pawnshop: A small lender that holds an item of value as collateral.

Payday lender: A company that provides cash in return for a postdated check.

Phillips curve: A negative relationship between inflation and unemployment; in its modern form, a relationship among inflation, cyclical unemployment, expected inflation, and supply shocks, derived from the short-run aggregate supply curve.

Pigou effect: The increase in consumer spending that results when a fall in the price level raises real money balances and, thereby, consumers' wealth.

Political business cycle: The fluctuations in output and employment resulting from the manipulation of the economy for electoral gain.

Present value: The amount today that is equivalent to an amount to be received in the future, taking into account the interest that could be earned over the interval of time; the value of a future dollar in terms of today's dollars; \$1 in n years = $\$1/(1 + i)^n$ today.

Price-earnings ratio (P/E ratio): A company's stock price divided by earnings per share over the recent past.

Primary markets: Financial markets in which firms and governments issue new securities.

Private loan: A loan negotiated between one borrower and one lender.

Private saving: Disposable income minus consumption.

Procyclical: Moving in the same direction as output, incomes, and employment over the business cycle; falling during recessions and rising during recoveries. (Cf. acyclical, countercyclical.)

Production function: The mathematical relationship showing how the quantities of the factors of production determine the quantity of goods and services produced; for example, $Y = F(K, L)$.

Profit: The income of firm owners; firm revenue minus firm costs. (Cf. accounting profit, economic profit.)

Public company: A firm that issues securities that are traded in financial markets.

Public saving: Government receipts minus government spending; the budget surplus.

Purchasing-power parity: The doctrine according to which goods must sell for the same price in every country, implying that the nominal exchange rate reflects differences in price levels.

Put option: An option to sell a security.

Quantity equation: The identity stating that the product of the money supply and the velocity of money equals nominal expenditure ($MV = PY$); coupled with the assumption of stable velocity, an explanation of nominal expenditure called the quantity theory of money.

Quantity theory of money: The doctrine emphasizing that changes in the quantity of money lead to changes in nominal expenditure.

Quota: *See* import quota.

Random variable: A variable whose value is determined by chance.

Random walk: The movements of a variable whose changes are unpredictable.

Rate of return: The return on a security as a percentage of its initial price.

Rational expectations: An approach that assumes that people optimally use all available information—including information about current and prospective policies—to forecast the future. (Cf. adaptive expectations.)

Real: Measured in constant dollars; adjusted for inflation. (Cf. nominal.)

Real exchange rate: The rate at which one country's goods trade for another country's goods. (Cf. exchange rate, nominal exchange rate.)

Real interest rate: The return to saving and the cost of borrowing after adjustment for inflation. (Cf. nominal interest rate.)

Real money balances: The quantity of money expressed in terms of the quantity of goods and services it can buy; the quantity of money divided by the price level (M/P).

Recession: A sustained period of falling real income.

Rental price of capital: The amount paid to rent one unit of capital.

Reserve requirements: Regulations imposed on banks by the central bank that specify a minimum reserve–deposit ratio.

Reserves: The money that banks have received from depositors but have not used to make loans; vault cash plus banks' deposits at the Federal Reserve.

Residential investment: New housing bought by people to live in and by landlords to rent out.

Return: The total earnings from a security; the capital gain or loss plus any direct payment (coupon payment or dividend).

Return on assets (ROA): The ratio of a bank's profits to its assets; ROA = profits/assets.

Return on equity (ROE): The ratio of a bank's profits to its capital; ROE = profits/capital.

Ricardian equivalence: The theory according to which forward-looking consumers fully anticipate the future taxes implied by government debt, so that government borrowing today coupled with a tax increase in the future to repay the debt has the same effect on the economy as a tax increase today.

Risk-adjusted interest rate: The sum of the risk-free interest rate and the risk premium on an asset, $i^{safe} + \varphi$; this determines the present value of expected income from the asset.

Risk premium (φ): The payment on an asset that compensates the owner for taking on risk.

Sacrifice ratio: The number of percentage points of a year's real GDP that must be forgone to reduce inflation by one percentage point.

Safe interest rate (i^{safe}): An interest rate that savers can receive for sure; also, *risk-free rate*.

Saving: *See* national saving, private saving, and public saving.

Savings institution: A type of bank created to accept savings deposits and make loans for home mortgages; also known as *savings banks* or *savings and loan associations* (*S&Ls*).

Seasonal adjustment: The removal of the regular fluctuations in an economic variable that occur as a function of the time of year.

Secondary markets: Financial markets in which existing securities are traded.

Sectoral shift: A change in the composition of demand among industries or regions.

Security: A claim on some future flow of income, such as a stock or bond.

Securities firm: A company whose primary purpose is to hold securities, trade them, or help others trade them.

Securitization: The process in which a financial institution buys a large number of bank loans, then issues securities entitling the holders to shares of payments on the loans.

Seigniorage: The revenue raised by the government through the creation of money; also called the inflation tax.

Shock: An exogenous change in an economic relationship, such as the aggregate demand or aggregate supply curve.

Shoeleather cost: The cost of inflation from reducing real money balances, such as the inconvenience of needing to make more frequent trips to the bank.

Small open economy: An open economy that takes its interest rate as given by world financial markets; an economy that, by virtue of its size, has a negligible impact on world markets and, in particular, on the world interest rate. (Cf. large open economy.)

Solow growth model: A model showing how saving, population growth, and technological progress determine the level of and growth in the standard of living.

Solow residual: The growth in total factor productivity, measured as the percentage change in output minus the percentage change in inputs, where the inputs are weighted by their factor shares. (Cf. total factor productivity.)

Specialist: A broker-dealer who manages the trading of a certain stock on an exchange.

Speculation: The use of financial markets to make bets on asset prices.

Stabilization policy: Public policy aimed at reducing the severity of short-run economic fluctuations.

Stagflation: A situation of falling output and rising prices; combination of stagnation and inflation.

Steady state: A condition in which key variables are not changing.

Sticky prices: Prices that adjust sluggishly and, therefore, do not always equilibrate supply and demand. (Cf. flexible prices.)

Sticky-price model: The model of aggregate supply emphasizing the slow adjustment of the prices of goods and services.

Stock: (*equity*) Ownership share in a corporation.

Stock market index: An average of prices for a group of stocks.

Store of value: A way of transferring purchasing power from the present to the future; one of the functions of money. (Cf. medium of exchange, unit of account.)

Structural unemployment: The unemployment resulting from wage rigidity and job rationing. (Cf. frictional unemployment.)

Subprime borrower: A borrower with lower income and assets and a weak credit history and thus higher risk of default.

Subprime lenders: Companies that lend to subprime borrowers.

Supply shocks: Exogenous events that shift the aggregate supply curve.

Tariff: A tax on imported goods.

Tax multiplier: The change in aggregate income resulting from a one-dollar change in taxes.

Taylor rule: A rule for monetary policy according to which the central bank sets the interest rate as a function of inflation and the deviation of output from its natural level.

Term premium (τ): Extra return on a long-term bond that compensates for its riskiness; τ_n denotes the term premium on an n-period bond.

Term structure of interest rates: Relationships among interest rates on bonds with different maturities.

Time inconsistency: The tendency of policymakers to announce policies in advance in order to influence the expectations of private decision-makers, and then to follow different policies after those expectations have been formed and acted upon.

Too big to fail (TBTF): The doctrine that large institutions with extensive links to other institutions must be saved to protect the financial system.

Total factor productivity: A measure of the level of technology; the amount of output per unit of input, where different inputs are combined on the basis of their factor shares. (Cf. Solow residual.)

Trade balance: The receipts from exports minus the payments for imports.

Transactions velocity of money: The ratio of the dollar value of all transactions to the quantity of money. (Cf. income velocity of money.)

Transfer payments: Payments from the government to individuals that are not in exchange for goods and services, such as Social Security payments. (Cf. government purchases.)

Underground economy: Economic transactions that are hidden in order to evade taxes or conceal illegal activity.

Undervalued asset: An asset with a price below the present value of the income it is expected to produce.

Underwriter: A financial institution that helps companies issue new securities.

Unemployment insurance: A government program under which unemployed workers can collect benefits for a certain period of time after losing their jobs.

Unemployment rate: The percentage of those in the labor force who do not have jobs.

Unit of account: The measure in which prices and other accounting records are recorded; one of the functions of money. (Cf. medium of exchange, store of value.)

Utility: A measure of household satisfaction.

Value added: The value of a firm's output minus the value of the intermediate goods the firm purchased.

Velocity of money: The ratio of nominal expenditure to the money supply; the rate at which money changes hands

Wage: The amount paid for one unit of labor.

Wage rigidity: The failure of wages to adjust to equilibrate labor supply and labor demand.

Worker-misperception model: The model of aggregate supply emphasizing that workers sometimes perceive incorrectly the overall level of prices.

World interest rate: The interest rate prevailing in world financial markets.

Yield to maturity: The interest rate that makes the present value of payments from a bond equal to its price.

Zero-bound problem: The potential inability of monetary policy to stimulate the economy due to the fact that nominal interest rates cannot be negative.

index